I0876494

THE HUNTER, THE CROWN, AND THE CAMERAS

McGill-Queen's/Beaverbrook Canadian Foundation Studies in Art History

MARTHA LANGFORD, SERIES EDITOR

Recognizing the need for a better understanding of Canada's artistic culture both at home and abroad, the Beaverbrook Canadian Foundation, through its generous support, makes possible the publication of innovative books that advance our understanding of Canadian art and Canada's visual and material culture. This series supports and stimulates such scholarship through the publication of original and rigorous peer-reviewed books that make significant contributions to the subject. We welcome submissions from Canadian and international scholars for book-length projects on historical and contemporary Canadian art and visual and material culture, including Native and Inuit art, architecture, photography, craft, design, and museum studies. Studies by Canadian scholars on non-Canadian themes will also be considered.

The Hunter, the Crown, and the Cameras

Joseph Idlout and the Image of Sangussaqtauliqtilluta

CAROL PAYNE

WITH TEXTS AND IMAGES BY
Joseph Idlout and Leah Idlout d'Argencourt Paulson

WITH CONTRIBUTIONS BY
Madeleine d'Argencourt and Augatnaaq Eccles

AND WITH THE WORDS OF
Paul Ullatitaq Idlout, Susan Salluviniq, Moses Idlout, Joshua Idlout, Ludy Pudluk, Jacob Anaviapik, Elisapee Ootoova, Ruth Sangoya, and Solomon Awa

McGill-Queen's University Press
Montreal & Kingston

ISBN 978-0-2280-2895-6 (cloth)
ISBN 978-0-2280-2982-3 (ePDF)
ISBN 978-0-2280-2957-1 (ePUB)

Legal deposit fourth quarter 2026
Bibliothèque et Archives nationales du Québec

Printed in Canada on acid-free paper

This book has been published with the help of a grant from the Federation for the Humanities and Social Sciences, through the Scholarly Book Awards, using funds provided by the Social Sciences and Humanities Research Council of Canada.

Funded by the Government of Canada | Financé par le gouvernement du Canada | Canada

Canada Council for the Arts | Conseil des arts du Canada

We acknowledge the support of the Canada Council for the Arts.

Nous remercions le Conseil des arts du Canada de son soutien.

McGill-Queen's University Press in Montreal is on land which long served as a site of meeting and exchange amongst Indigenous Peoples, including the Haudenosaunee and Anishinabeg nations. In Kingston it is situated on the territory of the Haudenosaunee and Anishinaabek. We acknowledge and thank the diverse Indigenous Peoples whose footsteps have marked these territories on which peoples of the world now gather.

Library and Archives Canada Cataloguing in Publication

Title: The hunter, the crown, and the cameras : Joseph Idlout and the image of Sangussaqtauliqtilluta / Carol Payne ; with texts and images by Jospeh Idlout and Leah Idlout d'Argencourt Paulson ; with contributions by Madeleine d'Argencourt and Augatnaat Eccles ; and with the words of Paul Ullatitaq Idlout, Susan Salluviniq, Moses Idlout, Joshua Idlout, Ludy Pudluk, Jacob Anaviapik, Elisapee Ootoova, Ruth Sangoya, and Solomon Awa.
Names: Payne, Carol J., author. | Idlout, Joseph, author, photographer.
Series: McGill-Queen's/Beaverbrook Canadian Foundation studies in art history.
Description: Series statement: McGill-Queen's/Beaverbrook Canadian Foundation studies in art history | Includes bibliographical references and index.
Identifiers: Canadiana (print) 20260176621 | Canadiana (ebook) 20260176672 | ISBN 9780228028956 (hardcover) | ISBN 9780228029823 (PDF) | ISBN 9780228029571 (EPUB)
Subjects: LCSH: Idlout, Joseph. | LCSH: Inuit—Social life and customs—20th century. | LCSH: Inuit—Social life and customs—20th century—Pictorial works. | LCSH: Photographers—Canada, Northern—Biography. | LCSH: Inuit hunters—Canada, Northern—Biography. | LCGFT: Biographies.
Classification: LCC E99.E7 P195 2026 | DDC 779.092—dc23

This book was designed and typeset by Garet Markvoort, zijn digital, in 10.5/14 Nexus Serif Pro with Nexus Sans Pro and Nexus Typewriter Pro. Copyediting by Robert Lewis.

McGill-Queen's University Press
Suite 1720, 1010 Sherbrooke St West, Montreal, QC, H3A 2R7

Authorized safety representative in the EU: Mare Nostrum Group BV, Doelen 72, 4831 GR Breda, the Netherlands, gpsr@mare-nostrum.co.uk

This book is dedicated to the Idlout family
– past, present, and future.

In memory of Paul Ullatitaq Idlout
(21 April 1935 to 31 December 2025)

Contents

FOREWORD

An Idlout Family Legacy

Madeleine d'Argencourt

Joseph Idlout and Kidlak were my grandparents. Their example shows us how to be strong, how to be tough, how to do so much for others. My sister and brother, my cousins, and the next generations, we have all learned that from their legacy.

I am my grandmother Kidlak's namesake. My aunt Susan Salluviniq calls me "mother," and I call her "daughter." My uncles used to bring me country food and say, "Here, Mama, it's for you! It's your favourite part." I got to know my grandmother's favourite foods through my uncles. It was awesome. I never got to meet her because she died before I was born. But we share many traits: Kidlak was bossy. She was precise. She was tough. My grandfather would go out for six weeks hunting, and my grandmother, Kidlak, would be at home with ten kids. I'm the same. When I was the chair of boards and an executive director, I had to prove myself. Kidlak is the boss, I thought. I was named well. I'm glad I was named after her.

My mother, my uncles, and my aunts told me stories about their parents. When my mother, Leah, mentioned her parents, she would start crying. We are an oral culture. I want the oral tradition to continue.

My grandfather, Joseph Idlout, did so much not only for his own family but for others too. He was among the first Inuit to have a Peterhead boat. He travelled to Kalaallit Nunaat/Greenland. I was told my grandmother had the first sewing machine in the area.

Idlout was so proud of his camera. My mother told me that he ordered a camera through Doug Wilkinson. My grandfather wanted that specific kind of camera. He was obsessed with it. Doug brought up other stuff, too, that my grandfather would order through him. They would write to each other back and forth. My grandfather gave him the money and asked him to get a camera. My mother and my aunts and uncles told me that my grandfather loved taking photos.

Joseph Idlout was a revolutionary. He was fierce. Idlout had no fear of polar bears and no fear of white people. No *illira*. White people came to his house and shook his hand.

Our family – Aunt Susan, Uncle Paul, me, my sister, my brother, our cousins – we have no fear too. My sister Lucie is a well-known musician and passionate advocate for Inuit; my brother Guy is a senior manager in the Government of Nunavut, fighting for Inuit; cousin Lori Idlout is the member of Parliament for Nunavut; cousin Joshua Idlout is the mayor of Pond Inlet/Mittimatalik; Rachel Qitsualik is a writer (quoted in this book); and all the other family members are fearless too.

My grandparents would be proud. Our family story tells us about togetherness and being strong, about the importance of language, and about pride in our culture. We used to be a proud people. We have been beaten down like dogs. Now, we steer our own ship. We are the kind of people who are innovative and resourceful. That is our legacy.

Madeleine d'Argencourt was a senior manager in the Government of Nunavut for over twenty years. She was on the board of the Aboriginal People's Television Network for ten years, including serving as its youngest and only female Inuk chair. She has also served as chair of the Inuit Broadcasting Corporation, chair of the Nunavut Film Development Corporation, executive director of the Nunavut Association of Municipalities, and executive director of the Qulliit Nunavut Status of Women Council, among other accomplishments.

Acknowledgments

This book is a complement to the online exhibition *Ajjiliurlagit ("Let me take your picture"): The Photographs of Joseph Idlout* (located at https://www.josephidlout photographs.ca/en and https://www.josephidloutphotographs.ca/iu/home). Both honour the hunter Joseph Idlout's life and his photographs, bringing them to broader audiences among Inuit and Qallunaat (or southerners). At the same time, the book aims to answer the call from the Qikiqtani Truth Commission for greater education in the south and among Inuit about the time of rapid colonial disruption that took place beginning in the 1950s. This history is told here through Idlout's photographs and other images, his wife Kidlak's and his family's experiences, as well as through Inuit oral history. Archival records and the experiences of Qallunaat, particularly Doug Wilkinson, are a part of this story too. It is a multivocal and visualized history that has been developed with the help of many. I am pleased to be able to express my gratitude publicly to the many people who contributed to this book.

The Hunter, the Crown, and the Cameras is dedicated to the extended Idlout family, and I offer my heartfelt gratitude to them. Just as the book was going into production, Idlout and Kidlak's eldest son, Bishop Paul Ullatitaq Idlout, passed away. I also dedicate the book to Paul, an inspiring Inuit leader, and feel very fortunate that Christina Williamson and I had an opportunity to speak with Bishop Idlout. Thank you to Susan Salluviniq (Idlout and Kidlak's youngest daughter), Elijah Erkloo and Daniel Komangapik (who were adopted by Idlout's parents, Arnaujaq and Akumalik), and Joshua Idlout (one of Idlout's grandsons), all of whom spoke with me. Many thanks to Idlout's granddaughter Madeleine d'Argencourt, who wrote the foreword and has shared family history with me. I am further grateful to grandchildren Eric Idlaut, Guy d'Argencourt, and Lucie Idlout for information. In writing this book, I have also learned much from the writing of granddaughter Rachel Qitsualik, who is quoted in these pages. Special thanks to Alexandra Anaviapik, a biological great-granddaughter of Joseph Idlout, who facilitated interviews with great skill. Alexandra, Christina Williamson, and I spoke to several members of the Idlout family as well as to community members in Pond Inlet/Mittimatalik, including Jacob Anaviapik, Ruth Sangoya, and Solomon Awa. We also had the honour to speak with Ludy Pudluk (who grew up at Idlout's camp) and with Elisapee Ootoova, both now deceased. This book honours their memories too. There are, of course, many Idlout family members and community members I have not been able to engage with, but I hope that the exhibition and this book will be valuable resources for them as well.

I have had the great pleasure of collaborating with Inuk historian, curator, artist, and educator Augatnaaq Eccles on both the exhibition *Ajjiliurlagit* and chapter 3 of this book. Thank you, Augatnaaq! I have learned so much from you.

In order to privilege Inuit memory (and to draw public attention to Inuit resources), this book reproduces some Inuit oral history transcripts and publications. Thank you to Madeleine d'Argencourt for permission to reproduce her mother Leah Idlout d'Argencourt Paulson's writing in *Inuit Today* magazine. And thank you to Inuit Tapiriit Kanatami for permission to reproduce Leah's *Inuit Today* articles and Idlout's 1959 *Inuktitut Magazine* article.

Thank you to the Qikiqtani Inuit Association for permission to reproduce materials from the Qikiqtani Truth Commission's websites and publications. Thanks, too, to Philip Goldring, a historian working with Julie Harris and Contentworks for the commission, who read over chapter 1. Thanks to Marquise Lepage of Productions du Cerf-Volant, who also read and commented on chapter 1 and provided permission to reproduce material from the *Iqqaumavara* history project.

Privileging Inuit memory and restorying history with Inuit words has also meant providing material in Inuktitut syllabics for the publications reproduced here as well as translations into English. I am grateful to Rhoda Kayakjuak and Nellie Erkloo for their translations. Thank you.

Idlout's photographs – and many related research materials – are housed in the Nunavut Archives. I am grateful to the archives and particularly to its former chief archivist, the late Ed Atkinson. Ed provided support and encouragement throughout research for this project, ensuring that even during the Covid-19 pandemic, I was able to access research materials. He is sadly missed. Thanks also to his colleagues Sharon Angnakak and Caroline Forcier-Holloway for their help. Special thanks also go to Philippa Ootoowak, archivist at the Pond Inlet Library and Archives Society (PILAS) at the Nattinak Visitors Centre in Pond Inlet/Mittimatalik. Research materials will be deposited at both the Nunavut Archives and PILAS.

I have conducted research at several other institutions that have provided materials and guidance. Thanks to the Anglican Church of Canada Archives (Toronto), the Bank of Canada Archives and Museum (Ottawa), the Hudson's Bay Company Archives (at the Archives of Manitoba, Winnipeg), Library and Archives Canada (Ottawa), the National Film Board of Canada Archives (Montreal), the Scott Polar Research Institute's archives (University of Cambridge), and the University of Toronto Archives. Finally, I gratefully acknowledge resources provided by the Social History of the Eastern Arctic Database (compiled by Frank Tester, Peter Kulchyski, and Paule McNicoll) at the University of British Columbia.

This book and the exhibition would not have been possible without generous support. I gratefully acknowledge an Insight Grant from the Social Sciences and Humanities Research Council of Canada, which funded the development of the online exhibition, honoraria to Inuit partners, research assistants, and travel. For sage guidance on grantsmanship and collegiality, thanks to Darlene Gilson, Kristin Bourassa, and Heather Steel. In addition, a Marston LaFrance Fellowship from the Faculty of Arts and Social Sciences at Carleton University provided me with uninterrupted time to write and conduct research.

I have greatly benefited from the insights and work of several Carleton University students and former students who provided research assistance. Many thanks to Christina Williamson, who travelled with me to Pond Inlet/Mittimatalik and to Iqaluit while still a doctoral student, conducting interviews with Alexandra Anaviapik and me. Christina subsequently collaborated as a colleague, co-editing the volume *Atiqput: Inuit Oral History and Project Naming* (2022) with Beth Greenhorn, Deborah Kigjugalik Webster, and me. Augatnaaq Eccles was also a student when she began working on the associated exhibition and continued working on Idlout's photographs in co-writing chapter 3, as noted above. Thanks to Nicole Naher for writing the alt text for the figures. Finally, I have benefited greatly from the insightful assistance of Katie Lydiatt, Evangeline Mann, and Theresa McAvoy. Many thanks.

Friends and colleagues have generously shared information, insights, feedback, permissions, and conversation, as well as invitations to speak about this material. Thanks to Anne Bowker, Michael Bravo, Jill Carrick, Janne Cleveland, Nancy Duff, Sandra Dyck, Matthew Farish, Brian Foss, Mitchell Frank, Beth Greenhorn, Kenn Harper, Anna Hoefnagels, Catherine Khordoc, Andrea Kunard, Martha Langford, Amy Lonetree, Johanna Mizgala, Gabrielle Moser, Sarah Parsons, Ruth Phillips, Leslie Reid, Jordan Reznick, Jeff Thomas, Brenda Vellino, Deborah Kigjugalik Webster, Ezlyn Whitaker, and Christina Williamson. Special thanks to Ellen Waterman and Carol Williams for close readings of excerpts and for sage advice. During an early stage in writing, I received invaluable feedback from fellow members of the School for Studies in Art and Culture's writing group at Carleton University, Alexis Luko, Charles O'Brien, Aboubakar Sanogo, and Michael Windover. Final edits were made with the quiet camaraderie of colleagues in the Faculty of Arts and Social Sciences' Writing Together group. Thank you all.

I have presented aspects of this work at various gatherings, including at the Universities Art Association of Canada (2015, 2017), University College Dublin (2015), the Photographic History Research Centre at De Montfort University in Leicester (2016), the Arctic University of Norway in Tromsø (2017), the Nunavut Research Institute in Iqaluit (2018), Concordia University in Montreal (2018), Carleton University in Ottawa (2018, 2019, 2020), the Canadian Historical Association (2019, 2022), the College Art Association (2020), the Institut national d'histoire de l'art in Paris (2022), and the working group Visual Cultures of the Circumpolar North at the Jackman Humanities Institute, University of Toronto (2024). Many thanks to the organizers and to audience members for their feedback.

Small sections of the manuscript have been published, although in different formats. A few pages of the introduction, chapter 3, and chapter 7 appear in the online exhibition. Thanks to Kelly Craver of Katittut, a division of Atiigo Media of Iqaluit, for designing the exhibition. A portion of chapter 5 appears in a different format in "Inuit, the Crown, and Racialized Visuality: Photographs from the 1956 Canadian Governor General's Arctic Tour," *Photography and Culture* 15, no. 4 (2022): 353–75, https://www.tandfonline.com/doi/full/10.1080/17514517.2022.2096280. I thank the anonymous readers of this article for their feedback.

At McGill-Queen's University Press, I have once again been fortunate to work with editor-in-chief Jonathan Crago. Thank you, Jonathan, for your support and sage advice throughout. I am grateful, also, to the press's anonymous readers for the time and care that they took in reviewing the manuscript. Their informed feedback and suggestions have been invaluable. The manuscript has benefited greatly from Robert Lewis's meticulous edits and patience. Finally, my gratitude to Kathleen Fraser, managing editor, and to all of her colleagues.

In working on the book and exhibition, I have learned much from the extended Idlout clan about the power and grace of family memory. This lesson is one that has been particularly poignant to me during what has been a period of loss for my own family. Early in the research, both my mother and mother-in-law passed away, and then, in an unkind symmetry, the last period of work coincided with the passing of my father and two years later my father-in-law. I honour their memories here. Throughout this difficult period, I have been so fortunate to have the love and close friendships of my sisters, Susan, Mary Ellen, and Elizabeth, as well as of my sisters-in-law, Blayne and Anne. And above all, I thank John, Meg, Alice, and Greg for love and encouragement.

A Note on Language, Spelling, and Names

Throughout this book, I have aimed to use language and names that are preferred by Inuit.

Today, the Government of Nunavut and the national organization Inuit Tapiriit Kanatami use the overarching term Inuktut to describe the languages spoken in Nunavut and across Inuit Nunangat (Inuit homelands).[1] Here, I largely use the term Inuktitut since it is the language spoken in the Qikiqtani region, where most of the events described in this book take place. But I occasionally use the term Inuktut when describing languages across Inuit Nunangat. As an oral language that has several dialects and has been transcribed into written forms only relatively recently, Inuktitut has many variant spellings. For Inuit names, I use the spellings employed by the Idlout family and other Inuit whenever known so that they are represented as they prefer. In making this determination, identifications through Project Naming of unnamed individuals in archival photographs in the collection of Library and Archives Canada have also been helpful. I have made every effort to get it right; apologies if there remain spelling errors. However, when quoting historical sources, I employ their spellings.

In the cases of the key communities in Inuit Nunangat discussed here, I have again strived to use the preferred usage of community residents. Many communities across the Qikiqtani region, including the Nunavut capital Iqaluit, are now known only by their Inuktitut names. In these cases, I use the Inuktitut place name in discussions about the community today, often followed by the English name. When discussing these communities decades ago, for historical accuracy, I use their temporary European name following the Inuktitut name, as in "Iqaluit/Frobisher Bay." For other communities, Inuit residents today more commonly use the European (usually English) names developed by settlers. I have maintained this practice but added the Inuktitut name afterward. For example, two of the key communities discussed in these pages are presented, following community usage, as Pond Inlet/Mittimatalik and Resolute/Qausuittuq.

Finally, I use the words "Inuit" and "Inuk" – "the people" and "a person" in Inuktitut. These are the terms used by those at the heart of this book. But when quoting archival material, for historical accuracy, I use the language employed by southerners at the time; however, I do not endorse that usage.

THE HUNTER, THE CROWN, AND THE CAMERAS

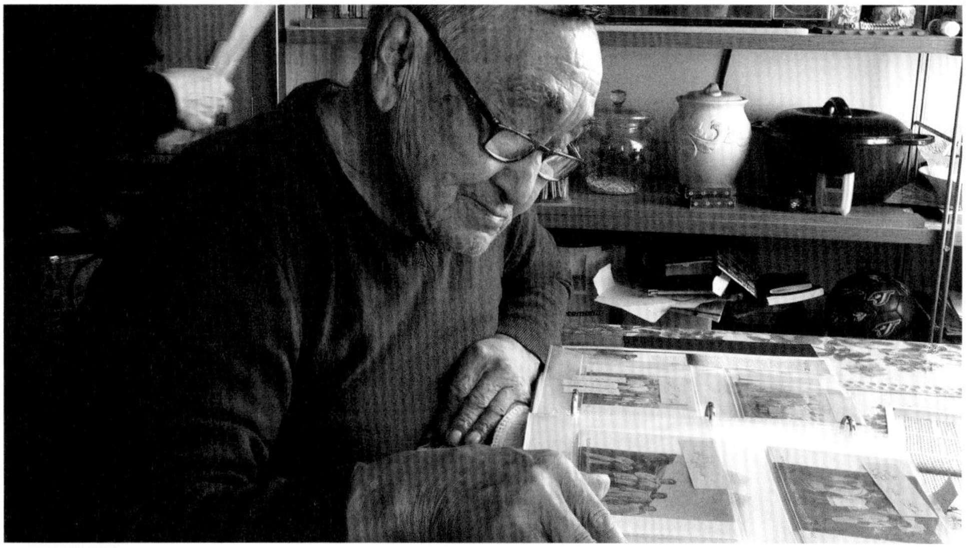

I.1 | Paul Ullatitaq Idlout, Apex, Baffin Island, May 2018. Photo: Christina Williamson.

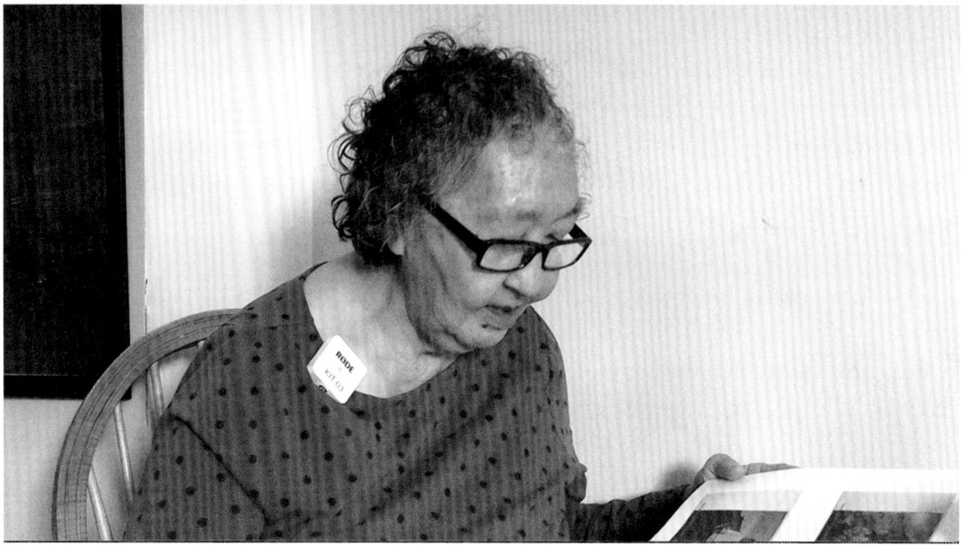

I.2 | Susan Salluviniq, Ottawa, April 2023. Video screen shot: Carol Payne and Augatnaaq Eccles.

INTRODUCTION

Joseph Idlout and the Image of Sangussaqtauliqtilluta

In 2018 and 2023, Inuit Elders Paul Ullatitaq Idlout and Susan Salluviniq pored over an album of photographs attributed to their father, the hunter Joseph Idlout (1912/13–1968). Both sat at kitchen tables while they leafed through the pages of an album filled with snapshots dating from 1951–58. Paul Ullatitaq Idlout was in his own kitchen in Apex, just outside of Iqaluit, sharing his recollections with historian Christina Williamson and me, whereas Paul's sister Susan sat at my kitchen table in Ottawa speaking with Inuk historian, curator, artist, and educator Augatnaaq Eccles and me (see figures I.1 and I.2).

The snapshots – some 300 in total, made with a mass-produced Kodak Duaflex camera – captivated the two Elders. Most of the pictures (about 232) represent life at Idlout's winter camp in Aulattivik on Curry Island near Eclipse Bay and at their spring camp in Nuvurulua about 50 kilometres west of Pond Inlet/Mittimatalik between 1951 and 1954.[1] These images form an intimate composite portrait of life at *ilagiit nunagivaktangat* (camp) in the years immediately before enforced settlement would dramatically change life for most Inuit, including Idlout's family (see figure I.3). In the snapshots, the twenty-nine members of the camp appear and reappear as familiar faces: Idlout's wife (Paul and Susan's mother), Kidlak,[2] most of their then eight children, and the other four family groups living together in the camp and visiting families from Arctic Bay/Ikpiarjuk. These pictures record the rhythms of life at camp, and in their attention to family, they visualize linked bonds, devotion to the environment, skill, and tradition. Other photographs from the same period focus on the collaborative drama of the hunt, demonstrating Idlout's and his community's prowess as hunters (see figure I.4). As Eccles and I discuss in these pages, Idlout's snapshots of camp illustrate Inuit cultural values, or Inuit Qaujimajatuqangit (IQ).

Other snapshots in the album picture southerners and visualize changes in Inuit culture. Visiting Qallunaat (as southerners, like me, are known in the Inuktitut language) also appear in the photographs from 1951 to 1954 (see figure I.5). They include officers of the Royal Canadian Mounted Police (RCMP) and staff of

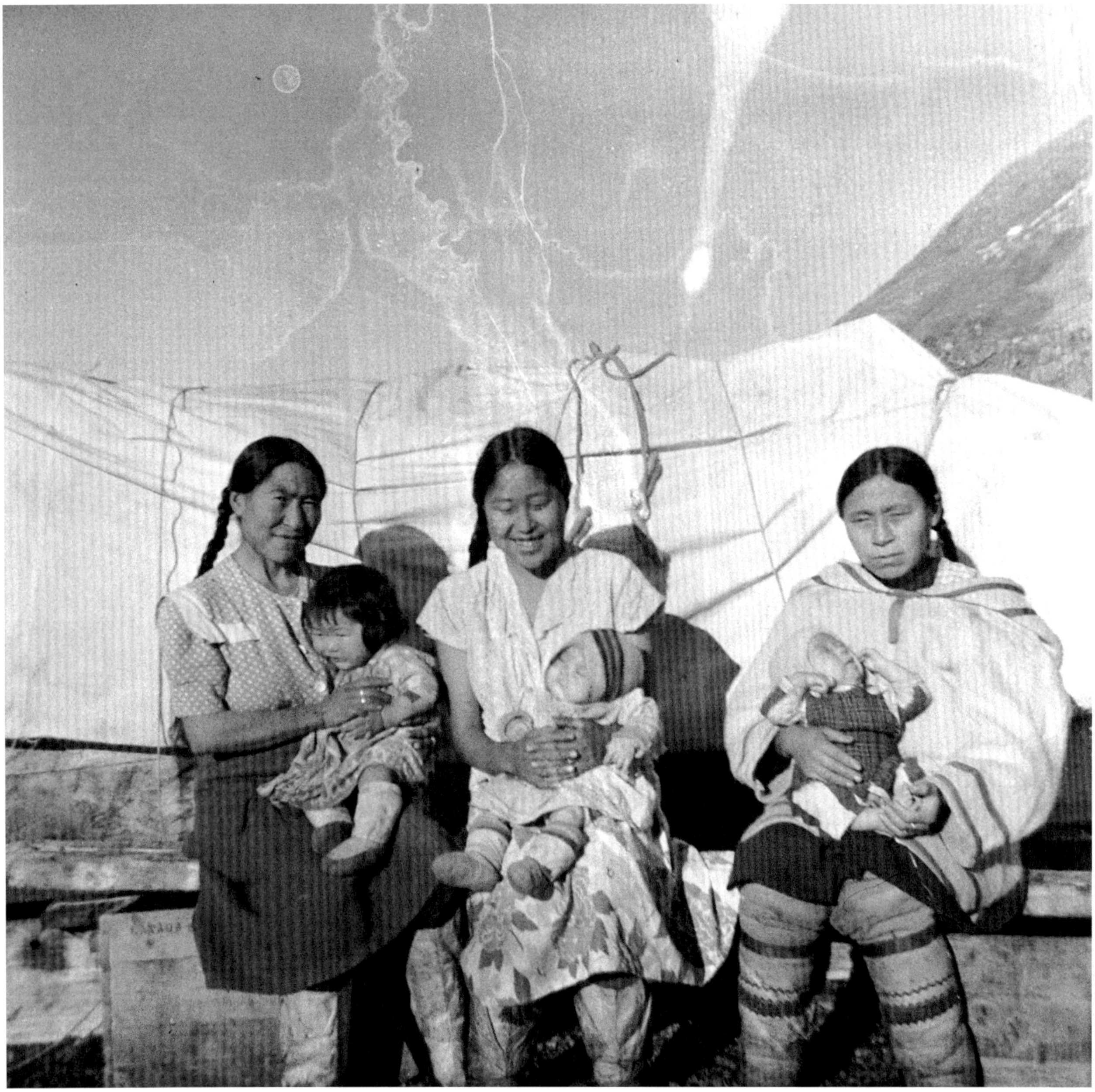

I.3 | New arrivals at Idlout's camp, Aulattivik, Eclipse Sound, North Baffin Island, June 1953. *Left to right*: Kidlak (Idlout's wife) with Ruth (Idlout's daughter), Rebecca (Idlout's daughter) with Rachael (Idlout's granddaughter), and Leetia (Kadluk's wife) with baby. A sod and wood house with canvas cover stands in the background. Photo: Joseph Idlout.

I.4 | Hunters cut up walrus on beach, Wollaston Islands shoreline, entrance to Navy Board Inlet, off Lancaster Sound, Bylot Island, September 1952. Photo: Joseph Idlout.

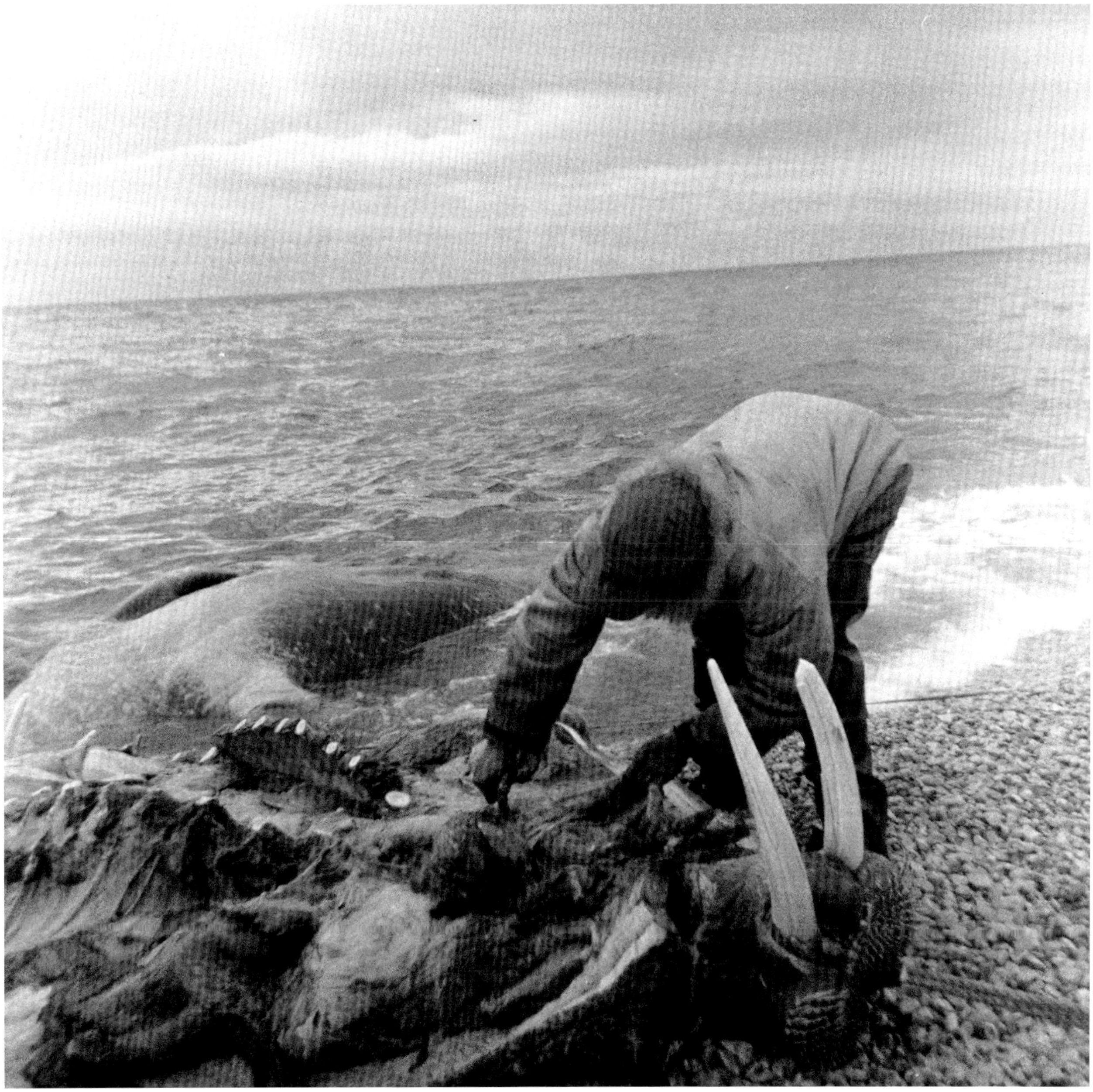

the Hudson's Bay Company, as well as Doug Wilkinson, the filmmaker, photographer, and Northern Service officer who first introduced Idlout to the camera and lived at his camp for several months. The 1950s, when the snapshots were taken, marked a period of accelerated contact and, with it, traumatizing changes in Inuit culture. This period is described by the Qikiqtani Truth Commission (QTC), the Inuit-led restorative justice body, with the Inuktitut word

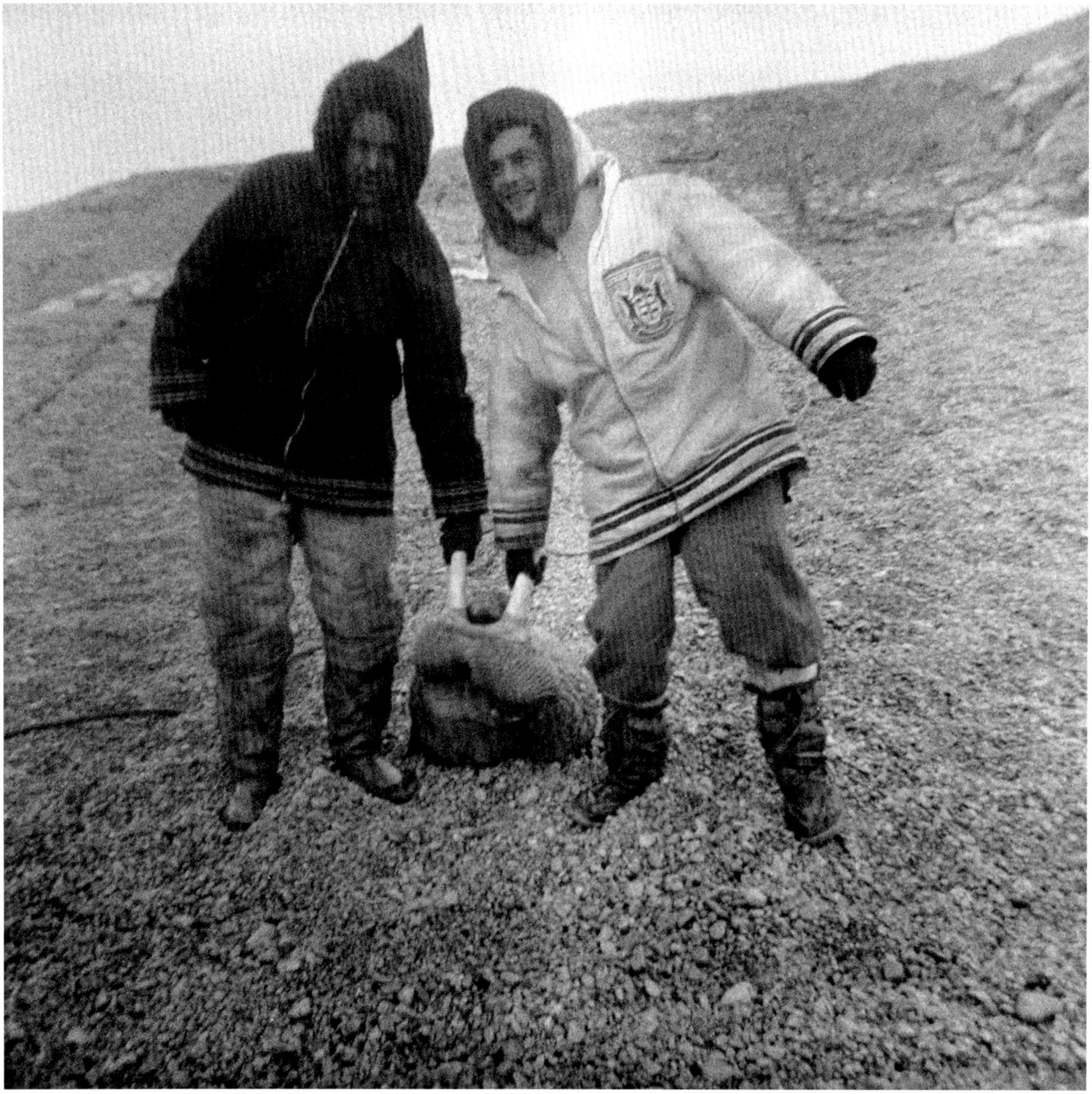

I.5 | Hunters carry walrus pieces to big boat on shore. Corporal Doug Moodie (RCMP) (*left*) and Bren Halloran (HBC), Wollaston Islands shoreline, entrance to Navy Board Inlet, off Lancaster Sound, Bylot Island, September 1952. Photo: Joseph Idlout.

I.6 | Four people posed for the camera in traditional Greenlandic Inuit clothing, Kalaallit Nunaat/Greenland, September 1958. Idlout travelled to settlements on the west coast of Kalaallit Nunaat/Greenland with nine other Canadian Inuit. The man in the centre is Charlie Smith of Aklavik, another delegate on the trip. Photo: Joseph Idlout.

"Sangussaqtauliqtilluta," translated as "disruption" or "the time when we started to be actively persuaded (or made to) detour (or switch modes)."[3]

The latest group of photographs, dating from 1958, venture farther into the circumpolar north. These dozens of photographs document a trip that Joseph Idlout took to Kalaallit Nunaat/Greenland (see figure I.6). Idlout and nine other Inuit men from across Inuit Nunangat were delegates on the trip sponsored by the Canadian Department of Northern Affairs and National Resources (DNANR). Idlout's camera fixed on the sights and peoples he encountered, connecting with

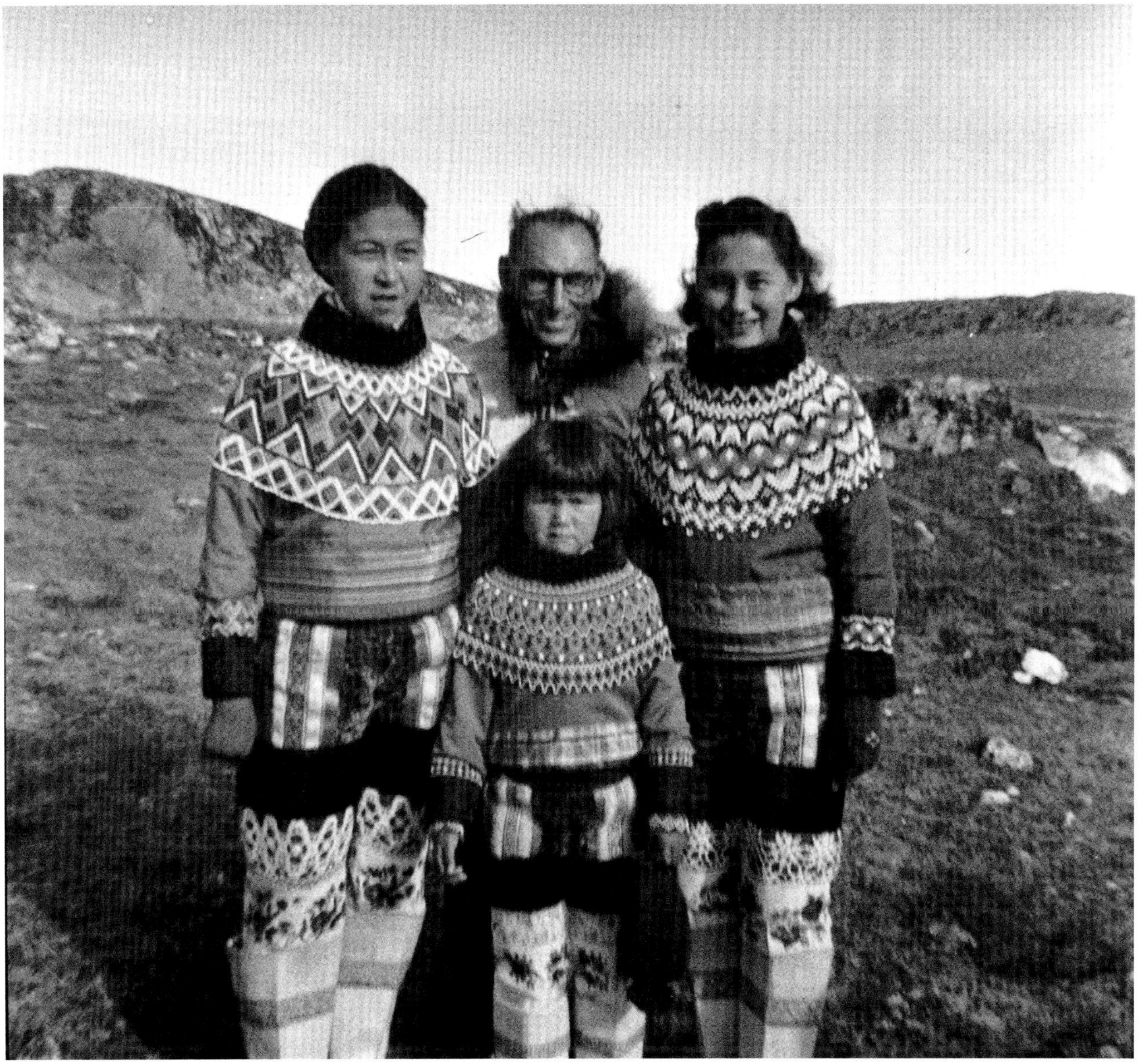

Greenlandic Inughuit, Tunumiit, and Kalaallit communities and contemplating the future.

Cameras had been present throughout Paul Ullatitaq Idlout's and Susan Salluviniq's childhoods and youths. Indeed, Idlout and his camp were portrayed in hundreds of photographs as well as films made by southerners and circulated globally. Most were taken by Doug Wilkinson for southern and international audiences. During one of his visits, Wilkinson brought Idlout the Kodak camera that had shot these images. For Idlout's camp – and perhaps for Inuit more broadly – cameras became both a tool of expression within the community and a form of intercultural contact with the south. During the 1970s, Idlout's daughter Leah, then the editor of *Inuit Today* magazine, published several of the hunter's photographs, as reproduced in this volume.[4]

Yet, as familiar as they were with photographic images of Idlout's camp in the 1950s, the two Elders – Idlout's eldest son and youngest daughter – had not seen many of these snapshots before or had not seen them in years. Viewing these images, they revisited long-lost family members and witnessed terrains that were central to their lives and family stories while witnessing their father's travels further afield. Paul Ullatitaq Idlout, Joseph Idlout's eldest child, was visible in dozens of images. In looking at the photographs, he was transported to his youth and life at camp. Susan, years younger, renewed stories of her family before their relocation in Resolute/Qausuittuq. The photographs sparked and animated memories – just as their recollections transformed the photographs themselves. Paul's and Susan's encounters were experiences in relationality, so central to Inuit and other Indigenous worldviews.[5] These photographs also demonstrate how the photographic image itself can be, in Elizabeth Edwards's terms, a "relational object" alongside material objects and social actors in a dynamic network of connections and interactions across time.[6]

Paul Ullatitaq Idlout's and Susan Salluviniq's encounters with these photographs in 2018 and 2023 crystallize many of the key issues addressed in this book. *The Hunter, the Crown, and the Cameras* tells the story of Sangussaqtauliqtilluta through images and through Inuit oral history. It is a study of intercultural exchange and a critique of settler colonialism focused on visual encounters between Inuit and Qallunaat during the tumultuous period of the 1950s and 1960s as well as its aftermath. At the centre of the book is Joseph Idlout. His life and his relationship with Doug Wilkinson are recounted through camera images, oral history, and archival documents. This book gathers the words of family and community members through oral histories and by reproducing articles written by Joseph Idlout himself and by Leah Idlout d'Argencourt Paulson, Idlout's daughter and the sister of Paul and Susan. These articles also include photographs by Joseph Idlout. I argue that attending to the visual and oral history record is an effective way to restory the past from Inuit perspectives, an approach that offers a methodology for settlers (like me) to respectfully share this history. In recounting a difficult history in a visualized and multivocal way,

I aim to answer the Qikiqtani Truth Commission's call for greater education in the south and among Inuit about the changes that took place during this period. Throughout, Joseph Idlout is the focus.

Joseph Idlout, Doug Wilkinson, the Camera, and Colonial Contact

It should come as no surprise that Joseph Idlout became a skilled photographer: he was, after all, probably the most extensively photographed and filmed Inuk of his time. Appearing in widely circulated documentary films (including a feature film and several newsreels) and in hundreds of photographs, Idlout became the face of Inuit culture for southern Canadians during the 1950s and afterward.[7] The experiences of performing for southern cameras taught Idlout, his family, and his extended community much about visuality both as a way to express Inuit culture and as a form of cultural contact with southerners. In turn, these photographs say much about both Idlout's own community and about his relations with outsiders, as his children Paul Ullatitaq Idlout and Susan Salluviniq discovered.

Idlout was certainly not the only Inuk photographing at this time. The best-known and most prolific contemporary Inuk photographer was Peter Pitseolak (1902–1973). Pitseolak first photographed around Kinngait/Cape Dorset in the 1930s, acquiring his own camera in the 1940s.[8] Today, about 2,000 photographs by Pitseolak are known, many made in collaboration with his second wife, Aggeok.[9] By the 1950s, it was not uncommon for Inuit, mainly Inuit men, to have cameras.[10] In 1958, the DNANR, the federal agency overseeing Inuit Nunangat at the time, published a guide for visiting southerners complete with a cover illustration of an Inuk man photographing.[11] Often cameras were gifted to Inuit men by visiting southerners.[12] The camera was, it seems, given as a form of transactional exchange like guns and boats; and as with such hunting equipment, exchanged cameras were often gendered masculine and coded in terms of class and fluency in southern culture. Yet Inuit photographers adapted the southern technology of the camera to Inuit culture.

Joseph Idlout's Kodak, too, was a gendered and culturally loaded item of exchange. As Idlout's granddaughter Madeleine d'Argencourt writes in the foreword to this book, the hunter asked Doug Wilkinson to bring him a camera from the south in 1951. Wilkinson, who worked and lived in Inuit Nunangat for years, maintained a long-standing and close association with Idlout. The southerner stayed at Idlout's camp for two extended periods in the early 1950s and maintained a correspondence with Idlout for years. Their relationship was forged through cameras. Idlout was the featured performer in Wilkinson's 1952 film *Land of the Long Day* as well as in newsreels, and he appeared in hundreds of still photographs shot by the southerner.[13] Wilkinson taught the Inuk hunter how to operate cameras – not just his own Kodak Duaflex but also a 16 mm movie camera – and the two apparently photographed side by side. The core section of this book takes their complex relationship – built on mutual dependence and respect yet deeply inequitable – as a case study of how visuality played a role in the entangled histories of Inuit and settlers in the Qikiqtani region during the 1950s and 1960s. It underscores how the camera was a tool for Idlout to express his own culture.

Photographs credited to Idlout are historically and culturally significant statements about Inuit life during the tumultuous period of the 1950s in the Qikiqtani region. As Augatnaaq Eccles and I argue in chapter 3, they demonstrate how Idlout and his community asserted not only their own culture – including values associated with Inuit Qaujimajatuqangit – but also their presence in negotiations between southern settler society and Inuit culture. Moreover, they recover an embodied Indigenous visual narrative on which to build Inuit stories and culture today, a visual record that – as I try to show in this book – responds to and counters southern pictorial treatments of Inuit life. In short, Idlout's photographs assert Inuit culture in direct, affecting ways that cannot be reduced to metaphors or solely seen as counternarratives of southern histories.[14] Yet these images also remain entangled with the south. In particular, they are inseparable from Idlout's close relationship with Doug Wilkinson. And, as with the relational and transhistorical nature of photographic meaning, questions of cultural entanglement remain relevant today. Indeed, I – a Qallunaaq researcher – am also entangled in these complex cultural dynamics.

Collaboration and Critique: The Larger Research Project and the Role of this Book

Although I am the principal author of this book, *The Hunter, the Crown, and the Cameras* is not only based on research collaboration but is also, as will become evident, committed to a critique of settler colonialism. It builds on my experiences as a Qallunaaq researcher who for two decades has had the privilege to work collaboratively with Inuit on photo-based history projects. For much of that time, I have been an affiliate of Project Naming, the photo-based Inuit history research program established by the Inuit school Nunavut Sivuniksavut in cooperation with Library and Archives Canada (LAC).[15] Hundreds of Inuit participants – often working across generations – have identified Inuit in archival photographs from LAC's collection, reclaiming Inuit knowledge and culture while pushing for change in official colonial archives.[16] This work culminated in a 2022 publication featuring twelve Inuit contributors, *Atiqput: Inuit Oral History and Project Naming*, which I co-edited with Beth Greenhorn, Deborah Kigjugalik Webster, and Christina Williamson.[17] I have subsequently worked collaboratively with anthropologist and knowledge keeper Deborah Kigjugalik Webster on other research projects.[18] My involvement in all of these collaborations has been inspired by the example of Onondaga photographer and curator Jeff Thomas, with whom I have collaborated.[19] I have also been inspired by Idlout's late daughter Leah Idlout d'Argencourt Paulson, whom I interviewed some twenty years ago and whose generous discussion of southern archival photographs of her community taught me much about how cultural positioning shapes visual perception.[20] Her words appear throughout this book in selections from her writing for the magazine *Inuit Today* and in other references. Learning from Jeff and Leah as well as participating in collaborations and community-engaged projects have shaped my understanding of recent histories recounted from the perspectives of Inuit and other Indigenous communities, and Indigenous perspectives have enlarged my own critiques of settler colonialism.

The research project from which this book emerges has two broad goals reflecting this formation. First, it aims to make photographs credited to Idlout widely accessible to Inuit communities – including, importantly, Idlout's descendants. The second goal of the research is rooted in the more conventional practice of a southern academic: to undertake a critical examination of Inuit and settler intercultural, visual encounters in the eastern Canadian Arctic during and since the 1950s and 1960s. Here, my decision to centre Idlout's experience as a maker of images and the subject of a southern gaze was influenced by all that I had learned from discussing his photographs with members of his family and other Inuit. Both goals are community-engaged, involving Idlout's family and community members in Pond Inlet/Mittimatalik as well as the Nunavut Archives. Throughout both aspects of the research, Augatnaaq Eccles also influenced my approach.

The first goal – rendering Idlout's photographs accessible – has culminated in the online exhibition *Ajjiliurlagit ("Let me take your picture"): The Photographs of Joseph Idlout*.[21] The exhibition was created in response to the interest of Idlout's family in making these historic photographs more widely accessible. The exhibition features Idlout's photography from the Nunavut Archives, which also encouraged the project to bring this part of its collection to many Inuit. Adopting an online format and making texts available in Inuktitut syllabics as well as English expanded the exhibition's accessibility. The online format was designed by Kelly Craver of Katittut, a division of Atiigo Media, an Inuit-owned design firm based in Iqaluit.

Augatnaaq Eccles and I collaborated on the online exhibition over a period of about eighteen months. At the time, Augatnaaq was a history student at Carleton University with experience as a curator and researcher. She has since been a teacher at Nunavut Sivuniksavut, an Ottawa-based Inuit post-secondary school, and in Rankin Inlet/Kangiqtiniq. Together, we selected images and drew on reflections from family members to illuminate Idlout's work.[22] Our organization of the exhibition followed a curatorial framework developed by Inuk art historian Heather Igloliorte, in which works are seen through the lens of the Inuit knowledge system known as Inuit Qaujimajatuqangit.[23] As discussed in chapter 3, which Augatnaaq and I co-authored, IQ provides a way of understanding how Inuit culture informed image making for Idlout. In the chapter, we also draw on the work of Rachel Qitsualik, one of Idlout's granddaughters and a knowledge keeper, author, and translator. In an essay on concepts of sovereignty, Qitsualik provides a holistic view of Inuit culture that complements IQ. The exhibition also includes an educational component, designed by Augatnaaq for teachers and students in Nunavut. In this way, we aim to bridge cultures, geography, and generations through images, texts, and pedagogical design.

The Hunter, the Crown, and the Cameras marks the second component of the larger research program. It has been edited and written to complement the online exhibition. Like the exhibition, while privileging Inuit voices throughout, this book features Joseph Idlout's photographs as well as images made of him. Grounded in community engagement, the book shows how cameras and camera-made images – photographs and films, in particular – were both forms for visualizing Inuit culture and points of contact between Inuit and the south: camera technology and representations may be understood both as tools of colonial control and as means of resistance and negotiation across time. The visual argument is supported by Inuit assertions. Published texts from the 1950s to the 1970s written by Joseph Idlout and his daughter Leah, which include photographs by Idlout, are reproduced throughout the book. Oral history accounts – gathered from interviews conducted for the exhibition and book or from other projects – build the narrative.

The book's materials have been compiled for audiences interested in Inuit cultural history, colonial critique, and visual culture. My hope is that the readership will include Inuit and other Indigenous scholars and students as well as non-Indigenous southern scholars and students. The material gathered and discussed here intentionally engages with decolonial discussions, proposing a hybrid methodology for historical analysis by combining visual culture analyses, oral history, collaborative work, and archival research. Importantly, as noted above, this restorying of the historical record responds to the Qikiqtani Truth Commission's call for increased education about the changes that took place in Inuit lives between the 1950s and 1970s.

As a whole, this book traces the entangled histories of Inuit and settlers in the Qikiqtani region during the 1950s and into the 1960s through camera-made images and the concept of visuality more broadly, while also following their transhistorical reception and the legacy of imaging the region today. Images made by Idlout and Wilkinson provide the key case studies, but the book also explores other individuals' images and texts that include Idlout and Wilkinson. Here, I focus on the 1950s – with some material related to the 1960s – a period that witnessed a remarkable acceleration of southern-Inuit interactions at all levels. The narrative geographically addresses the Qikiqtani region of present-day Nunavut and, more specifically, Joseph Idlout's communities around Pond Inlet/Mittimatalik and Resolute/Qausuittuq as a group that negotiated extensively with the south. I explore the broad changes in these areas and the corresponding resistance, as well as demonstrations of the resilience of Inuit culture.

At its core, this book concerns a period of "aggressive assimilation"[24] when Inuit were rapidly integrated – coerced – into the southern culture, often with disastrous results. Visuality, I show, played a role in the Inuit-Qallunaat entanglement of this period.

The first and most important guides to this history and its legacy come from Inuit communities themselves. Joseph Idlout's descendants – his son Paul Ullatitaq Idlout, his daughter Susan Salluviniq, his grandchildren and great-grandchildren as well as Inuit community members – have shared insights into this work. Among them, Alexandra Anaviapik, Joseph Idlout's biological great-granddaughter, played a particularly important role early on as part of the research team that liaised with the community and engaged in interviews, several conducted with historian Christina Williamson and me. Madeleine d'Argencourt, Lucie Idlout, and Eric Idlaut, three of Joseph's grandchildren, also provided invaluable advice and connections. Madeleine also wrote the powerful foreword to this book. The 2013 reports of the Qikiqtani Truth Commission (as discussed in chapter 1), the 2019 report of the National Inuit Strategy on Research Roundtable, prepared by Inuit Tapiriit Kanatami, and the 2007 guide *Negotiating Research Relationships with Inuit*, published by Inuit Tapiriit Kanatami and the Nunavut Research Institute, all provide models for ethical research that are culturally specific to Inuit and to Inuit relationships with southerners, like myself.[25] Inuit Qaujimajatuqangit and its eight principles are key guides to understanding this period and specifically Idlout's own images. "Inummarik: Self-Sovereignty in Classic Inuit Thought" (2013), an essay by Idlout's granddaughter Rachel Qitsualik, provides a holistic view of Inuit culture that informs the material here.[26] Accordingly, the book's narrative privileges Inuit oral and visual accounts. Joseph Idlout's own photographs, as well as his and his communities' gazes back at southerners and southern cameras, are central to the story told here. Indeed, one of my key arguments revolves around the importance of visuality as a complex and multidirectional circuit of Inuit cultural history. In addition to the richness of visuality, the history of this period is also told by Inuit throughout the book, which features seven little-known publications by the Idlout family: two published accounts written by Joseph Idlout in the late 1950s and early 1960s as well as five articles published by Idlout's daughter Leah Idlout d'Argencourt Paulson in the mid-1970s. Other sources, including testimonies from the Qikiqtani Truth Commission (2007–10), the *Iqqaumavara* history project (2014), and the Royal Commission on Aboriginal Peoples (1994), complement these published accounts by Idlout and family, as do recent interviews with Elders conducted either by Alexandra Anaviapik, Christina Williamson, and me or by Augatnaaq Eccles and me, as well as written correspondence and texts by Idlout and members of his family and community contained in archival records. More indirectly, I have also gathered Inuit accounts in archival material and images by listening intently for Inuit voices between the lines and through the images.[27] The book includes extensive references to and excerpts from visual, archival, and published historical records pertaining to Idlout's family and community and, more broadly, records sensitive to the management of Inuit Nunangat. Here, Douglas Wilkinson's records from the Nunavut Archives have been particularly important. But governmental records and other sources, including Hudson's Bay Company documents and missionaries' correspondence, are also woven into this story to foreground the complex cultural exchange that occurred during these years.[28] These disparate sources are brought together through "local storytelling," which – in Natalie Zemon Davis's classic terms – holds the possibility of "decentring" univocal historical authority.[29]

Joseph Idlout – the hunter of this book's title – is the central protagonist. He appears throughout as a performer and a maker of images as well as a cultural leader and a person impacted greatly by southern interventions. His family, community, and descendants also look back at the south within images and across the generations. Qallunaat appear, too, as contacts – both those with whom Idlout and his family closely interacted (like Doug Wilkinson) and more distant institutional and governmental authorities engaged personally and institutionally with Inuit, often through visualized forms. In examining these fraught relationships, this book offers a critical history of settler colonialism in Canada by examining visuality in the Qikiqtani region during the 1950s through the 1960s and by considering the long history of how Qallunaat-Inuit relationships have been viewed since then.[30] I argue that a close examination of visuality – visual representations, the gaze, and the visual as a form of social organization – exposes colonialist, racialized control of Inuit Nunangat while revealing the ways that Inuit refuted power through their actions and by returning the gaze. This approach and the material included here open historical analysis to multiple perspectives. At the same time, this book is specific and local: it tells Idlout's story – through images – to honour his life and that of his descendants.

Like the online exhibition *Ajjiliurlagit*, this book also constitutes a way for Qallunaat to work with and contribute to Inuit communities meaningfully and respectfully. As noted above, it foregrounds Inuit knowledge while pairing it with archival research. Inuit approaches to the past, particularly as articulated by the Qikiqtani Truth Commission, guide the structure of the work. In short, similar to the exhibition *Ajjiliurlagit*, this book is deeply informed by collaborations that centre Inuit voices and visions. In the broad context of efforts to understand and redress a difficult history and to respectfully advocate for and with Inuit culture, I believe that there is a role for Qallunaat analysis and historical investigation expressed in scholarly writing. Research and writing are contributions that settlers (like me) can make to furthering the aims of redress and advocacy. The work of decolonization and decolonial criticism is substantial and requires the respectful and supportive involvement of settlers as well as the input of Indigenous communities, particularly in writing histories of periods of prolonged encounter and cultural change. This book is the modest way that I have tried to share some of this work. It has been written, in part, to suggest ways that other settlers might also contribute. In short, this book aims not only to critically restory histories of a period previously framed by southern perspectives but also to propose a methodology that bridges visuality and Inuit oral history while reintroducing the Idlout archival resources for use by Inuit communities.

Sangussaqtauliqtilluta: A History of Disconnections and Disruption

Canada must acknowledge its past history of shameful treatment of Aboriginal peoples. It must acknowledge its racist legacy. It should not only acknowledge these facts, but also take steps to make sure that the country's history books reflect these realities ... Canadians must understand that their leaders had assimilation policies designed to kill Aboriginal cultures and traditions. In reference to Inuit, the *Report of the Royal Commission on Aboriginal Peoples* quoted an unnamed federal administrator as writing in a 1952 report, "Their civilization, because it is without hope of advancement, should be ruthlessly discouraged."
– John Amagoalik, 2012[31]

Although *The Hunter, the Crown and the Cameras* adopts a model of historical analysis that emphasizes Inuit contestation and reception across time, it is rooted temporally in the decades of the 1950s and 1960s. As Inuk leader John Amagoalik states above, this period advanced a "racist legacy" of assimilationist policies that have had devastating effects on Inuit and other Indigenous peoples across generations and into the present. In addressing this period, termed the "Sangussaqtauliqtilluta" by the Qikiqtani Truth Commission – particularly in chapter 1's detailed history narrated through Elders' testimonies – I respond to Amagoalik's call for history to "reflect these realities" of enforced assimilation, racism, and acculturation.

During the postwar years, particularly beginning in the 1950s, Inuit in the region came into more regular and sustained contact with southerners than they had in the preceding decades. In 1953, for example, the Canadian government, under Prime Minister Louis St-Laurent, established the Department of Northern Affairs and National Resources. As archivist Terry Cook has argued,[32] this administrative restructuring marked a significant shift, with St-Laurent intoning at the time that the departmental administration had moved its "centre of gravity ... north."[33] Indeed, by the mid-1950s, a southern presence in the north had rapidly escalated into what historian Philip Goldring terms a "more 'centralized' pattern" of contact established by the Canadian federal government.[34] That decade witnessed the rapid, often enforced, integration of Inuit into southern Canadian life, heightened by national economic interest in extracting resources from Arctic regions and by increased military and defensive activity in the Arctic in response to Cold War tensions. Inuit of the eastern Arctic experienced these external policies and programs through such dramatic changes as the removal of hundreds of Inuit to medical facilities in the south, the establishment of a cash economy, governmental administration of daily life, the mass conversion of Inuit (particularly by the Anglican and Catholic churches), the imposition of mandatory residential or federal day schools for Inuit children (led by government and church), the establishment of settled communities, and the relocation of several families – including Idlout's own – from Hudson's Bay and North Baffin Island to the High Arctic.

As Patrick Wolfe has argued, "Territoriality is settler colonialism's specific, irreducible element."[35] Yet, in Inuit Nunangat during the period addressed in this study, settler-colonial territoriality took distinctive forms.[36] The region was not extensively "settled" by outsiders; instead, often from a distance, government, military, and economic interests claimed territory in the region and domain over the lives of Inuit, in part through, paradoxically, moving Inuit themselves into settlements, where they were overseen by government agents. Practices of visuality – including photographs, films, and other forms of visual representation as well as the gaze and the surveillance of Inuit by southern authorities – supported southern assertions of control.[37]

The chief of the DNANR's Arctic Division at the time, R.A.J. Phillips, stated in 1957 that the government was trying "to hasten the day when in every respect the Eskimos can take their own places in the new kind of civilization which we – and they – are building in their country."[38] Here, Phillips – like other southern administrators – cloaked colonial authority and paternalism in the language of care.[39] This so-called "new kind of civilization" amounted to a relentless program of assimilation that within a few short years had transformed most Inuit in the region from nomadic hunters living in dispersed small family groups into sedentary members of a small number of settlements reliant on governmental assistance.[40] It was, as John Amagoalik intones, a "shameful treatment of Aboriginal peoples."

In this book, I try to strike a balance that acknowledges the historic fact of these injustices without letting them define the historical accounting expressed by Idlout, his family, and his community. In this way, I attend to Unangax scholar Eve Tuck's injunction to avoid "damage-centered research."[41] For Tuck, such research "operates, even benevolently, from a theory of change that establishes harm or injury in order to achieve reparation." It "looks to historical exploitation, domination, and colonization to explain contemporary brokenness, such as poverty, poor health, and low literacy. Common sense tells us this is a good thing, but the danger in damage-centered research is that it is a pathologizing approach in which the oppression singularly defines a community."[42] For Tuck, "damage-centered" research is rooted in a "theory of change" in which damage is documented in order to force accountability.[43] Addressing her comments to Indigenous communities, she acknowledges that "it is a powerful idea to think of [Indigenous peoples] as litigators, putting the world on trial, but *does it actually work*? Do the material and political wins come through? And, most importantly, are the wins worth the long-term costs of *thinking of ourselves as damaged*?"[44] Tuck recognizes that "particularly in Native communities, there was a need for research that exposed the uninhabitable, inhumane conditions in which people lived and continue to live," but she argues "that a time for a shift has come, that damage-centered narratives are no longer sufficient." [45] Instead, Tuck proposes "depathologizing work" focused on desires that are "concerned with understanding complexity, contradiction, and the self-determination of lived lives."[46]

Throughout this book, I report on how the "complexity, contradiction, and the self-determination" of Inuit lives may be gleaned in part through attention to the force of the returned gaze. This gaze is evident implicitly in representations of Idlout and his community in photographs and films (largely shot by Wilkinson) as well as evident in the archival record produced by Inuit. But more explicitly, Idlout's own photographs indicate an alternative vision and an assertion of agency. I have also structured the book to privilege contemporary Inuit voices, signalling how the issues addressed in these pages are still felt strongly today. Indeed, this story of colonial contestation in the Arctic is remarkably relevant in the 2020s as Canada and the world once again shift their "centre of gravity ... north."[47] In 2021, Canada installed Inuk journalist and Inuit rights activist Mary Simon as its first Indigenous governor general. Mary Simon's presence has increased awareness of Inuit culture widely, even during a fraught time when Arctic sovereignty, particularly in Kalaallit Nunaat/Greenland, has been threatened.

Writing Visual Culture in the North

The camera and other devices of visualization and display – technologies enlisted to aid the forced assimilation of Inuit and claims of Canadian national sovereignty over the Arctic – were witnesses to the dramatic changes that occurred during the Sangussaqtauliqtilluta period and have provided us with important historical records. Indeed, southern Canadian officials, who developed and instituted many of these changes, often knew of the Arctic, at least initially, solely through media, including visual media. For example, in his speech announcing the establishment of the DNANR, Prime Minister St-Laurent talked about being "quite impressed by what I have read and seen in films about the Eskimos."[48] He was not alone. Southern settlers were often introduced to Inuit culture through visual forms, and these representations shaped official attitudes and governmental programs. As I contend throughout this study, political and cultural tensions over the Arctic played out at this time in part through fields of visualization. These interventions included aerial mapping and radar technology employed by the US and Canadian militaries for the Distant Early Warning Line – what the US Army termed the "eyes and ears" of American defence – the designs of settled communities, displays like the DNANR's 1955 exhibition *Meet the North*, as well as ethnographic film and promotional photography commissioned by the Canadian government or produced through commercial media. Although visual art produced in the Qikiqtani region, particularly in Kinngait/

Cape Dorset, is the subject of a rich body of literature (as discussed below), the broader concept of visuality in the Arctic has not been explored extensively.

The Hunter, the Crown, and the Cameras builds on a multidisciplinary body of commentary and research about the period of Sangussaqtauliqtilluta in the Arctic, including visual media. Most important among this literature are oral histories conducted with Inuit Elders, including those gathered by the Qikiqtani Truth Commission.[49] Compiling oral histories has become a priority among many Inuit and southern researchers across Inuit Nunangat as a key means of maintaining cultural tradition and fostering Inuktitut language retention.[50] Consequently, as I have noted, these efforts are also political since these sources assert Inuit epistemologies – through the principles of Inuit Qaujimajatuqangit or traditional Inuit knowledges – over southern ways of knowing.[51] Although it is beyond the scope of this book to survey all Inuit oral history projects, I draw on several that are representative and that will lead the reader to more of the important oral history work undertaken in Inuit Nunangat. They include interviews that Alexandra Anaviapik, Christina Williamson, and I conducted with Elders in Iqaluit and Pond Inlet/Mittimatalik in 2018 as well as a more recent interview with Idlout's daughter Susan Salluviniq that Augatnaaq Eccles and I conducted. All interviews were centred on photographs credited to Joseph Idlout. In addition, testimony from the extensive oral histories gathered under the auspices of the QTC and the *Iqqaumavara* project opens the book, and Elders' responses to Idlout's photographs close it. The core of the book also regularly cites these observations as well as oral histories as key sources of historical information. In these ways, my aim is to prioritize Inuit accounts of the period. I also draw on several models for this work. For example, Julie Cruikshank's groundbreaking work in the western Arctic exemplifies oral history among Indigenous Elders in the north generally,[52] Emilie Cameron's subtle analyses of settler narratives about Inuit history inform the study,[53] Keavy Martin's innovative writing on the Inuit oral storytelling tradition as a literary form provides specific guide for addressing the Elders' stories discussed here, [54] and the Inuit Literatures website, developed by Daniel Chartier, makes available a wide array of sources.[55] My experience in working with Inuit oral histories was honed during my affiliation with Project Naming and while co-editing *Atiqput: Inuit Oral History and Project Naming* (2022).[56]

Also invaluable to this work has been a now-extensive body of scholarly and popular literature addressing the difficult history of the 1950s and 1960s in the Qikiqtani region and Inuit Nunangat broadly. The historical research led by historian Julie Harris of Contentworks for the Qikiqtani Truth Commission provides not only a wealth of information but also a model of collaborative research that bridges testimony and empirical historical research.[57] Frank Tester and Peter Kulchyski's volumes on Inuit relocations in the eastern Arctic and on game management are essential sources for any study of this period,[58] as are Alan Rudolph Marcus's histories of relocation and publications by Shelagh

D. Grant and P. Whitney Lackenbauer, among many others.[59] An indispensable resource has been Kenn Harper's work, notably "Taissumani," his periodic column for *Nunatsiaq News*.[60] My study is equally informed by a rich body of interdisciplinary literature, including approaches and insights emerging from Inuit studies, particularly in relation to anthropology and its critiques.[61] Recent interdisciplinary historical literature on the Arctic and colonial imaginaries has also provided important insights.[62]

As a study addressing visuality in the Arctic, *The Hunter, the Crown, and the Cameras*, of course, benefits greatly from scholarship on Inuit visual culture. The extensive literature on Inuit art examines the body of Inuit culture best known in the south and, therefore, offers important historical perspectives and critiques of settler engagement with art production.[63] Prominent among recent publications are Inuk art historian Heather Igloliorte's discussion of Inuit art and curation, Christine Lalonde's monograph on artist Pitseolak Ashoona, Norman Vorano's discussion of Inuit art's relation to the modern, the volume *Qummut Qukiria!* (2022), edited by Anna Hudson, Heather Igloliorte, and Jan-Erik Lundström, and a wealth of recent Inuit-led curatorial initiatives.[64] However, I want to be clear that this book is *not* a study of conventional forms of twentieth-century Inuit art – including carving, printmaking, fabric arts, and drawing. Nor is it engaged with questions of aesthetics; instead, it is a historical analysis of the camera as a tool for recording Inuit culture and as an intercultural connection. Explored here are the lesser-known ways that Idlout's camera-made images provided Inuit communities with a distinctive means to see themselves and to assert their culture, as well as how Idlout and his descendants responded to photographs and films during – and after – the Sangussaqtauliqtilluta period.

Scholarly writings on historical photography and filmmaking in the eastern Arctic, beginning with a groundbreaking survey essay by Richard Condon as well as J.C.H. King and Henrietta Lidchi's essential volume *Imaging the Arctic* (1998), provide crucial contexts for the emphasis on visuality during the 1950s.[65] Among the visual representations addressed by scholars – including Peter Geller in *Northern Exposures: Photographing and Filming the Canadian North, 1920–45* (2004) and Joan Sangster in *The Iconic North: Cultural Constructions of Aboriginal Life in Postwar Canada* (2016) – are ethnographic images made by or for the anthropologists Franz Boas and Diamond Jenness as well as the whaler and ethnographer Captain George Comer, photographs shot by settler residents in the north such as the Anglican missionary Bishop Archibald Lang Fleming and Geraldine Moodie, the wife of an RCMP officer, and Robert Flaherty's influential film *Nanook of the North* (1922).[66] Camera-made representations of Inuit by southerners dating from the nineteenth to the mid-twentieth centuries, like many ethnographic images of this era, are characterized by a salvage paradigm. Like the well-known work of the American photographer Edward S. Curtis, they ostensibly sought to preserve records of what southerners believed was a "vanishing culture." In the process, they represented Inuit culture as frozen in a past time, one to be superseded by the south.[67] Because historical camera-made images of Inuit replicate aspects of many colonialist and ethnographic representations of Indigenous peoples globally, this study is also informed by a larger, global body of scholarly literature critiquing ethnography and ethnographic representations.[68] Key among them are recent discussions of Indigenous sitters' agency before the lens, as articulated by Indigenous artists and scholars such as Jeff Thomas, Amy Lonetree, Celeste Pedri-Spade, Michelle Raheja, Gerald Vizenor, and Hulleah Tsinhnahjinnie, as well as by non-Indigenous scholars working in visual anthropology, film studies, and photo studies. Although these scholars acknowledge the camera as a colonizing tool, they reject conceptualizations of a passive sitter before an aggressive lens;[69] instead, they draw attention to signs of participation and resistance on the part of the Indigenous subjects of the camera's gaze.[70]

Although the literature on historical photographs that represent Inuit is substantial, the record of how Inuit themselves – like Joseph Idlout and members of his community – used the camera and responded to camera-made images remains little known before the 1970s. Work has been done over the past several years to recover the images made by historic photographers from other Indigenous groups,[71] but to date, there is only limited discussion of historical Inuit photographers of this period.[72] As noted above, photographer Peter Pitseolak (1902–1973), based in Kinngait/Cape Dorset, is the key exception to this neglect.[73] Other historic Inuit photographers have come to light, including Paulette Anerodluk, who photographed from the 1940s to the 1960s, as discussed by feminist historian Joan Sangster.[74] More recently, a growing number of Inuit photographers have developed new modes of expression with the camera, including Robert Kautuk, Jimmy Manning, Barry Pottle, and Katharine Takpannie, among many others.[75] And in cinema, the innovative and influential work of filmmaker Zacharias Kunuk of Isuma Productions, Alethea Arnaquq-Baril, and asinnajaq, among others, is redefining this medium in Inuit terms.[76]

Racialized Visuality

To address the history of Sangussaqtauliqtilluta, or disruption, and the visual forms that it often assumed, *The Hunter, the Crown, and the Cameras* adopts as one of its foundational concerns the intersections between racialization and visuality. As Marita Sturken and Lisa Cartwright state, "The concept of visuality refers to the ways that vision is shaped through social context and interaction."[77] Consequently, thinking in terms of visuality exposes the broader social implications of the visual than, for example, a study based solely on individualized physiological vision or visual representations alone would allow. The concept of visuality encompasses the gaze, visualizing devices, and visual representations. But visuality also extends to how social relations and space are organized visually and, indeed, to broader discourses of how the visual organizes society. For many scholars, the emphasis is on how visuality mediates the social. W.J.T. Mitchell, for example, proposes that we "treat visual culture and visual images as go-betweens in social transactions, as a repertoire of screen images or templates that structure our encounters with other human beings ... Images are the filters through which we recognize and of course misrecognize other people."[78] Similarly, visuality relates to what Gerald McMaster, Julia Lum, and Kaitlin McCormick term the "entangled gaze."[79] Adopting the capacious and flexible notion of visuality thus enables a multivalent discussion of the complex history of cultural interactions addressed here.

In his influential scholarship, Nicholas Mirzoeff emphasizes that visuality is inextricably linked to power and, more specifically, to imperialist assertions of authority.[80] As he states in *The Right to Look* (2011), "In a sense, all visuality was and is imperial visuality, the shaping of modernity from the point of view of the imperial powers ... Imperial visuality imagined a transhistorical genealogy of authority marked by a caesura of incommensurability between the 'indigenous' and the 'civilized.'"[81] According to Mirzoeff, the term "visuality" was coined in the 1830s by the Scottish historian Thomas Carlyle, a defender of European imperialism and vocal opponent of Abolition, who characterized visuality as the domain of European, masculine heroic leaders.[82] Mirzoeff argues that the conceptual model first articulated by Carlyle for "a coherent and intelligible picture of modernity that allowed for centralized and/or autocratic leadership" is witnessed in a series of complexes of visuality, including the slave plantation, European imperialism, and the contemporary military. In these historical cases, the "authority of coloniality has consistently required visuality to supplement its deployment of force. Visuality sutures authority to power and renders this association 'natural.'"[83] Yet, as Mitchell has asserted, "vision is never a one-way street, but a multiple intersection teeming with dialectical images."[84] This interest in intersectional and resistant vision has been taken up in critical anthropology and colonial critique too; as discussed in chapter 5, anthropologist Deborah Poole, for example, underscores the power of photographic contingencies and excesses to disrupt authority.[85] Mirzoeff also identifies a constellation of resistant responses to visuality. He defines these responses as "the assertion of the right to look, challenging the law that sustains visuality's authority in order to justify its own sense of 'right.'"[86] In this way, Mirzoeff conceptualizes visuality as embodying both authority and resistance.[87]

Drawing on Mirzoeff's conceptualizations, this book adopts visuality and resistance to it (or "the right to look") as key explanatory tools for approaching the complex history of settler-Inuit interactions in the eastern Arctic of the 1950s. The imposition of visualizing devices in support of settler-colonial and institutionalized federal efforts to assimilate Inuit marked a disconnection between southerners and an Inuit culture rooted not in visuality but in transgenerational oral tradition. In part, this book analyzes the Sangussaqtauliqtilluta period as a disconnection between Inuit oral tradition and the visuality of southern culture projected onto the north.

More specifically, I argue in these pages that the Qikiqtani region in the eastern Arctic during the 1950s and 1960s often marked a field of *racialized* visuality. That is to say that this complex of visuality often took the form of othering Inuit. As noted above, unlike other broad regions within what is now Canada, the Qikiqtani region was not physically settled extensively by outsiders. Instead, government, church, military, and economic institutions colonized the region and its peoples often from a distance. To generate settlement, this distant arm depended on the aid of technological devices – including visualizing technologies. Power was (and is) asserted through complexes of visuality that range from surveillance systems to the human gaze. These complexes included the presence of governmental representatives, such as Northern Service officers, and the enforced relocation of Inuit to settled communities, where they were managed by southern officials and institutions. As discussed in chapter 5, photo studies scholar Shawn Michelle Smith contends that "looking and seeing [are] racialized practices ... subjects are produced through practices of looking ... looking is learned, and ... seeing is culturally coded in terms of race."[88] Attention to the nexus of race and visuality in the Qikiqtani region, and in the eastern Arctic more broadly, during the 1950s and 1960s exposes systems of power and their contestations, including those articulated through Idlout's own photographic practice as a form of cultural assertion.

Cyclical Temporalities and Many Voices: Representing Inuit-Qallunaat Visual Entanglements during Sangussaqtauliqtilluta

The subject of this book – Inuit-Qallunaat visual entanglement during the Sangussaqtauliqtilluta period and in Inuit memory today – is complex. It includes visual images and orality to tell a history from decades ago that remains impactful today. How should the difficult history of these encounters be told? I have long recognized that a linear, distant, chronological narrative told in one voice is too inflexible, occupying an affective register that is too detached for the multivalent and engrossing experiences of visuality experienced by Inuit and addressed here. A distant view would not capture the textures of individual lives.[89] The tidiness of chronology would inevitably place the stress on a supposed moment of origin in the post–Second World War period and on the archival record of southern efforts at assimilation. Instead, *The Hunter, the Crown, and the Cameras* adopts a cyclical structure, and it combines documents – texts written or testimonies given by Idlout family members – with historical analysis.

The book opens and closes in the present with contemporary Inuit responses to the Sangussaqtauliqtilluta period and to its existing visual record. In this way, not only are Inuit perceptions and voices prominent in the narrative, but the structure also reflects cyclical conceptualizations of time in Inuit storytelling and culture in general.[90] Additionally, a cyclical narrative structure emphasizes how the history of disruption – in effect, the ongoing experience of trauma – continues to be relived and to impact life among many generations of Inuit. Rather than a conventional, linear history, this approach also allows for the exploration of multiple, nonchronological points of reception and production. The book tracks numerous photographs and films depicting Inuit in the Qikiqtani region of the eastern Arctic during the 1950s (and to a lesser degree, the 1960s) as well as Idlout's own photographs across several decades, providing the intersecting perspectives of sitters, image makers, viewers, institutions, and government. This approach traces transhistorical and transcultural relationships activated through visuality. In this way, the multiple interactions that constitute settler-colonial society – including interactions between Indigenous peoples, waves of settlers, and the metropole – are emphasized. My hope is that such a model resists the privileging of singular authority in conventional chronological historical narrative. The model opens a space for transcultural dialogue and critique while more clearly acknowledging Indigenous agency.

Key components of the history described in this book come from the Idlout family. As noted above, the book opens with a foreword written by Madeleine d'Argencourt, one of Idlout's granddaughters, who introduces her family and her grandparents' legacy. Interspersed throughout the book are six interludes under the title "In the Idlout Family's Words," with published historic texts by Joseph Idlout and by Leah Idlout d'Argencourt Paulson. Finally, the book is also filled with excerpts of testimonies by family members for the Sangussaqtauliqtilluta documentary project. These documents are central to the story told here, but the hope is that the words of Idlout family members will also be valuable resources for a diversity of contemporary and future readers.

The book adopts the intimate perspectives of microhistory. It offers a telling of Idlout's specific story and through his expressions and those of his family etches an understanding of how this period was experienced closely. Chapters 2 to 6, the core of the book, narrate the relationship between Idlout and Doug Wilkinson, a connection that I argue crystallizes the complex visual mediations between Inuit and southerners during the Sangussaqtauliqtilluta period. As noted above, Wilkinson maintained a close relationship with Idlout for many years. He lived at Idlout's camp during the summer of 1951 and cohabited with Idlout's family for one year from June 1953 until May 1954. In focusing on this specific relationship between Idlout and Wilkinson – that is, in adopting an approach indebted to microhistory – this study underscores their agency as historical actors while highlighting the everyday experiences of Sangussaqtauliqtilluta and the impact of the south in the north.[91]

These five core chapters also look at the racialized visuality of Sangussaqtauliqtilluta during the 1950s and 1960s using the microhistory of Idlout and Wilkinson's relationship in images. Attending to close readings of films and photographs, as well as to the encounter between the two, highlights the intimate texture of lives during this period of dramatic assimilationist policies. The five central chapters each highlight the relationship between Idlout and Wilkinson, as well as their relationship with the Crown through the Government of Canada, as played out through visuality. They follow a loose chronology from the late 1940s to the 1960s, with chapters examining overlapping periods within this range. In tracing this period through a relationship, these chapters offer a microhistory of Inuit-Qallunaat relations. The specificity of these chapters and the series of exchanged gazes that they narrate are social-historical in nature. That is to say that I am interested in conveying through Idlout and Wilkinson's relationship the intricate textures of settler-Inuit interactions and lived experience at this tumultuous time. But the five core chapters also move from individual experiences to the institutional. I try to demonstrate, for example, how Wilkinson's and others' visualizations of Inuit Nunangat became increasingly ensconced in the settler bureaucratization of Inuit lives in the region.

Together, these chapters and the republished texts by Joseph Idlout and Leah Idlout d'Argencourt Paulson provide a cyclical, visual, multivocal, and intimate history of Sangussaqtauliqtilluta.

Chapter 1, "Elders Narrate the History of Sangussaqtauliqtilluta: Telling the Story of Disruption for the Qikiqtani Truth Commission and *Iqqaumavara*," recounts the history of disruption and its transgenerational impact on Inuit of the Qikiqtani region. It opens with a discussion of testimonies given by Idlout's adult children Paul Ullatitaq Idlout, Moses Idlout, and Susan Salluviniq for the Inuit-Qallunaat collaborative history project *Iqqaumavara*. The rest of the chapter continues to tell this difficult history through Inuit Elders' memories by drawing on oral histories amassed by the Qikiqtani Truth Commission, the Inuit-led Qikiqtani restorative justice body active from 2007 to 2010, and by the *Iqqaumavara* project from 2011 to 2013. In this way, the chapter introduces historical and methodological grounding for the rest of the book. By conveying relatively recent Inuit testimonies, it also privileges Inuit experience *today* and cyclical approaches to historical representation.

Chapter 1 is followed by an excerpt from Leah Idlout d'Argencourt Paulson's article "C.D. Howe I," *Inuit Today* 6, no. 5 (June 1977): 30–45. In the mid-1970s, Leah was the editor of *Inuit Today*, a journal published in Inuktitut syllabics and English. She periodically published reflections on her own experiences, which provide invaluable insights into life during her childhood and the Inuit experience of Sangussaqtauliqtilluta. This excerpt is drawn from a five-part article published in the June, July–August, October, and November 1977 issues of *Inuit Today*. It recounts Leah's experience as a tuberculosis patient taken from her family for treatment in the south and transported there on board the CGS *C.D. Howe*, an Eastern Arctic Patrol vessel.

Chapter 2, "The Hunter and the Cameras: Joseph Idlout and Doug Wilkinson Meet (1952)," narrates Idlout's early life and Wilkinson's time with the National

Film Board of Canada in the Arctic from 1948 to 1952. The chapter culminates with a detailed analysis of Wilkinson's most influential film, *Land of the Long Day* (1952). Idlout stars in this popular ethnographic film as an updated version of Flaherty's character Nanook (originally performed by Allakariallak). In my analysis of *Land of the Long Day*, as well as Wilkinson's earlier films, I highlight the agency of Inuit performers, an agency that often disrupts conventional colonial positions. The response of Wilkinson's Inuit actors to his image of Inuit culture was always already integrated into his productions; in *Land of the Long Day* and Wilkinson's other films and still images, Inuit were collaborators and active agents in his imaging of their people and land.

Two Idlout family publications bridge chapters 2 and 3, providing accounts of camp life. The first is a letter from Joseph Idlout, published in 1961, that lists "ten uses for the seal." The letter underscores Idlout's skill as a hunter, his stewardship of the *nuna* (land), and his ability to provide for his community. The second document is Leah Idlout d'Argencourt Paulson's 1976 *Inuit Today* article "Spring," which recalls her family's move from their winter camp to the spring camp, providing rich detail about camp life and how the family worked together harmoniously. Both of these essays reflect Inuit Qaujimajatuqangit principles – particularly *piliriqatigiinniq/ikajuqtigiinniq*, the value of working together and maintaining harmony, and *pijitsirniq*, serving and providing for family and the community – which are central to the subsequent chapter.

Chapter 3, "The Hunter: Joseph Idlout's Photographs at *Ilagiit Nunagivaktangat* (Camp) and Inuit Qaujimajatuqangit (IQ) (1951–54)," co-written with Augatnaaq Eccles, is drawn from and expands on text prepared for the online exhibition *Ajjiliurlagit*. Here, we look at Idlout's photographs made between 1951 to 1954 at the hunter's camps on North Baffin Island.[92] The core of the chapter argues that Idlout's photographs – like the two essays preceding the chapter – reflect IQ values. As noted above, we also discuss how they reflect the holistic view of Inuit knowledge keeper, writer, and Idlout granddaughter Rachel Qitsualik. To preface this argument, we discuss the methodology for our own collaboration, one that we have come to recognize reflects the IQ principle of *aajiiqatigiinniq*, decision making through discussion and consensus.

Leah Idlout d'Argencourt Paulson's November 1976 *Inuit Today* article "Merry Christmas!" follows the discussion of Idlout's photography. This essay recalls Leah's excitement as a child on Christmas day at Aulatsivik (Leah's spelling of Aulattivik). Again, her story demonstrates how the family worked together, reflecting IQ principles evident in Idlout's photographs, some of which illustrated this 1976 article.

Chapter 4, "Exchanged Gazes and Oversight: Joseph Idlout and Doug Wilkinson (1953–55)," closely examines the period of almost one year when Wilkinson lived with Idlout's family at his camp on North Baffin Island as well as the publications and films resulting from the trip. Wilkinson undertook the extended stay as a form of immersion in Inuit culture in the months before he became a

Northern Service officer working for the federal government. He advocated for modified governmental intervention in Inuit lives, but he also asserted strongly that it would be effective only if southerners fully understood Inuit culture. Wilkinson proposed staying a year at Idlout's camp as a case study for this intensive Inuit education of southerners. The encounter is narrated in Wilkinson's correspondence, reports, field notes, and publications as well as in newsreels and still photographs. Embedded in this archival material are Wilkinson's own nascent thoughts on the south's management of Inuit lives. But these representational forms and musings by Wilkinson are also disrupted by Idlout's own images of Wilkinson and other southerners as well as by the hunter's voice heard in Wilkinson's accounts.

Following chapter 4 is the fifth and final instalment of Leah Idlout d'Argencourt Paulson's 1977 memoir. It reflects on her excitement upon returning to the Qikiqtani region following tuberculosis treatment in the south. Titled "C.D. Howe V: Trip Back Home," the essay expresses the closeness of the Idlout family amid dramatic change.

Chapter 5, "The Crown: Connections, Disconnections, and Racialized Visuality in Governor General Vincent Massey's Tour of the North (1956)," situates Idlout and Wilkinson within the context of one spectacularized governmental intervention in the Arctic. This chapter extends *The Hunter, the Crown, and the Camera*'s overarching exploration of racially coded visuality in the Qikiqtani region during the 1950s through a close examination of visual representations – photographs, film, and news accounts – depicting Massey's 1956 tour of the north. Both Idlout and Wilkinson participated in the tour, Idlout as part of a greeting committee in Resolute/Qausuittuq and Wilkinson as the coordinator of activities in Iqaluit/Frobisher Bay. As I argue, the visual record of the 1956 tour thematizes visuality itself. In image after image, it declares settler-colonial authority through claims of visual mastery even while photographic contingencies and excesses, seen in part in the returned gazes of the Inuit sitters, including Idlout, assert their own challenges. I suggest here that an attention to the nexus of race and visuality exposes complex ways that racial constructions are performed with and for the camera in these images.

Joseph Idlout's 1959 *Inuktitut Magazine* article "Resolute Bay Man Visiting Greenland," offers first-person reflections on the hunter's voyage to Kalaallit Nunaat/Greenland. This trip is the central topic of the subsequent chapter. Idlout's own published account – illustrated by his snapshots from the trip – provides insights into circumpolar Inuit experience at this time. The book includes an English transcript of the article by translator Rhoda Kayakjuak alongside the article as originally published in Inuktitut syllabics.

The microhistory of Idlout's relationship with Wilkinson closes in chapter 6, "The Hunter in Exile: A View from Kalaallit Nunaat/Greenland and Resolute/Qausuittuq (1958–68)." This chapter narrates the final years of Idlout's life as a High Arctic exile and his growing resistance to assimilationist policies at that time. In 1955, Idlout and his family relocated to Resolute/Qausuittuq as part of an effort that had begun in 1953 when several families were moved to the High Arctic from the area around Inukjuak/Port Harrison as well as from Pond Inlet/Mittimatalik.[93] Idlout and his family were moved to Resolute/Qausuittuq ostensibly to guide the other families (from more southerly areas) in regional hunting practices. Idlout, expecting to hold an elevated position because of his expertise as a hunter and long associations with southerners, undertook the move with confidence. The reality was otherwise. But to contextualize the relocations, chapter 6 looks closely at a remarkable 1958 trip that Idlout took during this period to Kalaallit Nunaat/Greenland with nine other Inuit delegates and southern officials. Idlout (and others borrowing his camera) took snapshots throughout the trip and – as seen in the reproduction preceding this chapter – wrote a 1959 article for *Inuktitut Magazine* about the trip.[94] I argue that a close reading of the photographs, *Inuktitut* article, and government documents reveals growing resistance to assimilationist policies. The final section of chapter 6 returns to Resolute/Qausuittuq, where Idlout continued to be the object of Doug Wilkinson's camera and, through correspondence with government, continued to advocate for Inuit authority.

Leah Idlout d'Argencourt Paulson's October 1975 *Inuit Today* article, "First Inuit Picture on Canadian Money," follows chapter 6. It provides Leah's detailed and personal analysis of the most widely circulated image of Idlout family and camp members: an image of men and boys from the camp reproduced on the Canadian two-dollar bill, which was in circulation when Leah published this article. Whereas the piece of currency reproduced a photograph by Doug Wilkinson, Leah illustrates her own article with photographs taken by Idlout's camera.

Leah Idlout d'Argencourt Paulson's article about the Canadian two-dollar bill ushers in chapter 7, "The Hunter Returns: 1975 · 1990 · 2018–23." In this chapter, the cyclical narrative returns to more recent history, with Inuit voices and images addressing the memory of Sangussaqtauliqtillut by examining the afterlives of both Idlout's image and those photographs attributed to him. Here, I revisit the notion of a photograph's cultural biography, making use of Elizabeth Edwards's discussion of photographs as social or relational objects, as sketched earlier in this introduction.[95] Beginning with a discussion of Leah's October 1975 article, I trace the ways that images depicting Idlout circulated over time, their meanings shifting with reception from different perspectives. Idlout's image – appearing in films, publications, and even, as Leah describes, on a piece of currency – became, at different moments, a marker of a southern perception of idealized Indigeneity and Canadian settler sovereignty over the High Arctic as well as a sign of Inuit resistance during the Sangussaqtauliqtillut period. The chapter culminates with a discussion of how Idlout's descendants and community members are reactivating the hunter's own photographs today. Rather than offering a conventional conclusion, the book ends – as it began – with Idlout family members' words and recollections.

1 Elders Narrate the History of Sangussaqtauliqtilluta

Telling the Story of Disruption for the Qikiqtani Truth Commission and *Iqqaumavara*

When one grows up in a place, that land becomes a part of that person. The land is a part of that person. When these people left their very own blood relatives and the land they're connected to, to never return, that had a big impact.
– Moses Idlout, 2011[1]

A few years before Paul Ullatitaq Idlout and Susan Salluviniq looked at their father's snapshots, the two Elders and their late brother Moses Idlout sat before video cameras discussing their personal experiences during the Sangussaqtauliqtilluta (disruption) period. Their interviews were videotaped for *Iqqaumavara* (I remember), a public history project and website examining the High Arctic relocations of 1953–55 through Elders' memories.[2] Moses Idlout was interviewed in 2011 at Inukjuak/Port Harrison, his wife's birthplace and their home since 1977 (see figure 1.1); the interviews with his brother Paul Ullatitaq Idlout (see figure 1.2) and sister Susan Salluviniq were filmed two years later in Pond Inlet/Mittimatalik.

In the videos, the Elders face the camera, speaking in Inuktitut with great poignancy about their relocation to Resolute/Qausuittuq in 1955. The Elders recall in vivid detail the coerced relocation that led them to the High Arctic and how bleak life often was there at first, noting the unfamiliar hunting grounds and foods, the tense relations both with military personnel and between different groups of exiles, and the disciplinary schooling. Telling their stories was important in exposing these hardships. As Moses Idlout states, perhaps hopefully, "This harsh relocation the government did will never be repeated because of the awareness of the story."[3]

In these videos, Paul Ullatitaq Idlout, Moses Idlout, and Susan Salluviniq tell histories of the Sangussaqtauliqtilluta period through *unikkaat*, which Keavy Martin has defined as memories or life stories that are told through personal experiences.[4] In recent years, *unikkaat* material recorded by Elders has become a key tool for maintaining and strengthening Inuit cultural traditions. Indeed, as Beth Greenhorn, Deborah Kigjugalik Webster, Christina Williamson, and I

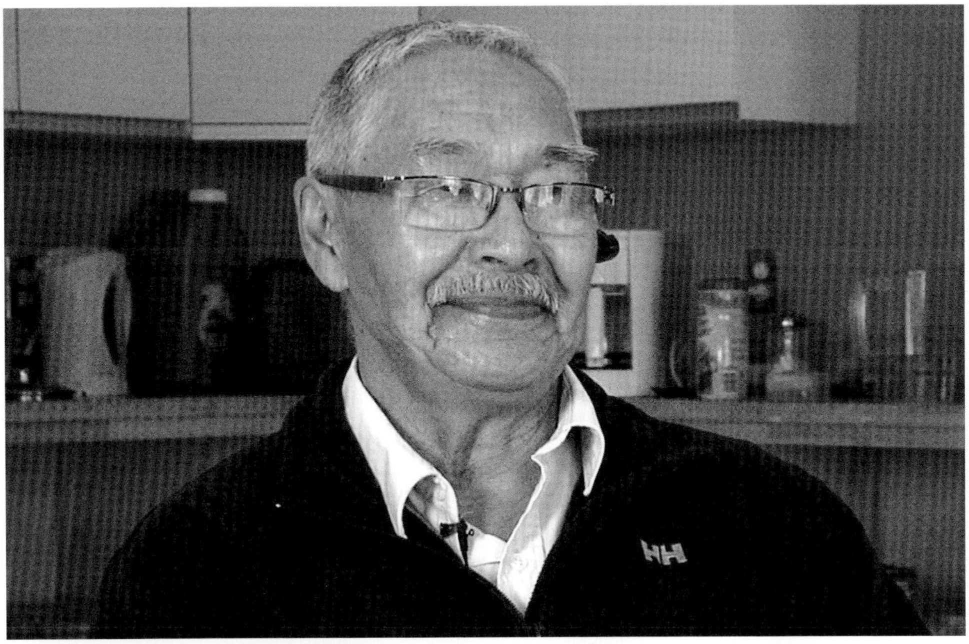

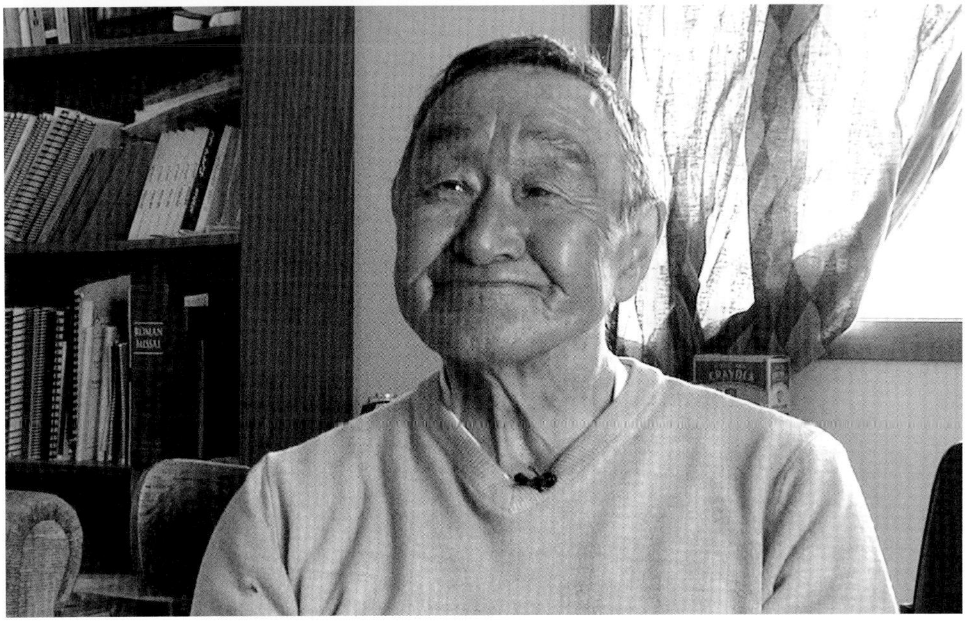

1.1 | Moses Idlout, 2011, from *Iqqaumavara* interview video recording.

1.2 | Paul Ullatitaq Idlout, 2011, from *Iqqaumavara* interview video recording.

have noted, a rich body of this literature has emerged from the influential oral history projects developed, for example, by Nunavut Arctic College and by the Igloolik Oral History Centre as well as in such publications as *Uqalurait: An Oral History of Nunavut*, among other initiatives.[5] *Unikkaat* has also been crucial in telling the history of Sangussaqtauliqtilluta from Inuit perspectives.

This chapter provides historical and methodological grounding for the rest of the book by recounting the history of southern interventions during the 1950s and 1960s in the Qikiqtani region, but it does so by drawing on *unikkaat* in the form of Inuit Elders recounting their own experiences. Specifically, the Elders' accounts referenced or reproduced here were recorded either for the *Iqqaumavara* history project from 2011 to 2013, including the interviews with Paul Ullatitaq Idlout, Moses Idlout, and Susan Salluviniq, or for the Qikiqtani Truth Commission (QTC), the Inuit-led restorative justice program, from 2007 to 2010.

Drawing on these relatively recent Inuit discussions, I have three broad goals in mind: to provide the reader with a historical overview of the Sangussaqtauliqtilluta period as recalled by Inuit themselves, including the Qikiqtani region's inhabitants, called Qikiqtaalungmiut; to discuss methodological and ethical considerations; and to signal how past cultural disruptions continue to impact the lives of Inuit in the region. In these ways, this chapter opens the book's history of visuality during the period of disruption through a discussion of reflections by Inuit *today* and initiates the book's cyclical structure. In eschewing more conventional authoritative, distant, and singular narratives that might easily privilege southern perspectives, I foreground *Inuit* experiences and political agency today by focusing on how the history of Sangussaqtauliqtilluta has been recalled recently by Inuit Elders and presented both by the Inuit-led QTC and by the Inuit-Qallunaat collaboration *Iqqaumavara*. These two initiatives also provide methodological models for privileging Inuit voices, working collaboratively, and combining oral history with archival research in this chapter and throughout the book. Most of the content is drawn specifically from material that the commission and *Iqqaumavara* gathered in relation to Pond Inlet/Mittimatalik and Resolute/Qausuittuq, regions and communities where Joseph Idlout and his family lived.

The chapter first introduces the QTC and *Iqqaumavara*, including discussions of their mandates, methodologies, and findings. These overviews are interspersed with a few lengthy quotations from the organizations' oral histories. The body of the chapter, as described above, is comprised almost entirely of excerpts from oral history interviews to outline the story of Sangussaqtauliqtilluta through Elders' own words. Specifically, this chapter quotes from Elders speaking about their experiences mainly in the areas where Joseph Idlout and his family lived. The chapter closes with a return to the book's overall theme of visuality during the Sangussaqtauliqtilluta period by considering the role of images in both the QTC's and *Iqqaumavara*'s historical representations.

For permission to quote, I am grateful to the Qikiqtani Inuit Association and to Marquise Lepage of Productions du Cerf-Volant, the producer of *Iqqaumavara*. Above all, I thank the Elders quoted here; by sharing their words through the two projects discussed in this chapter, they have paid tribute to Inuit culture and informed the world of this history. The QTC and *Iqqaumavara* websites provide a larger group of Elders' accounts and findings. I encourage readers to turn to these rich resources.[6]

The Qikiqtani Truth Commission

This period of recent history is very much alive to Qikiqtaalungmiut, and through testifying at the Commission, Inuit spoke of our experience of that time.
– J. Okalik Eegeesiak, president of the Qikiqtani Inuit Association, 2013[7]

The Qikiqtani Truth Commission, one of the most significant responses to the Sangussaqtauliqtilluta period and its ongoing impact, was founded as an act of contestation both against historic human rights abuses and against earlier governmental findings. It originated in 2000 with a call for a public inquiry into the mass killing of *qimmiit* (sled dogs) by the Royal Canadian Mounted Police (RCMP) from 1950 to 1975. This call was made jointly by the Qikiqtani Inuit Association (QIA), which represents Inuit of the Qikiqtani region, whose communities extend from Sanikiluaq/Belcher Islands in the south to Grise Fiord/Ausuittuq in the north, and by the Makivik Corporation, representing Nunavik. The killing of *qimmiit* by the RCMP, either independently or as legislated through a territorial ordinance, prevented Inuit from hunting and living off the land, effectively keeping them hostage in settled communities and preventing traditional patterns of life.[8]

In response to the joint call of the QIA and the Makivik Corporation, the Canadian government requested that the RCMP conduct its own investigation into the slaughters. RCMP investigators largely drew on the police force's internal records, other governmental records, and interviews with Qallunaat in the region; very few insights from Inuit themselves were consulted.[9] Although the RCMP acknowledged that *qimmiit* had been killed by its officers, it suggested that this culling was done for "public health and safety reasons, in accordance with the law." The 2006 final report concluded, "The RCMP review team did not uncover any evidence to support the allegations, within the large volume of information collected, of an organized mass slaughter of Inuit sled dogs by RCMP members in Nunavik and Nunavut between 1950 and 1970, carried out at the direction of the Government, or on the RCMP's own initiative."[10] The QIA and the Makivik Corporation immediately rejected the RCMP's findings and methodology.[11] As Thomasie Alikatuktuk, president of the QIA responded, "The slaughter of the sled dogs caused physical and emotional hardship that endangered the very survival of Inuit who lost their dogs. It scarred us and our families. What the RCMP claim as truth is not the truth that Inuit lived. I know this because I have seen it with my own eyes."[12]

The QIA decided to establish its own truth commission, initially to investigate the slaughter of *qimmiit* specifically. The commission was modelled after restorative justice bodies globally – including, most prominently, the South African Truth and Reconciliation Commission of the 1990s. Closer to home, it was situated in relation to the almost concurrent Truth and Reconciliation Commission of Canada, which conducted an investigation of Indian residential schools from 2008 to 2015.[13]

In contrast to the RCMP inquiry, the QTC was firmly Inuit-centred. Established by the Qikiqtani Inuit Association, the commission was headed by Nunatsiavut Inuk and former district court judge James Igloliorte. Madeleine Redfern, who would become mayor of Iqaluit in 2010, was the QTC's executive director, and Joanasie Akumalik was its executive assistant, which involved working with community liaisons across the Qikiqtani region.[14] And above all, the findings were based on Elders' experiences, as recounted through *unikkaat*. As the QTC stated, its findings "represent the Inuit experience during this colonial period, as told by Inuit."[15] In these ways – by economically funding the commission, maintaining its Inuit management, and stressing Inuit oral tradition – the QIA rendered the form of a southern judicial body, a commission, in Inuit terms.[16]

The Qikiqtani Inuit Association gave the commission team a broad mandate to examine the effects of assimilationist policies from 1950 to 1975. They were asked "to create a more accurate and balanced history of the decisions and events that affected Inuit living in the Qikiqtani region in the decades following 1950, and to document the impacts on Inuit life."[17] This mandate exceeded the initial inquiries into the slaughter of sled dogs, but it marked a recognition that the killings were part of a larger colonial system of acculturation. The QIA and the commission decided to exclude certain prominent concerns being addressed by other bodies. For example, it did not explicitly address the question of residential schools, which was the mandate of the Truth and Reconciliation Commission of Canada. Nor did the QTC focus explicitly on the High Arctic relocations, which had been the subject of the Royal Commission on Aboriginal Peoples in the 1990s and, as discussed below, would later be the subject of *Iqqaumavara*'s public history accounts. However, references to the relocations and enforced schooling were made in the hearings and are evident in the commission's reports.

In answering the call for a "more accurate and balanced history," Igloliorte and the commission chose to recount this period principally from Inuit perspectives. As the commission describes its approach, "As an Inuit-led project, the Qikiqtani Truth Commission recognizes the importance of oral history to our understanding of what happened in the past. The stories of Inuit elders, told in their own words and the words of their children and grandchildren, allow all Canadians to see and interpret the multiple truths of their lived experiences, through their eyes. Their personal accounts, within the context of this truth commission, have been gathered, recorded and weighed along with the written records found in archives across Canada."[18] Hearing, recording, and disseminating Inuit Elders' testimonials, which took the form of *unikkaat*, was the cornerstone of the QTC's approach. The commission held hearings at the thirteen settled communities of the Qikitaaluk region, visiting two of these communities – Kimmirut and Sanikiluaq/Belcher Islands – twice. Interviews were also conducted in Ottawa and Edmonton. In total, 295 testimonies were video recorded. The vast majority were given by Inuit Elders, although members of younger generations of Inuit also testified; an additional fourteen of the interviews were conducted with Qallunaat who live in the Qikiqtani region or have extensive experience there.[19] In addition, for its findings, the commission drew on testimonies gathered by the Qikiqtani Inuit Association between 2004 and 2006.

As the commission noted, the testimonies comprised vivid personal accounts. Elders discussed "relocations from *ilagiit nunagivaktangit* [camps on the land] to established settlements; the deaths of *qimmiit*, which reduced their ability to hunt and support their families; the removal of Inuit children from families for extended periods of time; and the tragic separation of families due to the lack of medical services in the North."[20] Watching the videotaped interviews, one is struck by the detailed recollections and the depth of feeling that the Elders possess. The format of these Inuit-led hearings is equally moving. Igloliorte models an approach built on respect. Elders are not interrupted with numerous questions; they speak at length. And each interview ends with the judge thanking the Elder for the specific details of their testimony and for their willingness to speak. There is a sense that, perhaps for the first time, Elders have been heard.

Secondary to oral testimonies by Inuit Elders, the QTC also drew on archival research. This work was undertaken by Contentworks, a heritage and public history organization led by the historian Julie Harris. As Philip Goldring, a historian on the project, recalled in a published reflection, "The QTC's and QIA's decision to work with a team of professional historians from the outset underlined the importance they saw in finding a balance in the collection and use of historical information."[21] In this way, the QTC provides a model for settler research about the period. As Goldring has articulated, the commission "began by asserting memory as a source" and then combined the testimonies with detailed archival research, which corroborated Inuit memory.[22] The commission, in effect, developed an approach that brought together Inuit oral tradition with conventional (southern) historical research. Further, it privileged *unikkaat*, rooted in oral tradition, as a historical source.

Testimonies and research conducted for the QTC were in turn used to produce a series of publicly accessible reports and a database. Igloliorte's final report – subtitled *Achieving Saimaqatigiingniq*, defined as "a new relationship 'when past opponents get back together, meet in the middle, and are at peace'"[23] – provided a detailed summary of what the commission had learned and its recommendations. In addition, nine reports were published, each addressing a prominent theme that the commission had identified: *Aaniajurliriniq: Health Care in the Qikiqtani Region*; *Igluliriniq: Housing in the Qikiqtani Region*; *Illinniarniq: Schooling in the Qikiqtani Region*; *Nuutauniq: Moves in Inuit Life in the Qikiqtani Region*; *The Official Mind of Canadian Colonialism*; *Paliisikkut: Policing in the Qikiqtani Region*; *Pivalliajuliriniq: Economic Development in the Qikiqtani Region*; *Qimmiliriniq: Inuit Sled

Dogs in the Qikiqtani Region; and *Analysis of the RCMP Sled Dog Report*.[24] Finally, the commission published community histories for each of the thirteen communities that it visited in the Qikiqtani region. All of these histories combine Qikiqtaalungmiut testimonies to the commission with archival and secondary research conducted by the commission's team of historians.

In its summary statements, the Qikiqtani Truth Commission acknowledges that the history unearthed through oral testimony and archival research is multivalent and complex. In a preface to its key findings, the commission states, "Our interviews and research have shown us that no single truth will explain the changes Qikiqtani Inuit experienced from 1950 to 1975: nor are there easily identified villains and victims. It is a history of displaced families, inadequate housing, coercive government relations, tuberculosis epidemics, residential schools and the killing of *qimmiit*, or sled dogs. But it is also a history of increased opportunity, new social programs and mutual – if often misguided and inappropriate – efforts to reconcile two very different cultures: those of the North and the South, Inuit and Qallunaat."[25] As a result, the QTC's recommendations, like its summary reports, reflect this complexity. The commission's final recommendations are organized into four broad categories, each an umbrella for more specific findings. First, it recommends governmental acknowledgment and responsibility: "The Government of Canada should acknowledge that the effects of many of its decisions led to unnecessary hardship and poor social, health, and education outcomes for Inuit, and both southern Canadians and younger Inuit should learn more about the changes that occurred in the 1950 to 1975 period in the Qikiqtani region." As part of this first recommendation, the QTC also calls for "concrete steps to promote healing for those affected." Second, the commission urges that "Inuit governance must be strengthened so that political, social, and economic decisions truly reflect Inuit culture and needs"; this action is seen as important in avoiding a repetition of the mistakes that occurred during Sangussaqtauliqtilluta. The QTC's third series of recommendations calls for "strengthening Inuit culture." The fourth and final group of recommendations issued by the commission looks to the detrimental and long-term impacts of assimilation policies; under the rubric "Creating Healthy Communities," it calls for culturally appropriate steps to address a "number of serious social ills."[26]

Iqqaumavara

> What happened to our story was [a] monumental saga in the Canadian history … that should not be forgotten. Let's do something about the history and let it be known properly that our relocation story is very important. It has to be known.
> – Larry Audlaluk, 2014[27]

Like the Qikiqtani Truth Commission, *Iqqaumavara* employs *unikkaat* from Inuit Elders to expose the difficult history of Sangussaqtauliqtilluta. But whereas the QTC's mandate was broadly framed by various aspects of Sangussaqtauliqtilluta,

Iqqaumavara is focused specifically on the High Arctic relocations. The *Iqqaumavara* website states that the project has amassed the "largest online source of information dedicated to the 1953 and 1955 forced relocation of Inuit families to the High Arctic."[28]

The *Iqqaumavara* website is a Qallunaat-led collaboration with Inuit. As Marquise Lepage of Productions du Cerf-Volant wrote to me, "This site was created specifically to preserve the memory of those who had experienced the terrible relocation of the 1950s."[29] Évangéline De Pas and Geneviève Thibert, also of Productions du Cerf-Volant, worked with Lepage for four years from an original idea that she and Martha Flaherty had developed.[30]

That idea had germinated in the wake of the 2009 film *Martha of the North*, co-produced by Virage, Cerf-Volant, and the National Film Board of Canada. Directed by Lepage and written by Flaherty and Lepage, *Martha of the North* tells Flaherty's life story in her own words (while drawing on interviews with other exiles) as she recalls her childhood as one of the High Arctic exiles relocated from Inukjuak/Port Harrison to Grise Fiord/Ausuittuq on Ellesmere Island, the northernmost community in Canada.[31] The title of the film is a play on Robert Flaherty's celebrated 1922 production *Nanook of the North*, which was filmed in Inukjuak/Port Harrison; indeed, Martha Flaherty is the biological granddaughter of the American filmmaker. Incorporating archival photographs and film footage, along with contemporary footage shot by Lepage and her team, the 2009 film follows Martha Flaherty as she recalls her early life in Inukjuak/Port Harrison and her family's traumatic relocation to Grise Fiord/Ausuittuq in 1955. As Lepage recounted to me, *Martha of the North* "inspired the Canadian authorities to make an official apology to the Inuit, for the suffering endured. Moreover, Minister John Duncan, then Minister of Indigenous and Northern Affairs, by his own admission, took a lot on the content of the film to write the letter of apology from the Canadian government."[32] On the *Iqqaumavara* website, Lepage goes on to write about the aftermath of *Martha of the North* as the impetus for an extended project:

> After the movie was finished, we had the chance to present it to various communities in Nunavik and Nunavut. Watching the film inspired several people to approach us and share some of their childhood memories, as well as open up about the traumatic events of their own relocation. Shaken by all those revelations, Martha and I began dreaming of gathering their stories. We wanted to offer a space where the people and families involved in the relocations of 1953 and 1955 could open up about their suffering. A space where their descendants could learn about their family's history. A site to collectively remember this human tragedy.[33]

Iqqaumavara was grounded, therefore, in that sense of wanting to create a site for collective remembrance.

Iqqaumavara takes the form of a website that combines multiple narratives across different formats in order to tell the multivalent story of the High Arctic relocations for diverse audiences. The site is trilingual, with information available in Inuktut syllabics, French, and English. It presents five different bodies of material: a timeline, which in turn includes archival documents;[34] a collection of archival photographs depicting High Arctic exiles; introductions to five communities, including short films made by youth;[35] videotaped interviews with forty exiles; and twelve short, sequential films. Reflecting Lepage's, De Pas's, and Thibert's cinematic backgrounds and the origins of the project in filmmaking, the brief films form the centrepiece of *Iqqaumavara.* They sequentially narrate the story of the High Arctic relocations through contemporary film footage paired with the video interviews and archival materials also available on the site. As each film is between only three and eight minutes, the cinematic narrative is relatively accessible in the north, where broadband is limited. Each of the twelve films addresses a key event or concern: *They Remember, Why?, Promises, The Trip, Cold and Hunger, Forsaken, The Impacts, Their Homeland, The Help from Pond Inlet, The Apology, The Healing,* and *The Future.*[36]

Unikkaat – in the form of Inuit Elders recounting their own personal experience – is central to the *Iqqaumavara* project. Not only are forty videotaped interviews presented, but these interviews comprise the bulk of the twelve brief films. Although the interviews are edited to fit into the films' relatively linear narratives, the prominence of Elders' words signals that the history told by *Iqqaumavara* is based on Inuit perspectives. In this way, *Iqqaumavara* shares an emphasis on Inuit *unikkaat* with the QTC, although *Iqqaumavara* is a Qallunaat-Inuit collaboration, takes a more cinematic approach, and aims to convey public history in a narrative format.

"The truth that Inuit lived":[37] The Sangussaqtauliqtilluta Period in Inuit Elders' Words

Well, I have all kinds of memories that are good but I've also experienced many things that bring pain to myself and my people.
– John Amagoalik, 2008[38]

In telling the story of Sangussaqtauliqtilluta from their own perspectives, Inuit Elders testifying before the Qikiqtani Truth Commission and participating in *Iqqaumavara* oral histories reflected on the complexity of that period and, indeed, the complexity of memory. In this section, to provide the reader with a broader context for the events that unfold in the core of this book, I recount material culled from some testimonies that offer Inuit perspectives.

Ethical concerns are also at stake. Testimonies gathered by restorative justice bodies, including the QTC, and documentary accounts, like those presented by the *Iqqaumavara* project, speak of trauma. The brave people testifying publicly expose the violence that they have experienced and continue to experience. They stand vulnerable before witnesses and audiences. In their testimonies, they demand justice by speaking directly against oppression, yet simultaneously, those giving and hearing testimony relive atrocities and hardships. How, then, can a difficult history, like the Sangussaqtauliqtilluta period, be recounted in a way that both honours Inuit memory and avoids retraumatizing?

On the one hand, recounting this history answers the QTC's own recommendation that "both southern Canadians and younger Inuit should learn more about the changes that occurred in the 1950 to 1975 period in the Qikiqtani region."[39] In Paulette Regan's words, this account "restories" Canadian settler history with the experiences of those whom histories have often overlooked entirely or marginalized.[40] Quoting Inuit testimony also conveys this history in ways that honour specific Inuit knowledge by privileging an Inuit approach to historical consciousness – one that emphasizes oral tradition handed down through generations and sees the past lived in the present. Further, these personal testimonies, which recreate the past in rich detail and emotion, answer back to colonization (past and present) and can impact non-Indigenous audiences powerfully. In a discussion of the Truth and Reconciliation Commission of Canada, Anna Cook, for example, draws on Dian Million's "felt theory" to argue for the potential of testimonies to disrupt settler narratives in meaningful ways.[41] Cook advocates for the "possibility of hearing the experiential, subjective, and emotionally charged testimonies in *unsettling* ways. That is to say, felt knowledge can provoke settlers to become ethical witnesses and learn to listen differently – with a decolonizing ear."[42]

Yet, on the other hand, in quoting from restorative justice testimony and from oral accounts of difficult histories, there is an ever-present danger of retraumatizing. For example, in her discussion of historians' use of testimony from the South African Truth and Reconciliation Commission, Monica Patterson cautions, "It is important to acknowledge the *ethical murk* that defines our engagements with past violence. Signed consent forms cannot guarantee that interviewees will not be hurt or negatively affected by how we choose to portray them, or the (often unpredictable) circulations and afterlives of these portrayals ... In engaging with the past and probing into people's memories, oral historians can also generate new pain or reopen old wounds. It is important to hold this possibility up alongside the more celebratory characterizations that have papered over the ethical murk at the heart of all oral historical inquiry."[43] The reuse of sensitive testimony always runs the danger of opening new wounds and altering meanings. As articulated by oral historian Steven High, another concern with one scholar harvesting oral histories conducted and archived by others is that "intellectual labour ... [is] rendered invisible or inaudible." In the case of material in this chapter, I have been mindful of this concern by noting the QTC's and *Iqqaumavara*'s role in gathering testimonies and their methodologies.[44]

With these debates in mind, I have decided to recount the story of Sangussaqtauliqtilluta told through the testimonies gathered by the QTC and the *Iqqaumavara* project. This approach is one, I hope, that honours the Inuit-centred emphasis on orality and highlights the affective impact of Elders' memory while avoiding potential retraumatization. In what follows, I quote from several accounts but paraphrase and anonymize other testimonies with sensitive information. I have added references from the QTC and historical sources to provide further context for Elders' quotations. I also recognize that not all knowledge of this trauma will be accessible. My hope is that presenting this period through Elders' words can provide a fulsome historical picture that privileges Inuit culture and resilience and that does not define Inuit solely in terms of the traumas that they have endured.[45] The following historical overview is organized around some of the key themes identified by the QTC: life at *ilagiit nunagivaktangat* (camp), the move to permanent settlements overseen by Qallunaat, the relocation to the High Arctic, health care, schooling, housing, interactions with Qallunaat, and *qimmiit.* Because the *Iqqaumavara* project focused largely on the High Arctic relocations, its quotations are more limited than those of the QTC. Across all of these themes, I focus the discussion on testimonies and reports amassed by the QTC that relate mainly to Pond Inlet/Mittimatalik and Resolute/Qausuittuq, communities where Joseph Idlout lived. When Inuit Elders recall the history of Sangussaqtauliqtilluta, they speak of vivid personal experiences, *not* primarily of governmental policy. And although they unflinchingly outline the impact of Ottawa-led changes, their narratives insist on the importance of Inuit community and culture. For example, their testimonies are usually rooted in memories of *ilagiit nunagivaktangat* before the cultural disruptions. Elders recall travelling long distances and working together to hunt, sew, fish, and build sod houses. Often memories of life on the land are fond, as the focus is not on dramatic moments but on the comforting routines of life and an important sense of interconnectedness.[46] As Elder Elisapee Ootoova told QTC commissioner James Igloliorte, "We were only few of us. We had no choice but to help each other out. That's our culture. We help each other out always."[47]

The move to permanent settlements overseen by Qallunaat marked a period of difficult transition for Qikiqtaalungmiut. As one of the QTC's reports discusses in detail, the Inuit who lived in small groups at more than 100 *ilagiit nunagivaktangit* across the Qikiqtani region in 1950 had been concentrated into thirteen communities by 1975.[48] Inuit were often pressured to move, although some accepted the relocations as opportunities. The QTC's findings demonstrate that Inuit "consent" to the moves marked heightened cultural disjunctures or misreadings: what Qallunaat interpreted as willing agreement may have been prompted by fear or inhibitions in the face of stark power inequities.[49] Existence at settled communities was dramatically different from life at *ilagiit nunagivaktangat.* One Elder talked in depth about the change. At *ilagiit nunagivaktangat,* there was a small and close community, food was sufficient, and the family members were warm. Once at Pond Inlet/Mittimatalik, they lived in a tent without adequate heat, and country food (or wild game) was no longer available. The family's usual activities – sewing, hunting, and handiwork – were abandoned.[50] As Elder Isaac Qiyuapik summarized, "The transition from our life on the land to life today is completely a polar opposite of our lifestyle."[51]

For Inuit relocated to the High Arctic, those transitions were even more harsh. As discussed in detail by the *Iqqaumavara* project as well as in detailed scholarly studies, dozens of Inuit were coerced to move in 1953 from Inukjuak/Port Harrison (in what was then northern Quebec) to settlements established by the government in Resolute/Qausuittuq and Grise Fiord/Ausuittuq. In 1955, more Inuit would join them from Inukjuak/Port Harrison and Pond Inlet/Mittimatalik, including Idlout and his family.[52] Others would follow in subsequent years. The Canadian government deemed the relocations an "experiment"[53] that, as many Inuit and scholars have demonstrated, was motivated by the desire to assert sovereignty over the Arctic.[54] As one of Joseph Idlout's granddaughters, the musician Lucie Idlout, summarized in a 2014 interview with the Canadian Broadcasting Corporation, "We were basically human flagpoles."[55] The phrase "human flagpoles" has become a touchstone to describe the relocations.[56] Elder Markoosie Patsauq told the *Iqqaumavara* project,

> When I found out that this relocation was an experiment, I said to myself: there is something wrong there somewhere: Experimenting with the people, without their consent was forbidden by international law and … we have something to settle with the federal government. They need some explaining to do. Why they didn't tell us that this one was an experiment? And it was not for, it was not two years, it was more than that. They had a hidden motive. They didn't tell us that they were planning to make us stay up there for many many years. So that's another thing that angers me.
>
> Because using us as experimental objects was not legal, I would say. It was illegal according to the international law. So I said to myself, I think we have something against the federal government that will stand in court. But the federal government they kind of say: You volunteered. And it wasn't so. We didn't volunteer. Federal government just came into this area and said they have to send us up to the high arctic for two years. Two years was not bad. We could survive that. We could be away from the family for two years, away from the homeland for two years, hunt and come back in two years. That was not a bad idea. Beside they tell us they gonna support us all the way. Which was not the truth.[57]

In interviews for the *Iqqaumavara* project, Elders described how their families had been manipulated to move, often very unwillingly. As John Amagoalik, who was relocated as a child from northern Quebec to Resolute/Qausuittuq, told the *Iqqaumavara* researchers,

> I do remember the RCMP visiting our small camp when I was about five years old. And I do remember the relocation itself, I was almost six then. Well, they came to our camp, I remember that and they had some very intense conversations with my parents and I could understand that they were talking about being relocated to some other place, so I could understand the subject that was being discussed and I could understand that the RCMP were very determined to carry this project out and that my parents had a lot of reservations and they didn't want to take part at all when they first responded to the RCMP request. And I remember the RCMP went away, I don't know for how long but they came back and made the same request. They did that two or three times and I could sense that they were not willing to take no for an answer. And I remember my father finally agreed to the project under certain conditions. My father insisted that they would be allowed to return if they didn't like this new place and that the whole group would not be separated, that they would stay together.[58]

Leaving behind familiar environments and moving to the High Arctic was also a shock. As Joseph Idlout's son Moses explained to the *Iqqaumavara* researchers,

> When we arrived there, Qausuittuq is different than all the other places. It's not the same as Mittimatalik. When we arrived in Resolute it was ice. Maybe this height here, seven feet, was about the thickness of the ice on the bay. When we arrived in the middle of August by ship, the ship broke the ice. It was snowing the next day. Fall season was starting. It's very different from Mittimatalik. It was a lot colder. It was very different when we arrived there ... When one grows up in a place, that land becomes a part of that person. The land is a part of that person. When these people left their very own blood relatives and the land they're connected to, to never return, that had a big impact.[59]

Feeling abandoned and ill-equipped for the new environment, they feared for their survival. When the exiles told the RCMP that they wanted to return to their home communities, they were informed that they had to stay.

Inuit were also taken away to the south for health care, particularly those treated for tuberculosis during outbreaks. Although nursing stations were established at some communities, health care was more often provided on board the CGS *C.D. Howe*, an Eastern Arctic Patrol vessel that travelled across the Qikiqtani region.[60] Visits to the ship were often traumatic for Inuit.[61] Those diagnosed with tuberculosis were immediately taken away from their families and sent to sanatoria thousands of kilometres away in the south. As described in relation to the Nanilavut initiative, "an estimated one-third of all Inuit were infected with tuberculosis between the 1940s and 1960s."[62] One Elder, for example, remembered being sent to Manitoba for tuberculosis treatment. About eleven years old at the time, she and others were taken off the *C.D. Howe* at Kuujjuaq/Fort Chimo during the long voyage from Inukjuak/Port Harrison to Resolute/Qausuittuq. The girls remained there for two years. The foreign environment, filled with non-Inuit and unfamiliar food, was frightening to her. Compounding this anxiety, she was not at first returned to her parents in Resolute/Qausuittuq but instead sent by ship back to Inukjuak/Port Harrison in northern Quebec. It took months to be reunited with her family.[63] In *Martha of the North*, Martha Flaherty recalls her sister Mary having a similar experience in the south.[64]

Inuit were changed by the experience of hospitalization in the south. One Elder testified, for example, that after a year in hospital in Quebec City, he learned English but had lost many traditional skills. Upon returning north, he had to relearn to hunt.[65] Some Inuit taken south for health care never returned. Their families mourned without information about what happened to their loved ones or where they were buried.[66] Discussions of being taken to health care facilities in the south or watching family taken away marked painful parts of Elders' testimonies. Indeed, the hurt of these losses is palpable in the videotaped recordings as Elders recall parents and siblings taken away on the *C.D. Howe*.

The Idlout family, too, was impacted directly by southern interventions in health care. This book includes excerpts from Leah Idlout's personal experience as a tuberculosis patient on the *C.D. Howe* and at the Parc Savard Hospital in Quebec City in 1951–52.[67]

Like health care, schooling also fell under southern control and was referenced in testimonies before the Qikiqtani Truth Commission. Although the QTC did not explicitly address residential and federal day schooling, which were investigated nationally by the Truth and Reconciliation Commission of Canada, Elders testifying discussed their school experiences, and these accounts are referenced in commission reports. Often the legal requirement to attend school was used to pressure Inuit to move into settlements. RCMP and other officials threatened Inuit, telling them that they were legally required to send their children to school and that the governmental support that they needed so badly was contingent on compliance with this regulation.[68] A school was established in the community of Pond Inlet/Mittimatalik, for example, and Inuit in the surrounding area were told that they had to come into the community so that their children could attend school. One Elder told the commission of her own painful experience as a mother watching her children leave for school.[69] School itself became another arena of cultural conflict for children and their families. Elders described, for example, corporal punishment at school for speaking in Inuktitut.[70]

Other Inuit children were sent far away to residential schools.[71] Some from the Qikiqtani region were sent to Churchill or Iqaluit/Frobisher Bay to attend school.[72] The experience resulted in cultural loss for many. One Elder testified that he lost a sense of cultural foundation: "We missed out on the actual survival experiences because we were shipped off to systems that were foreign to Inuit."[73]

For family members at home in the Qikiqtani region, the absence of children sent to residential school was also disruptive. One Elder recalled growing up without older siblings who had been sent away to school and became strangers.[74]

Housing was another source of great strain and contributed to illnesses. For example, several Elders described in detail a housing shortage when they arrived in Pond Inlet/Mittimatalik in the 1950s.[75] They recalled spending the first winter living in a tent without adequate heat.[76] Once housing was finally secured, several families at times lived together in very crowded conditions. Every floor space would be covered with bedding.[77] Housing conditions in Resolute/Qausuittuq were even more austere. Those who arrived in the later 1950s often had nowhere to live. One Elder recalled a family of eleven living in a tent throughout the High Arctic winter. The following spring and summer, they built a makeshift home out of wood found at the dump.[78]

Qallunaat, with whom contact had previously been only periodic, were now a larger presence in Inuit lives. Hudson's Bay Company staff, missionaries, and especially officers of the RCMP figured prominently in Elder's recollections of this period. In testimonies, Elders spoke of their fear and mixed feelings about southerners. They described Qallunaat as "bossy and controlling."[79] Others testifying were more blunt. One stated, "In those days we were treated pretty much like dogs, we had to follow everything they said, we were treated like second class citizens back then. They were the big bosses in those days."[80] Tensions and racialized hierarchies often characterized the relationships between Inuit and southerners.

Among Qallunaat in the Qikiqtani region, the RCMP, which had a post in Pond Inlet/Mittimatalik as early as 1922, carried out a range of duties. Inadequately trained for life in the Arctic, authoritative, and erratic, RCMP officers exemplified the controlling Qallunaat for many Inuit. Inuit periodically encountered officers long before moving to settlements during their routine, annual patrols to *ilagiit nunagivaktangat* to gather information about Inuit and game.[81] As the QTC reports, around RCMP officers, Inuit often felt "*ilira*, the Inukitut term to describe a sense of fear, intimidation, and embarrassment."[82] Once Inuit had moved to permanent settlements, RCMP officer wielded more constant authority over them. But, paradoxically, they were also completely dependent on Inuit for survival. Indeed, in speaking to the QTC, several Elders characterized Qallunaat as childlike in their dependence on Inuit.[83] One Elder wanted to correct the prevailing historical record by stating,

> If the RCMP had ever tried to do this individually without the assistance of Inuit, they would never have survived without their assistance. These non-Inuit would have been dead. I think that this is something that southerners have to understand, especially from a historical perspective because we see a lot of old RCMP officers' stories about how heroic they were. But from our perspective without the Inuit looking after them hand and foot, they would not have survived … These people seem like they

were not on the same trips we were … We had to look after them like little kids … As people who couldn't look after themselves, they had to be clothed, fed, and kept in warm spots by the Inuit helpers. It was pretty much like looking after a five or six year old kid … Those Inuit really had a hard time because they didn't only have to look after themselves but after the RCMP.[84]

Among the Inuit on whom officers depended were those who worked for the RCMP as special constables – culture brokers employed in various capacities, including as guides and translators both of language and of Inuit ways.[85] The pressure on special constables and their families was enormous. As the daughter of a special constable reported to the QTC, her father "was expected to do everything, feed dogs, keep dogs quiet. I remember my father getting up in the middle of the night trying to keep the dogs quiet so the RCMP could sleep in peace. My mother was expected to make two sets of complete clothing for different seasons. All the special constables' wives were expected to do such thing[s] but that's on top of making all of the clothes for their large families. Apparently, they weren't paid for a long time. Some never received pay."[86]

Qimmiit became particular points of tension between Inuit and RCMP officers (as well as other Qallunaat) at settlements. Elders talked about the importance of dog teams to identity. For many Inuit men who hunted on the land, dogs were "partners."[87] In contrast, Qallunaat often saw dogs as threatening. The Ordinance Respecting Dogs required that dogs be tied up and muzzled in communities and that children not oversee dogs. These measures were all inconsistent with Inuit traditional practices. Significantly, the ordinance endorsed officers' right to destroy dogs "for humane reasons or reasons of safety" at the RCMP's discretion.[88] Numerous Elders testified to the QTC about dog shootings; indeed, as noted above, the commission was established to address the killings. The loss of dogs altered Inuit lives immediately and profoundly. Without dog teams (at a time when most could not afford snowmobiles), Inuit could not travel to *ilagiit nunagivaktangat* and hunt. The killings effectively kept them hostage in the communities established by government. As one Elder testified,

I spent more time in the community but was one of the last men to retain a dog team, most were advised not to keep a dog team at that time. We knew as long as they were tied up, we could keep them. We knew that any loose dogs would be shot. That was distressing because income was almost impossible. When that loose dog policy came around, it was disturbing because most of us had our dogs as transportation and most of us could not afford snowmobiles. These were the only ways to provide sustenance to our families because we were still in a subsistence form of life.[89]

In another testimony, the QTC was told of RCMP officers luring loose dogs with food and then shooting the animals.[90] At times, officers tasked Inuit – especially special constables – with killing dogs. This caused further discord within communities still alluded to today. As one Elder observed, "In hindsight, sometimes I reflect on the fact that the government and RCMP tried to change the accountability of dog shooting by tasking it to the local Inuit. What we underwent in this experience was quite traumatic."[91]

The killing of dogs compounded the other changes in society and had particular impact for the traditional gendered roles held by men in Inuit culture. As one Elder explained in his testimony,

> Back in those days prior to the transition, the status symbols of Inuit changed ... With the influx of the fur trade, the status symbol of an Eskimo man was self-reliance and the ability to maintain a team of twelve dogs. Twelve dogs was the magic number that Inuit tried to attain. Every man had to prove his ability to look after himself, his family, his dogs, and his clan. The ultimate pinnacle of that, the proof in the pudding as the white man have that saying, is having twelve dogs, caring for your family, and being a good hunter ... The transition resulted in a loss of status, and the reverberations have impacted us to date. Men, especially, lost their entire status. They went from independent, proud, self-fulfilled men to when they were moved to the community, to less than a man like a teenage boy. In the Inuit world, that would be akin to chopping off one leg at the knee and your other arm. When we got into the community, it was in a period of transition. It was a very mixed up community. A lot of Inuit men, especially, were unsure of their new roles. All you could see especially was a pallor of despair, hopelessness, and you could definitely feel the loss of cultural identity and pride and the fact that the men and the elders had lost their place in Inuit society. Another one of the developments I noticed was that all of a sudden, men who had been busy from waking up to bed time, constantly busy, all of a sudden had time on their hands. Time to reflect.[92]

In listening to Elders in a public forum, the Qikiqtani Truth Commission honoured their grief and their telling of the past. As QTC commissioner James Igloliorte stated in the QTC's final report, "Time and again, we were told the value of having accounts of events shared for the first time to an official Inuit-led body, which greatly aided in unburdening a heavy heart. There was also visible evidence that many of the speakers were at peace after testifying, or on their way towards healing."[93] By making recorded public testimonies like those quoted or paraphrased above, as well as by producing public histories, *Iqqaumavara* and the Qikiqtani Truth Commission also restoried the historical record. In insisting that the story of Sangussaqtauliqtilluta be told through Inuit experiences, it validated orality as a historical source while also demonstrating that oral history and conventional archival research can be complementary.[94]

Visuality and *Unikkaat*

Be mindful of the fact that what you think you see in these historical photographs does not reveal the context in which the photograph was taken.
– Qikiqtani Truth Commission, 2015[95]

Among the moving testimonies and archival documents amassed by the QTC and by *Iqqaumavara* are numerous images, including videos of Elders speaking as well as footage and still photographs documenting both organizations' work. This material is augmented by collections of archival images and by family snapshots dating from the 1950s through the 1970s, some taken by Elders who were interviewed or by their families. *Iqqaumavara*'s short films include numerous archival images, and the QTC's published reports are illustrated with archival images too. In their use of photographs and filmed footage, the QTC and *Iqqaumavara* implicitly acknowledge camera-made images as part of the ongoing story of Sangussaqtauliqtilluta.

Indeed, as I show throughout this book, cameras were ubiquitous in the Qikiqitani region during the 1950s and 1960s. Usually, they were wielded by visiting southerners. Missionaries, government officials, military personnel, and researchers, for example, often photographed and filmed the Arctic landscape and the Inuit they encountered. As Inuk leader John Amagoalik recalled, "The Inuit are probably the most photographed race of people on earth. The first time I saw a white man, he had a camera and it seems that whenever government officials or tourists came North, they always had cameras and they projected what we considered to be the wrong images of the Inuit – the Hollywood image or the stereotype image."[96] Like John Amagoalik, Inuit were accustomed to the camera as a key technology mediating the intercultural encounters between north and south, including the difficult histories that Elders narrate of that time.

John Amagoalik's – and other Inuit's – experiences of encountering southern culture through camera vision call to mind Mary Louise Pratt's familiar concept of the "contact zone."[97] When Pratt first used the term, she was examining travel writing from locations at particular historical moments when cross cultural interactions had occurred. For Pratt, the "contact zone" invokes "the spatial and temporal copresence of subjects previously separated by geographic and historical disjunctures, and whose trajectories now intersect ... A 'contact' perspective emphasizes how subjects are constituted in and by their relations to each other ... in terms of copresence, interaction, interlocking understandings and practices, often within radically asymmetrical relations of power."[98] Certainly, the Qikiqtani region of the 1950s and 1960s constituted a "contact zone." But I contend that camera vision and the images that cameras produced could also be understood productively as sites of "copresence, interaction, interlocking understandings and practices." In short, the manifold experiences of cultural encounter during the Sangussaqtauliqtilluta period took place, in part, through cameras.

By including a selection of the many camera-made images from this period in their historical critiques, the QTC and *Iqqaumavara* not only acknowledge the role of visuality in this difficult history but also reveal the complex layers of meaning in visual representations and visuality more broadly. For example, the *Guide to the Community Histories and Special Studies of the Qikiqtani Truth Commission*, a publication indexing the QTC's various individual reports, opens with a preface entitled "About the Photographs."[99] Here, the authors caution readers that "visual representation, through film and photography, is not objective. Viewers have no idea what occurred in the moments just before or just after a photo was taken, nor are they privy to what was left on the cutting-room floor. The context in which a photo was taken can affect or change what viewers feel when they engage with the photograph ... Readers are asked to be mindful of the fact that what you think you see in these historical photographs does not reveal the context in which the photograph was taken."[100] Although the QTC was at pains to dispel notions of photographic objectivity, it also included numerous images shot during the 1950s and 1960s of the Qikiqtani region. The inclusion of these images and related filmic imagery implicitly acknowledge that image meaning is always pliant, never fixed. Not only does the "context in which a photo was taken" or a film was shot contribute to its meaning, but the context of its reception also shapes meaning. Within records produced by the QTC and by *Iqqaumavara*, images take on new meanings. No longer visual records endorsing assimilation, they are transformed through the brave and moving words of Elders into visual evidence of resilience, or what Minnesota Chippewa scholar Gerald Vizenor terms "survivance."[101]

As I argue throughout *The Hunter, the Crown, and the Cameras*, assimilation policies and programs of this time were both enacted and resisted in part through images (and the varied experiences of visuality). The chapters that follow narrate a series of incidents revolving around visuality and Sangussaqtauliqtilluta. As a specific case study, I look at the complex relationship between Joseph Idlout and Doug Wilkinson as it played out visually in film and newsreel productions as well as in still photographs shot by the hunter Idlout, his Qallunaat friend Wilkinson, or others. Here, visuality also extends to the ways that Inuit lives were managed and categorized through the functions of the gaze and the bureaucratic organization of Inuit lives. As stated by J. Okalik Eegeesiak, president of the Qikiqtani Inuit Association, "This period of recent history is very much alive to Qikiqtaalungmiut."[102] The historical narrative that follows is told through images but also illuminated by the Inuit recollections cited in this chapter and by the publications written in the 1970s by Idlout's daughter Leah Idlout d'Argencourt Paulson and during the 1950s and 1960s by Idlout himself, both of which are reproduced throughout the book. Immediately following this chapter is an excerpt from the first part of Leah's 1977 five-part article on her experiences as a tuberculosis patient sent to the south for treatment. Leah's words make the disruption vivid.[103]

In the Idlout Family's Words 1

Excerpt from Leah Idlout d'Argencourt, "C.D. Howe I," *Inuit Today* 6, no. 5 (June 1977): 30–45, excerpt at 30–7

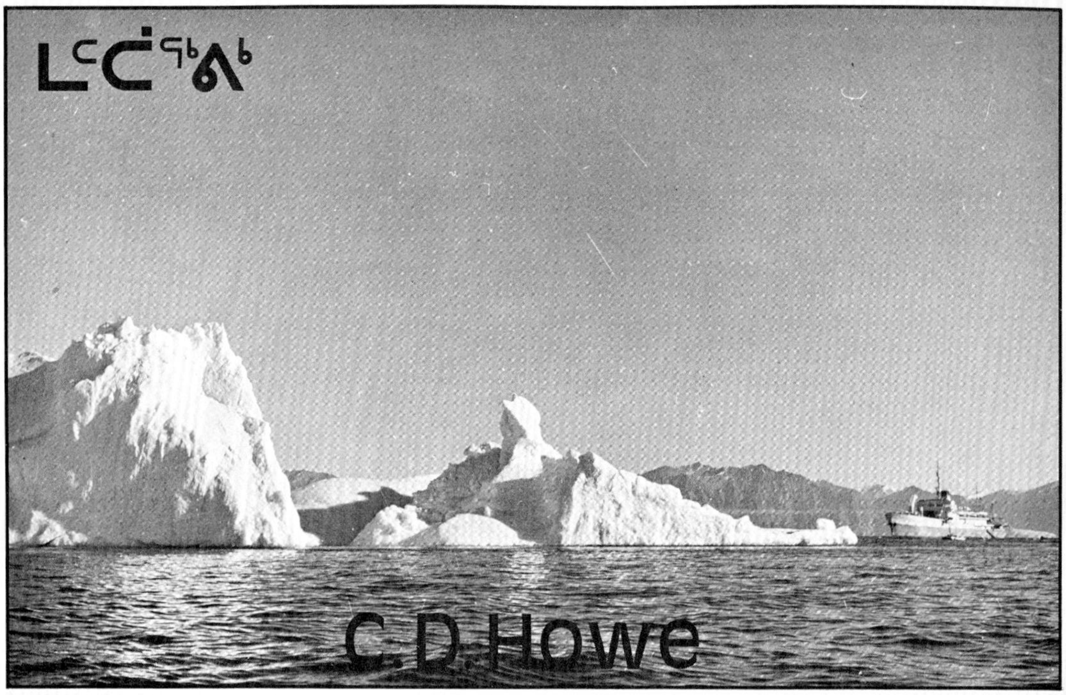

All photos in this article, unless otherwise stated, were taken by W. Doucette and are courtesy of the Public Archives of Canada.

by Leah Idlout d'Argencourt

ᓕᐊ ᐃᖕᓚᐅᒥᑦ

ᐃᓄᖕᓚᓇᐅᕐᑲᑕᐅᓯᒪᒐᒪ, ᐃᓅᓕᓚᐅᕐᓯᒪᖕᓗᖅᒪ ᐱᕈᕐᕕᒥᓯᒪᖕᓗᒍᓗ ᕐᑲᐅᓯᐃᑦᑐᓂᖅᕐ ᑕᐅᓲᒥ. ᐊᕐᖂᒍᑦ 17 ᓈᓕᕐᐸᑦ ᕐᑲᖕᓗᓈᑦ ᓄᓇᖅᒪᑦᓃᑦᓗᖅᒪ.

ᑕᕙᕋ ᑕᒪᒃᑯᐊ ᐱᓇᓱᕐᑲᑦᑕᕐᓯᒪᔾᒃᑲ ᓇᓂᑐᐃᑦᓇᕐᓗ ᓲᕐᑲᐃᒻᒪ ᓄᓇᓕᖅᓄᑦ ᓇᒧᑐᐃᑦᓇᖕ ᐊᐃᕐᑲᑦᑕᕐᓯᒪᒪᒪ ᐊᑭᐊᓂᒥᐅᓂᓗ ᐋᓂᒥᐊᕐᓗ ᐅᑭᐅᕐᑕᕐᑐᒥᐅᓂᕐᓴᖕ, ᑲᓇᑕᐅᖕᓗ ᓄᓇᖅᒪᓂ. ᐅᓄᕐᑐᐊᕐᑎᕐᑐᓄᑦ ᓇᕈᓇᒃᑎᖕᓗᖅᒪ, ᐊᐱᕐᓲᕐᑕᐅᕐᑲᑦᑕᕐᓯᒪᒪᒪ ᓇᓂᒥᐅᑕᐅᖅᒪᖅᒫᕐᒪ ᓇᓂᓗ ᐃᓅᓕᓚᐅᕐᓯᒪᔪᓇᐊᒃᓴᖕ, ᕐᑲᖅᒪᓗ ᕐᑲᖕᓘᓈᑦ ᓄᓇᖅᒪᑦᓄᖕᖅ ᑲᓇᐊᕐᖅ ᒪᐅᓯᓇᓚᐅᕐᑕᑦᓂᒃ, ᓇᓂᓗ ᐃᓕᑦᓂᐊᓴᐊᓚᐅᕐᓯᒪᖅᒪᖅᒫᕐᒪ, ᐊᓯᕈᓘᔭᖅᒥᑦᓂᒃ ᓗᑦᑕᐅᖕ.

ᑭᐅᔭᖂᖅᒪᒃᑭᑦ ᐊᐱᕐᓲᕐᑕᐅᔪᑦ, ᑭᓇᒃᑯᑐᐃᑦᓇᕐᓄᑦ ᐅᕐᑲᐅᖕᔭᐅᒡᒍᒪᒪ, ᕐᑲᓄᐃᒻᒪᑦ ᑎᑎᕋᕐᓯᒪᖖᒥᑦᑕᓇᐊᒃᓴᑦᓂᒃ ᐅᓂᒃ ᑳᓕᐅᕐᓗᖅᒪ ᐅᕐ ᑲᓖᒪᒃᓴᓂᒃ ᐅᕐ ᑲᐅᑎᔭᐅᔭᖂᖅ ᒪᒪ ᑕᐃᒪᑦᓇ ᐃᖅᑲᐃᑎᑕᐅᒡᒍᒪᒪ ᐃᓱᒪᓕᕐᑎᑕᐅᕙᒃᓗᖅᒪ, "ᐄᓛᒃ, ᓱᖅᒪᑦ, ᐅᕐ ᑲᓖᒪ ᒪᓕᐅᖕᖅᒥᓚᖅᒪ?

ᑕᕙᕋ ᑎᑎᕋᕐᑲᑦᑕᕐᓂᐊᕐᒪ ᑭᖅᑯᓕᓈᒃ ᑕᕐᓂᐊᕐᑐᓂᒃ ᐃᓄᐃᑦ ᐅᖕᓗᒥᒥ, ᐱᓇᓱᒃᕕᒥᓯᒪᓕᕐᓗᒥᑦ ᐅᑭᐅᐸ ᐅᖅᒪᑖᓄᑦ ᐋᖅᑭᒃᓱᐃᔪᐅᖕᓗᖅᒪ. ᑕᕙᕋ ᐅᕙᑦᓂᖕᓚᓇᒃ ᐱᔪᒪᒪᓗᐊᕐᓗᑎᒃ ᐅᓂᒃᑳᕐᓂᐊᕐᑐᑦ, ᑭᓯᐊᓂᑦᑕᐅᖅ ᐃᓅᕐᑲᑎᒃᑲ ᐊᑐᕐᓯᒪᔭᖅᒥᑎᒍᑦ ᐃᖅᑲᐃᕐᑲᑦᑕᕐᓂᐊᕐᑐᒃᓴᐅᖅᒪᑕ ᐃᓄᐃᑦ ᓄᓇᖅᒪᑦᓂ ᐊᒻᒪᓗ ᕐᑲᖕᓗᓈᑦ

I, an Inuk born and raised in the High Arctic, have spent the 17 last years of my life living in the south of Canada. During those years, I have held several jobs which have taken me, in the course of my work, to settlements from one side of the Arctic to the other, as well as to many parts of southern Canada. Many times during those trips, people have asked me questions about the place and circumstances of my birth, my first trip south, my schooling, and so on.

In answering such questions, I have related time after time stories of my life and experiences I have had. After listening to these stories, so often people have asked, "Why don't you write a book?" Each time this has been suggested to me, it has made me think, "Yes, why not, why don't I write a book about my life and the experiences I have had?"

Now I am ready to tell my story. I plan to tell it in a series of articles

ᓄᓇᖕ ᒪᑦᓄᐊᕐᓯᒪᕙᒃ ᑐᕕᓂᕐᓂᒃ. ᐊᑐᕐᓯᒪᔪᕐᔪᐊᕆᖕᓂᒃ ᑎᑎᕋᕐᑕᐅᓯᒪᕙᓐᖕᒋᑦᑐᓂᒃ. ᐃᓄᕐ ᑲᑎᒃ ᑲᔪ ᐱᓪᓗᒋᑦ ᑎᑎᕋᓐᓇᐊᕐᓯᔭᒃ ᑲ ᐃᓄᖕᓄᑦ ᓇᖕᒥᓂᖅ ᑎᑎᕋᕐᑕᐅᓯᒪᔪᓂᒃ ᐅᓂᒃ ᑳᓚᐅᕐᓯᒪᔪᕐ ᑲᑦᑎᐊᓐᖕᒋᒪᒪᑦ ᒫᑦᓇᐅᔪᖅ. ᑕᑯᓯᒪᔭᒃ ᑲᔪ ᕐᑲᓪᓗᓈᑎᑐᑦ ᐅᕐ ᑲᐱ ᑦᓇᓐᖕᒋᔪᖕ ᒪᕐᓗᖕ ᒪ ᐱᒋᐊᕐᓗᒋᑦ ᐅᓂᒃ ᑳᑦᑎᐊᐱᒪᒪᓗᐊᕐ ᑐᖕ ᒪ ᐅᐊᑦᑎ ᐊᐱᕕᓂᕐᑐᑦ ᐅᑎᕐᑎᑦᓇᔪᖕᓂᕐ ᑑᓐᖕᒋᑦᑑᒪᓗᐊᖅ ᑎᑎᕐᕐᓯᒪᔫᕐ ᑯᑎᕐ ᑲᑦᑎᐊᓐᖕᒋᓗᐊᕐᑦᑕ ᑭᓯᐊᓂ ᐃᓅᓪᓗᑕ.

ᓯᕗᓪᓕᕐᐸᐅᓪᔨᓂᐊᕐᑐᖕ ᒪ ᒪᑦᑖᕐᕕᒃ ᑰᐸᓯᓐᓚᐅᕐᓯᒪᔭᑦᓂᒃ, ᐆᓪᓚᓇᐊᓐᖕ ᒪᐅᓯᓐᓚᓚᐅᕐᓯᒪᔭᑦᓂᒃ ᐋ ᒪᔪᖅᑳᑦᓂᒃ ᕐᑭᒪᐃᓪᓗᖕ ᒪ ᓯᕗᓪᓕᕐᐹᑦᑎᐊᒥᒃ. 12-ᓂᒃ ᐊᕐᖁᕐ ᑲᓚᕐᓗᖕ ᒪ ᐃᓅᓯᕐ ᐊᔾᔨᕐᑎᑕᐅᖅᑯ ᓴᓚᐅᕐᓯᒪᖕᒪᑦ ᐊᒻᒪᓗ ᐊᑲᐅᕐ ᑲᑦᑕᐱᑦᓂᕐᒪᑦ ᒪᑦᓇ.

in Inuit Today, of which I have been editor for over a year. This is my personal story, but it is also one with which so many Inuit will be able to identify. It is a story dedicated to the Inuit of the North.

I am starting with an account of my first trip on the ship, the C.D. Howe, for it was this unexpected adventure at the early age of 12 that changed my life so completely and made it difficult for me to remain a full Inuk living in the North.

ᐊᑖᑕ, ᔫᓯᐱ ᐃᓪᓚᐅᖅ, ᓄᓇᓕᖕᓂ ᐃᓯᒪᓕᒃ ᑕᐅᓚᐅᕐᓯᒪᖕᒪᑦ, ᓄᕗᕈᓗᐊᓂ, ᕐᑲᓂᖅᔭᓂ ᒥᑦᑎᒪᑕᓕᐅ< ᐅᐱᕐᖕᒥᕕᑦᑎᑦᓂ ᕐᑭᑭᕐᑖᓗ< ᐃᓯᐊᓂ. ᐃᓪᓗᐅᕐᓯᒪᔪᖕᒪᓕ ᐸᒥᐅᔭᒥ ᓄᕗᕈᓗᐊᑕ ᕐᑲᓂᖅᔭᓂ, ᓄᕗᕈᓗᐊᓂᓕ ᐅᐱᕐᖕᒥᑦᓗᐊᑕᕐᐸᓚᐅᕐᓯᒪᓚᐅᑦᑕ ᐆᓚᑦᑎᕕᖕᒥᓗ ᐱᕆᕐᕕᒥᓕᓚᐅᕐᓯᒪᔭᕐ ᐃᓚᒃ ᑲᓗ ᐃᓚᐃᑦᓇᑦᑎᑦᓂᒃ ᓄᓇᑦ ᑲᑎᕐ ᑲᖕ<ᒃᑎᓪᓗᑕ. ᓱᖕᑯᐃᓱᑦᓚᓐᓄᑎᒥᓕᕐᓗᒋᑦ ᑕᐃᑦᓱᒪᓂᐅᑎᓪᓗᒍ ᐅᒥᐊᕐᔪᐊᕐ ᑕᕐ ᑲᐅᓯᓐᖕᒪᒃ ᑕᖕ ᒪᓂ, ᑕᐃᑦᓇᓗ ᒪᑦᑳᕐᕕᒃ ᓰᑏᕼᐆ.

ᐅᐱᕐᖕᒪᓇᐊᑕᒫᑦ, ᓯᑯᐃᔭᕐᓯᒪᓕᕐᑎᓪᓗᒍ, ᕐᑲᓪᓗᓇᑦᓯᐊᖅᒥᑦᓇᕐ<ᓚᐅᕐᓯᒪᖕᒪᑦ ᐊᑖᑕ ᐅᐱᕐᖕᒥᕕᑦᑎᑦᓂᑦ ᒥᑦᑎᒪᑕᓕᖕᒍᑦ ᒫᑦᑳᕐᕕᒃᓯᐅᓇᐊᕐ ᑐᕐᓗᓂ, ᐅᒥᐊᕐᑲᕐᒥ ᐆᓚᐅᑎᓕᖕᒥᒃ ᐊᑐᕐ ᑕᐅᔭᓐᐊᕐ ᑲᕐᑲᑦᑕᓚᐅᕐᓯᒪᖕᒪᑦ ᕐᑲᓪᓗᓈᑦ ᐅᒥᐊᕐᔪᐊᓕᐊᕐᑲᑦᑕᕐᑐᓄᑦ ᓄᓇᓕᓕᐊᕆ ᑦᓴᕐᑲᑦᑕᕐᓗᓂᓗ ᐅᓯᒃᑕᕐᑲᑕᐅᕐᑲᑦᑕᕐᓗᓂᓗ ᓄᓇᓕᖕᓄᑦ ᓂᐅᕐᑦᑕᐅᔪᓂᒃ, ᑕᑯᓪᓗᓂᓗ ᕐᑲᓪᓗᓈᑦ ᑎᑭᑕᐅᓕᑕᐃᑦᓇᕐᒥᑲᒥᒃ ᐅᑭᐅᓕᒫᒧᑦ ᓈᓴᓂᐊᕐᑐᓂᒃ ᑭᓱᒃᓴᕐ ᑖᑕᐃᑦᓇᕐ<ᓚᐅᕐᓯᒪᖕᒪᑕ. ᓂᐅᕕᕐᖃᕐᓗᓂ ᓂᕐᑭᒃᓴᕐᑎᑦᓂᒃ ᐆᔭᖅ ᐅᑭᐊᒃᓵᓗᓪᓗ ᓯᑯᓐᖕᒥᑦᓂᓕᒫᖕᒪᓄᑦ. ᓇᒃᓴᕐ<ᓚᐅᕐᓯᒪᖕᒪᑎᒍᑦ ᐃᓚᒦᓕᒫᑎᒍᑦ ᐃᓚᒃ ᕐᑭᑐᕐᖕᒪᓕᒫᓂ ᐊᖕᓇᒪᓗ ᐃᓚᐅᓕᑕᐃᑦᓇᕐᓗᑕ, ᐆᑦᓖᑦᑎᐊᕐ ᑐᐊᑦᓅᕐ ᑲᑦᑕᐅᕐ ᑲᑦᑕᓚᐅᕐᓯᒪᔪᒍᑦ ᐅᖕᒪᔪᖕᑰᓴᕙᒃᓗᓂᓗ ᐅᐱᕐᖕᒥᕕᑦᑕ ᐊᑯᑦᓂᖕᒪᓂ ᒥᑦᑎᒪᑕᓕᖕᒥᐅᑦᓗ ᕐᑲᓪᓗᓈᓕᑦ.

ᓂᖕᒥᒡᔭᒃ ᑯᒃᑲᓕ, ᐸᓂᐸᐱᒃ ᑯᒃᑲᓗ — ᓄᓇᑦᑎᑦᓄᔪᑎᓚᐅᕐᓯᒪᔭᖕ ᒪ ᐃᑲᔪᕐᑎᒋᔪᒪᓪᓗᓂᐅᒃ ᐊᒃᑲᒪ, ᐊᑖᑕᒪ ᓄᑲᑐᐊᑦᑎᐊᖕ ᒪ ᑐᕐ ᑯᑎᓪᓗᒍ — ᐊᒻᒪᓗ ᐊᐃᒪ ᑕᐃᑯᓂ ᓄᓇᑦᑎᑦᓂ ᕐᑭᒪᒃᓗᑎᒍ ᓇᑦᑎᕐᓱᖕᓂᐊᕐᒪᑕ ᕐᑭᖕᓂᔭᒃᓴᓂᒃ ᐅᑭᐅᒃᑯᑦ ᓂᕐᑭᒃᓴᓇᓂᐊᕐ ᑕᑦᑎᑦᓂᒃ

ᑕᐃᑯᓂ, ᒥᑦᑎᒪᑕᓕᖕᒥ, ᐅᑕᖕᑭᓕᕐ ᑲᑦᑕᓚᐅᕐᓯᒪᔪᒍᑦ ᒪᑦᑳᕐᕕᒥᒃ. ᑕᐃᑦᓱᒪᓂᐅᑎᓪᓗᒍ, ᑎᑭᕐᑲᑦᑕᕐᓂᓴᔭᖕ ᒪ ᒫᑦᑳᕐᕕᐅ< ᐱᕕᖕᔪᐊᓴᔭᐅᕐᑲᑦᑕᓚᐅᕐᓯᒪᖕᒪᑦ ᑭᓇᒃᑯᑐᐃᑦᓇᕐᓄᑦ, ᕐᑲᓪᓗᓈᓄᐊᓐᖕᒍᐊᒃ, ᕐᑭᑭᕐᑖᓗᖕᒥᐅᑕᔪᖕᓄᑦ ᓄᓇᓕᖕᓂᑦᑐᓄᑦ. ᑕᐃᑦᓱᒪᓂᐅᑎᓪᓗᒍ, ᐅᒥᐊᕐᔪᐊᒃ ᐊᒃᑯᑎᑐᐊᖕᒍᕐᑲᑦᑕᓚᐅᕐᓯᒪᖕᒪᑦ ᓄᓇᓕᖕᓄᑦ ᕐᑭᑭᕐᑖᓗᖕᒥᐅᓄᑦ ᐊᔪᖕᒥᑦᓄᑦᓗ ᐊᑭᐊᒥᐅᑦ ᐃᓚᖕᒥᑦᓄᐊᕐ ᑲᑦᑕᕐᑐᓂ ᕐᑲᓪᓗᓈᓂᓐᖕ ᑰᕐᑐᓂ. ᐅᐱᕐᖕᒪᓇᐊᑕᒫᑦ, ᒪᓐᑐᓇᐊᒥᓐᖕ ᑰᕐᑐᓂ, ᐅᓯᕐ ᑲᑦᑕᓚᐅᕐᓯᒪᖕᒪᑦ ᓂᐅᕕᐊᒃᓴᓂᒃ ᕐᑲᓪᓗᓈᓪᓗ ᐱᒃᓴᖕᒥᑦᓂᒃ ᓄᓇᓕᖕᓄᐊᕐ ᑐᓂᒃ — ᓄᓇᓕᑦᓴᖕᓄᑦ ᐅᑭᐅᓕᒫᒧᑦ ᓈᓪᓗᒪᔪᒃ ᑐᓂᒃ ᐊᕐᖁᒍᓕᕐᒥᖕ<ᑦ ᑭᓯᐊᓂ ᑕᐅᐅ ᑎᑭᑕᐃᑦᓇᐱᒫᕐᒥᖕᒪᑦ. ᕐᑲᓪᓗᓈᕐ ᑲᖕᒍᐅᓪᓕᐊᔪᓂᒃᓗ ᑎᑭᐅᑦᓴᕐ ᑲᑦᑕᐅᕐᓯᒪᖕᒪᑦ — ᓂᐅᕕᕐᑎᒃᑯ

My father, Joseph Idlout, was the leader of our camp, Nuvurulua, which was near Pond Inlet on the northern tip of Baffin Island. I was born at Tay Sound near Nuvurulua, and it was at Nuvurulua that I spent my early years with my family and other close relatives. Among my most vivid memories of those days were the visits of that legendary ship, the C.D. Howe.

Each spring, after the ice had broken up, my father would travel from our camp to Pond Inlet to take part in the annual visit of the C.D. Howe. His motor boat was used to transport the white people in the settlement to and from the ship and to help unload supplies for the coming year. This was also the time for my father to purchase food for the summer and fall to last us until freeze up. He would take our whole family with him, and the trip between the camp and the settlement was a long but enjoyable one for all of us.

My grandparents, my second cousin - who my father brought to our camp to help him after my uncle, my father's only brother died - and my brother-in-law would stay behind to continue hunting seals to cache for winter food.

There, in Pond Inlet, we would wait for the arrival of the C.D. Howe. In those early years, the annual visits of the C.D. Howe formed a very important part in the lives of people, especially white, living in the Eastern Arctic settlements. At that time, the ship was the only transportation link between the settlements of the Eastern Arctic and the south. Each spring, travelling from Montreal, it sailed north to deliver goods and supplies to the settlements - goods which would have to last the people of

31

ᑦᓂᒃ, ᐸᓖᓯᒃᑯᑦᓂᒃ, ᐊᔪᕿᖅᑐᐃᔨᒃᑯᑦᓂᒃ — ᐊᖅ ᐅᑎᔫᕐᓗᓂ ᓄᓇᓕᖕᓄᑦ ᐊᐅᕐᓚᕈᑕᐅᖅᑲᑦᑕᖅᓗᓂᓗ ᖅᑲᕐᓗᓈᑦ ᓄᓇᖕᒪᑦᓄᑦ ᐅᓯᕐᔪᖅᑲᑦᑕᓚᐅᖅᓯᒪᖕᒪᑦ.

ᑎᑭᑦᓂᖕᒪ ᒪᑦᑳᖅᕕᐅᑉ ᐊᒻᒪᑦᑕᐅᖅ ᐋᓐᓂᐊᖅᓯᐅᖅᑲᑦᑕᓚᐅᖅᓯᒪᖕᒪᑦ ᑕᑉᐸ ᐋᓐᓂᐊᖅᓯᐅᓕᑕᐅᑕᐃᑦᓇᖅᓗᑕ. ᑕᑉᐸᓗ ᓂᐅᖅᐃᓇᓯᓕᖅᓗᓂ ᐅᓯᔪᐋᓗᒪᒥ ᐅᒥᐊᖅᔪᐊᖅ, ᓘᒃᑖᑦ ᑭᒍᓯᕆᔨᓗ ᐋᓐᓂᐊᖅᓯᐅᓇᕈᓘᔭᑲᐅᖅᑐᖅᑲᑦᑕᖅᓗᑎᒃ ᑎᑭᓯᒪᓚᐅᕐᐱᕐᓛᖅᔪᓂᖅ ᓚᓂ ᐃᓄᓕᒫᓂᒃ ᖅᑲᕐᓗᓇᕐᓯᐊᖅᓯᒪᔪᓂᒃ ᓄᓇᖕᖕᓂᑦᑕᐅᖅ ᖅᑲᕐᓗᓈᖅ ᑲᓐᖕᒥᑦᑐᖅᒥᐅᓂᒃ ᐃᓚᒥᓚᐅᕐᓯᕐᓗᓂ.

ᑎᑭᑐᐊᖅᑦᑕ ᖅᑲᕐᓗᓇᑦᓯᐊᖅᓗᑕ ᒥᑦᑎᒪᑕᓕᖕᒧᑦ, ᐊᑖᑕᒐ ᓂᐅᕕᖅᐸᓚᐅᖅᒪᑦ ᐊᑦᓄᕆᒃᓴᓂᒃ ᓂᐅᕕᖅᑎᒃᑯᓂᑦ ᓂᐅᕕᖅᑎᔫᑎᕐᓗᒥᑦᑕᐅᖅ ᓄᑖᓂᒃ ᐊᑦᓄᖁᑖᓇᓂᐊᖅ ᑕᑦᑎᑦᑲᓂᒃ ᐅᒥᐊᖅᔪᐊᖅᓯᐅᑎᒥᓂᐊᖅᓗᑎᒍ. ᓄᑖᓂᒃ ᐊᑦᓄᖁᖅᑖᓇᓂᐊᖅᑕᑦᑎᑦᓂᒃ ᐋᓈᒐ ᐊᑦᓄᖁᓚᐅᖅᑐᐊᓖᖅᐸᓚᐅᖅᓯᒪᖕᒪᑦ ᖅᑯᓕᑦᑕᐅᔭᓚᐅᖅᓗᓂᑎᒍᑦ ᐊᖅᓯᑖᖅᑐᖅᓗᑕᓗ, ᐅᕕᓂᕈᖅᑖᖅᑐᖅᓗᑎᒃᓗ ᐊᓂᒃᑲ ᖅᑲᖅᓚᖅᑖᖅᑐᖅᓗᑎᒃᓗ. ᓇᑦᑎᖅᕕᓂᖅᓂᒃᓘᑦᓃᑦ ᑲᒥᒃᑖᖅᑐᖅᓗᑕ ᐱᕙᓚᐅᖅᑦᑕ. ᐊᖅᑫᒍᖅᑲᓕᖅᓗᖕᒪ 11-ᓂᓂᒃ, ᐃᑲᔪᕈᑦᓇᖅᓯᓚᐅᖅᓯᒪᓕᒪ ᖅᑯᓕᑦᑕᐅᔭᒃᓵᖕᓂᒃ ᐊᖅᓯᓕᐅᕆᐅᖅᓗᖕᒪ, ᐅᕕᓂᕈᓕᐅᕈᐅᑦᓇᖅᓯᕐᓗᖕᒪᓗ ᐊᒻᒪᓗ ᖅᑯᓕᑦᑕᐅᔭᐅᑉ ᖅᑲᓖᖕᒥᑦᓂᒃ ᐊᓂᑦᓄᑦ. ᒥᖅᓱᕆᐊᒃᓴᖅ ᖅᑯᕕᐊᒥᒻᒪᕆᒃᐸᓚᐅᖅᑲᒃᑯ, ᒥᖅᓲᒪᒥᒃ ᐊᑐᕆᐊᒃᓴᖅ ᖅᑯᕕᐊᒥᓗᐊᖅᑲᑦᑕᓚᐅᖅᓯᒪᒐᒃᑯ, ᐋᓈᒐ ᐊᑦᓄᖅᕐᓯᐅᖅᑎᕐᓗᒍ ᒥᑭᑦᓂᑦᓂᑦ ᑲᕐᔮᕆᐸᓚᐅᖅᓯᒪᒐᒃᑯ ᓄᑖᓂᒃ ᐊᑦᓄᖅᕐᓯᐅᖅᑎᕐᓗᒍ.

ᐱᓕᕆᔪᐃᑦᓈᓗᓕᖅᐸᓚᐅᖅᓯᒪᖕᒪᑕ ᐱᓇᓱᒃᑐᐃᑦᓈᓗᓕᖅᓗᑎᒃ, ᐋᓈᒐᓗᐋᖅᓗᒃ, ᐊᒻᒪᓗ ᐸᐃᓐᔭᕆᐊᖅ ᑲᐃᑦᓇᓕᖅᐸᓚᐅᖅᓯᒪᖕᒪᑦ ᐊᓂᒐᓚᑦᑲᓂᒃ ᓄᑲᖅᓕᖅᓂᒃ, ᑕᑉᐸ ᑕᒪᑦᓇᐅᓕᖅᑎᕐᓗᒍ ᐆᔪᐸᐅᖅᓯᒪᔪᓂᒃ ᓂᖅᑭᑕᖅᑲᑦᑎᐊᕈᓃᓚᐅᖅᓯᒪᖕᒪᑦ ᓂᖅᑭᕐᓚᕆᒃᑕᖅᑦᑎᐊᕈᑦᓇᓚᐅᖅᓯᒪᓇᓂᓗ ᖅᑲᕐᓗᓈᓕᖕᓂ ᓄᓇᓕᖕᓂ, ᑳᖕᒥᑦᓇᕈᓘᖕᓇᖅᓯᐸᓚᐅᖅᓯᒪᔪᖅ.

ᐊᑯᓚᐃᐸᓗᒃᑐᒥᒃ, ᐊᑖᑕᒐ ᓂᐅᕕᖅᑎᒃᑯᓕᐊᖅᐸᓕᐅᖅᓯᒪᔪᖅ ᒪᑦᑳᖅᕕᒃ ᓈᓂᕐᓗᐊᓕᖅᓯᒪᖕᓖᑦ. ᓂᐅᕕᖅᑎᒃᑯᑦ ᐊᖕᒪᔪᖅᑳᖕᒪᑦ ᓈᓚᐅᑎᓕᔫᐸᓚᐅᖅᓯᒪᖕᒪᑦ ᐊᐅᓚᖅᑎᕐᔫᕐᓗᓂᓗ. ᑕᐃᑦᓯᒪᓂᐅᑎᕐᓗᒍᓕ ᑕᒪᒃᑯᐊ ᓄᓇᓖᑦ ᑐᓴᖅᔪᒃᑕᑐᐊᕆᓚᐅᖅᓯᒪᒐᒃᑭᑦ, ᐃᒡᓗᓕᒃ, ᐃᒃᐱᐊᖅᔪᒃ, ᐸᖕᓂᖅᑑᖅ ᐊᒻᒪᓗ ᑲᖕᖕᒥᖅᓗᓖᐱᒃ. ᖅᑲᐅᓴᒪᕐᓗᖕᒪ ᑕᐃᒪ ᑲᖕᒥᖅᓗᓖᐱᒃ ᑭᖕᒍᕐᓕᖅᐹᒥᒃ ᑎᑭᓚᐅᖅᓂ ᖅᑲᓂᑦᓂᖅᐸᐅᖕᒪᑦ ᓄᖅᑲᖅᕕᒥᔭᑐᐊᕆᓂᐊᖅᓗᓂᐅᒃ ᐅᒥᐊᖅᔪᐊᖅ, ᒥᑦᑎᒪᑕᓕᖕᒧᑦ ᑎᑭᓐᖕᒥᓚᐅᕈᑎᑐᐊᕆᓕᖅᓗᓂᐅᒃ.

ᐊᓯᐃᓛᖅᓗᒃ ᑕᐃᒪ, ᐳᓛᕆᐊᑦᓱᔭᖅᐸᓚᐅᖅᓗᓂ, ᐊᑖᑕᒐ ᐅᑎᖅᒥ ᐊᓯᐃᓛᒃ ᐅᖅᑲᐅᑎᐸᓚᐅᖅᓯᒪᖕᒪᑎᒍᑦ ᓰᑏᕼᐊᐅᔫᖅ ᑐᖕᒥᒍᒥᐊᓯᕗᖅ ᑎᑭᑦᓂᐊᓕᖅᓗᓂ ᑕᑉᐸ ᐃᑲᖅᖅᐃᑦ ᐅᓄᖕᖕᒥᑦᑐᑯᓗᐃᑦ ᓈᑐᐊᖅᐸᑕ. ᑕᑉᐸ ᐊᑯᓂᐊᓘᖅᑰᕐᔫᑦ ᐅᑕᖅᑭᑦᓱᔭᓚᐅᖅᓗᑕ ᐱᖅᓚᕈᔫᒃᑐᐋᓗᓕᖅᓗᑕ ᓇᐅᑦᑎᖅᓱᑦᓱᔭᖅᐸᓚᐅᖅᓗᑕᓗ, ᐅᒥᐊᖅᔪᐊᖅᓗᒃ ᐊᓚᒃᑲᑦᓚᖅᐳᖅ.

ᓴᖅᑭᑦᓂᐊᓗᐊ ᑲᒪᓇᖅᐸᓚᐅᖅᓯᒪᖕᒪᑦ ᓰᑏᕼᐊᐅᑉ. ᖅᑲᖅᑳᓗᐃᑦ ᐊᑯᑦᓂᖕᒪᒍᑦ ᓄᐃᓯᕐᓛᖅᒪᑦ ᓴᖅᑦᑐᐊᓗᒃ ᐅᐊᑲᕐᓚᓖᖕᒍᐸᓚᐅᖅᓯᒪᖕᒪᑦ. ᐅᒃᐱᖅᓇᑦᑎᐊᖅᑰᓯᐸᓚᐅᖅᓯᒪᖕᖕᒥᒻᒪᕐᔫᑦᓃᑦ ᐊᖕᒥᔪᕐᓚᖔᖅᑰᓯᐸᓚᐅᖅᓯᒪᖕᒪᑦ ᐃᖕᒥᖅᖅᓯᔪᐊᓗᒃ ᐊᐅᓚᐅᑎᒥᓄᑦ ᐃᓐᖕᒥᖅᖅᑕᐅᕐᓗᐊᖅᑰᓯᓇᓂ. ᓯᕗᐊᓗᐊ ᖅᑲᑯᑲᕐᓚᒃᓗᓂ ᖅᑲᓖᖅᑎᓇᕐᓚᑦᑖᖅᑐᖅ ᐃᖕᒥᖅᖅᓂᐊᓗᖕᒥᓄᑦ ᓯᖅᓗ ᓴᕕᒃ ᑲᐱᐸᕐᓕᐊᕐᓚᑦᑖᖅᑰ

the communities and surrounding areas for the whole of the following year. And it carried the white people - traders, R.C.M.P., missionaries - to and fro between the communities in which they were serving and the south.

The visits of the C.D. Howe also served an important medical purpose. At the same time as the cargo was being unloaded from the ship, doctors and a dentist on board made quick examinations of the white people in the settlement and all the Inuit who had gathered there from the surrounding area.

As soon as we reached Pond Inlet, my father would purchase materials from the Hudson's Bay store for my mother to make us new clothing before the ship arrived. Out of the new material my mother would quickly produce duffle parkas and socks, shirts for my brothers and pairs of pants. We would even get new seal skin boots. At age 11, I was old enough by then to help make the duffle socks, shirts and parka covers for my brothers. I really liked sewing, especially using the sewing machine, for I had watched my mother closely for many years as she made new clothing for us.

Everyone would be so busy, especially my mother, and I had to look after my younger brothers too. During this time, we would hardly get any cooked meals for there was not much Inuit food available in the settlement.

Once in awhile, my father would go to the Hudson's Bay to check on the whereabouts of the C.D.Howe. The manager there was the owner and operator of the only HF radio in the settlement. At that time, I had only heard the names of settlements like Igloolik, Arctic Bay, Pangnirtung and Clyde River. I knew that Clyde River was the last stop before Pond Inlet.

Finally, after several visits, my father would return to tell us that the C.D. Howe was on its way and would be arriving at such and such an hour. Then, after what seemed like hours of waiting and watching, the ship would loom into sight.

The first glimpse we had of the C.D. Howe was always amazing to me. Rounding the side of a steep cliff, she would suddenly appear in view. I found it hard to believe that a thing so enormous could move so fast. Her white bow seemed to cut through the water like a knife,

ᓯᕗᖅ, ᐃᖕ ᒥᐅᓕᒐᕗᐊᕐᑎᑦᑎᐊᔪᓕᕐᔪᓂᔪ ᐃᒪᕐᒥᒃ ᕿᓴ ᕐᕕᒥᓂᐊᕐ ᑕᒥᓄᑦ ᐊᐃᕗᐊᔪᒃ.

ᐊᒻᒪᑦᑕᐅᖅ ᐅᐊᒃᑰᓚᒥᕐ ᑲᑦᑕᓚᐅᕐᓯᒪᖕᒥᔭᕐ ᓰᑏH ᐅ ᒪᑦᑖᕐᕕᐅᐸ ᐅᓯᒃ ᑲᐅᓂᐊᓗᐊ ᐃᓄᒥᐊᔭᒐᕗᐊᓂᒃ. ᕐᑯᓂᒥᑰᓂᕐ ᑲᒻᒪᕆᒃᔪᓂ ᐊᒡᓛᑦ ᒥᑦᑕᕐᕕᕐ ᑲᒻᒪᕆᒃᔪᓂ ᕐᑲᖕᒐᑦᑕᕐᑐᑯᖕᒪᑦ ᕐᑭᓚᒃᑰᕐᑐᖅ ᑕᖁᑲ ᕐᑲᖅᑳᔪ ᐃᑦ ᕐᑯᓚᐅᑕᑯᔪᒥᐤᔪᓂᒥᑦ. ᐊᒡᒥᕐᑐᑯᔪᒃ ᑕᖁᑲ ᕐ ᕿᓚᒃᑯᑦ ᓲᕐᔫᓂ ᐸᖕᓇ ᕿᒃᑐᕙᐊᑯᔪᒃ, ᒥᑦᔪᓂ ᐊᓯᐃ ᓛᒃ ᑕᕝᕙ ᓄᓇᓖᑦ ᓴᑦᑎᐊᖕᒐᑦᓄᑦ ᐊᑯᑦᓂᖕᒐᑦᓄᑦ. ᑕᒪᑦᓴ ᑲᒪᕗᑦ ᐅᐊᒃᑰᓚᑐᓯᒃᑐᑦ ᑕᑯᔭᕐᑐᕐᑐᐋᓂᕐᔪ ᑎᒃ ᐃᓄᒥᐊᒃᓯᑲᐅᑎᒥᕐ ᑲᑦᑕᓚᐅᕐᓯᒪᕗᑦ ᓄᐊᑦᑐᑦ ᑕᕙ ᕗᖕᒐ ᕐᑯᓂᒦᑰᓂᑰᐸ ᒥᕙᕕᒥᔭᖕᒐᓄᑦ ᓂᐅᕙᕕᐅᓇᐊᕐᑐ ᐅᕐᑲᓇᐊᕐᑐᕐᑐᒥᒃ ᒪᑦᑖᕐᑎᑕᐅᔭᕐᑐᕐᓂᐊᕐᑐᑦ ᐋᖅᑭᒃ ᓱᕐᑕᐅᓕᕐᑎᓐᑐᒥᑦ.

sending huge waves that hissed and rolled all the way to where we would be waiting at the water's edge.

It amazed me also to think that the C.D. Howe could carry so many people all at the same time. She even carried a helicopter on the front top deck that would fly up into the sky at the same time as the ship appeared from behind the cliff. The helicopter would hover in the sky like a hugh mosquito, and then land right in the middle of the settlement. A crowd of eager spectators would quickly gather while officials disembarked to begin making arrangements for the medical examinations.

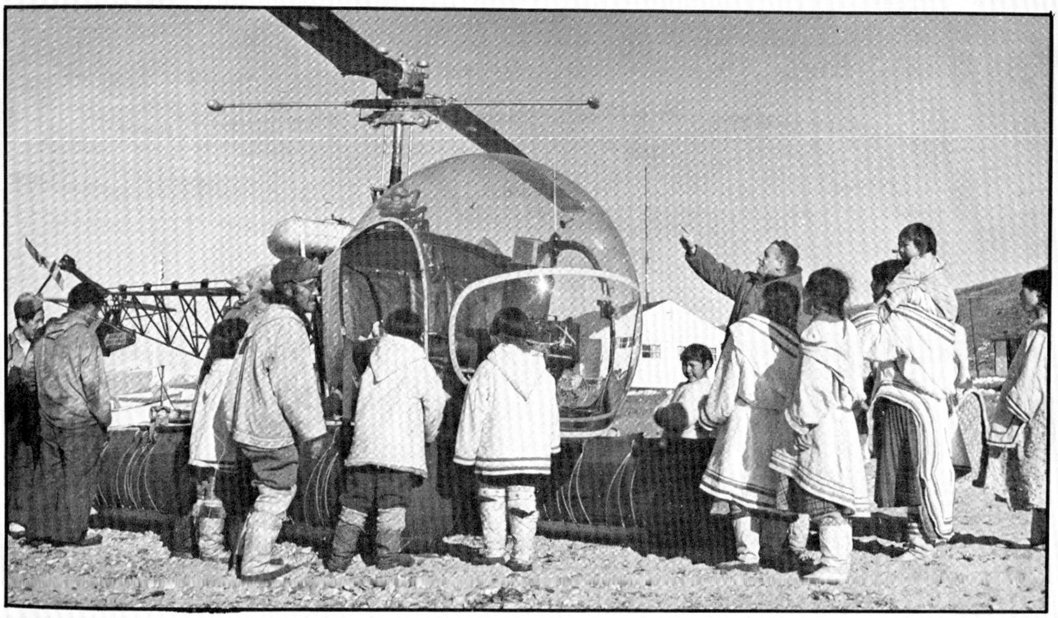

Alex Stevenson explaining the Bell Helicopter to Inuit at Pond Inlet, July 1951.

ᐅᒥᐊᕐᔪᐊᖅ ᕿᓴᕐᔪᓂ ᐅᖕ ᒐᓯᐸᔪᒃ ᑐᑭᔪᖕᔫᑦ ᓵᑦᑎ ᑦᓄᑦ. ᕿᓴᕐᕙᔪᐊᓗᐊ ᐅᒃ ᐱᕐᕚᓚᕙᓕᑦᑎᔪᒻᒪᕆᐋᔪ ᕐᑲᑦᑕᓚᐅᕐᓯᒪᖕᒪᑦ, ᐱᕐᑲᔪᔭᑭᔪᒃᑐᑦ ᓯᖅᑲᐸᓕᑦᑎᔪ ᐋᔪᖅᑰᓯᓐᔪᓂ. ᑕᕙᕚᑦᑕᐃᑦᓇᒻᒪᕆᑯᔪᒃ ᑕᕙᕚᔪ ᓂᐅ ᖅᐃᑦᔪᑎᑭᔪᖕᒥᒃ ᐃᒫᕐᑕᐅᔭᕆᕐᔪᑎᒃ ᑕᕐᑕᕐᑐᑭᔪᐃᑦ ᓯᐋᑭᔪᐃᑦ ᓂᐅᖅᐃᓇᓯᓚᕆᕐᔪᑎᒃᔪ ᓄᓇᓖᖕᓅᕐᑐᒃᓴᓂᒃ.

ᓄᖅᑲᓚᐅᖕᖕᒥᑦᓂᖕᒐᓂ ᓯᓚ ᐅᒥᐊᕐᔪᐊᖅ, ᐃᓖᑦ ᑕᒪᑦᓴ ᐸᕐᓇᔪᕕᕐᑐᑦ ᐅᒥᐊᒃᑯᑦ ᐊᑎᕐᓂᐊᖅᒥᒃ. ᐅᕐᑲᐅᖕᔭᐅᓯᒪᕚᕕᕐᔪᑎᒃ ᕿᓇᒃᑯᑦ ᒪᑦᑖᕐᑎᑕᐅᔭᕐᑐᖅ ᑳᕐᓂᐊᕐᒪᖕᑏᑕ ᓂᐅᕕᕐᑎᒃᑯᑦ ᐊᖕᒐᔪᖅᑳᖕᒐᑦᓄᑦ ᓄᓇ ᓚᖕᓄᑦ ᑕᕙᕚ ᐊᖕᒐᔪᖅᑲᐅᒐᒥ. ᐃᓚᒃ ᑲ ᓯᕗᓪᓕᕐᐸᐅᑎ ᑕᕆᕙᓚᐅᕐᓯᒪᖕᒪᑕ ᐊᑖᑕᒐ ᐅᓯᕚᒃᑲᒥ ᕐᑲᓪᓘᓇᓂᒃ ᐅ ᒥᐊᕐᔪᐊᕆᐊᕈᓪᓗᓂ ᓄᓇᓕᖕᓂᑦ ᐅᓰᑦᓇᕐᐸᓚᐅᕐᓯᒪᒐ ᒥ ᐅᒥᐊᕐᔪᐊᕆᐊᑦᓚᐅᑎᓕᕗᒪᔪᓂᒃ.

The ship dropped anchor some distance from shore. You could hear the anchor rumble as it hit ground, like an iceberg breaking up. Almost immediately, two barges would be dropped from the deck and the crew would start to unload supplies for the settlement.

Even before she came to a stop, the families would be all prepared to take their boats out to meet her. Usually, they had already been told by the Hudson's Bay manager, who was the boss of the whole community, the order in which the families were to leave for the ship.

33

ᑎᑭᑦᓇᕐᑎᒍ ᐅᒥᐊᕐᔪᐊᖅ ᒪᔪᕐᐅᑎᕈᓗᖕᓯᑎᓘᕐᐸᓚᐅᕐᓯᒪᒐᑦᑕ ᓰᕐᑲᐃᒻᒪ ᒪᑦᑖᕐᐱᒥᓂᐊᕐ ᑕᑦᑎᑦᓄᑦ. ᒪᔪᕐᐅᑎᕈᓗᖕᒥᑦ ᓴᐱᕐᔭᐅᕙᓚᐅᕐᓯᒪᖕᒪᑕ ᐅᓈᒃᓴᔭᑎᑐᕐᑐᐊᑦᑐᓂᒃ ᐆᓛᔮᕐᓗᑎᒃ ᒪᔪᕐᐅᑎᒥᓕᕐᓗᒥᑦ ᐊᒃᓗᓈᔭᒍᑦ ᐊᑕᐅᑎᕐᑲᖅᓗᑎᒃ ᓇᖕᒥᐊᕐᓇᕐ ᑐᐊᓘᕐᑲᑦᑕᓚᐅᕐᓯᒪᖕᒪᑕ. ᑐᑎᒥᐊᑕᒫᑦ ᐆᓚᔮᖕᔪᔭᕐᓗᑎᒃ ᑕᕝᕙ ᐃᒪᖅ ᐊᑖᒍᑦ ᐃᖅᑲᕐᑲᖕᒥᑦᑐᐊᓗᒃ ᑖᑦᓗᑐᑦ ᑕᑯᒃᓴᐅᓐᓗᓂ ᑲᑕᒃᕕᒃᑯᒥᓇᖕᒥᑦᑐᐊᓗᒃ, ᕐᑯᐃᓕᕐ ᑕᓇᒻᒪᓇᒃᐸᓚᐅᕐᓯᒪᖕᒪᑦ.

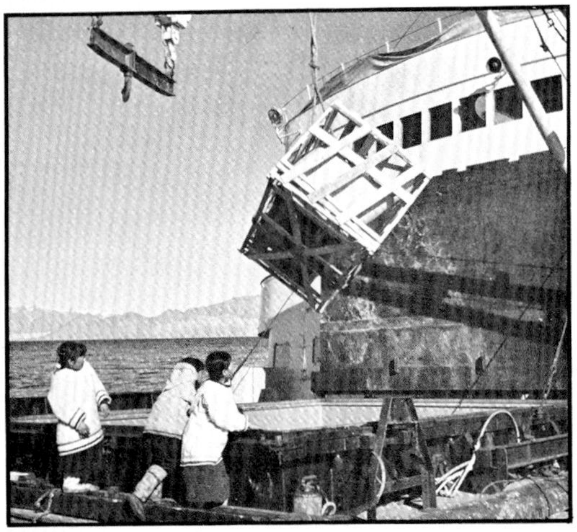

ᒪᔪᕐᑦᑕ ᐅᒥᐊᕐᔪᐊᒧᑦ, ᐃᓯᕐᑎᑕᐅᓐᓗᑕ ᑕᕝᕙ ᒪᑦᑖᕐᑎᑕᐅᕙᐱᒥᓂᐊᕐ ᑕᑦᑎᑦᓄᑦ, ᐊᒻᒪᓗ ᑕᕝᕙ ᕐᑯᓕᑦᑕᐅᔭᐃᕐᑎᓕᕐᓗᑕ, ᓯᕗᓐᓕᕐᒥᒃ ᑎᑎᕋᕐᑕᐅᔭᓇᐊᕐᑲᕐᑲᑦᑕᓚᐅᕐᓯᒪᒐᑦᑕ, ᐊᑎᕐᐳᑦ ᑕᕝᕙ ᑎᑎᕋᕐᑕᐅᓯᒪᓕᓈᕋᓗᐊᕐᑎᓐᓗᒥᑦ ᐃᓚᒦᑦ ᓂᐅᕕᕐᑎᐅᑉ ᓄᓕᐊᖓ ᒐᑕ ᓄᓇᓕᖕᓃᓯᖕᒐᕐᑎᓐᓗᑕᓕ. ᒪᑦᑕᕐᑎᓕᕐᓗᑕ ᑕᕝᕙ ᐊᔨᐃᓛᒃ ᐅᕐᑲᐅᑎᔭᐅᓐᓗᑕᓗ, "ᐆᒪ ᕐᑳᖕᒐᓅᕐᓗᑎᑦ —ᓂᐅᓇᑦ ᓄᖅᑲᓇᑦ. ᑕᐃᒪ!" ᓘᒃᑖᖅ ᑕᕝᕙ ᕐᑲᐃᒐᒥ ᐊᑕᔪᕐᓯᒪᑲᓐᓚᒃᓗᓂ ᕐᑲᑯᑦᑕᒥᒃ ᐊᕐᓇᑎᑐᑦ. ᐳᐸᓐᓄᑦ ᓈᓚᐅᑎᓕᔭᕐᓗᑎᒃ, ᓴᒡᕕᑦᑎᒍᑦ ᓈᓚᑦᓰᔮᓗᕐᑲᑦᑕᕐᓗᓂ, ᑐᓄᒃᑯᑦᓗ, ᐊᑯᓂᕈᓗᒃ. ᕐᑯᖕᒐᓚᐅᐱᑦᓚᒃᐸᒃᓗᓂ, ᓂᑦᓕᓚᐅᕐᓯᒪᑦᓚᕐᓂ.

ᑕᐃᒪᑕᐃᑦᓇᖅ, ᑭᒍᑎᓕᓇᓂᓘᔨᓐᓚᓇᕗᒍᑦ, ᑕᕝᕙᑦᑕ ᐅᖅ ᐊᑕᔪᕐᓯᒪᑲᓐᓚᒃᑭᑦᓗᓂ ᕐᑲᑯᕐᑕᒥᒃ, ᑭᔨᐊᓂᓕᕐᑲᐅᖅᒥᒍᑦ ᐃᑯᒪᔪᒥᒃ ᓇᓴᕐᓯᒪᖅᑰᔨᓐᓗᓂ. ᐃᖕᓯᑎᑦᓗᓂᑎᒍᑦ ᐃᓗᕐᓇᓇᕐ ᑐᐊᑦᓄᖕᒍᑦ ᐃᑯᒫᓗᖕᓘᑦᓇ ᕐᑲᐅᒪᒪᖅᑯᑎᖕᒐ ᓵᑦᑎᐊᑯᓗᐊᓂ, ᐊᐃᑦᑕᕐ ᑯᔨᕙᒃᓗᓂ ᐊᒃᔪᓐᓛᓗᒃ ᐊᐃᑦᑕᕐᑎᑦᑎᑦᓛᓗᒃᐸᒃᓗᓂ. ᕐᑲᐅᔨᓴᓚᐅᐱᓐᓚᕐᔪᑯᓗᒃᓗᒃᓂ, ᓂᐅᕐᑐᕐᑐᐊᓘᑦᓯᕐᓗᓂ ᑭᒍᑎᓂᒃ ᕐᑯᐊᖅᓵᕐᓇᕈᑦᔪᑦᑐᑦ ᐆᓚᐅᑎᒍᕐᑐᒍᑦ. ᐃᖅᑲᐅᒪᔭᕈᓗᒐ ᓱᓕ ᐊᒡᒐᑯᑦᓯᐊᓗᖕᒥᑦᓄᑦ ᑎᒍᒥᐊᕐ ᑐᐊᓗᐃᑦ ᓂᐅᕐᔫᑎᒥᒃ. ᒥᓇᒥᕐᓂᐊᖕᒍᕐᓇᒻᒪᓇᕐᑲᑦᑕᐅᕐᓯᒪᖕᒪᑦ ᐅᓯᐅᒪᓗ ᐃᒃᓯᕙᐅᑕᓇᔭᒧᑦ.

ᑲᐸᐊᓗᕈᔪᐃᑦᓇᕐᑎᑕᐅᕐᑲᑦᑕᐅᕐᓯᒪᖕᒪᑦ ᑕᒪᕐᑎᑦᓄᑦ. ᓄᑕᕐᑯᓗᐃᑦᓗ ᒪᑯᐊ ᑲᐸᐊᔪᒃᑐᑯᓗᐃᑦ ᕐᑭᐊᖕᒐᔭᒃᑐᑦ ᑲᐳᕐᑕᐅᔪᑦ; ᐊᒻᒪᓗ ᒪᑯᐊ ᐃᓄᒥᐊᔭᕈᔮᔭᓕᕐᑐᑦ ᑲᑎᑕᐅᒐᑦᑕ ᕐᑯᑦᓇᐅᔮᖕᒐᓂ ᐅᑕᖅᑭᐅᕐᑐᑦ, ᐆᒪᑦᔭᑎᕆᓐᓗᑎᒃ ᐊᑦᓄᕐᒥᖕᓂᒃ ᑎᒍᒥᐊᖅᑲᕐᑐᑦ.

Our family was always the first to go because my father carried an extra load of white people from the settlement in our boat.

When we reached the side of the ship, we had to climb up a ladder to the lower deck. The ladder had metal stairs and railings on either side of rope and metal. With each step it bounced and swayed over the icy water which surged menacingly below.

Once on board, we entered the section where we were to receive our medical examination, and we removed our outer clothing. First, we had to be registered, even though a list of our names had already been provided by the wife of the Hudson's Bay manager. Then, we removed our tops, and an attendant would say, "Stand up here - take a big, deep breath - hold it. That's it!" A doctor would then appear dressed in a funny white gown that looked like a woman's dress. Using a stethoscope, he listened to our chests, front and back, over and over again. He smiled once in awhile, without saying a word.

Finally, the dentist would take over, wearing the same white gown, but with a light attached to his forehead. He would sit each of us down in turn in a comfortable chair with a light shining directly in front, and ask us to open our mouths wide. After a quick examination, he would start to drill into some of the teeth. I can still remember his huge hands holding the drill. Sometimes I was afraid I'd be sick right there in that chair.

It was a scary experience for all of us. The small children would be frightened and would cry from getting needles; and there would be so many people crowded into the hallway, prespiring and holding on tightly to their clothing.

This year, as usual, the members of my family were examined one after the other. After my examination, the doctor asked my parents many questions about any sicknesses I had had, or if I had any complications now. Everything seemed to happen pretty much as it had the year before.

Then, an unusual thing took place. Scarcely an hour after we returned to the settlement, my father loaded us back on his boat and we set out again for the C.D. Howe. Never before had my father

ᑕᕙᕘᓂ ᐊᕐᕿᒎᑎᓐᓄᒍ, ᐃᓕᖅᑯᓯᕐ ᑕᖅ ᓚᓂᖅ ᓛᓯᑦ, ᐃᓚᒃᑲ ᕐᑲᐅᓱᔅᕐ ᑕᐅᓕᕐᒥᑎᓐᓄᒥᑦ ᒪᑦᑖᕐᕕᖅᒧᑦ ᑮᖅ ᔫᓕᓃᒃᑕᕐᓄᑕ. ᕐᑲᐅᓱᔅᕐ ᑕᐅᕐᑖᓄᖅᓚ, ᓅᒃᑖᒧᑦ ᐊᑖ ᑕᒃᑯᒃᑲ ᐊᐱᕐᓯᕐ ᑕᐅᑦᓲᔅᓕᕐᓄᑎᒃ ᐋᑦᓂᐊᓴᕐᑲᑦᑕᕐᓯ ᒪᔪᑦᓂᒃ, ᕐᑲᓂᒪᓄᐊᕐ ᑐᐋᓘᓚᐅᓇᐊᒃᓴᒪᓄ. ᐊᕐᕿᓂᓂᑐ ᓯᓕ ᑕᐃᒪᑦᓇ ᐱᓕᓇᑦᓄᑎᒃ.

ᑕᐃᒪᓕ, ᒪᓄᒃᓇᕐᓯᓚᐅᕐᓯᒪᖅᒪᑕ. ᐅᑦᓯᕐᓇᑦᑎᐊᓐ ᖅᒥᓄᓂ ᐅᑎᕐᓯᒪᓕᕐᓄᑕ ᓄᓇᓕᐊᕐᓯᒪᓕᕐᓄᑕ ᐃᑲᕿᕐᕿᓐᓄ ᐊᑰᖅᑯᕐᑐᒥᒃ, ᐊᑖᑕᒪ ᐅᒥᐊᕐᔪᐊᓕᐊᕈᑎᒃᑲᑦᓂᓕᓚᐅ ᕐᓯᒪᖅᒪᑎᑯᑦ ᐅᒥᐊᒥᑯᑦ. ᐅᒥᐊᕐᔪᐊᓕᐊᕈᑎᔭᐅᒃᑲᑦᓂ ᕈᑦᓃᕐᐸᓚᐅᕐᓯᒪᓚᑦᑕᓕ. ᓄᑕᖅᑎᑯᑦ ᐊᒡᕕᐊᑐᐃᑦᓇᕐᑲ ᑦᑕᕐᓂᐊᕿᑦᑕ ᐱᓇᓱᕐᑲᑕᐅᑎᑦᓄᑯ ᒪᓕᒃᑲᑦᓂᕐᐸᓚᐅᕐᓯ ᒪᙳᕐᒥᑦᓇᑦᑕ.

ᐊᑯᓂᐅᙳᕐᒥᑦᑐᖅ ᕐᑲᐅᓱᓕᕐᑐᖅᓚ ᐅᑦᓯᕐᓇᕐᓯᖅᒪᑦ ᑕᒪᑐᒪᓂ ᕐᑲᓄᐃᕈᔫᖅᑰᓱᓕᕿᑦᑕ. ᐋᑦᓂᐊᓃᕿᕐ ᑕᐅᓐᓄ ᖅᓚ ᐊᒻᒪᓄ ᑕᐃᒪ ᐃᓚᑦᓂ ᕐᑭᒪᐃᓂᐊᕐᓂᕿᕐ ᑕᐅᓕᓚᐅᕐ ᓯᒪᓚᓚ ᑕᕙᕘ ᓯᓕ ᐅᓐᓅᐸ ᐃᓚᖅᓚᒍᑦ ᐅᖅᓚᓯᒃᑐᐊᓄᖅ ᒧᑦ ᐆᓐᓚᕐᓂᐊᕐᓂᕿᕐ ᑕᐅᓕᕿᒪ ᐋᑦᓂᐊᕕᓕᐊᕐᓄᖅᓚᒎᖅ ᕐᑲᓐᓅᓈᑦ ᓄᓇᖅᓚᑦᓅᑦ.

ᑕᕙᕘᑦᑕᐃᑦᓇᓄᐊᑰᖅᒪᑦ, ᐃᓯᒪᔪᑦᓇᑦᑎᐊᓚᐅᓐᖅᒥ ᑦᑐᖅᓛᑦᓃᑦ. ᑕᐃᒪ ᐅᒥᐊᕐᔪᐋᕿᑦᑕ, ᓇᓄᔪᑦᓃᓚᐅ ᕐᑐᖅᓚ, ᐅᒃᐱᕈᓯᓕᑦᓇᓴᑦᑎᐊᓕᕐᓄᖅᓚᓄ ᐆᑦᓚᕐᓂᐊ ᓴᐊᒃᓴᖅ, ᐸᖅᓇᕐ ᑕᐅᓯᒪᓐᖅᒥᑦᑎᐊᕿᓄᐊᕐᓄᖅᓚ ᐊᒻᒪᓄ ᐃᓪᓕᕐᕕᒥᓕᓚᓐᖅᒥᑦᓄᖅᓚ. ᐊᓂᕈᓗᑦᑕᐅᖅ, ᐸᓂᓗᒃ, ᕐᑮᖅᓱᕐᑲᑦᑕᕿᒥ, ᐆᑦᓚᓕᓚᒥᓐᓄᓂ, ᕐᑲᓄᐃᒻᒪᓐᓕᑭ ᐊᖅ ᐆᓐᓚᕈᑦᓃᓚᐅᕐᓯᒪᖅᒪᑦᓕ ᐁᑦᑖᖅᔪᓚᐅᕿᓄᐊᕐ ᐳᖅ.

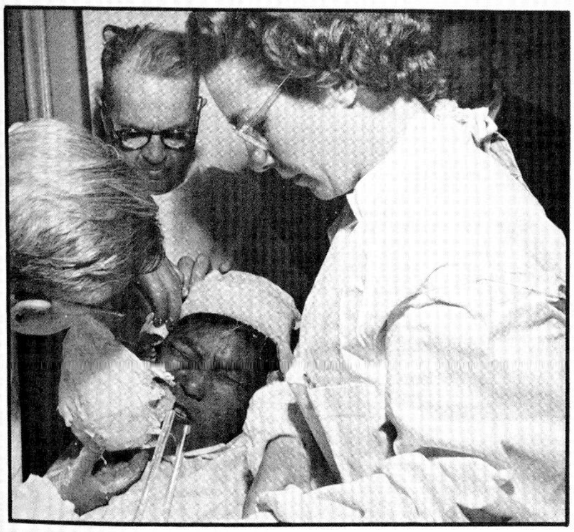

Dr. Davies, head of the eye survey party removing plaster from the face of an Inuk girl aboard the C.D.Howe ship, such masks are used to design frames for the difficult to fit Inuit face.

ᓅᒃᑖᖅ ᐃᓱᓕᓴᓱᓄᑦ ᐱᐃᔭᑎᓴᔪᖅ ᑭᐃᓇᕐᒧᑦ ᓇᒻᒪᒃᑎᓴᑦᔪᑕᐅᔪᒥᒃ ᐃᓄᐃᑦ ᐃᒡᒐᓕᐅᕐᑕᐅᑦ ᔪᐃᑎᒃᓴᖅ ᓚᓂᒃ.

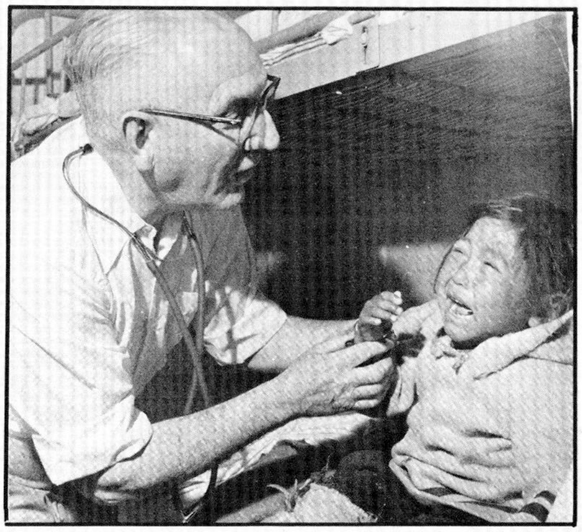

Dr.Campbell examining an Eskimo boy of the Lake Harbour area aboard C.D.Howe ship, July 1951.

ᓅᒃᑗᖅ ᕐᑲᐅᓱᔅᕐᑐᖅ ᑭᖅᒥᕈᒪᒥ ᒪᑦᑗᕐᕕᒃ ᕉᑎᕼᐆ ᐃᓄᖅᓄᐊᕐᓯᒪᑎᓐᓄᒍ ᔪᓚ 1951.

allowed us to return with him a second time to the ship. We kids would just get in the way and he had work to do, he said.

It wasn't long before I learned that there was something very wrong this time. I was sick and would have to leave my family that very day and go far away to the hospital in the south.

It all happened so fast, I scarcely had time to think. By the time we arrived back on the ship, I knew for sure that it was true, that I was really going, although I was totally unprepared and didn't even have any bagage to take along. And my brother, Paniloo, who suffered from epilepsy, was supposed to come along too, although for some reason he didn't in the end.

I hardly remember anything that was happening or being said to me at the time of departure, except that my dear oldest sister Rebecca (Qitsualik) was crying. Was I going away for good? I didn't feel sick. Was I going to die in the white man's hospital? It terrified me to think of these things. Several years before, my sister Rebecca had spent a year in England, but she had not been sick or been hospitalized. Why was she crying for me now?

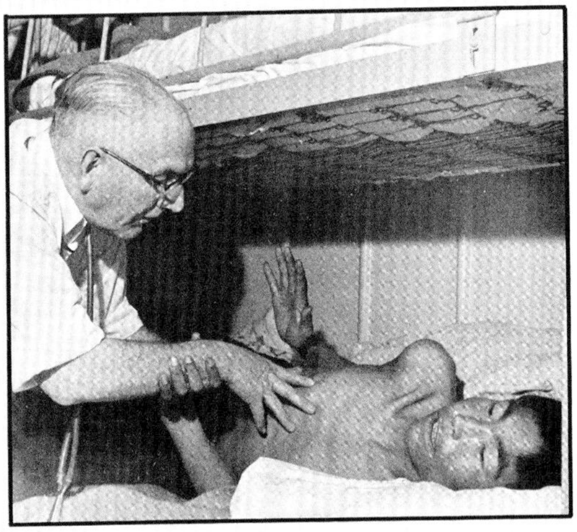

Dr. Campbell examining a sick Eskimo hunter aboard the C.D.Howe ship, picked up at Cape Hoped Advance.

ᐊᓐᓂᓕᐊᕕᓂᖓ ᔫᓯᐱ ᐃᓪᓚᐅᑉ

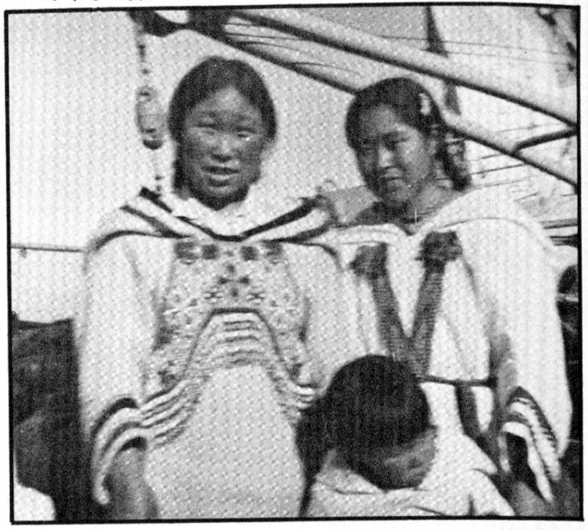

Photo: Joseph Idlout

Mrs. Martha Nasuk, Rebecca my sister Maudie Qitsualik, C.D.Howe, July 1951.

ᒫᑕ ᓇᓱᒃ, ᕆᐱᑲᓗ ᐊᖓᔪᑯᓗᒐ ᐊᓪᓚᓗ ᒨᑎ ᕿᑦᓱᐊᓕᒃ, ᓰᑏᕼᐋᐅᒥ, ᔪᓚᐃ 1951.

ᐃᖅᑲᐅᒪᑦᑎᓐᓈᕐᒥᑦᑐᖓ ᖃᓄᐃᓕᕐᓱᐊᕐᓂᕐᒪᖓ ᑳᑦᑎᑦᓂᒃ ᐅᕙᑦᑑᓂᑦ ᐅᕐᑲᖅᑕᐅᔪᙵᓂᐅᒐᓗᐊᓂᒃ ᐋᓐᓚᓇᐊᓚᑦᑎᓐᓗᑕ, ᑕᕙᕙᑐᐊᖅ ᐊᖓᔪᑯᓗᒐ ᓇᐱᑲ (ᕿᑦᓱᐊᓚᒃ) ᕿᐋᓚᐅᕐᓯᒪᖕᒪᑦ. ᐋᓐᓚᐃᑦᓇᖑᐊᕐ ᑐᙵᓂᐅᓚᕐᑐᖕ ᒐᓚᕐ ᑲᐃ? ᖃᓂᒪᖅᑯᓕᕈᓐᓂᖅ ᒥᑦᑎᐊᕐ ᓗᖕ ᒐᓗ. ᑑᕐ ᑯᔭᕘᑐᐃᑦᓇᕐ ᑐᒃᓴᐅᔫᓚᕐᓂᖅᒪ ᐋᑦᓂᐊᙱᓚᐊᕐᓂᐊᕈᒪ ᖁᓚᑦᓇᕐᓯᔪᒃᓴᐅᑦᓂᖅᒪ? ᑲᐸᐃᐋᕐᓯᓛᕐᓯᒪᑦᓚᕐᐳᖅ ᑕᒪᒃᑯᐊ ᐃᓱᒪᒥᑦᓂᕈᒃᑭᑦ. ᐊᖓᔪᑯᓗᒐ ᓈᐱᑲ ᑕᕙᕙᑎᑭᖅᑖᐸᓗᓚᐅᕐᓗᓂ ᐊᕐᖁᒍ ᓈᓐᓗᒍ ᑯᐃᐸ ᓄᓇᖕᒐᓂᑦ ᐋᑦᓂᐊᕆᐊᕐ ᑐᓐᖕᒥᑦᓗᓂᓕ ᐋᓐᓚᕐᓯᒪᓛᕐᓯᒪᖕᒪᑦ ᐊᕐᖁᒍ ᓈᓐᓗᒍ ᐋᑦᓂᐊᙱᓚᐊᓐᖕᒥᒃᑲᓗᐊᕐᓗᓂᓕ. ᖃᓄᐃᒻᒪᓐᓕᑭᐊᕐᖕᒥᑦᓇ ᕿᐊᖅ ᒐᔭᐅᑎᒥᓐᓚᕐᓂᕐᑳᖕᒐᐃ?

ᐃᖅᑲᐅᒪᔭᑐᐊᒃᑲ ᑕᐃᒪ ᐊᑖᑕᒪ ᐅᒥᐊᖅᒐ ᑕᑯᔪᑦᓇᐃᓐᓕᑦᓗᒍ ᐃᓲᒃᑲᒃ ᑕᒃᓯᕐ ᑐᐋᓛᕐᒪᑎᒃ, ᕿᑯᕙᐅᕐ ᑐᐋᓛᕐᒪ ᐅᓗᐊᒃᑯᑦ ᑲᑕᒑᐅᔫᕐᔪᒃᓗᑎᒃ. ᕿᑯᕙᒥᔭᐳᑦᓈᖕᒥᑦᓗᖕᒐᓗ, ᑭᓇᒃᑯᑐᐃᑦᓇᕐᓄᑦ ᖃᐅᓯᔭᐅᑐᐃᑦᓇᕐᓂᐊᕐᒪ ᕿᖕᒐᔭᒃᑐᖕᒐ. ᐃᓄᒥᐊᑉᐳᐃᑦ ᑕᒪᑦᔭᖃᓐᓈᑉᐴᔫᖕᒪᑕ ᓴᐃᒍᕐᓯᒪᐅᕐᑐᑦ ᐅᒥᐊᕐᔪᐊᐸ ᓯᓈᓂ, ᖁᓐᖕᒥᐊᕐ ᑐᐋᓗᐃᑦ ᒪᑦᑳᕐᖃᒃ ᐃᖕᒥᕐᖁᓯᓚᕐᑎᓐᓗᒍ ᓄᓇᓕᖕᓂᑦ. ᕿᕙᐃᐅᕐ ᑕᐃᓚᒪᓇᔪᓐᓚᒃ ᑐᐋᓐᒐᓗᐊᕐᓗᖕᒐ, ᖁᓐᖕᒥᐊᕐᔪᒃᑭᓐᖕᒐᓗᑦᑕᐅᖅ ᐊᑖᑕᒪ ᐅᒥᐊᖕᒐᓂᒃ ᐃᓚᓴᕐᓯᔪᑦᓇᐃᓐᓚᑦᓗᖕᒐᓗ ᓇᓐᓚᐊᖕᒍᒐᓗᐊᕐᒪᖕᑳᑎᒃ ᐋᓈᓇᒐᓗ ᐊᑖᑕᒐᓗ.

ᑕᐃᒪ ᒪᔪᕐᖁᐅᑎᑦ ᖁᕙᕙᕐ ᑕᐅᓐᓚᕐᐸᑦ ᐃᓂᒥᓄᐊᕐᑕᐅᓐᓗᑎᒃ, ᑕᕙᕙ ᐅᒥᐊᕐᔪᐊᑦ ᓂᐅᔪᕐᑲᒃᑲᑦᓂᓐᖁᔾᔪᑦᓃᕐᒪᑦ ᑭᖕᑯᓐᓚᕐᒥᒃ ᑭᓯᐊᓂ ᓄᓇᓕᖕᓄᑦ ᓄᖅᑲᕐᒥᒍᑦᑕ, ᓄᖅᑲᒃᑲᑦᓂᓛᕐᓯᒪᓂᐊᕐᓗᐊᕈᑦᑕ ᖃᐅᓈᑦ ᓄᓇᖕᒐᑦᓄᑦ ᑎᑭᓛᖅᑳᕐᑕ. ᐅᒥᐊᕐᔪᐊᒃ ᑰᓚᐅᕐᓯᒪᓐᖕᒥᑦ ᓇᒪᓗ ᖃᐅᔨᒪᓐᓇᖕᒐ ᖃᓄᐃᒃ ᑲᓗᐊᕐᒪᖕᑳᑦ ᐅᒥᐊᕐᔪᐊᒃ ᑯᓇᐊᒃᓴᖅ ᐊᑯᓂᐊᓘᙱᐊᒃᓴᕐᔫᑦᓃᑦ. ᓄᓇᓕᖕᓂᑦᓗ ᑕᕙᕙ ᓄᓇᑦᑎᑦᓂᑦ ᐊᑎᕐ ᑐᕐ ᑲᒃᑲᑦᓂᑦᔾᔪᑦᓃᕐᓗᓂ ᐅᒥᐊᕐᔪᐊᒧᑦᑦᓃᑦ ᒪᔪᕐ ᑐᕐ ᑲᒃᑲᑦᓂᑦᔾᔪᑦᓃᓗᓂ. ᐱᔭᕇᖁᒥᒃᓚ ᑕᐃᒪ ᖃᓄᐃᓕᒃᑲᑦᓂᑦᔾᔪᑦᓃᕐᒥᖕᒪᑕ ᓴᐱᕐᓇᕐᓯᓐᒪᓐᓗ.

All I can remember was my father's boat that I could hardly see anymore through my foggy eyes, so many tears were flooding warmly down my cheeks. And I couldn't wipe them away, for if I did, everyone would notice me crying there. There were so many white people lined up on the upper deck, watching as the C.D. Howe moved away from the settlement. I tried hard to hold back my tears, at the same time straining to keep sight of my father's boat until I could hardly tell which one was my mom or dad.

Then the ladders folded back into place, which meant that nobody would be able to leave the ship again until it reached the next settlement, that is if it was going to stop again before arriving in the white man's land. I had no idea or picture in my mind of what it would be like to travel on the big ship for a long trip. Now nobody from the settlement was ever again going to be able to climb back on board with us. Done is done.

I was not going to jump to the salt water either in order to get back with my family. Even though I so badly wanted to stay and never go away, I was far too terrified of the deep dark blue sea water below. I had never ever wanted to leave my family, not even to go to other camps. I did go alone with my father to the settlement once. At that time I was so mise-

ᕐᑭᒡᒥᐅᔮᓐᖅᒐᓗ ᑕᓇᐅᕐᔪᑦ ᐅᑎᕐᓯᐊᕐᔪᖅᒐ ᐃᓚᑦᓄᑦ. ᐆᐤᓚᕈᒪᓐᖅᒥᑦᑐᐤᓛᒪᓇᐋᓗᐋᕐᑐᖅᒐ ᕐᑭᒪᐃᔪᒪᐸᑐᐊᕐᔪᓚᐅᕐᓯᒪᓐᖅᒥᑦᓇᒪ ᐃᓚᑦᓂᑦ, ᓇᖅᒥᐊᑐᐊᕐᑐᐋᓗᒪᒪ ᐃᑎᔪᕈᑐᖅᒥᒃ ᑖᑦᑐᑐᕐᑐᒥᒃ ᑕᓇᐅᒥᒃ. ᕐᑭᒪᐃᔪᒪᐸᑐᐊᕐᔪᑯᓚᐅᕐᓯᒪᓐᖅᒥᑦᓇᒪ ᐃᓚᑦᓂᒃ, ᓄᓇᓕᖅᓄᐊᕐᑐᖅᒐᑑᑦᓃᑦ ᐊᓯᓄᑦ ᕐᑲᐤᑐᓈᕐᑳᖅᒥᑦᑑᒐᑐᐊᓄᑦ ᐊᑖᑕᓄᑦ ᐃᓚᐅᓚᐅᕐᓯᒪᒐᑐᐊᕐᓴᒪ ᕐᑲᐤᑐᓇᑦᓯᐊᕐᑎᐤᑐᔪ ᕐᑲᐱᓚᓇᑐᐊᕐ ᑐᐋᖅᒪᑦ ᐃᓛᐤᑐ ᑕᒪᒃᑭᓴᑕ ᐊᑖᑕᒪ ᐃᓚᐅᑎᒃᑲᑦᓂᕈ ᑦᓃᓚᐅᕐᓯᒪᖅᒪᖅᒐ.

ᐃᒃᕐᓴᐃᑦ ᓯᓂ ᒪᕐᕈᒃ ᐱᖅᒐᓱᐤᑑᑦᓃᑦ ᑕᕙᕙ ᐆᐤᓚᕐᓂᐊᕐᓂᖕᒃᑲᐅᔭᑦᓂᒃ ᕐᑲᐅᔨᓚᐅᕐᑐᖅᒐ ᐃᑭᒪᓕᓴᒪ ᒪᑦᑖᕐᓴᕕᒃ ᑎᑦᑑᕈᑐᓯᑦᓚᕐᐳᖅ ᐆᑦᓚᕐᓂᐊᓖᖅᒐᒥ ᓄᓇᓕᖅᓂᑦ ᑕᐃᒪᑦᓇ ᑎᑦᑑᓰᖅᔪᒐᒥ. ᕐᕈᒪᒥᖅ ᓄᓕᐊᖅᒐᑐ ᐊᒪᐅᓕᓘᖅ ᐆᑦᓚᓕᓚᐅᕐᓯᒪᖅᒥᖅᒪᑎᒃ ᑕᐃᑦᓯᒪᓂ ᐅᑮᐸᑦᑎᑦᓂ ᐅᐱᕐᖅᒥᐸᑦᑎᑦᓃᓚᐅᕐᑐᑎᒃᑐ ᑕᖅᑭᓂᒃ ᐱᖅᒐᓯᓂᐅᖅᔲᖅᑐᖅ, ᑕᕙᕙᑐᐊᖅ ᓄᓇᑦᑎᑦᓂ ᕐᑲᐤᑐᓈᑐ ᐊᓯᓯᒪᐤᑐᑎᔪᑦ. ᕐᑭᒪᒥᐅᐸ ᓄᓯᒃᑐᓂᖅᒐ ᒪᔪᕐᑐᑎᑦ ᐊᑖᓄᑦ, ᓯᕈᔪᐊᑐᒃ ᑲᑕᒐᕐᒪᑦ ᒪᕐᑯᒃᑐᑎᑐᑦ ᑎᑦᑐᓚ ᕐᑐᒥᑦ. ᕐᑲᓄᐃᒃᓴᐸᑐᐊᕐᔪᓐᖅᒥᑦᑎᐊᕐᑎᑦᑐᖅᒐᒥ ᐃᐱᕈᕈᑐᒃᑲᑐᐊᕈᒪ ᐋᑖᑕᒪ ᐅᒥᐊᖅᒐ ᑕᑯᑦᓇᒃ ᑲᓂᓚᐅᓯᖅᒐ ᕈᒃᑯ. ᑕᐃᑦᓯᒪᓂᐅᑎᐤᑐᔪ, ᑕᕙᕙᑐᐊᖅᔪᓚᐅᕐᓯᒪᖅᒪᑦ. ᐃᑐᐃᑦᓕᕐᑐᐤᓛᑐᓚᐅᕐᓯᒪᒐᒪ, ᓴᕐᑐᓯ ᓇᑦᑎᐊᑯᑑᔪᖅᒐ ᐋᓈᓇᐃᕈ ᑦᓴᑯᑐᒃ.

ᐃᒻᒪᕐᑳ ᐅᒥᐊᕐᔪᐊᕐᒥᐅᑐᒃ ᑖᑯᑐᐃᑦ ᕐᑯᓐᖅᒥᐊᓚᐅᕐᓯᒪᓐᖅᒪᑕ ᐅᒥᐊᕐᔪᐊᒥᒃ ᐃᖅᒥᕐᓴᓯᒥᐊᕐᑐᒥᒃ ᕐᑭᒪᐃᓂᕐᑎᐤᑐᔪ ᓄᓇᓕᖅᓂᒃ. ᐃᓚᐅᒥ ᔪᓂ ᒪᑭ ᐊᖑᑎᕐᔪᐊᖅ, ᓂᖅᒥᐅᕐᒪ ᐊᓂᑐᐊᑯᑐᐊ ᐃᑦᑐᕐ, ᐊᒻᒪᓗ ᑯᐤᑐ ᐃᒃᓯᕐᕐᔪᐊᒃᑯᑦ ᐃᓄᖅᒐᑦ, ᑕᒪᕐᒥᒃᓂ ᐋᐤᓂᐊᕕᓂᐋᐅᕐᓯᒪᓐᖅᒥᒐᒥᒃ ᒥᑦᑎᒪᑕᓂᖅᒥ, ᑐᕐᑯᑐᐅᕐᓯᒪᔪᒃ ᐋᐤᓂᐊᕕᖅᒦᑦᑐᑎᒃ ᑯᐱᒃ ᓯᑎᒥ. ᕐᑲᐅᔨᑐᐅᕐᓯᒪᓐᖅᒥᑦᑎᐊᕐᑐᖅᒐ ᑕᕙᕙ ᕐᑲᐤᑐᓈᑦ ᓄᓇᖅᒐᑦᓄᑦ ᐋᑦᓂᐊᕕᓂᐊᕐᑐᕐᑲᑐᐅᕐᓯᒪᖅᒪᖅᑮᑦ ᒥᑦᑎᒪᑕᓂᖅᒥᐅᑕᕐᒥᒃ.

ᐊᐤᓄᕐᒃᑲᑦᓂᒐᒥᓐᖅᒥᑦᑎᐊᕐᑐᖅᒐ, ᑭᓯᐊᓂᓂ ᑕᕙᕙ ᐊᑐᕐᑕᑐᐊᒃᑲ: ᐊᑕᔪᑯᒃᑳᓯᒪᐤᑐᖅᒐ ᐃᑐᑦᓂᕐᒥᒃ, ᕐᑲᖅᓂᒃᑲᒐᑐ ᐊᕐᓇᑦᓇᐅᕙᑐᐅᕐᓯᒪᔪᑦ ᑕᓯᔪᐋᓂᑦ ᑐᖅᔪ ᔪᕐᑕᐃᑦ ᐆᐸᔪᒃᑐᐃᑦᑑᑦᓃᑦ, ᐊᑕᔪᕐᓯᒪᐤᑐᖅᒐᑐ, ᕐᑯᓂᑦᑕᐅᔭᕐᓯᒪᐤᑐᖅᒐᑐ ᕐᑲᑯᕐᑕᒥᒃ ᕐᑲᓂᐹᕐᑲᖅᑐᓂ ᓇᑦᑎᕐᓴᕕᓃᒐᓂᒃᑐ ᑲᒥᒃᓯᒪᐤᑐᖅᒐ ᕐᑯᓂᑦᑕᐅᔭᒃᓭᒐᓂᒃᑐ ᐊᓂᕐᓯᒃᓯᒪᐤᑐᖅᒐ, ᑲᔾᔭᖅᓂᒃᑐ ᓄᕕᕐᓵᖅᓂᒃ ᐊᓂᕐᓯᑯᑖᒃᓯᒪᐤᑐᖅᒐ. ᐃᓄᒃᑎᑐᐤᑐ ᐃᔾᔪᕐ ᑯᑎᒥᕐᑐᖅᒐ ᕐᑭᔪᖅᓂᒃᑐ ᐃᓅᓴᒐᒥᕐᑐᖅᒐ.

ᐅᕙᒍᑦ — ᐃᓄᒃᑎᒍᑦ — ᓯᕗᐊᓄᐊᕈ ᑦᓴᐅᑐᐅᕐᓯᒪᔪᔪᑦ ᒪᑦᑖᕐᓴᕕᐅᐸ. ᒪᑐᕐ ᑲᖅᑐᓂ, ᑐᕐᓵᓂᐅᕐᓯᒪᓴᑦᔪᖅ ᑏᓯᔪᒥᒃ. ᐃᓯᓇᐊᕐ ᑲᓴᑦᑕ ᑕᕙᓇ ᐹᖅᒐᔪᑦ ᐊᖅᑲᕐᑎᕐᑐᑕ ᐊᒻᒪᖅᒐᑦᑎᐊᕐ ᑐᒃᑯᑦ ᒪᔪᕐᓴᐅᑎᑎᔪᑦ ᐃᓂᒥᓂᐊᕐ

ᑕᑦᑎᑦᓄᑦ ᐊᖅᒥᕐᓴᓇᓂᐊᕐᑕ ᑕᑦᑎᑦᓄᑦ ᑕᖅᑭᒐᓴᖅᓂᒃ.

ᑖᕐᑐᐤᑑᓗᒪᑦ ᐃᓯᓕᕐ ᑕᕗᑦ ᐊᒃᐸᓯᖅᒪᑦ ᐅᒥᐊᕐᔪᐊᒥ, ᐃᓚᑦᕐ ᑲᑦᓇᔪᒃ ᑲᑐᐊᕐᑐᓂ ᐊᖅᒪᑐᕐ ᑕᓂᒃ ᐊᕙᑎᖅ ᒥᒃᑎᒃᑯᑦ ᐊᑐᓂᑦ. ᐅᐃᑦᑎᐊᕐᔫᒥ ᑕᐃᑦᓇᕐᓴᒪ, ᕐᑯᓕᓇ ᒪᑯᐊ ᐃᓚᑮᑦ, ᑭᑭᐊᒃᑐᕐᓯᒪᐅᕐᑐᑦ ᕐᑭᐅᔮᓕᖅᓄᑦ ᐊᑕᐅᓯᐊᓗᖅᒦᐤᑐᑎᒃ. ᐊᑕᐅᓯᑯᖅᒥᒃ ᕐᑯᐃᔭᕐᑐᕐᕕᕐᑲᖅᑐᓂ ᑯᕕᔭᕐᑐᒥᒃ ᐅᐊᓴᕐᕕᑯᑐᕐ ᑲᖅᑐᓂ ᐊᓗᖅᑐᑦ, ᓵᑯᑖᑐᕐᑲᖅᑐᓂᑐ ᐊᑕᐅᓯᐊᑐᖅᒥᒃ ᐃᒡᑐᕐᖅᓂᒃ ᐅᐊᓴᕐᑐᓂ ᐊᑕᔪᒥᒃ ᐃᒡᑐᕆᖅᓂᒃ ᐊᒻᒪᑐ ᓂᕐᓇᑎᓄᑦ ᐅᐊᓴᕐᕕᕐᑲᖅᑐᓂ ᐊᑦᓄᑳᕐᓯᐅᑎᑭᖅᑐᖅᒥᒃ. ᑕᕙᕙ ᐃᓂᒥᓂᐊᕐᑕᕗᑦ ᓯᕗᔪᒐᔪᖅᓂᓚᑳᕐᑐᑦᑎᑦᓄᑦ, ᕐᑲᓂᓚᔪᓚᓛᓄᑦ ᐃᓛᐋᑦᓂᐊᓚᓛᓄᑦ ᐊᑐᕐ ᑕᒃᓴᓪᓚᖅᔪᕐᑎᑕᐅᓯᒪᔪᕐ ᑕᕙᕙᐅᓇ ᐊᖅᔪᑎᓄᑦ, ᐊᕐᓇᓄᑦᑐ ᐊᒻᒪᓗ ᓄᑕᖅᓄᑦ ᑕᒪᒃᑭᐅᒪᔪ

rable to be away from the camp and my whole family that my father never took me away again.

No more than two or three hours after I first learned that I too would be a passenger this time, the C.D. Howe gave a whistle like she always did when she was leaving the settlement. Doug Wilkinson and his wife Vivian were leaving at the same time after having spent three months with us at the camp. They were the only white people who had ever lived with us there. Doug pulled me back under the ladders, because of the dirt that was dropping down like rain from the whistling ship. I couldn't care less if I got dirty or not, just as long as I could see my father's boat. At that moment, that was all that mattered. I was feeling so full of loss, like a baby seal without its mother.

Probably every single passenger on board was out watching the ship pull away from the settlement. Among them was Maki Angutirjuaq, my grandmother's only living brother, and Kudlu, a Roman Catholic servant, both who were going to the hospital from Pond Inlet. Both of them eventually died in the hospital and were buried in Quebec City. From what I knew at that time, nobody had ever gone away to the hospital before from Pond Inlet.

I didn't bring any extra clothing with me, but had only the things I was wearing: long underwear, bloomers, a dress, a duffle parka with white cover, seal skin boots with duffle socks and long, brown woolen stockings. I also had my Inuktitut New Testament and my handmade wooden dolls.

We - the Inuit passengers - were taken to the front of the C.D. Howe. There was a door there, standing up like a little porch. We had to enter that door and climb straight down an upright ladder to the place that would be our home for the next few months.

It was very dark inside when we entered the lower level of the ship, even though there were port holes on either side. When my eyes finally adjusted to the dark, I could see beds screwed to the wall, one on top of the other like bunk beds, all in one open space. There was also one flush toilet room with a sink, a long table with benches on either side and a laundry sink to wash dishes.

2 The Hunter and the Cameras

Joseph Idlout and Doug Wilkinson Meet (1952)

By 1952, Joseph Idlout's image was known around the globe (see figure 2.1). Idlout had been featured in the National Film Board of Canada production *Land of the Long Day*, released that year, and in a series of still photographs taken during the film shoot. Director Douglas Wilkinson modelled the film loosely after Robert Flaherty's influential 1922 ethnographic film *Nanook of the North*.[1] Like that earlier film, *Land of the Long Day* reconstructs pre-contact life at *ilagiit nunagivaktangat* (camp) with dramatic hunting scenes driving a narrative centred on one archetypal Inuk. As Alan Rudolph Marcus has shown, Idlout is presented as the new Nanook.[2] Idlout appears throughout the film as a heroic figure. The hunter is seen stalking a seal with slow and careful deliberation and taking chase in a *qajaq*. And this heroic image was circulated widely. London's *Picture Post* and *Time* magazine in the United States reproduced stills, and the film was screened at festivals internationally.[3]

Land of the Long Day was a product of intercultural contact and the beginning of a decades-long connection between Idlout and Wilkinson. This connection was forged with and through cameras. *Land of the Long Day* and Wilkinson's other cinematic works of the time exemplify the ways that the north and Inuit life were imagined, imaged, and consumed by Qallunaat. But these films were *never* solely the products of southern imaginings. Idlout and other members of his camp were active collaborators in the making of Wilkinson's films. Indeed, these productions would not have been possible without Inuit guidance. The completed films, too, bear the traces of their agency and their presence.[4]

This chapter, the first of the five in the book's core section on visuality in the Sangussaqtauliqtilluta period, narrates a microhistory of Inuit-Qallunaat contact through Joseph Idlout's relationship with the filmmaker Douglas Wilkinson. I open with a discussion of Idlout's life and community history. Wilkinson's experiences as a filmmaker in the north follow. Here, I analyze several of his productions. I suggest that Wilkinson's work in the eastern Arctic – apparent specifically in his depictions of Idlout in photographs and films, particularly *Land of the Long Day* – crystallizes the colonial relationship between southern Canada and Inuit during the late 1940s and early 1950s. This work also shows how these complex interactions were played out visually. The chapter culminates with a detailed analysis of *Land of the Long Day*, where I argue that Idlout and his fellow performers were active agents in the production.

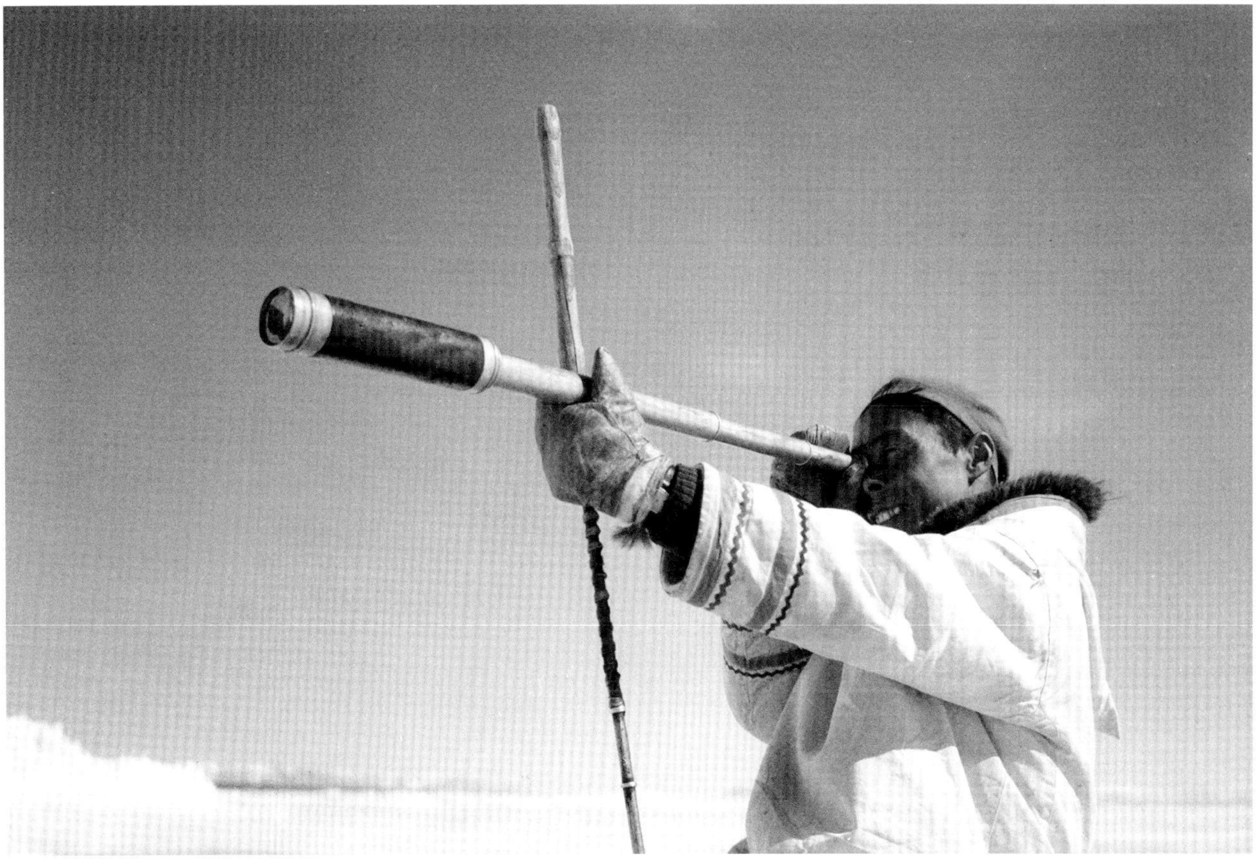

2.1 | Joseph Idlout looks for seals sleeping on the sea ice, Bylot Island, October 1952. Photo: Doug Wilkinson.

Idlout: A Life on the Land and in Contact

By the early 1950s, when he met Doug Wilkinson, Joseph Idlout was in his late thirties or early forties. Oral history accounts provide invaluable information about his life as head of camp, husband of Kidlak,[5] father of a large family, and son of Arnaujaq and Akumalik. Elders' oral history accounts also indicate that Idlout was well established as a respected leader among the Tununirmiut. Translated from Inuktitut by the Qikiqtani Truth Commission and others, Tununirmiut means "people of the shaded place," a reference to its location near present-day Pond Inlet/Mittimatalik on the less sunny eastern shore of Eclipse Sound on North Baffin Island. The area had been occupied for thousands of years and was known as a rich hunting ground for fish and sea mammals.[6] It was also an area of contact with southerners – Qallunaat – which had long been a periodic feature of Inuit life in on northern Baffin Island.

Idlout's father, Akumalik, taught him the many intricate hunting skills needed to survive and to support a large family. According to historian Kenn Harper, Akumalik was born around 1890 in Tununiq.[7] Idlout succeeded his father as head of camp, a testament to his prowess as a hunter. But he also learned – from his father and other Tununirmiut – how to navigate encounters with southerners skilfully. Idlout's sphere of influence and interactions always extended beyond his own Inuit community. Indeed, some of his descendants, including his daughter Susan Salluviniq, believe that Idlout may have been the biological son of whaler Joseph-Elzéar Bernier.[8] By the time Idlout became acquainted with Wilkinson, contact with Qallunaat was familiar and the camera was often part of these intercultural encounters.

Outsiders may have visited what is now known as the northern Qikiqtani region of Nunavut as early as the fourteenth century, when the presence of Norsemen from Kalaallit Nunaat/Greenland in the area is indicated by some research. As historian Shelagh D. Grant has shown, the British ship *The Discovery* is known to have sailed in the area in 1616, but the so-called Little Ice Age subsequently prevented outsider travel for about two centuries. In the early nineteenth century, British expeditions led by John Ross in 1818 and by William Edward Parry in 1819 renewed efforts at European exploration and conquest.[9] Indeed, the English names still commonly used for various sites in the region – including Baffin Island, Pond (or Pond's) Inlet, and Bylot Island – were established by British explorers in a common colonial effort to claim territory linguistically and through cartography. At the same time, whalers – particularly Scottish whalers – started to come to the Arctic in large numbers.[10] However, it was only around 1854 that whalers began to enter Eclipse Sound and that interactions, including trade, with whalers became a common seasonal feature of life. Indeed, whalers were known to have fathered children in the Inuit communities that they visited.

Contact between the Tununirmiut people and outsiders increased in the early years of the twentieth century. In 1903, the Dundee Whaling Company established a land-based whaling station nearby on Eclipse Sound.[11] The establishment of the relatively short-lived whaling station paved the way for more Qallunaat commercial and institutional presence in the region. The Hudson's Bay Company (HBC) established a post at the present site of Pond Inlet/Mittimatalik in 1921 and by 1923 had become the sole trader operating in the vicinity. In 1922, the Royal Canadian Mounted Police established a post at Pond Inlet/Mittimatalik, the first in the Qikiqtani region, and seven years later Anglican and Catholic churches set up missions there.[12]

Records left by Qallunaat officials at Pond Inlet/Mittimatalik provide invaluable information about Idlout, his family, and other Tununirmiut. Reading between the lines of their correspondence and ledgers reveals much about how the Tununirmiut negotiated with – and, at times, subverted – the south.

Idlout and his father, Akumalik, regularly traded with and periodically worked for the HBC. The company's ledgers mention Akumalik beginning in 1922, shortly after the establishment of the post.[13] It is clear that Idlout's father was one of the key hunters the post relied on for trade. He is mentioned periodically as a hunter, sometimes travelling with Mukkee (the primary Inuk employee at the HBC post) and assisting police officers. By 1929, Idlout himself begins to appear in the HBC ledgers. Although fur stocks had diminished by the mid-1940s, HBC records indicate that Idlout was one of the most successful hunters trading at the post. In May 1946, he is listed as the top trapper in the region, with 103 foxes.[14]

Anglican mission records yield even more information about Idlout and his family. Although both Roman Catholics and Anglicans were long active in the Arctic – including in Pond Inlet/Mittimatalik by 1929 – Idlout's family were closely associated with the Anglican Church. Anglican missionaries had been present in what is now Nunavut as early as 1853.[15] They were responsible for converting the Inuit they encountered and, to that end, also took on some educational services, teaching their congregants to read syllabics, often based on biblical and liturgical texts that the missionaries translated themselves. Idlout, for example, was christened with the biblical name Joseph and taught to read Inuktitut syllabics by missionaries.

But Idlout was no doubt introduced to Christianity by his father. In a 2020 article, Kenn Harper discusses Akumalik's own conversion to Christianity in the early twentieth century and his activities proselytizing among Inuit for years. According to Harper, at that time, Inuit on North Baffin Island melded Christian practice with Inuit spiritual beliefs and rituals.[16]

When Qallunaat missionaries arrived in Pond Inlet/Mittimatalik in 1929,[17] religious practice adopted more southern and colonial approaches. Rev. (later Canon) John ("Jack") Hudspith Turner established the Anglican mission at Pond Inlet/Mittimatalik with funding from the Bible Churchmen's Missionary Society. Turner remained there until 1945, when he moved to Moffat Inlet, where he died in 1947.[18] Idlout's eldest daughter, Rebecca, lived with Turner's family for several years, and the Turners attempted to adopt her in the mid-1940s.[19] Idlout's father, who was particularly devout, worked as an assistant and unofficial catechist[20] to Turner and his successors.[21] Yet the archival record also indicates that Akumalik and other Inuit in the region were not submissive to the missionaries or to the demands of the church but used the association to their own ends. In journal entries during the early 1930s, Rev. Harold Duncan, for example, periodically complains of Akumalik deceiving him for material goods.[22] As the missionary Rev. Thomas Daulby lamented in 1950, "It was most grievous to hear our own helper [Nasook], to whom the Eskimos look as one of their spiritual leaders, say, 'When we are here we believe what you say, and when we go elsewhere we believe what other people tell us.' On their own admission, they want to please everybody, and one of them said it would be much better if all the white people thought alike! No doubt this state of affairs has remained unchanged for years."[23] Even Tununirmiut who were observant Christians, like Idlout's family and Nasook, maintained their independence from missionaries.[24]

With the presence of missionaries, traders, and government officials, life for Inuit in the region became increasingly institutionalized. Beginning in 1941,

Inuit in the region were issued identification numbers by the government. Idlout's number – E5-766 – indicates that he was from the region classified as the eastern Arctic (E) and from the area of Pond Inlet/Mittimatalik (5). Around the same time, the introduction of family allowances encouraged Inuit to visit settlements more frequently.

Waves of southern visitors interacted with the Tununirmiut in part by means of camera-made images, which reveal – through multidirectional gazes – the complexity of these early encounters as experienced by both the subjects and the makers of the images.[25] For example, in 1904, a year after the Dundee Whaling Company station had been founded, A.P. Low of the Geological Survey of Canada led an expedition that included a photographer and travelled to Pond Inlet/Mittimatalik.[26] The mariner Joseph-Elzéar Bernier – Idlout's possible biological father – sailed in the Arctic and visited Pond Inlet/Mittimatalik several times, including as commander of government expeditions in the region from 1904 to 1911 and as captain of an Eastern Arctic Patrol vessel, the CGS *Arctic*, in the early 1920s.[27] Photographs shot by Paul Levasseur of Inuit posing by Bernier's ship in 1907 and fifteen years later by William H. Grant of Inuit aboard the ship in 1922 attest to the crew's engagement with Inuit (see figure 2.2).

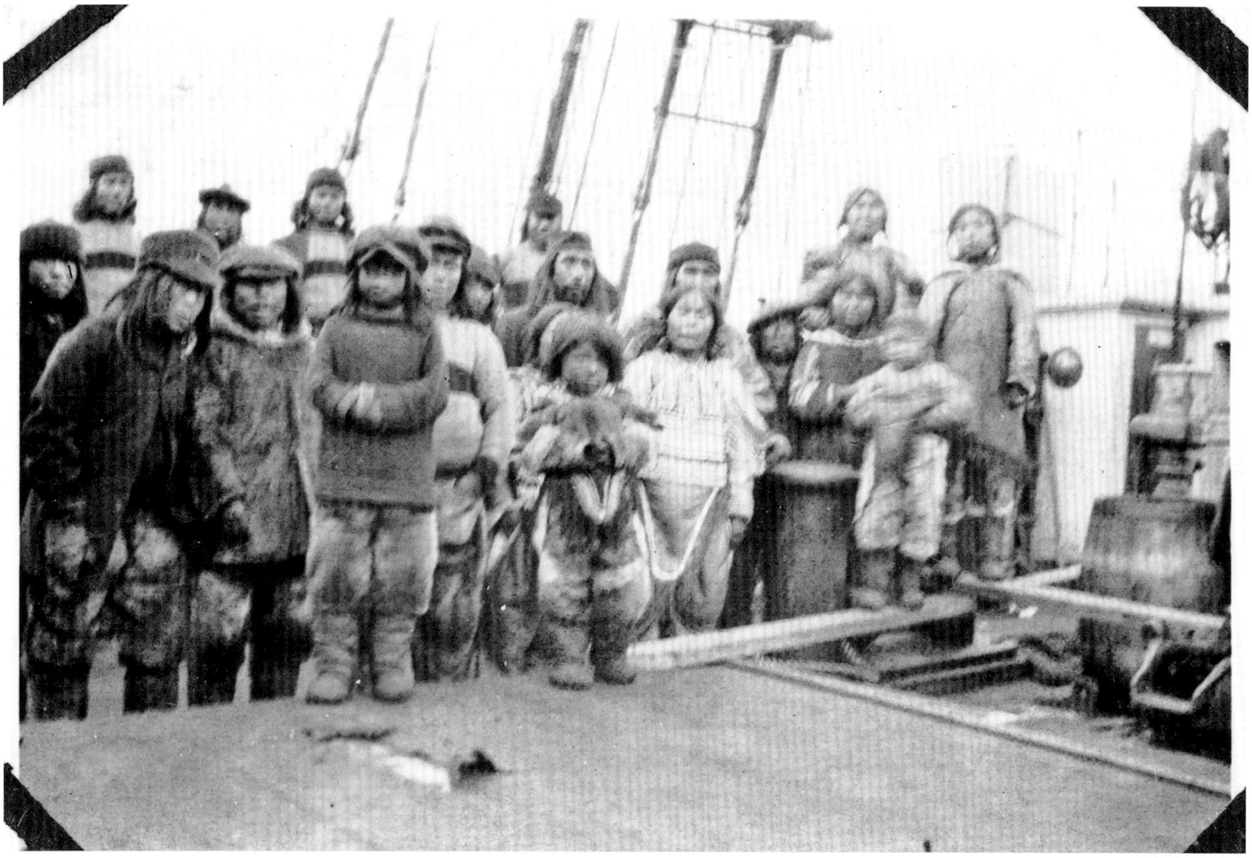

2.2 | Inuit from Pond Inlet/Mittimatalik on board the CGS *Arctic*, 2 September 1922. Photo: William H. Grant.

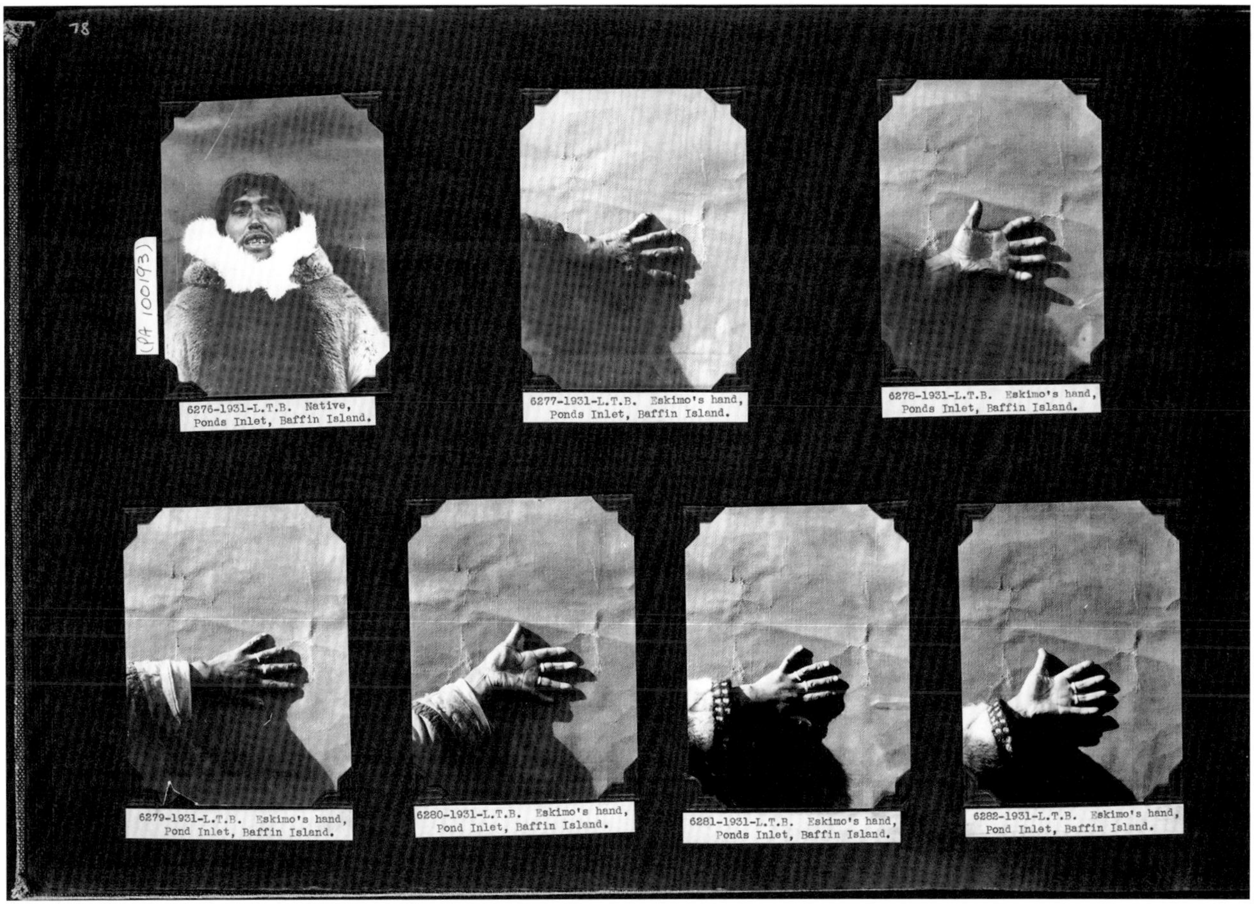

2.3 | "Native and hands," Pond Inlet/Mittimatalik, North Baffin Island, 1931. The unidentified "native" is Iqaqsaq of Pond Inlet/Mittimatalik. Photos: L.T. Burwash.

As historian Peter Geller has shown, by the 1920s, the Inuit of Pond Inlet/Mittimatalik were also photographed as part of the official reports made by Major Lachlan Taylor Burwash for the Department of the Interior.[28] Burwash produced a systemic series depicting Inuit at the settlement. The images include portraits of unnamed Inuit, often posed in clothing supplied for the shoot. Like Levasseur's earlier images, they emphasize frontality and position their subjects in standardized poses against a neutral backdrop. Within the photo albums that accompanied Burwash's reports, these likenesses are placed beside images of Inuit hands. Truncated and decontextualized in a manner adapted from the techniques of physical anthropology, Inuit lives are reduced by such images to mere bodies, physiognomic types.[29] It is only more recently that the names of the sitters have been returned to them. In this case, through the reidentification initiative Project Naming, the man seen in figure 2.3, for example, has been recognized as Iqaqsaq, an Inuk who helped to build the Anglican mission.[30]

In other images by Burwash, the Tununirmiut return the southerner's gaze and demonstrate their familiarity in negotiating with southerners. A photograph dated to 1924, for example, shows Akumalik and his family posing outside

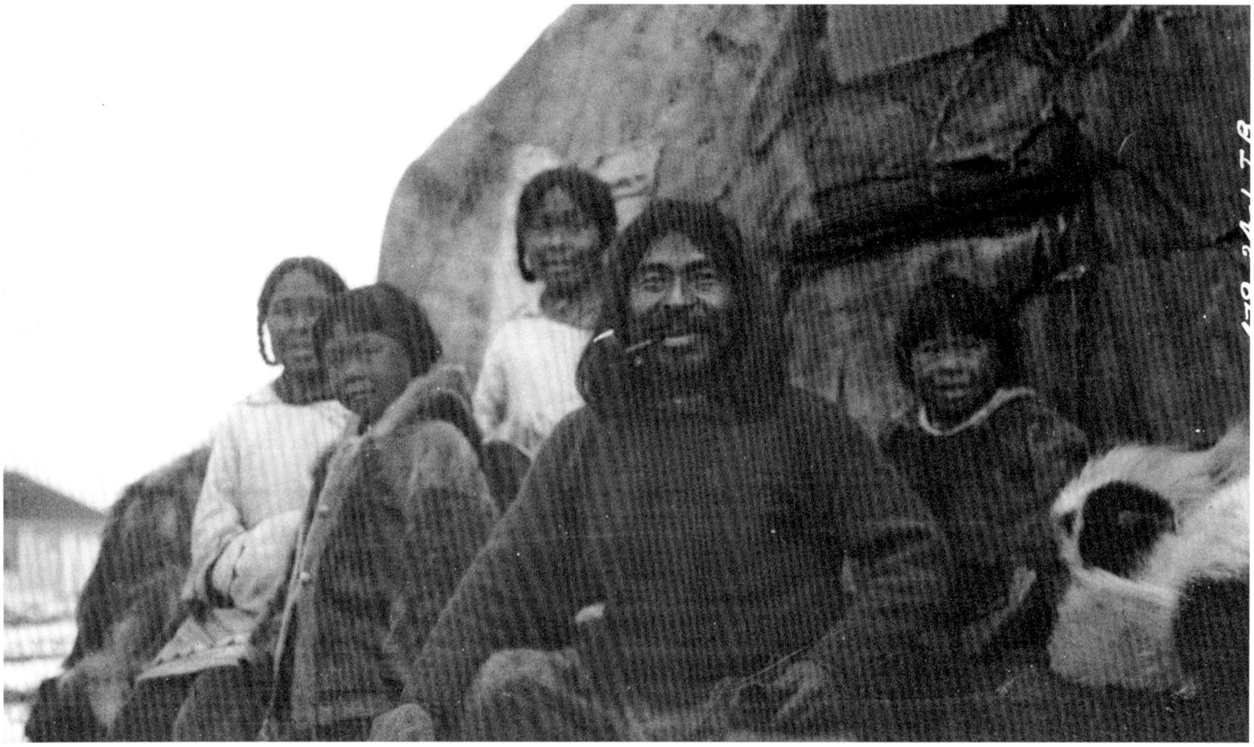

2.4 | Northeast coast of Baffin Island, 17 September 1924, outside of Akumalik's home. *Left to right*: Arnaujaq, Illauq, Niigug Inuujaq, Akumalik, and either Moses Ittukusuk or Idlout. Photo: L.T. Burwash.

their tent (see figure 2.4). Akumalik, the Anglican catechist and successful hunter, smokes his pipe and smiles broadly. Surrounded by his wife and children, he appears to be at confident ease – an equal in relation to the visiting photographer. At the right side of the frame, a young boy – possibly Idlout himself – peers over Akumalik's elbow at the camera. Although still a young child, he is already learning about the camera as a site of cultural encounter and negotiation.

Going North: Wilkinson's Early Film Work and the Arctic, 1946–49

Like Idlout, Doug Wilkinson (1919–2008) learned that the camera could be a contact zone between Inuit and Qallunaat. Born and raised in Toronto, Wilkinson first travelled north in the 1940s following military service, where he had been introduced to photography.[31] He would remain devoted to the north throughout his life.[32] Wilkinson leveraged his early military training in photography to land jobs with the National Film Board of Canada (NFB) on two productions made in collaboration with the Canadian military. In 1946, Wilkinson was based out of Churchill, Manitoba,[33] as a film editor and director with the team filming *Exercise Musk-Ox*, named for a nontactical Cold War operation undertaken jointly by the Canadian Army and the Royal Canadian Air Force to test travel capabilities in the Arctic during the winter.[34] The team of forty-seven military personnel travelled a remarkable 5,000 kilometres between February and May

1946 in tank-like snowmobiles from Churchill northwest to Cambridge Bay/Iqaluktuuttiaq, then southwest to Norman Wells, and finally southeast to Edmonton.[35] The exercise was extensively documented by the military and the NFB, culminating in a fifty-eight-minute, four-reel 16 mm film, which was promoted as a "record" of the expedition.[36] Next, Wilkinson directed another NFB-military collaboration in the Arctic and Subarctic, the forty-one-minute 16 mm film *Going North* (1948).[37] Shot in Arviat/Eskimo Point in 1947–48 and produced by the NFB for the Department of National Defence and the Canadian Army in cooperation with the National Research Board,[38] *Going North* was made largely

2.5 | *Top left to bottom right*: Gunnar Ingebrigtson seen through the haze of a severe ground drift; aerial view from a plane; Corporal McLaughlan and family; Mrs Corporal McLaughlan; Doug Wilkinson, Dr Carter Storr, and Dr Simpson walking through a severe ground drift; Inuit family in the entrance to their home, 1949. Photos: S.J. Bailey.

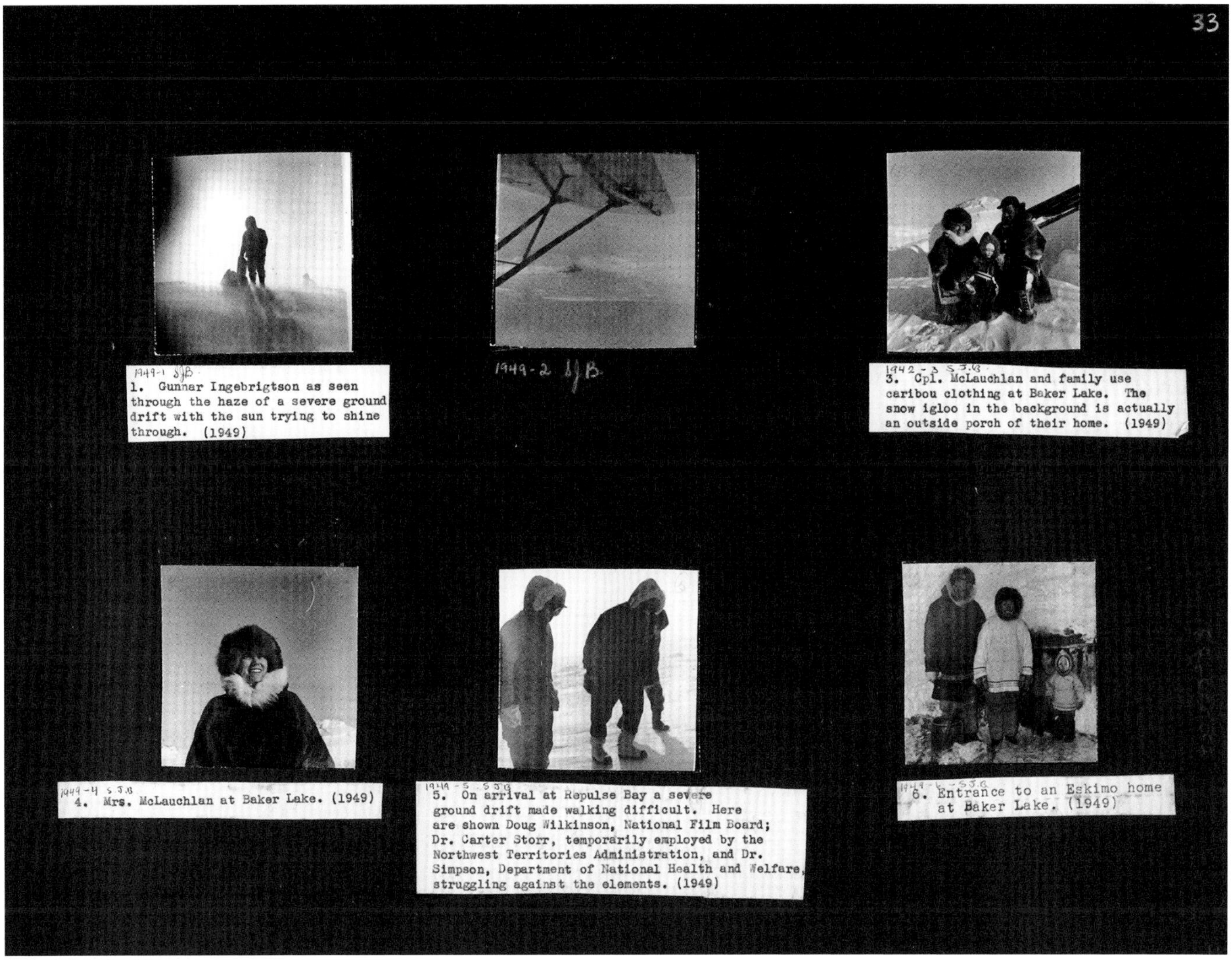

for military personnel and billed as a "winter training film which introduces the climate, resources and living problems of Canada's north."[39] The film constitutes a classic example of NFB expository documentary: a male voice-of-God narrative and "evidentiary editing" create the semblance of a seamless narrative in which rational, clear procedures are offered as solutions to the problem of military manoeuvres in harsh winter conditions.[40] However, although the film's emphasis is on how the military can adapt to northern environments, *Going North* also introduces the life of Inuit and other Indigenous peoples in the regions, even if no Indigenous peoples are named. Inuit adaptation to severe cold is highlighted through one ethnographic-style sequence in the film as a model for military in the region.[41] In addition to these two films, Wilkinson worked for the NFB shooting still photographs for albums documenting the Eastern Arctic Patrol flight from Churchill to North Baffin Island (see figure 2.5).[42]

In 1949, Wilkinson contributed to the post-production of three short films for the NFB's Arctic Notebook series, which were made from existing footage: *Arctic Dog Team, Across Arctic Ungava*, and *How to Build an Igloo*. All were intended for classroom use,[43] and like his earlier military films, this series reflects the authority and overt didacticism of the expository mode of documentary.

Across Arctic Ungava (1949), produced in cooperation with the National Museum of Canada, was shot entirely by archaeologist and ethnographer Jean Michéa, with Wilkinson editing the film and writing the script (see figure 2.6).[44] The

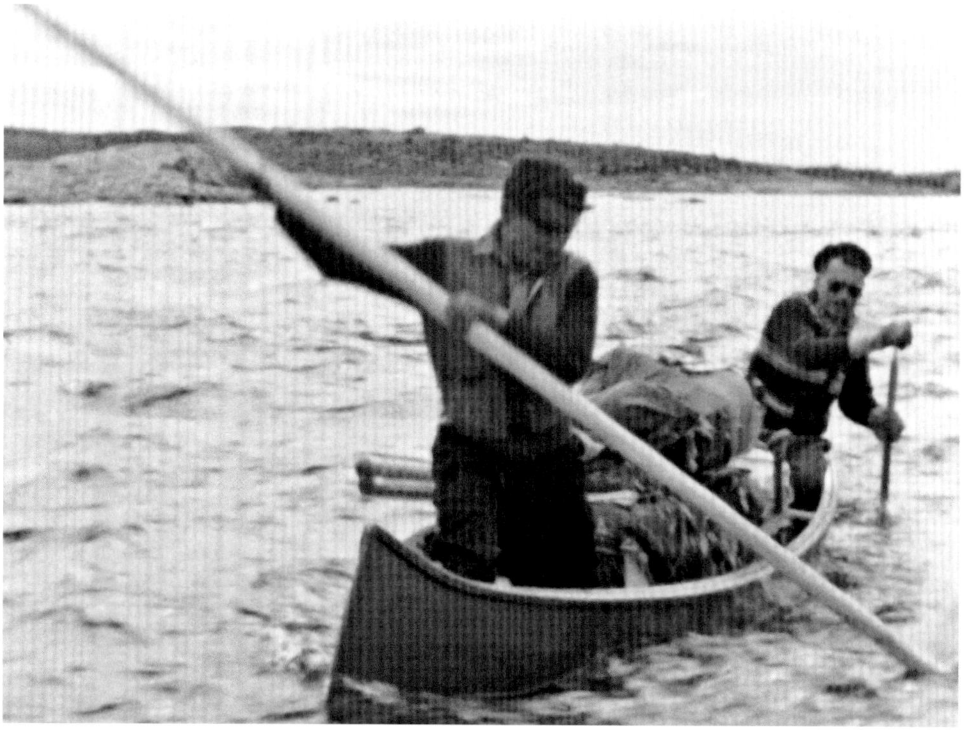

2.6 | From the documentary *Across Arctic Ungava*, 1949, National Film Board of Canada.

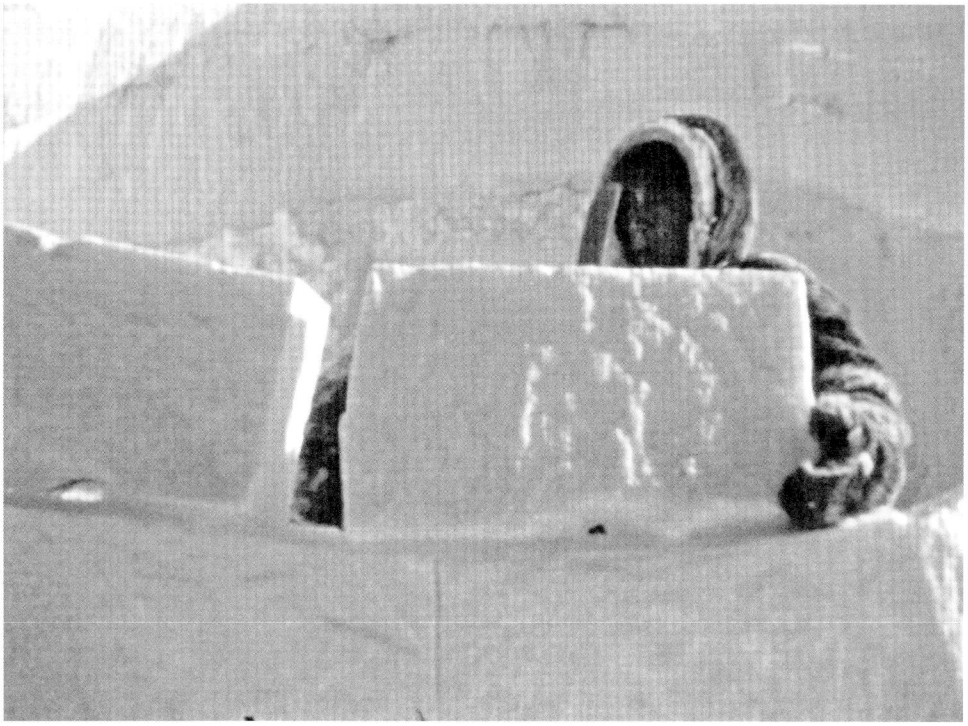

2.7 | From *How to Build an Igloo*, 1949, National Film Board of Canada.

nineteen-minute film follows a research trip that Michéa took with Dr Jacques Rousseau, director of the Montreal Botanical Gardens, who was the expedition's lead; Pierre Gadbois, a geographer; Dr Edgar Aubert de la Rue, a geologist; and four Indigenous men, who are unnamed throughout the film and in subsequent reports by the scientists.[45] The eight canoed across Ungava on the Kogaluk and Payne Rivers. Back in Ottawa, Michéa's raw footage was crafted into a seamless travelogue recording information about the scientists' research into Indigenous life, botany, soil, geographical terrain, and birds amid onslaughts of mosquitoes. Here, the voice-over narrative (written in English by Wilkinson in Ottawa) is performed by an unidentified narrator awkwardly imitating a French accent as though the scientist Michéa were speaking directly to the audience.

How to Build an Igloo and *Arctic Dog Team*, the other two films in the 1949 series, are both ten-minute reels made from colour footage shot in Arviat/Eskimo Point during the filming of *Going North*. Chester Kissick of the US Army base at Churchill shot the raw footage during a leave; however, he asked that he not be credited by name.[46] Wilkinson is credited with "technical supervision and commentary," and Neil Harris was the editor.[47] *How to Build an Igloo*, which remains a popular film in the NFB's Arctic catalogue, follows two Inuit men, identified as Tupak and Akivtak, as they construct an *iglu* (igloo) (see figure 2.7). The camera follows them with graphics interspersed to further explain the building process. The disembodied, southern male voice-of-God narration was scripted by

Wilkinson. It explains the building process in language accessible to the target audience, school children:[48] "The Eskimo word 'igloo' means house, and to the natives of the Canadian Eastern Arctic, igloo is the snow house. Built of snow blocks cut from the hard packed drifts, an igloo provides the Eskimo with shelter during the long winter months. Easy to build, once you know how, his home is compact and strong."[49] As the architect and architectural historian Samuel Dubois has argued, *How to Build an Igloo* reinforces several southern myths.[50]

The film *Arctic Dog Team* is similarly didactic, offering an introduction to husky dog teams with some commentary on Inuit life on the land.[51] The film opens with the narrator announcing, "The Eskimo is a nomadic hunter, constantly on the move in search of food; food for himself, his family and his dogs. Without dogs he could not travel, and to the extent that he must travel to find food, his life depends on his dog team."[52] But a southern presence is also evident throughout the film in the figure of Father Henri-Paul Dionne, the Catholic missionary stationed in Arviat/Eskimo Point, with whom Wilkinson stayed during the filming of *Going North*. The film follows Father Dionne as he prepares his dog team for a trip to an Inuit encampment.

The National Film Board Arctic Project

While engaged in post-production for the Arctic Notebook series,[53] Wilkinson was already planning a more ambitious ethnographic film program, an "opus on Eskimo life," as the NFB's Tom Daly would characterize it.[54] Eventually, Idlout would become the star of this undertaking. A 1950 article in the journal *The Arctic Circular* – uncredited but likely written by Wilkinson himself – describes the National Film Board Arctic Project as a series of six films addressing "The Eskimo," "The Eskimo Child," "The Natural Economy of the Arctic," "Arctic Weather Station," "Birds in the Arctic," and "Arctic Settlement."[55] In contrast to what Wilkinson deemed the largely inadequate state of filmmaking in the region, these films were to provide "an accurate and complete record of the country and of the Eskimo."[56] Although *The Arctic Circular* article appears to be critical of much amateur filmmaking in the north, it makes exceptions for those productions "made for the Department of National Defence, or made by professional cameramen of the silent movie era."[57] These exceptions, although unnamed, are clearly Wilkinson's own military collaborations and Robert Flaherty's celebrated silent-film era production *Nanook of the North* (1922).[58] As Wilkinson later wrote, "Until 1951 the Eskimo presented a problem in film. Outside of Flaherty's famous *Nanook of the North*, no film on the Eskimos had attempted to be anything but a very superficial coverage of an interesting and remote primitive people."[59]

In modelling his filmmaking in 1950–51 on *Nanook of the North*, Wilkinson was expressing his own ambitions as a filmmaker and amateur ethnographer. Flaherty's film has long been cited as a "foundational work in the histories of documentary and ethnographic cinema."[60] Wilkinson, like many early and mid-twentieth-century ethnographic filmmakers, prized *Nanook* as the product of a sustained and, therefore, more seemingly "authentic" settler engagement with an Indigenous community.[61] Beginning in 1910, Flaherty travelled to areas around Hudson Bay and the Ungava Peninsula several times, first bringing a film camera with him in 1913 on his third expedition. In 1920, with his initial film badly damaged, Flaherty returned to Sanikiluaq/Belcher Islands in Hudson Bay for a period of months to film *Nanook of the North.*[62] As a result, Flaherty's relatively long-term experiences among Inuit – particularly those of Sanikiluaq/Belcher Islands, including Allakariallak, who performs the title role – reflects immersive anthropological fieldwork, as first popularized by Bronislaw Malinowski. The subsequent reception of *Nanook of the North* has been complex. By the 1990s, although revered for decades, the film came to exemplify the ways that ethnographic cinema was exploitative and imperialist.[63] And in another

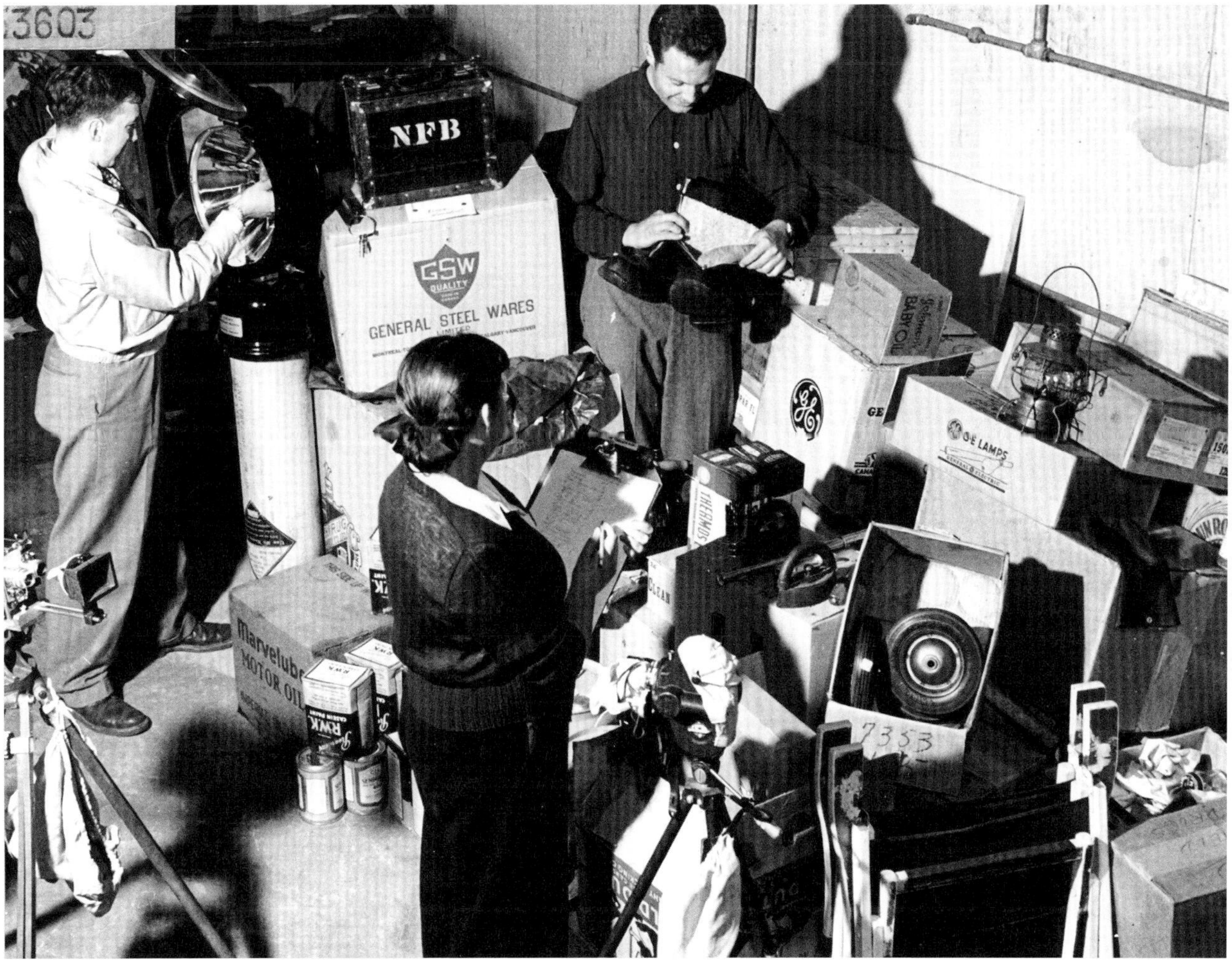

2.8 | Jean Roy, Vivian Wilkinson, and Doug Wilkinson with film equipment, 1950. Photo: G. Blouin.

twist in the film's long history of reception, recent Indigenous scholars and artists have drawn on *Nanook of the North* in efforts to reassert the agency of cinema's Indigenous subjects while also critiquing the larger colonialist project of ethnography.[64] But for Wilkinson in the early 1950s, the film constituted, however problematically, a model of respectful, cultural engagement. In attempting to produce an updated *Nanook of the North,* Wilkinson sought a way to visualize deep, immersive cultural contact with Inuit. However, as with the earlier film, the results and responses were complex and problematic.

With support from the NFB, Wilkinson travelled for a period of fifteen months, accompanied by his wife, Vivian, and cameraman Jean Roy (see figure 2.8).[65] The Wilkinsons and Roy boarded the Easter Arctic Patrol ship MV *Regina Polaris* in Montreal on 7 July 1950.[66] After almost four weeks at sea, they established a base at Chesterfield Inlet/Igluligaarjuk, where they stayed until April 1951 before continuing to North Baffin Island for the remaining five months of the trip.

Conditions in Chesterfield Inlet/Igluligaarjuk were challenging. Food supplies arrived weeks after expected,[67] and the filming schedule, already "flexible," had to be constantly adapted.[68] Wilkinson and Roy spent weeks travelling from Chesterfield Inlet/Igluligaarjuk Inlet to shoot footage of the caribou migration only to miss the herd due to weather and mechanical difficulties (see figure 2.9).[69] And an *iglu* specially constructed for filming collapsed during a warm spell, requiring reconstruction.[70] Roy later recalled, "We learned to make films with very little. For instance, in the Arctic, our gear was very basic. We used 16 mm colour film stock. There was no lab. We proceeded blindly, for months on end. There were no rushes. So, I developed small segments in a stop bath to see if we'd captured anything. But that's all."[71] The choice of 16 mm was practical: the equipment would be lighter and easier to transport than 35 mm cameras and film.[72] But the limited amount of equipment that they brought also prohibited showing participants all of the work in progress – as Flaherty, for example, had done during the filming of *Nanook of the North.*[73]

In the end, however, Wilkinson would boast that the team had filmed 2,500 feet of film in addition to photographing dozens of stills.[74] Footage, shot by Roy and directed by Wilkinson, was used for two short films in the NFB's monthly newsreel series Eye Witness (Coup d'oeil in French). *Sister Pelagie* (1951) documents the ceremony in which a seventeen-year-old identified as Poovlalerak took vows in Chesterfield Inlet/Igluligaarjuk to become the first Inuk Grey Nun.[75] And *Arctic Lifeline* (1952), filmed during Wilkinson and Roy's return voyage in September 1951, profiles the medical vessel CGS *C.D. Howe* during its inaugural annual trip to the Arctic.[76] In addition, Roy and Wilkinson filmed northern wildlife, including muskox, wolves, grizzlies, walruses, and polar bears, as well as various flora of the region.[77] And the pair shot dozens of still images at various locations and during filming. But the expedition's major accomplishments were two longer films released in colour as well as black and white: *Land of the Long Day* (1952) and *Angotee: Story of an Eskimo Boy* (1953).[78]

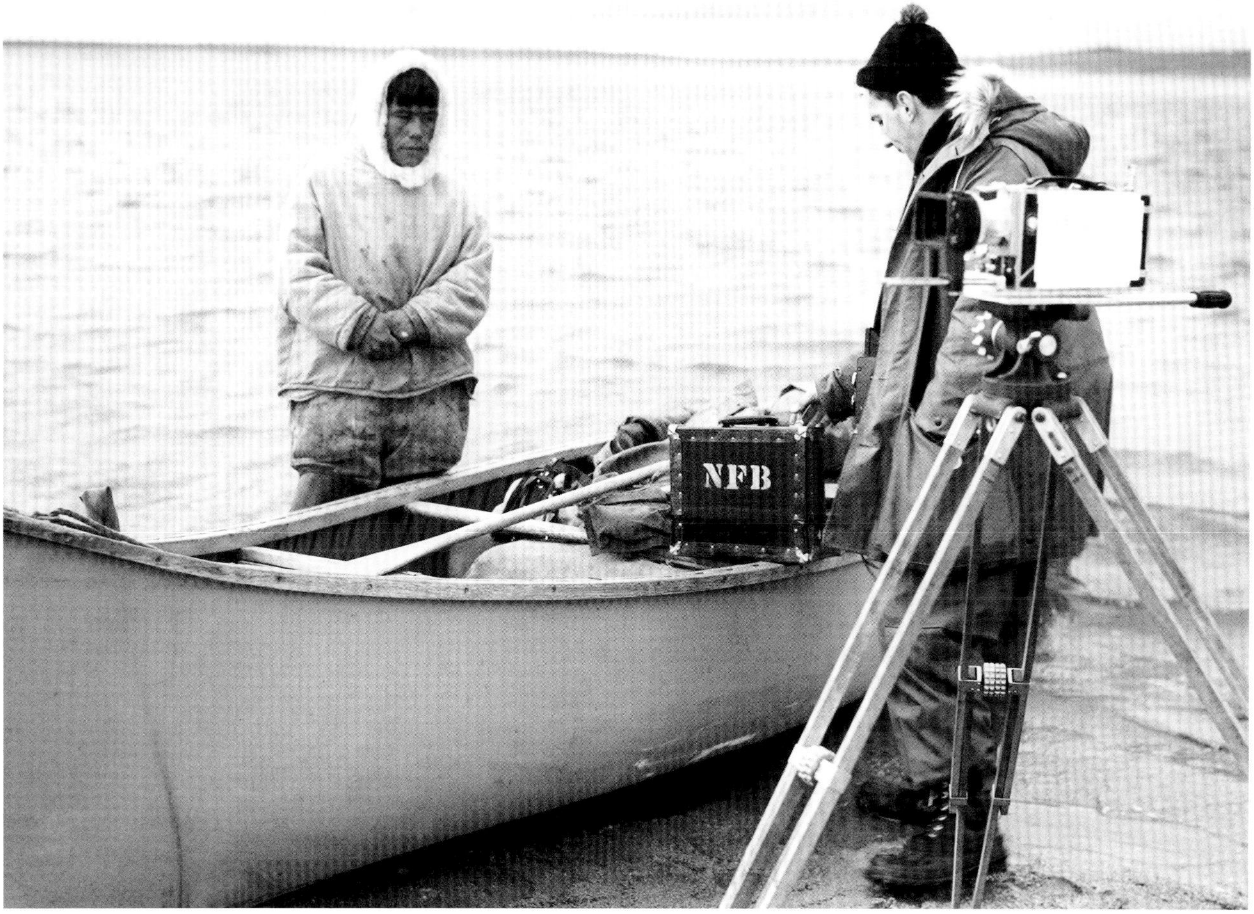

2.9 | Cinematographer Jean Roy and an Inuk guide identified as Cogiakuk during filming of *Land of the Long Day* in Igluligaarjuk/Chesterfield Inlet, 1951. Photo: Doug Wilkinson.

Angotee, as the film on "The Eskimo Child" came to be called, follows the life of a fictional Inuk boy from birth to young adulthood, when he becomes the father of a son himself (see figure 2.10). Shot around Chesterfield Inlet/Igluligaarjuk from January to March 1951, after weeks of pre-production, the film draws a correspondence between Angotee's growth and the changing seasons. The twenty-nine-minute film, released in 1953, features several Inuit as actors often performing in a reconstructed and oversized *iglu*, perhaps modelled after the *iglu* that Flaherty had constructed to film *Nanook of the North*.[79] A total of five actors performed the title role at different ages: in infancy and at two, seven, twelve, and eighteen. As Wilkinson recounted years later, the lead character was given the name Angotee as a tribute to an Elder who had died in a polio epidemic.[80] The young actor portraying the character at two years of age is also named Angotee, presumably after the Elder. Tooga, the child portraying Angotee's younger

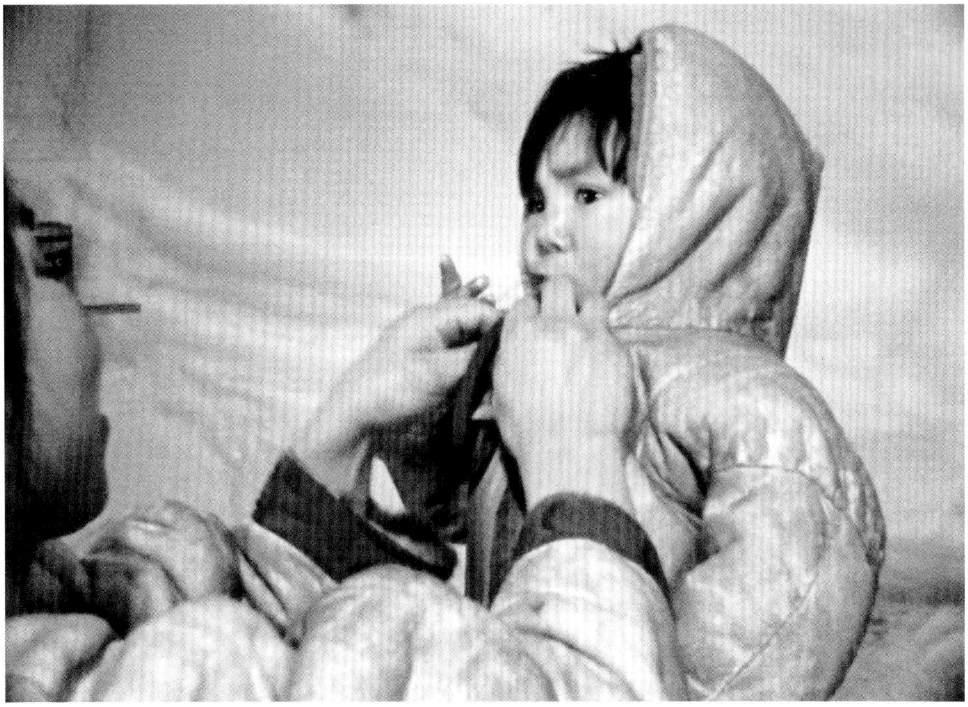

2.10 | From *Angotee*, 1953, National Film Board of Canada. The young actor is named Angotee.

sister in the early scenes, also takes the role of Angotee at age seven.[81] They were paid as nonprofessional actors.[82] Wilkinson stated, "The highlight of this work was the photographing of the birth of a baby in an igloo."[83] Stills from the birth scene appeared widely in the international press, including a four-page spread in London's *Picture Post*.[84]

Like *How to Build an Igloo* and *Arctic Dog Team*, *Angotee* was produced as a work of popular anthropology informed by salvage ethnography. The film employs the familiar structure and narrative authority of expository film ostensibly to teach its (southern) audience about Inuit life. Like many NFB productions of the time, it seems aimed at juvenile audiences, who might be able to relate to Angotee's youth. A press release explains, "In telling the story of Angotee, the film describes the life and customs of an Eskimo family, the typical upbringing of an Eskimo boy and the favored place he occupies in the family. It is a picture of domesticity, involving not only the immediate family but also the aged grandmother and other members of the community as well."[85] However, as the contemporary filmmaker Alethea Arnaquq-Baril notes, *Angotee* (like *How to Build an Igloo*) presents "a falsely romantic and ahistorical image of Inuit life, suggesting a people frozen in time, a culture destined to disappear."[86]

Angotee also briefly introduces new federal interventions in Inuit life. In a two-minute scene, the infant Angotee and his family travel for four days to visit an unnamed settlement (clearly Chesterfield Inlet/Igluligaarjuk).[87] Once there, his sisters, Kowna and Amuk, explore a new school under construction. Voice-over narration pronounces that "this is where Eskimo children can learn to read and write, just like the children in the land of the white man." Kowna and Amuk happen upon two white builders preparing a classroom for use; giggling with surprise at seeing the men, the girls race out of the building. The narrator intones, "A strange place ... for shy little girls." Meanwhile, their parents, Attootoo and Koonuk, visit the Hudson's Bay Company post to trade skins, receive family allowance, and buy food, including pablum.[88] These episodes are clearly intended to promote new governmental policies among Inuit. However, viewed from the perspective of twenty-first-century knowledge of the trauma inflicted through enforced settlement and schooling, they are ominous. In one of the film's final scenes, Angotee, now an adult, returns to the settlement. This time, he travels in order to marry at the Roman Catholic church.[89] The film lingers over the ceremony as Angotee and his new wife, Shikeetna, exchange vows. The two short scenes at the settlement bookend life on the land with the presence of southern institutions. In this way, although largely a work of salvage ethnography, *Angotee* also seems to advocate for the assimilation of Inuit into the southern welfare state. However, within five years, Wilkinson would recall, "At Chesterfield I saw much of the demoralizing effect of close contact with the white man on the local Eskimo population."[90]

Idlout, the New Nanook

In April 1951, after the filming of *Angotee*, the Wilkinsons and Roy travelled by plane to the settlement of Pond Inlet/Mittimatalik on North Baffin Island. There, they would join Idlout's camp for the shoot. In contrast to the tensions that Wilkinson alluded to in Chesterfield Inlet/Igluligaarjuk, he wrote later that "it was not until I got to Pond Inlet that I began to discover something of how an Eskimo could live in his land."[91]

At the time, the camp comprised a community of five families. Idlout and Kidlak lived with their five youngest children: Paniloo, Leah, Moses, Paul, and Noah. Following custom, their eldest son, Paul Ullatitaq had been raised by his grandparents, Arnaujaq and Akumalik. Ullatitaq, in turn, married during the summer of 1951 when the Wilkinsons and Roy were present. The eldest daughter, Rebecca, after living until 1948 with Anglican missionary Rev. Jack Turner and his wife Joan Hobart Turner, married Gideon Qitsualik and returned with her husband to North Baffin. The camp also included the family of Leetia and Kadloo, the latter being the son of Hudson's Bay Company trader Gaston Herodier.[92]

As head of camp, Idlout was responsible for the welfare of all five families. David Kalluk (Kadloo), who lived in Idlout's camp as a child, explained to the Qikiqtani Truth Commission in December 2008, "You have to have a leader when you're in the camp so things go smoothly ... working with the people to make the camp smoother, to make it survive ... We never really got hungry. Our leader was a good hunter."[93] Within the gendered hierarchy of camp life, the head – always a man – had to be an expert hunter; he was responsible for ensuring sufficient food and other resources. Another son of Kadloo and Leetia, Ludy Pudluk, who also spent his childhood at Idlout's camp, told the Qikiqtani Truth Commission that Idlout as head of camp was responsible for

> pushing the hunters to go out as much as they could to prevent starving. He was a good leader in the camp. There was about four dog teams in that camp, and each eat a lot of food, and us had to eat food too. Sometimes, if we were eating too much, he would say that's enough so we would have enough for the whole winter ... Idlout was a good hunter and would support the family and the camp. There was another camp about 25 miles from us, and they almost ran out of food but sometimes [had] no food and no oil to warm their sod house. They always came to our camp, and Joseph Idlout would give them just enough for a one-week supply because we needed that too at our camp, but we shared what we had. We would sometimes get more in the summer in case another camp would need some help. He was a funny guy. When the other camp would come three or four times a year, he would say, "No more, we have to have enough for our camp to survive. Why don't you go out and hunt yourself?" He was nice and patient, but a couple times that same person would keep coming back, and he would say, "No."[94]

Idlout was accustomed to leading not only the people at his camp but also visiting Inuit.

In the film that Wilkinson was shooting, Idlout became both the southerner's guide and a featured performer (see figure 2.11). Just as Flaherty, in making *Nanook of the North*, had decided "to take a single character [played by Allakariallak] and make him typify the Eskimos," Wilkinson selected Idlout as the archetypal Inuk, casting him as the new Nanook, as Alan Rudolph Marcus has argued.[95]

After meeting Idlout, the Wilkinsons and Roy moved to the camp in Aulattivik at the eastern end of Eclipse Sound some 100 kilometres from Pond Inlet/Mittimatalik. They would remain there for the duration of the shoot until September 1951. At camp, they lived among the community of about thirty people in the five family groups.

During the filming of *Land of the Long Day*, the Wilkinsons and Roy were completely dependent on Idlout and fellow camp members for survival; as a result, camp members also became essential (if uncredited) members of the production team.[96] Wilkinson later stated that he paid performers as nonprofessional actors,[97] but one of the performers – Gideon Qitsualik, referred to as Kitsooalik by Wilkinson – recalled in 1978 that he had never been paid and thought that only Idlout had received remuneration.[98] Yet, whether remunerated or not, Inuit were burdened by the presence of these southerners.[99] Members of the camp were called upon to perform film roles and to pose for still photographs. Roy and Wilkinson spent weeks staging and shooting scenes featuring Idlout's family – including his wife, Kidlak, parents, and children – while the film's climatic hunting scenes, filmed throughout the month of August, starred Idlout, his son Paniloo, the hunter Kadloo, and other male members of the camp.[100] Gideon Qitsualik remembered, "We always had to rehearse a lot for the film, almost every day in spring and summer months when there were no clouds in the sky ... It was time-consuming and we really got bossed around. Sometimes we felt like slaves."[101] Moreover, with limited film processing onsite and no projecting equipment to show them the results of their efforts, they "proceeded blindly, for months on end" in their performances.[102] Wilkinson and Roy also filmed scenery and wildlife, travelling to the floe edge off Button Point and to Bylot Island to photograph Arctic birds, sea mammals, the breakup of sea ice, and the region's mountainous terrain.[103] Although human actors do not appear in these travelogue-like scenes, they also required the active participation of camp members, who transported, guided, fed, and aided the southern filmmakers. Serving both as performers and as unacknowledged members of the crew, Idlout and the rest of the camp were active agents in the production.

2.11 | National Film Board photographers setting up during filming of *Land of the Long Day*, 1951. Likely Jean Roy and Joseph Idlout. Uncredited photo likely by Doug Wilkinson.

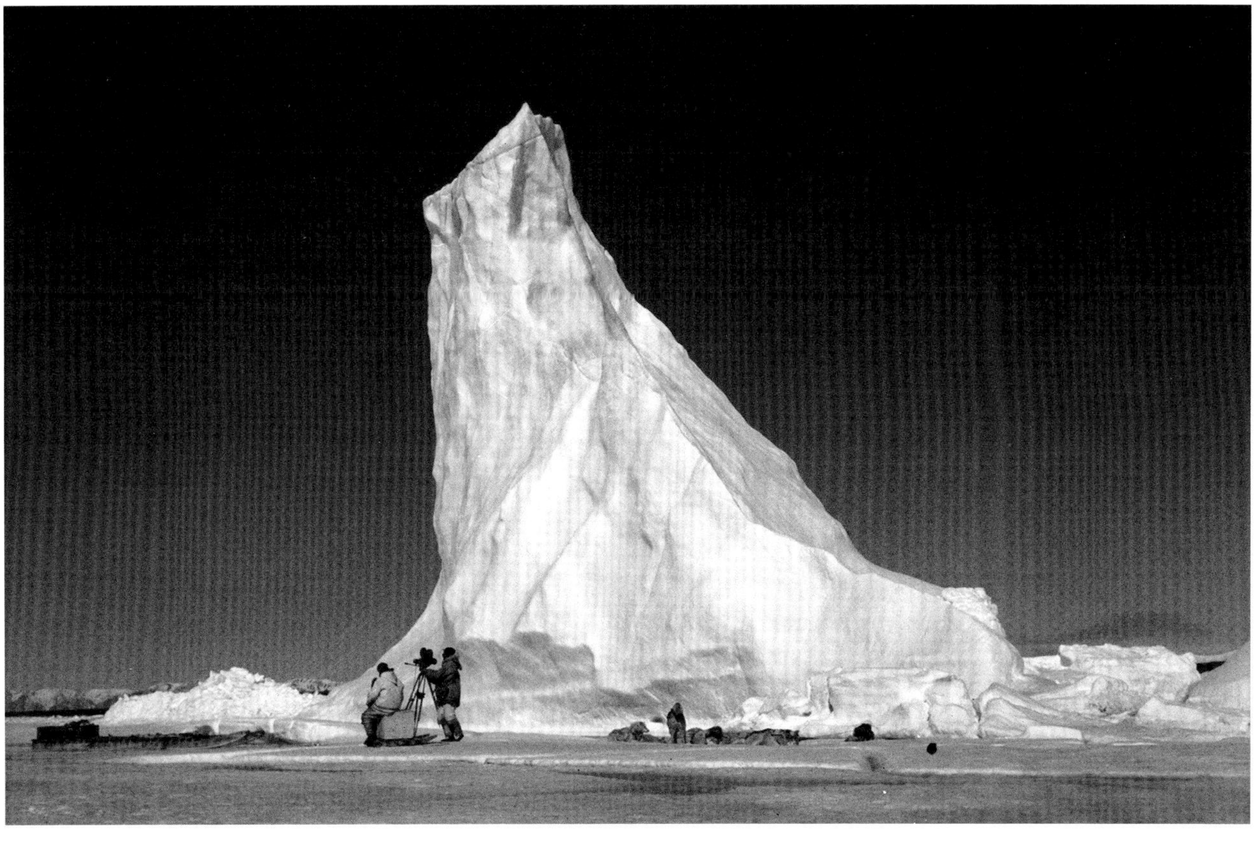

Land of the Long Day

The raw footage shot on North Baffin Island became *Land of the Long Day*. After months of post-production in Ottawa, it was released in 1952 as a thirty-seven-minute, four-reel, 16 mm narrative film. Wilkinson clearly came to see this film as the most significant production of his time spent in the Arctic. Indeed, it would come more closely to Wilkinson's model, *Nanook of the North*, than his other cinematic productions. In November 1951, he requested that the then substantial sum of $1,000 be moved from the budget for *Angotee* to that of *Land of the Long Day*.[104] The NFB shared Wilkinson's enthusiasm, widely promoting *Land of the Long Day* and attempting to reach even larger audiences through the distribution of a shorter eleven-minute version for newsreels.[105]

The film's title, *Land of the Long Day*, announces its central temporal framing. Ostensibly it follows the passage of one year on North Baffin Island, beginning and ending in the darkness of winter. The change of seasons is marked by views of Arctic scenery as Roy's camera pans across terrain and sea, at times accompanied by audio clips of waterfowl and huskies baying.[106] Simultaneously, these sweeping shots present the film's protagonists – Idlout and members of his camp – as a people at one with the rhythms of nature.

Unlike *Angotee*, *Land of the Long Day* eschews references to southern culture. All action takes place at camp. Neither the southern filmmakers nor Idlout's and his community's long-standing links with Qallunaat at Pond Inlet/Mittimatalik are seen or mentioned. Wilkinson was careful to excise most references to the south; even common consumer products like Red Rose Tea, then a staple of Inuit camp life, are nowhere to be seen.[107] Southern-manufactured hunting equipment marks an exception to this re-creation of pre-contact life: a dory, a rope, rifles, and a retractable telescope, all manufactured in the south, appear throughout the film. Yet here, too, the narration is quick to minimize Inuit dependence on southern technology. For example, although the hunters Idlout and Kadloo carry rifles in their *qajait* (kayaks) during a whale hunt, they end up killing with harpoons. And even if the narration admits that the rope has been purchased from a trader, it quickly – almost defensively – adds that "we make the net ourselves." In short, *Land of the Long Day* exemplifies salvage ethnography in its performance of pre-contact Inuit life.

The debt to the visual culture of salvage ethnography is clear from *Land of the Long Day*'s opening. The title itself not only references the temporal but also echoes Edward S. Curtis's *In the Land of the Head Hunters*, a 1914 film made with the Kwakwa̱ka̱'wakw of the West Coast.[108] But, without question, *Land of the Long Day*'s key source within the history of ethnographic cinema remained *Nanook of the North*, which, as noted above, Wilkinson references in various archival records and publications.[109]

Within its first few frames, *Land of the Long Day* pays homage to *Nanook of the North*. Wilkinson's film opens with two brief intertitles overlaid onto the image of a piece of caribou skin. They contextualize the setting and introduce the film's hero: "In the Pond Inlet area of North Baffin Island live the most northerly group of Eskimos in Canada, the Tununirmiut. This is their story, set in the hunting territory around the Island of Alukseevee, and told as Idlouk would have told it in his native Eskimo." For audiences familiar with the history of documentary cinema, the subject of the film and these intertitles specifically call to mind *Nanook of the North*, which also opens with contextual information and an introduction to the film's protagonist.[110] *Land of the Long Day*, however, departs from its silent-film model in tone. Whereas Flaherty characterizes the setting and subjects of *Nanook of the North* in melodramatic verbiage, describing "the mysterious Barren Lands – desolate, boulder strewn, wind-swept – illimitable spaces which top the world" and the "fearless, lovable, happy-go-lucky Eskimo," *Land of the Long Day*'s introductory intertitles adopt the sober, didactic restraint of NFB expository film.

Although understated, *Land of the Long Day*'s opening intertitles establish a sense of ostensible authenticity for the intended (southern) audience. In announcing that "this is their story ... as Idlouk would have told it in his native Eskimo," the intertitles propose that the film offers audiences a direct encounter with Inuit culture. Roy's camera provides viewers with voyeuristic glimpses of camp life and scopic mastery of the terrain and sea.

Audio also contributed to the film's seeming authenticity. Recordings of Inuktitut songs and conversation are periodically interspersed into the soundtrack composed by Louis Applebaum to indicate the voices of various actors and "as a guide to Eskimo song melody."[111] Wilkinson and two film production crew members recorded Inuit voices at the Parc Savard Hospital in Quebec City, where Idlout's daughter Leah was among numerous Inuit being treated for tuberculosis.[112] Wilkinson had travelled to Quebec City during one of the recording trips to bring her back to his home in Gatineau, north of Ottawa, for four months of convalescence with his family.[113] As Leah recalled in a 1977 article in the magazine *Inuit Today*, "Different Inuit at the hospital did the voices of the various members of my family. Qarjugaarjuk from Cape Dorset did the voice of my grandmother Mary Arnaujaq, Elisapie from Pangnirtung was my mother Rebecca Kidlak [Kidla], Kublu from Pond Inlet was my father Joseph Idlout and my grandfather Abraham Akumalik, Suujuq was my brother Paul Idlout, Sanguja was my brother Peter Lazarus Paniloo, and an Inuk from Cape Dorset was my little brother Noah Idlout."[114]

However, audiences chiefly experience this seemingly direct encounter with Inuit camp life through the film's voice-over narration "as Idlouk would have told it." Unlike the intertitles, the narration is spoken in the first-person ostensibly from Idlout's own point of view, underscoring his role as the film's singular hero. The narration unifies the various scenes into a cohesive story about the cycle of the seasons in the life of this Inuit group. Over the sound of howling dogs, we are told, "In winter only the moon shines over my land. Between

November and February, the sun has gone away. We live out our winter lives hunting and trapping by the light of our friend, the moon. One day in January, daylight comes back. It only stays for a little while, then it is gone again. But it is back the next day, and the next, getting stronger and brighter each day. The sun has come back to us again." The gentle cadences of the voice and poetic text paired with footage of the receding sun draw the audience into the sensations of Arctic life. But, in fact, the voice-over narration is a highly choreographed simulation. The speaker is *not* Idlout but, instead, the southern Canadian actor John Drainie, who imitated an Inuk accent in performing the narrative. The text itself was entirely scripted by Wilkinson.[115] Indeed, archival documents show that the script was carefully edited to construct a semblance of otherness and to excise any "white man's talk" from the narration. In his edits of the script, Les McFarlane of the NFB urged Wilkinson toward "an effect of simplicity which should be primitive, elemental and yet with a certain poetry of simplicity."[116]

Across the seasons of the year, *Land of the Long Day* presents Idlout and his community in ways that reflect the assumed values of the NFB's target southern and middle-class audiences. Although the camp comprised five family groups living together communally, the film highlights Idlout's own immediate family. His parents, wife, and children are presented as a nuclear family group. They are portrayed as an industrious and thrifty people. In an early scene describing the spring thaw, for example, the camp moves to a dry beach. This allows the filmmakers to record the harnessing of sled dogs, drawing on didactic information that Wilkinson had used in the 1949 film *Arctic Dog Team*. A later scene from reel three of *Land of the Long Day* introduces members of Idlout's immediate family through their labours. Following the narration's announcement that "everyone at my camp works hard, and everyone has a job to do," we watch Kidlak (Idlout's wife) mending *kamiik* (boots), Arnaujaq (his mother) drying sealskin, and Akumalik (his father) scraping sealskin lines to be used as dog traces and for harpoons (see figure 2.12). Medium shots are interspersed with close-ups to create a sense of intimate familiarity between the audience and Idlout's family. Brief scenes of children at play, huskie puppies, and a young seal sliding into the water provide comic relief from the heavy demands of camp life.[117]

Above all, *Land of the Long Day* focuses on the masculine world of the hunt and on Idlout's prowess as a hunter. As the narration states, "We are Eskimo. Our life is the hunt." The film features two lengthy hunting scenes. The first opens with Idlout crouching on an iceberg surveying the ice-covered sea with his telescope. The accompanying narrative teases, "Next to the polar bear, the seal's biggest enemy is, uh, me." The camera moves in to a close-up of Idlout peering through the telescope (see figure 2.1). With the sound of gentle Inuktitut humming in the background, the camera adopts a point-of-view shot, scanning the ice as though from Idlout's perspective. A dark form appears on the ice. The scene cuts back to Idlout calling to his son Paniloo. The hunt begins. In the five-minute scene, editing and sound establish a sense of intense concentration and slowly building

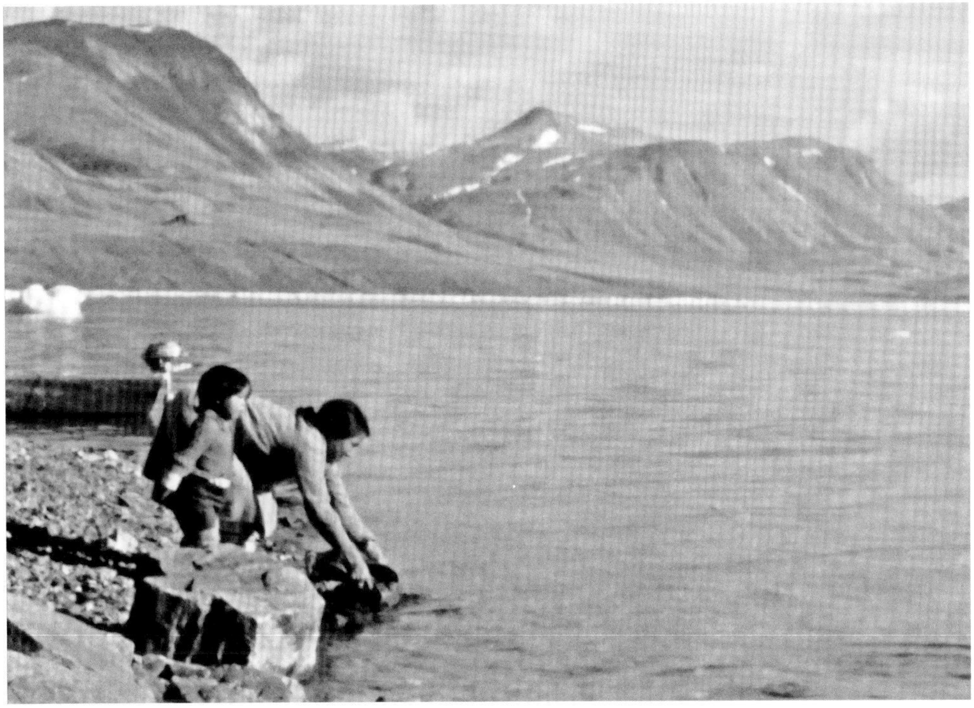

2.12 | Kidlak softening boots with Moses, from *Land of the Long Day*, 1952, National Film Board of Canada.

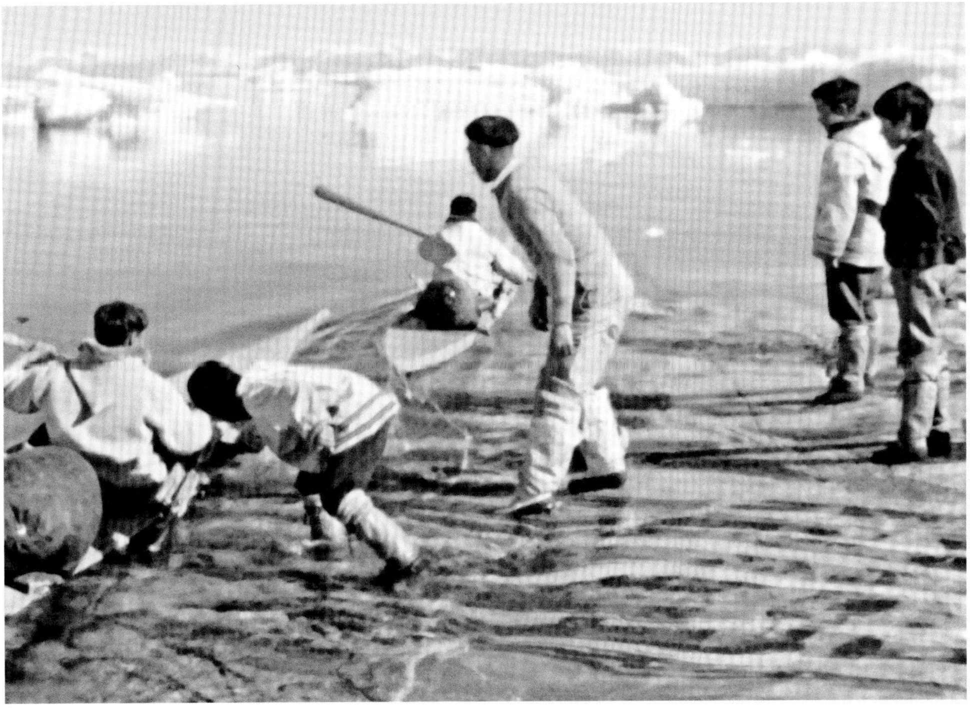

2.13 | Idlout and Kadloo in *qajait* with Qitsualik and boys of the camp, from *Land of the Long Day*, 1952, National Film Board of Canada.

drama. The camera shifts between medium shots, medium close-ups, point-of-view shots, and reverse shots (even, at times, as though from the seal's perspective).[118] Applebaum's score builds to a crescendo as Idlout furtively approaches the seal from behind a screen and fires his rifle.

The second hunting scene provides the film's dramatic climax. Idlout and Kadloo hunt a pod of white whales and narwhals from their *qajait* (see figure 2.13). Gideon Qitsualik and a group of boys follow behind in the dory. This scene is more fast-paced than Idlout and Paniloo's seal hunt. The quick tempo of the score and edits combine to build dramatic tension as Idlout strikes the whale with his harpoon. Seamless editing of footage shot at different times and credible re-enactments provide a sense of immersion in the immediacy of the hunt. This scene most closely replicates the popular drama of *Nanook of the North*. But it was less convincing for those familiar with camp life. Gideon Qitsualik recalled seeing Roy film a hunter as he threw his harpoon into water where there were no whales; later, in watching *Land of the Long Day*, Qitsualik was surprised when, through the wonders of editing, a whale appeared at the end of the harpoon.[119]

With the hunt successful, *Land of the Long Day* reaches its conclusion. Shots of ice forming on the sea and the setting sun provide visual closure while the narrative intones, "And with the stinging cold of the October blizzards, our long day is drawing to a close. Our daylight is dying. Each day the sun comes up a little later, sets a little earlier. One day the sun barely rises over our land. Tomorrow it will set and be gone. But we don't mind. Our meat caches are full. This winter we shall not be hungry. Life will be good in our land." As with the film's introduction, the people of Idlout's camp are presented as integrated into the rhythms of nature.

Conclusion: Unsettling *Land of the Long Day*

Land of the Long Day captivated southern audiences. The NFB distributed the film (and its shorter version, *Arctic Saga*) internationally to largely enthusiastic audiences.[120] *Land of the Long Day* went on to win several awards, including – no doubt to Wilkinson's great satisfaction – being one of three films tied for the top prize at the Robert J. Flaherty Film Awards in New York.[121] Stills from the film and from *Angotee* were reproduced in London's *Picture Post* and in the American magazines *Argosy* and *Time*, among others.[122]

However, other viewers were unsettled. Some recognized cultural disconnections in the film's production. At a test screening for the Toronto Film Society, for example, several audience members identified the narrator as non-Inuk and registered objections to his appropriation of an Inuk accent. When asked what they disliked specifically about the film, several viewers at a test screening by the Toronto Film Society, for example, cited the southern narrator's imitation of an Inuk accent. One responded, "I objected to the commentator trying to talk like an Eskimo," and another described the commentary as "mawkish, infantile, affected."[123]

Others perceived a greater degree of Inuit-Qallunaat interchange than the film explicitly acknowledged. A film-use report, written following a May 1953 Vancouver screening, suggested that "perhaps some part of the dialogue could have included the fact of the white man's infiltration and inter-marriage."[124] As producer Michael Spencer noted in correspondence about the report, this comment "refers of course to the two members of Idlouk's family group who are 50% white ... We gave a lot of consideration to this point and we realized that this situation could arise. However, since the commentary is spoken by Idlouk himself we could hardly have him make a reference to the admixture of white blood. What we did was to have the commentator say, over a big closeup of one of the two men, 'for we are Eskimo.'"[125] The two men, Kadloo and Qitsualik, were indeed biracial. Their appearance, particularly the close-up of Kadloo that Spencer references,[126] would have disrupted expectations of Inuit exoticism held by most southern settler audiences. Kadloo's face, with light skin and European features, looks out at the film's southern audiences: not so much a distant other as a mirror image reflected back to southern viewers. His image registers the instability of racialized categories (see figure 2.14).

In such subtle ways, Idlout, Kadloo, and the other members of the camp cannot be contained within *Land of the Long Day*'s restrictive fantasy of salvage

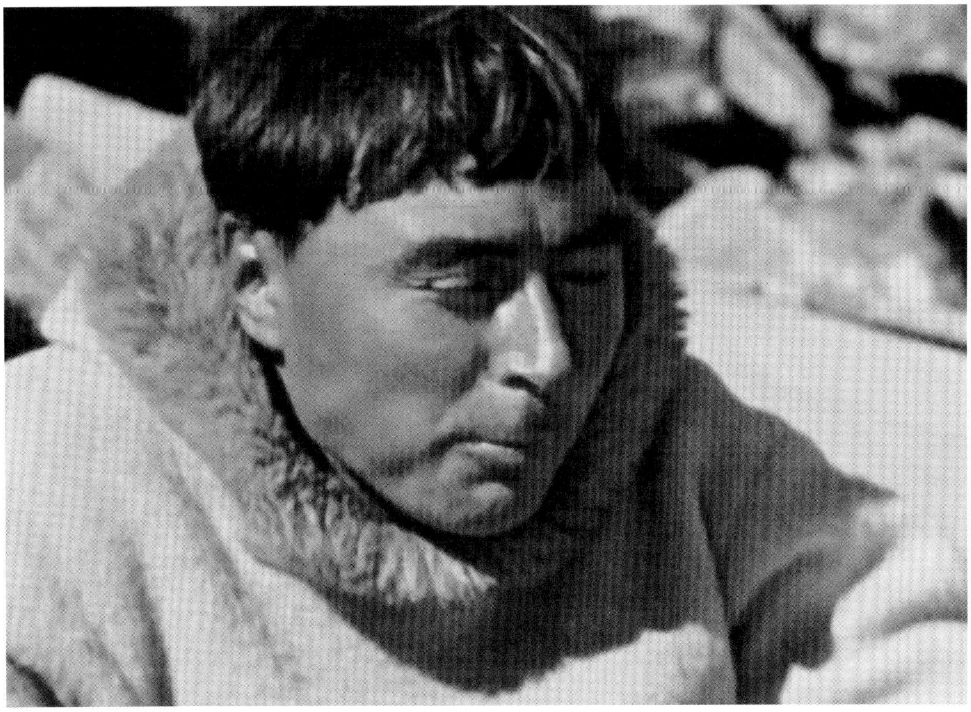

2.14 | Kadloo, from *Land of the Long Day*, 1952, National Film Board of Canada.

ethnography. Their very appearance contradicted the film's claims of otherness. As a result, they disrupt what the filmmaker Arnaquq-Baril terms "a falsely romantic and ahistorical image of Inuit life" and what the anthropologist Johannes Fabian familiarly describes as the "denial of coevalness," anthropology's tendency to present non-Western subjects temporally as living outside the modern.[127] Instead, members of the camp were active agents who collaborated in the making of these films. Indeed, years later in an interview, Wilkinson acknowledged the collaborative nature of his Arctic filmmaking at the time. In discussing the production of *Angotee*, he stated,

> The scripting of it was done with the Eskimo people and what I would do, what we would really do, and Jean Roy as well, would be to simply invite a group of people to come in almost every night and we would go over the sequences in the film and they would tell me how this was done, and how that was done, how babies were born and all, they would go, simply lay them out on the kitchen table, floor and everybody would get into it and that, and they'd do a little acting show for us, and so we had everything plotted out on the floor of our living room in this house. Mainly, the Eskimo people themselves were really doing the script for me in a kind of way ... and then I would translate this into shots, close-ups, mediums, long-shots, tracking shots or whatever the case may be.[128]

The agency of Idlout and his family is underscored in the two publications that follow this chapter. A letter from Joseph Idlout to R.G.H. Williamson – then head of Linguistic Services, Welfare Division, Department of Northern Affairs and National Resources – was translated by Williamson and published in 1961 in an obscure journal under the title "Ten Uses for the Seal."[129] Although translated, it provides a rich sense of Idlout the hunter in his own words, and the detailed cultural information indicates that it is a credible translation. Leah Idlout d'Argencourt Paulson's article "Spring," which appeared in a 1976 edition of the magazine *Inuit Today*, looks back on her childhood and the Idlout family's close relationship to the land.[130] Together, these two pieces of writing also signal how the Idlout family's life reflected the principles of Inuit Qaujimajatuqangit, or Inuit traditional knowledge.

In the Idlout Family's Words 2

Joseph Idlout, "Letter to an Administrator (Idlout's 10 Uses for the Seal)," *Plywood World* 1, no. 4 (1961)

LETTER TO AN ADMINISTRATOR

To the fair one:

You haven't written to me and it is difficult to know just how you are but you are still lovable. I have just arrived today, and there is no ice forming yet. I wonder the reason for our land being like the whiteman's. Just imagine, the white people are making houses in the middle of the winter. They are building five houses for some teachers when it is cold outside. The Eskimos probably would find difficulty in building on a cold day although the whiteman do have eight Eskimo helpers. We are quite alright in our land but I think there will be fewer fox than there were last year because there are no fox tracks. I do not think my pipe will be full this winter.

I am now working with the Air Force with two other Eskimo companions. I will be helping all the time through the Eskimos, and sometimes I will be able to go hunting for a whole week. Sometimes this will be enough but probably at the end of next year my pipe will be full.

I am going to write about different thing I have done and about what I know such as animals. If you are going to worry much of what I am going to say, even though you know about it, I am just going to write about it anyway. I have been living by seal for so long. I have been living by seal more than I have other food through my life. When I used to live in Pond's Inlet, I used to catch about 200 seals in one whole year, but nowadays I have not been getting enough because I am becoming an old man. I understand now that the seal is the most useful thing that the Eskimos use in our land. Even though I will not see these things happen this winter, I am just writing about it, and you also know about this because no wonder, they belong to God. We all know that the Ten Commandments consist of ten and that is how many uses a seal has too, but of course I am telling a story: my best regards to you.

Idlout's ten uses for the seal:

1. *We use the seal as our food, by boiling it, eat it raw, eat it frozen, and also use it as dog food; the bladder, the gall-bladder,*

and these are our only food, so we eat it with delight with our eyes closed when it is boiled.

2. *The oil from the fat is used on the kudlik (oil lamp) and if you get one big seal, the oil will be enough for five days. The other uses are also to grease the seal skin ropes and also was used to wash faces by our ancestors.*
3. *The seal's skin is the most useful part of all with the fur. taken off because we use it as boots taking out the fat membrane and leaving the outer black membrane on it and also it is useful for the use of mitts. By leaving part of the fattish membrane on, we can make use of it as a harness for the dogs, and also can be used as a rope to tie and pack up the sled.*
4. *When you soak the skin in water, it makes a good boot and very good mitts when the black membrane is taken off and making it white and also without the fat membrane on it; also the parts of the seal's skin are used as a long string to tie parts of other ropes together.*
5. *Also without the fur, the whole skin taken off carefully from the seal, can be blown up and used as a float for the kayak. The float can also be used as a fat container for oil. The skin can also be used for a rope for tying parts of the sled together to make it strong and flexible.*
6. *The skin, when it is aged and half decayed and the fur taken off from being in the water, it can be used to make kayaks and umiaks (boats).*
7. *The skin with the fur on it can be used as tents without the fattish membrane on it. Five big seals can be used as tents for the Eskimos, and this can be used by five people who can sleep in it.*
8. *When fur is not taken off, we use as pants, parkas, mitts and boots without the fattish membrane, so this also is very warm.*
9. *The baby seals are the very best but you should leave the fur on because it makes good pants and also very good parkas and also very good boats when it is sewn well and attractively.*
10. *The parkas, when it is made by the baby seal's fur, is very good and attractive to look at. When the fur is close to the skin, on the pants, it is very warm.*

Written by Idlout, an Eskimo living at Resolute Bay, to R. G. H. Williamson, whose translation is a faithful rendering of the writer's style of expression. Mr. Williamson received the letter as Head of the Linguistic Services, Welfare Division, Department of Northern Affairs and Natural Resources. He is now supervising the Rehabilitation Centre at Rankin Inlet, N.W.T.

ᐅᐱᕐᖕᑲᖅ SPRING

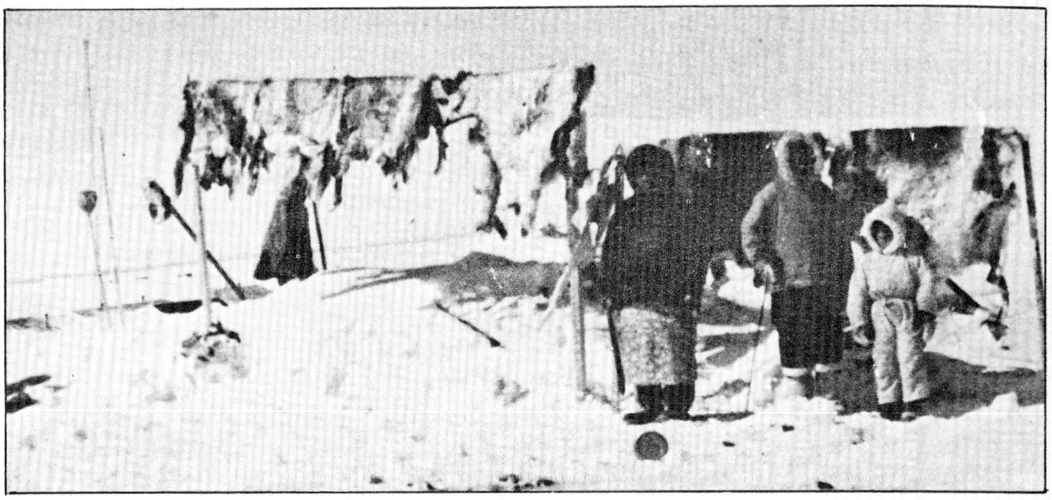

ᓕᐊ ᐃᐤᓚᐅᕝ ᑕᕐᔭᓐᑯᕐ

By LEAH D'ARGENCOURT

ᐅᑭᐅᑦᑐᕐ ᑲᐅᔪᓗᐅᕐᑎᕐᓗᒍ ᐊᒃᓱᕈᓴᖅᓇᓚᐅᕐᓗᓂ, ᐅᐱᕐᖅᒪᖅᕐᓂᒃ ᐅᑭᐅᕐᑕᕐᑐᒥ ᑲᕐᔪᕐᓇᕐᓯᕕᖅᓴᐊᓱᖅᑐᕙᓚᐅᕐᓯᒪᕗᖅ ᐅᑭᐅᓗᒃᑕᐸ ᐊᓯᖅᒥᕐᓂᕐ ᐃᓚᒥᓕᒪᓂᕐ, ᐊᓯᖅᒥᕐᓄᕐᓗ ᐃᓚᒥᔪᐅᓴᓄᕐ ᑕᒪᑐᒥᖅᒪ ᐃᓄᕐᑲᖅᖅᒥᕐᑐᕐᒥ ᐅᓄᕐ ᑲᕐᔪᕐᓇᕐᓯᕕᒃᓴᐊᕐᐸᓚᐅᕐᓯᒪᕗᖅ. ᑕᐃᒪᐃᓕᕐᖁᐃᖅᒪᕐ ᐃᓚᔫᕐ ᓄᓇᕐᑲᑎᒍᕐᓗ ᐆᕐᓚᓇᐊᕐ ᑲᓕᕐᐸᓚᐅᕐᓯᒪᒪᕐᑕ ᐅᐱᕐᖅᒥᕕᕐᑎᕐᓄᕐ ᐋᑐᓇᓱᖅᕕᒃᓴᕐᑎᐋᕆᐅᓴᕐᓇᕐᑐᒍᕐ.

ᕐᑲᐅᒃᐸᓕᕐᓗᓂ ᐃᓚᒥᓕᒪᑎᒍᕐᓄᕐ ᐸᖅᓇᔭᒪᓱᓕᕐᓗᓂ ᕐᑭᒍᒃᓯᕐᓂᒥᕐᓗᓂ, ᐃᕐᓇᕐᑎᕐᓇᕐᐸᓕᓚᐅᕐᓯᒪᔭᕝ ᐃᓱᒪᕈᓗᔪᓕᕐᓗᓂ ᓯᕐᓇᒃ ᑐᒪᓕᕐᓗᓂᓗ. ᓇᔭᒪᓇᕐᓇᓕᑲᐃᕐᓇᓂ ᐊᓴᐊᒃᓴᕝ ᐅᐱᕐᖅᒪᓕᒪᒍᕐ ᐆᔪᕐᓗᒍ. ᑕᕙᕙ ᑲᕐᔪᕐᓇᕈᓯᓇᓚᐅᕐᑕᖅᒪ, ᐱᓱᔭᕐ ᑲᕐᑕᓚᓕᓇᐊᒃᓴᕝ ᓇᒧᑐᐃᕐᓇᕐᓯᐊᕝ, ᐅᕐᑯᒃᓴᕐᓯᒪᐃᕐᓇᓗᒍᕐᓂᕐᓗᓂ, ᐱᑭᐅᓯᐅᓇᐊᕐᑲᕐᑕᕐᓗᓂ, ᐆᓚᓴᕐᑲᕐᑕᕐᓗᓂᓗ ᑲᓇᔨᕈᖅᓂᒃ ᐅᒪᑯᓗᖅᓂᒃᓗ, ᑭᓱᑐᐃᕐᓇᕈᓗᔭᕐᓂᒃᓗᓂᕐ ᓄᓇᒥᐅᑕᕐᓂᒃ ᐃᒪᕐᒥᐅᑕᕐᓂᒃᓗ ᓇᒻᐸᕈᓗᔭᓕᕐᑲᕐᑕᕐᓂᐊᕐᓗᓂ.

ᐃᓚᒥᓕᒪᕐ ᐅᕐᓚᕈᕐᓂᐊᓕᕐᓗᑎᒃ ᐅᔪᕐᑐᕐᓗᑕᓗ ᓇᕐᑎᕐᒥᒃ ᐅᕐᓚᕈᒥᑕᓇᓗᒍ. ᑕᐃᒪ ᐸᕐᓇᔪᒥᐊᓱᕗᒍᕐ ᐳᖅᑲᐃᓕᒪᓇᒃᓗᑕᓗ ᐃᒃᐱᐊᕐᔫᖅᓄᕐ ᐊᓇᓇᒍᕐ ᓴᓇᔭᕕᓂᕐᓂᒃ ᑐᐱᒃᓴᒍᕐ. ᑕᐅᑐᔭᕐᔫᒃᓗᒍ ᐳᖅᑲᐃᔫᖅ ᕐᑯᕕᐊᓇᕐᐸᓚᐅᕐᓯᒪᔫᖅ, ᐊᕐᓄᖁᑐᐊᑯᓗᖅᓂᒃ ᐳᖅᑲᕐᑕᐅᑎᕐᓗᒥᕐ, ᑐᒃᑐᖁᔭᐃᕐ ᕐᑭᒪᓚᑲᐅᕐᓗᑎᒃ ᐅᑭᐅᕐᓯᐅᑎᐅᔫᕐ ᑕᑯᓂᐊᑭᕐᓂᕐᓗᒥᕐ ᑕᐃᒪ ᐅᑭᐊᒃᓴᐅᓚᕐᑐᒥ ᐅᑭᐅᖅᑯᓚᕐᑐᒥᓗᕐᓂᕐ ᑭᓯᐊᓂ ᐊᓇᓇ ᐸᕐᓇᔫᕐᒥᒃᐸᕐ ᐅᑭᐅᒍᕐ ᑕᑯᑕᐃᕐᓇᑭᒪᓕᓇᕐᓗᒥᕐ.

ᐊᑕᑕᒪ ᓯᕗᔫᒃ ᑯᕕᖅᒥᒃ ᐳᖅᐃᑎᕐᓗᑕ ᓴᕕᒃ ᑯᕕᖅᒥᓂᒃ ᐸᕐᓇᔫᔭᕐᔫᒃᓗᓂ ᐆᕐᓚᕐᑲᕐᑕᕐᑐᕐᓯᐅᑎᒥᓂᒃ ᐋᓇᒪᓗᕐᓂᕐ ᐅᖅᑎᒪᓗᕐᓂᕐ ᑕᕐᑯᐊᒃᓴᔪᕐ ᐱᔭᓇᔭᕐᓂᐊᕐᓗᑎᒃᑯ

After the long struggling winter, spring in the Arctic was the most exciting of all the seasons for the whole family, and for all those who were around to enjoy the nature of things. It was the time when our family and neighbours would move to our spring camp where the best hunting was to be found.

The day before the whole family was to set out by dog team, I would go to bed and dream all kinds of dreams. I would plan where our new home was going to be for the spring and the summer. I would recall how much fun it was going to be, wandering around anywhere I wanted to go without heavy winter clothing, looking for birds' nests, fishing for ugly-looking sculpins and codfish, or looking for whatever I could find on the land or at sea.

The family would get up early in the morning and have seal meat cooked for breakfast. Then we would start packing with bags made by my mother out of canvas material. Watching her was fun, seeing her pack

ᓱᕙᔪᕐᓗ, ᑎᓕᐅᑭᑦᓗ, ᐃᕐᖕᔪᓯᑦᓗ ᐃᓚᒥᖕᖏᑦ ᐊᑐᓂᑦ ᓇᒪᒃᑎᕐᓯᒪᑦᓗᑎᒃ ᐊᑐᓂᕐᖕ, ᓱᒃᑲᕐᒥᒃᓗ, ᐸᓚᐅᒐᕐᒥᒃᓗ ᑎᒥᒃᓗ, ᐸᑕᒥᒃᓗ, ᓴᑕᕐᑲᑐᐊᕐᐸᑦᓗ ᓴᒥ ᐅᓗᒥᒃᓗ.

ᑕᐃᒪᓕ ᐊᑕᑕ ᐊᑦᖁᕐᕐᑐᓕᕐᑐᖅ ᕐᑭᒍᒃᓯᔪᑐᕐᓯᐅᑎᒥᓂᒃ ᕐᑯᐱᐊᓇᓗᐊᒃ ᑲᑦᓂᕐᒥᔪᖅ, ᑕᐃᐸ ᐊᓯᐃᓚᒃ ᐊᐅᑦᓚᕐᓂᐊᕐᑐᐁᑦᖁᓕᓐᐊᒃᓴᖅ ᓇᓗᓇᑭᑦᓂᕐᓗᓂ ᐅᐱᕐᖕᒥᐱᑦᑎᑦᖁᑦ. ᐱᔭᓐᕐᒥ ᐊᓂᑦᓗᓂ ᐅᓯᓕᕐᑐᓐᐊᕐᑐᓕᕐᑐᖅ ᕐᑲᒍᑎᖕᓂᒃ ᐊᒃᔭᑲᑦᑕᕐᐱᒥᑦᓗᒍ ᐋᓇᒍᑦ ᕐᑲᐃᑕᐅᑭᓗᑐᐃᑦᓇᕐᑐᓂᒃ, ᑎᑭᖅᑲᖅᑯᓴᐅᑦᔪᐊᕐᐸᒃᓗᑕ ᖁᑲᒪᓇᒃᑲᓗ, ᐅᐱᖕᒍᐊᕐᐱᒃᐸᒃᑲᑦᑕ ᓴᖕᖕᒥᓂᕐᕐᑕᐅᓱᖕ ᒪᕐᖕᒪᑦᑕ ᑲᔪᒥᓐᐊᑦᓚᒃᐸᓚᐅᕐᑐᒍᑦ ᐱᒃᑲᐅᑦᓚᐱᓕᕐᑦᑕ ᐊᒃᓴᕐᑐᓐᐊᒃ ᑲᑦᓂᕐᐸᓚᐅᕐᑐᒍᑦ.

ᐋᒪᔪᒃᓕᕐᐸᐅᑦ ᖁᑲᖕᒪᖕᒪᓗᑦᓂᑦ ᐊᓂᒪ ᐊᑕᑕᑦᑎᑦᓂᒃ ᐃᑲᔪᕐᓂᐊᕐᓗᓂ, ᐅᓯᓕᕐᓱᕐᓗᑎᒃ ᓇᕐᑭᑕᓐᓗᑎᒃᓗ ᐊᓇᓐᓗᑎᒃᓗ ᕐᑭᒻᒥᓂᒃ ᕐᑲᓕᖕᒍᓕᕐᑲᑦᑕᐅᐃᐸᒃᓗᑎᒃ ᐸᓴᔪᑭᔪᓕᕐᐸᒃᓗᑎᒃᓗ ᐃᖕᒥᖕᖏᑦ. ᑕᒪᕐᒥᓕᒪᑦᑎᐊᖅ ᕐᑯᐱᐊᓯᑭᓗᓴᓕᕐᓗᑎᒃ ᐱᕐᑲᑦᓇᓐᐅᑎᑦᑎᐊᓕᕐᓗᑕᓗ ᐱᓇᓯᑭᓗᓴᕐᑲᑎᒥᓕᕐᓗᑕᓗ. ᐊᐱᕐᓱᓗᓴᐃᑦᓇᓕᕐᓗᑎᒃᓗ ᖁᑲᕐᓯᐊᓂᒃᑲ ᐊᑦᖁᕐᕐᑐᕐᓱᒃᓗᒥᑦ ᐸᕐᓇᒐᓗᐊᕐᓗᒥᑦ, ᐊᐱᕐᑯᑕᐅᒪᔪᒃᑐᖅ ᓇᔪᖕᖕᒪᕐᓂᐊᕐᑐᐊᓗᓕᓐᐊᒃᓴᑦᑎᑦᓂᒃ.

ᑭᖕᔪᑦᓕᕐᐸᐅᓕᕐᑐᒥᒃ, ᐋᓇᒪ ᕐᑲᐅᓯᓴᒃᑲᑦᓂᓐᑦᓗᓂ ᕐᑭᒪᐃᖕᖕᒥᒃᑲᓗᐋᓐᐊᒃᓴᑦᑎᑦᓂᒃ ᓇᒃᓴᑭᒪᔭᓕᒪᒥᓂᒃᓗ ᐱᒪᓗᐋᓐᐊᒃᓴᒥᓂᒃ ᐃᒪᓗᑦᑎᑦᓂᑦ. ᐊᓯᐃᓚᒃ ᑕᐃᐊ ᐊᑕᑕᒥᔭᖅ ᐊᐅᑦᓚᕐᓴᐃᓯᑦᓗᓂ ᕐᑭᒪᒥᓂᒃ. ᐊᓯᐃᓚᒃ, ᐃᖕᒥᕐᖁᓯᑲᑦᓚᒃᑐᐋᓗᒪᑦᑕ ᓯᒃᓴᑭᓗᒃᑯᑦ ᒪᓂᖁᐅᖕᖕᒥᑦ ᑐᐋᓗᓗᑦᓂ ᕐᑭᑭᑦ ᓂᐸᕐᑭᓴᑭᓗᓴᕐᓗᑎᒃ ᐅᐊᒃ ᐊᐅᑦᓚᕐᓯᕐᑐᐋᓗᐃᑦ ᖁᓯᒃᓯᑲᑦᓚᒃᓗᑎᒃ ᓇᖕᒥᐊᕐᓇᕐᐸᓚᐅᕐᓯᒪᔪᕐᑭᒪᒪᐅᑲᑦᓚᖕᓂᐊᕐᓯᓱᒥᑦᓗᓂᓗ ᐊᐅᑦᓚᕐᑲᑦᑕᓕᓂᐅᓇᓂ.

ᑕᐃᑦᓱᒪᓂᐅᑎᑦᓗᒍ, ᓱᕐᓗᓕ ᖁᓇᒍᑦ ᐊᔪᐋᓗᐋᖁᑦ ᐊᐅᑦᓚᕐᓂᐊᕐ ᑯᓱᓇᕐᐸᓚᐅᕐᓯᒪᖕᒪᑦ ᓯᓚᔪᐊᒍᑦ, ᓯᓚᕐᔪᐊᒥᒃ ᕐᑲᐅᓱᒪᓕᓂᐅᖕᖕᒥᓱᖕᒪᕐᓗᓂ.

ᕐᑭᒪᐃᓕᕐᓗᓂ, ᐅᑭᐅᖅ ᓇᔪᐃᑦᓇᕐᑕᐱᓂᕐᒥᒃ ᐃᓱᒪᑭᓗᓴᓕᕐᓇᕐᐸᓚᐅᕐᒥᔪᖅ. ᑕᐅᑐᓴᕐᔪᒃᓗᒍ ᕐᑭᒪᒃᐸᑦᓕᐳᓴ ᓱᒃᑲᐃᑦᑐᑯᓗᑦᓗᓂ ᑕᓕᐸᑦᓕᐋᔪᓴᕐᔪᓕᕐᑐᖅ ᐃᖕᒥᕐᖁᐅᓴᕐᔪᒃᓗᓂ ᑕᐃᐊ ᑐᐱᖅ ᓇᔪᒪᒃᓴᑐᐊᖅ ᓇᒃᓴᕐᑕᑐᐋᑦᓗᒍ ᐃᓂᒃᓴᑐᐋᓂᐊᕐᑕᐅᑦ ᐅᐱᕐᖕᒪᓕᒪᖅ ᐊᐅᓴᕐᓗ. ᐊᐱᕐᓱᑭᑦᓇᕐᑕᓗ ᐋᒪᔪᖅᑲᑦᑎᑦᖁᑦ ᕐᑲᖁᐃᑦᓂᐊ

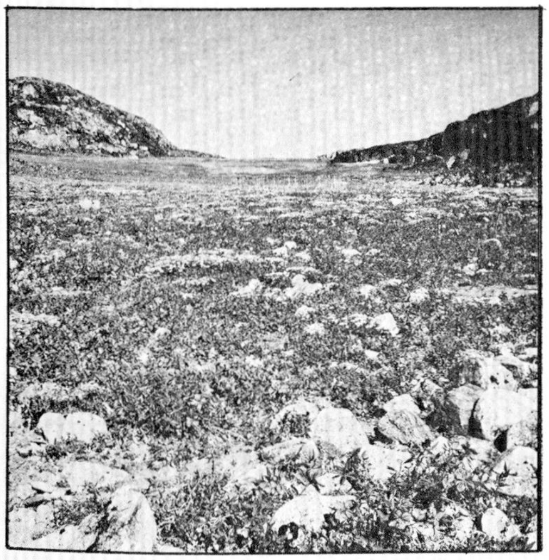

only a few articles of clothing, leaving the caribou winter clothing behind that we were not going to see until the next fall or winter, when she would start preparing for the winter once again.

My father would prepare the grub box with his own hunting belongings and I or my mother would finish the packing with another wooden box. Into it would go the primus stove, kettle, mugs enough for each of us, sugar, bannock, tea, butter, jam if we were lucky enough to have it, and the ulu.

Then, to see my father dressing up in his hunting clothing was fun too, to know he was really taking us on a trip to the spring camp. Soon he would go out to start loading the dog-sled and I would bring him whatever my mother asked me to carry, racing with my younger brothers, while we told each other how strong we were. And our rivalry would keep us even busier.

The older children would help father as usual, loading and harnessing the dogs that were yelping and frisking with each other. Everyone would become friendlier than ever, and full of laughter as we shared each others' work. And so many questions would be asked by the younger brothers as we helped them dress up for the trip, most of all of course about where we were going.

Right at the last minute, my mother would check once again to see that she had packed everything she wanted, or she thought we needed from the house. Finally, father would start mushing and calling the dogs. Then, the sudden taking off on the rough beach, with the yelping and anxious dogs pulling us off. It was always a little scary at first, when we were not yet used to travelling much.

In those days, it was always like going to a new world, when we didn't know too much about what the world was like.

Leaving the old, long winter of hiberation made one imagine all kinds of things. Watching it slowly

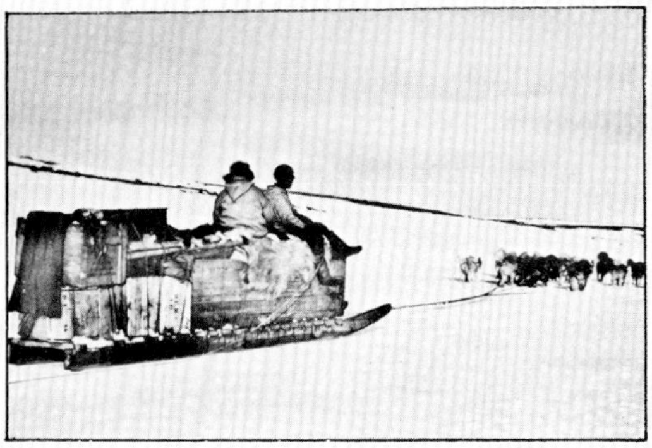

ᖅᖅᒥᒃ ᑲᓗᐊᓴᐊᒃᓴᑦᑎᑦᓂᒃ, ᕐᑲᐅᔨᒪᑦᑎᐊᕐᐸᓚᐅᕐᒥᒃᓚ ᐱᖅᒥᒃᓇᕐᑭᖅᖅᒥᑦᓇᑦᑕ. ᐊᔪᖅᒥᑦᓄᑦᓗ ᓴᑦᑐᑦᓇᕐᐸᓚ ᐅᒃᖅᒥᑦᓇᑦᑕ ᑕᕙᕙᑐᐊᓴᓚᑦᑎᒍᑦ.

ᑎᑭᑕᐃᑦᓇᕐᓗᑕ ᐅᐱᕐᖅᒥᕕᑦᑎᑦᓄᑦ, ᑕᕙᕗᖅᓚᑦᓴᐃ ᑦᓇᖅ ᐅᐸᒃᐸᒃᑕᑦᑎᑦᓄᑦ ᐅᐱᕐᖅᓚᕐᖅᓚᑦ ᐊᕐᕋᑐᑕᒪᑦ ᐋᒃ ᐅᑭᕕᑦᑎᑦᓂᑦ ᐊᑦᔨᐅᕙᓚᐅᖅᖅᒥᒪᒥᒃᒪᑦ ᕐᑭᒪᕐ ᑕᕐ ᑕᑦᑎᑦᓂᑦ ᐱᖅᖅᒍᐊᕐᕕᒥᕐ ᑲᑦᑕᕐ ᑕᐃᑦᓄᒥᓕᕐ ᑕᑦᑎᑦᓄ ᐅᓂᕐᐁᑦᓗᑦᓂᑦ ᐃᓕᑕᕐᓇᕐᓗᑎᒃ, ᔨᒐᔭᕐᓗ ᕐᑲᕐᑲᐃᑦᓗ ᐱᖅᒍᐃᑦᓗᑦᓂᑦ ᐱᔪᔪᒐᕕᒥᕐ ᑲᑦᑕᕐᓂᐊᕐᑕᕗᑦ. ᑕᕙᕙ ᑕᒪᕐᒥᓕᒪᖅ ᕐᑯᕕᐊᓇᕐ ᑐᐃᑦᓇᐅᑎᐊᓕᕐᓗᑎᒃ ᐃᒥᕐᑕᕐᓂ ᕐᓗᓂᑦ ᑲᑭᐊᒃ ᑐᐊᑦᓄᖅᒥᒃ ᓂᓚᒃ ᑕᖅᖅᒥᖅᓚᕐ ᑲᑦᑕᓕᕐᓗᑕ ᐃᓚᓕᒪᑦᑎᑦᓄᑦ ᐃᓗᑦᓇᓕᒪᖅᒥᑦ ᓄᑕᐅᔪᐃᑦᓇᐅᓕᓴᑦᓗᑎ ᐊᕐᕋᓂᑐᐃᑦᓇᐅᓚᓗᐊᓂᑦ.

ᑕᐃᒪ ᐊᓇᓇ ᐊᑕᑕᓗ ᑐᐱᕐᕕᒃᓴᕐᔨᐅᓕᕐᓗᑎᒃ, ᓇᕐᑭ ᑕᖅᒥᐊᕐᑎᓕᕐᓗᑕᓗ ᐅᑦᓚᖅ ᐅᔨᓕᕐᔪᕐ ᑕᐅᕋᑕᕐᑐᕕᓂᕐᓂᒃ ᑐᐱᖅ ᓇᕚᕐ ᑕᐅᖅᒪᑦ, ᐊᓇᓇᒥᔭᖅ ᐅᔪᓕᐅᕐᓂᐊᓕᕐᓗᓂ ᐊᖅᑯᑎᑦᑎᓂ ᓇᑦᑎᕐ ᑕᐅᕋᑕᕐᑐᕕᓂᐊᑦᓄᖅᒥᒃ. ᐊᓂᒥᔭᐃ ᐱᖅᖅᒍᐊᖅ ᒍᔭᕐᔪᓕᓐᕐᓗᑎᒃ ᔨᓚᒥ ᑐᐱᕐᒥᑦ ᑐᓴᕐᓴᐅᑦᓗ ᑎᒃ ᐅᕐᑲᑦᓚᕐᑲᑎᒥᖅᒍᔭᕐᔪᒃᑐᑦ ᐃᒡᓚᕋᓚᒃᑐᑦᓗᓂᑦ. ᔨᕐᑭᑦᓂᐅᔭᕐᔪᒃᓗᓂᓗ, ᔨᓚᑦᑎᐊᕐᕙᐅᓂᖅᓚᓂ ᐆᑦᓚᕐᕕᕐ ᑲᕋᑦᑕ ᐊᓇᓇᓚᓗ ᐱᔭᐅᓗᐊᕐᑯᕐᓗᓂ ᐱᓕᕆᐊᒃᓴᓕᓚᑦᓗᓕ ᒥᖅᒪᑦ ᐃᓚᒥᐊᑐᓚᑦᑕ.

ᓄᑕᒥᒃ ᐊᑐᓕᕐᒥᔭᕗᑦ ᒪᓂᕋᕐᓗ ᐆᒃ ᑐᐊᑦᓄᓕᕐᓗᓂ ᐊᐅᑎᕐ ᑲᑦᑎᐊᕈ ᑦᓂᕐᐸᑦᓕᐊᖅ ᒍᔭᕐᔪᓕᕐᓗᓂ. ᐃᓚᒥᓕᒪ ᑯᓗᒃᑎᒍᑦ ᕐᑯᓚᖅᒥᕐᔨᕐ ᑲᑦᑕᕐᓂᐊᓕᕐᓗᑕ ᐊᑕᐅᑦᑎᒃᑯ ᐅᖅᒥᐅᕐᐸᕐᓗᑦᓂᕐ ᐃᕐᑐᕐᐸᕐᓗ ᐃᓚᐅᑎᕐᓗᒥᕐ, ᐊᓂᕐ ᓗᐊᑦᑯᒃᑲᓗ, ᓄᓇᖅᑲᑎᐸᑦᓗ. ᑕᐃᒪ ᓄᑕᕐ ᑐᒪᓂᐊᕐ ᑐ ᐊᑦᓄᓕᕐᓗᑕ ᓂᕐᑭᓂᒃ, ᓄᑕᓂᒃᓗ ᓇᑦᑎᕐᕕᓂᕐᓂᒃ ᑲᒥ ᒃᑕᕐᑐᕐᓗᑕ ᑲᒥᒃᑕᕐᑐᕐᑐᐃᑦᓇᐅᓗᑕ.

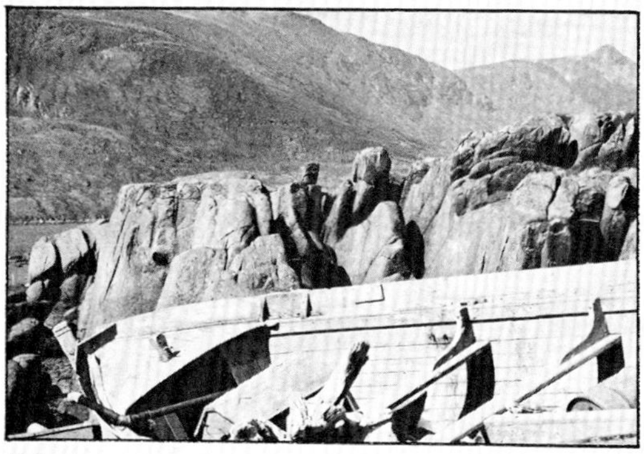

50

disappear from sight as we moved along, and all we were taking with us as a shelter for the whole spring and summer was a portable canvas tent. Moving to a place that was out in almost nowhere, until we became used to our whole new environment once again. And we couldn't even ask our own parents if everything was going to be all right, because they knew what they were doing and they were everything to us. There was no one else to turn to but them.

Then, finally we would arrive at the new spring camp, and it was the same place we came every year in spring time. It was completely different from the camp we had left behind, and it was the most exciting experience to see the old playgrounds, stones, the same beach and hills where we would take long hikes. Then everything began to be so much fun again; even fetching pure water instead of ice for the whole family was something new again from the year just past.

Soon mother and father would start examining the ground for a good place to erect the tent, then start unloading the same belongings that we had loaded that same morning. When the tent was up, mother would prepare a hot meal with the seal freshly caught on the trail. The younger brothers would already be playing outdoors and you could hear them clearly from inside the tent with their happy sounds, talking and laughing with each other. And the sun would be happily shining, as a clear day was always chosen by my father for travelling with the whole family. Probably especially for my mother who had so much work ahead of her to do during the spring for her big family.

With the new life, everything on the ground would begin to appear, as the snow melted gradually away. Then the whole family would go out hunting for seal altogether, even the grandparents, cousins, and the neighbours. That meant we would have more fresh meat to eat regularily, and new seal skin boots for everyone.

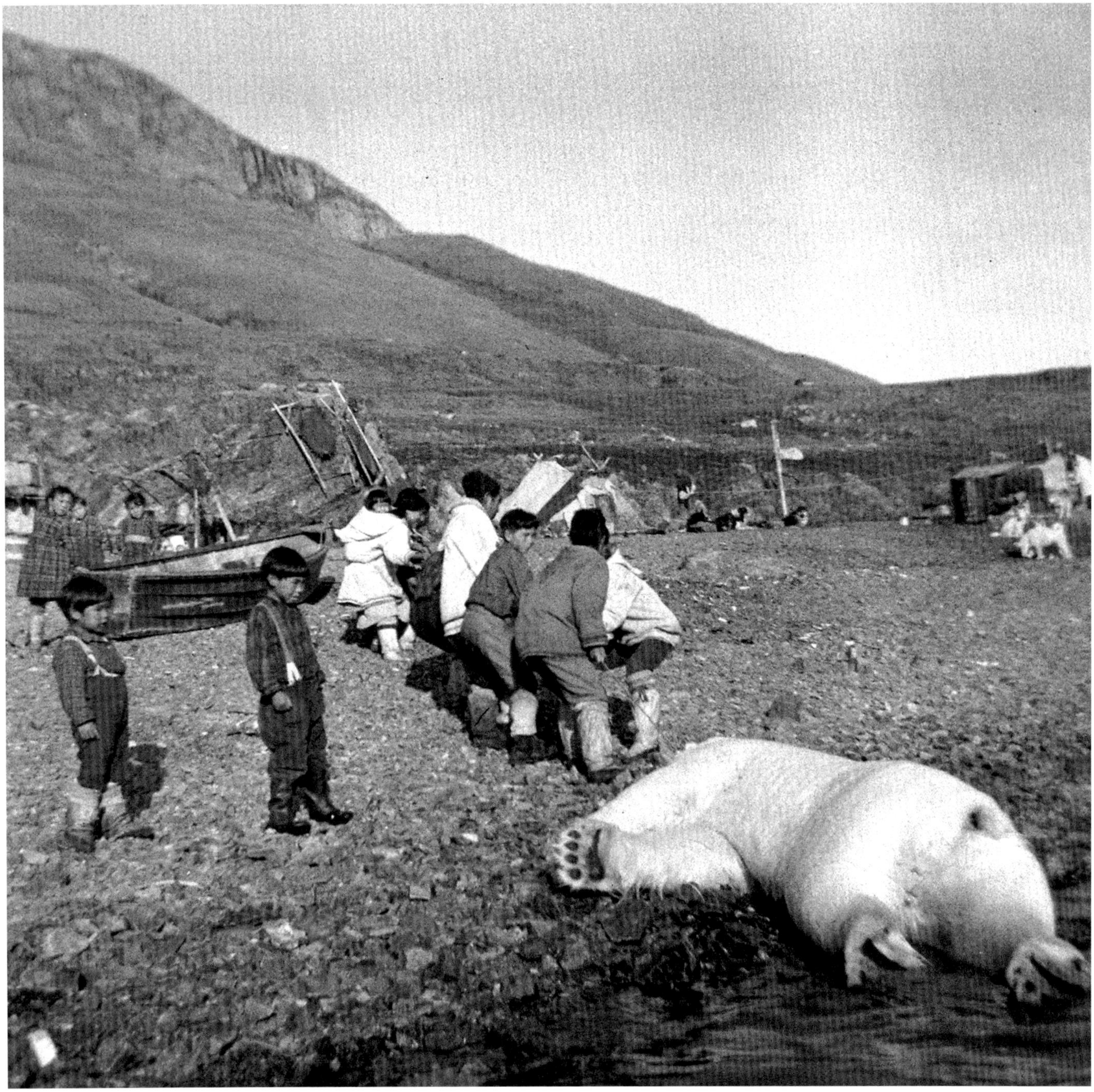

3.1 | Hunters drag a bear carcass up the beach at Idlout's camp, Aulattivik, Eclipse Sound, North Baffin Island, August 1952. Winter sod and wood houses stand in the background. Pictured are Noah, Pauloosee, Kidlak with Ruth, Paul Ullatitaq, Ludy Pudluk, and Lazarus Paneeluk. Uncredited photo likely by Joseph Idlout.

3

The Hunter

Joseph Idlout's Photographs at *Ilagiit Nunagivaktangat* (Camp) and Inuit Qaujimajatuqangit (IQ) (1951–54)

Augatnaaq Eccles and Carol Payne

In Joseph Idlout's and Leah Idlout d'Argencourt Paulson's words, in the two texts preceding this chapter, the family's experiences at *ilagiit nunagivaktangat* (camp) come alive. Idlout's daughter Leah, in a spring 1976 article for *Inuit Today*, recalls the family's annual move from their winter camp in Aulattivik to their spring camp in Nuvurulua, about 50 kilometres west of Pond Inlet/Mittimatalik.[1] With breathless excitement, she dreams of the new camp and recounts how the whole family worked together during the move:

> To see my father dressing up in his hunting clothing was fun too, to know he was really taking us on a trip to the spring camp. Soon he would go out to start loading the dog-sled and I would bring him whatever my mother asked me to carry, racing with my younger brothers, while we told each other how strong we were. And our rivalry would keep us even busier.
>
> The older children would help father as usual, loading and harnessing the dogs that were yelping and frisking with each other. Everyone would become friendlier than ever, and full of laughter as we shared each other's work. And so many questions would be asked by the younger brothers as we helped them dress up for the trip, most of all of course about where we were going.[2]

In a letter published in 1961, Joseph Idlout also illuminates camp life by telling a story about ten uses for the seal. The letter was written to government official R.G.H. Williamson, who translated it from Inuktitut syllabics. In the letter, Idlout lists how seals provide food, oil, shelter, and clothing, among other necessities. He states, "I understand now that the seal is the most useful thing that Inuit use in our land."[3] Together, Idlout's and Leah's texts demonstrate how camp life was built on families and communities working together with one another and in harmony with nature. In short, these two essays reflect some of the values and key principles of Inuit Qaujimajatuqangit (IQ).[4]

IQ encompasses Inuit knowledge. According to Shirley Tagalik, the term "translates directly as 'that which Inuit have always known to be true' … Inuit Qaujimajatuqangit is recognized to be a unified system of beliefs and knowledge characteristic of the Inuit culture."[5] This knowledge was built and shaped by the Arctic environment and by lived experiences passed on through generations. The harsh environment makes it necessary to live in harmony. Senseless fighting, exploiting nature and animals, and being selfish would make life more difficult than it already is. Inuit believe that things come back to you full circle. That is why they are taught to be welcoming, to help others, to take only what you need, to deal with conflict respectfully, and so on. In these ways, IQ values serve a very practical purpose.

The Government of Nunavut draws on IQ as a worldview comprised of a set of eight guiding principles:

- *Inuuqatigiitsiarniq*: Respecting others, relationships, and caring for people.
- *Tunnganarniq*: Fostering good spirits by being open, welcoming, and inclusive.
- *Pijitsirniq*: Serving and providing for family and/or community.
- *Aajiiqatigiinniq*: Decision making through discussion and consensus.
- *Pilimmaksarniq/Pijariuqsarniq*: Development of skills through observation, mentoring, practice, and effort.
- *Piliriqatigiinniq/Ikajuqtigiinniq*: Working together for a common cause.
- *Qanuqtuurniq*: Being innovative and resourceful.
- *Avatittinnik Kamatsiarniq*: Respect and care for the land, animals, and the environment.[6]

Inuit Qaujimajatuqangit could be seen as guidelines on how to live a "good life" – that is, one in harmony with both the environment and the people around you. Inuit believe that although hard times are unavoidable, practising these beliefs ensures that you do not add to hardship. Instead, you create a foundation for a community that can persevere in spite of hardship, and when good times come, which they eventually do, they are shared and contributed to by all.

The values represented by IQ principles infused all aspects of life at Idlout's camp. Respect for the environment and animals, resourcefulness, developing skills through observation, welcoming and caring relationships, and working together toward common goals were values that guided everyone and all aspects of life at camp. By being resourceful, you also contribute to the success of the community and enhance your ability to contribute. This is done not just for individual benefit. These values are evident in Joseph Idlout's and Leah Idlout d'Argencourt Paulson's words in the essays reproduced here. And, as we argue in this co-authored chapter, IQ also infused Idlout's own practice as a photographer. That is seen, for example, in the photograph that opens this chapter of camp members working in unison to haul a polar bear to shore, an image that Leah also reproduced in her 1975 article "First Inuit Picture on Canadian Money," reproduced following chapter 6 (see figure 3.1).[7]

This chapter looks closely at the earliest photographs credited to Joseph Idlout. These images date from 1951 to 1954 and depict life at Idlout's camps in the Qikiqtani region in Aulattivik and in Nuvurulua.[8] They provide distinctly Inuit views of life on the land that differ significantly from the perspective of Doug Wilkinson's film *Land of the Long Day* (1952). We argue that viewing the Idlout photographs through IQ allows us to understand relationships between Inuit and with the *nuna* (land). We adapt this approach from the work of Inuk art historian Heather Igloliorte. In her essay "Curating Inuit Qaujimajatuqangit: Inuit Knowledge in the Qallunaat Art Museum" (2017), Igloliorte outlines how IQ can be used to deepen our understanding of Inuit art.[9] Here, this approach provides us with a culturally specific lens to look at Idlout's photographs and to understand his community more deeply.

IQ values – particularly, the principle of *aajiiqatigiinniq* (decision making through discussion and consensus) – also inform this chapter, co-written by Augatnaaq Eccles, an Inuk historian, curator, artist, and educator born and raised in Rankin Inlet/Kangiqtiniq, and Carol Payne, a photo studies scholar and lead on this larger research project. Together, we collaborated on the online exhibition of Idlout's photographs from the Nunavut Archives entitled *Ajjiliurlagit ("Let me take your picture"): The Photographs of Joseph Idlout,*[10] which is the basis of our thinking for this chapter. What follows is drawn from collaborative research and discussions that we had over a period of about eighteen months while preparing the exhibition as well as further discussions and writing over two periods of a few weeks when adapting material from the exhibition for this chapter. To clarify our process of working, this brief introduction is followed by a co-written section on our methodology in developing the exhibition. Subsequently, Carol provides a discussion of Idlout's introduction to photography through his relationship with Doug Wilkinson. The core of the chapter follows with an analysis of Idlout's photography from this period viewed through the lens of IQ. Augatnaaq is the lead author for the IQ analysis, with contributions from Carol. The chapter has been developed in conversation but also with each of our voices coming in and out of focus.

Aajiiqatigiinniq: An Approach to Idlout's Photographs

Our shared understanding of Idlout's photography grew out of our collaboration on the online exhibition *Ajjiliurlagit*. As noted, the foundation for this chapter is provided by that exhibition, with its emphasis on IQ as a lens through which to illuminate Idlout's photographs and through them to deepen an understanding of *ilagiit nunagivaktangat*. Here, we look specifically at his photographs of camp life from 1951 to 1954. In what follows, we outline our working method, which – as we later recognized and discuss below – approximates the IQ principle of *aajiiqatigiinniq*.

In early discussions, working with Alexandra Anaviapik and Christina Williamson, Idlout family members expressed an interest in making photographs credited to Joseph Idlout widely accessible.[11] With the Covid-19 pandemic slowing in-person research yet also illustrating daily that online platforms could be effective in reaching audiences, a digital exhibition seemed to be ideal for access by Inuit in the Qikiqtani region as well as throughout Inuit Nunangat. Making text available in both Inuktitut syllabics and English would help to reach more Inuit while aiding language retention. Throughout, Idlout family members and the Nunavut Archives – then led by archivist Ed Atkinson – supported the initiative. Carol's previous work with online platforms also showed their positive possibilities.

In early 2022, Augatnaaq Eccles began working on the project. Augatnaaq has taught Inuit history and an Inuktitut language course at the Inuit college Nunavut Sivuniksavut, curated the award-winning exhibition *Seasons of the Sun* (2023) at the Carleton University Art Gallery, and is the creator of the *Tuberculosis Parka* (2020) art piece, which explores the history and experiences of Inuit and tuberculosis hospitals. She is a master's of education student at the University of Ottawa.

Our working method aims to follow the very IQ principles through which we viewed Idlout's photographs themselves. The online exhibition's development was grounded in shared conversations, collaborative work, and consensus decision making. In this way, our work together – although based on one body of work in an online exhibition – harmonizes with Heather Campbell and Reilly Bishop-Stall's broader proposal for an "Inuit approach to archival work" that overhauls the colonial archive by following IQ principles.[12]

In particular, *aajiiqatigiinniq* became our approach to the exhibition. This principle underscored life at camp, yet it seemed too abstract to present as a visualized component of the exhibition. A reader of this text pointed out that *aajiiqatigiinniq* aptly describes the transgenerational discussions and various consultations through which we developed the exhibition itself.[13] In this way, our work together reflects a growing movement toward challenging some conventional southern models of academic mentorship in arts and humanities disciplines. Carol hired Augatnaaq with funding from the Social Sciences and Humanities Research Council of Canada, but we developed a dialogic model of working. Decisions were made through discussion, and tasks were divided. Arguably, curatorial work lends itself to this approach: exhibitions propose a more open-ended experience for a visitor than academic writing usually does for a reader, and by design, organizing an exhibition requires a team with complementary skills and negotiation. Augatnaaq's and Carol's previous experiences provided models both for curatorial work and for collaboration. As noted, Augatnaaq had recently curated the exhibition *Seasons of the Sun* at the Carleton

University Art Gallery as part of the Inuit Futures initiative and had collaborated with medical historian Lori Jones. And Carol's earlier work as a curator and in previous academic collaborations illuminated the importance of working together.

Our first task was to find a way of presenting Idlout's photographs within a digital exhibition. With a full collection of some 300 individual photographs, we agreed that selections would have to be made. Which images had been most meaningful to Idlout's family during interviews? Which provided information about Inuit life at the time? How would they be organized? To make these choices, we spent a lot of time looking closely, ironically with the aid of a very analogue approach. We printed the digital files out onto sheets of 8½ × 11 inches so that they were large enough to see in detail, and we reserved access to a table 12 feet long where the images could be viewed together. Over a couple of sessions, we arranged and rearranged the images in different configurations. Looking also involved talking about what we saw in individual images and what we saw in different groupings. We noted that identifying the sitters and providing a sense of camp life was important to the community and to Idlout's family. Carol suggested organizing images by subject matter important to the community: hunting, housing, family, landscapes, and visitors. We rearranged photographs around these visible themes. Augatnaaq added that she identified suggestions of two IQ principles in several of the photographs: *pijitsirniq* (serving and providing for family and/or community) and *pilimmaksarniq/pijariuqsarniq* (development of skills through observation, mentoring, practice, and effort). As Augatnaaq explained, *pijitsirniq* underscores images from the hunt and of food and clothing preparation, which in turn are closely related to the hunt; and *pilimmaksarniq/pijariuqsarniq* offers a way of understanding the many images of children observing and helping Elders with tasks. Again, we reorganized images to include these two new groupings and then looked over the whole.

Collaboration invites participants to see the world in new ways as they learn to look with heightened awareness of their research partner's perceptions and experiences. For Carol, Augatnaaq's suggestion – to organize some of the work around two IQ principles – completely changed the way she saw the print-outs on the table. Images that on the surface seemed to picture very distinct activities now rhymed. With the two new groupings in front of us, we paused to talk about how they had changed the meanings of the photographs. *Pijitsirniq* and *pilimmaksarniq/pijariuqsarniq* did not so much describe overt or visible subject matter as emphasize underlying relationships – between people and with the *nuna*. These two groupings invited a new level of cultural understanding of the photographs, hinted at but not fully defined by the visual.

With Augatnaaq's intervention, the exhibition moved in a new direction. We wondered what would happen if we jettisoned the descriptive categories and instead organized the whole exhibition around IQ.[14] That would still enable us to include photographs that were most meaningful to the Idlout family but arranged differently. At this point, we turned to information available on IQ.[15] Carol introduced Augatnaaq to Heather Igloliorte's article "Curating Inuit Qaujimajatuqangit: Inuit Knowledge in the Qallunaat Art Museum" as a model. In the article, Igloliorte proposes that IQ can deepen an understanding of Inuit art, and she demonstrates this idea through her own exhibition *Illippunga: I Have Learned*, a 2016 reinstallation of the permanent collection of Inuit art amassed by Raymond Brousseau at the Musée national des beaux-arts du Québec.[16] As Igloliorte writes, "The implementation of IQ by the Government of Nunavut and other organizations makes a statement that, despite its ancient roots, Inuit Qaujimajatuqangit is not without relevance or application in modern Inuit life; it is a living knowledge. At the center of this philosophy is respect for relationships: the relationship with the land; the relationship with Arctic flora and fauna; and, especially, the relationship between family members and community members as to their responsibilities to each other, as well as their responsibility to pass on knowledge between generations."[17] Igloliorte's article and the application of IQ provided a culturally appropriate guide for presenting Joseph Idlout's photographs. As Augatnaaq notes in the online exhibition's text, "IQ shapes the Inuit worldview and it would have shaped the way Idlout, and other Inuit would have seen and interacted with the world around them. We chose to organize this exhibition according to this framework because we found that when we looked at Idlout's photographs, Inuit Qaujimajatuqangit principles could be identified within each image."[18]

With this model, we reorganized the exhibition entirely around IQ principles. By the time we worked on the online exhibition, the Government of Nunavut had expanded the IQ principles from six (as highlighted in Igloliorte's article) to eight. Augatnaaq wrote the curatorial essays introducing the exhibition and the different IQ principles. Carol edited as well as contributed biographical and archival material used in the exhibition. Consultations were important too. We interviewed Idlout's youngest daughter, Elder Susan Salluviniq, and spoke with other Idlout family members. Augatnaaq's aunt Nancy Karetak-Lindell and mother, Selma Eccles, also edited and reviewed the numerous texts that accompany each theme. Carleton graduate student Evangeline Mann edited some of the biographical texts. Robert Evans, interpretive planner with the Canadian Museum of Human Rights, also consulted with us about best practices for online exhibitions. Finally, Augatnaaq developed a guide for educators to bring *Ajjiliurlagit* to classrooms in Nunavut. This guide includes a brief overview of the exhibition and a lesson plan with questions and activities aimed at facilitating conversations and getting students to think critically about the exhibition and its themes.[19] This educational component was developed in part with a few students from Nunavut Sivuniksavut who participated in a pilot demonstration of the lesson plan. We contracted translator Rhoda Kayakjuak to translate all English texts into Inuktitut syllabics so that everything was available in both languages. The online exhibition itself was developed by Kelly Craver of Katittut, a division of Atiigo Media, an Inuit-owned design firm based in Iqaluit/Frobisher

Bay. Again, our work with Kelly followed a similar model of discussions, samples, and consultations.

One IQ principle proved challenging to visualize in the exhibition yet, ironically, defined our own collaboration. In our many discussions, we thought that *aajiiqatigiinniq* underscored life at camp yet was too difficult to illustrate visually in the exhibition. As noted, a reader of this text pointed out that *aajiiqatigiinniq* described the process of our own work together and other consultations, including our work on this chapter. As with the exhibition, this chapter emerged from discussions, drafts, edits, and more discussions to which both of us contributed, with each voice rising to the fore in certain sections.

Idlout behind the Camera: A Visual Dialogue with Doug Wilkinson

Joseph Idlout's photography – the subject of the online exhibition *Ajjiliurlagit* – is not well known, although Idlout himself was the subject of hundreds of photographs and moving images throughout his life. Oral history accounts attest to his prolific activity as a photographer.[20] Photographs from the 1950s made by southern visitors to the north and archival records also document Idlout with his camera.[21] As reproduced in this volume, some of Idlout's photographs were used to illustrate his daughter Leah's articles for *Inuit Today* magazine.[22] Yet the negatives and photographic prints themselves have remained largely unseen.[23] The online exhibition and this book are intended to bring these images to light. As we argue throughout this chapter, Idlout's photography reflects IQ values, but it is also entangled with the south, particularly through his relationship with Doug Wilkinson.

Idlout's practice as a photographer is intertwined in his relationship with Doug Wilkinson. As Madeleine d'Argencourt recounts in the foreword to this book, her grandfather Joseph Idlout asked Wilkinson to bring him a camera. In 1954, Wilkinson wrote the only published account of Idlout as a photographer (using an alternative spelling of his name) during the hunter's lifetime.[24] "Idlouk – Arctic Amateur" appeared in a 1954 issue of the popular hobbyist magazine *Photography* (see figure 3.2). It narrates Idlout's introduction to photography and, as a result, can be read as a complement to Wilkinson's publications of the mid-1950s about his own sojourns in the north.[25] Wilkinson's text is couched in primitivizing language typical of the time. Following familiar tropes of "allochronism,"[26] Wilkinson describes Idlout and the members of his camp as "primitives" and as "hunters and trappers living a way of life that has come down unchanged through the past ten thousand years."[27] The article includes thirteen photographs credited to Idlout and dated to the period 1951–52 and two by Wilkinson of Idlout posing with his camera. It also claims to reproduce a letter, dated 1 September 1952, written in Inuktitut syllabics, credited to Idlout, along with what is presented as its English translation (see figure 3.3). Wilkinson states that the letter was sent with the exposed film, with the translation partly recounting Idlout's experience photographing.

Next four pages

3.2 (*first spread*) | Doug Wilkinson, "Idlouk – Arctic Amateur," *Photography*, April 1954, 38–9.

3.3 (*second spread*) | Doug Wilkinson, "Idlouk – Arctic Amateur," *Photography*, April 1954, 40–1.

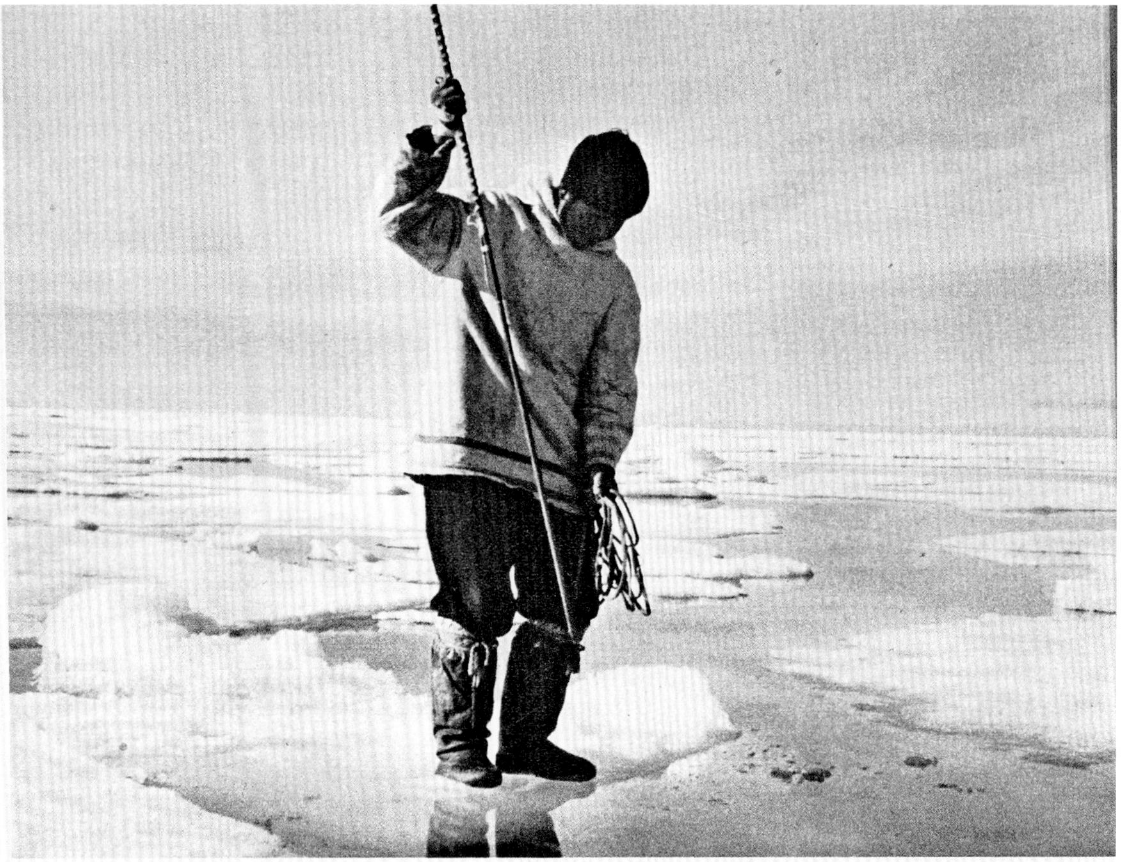

Photographer Idlouk, far within the Arctic Circle on northern Baffin Island, gets a picture of a kinsman spearing dinner for his family.

IDLOUK — arctic

This Eskimo snapshooter has to wait a whole year to see how his

"Adgeekoloogneeat takoogneeakpookah oomeeakjuak tikeeput," said Idlouk to his wife, Kidlik, "Alleeani!"
("We will see the pictures when the boat arrives," said Idlouk to his wife, Kidlik, "What pleasure!")

NOT many of us have to wait until a boat arrives before we can see our finished prints, particularly a boat that calls only once a year. But to Idlouk this is quite an ordinary occurrence. For Idlouk is an Eskimo. He lives with his wife and family on north Baffin Island in the Canadian Eastern Arctic. His people, the Tununermiut group, are the most northerly permanent inhabitants on the North American continent, hunters and trappers living a way of life that has come down unchanged through the past ten thousand years.

Idlouk and his people are primitives. Until 1930 when the Hudson's Bay Company, the Royal Canadian Mounted Police, and the Anglican Mission established a post in this area, their only contact with the outside world had been through the early explorers and whalers. Even now there are children at the outlying camps who have never seen a white man. And, although today they use high-powered rifles and gas-powered boats, their life is still the hunt. Their highest reward in life is still a full stomach.

Among his people Idlouk is a remarkable person, intelligent, enterprising, and resourceful. With money procured by trapping and then trading the skin of the white fox to the Hudson's Bay Company, he has managed to buy a great many things that the Eskimos of his area do not usually have: a forty-foot motor boat, eighteen-foot canoe and outboard motor, rifles of various calibres, telescope, barometer. His camp always has lots of food, both the meat that he

38

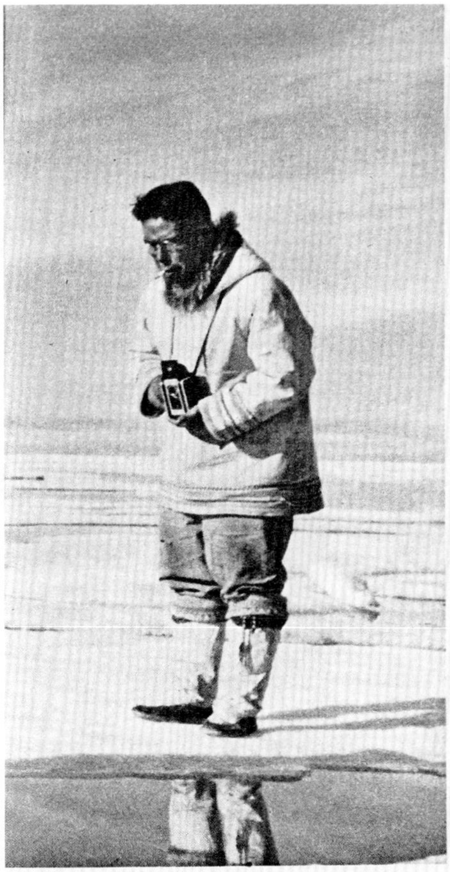

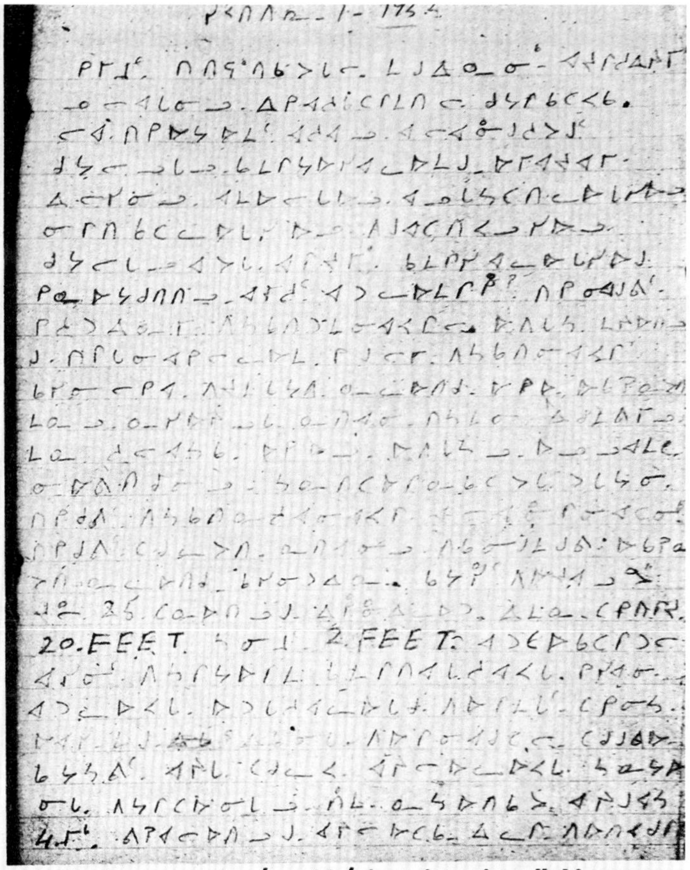

Idlouk's letter to the 'outside' is written in syllabic Eskimo alphabet. For a translation of it, and some of the pictures that came with it, turn page

amateur

By DOUG WILKINSON

pictures will turn out

gets by hunting, and the tea and biscuits that he buys from the trader. Each year he tries to add to the equipment of the camp, and if he has any money left over after the essentials have been purchased he will buy anything that may catch his eye.

In 1951 my camera caught his eye, and today Idlouk is fast becoming an enthusiastic amateur photographer, probably the first his land has ever produced.

I first met Idlouk in the spring of 1951 when my wife and I flew north to make a film on the life of the Tununermiut Eskimos. For five months we lived with Idlouk and (*Continued on page* 106)

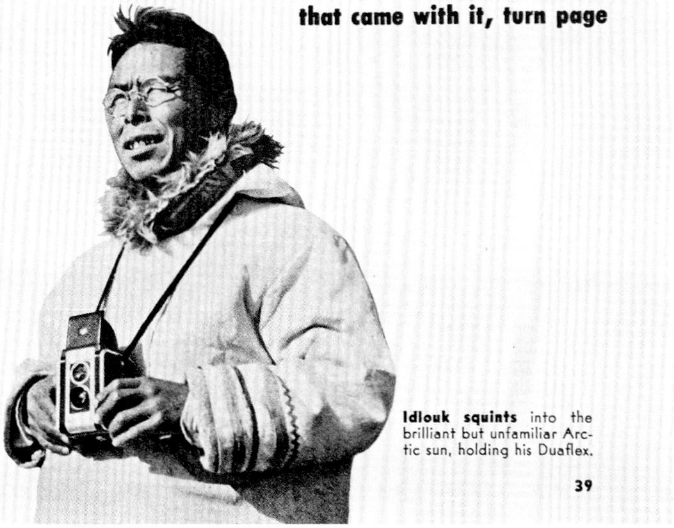

Idlouk squints into the brilliant but unfamiliar Arctic sun, holding his Duaflex.

39

This is what Idlouk wrote— and these are the pictures he sent

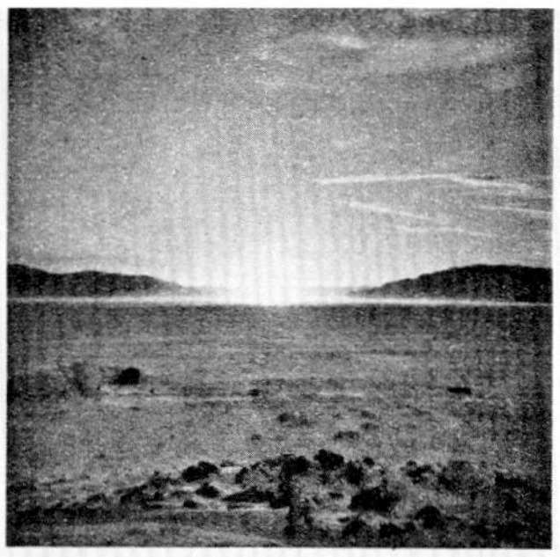

"The sun came back to us in February. We hadn't seen him for three months."

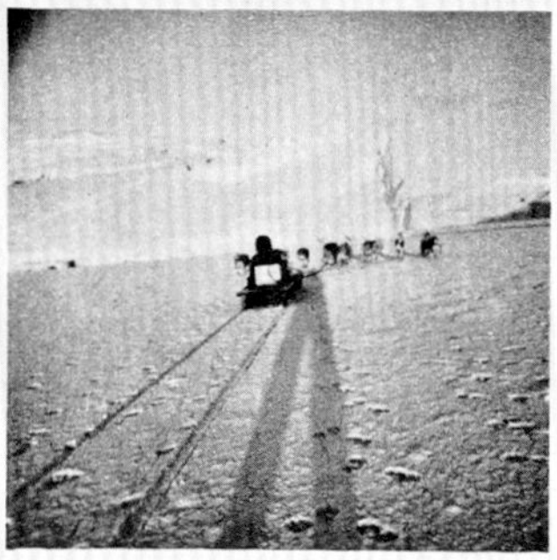

"My shadow was very long. I could not get it out of the picture."

Idlouk to Kingmik:

Alleeani! Tomorrow the policeman is going on patrol. He will take my pictures and have them sent to you on the aeroplane. I am glad. I would like to see some of my pictures. You can make them for me and send them on the big boat in the summer.

Last autumn I was too busy to take many pictures. I had to hunt and fish all the time so that our caches would be full of meat for the dark months. When we were fishing my hands were too wet and cold for me to hold the camera and push the button. But I took a picture of Oodlootituk and Panneeloo and Elijah with some of the fish we brought back to camp. They were frozen stiff, the fish.

And I hunted caribou to get skins for warm winter clothing. I shot four. Now we have warm clothes. But I did not take any pictures. Too bad. But I could not carry my camera on this hunt. For we had to move very fast, and be very careful.

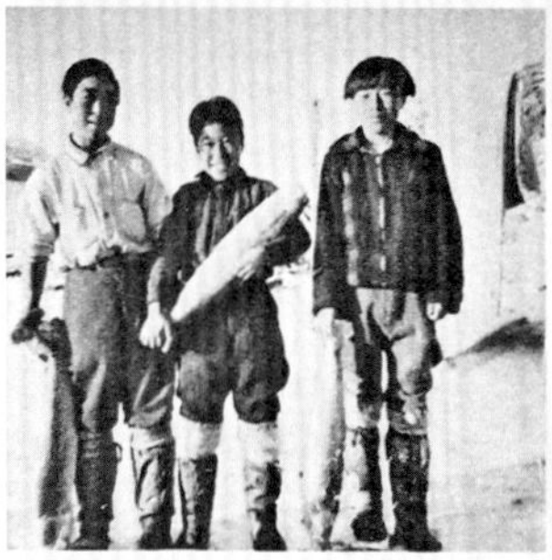

"I took a picture of Oodlootituk and Panneeloo and Elijah with some of the fish . . . frozen stiff."

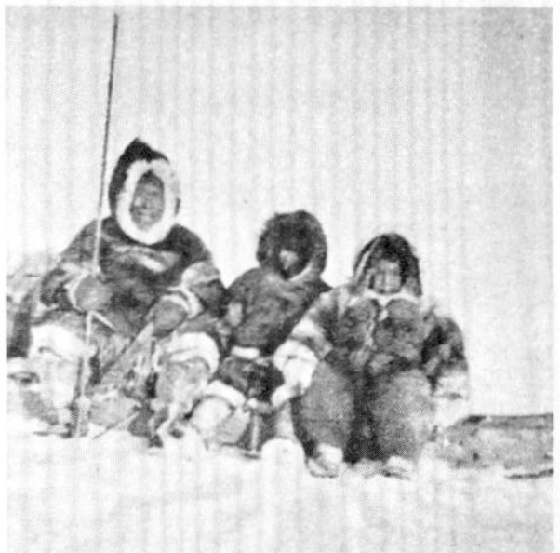

"I hunted caribou to get skins for warm winter clothing. I shot four. Now we have warm clothes."

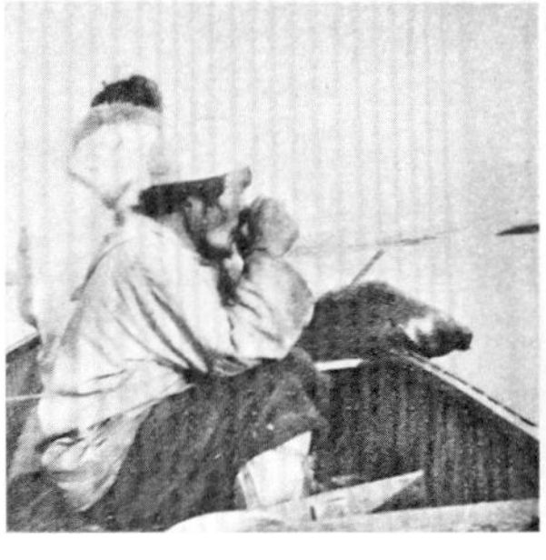

"We hunted seal from my canoe. We drank lots of tea, especially Alaloo . . . how he likes tea!"

We hunted seal from my canoe. It was very cold on the water. We drank lots of tea, especially Alaloo. You remember how he likes tea. I found it was hard to take pictures when I was hunting or fishing. My hands got covered with blood and fat. Then I did not like to touch my camera. It would get dirty and perhaps be no good.

After the sun had gone I took only one picture. It was in my igloo. I don't think it will be good. [It wasn't.] The glass kept getting covered with fog. Our igloos are very damp when it is cold. The seal oil lamps are not very good.

The sun came back to us in February. We hadn't seen him for three months so I took his picture. I had to be quick for he didn't climb very high and was gone again in a few minutes.

I was very happy at being able to use my camera again. I turned around quickly and took another picture of Panneeloo with the sled and dogs. And I almost forgot to turn the film to the next number. It is so easy to forget. And my shadow was very long. I could not get it out of the picture. I hope it does not matter. It looks funny, don't you think?

After the sun came back I tried to take pictures every day. But sometimes my camera was bad. It got cold very quickly and often wouldn't click at all. Now when it is cold I keep the camera under my parkha and only bring it out to take the picture. Once I turned the knob too quickly when I was winding the film. It broke the film. I remember what you told me about the film getting hard (brittle) when it is cold. I will be more careful.

One day I put the camera down on the ice and one of my dogs lifted his leg to it. What a mess. It was frozen stiff. I was very angry. I beat the dog until he howled. But I'll show him. I won't take his picture.

We were all very happy to see the sun come back. My mother said, "Take a picture today and send it to Kingmik to let him know that we are all happy and well fed and that there is no sickness in the camp."

This winter past there were not many foxes.

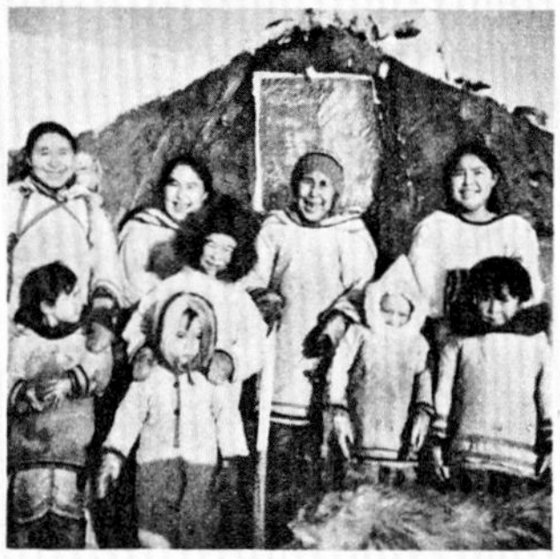

"My mother said, 'Take a picture today and send it to Kingmik . . .' "

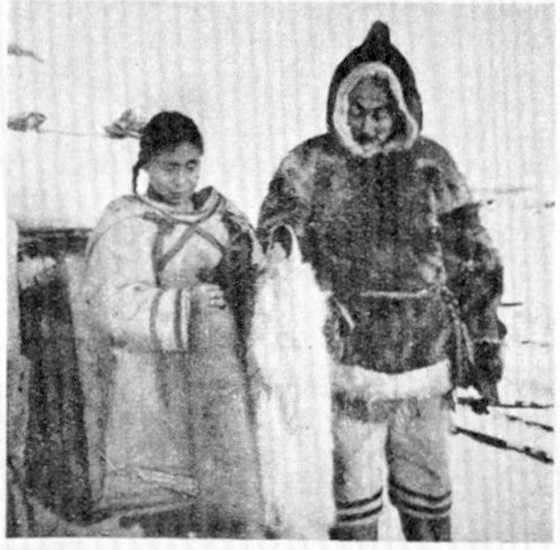

"There were not many foxes. Kadloo got two in February. He wanted to buy a camera but I said food came first."

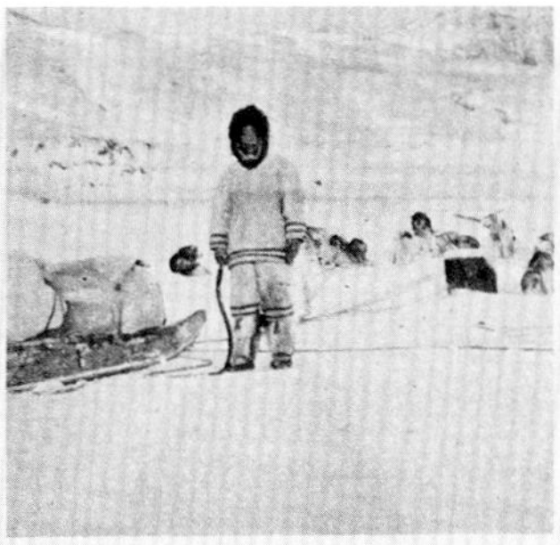

"I took pictures of Panneeloo bringing a load of ice from the iceberg. This is for our drinking water."

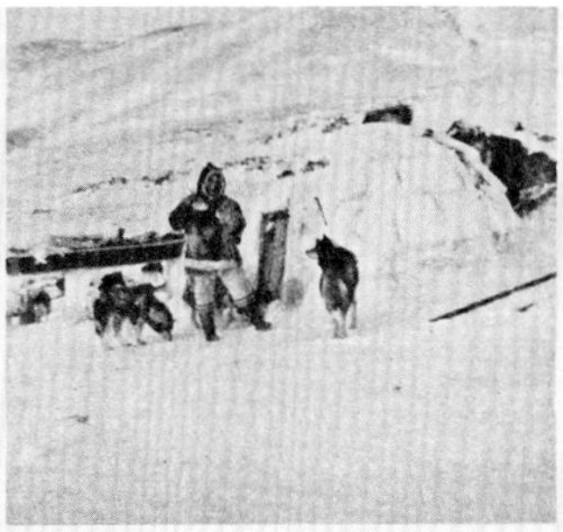

"I took another of the snowhouse Kadloo built as a porch for his igloo."

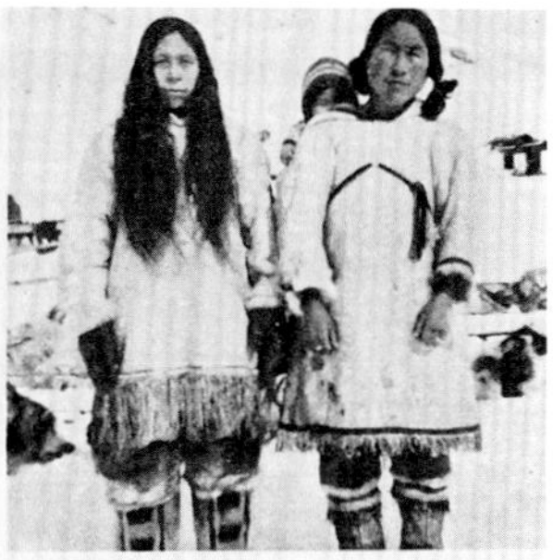

"My wife and Kadloo's wife wanted to play a joke with you. They let down their hair and marked their faces as our women did long ago."

Kadloo got only two in January. He wanted to buy a camera but I said bullets and food came first. He didn't have enough money. Perhaps next year will be better, there may be more foxes and more money. We will see.

In the spring I took a lot of pictures. It was good to have the daylight all the time. And I remembered what you said about taking pictures at night when the sun is not so strong on the snow. In the spring the daytime sun is very strong when it shines on the snow. Perhaps I will have a camera like yours one day. Then I can take pictures at any time.

I took pictures of Panneeloo bringing a load of ice from the iceberg. This is for our drinking water. And I took another of the snowhouse Kadloo built as a porch for his igloo. Then my wife and Kadloo's wife wanted to play a joke with you. They let down their hair and marked their faces the way our women did long ago, then they made me take their picture. They had a hard time to keep from laughing. I did too. I was afraid I would jiggle the camera and spoil the picture. I hope not.

But I had to be careful. I was taking a lot of pictures. I did not want to use up all my film too soon. The trader is going to have film in his store for me next year, but it is a long time yet before the boat will be here.

This year we haven't much money but we have lots of food at my camp. Each day we cut up fresh seal for food. And soon the whales will be here.

Alleeani! I almost forgot. I have a new baby daughter. She was born just after you left. I was very happy for I have enough sons. She is called Ruthee. If you come back to my land you will see her. She is as fat as a baby seal.

Alleeani again! Yesterday my son Oodlootituk was married at the Mission house. His wife is Ishoogituk, you will remember her. She will be a good wife, for she is a good cook and a good sewer. I wore my white man's clothes to the Mission. So did Oodlootituk. And after the service the missionaries wife took our picture. Everyone looked happy but the new husband and wife.

Now I will send the pictures to you, and you can have them made for me. Perhaps I can have them on the boat this summer. I would like to see them. I don't think they will be very good for I am not *Adgeleeuktee* [the one who takes pictures]. Perhaps I will throw my camera away if they are no good. We will see.

Goodbye to you and to Amouleegah. I will not forget you.—

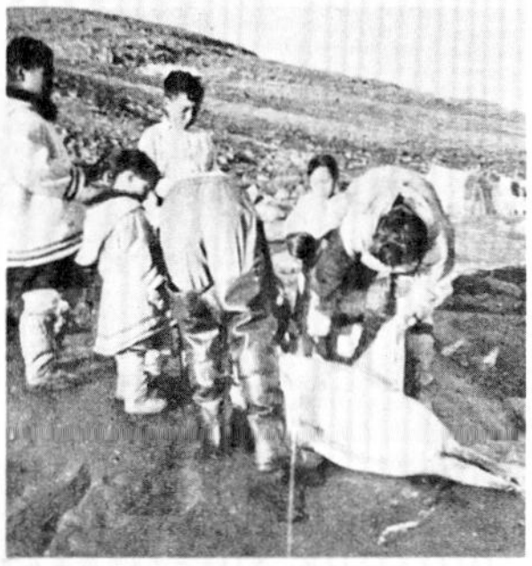

"Each day we cut up a fresh seal. And soon the whales will be here."

Note: "Kingmik" is Wilkinson's Eskimo name. It means "dog"; this is as close as the Eskimo alphabet can come to "Doug." "Amouleegah" is Wilkinson's wife; the name means "snow bunting," a small bird.

"Yesterday my son Oodlootituk was married at the Mission. His wife is Ishoogituk."

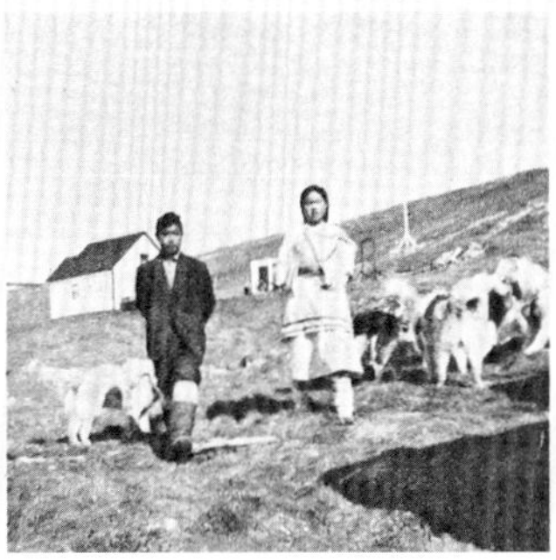

"After the service the missionary's wife took our picture."

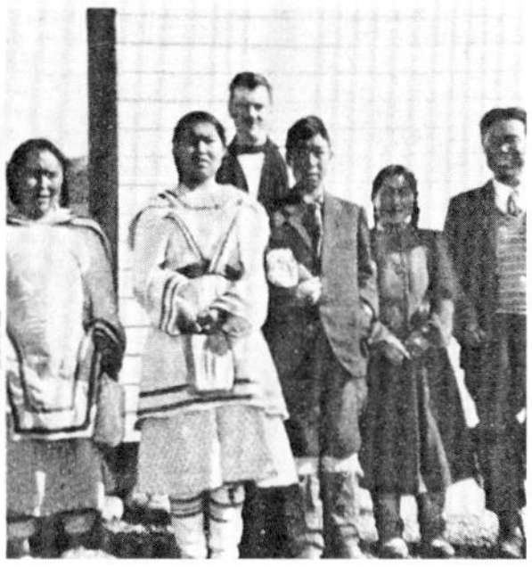

But here Wilkinson proves to be a somewhat unreliable narrator. His supposed translation of the letter in syllabics from Idlout does not represent the note reproduced in the article at all. According to Inuktitut translators Rhoda Kayakjuak and Nellie Erkloo, the letter discusses the return of his daughter Leah after her treatment in the south for tuberculosis and a stay with Wilkinson's family. (These same events are narrated by Leah herself in the five-part article "C.D. Howe," with excerpts reproduced in this book.)[28] In his 1954 article, Wilkinson goes on to discuss a *qajaq* (kayak) that Akumalik, Idlout's father, built for Wilkinson to use during his upcoming stay with Idlout's camp.[29] Idlout does say that he photographed the wood for the *qajaq*, but otherwise the note does not discuss his photography.[30] Although Wilkinson's translation could be based on another letter from Idlout, the presentation here suggests that Wilkinson's account – like his narration in Idlout's voice for *Land of the Long Day* – was fabricated. Although the article is the only contemporary published source of information on Idlout's photography, it is clearly problematic. As we argue here, Idlout's photographs should be seen as collaborative. Reflecting the values of Inuit Qaujimajatuqangit, they show the integral interconnections of and harmony in the community at camp. Yet, at the same time, these images, the products of a southern-made technology, are also entangled with Wilkinson and, by extension, with southern settler culture more broadly.

Nonetheless, it is clear that after meeting in 1951, Idlout and Wilkinson seem to have developed a comradery born not only out of living on the land together but also out of a mutual interest in technology. Whereas the film *Land of the Long Day* details Idlout's expert use of "traditional" Inuit technologies, Wilkinson's subsequent publications also laud Idlout's adoption of southern technologies and consumer culture. In the 1954 *Photography* article, for example, Wilkinson states, "Among his people Idlouk is a remarkable person, intelligent, enterprising and resourceful. With money procured by trapping and then trading the skin of the white fox to the Hudson's Bay Company, he has managed to buy a great many things that the Eskimos of his area do not usually have: a forty-foot motor boat, eighteen-foot canoe and outboard motor, rifles of various calibres, telescope, barometer."[31] Wilkinson goes on to say of Idlout that the camera was another technology that "caught his eye."[32] In this passage, it is clear that the camera – like a rifle or a motorboat – was coded in terms of gender as a masculinized tool.

According to the 1954 account, Wilkinson introduced Idlout to photography in the spring of 1951 during the filming of *Land of the Long Day* and brought him a Kodak Duaflex camera with six rolls of film.[33] The Duaflex was a "pseudo twin-reflex camera" both manufactured to resemble and marketed to capitalize on the popularity of the twin-reflex Rolleiflex; however, the Duaflex had the same basic mechanism and limited focal range as Kodak's popular snapshot camera, the Brownie. Using 620 film, the Duaflex also produced 6 centimetre square negatives.[34] Wilkinson recounts that he had only limited time to instruct Idlout in using the camera before departing with his wife and Roy for the south. He writes that in July 1952, Idlout sent him the six rolls of film, now exposed, for processing in Ottawa.[35] The following year when Wilkinson arrived to spend fifteen months with Idlout, he packed a developing and printing kit as a gift for Idlout.[36] Archival records also indicate that during his 1953–54 stay in the north, Wilkinson introduced Idlout to using a motion picture camera. Idlout, for example, is credited as the cameraman for a 1954 newsreel on Wilkinson's sojourn in northern Baffin.[37]

Today, decades after Joseph Idlout and his community took these photographs, they still remain entangled in his relationship with Doug Wilkinson. As noted earlier, the approximately 300 extant photographs credited to Idlout – including negatives shot between 1951 and 1954, as well as a group of negatives shot in 1958 (discussed in chapter 6) – are now part of the larger Douglas E. Wilkinson fonds in the Nunavut Archives. There, they are interspersed among 5,000 of Wilkinson's own still photographs.[38] Wilkinson donated Idlout's negatives, along with his own images, films, and documents, beginning in the 1970s.[39] Negatives by Idlout are identifiable through item-level descriptions based on Wilkinson's own records. But they are also distinguishable from Wilkinson's photographs by technology: Idlout's 6 centimetre square negatives, with limited focal range,[40] stand in stark contrast to the wider vistas, expanded focal range, and greater detail achieved by Wilkinson's equipment. Yet, despite using a rudimentary snapshot camera, Idlout was able to create images of intelligence and beauty that were – most importantly – deeply embedded in Inuit culture.

Picturing Inuit Qaujimajatuqangit: Idlout's Photographs of *Ilagiit Nunagivaktangat* (Camp)

Between 1951 and 1954, about 232 negatives were shot with Idlout's camera. Most represent life at the winter camp in Aulattivik or at the spring camp in Nuvurulua, featuring the *nuna*, sea, and sky. Through the lens of Inuit Qaujimajatuqangit, these photographs not only showcase life at *ilagiit nunagivaktangat* but also convey the Inuit values that shaped daily life.

In some ways, Idlout's camerawork resembles the well-known photography of Peter Pitseolak. As noted in the introductory chapter, Pitseolak, from around Kinngait/Cape Dorset, was the most prolific Inuk photographer of his time. He had been introduced to the camera in the second decade of the twentieth century when he met Robert Flaherty in 1912.[41] Pitseolak first photographed in the 1930s, acquiring his own camera a decade later. In total, about 2,000 negatives by Pitseolak are known today, many made in collaboration with his second wife, Aggeok.[42] These photographs largely document their own community. They include numerous portraits as well as hunting scenes. In oral histories, Pitseolak

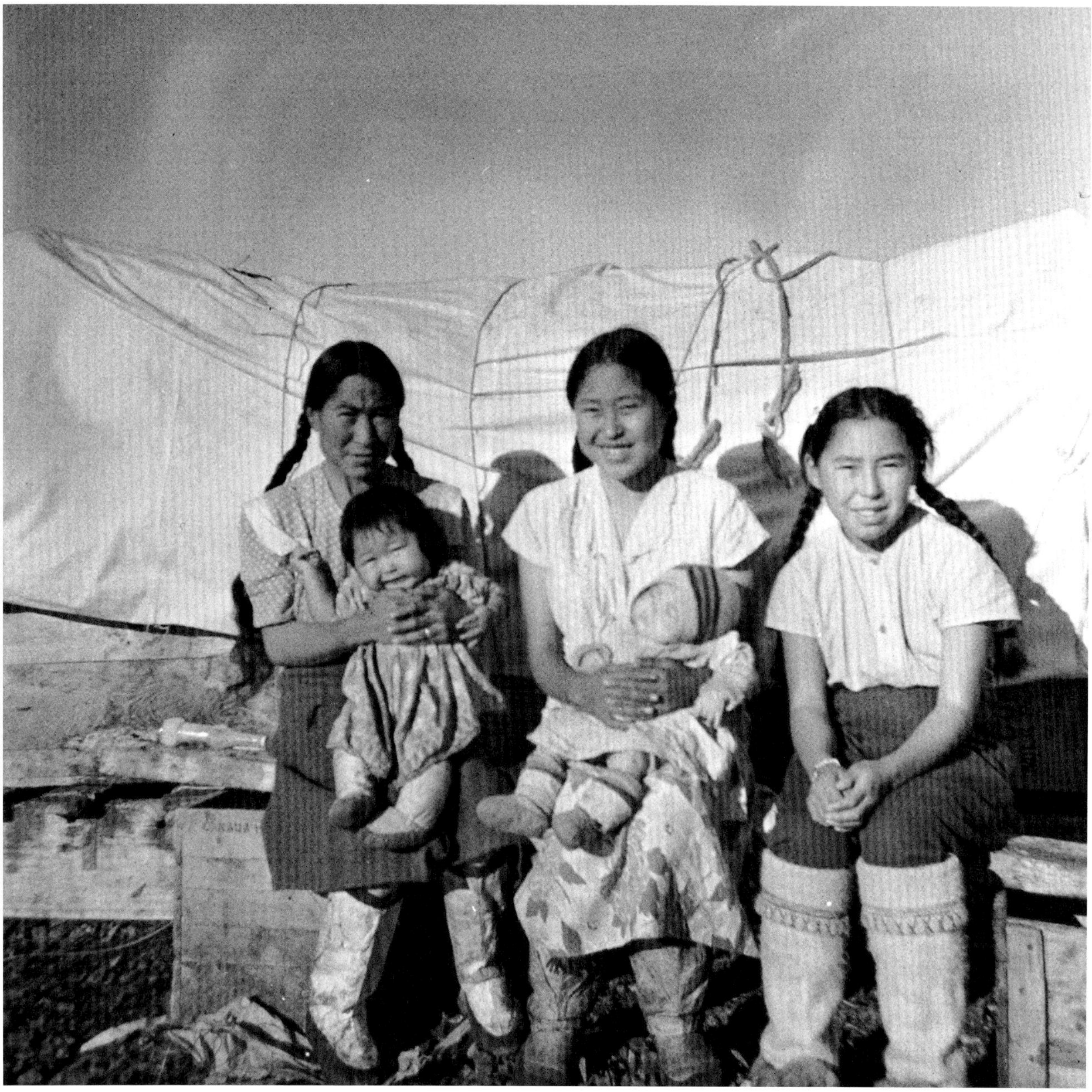

3.4 | Idlout family members at Idlout's camp, Aulattivik, Eclipse Sound, North Baffin Island, June 1953. *Left to right*: Kidlak (Idlout's wife) with Ruth (Idlout's daughter), Rebecca (Idlout's daughter) with Rachael (Idlout's granddaughter), and Leah (Idlout's daughter). A sod and wood house with a canvass cover stands in the background. Photo: Joseph Idlout.

3.5 | Joseph Idlout, wife Kidlak, and daughter Ruth pose for the camera at camp, Aulattivik, Eclipse Sound, North Baffin Island, May 1952. Uncredited photo taken with Idlout's camera.

remarked that he made the photographs for his grandchildren as a record of life.[43] Additionally, as Dorothy Eber argues, the photographs were templates for Pitseolak's drawings.[44]

Like Peter Pitseolak, the most frequent subjects of Idlout's photographs are his family and Inuit community as seen at camp. Before the camera, the twenty-nine members of the camp appear and reappear as familiar faces: Idlout's wife, Kidlak, and most of their then eight children, the other four family groups living together in the camp, and visiting families from Arctic Bay/Ikpiarjuk (see figure 3.4). Occasionally, Idlout himself makes an appearance in the group portraits, at times seen from a low vantage point, possibly with a child briefly wielding the Duaflex (see figure 3.5). Indeed, it is clear that the camera, like all technologies at camp, was shared and that pictures were made collaboratively.

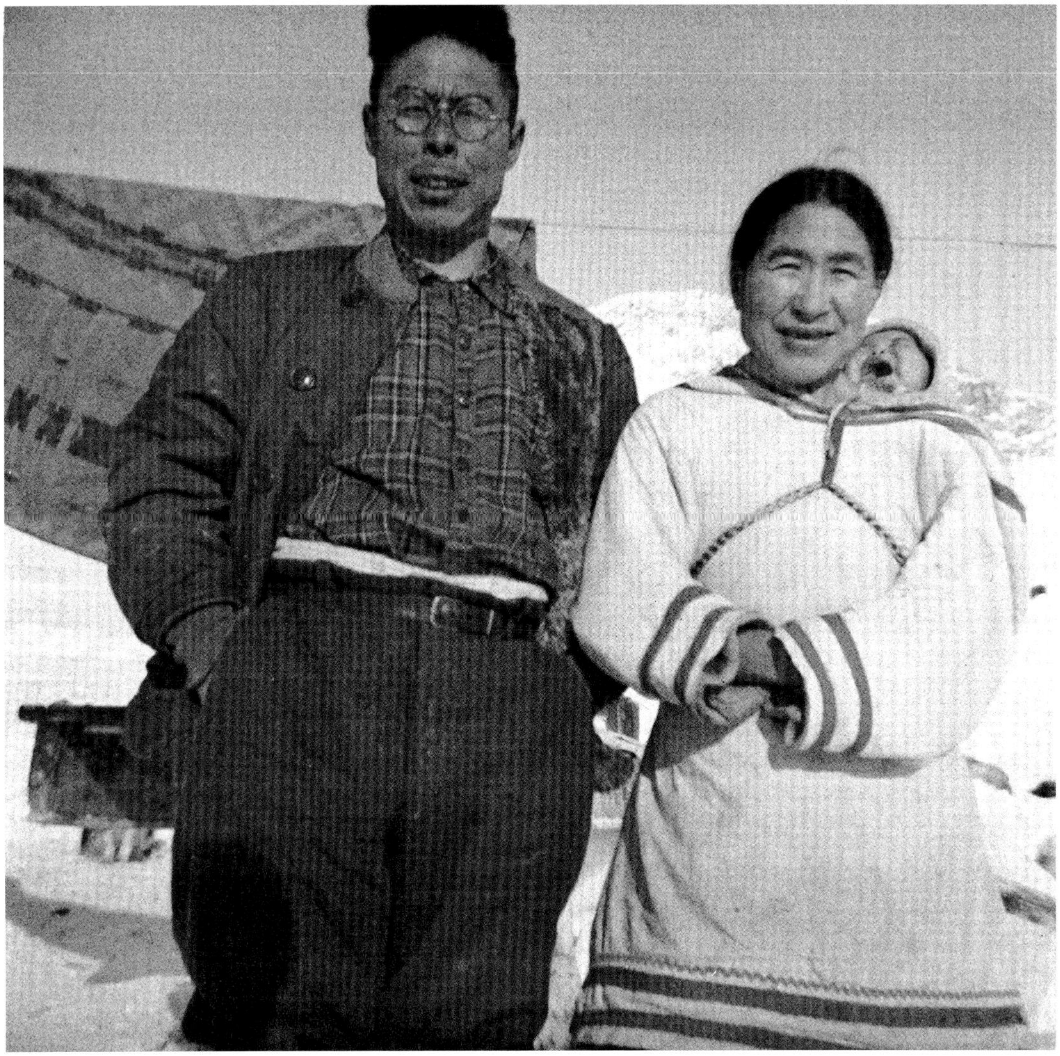

Occasionally, Inuit visitors from around Arctic Bay/Ikpiarjuk, about 150 kilometres northwest of Idlout's camp, also appear as guests of the camp. Composed with great deliberation, Idlout's studies of the people in Aulattivik and in Nuvurulua are neither the spontaneous snapshots for which his mass-produced Kodak was marketed in the south nor the emblematic tableaux that were shot and circulated by Wilkinson. Instead, Idlout's photographs record the rhythms of life at camp and, in their attention to family, visualize linked bonds, devotion, skill, and tradition.

In other photographs, the Arctic terrain unfolds before the camera: sea ice, vast terrain, and an ever-shifting sky. The majority of these photographs depict the hunt; they are the most dramatic of these images. The photographs illustrate and perform Idlout's and his community's prowess as hunters. Photographs of the polar bear hunt from the sequence below include figure 3.1.

The hunting photographs stalk prey visually, reaching a narrative climax in trophy images of a narwhal, a seal, and a polar bear after capture (see figures 3.6, 3.7, 3.8, and 7.7). Idlout's camera fully takes in the visceral bloodiness of the carcasses and displays of triumph by the hunters. These images stress the collaborative efforts needed for the hunt. Whereas Doug Wilkinson created visual *emblems* of the hunt in his still images and in film, Idlout's photographs seem to exist *within* a direct, embodied, and communal experience of hunting. The photographs often replicate a hunter's-eye view, reproducing an intense focus on prey as well as the hunter's perspective from a *qajaq* or a *qamutik* (sled) (see figure 3.9). But the hunt was not only a masculinized effort. As Christina Williamson has argued, women's work at camp was crucial to the hunt and considered an integral part of hunting culture.[45] The photographs depict women's work creating clothing from prey and preparing food from the hunt. Idlout's camera captured the many aspects of hunting in Aulattivik and in Nuvurulua, envisioning it through IQ.

Together, these photographs – portraits of camp members and Inuit visitors as well as images of terrain and the hunt – represent what it means to be an Inuit community and how Inuit culture takes form in daily life. In short, these photographs seem to visualize many aspects of Inuit cultural values, principally including Inuit Qaujimajatuqangit.

Inuit Qaujimajatuqangit is described by Inuit in many ways but can be understood generally as a culmination of wisdom passed down from generation to generation. Its acronym, IQ, is an "Inuktized"[46] play on "intelligence quotient," and as such, it indicates culturally specific Inuit intelligence. Jaypeetee Arnakak defines IQ as "a means of rationalizing thought and action, a means of organizing tasks and resources, a means of organizing family and society into coherent wholes."[47] The late Elder Mariano Aupilaarjuk described the foundation of IQ as "the truths of Inuit culture and the desire to live in harmony. Living in harmony like that we can expect a better world to surround us."[48] As discussed by the

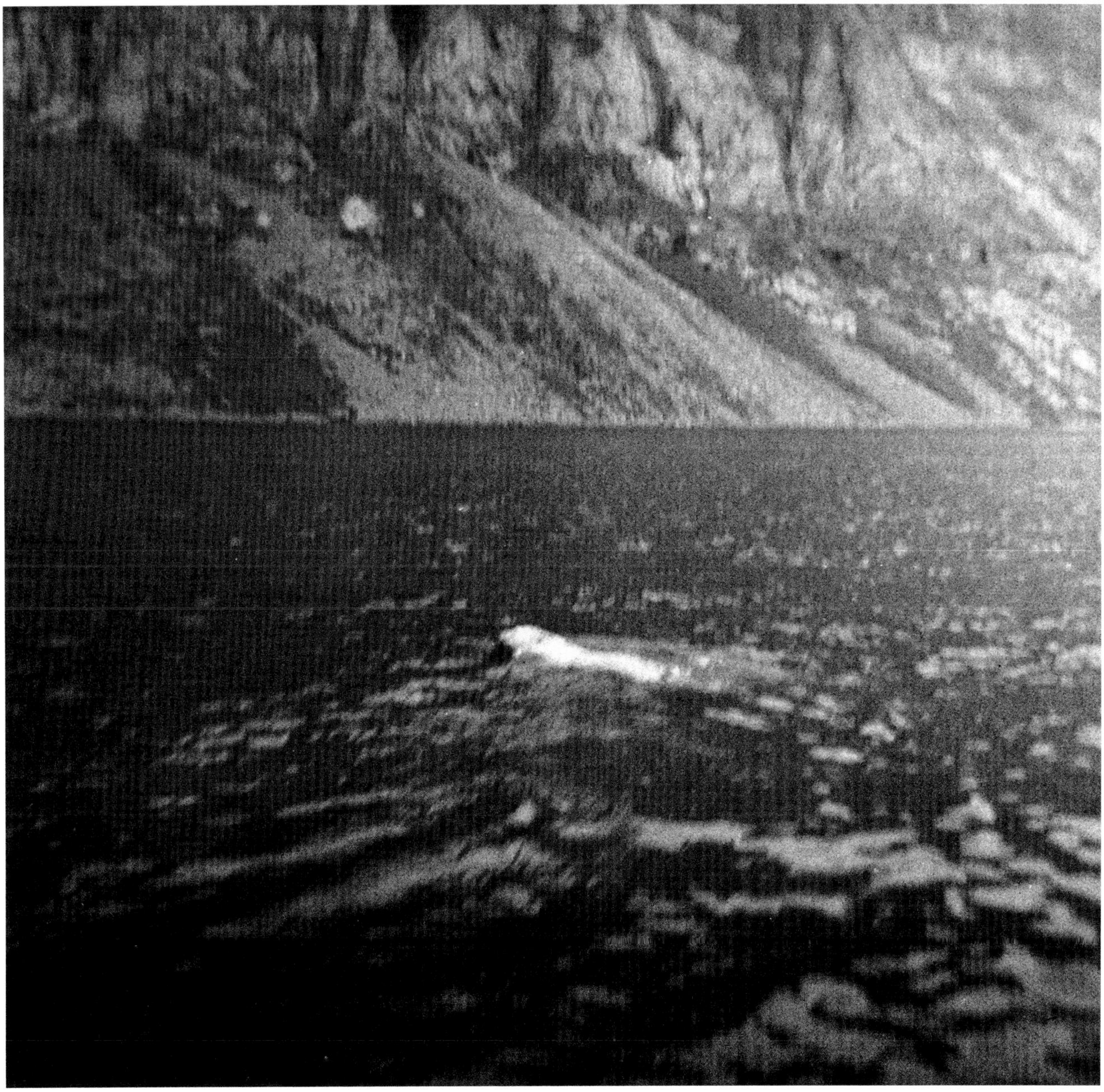

3.6 | Hunting a polar bear in the water from Idlout's big boat, White Bay, off Eclipse Sound, North Baffin Island, August 1952. Photo: Joseph Idlout.

Government of Nunavut, IQ is comprised of the eight guiding principles noted earlier, which apply to different aspects of life.

The values upheld by the IQ principles also coalesce with important discussions of Inuit culture by Inuk knowledge keeper, author, and translator Rachel Qitsualik. Notably, Qitsualik is also a granddaughter of Idlout, her mother being Idlout's eldest daughter, Rebecca. In an essay on the Inuit relationship to notions of sovereignty, Qitsualik describes the holistic Inuit worldview, where everything is connected and Inuit values create a "system of self-perpetuating health."[49] For Qitsualik, an Inummarik (lit. "true human") is nonanthropogenic in rejecting southern notions of human primacy over nature. Instead, an Inummarik lives harmoniously with the elements of *imaq* (water), *nuna* (land), and *sila* (sky). She explains that nonanthropogenic "attitudes allow" Inuit "to

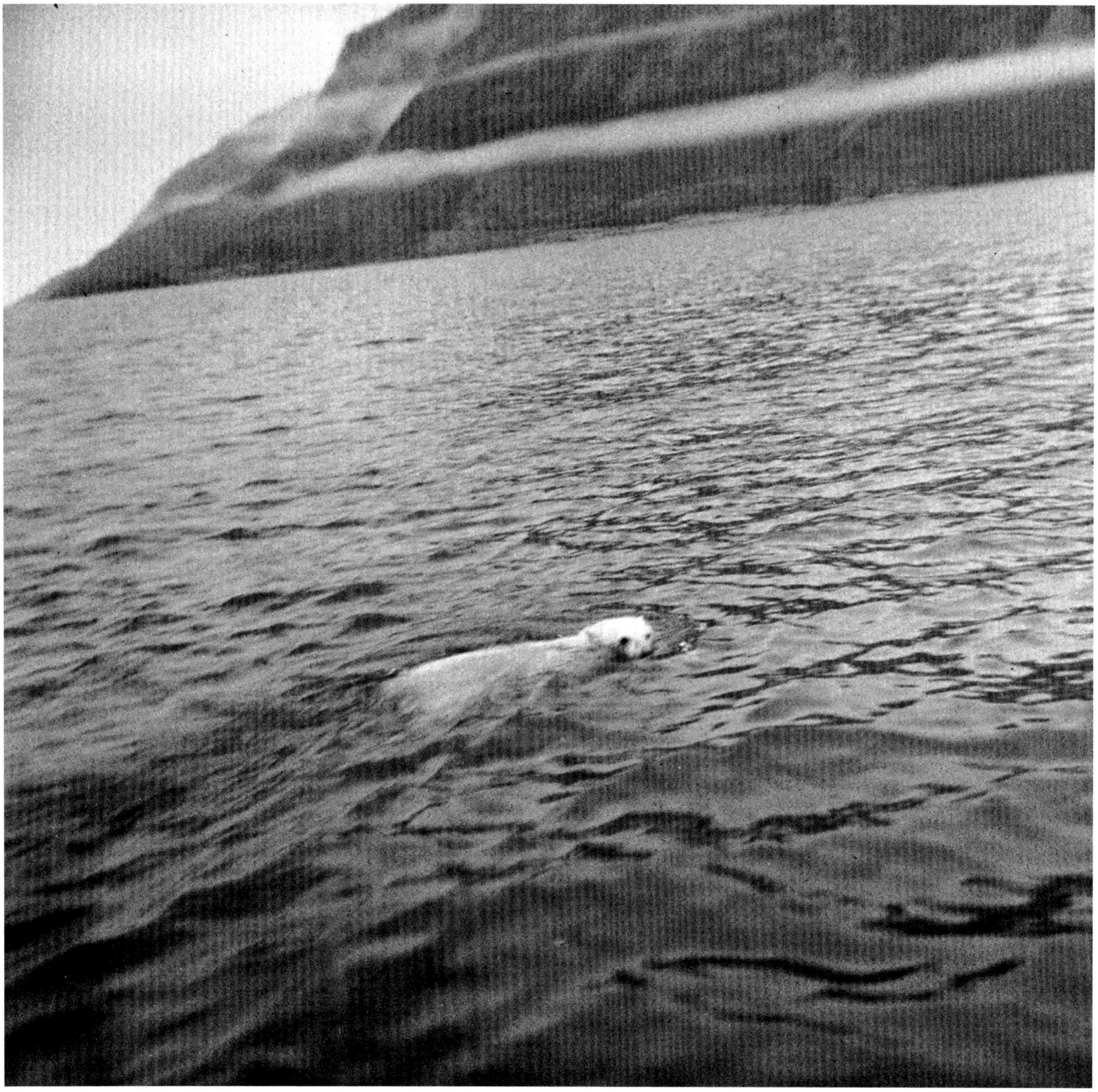

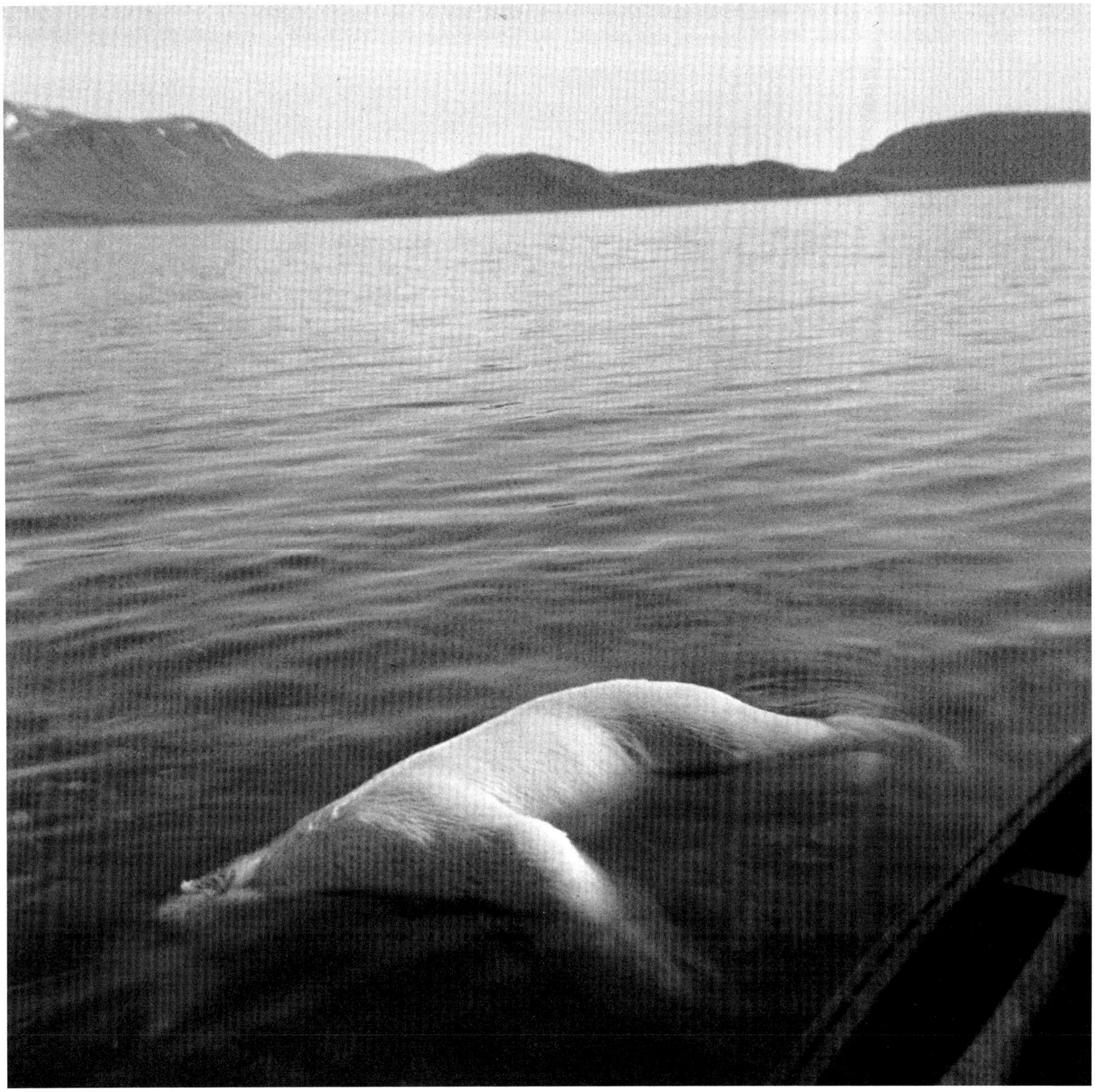

3.7 | Hunting a polar bear in the water from Idlout's big boat, White Bay, off Eclipse Sound, North Baffin Island, August 1952. Photo: Joseph Idlout.

3.8 | A dead polar bear in the shallows, hunted in the water from Idlout's big boat, White Bay, off Eclipse Sound, North Baffin Island, August 1952. Photo: Joseph Idlout.

look toward Water, Land, and Sky for cues as to how human beings may remain healthy ... The healthful human pattern cultivates awareness (e.g., inua), rather than mere behaviour."[50]

In viewing these images through the lens of IQ, with attention to Qitsualik's discussion of the holistic Inuit worldview, we are following Heather Igloliorte's influential work. Igloliorte proposes IQ "as the basis for understanding Inuit artistic productions."[51] She argues that Inuit artworks – including a vast array of cultural production – "demonstrate how lived experiences, values, and

3.9 | Seal hunt from a canoe, Eclipse Sound, North Baffin Island, October 1951. A man, possibly Herodier Kadluk, prepares to harpoon a seal. Photo: Joseph Idlout.

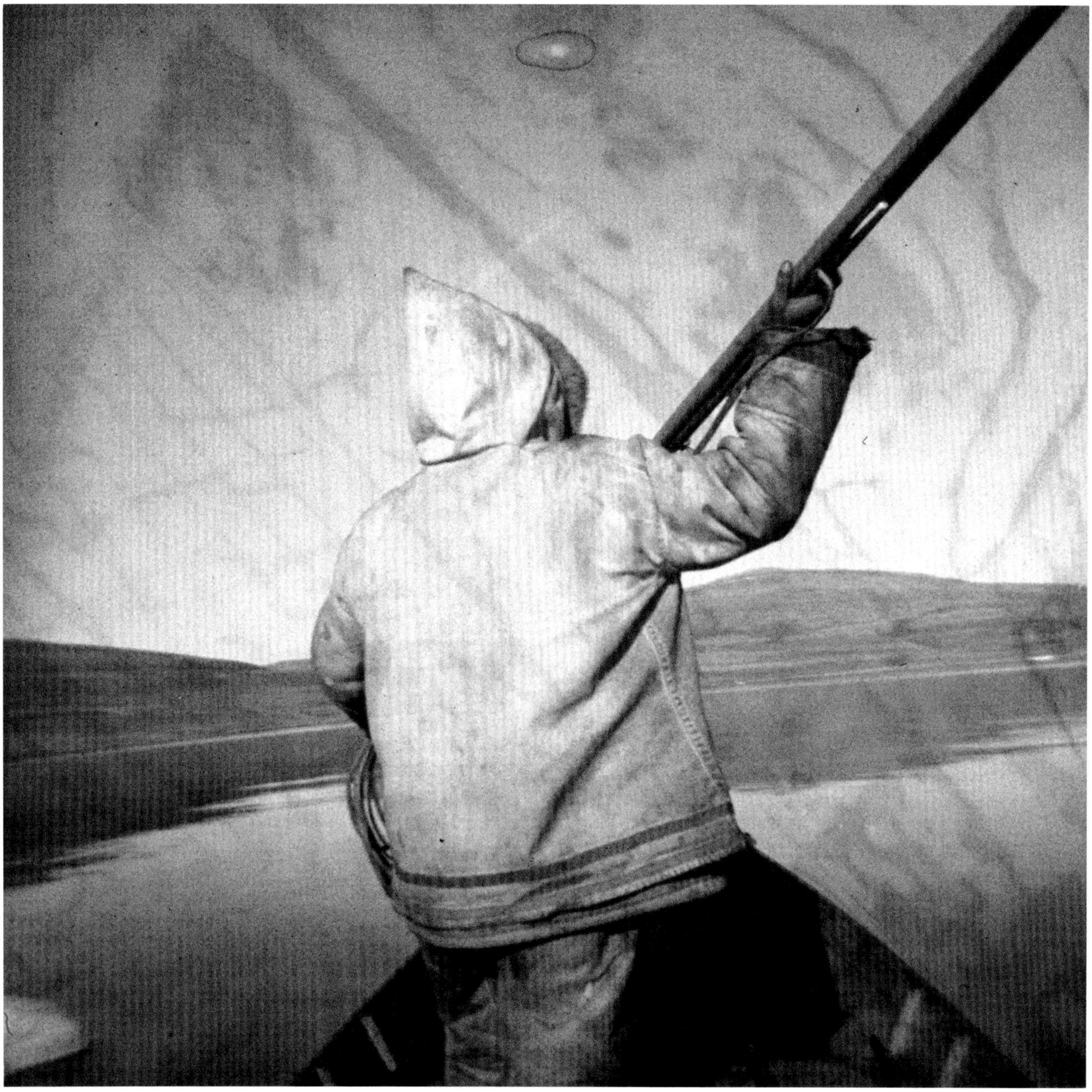

knowledge are embedded and apparent in a variety of complex and interrelated ways, even if it is not always apparent to southern audiences."[52]

Inuit Qaujimajatuqangit principles, built upon holistic unity and regard for others, are foundational to Inuit societal structures. *Inuuqatigiitsiarniq*, for example, is defined as the principle of respecting others, including relationships and caring for people. Following this principle ensures the well-being of the community as a whole through the reciprocation of kindness and respect. Idlout's photographs represent and reinforce the close-knit relationships between family, different generations, and friends in Aulattivik and in Nuvurulua. Although all relationships are valuable to Inuit, the family unit is the most important. For Inuit, family extends beyond southern notions of the nuclear family. As seen in many of Idlout's photographs, community is built on family. In Inuit culture, it is important that children grow up knowing who their relatives are, down to their distant cousins and past generations. Through this knowledge, children learn where they come from and who they are. The Inuit naming system is one way of creating this bond between the families and all Inuit across generations.[53] Naming is a way to build kinship where there have been no previous familial ties, and families often treat the child named after a loved one with the respect shown their namesake. *Inuuqatigiitsiarniq* is instilled in children from a young age by teaching them to respect others and to heed and respect adults, especially Elders, who hold the most knowledge. In accordance with *inuuqatigiitsiarniq*, competition and hateful or jealous behaviours that create unnecessary strife are seen as inappropriate because they threaten the vitality of the community. Inuit strive to live a good and happy life, and part of this undertaking involves being a good person. It is for this reason that, historically, Inuit often resorted to solving disagreements through friendly competitions such as throat singing, Inuit games, or song duels. Although these methods are no longer widely practised as a form of conflict resolution, Inuit continue to encourage treating others with dignity and respect as well as working through disagreements immediately so as not to carry a grudge.

The eight IQ principles are intertwined. *Inuuqatigiitsiarniq*, for example, intersects particularly closely with *tunnganarniq*, *piliriqatigiinniq/ikajuqtigiinniq*, and *aajiiqatigiinniq*. All three principles encourage living in harmony with each other and creating communities of care. *Tunnganarniq* specifically represents fostering good spirit by being open, welcoming, and inclusive. In Inuit culture, it is important to be welcoming, and people can take pride in the fact that they can welcome guests into their home and share a meal or provide visitors with anything that they may need. Traditionally, the cultural value of being welcoming meant that if Inuit were travelling to another camp, they would likely be taken care of. *Tunnganarniq* supports community wellness by creating a safe environment where people feel comfortable seeking support and creating meaningful relationships. *Tunnganarniq* can be seen as the starting point for fostering good relations with one another and is a value that requires reciprocation.

Idlout's photographs are filled with encounters that reveal *tunnganarniq*. They include photographs of other Inuit who welcomed Idlout or who were welcomed to Idlout's camp.

The IQ principle of *piliriqatigiinniq/ikajuqtigiinniq* represents working together for a common cause and was integral to keeping harmony in the camp. Inuit recognize the significance of collaborative effort, especially in relation to the harsh Arctic environment where it would have been impossible to survive without the help and cooperation of one another (see figure 3.10). Inuit children are often taught to help others whenever possible, without the expectation of receiving anything or recognition in return. In practice, *piliriqatigiinniq/ikajuqtigiinniq* comes full circle: help will be available if needed. Helping each other also ensures the well-being and success of the community, as more can be accomplished with the help of others. Several of Idlout's photographs depict community members working together, reflecting *piliriqatigiinniq/ikajuqtigiinniq*. This principle is seen, for example, in a sequence of images focused on building a shelter, likely for storing food, where the men and boys of the camp cooperate in cutting blocks of snow and transporting them (see figure 3.11).[54]

Aajiiqatigiinniq, the principle of decision making through discussion and consensus, provides protocols for aspects of *inuuqatigiitsiarniq*, *tunnganarniq*, and *piliriqatigiinniq/ikajuqtigiinniq*. The decision-making process of Inuit, especially before colonization, differed from that of many other cultures in the fact that there was no one leader, one gender, or one demographic of people who made decisions on behalf of the entire community. There may have been one or a few particular people whom many in the camp looked to for advice. Idlout, for example, served in this way at his camp. But, overall, Inuit leadership was fluid and could change depending on expertise and the problem at hand. Following *aajiiqatigiinniq* decreased the possibility of major conflicts, as decisions were made through the input of all adults and Elders in the camp, with the community's best interests in mind. As we noted above, the principle of *aajiiqatigiinniq* cannot be illustrated through the lens of a camera as explicitly as the other Inuit Qaujimajatuqangit principles. Yet it undergirds all of Idlout's scenes of hunting and camp life.

Like *inuuqatigiitsiarniq*, *tunnganarniq*, *piliriqatigiinniq/ikajuqtigiinniq*, and *aajiiqatigiinniq*, the remaining four IQ principles address care but now extended to learning, skill development, stewardship of the *nuna*, and providing for community. For example, the IQ principle of *pijitsirniq*, serving and providing for family and the community, is reflected in Idlout's photographs that depict members of camp engaging in hunting, caretaking, butchering, and preparing skins. For Inuit, very few actions are accomplished solely for the self; when a hunter catches an animal, its meat is often distributed beyond his own family and shared with those who have less. Prior to the widespread availability of southern fabrics, the skin from catches would be used to clothe entire families. *Pijitsirniq* contrasts greatly with southern ideas of individualism, which carry the expectations that

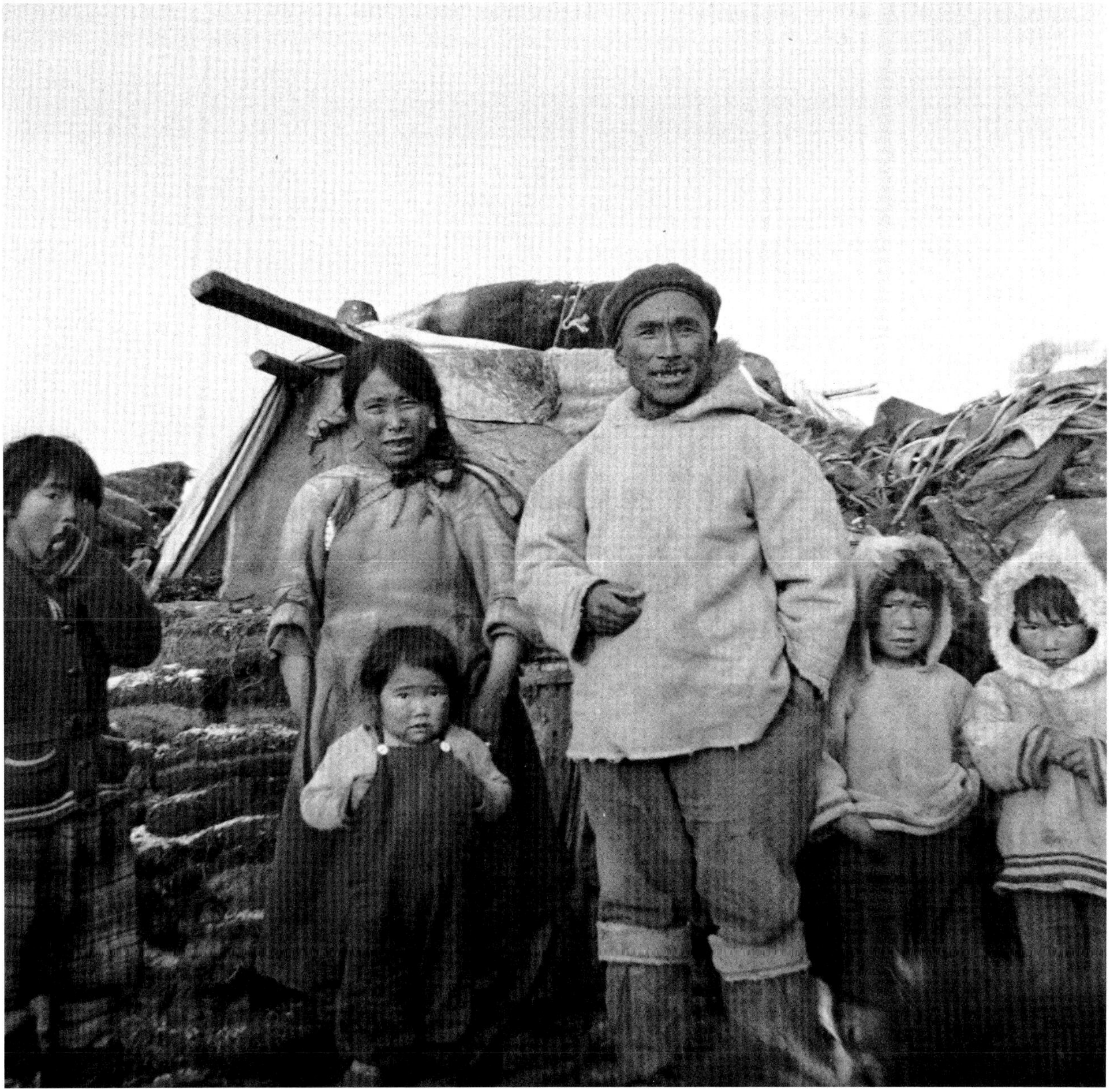

3.10 | Hunter Simon Anaviapik and family on Eclipse Sound, possibly in Qimmivik or in Aulattivik, May 1952. *Left to right*: Daniki Olayuk, Rebecca Anaviapik, Susie (in front), Simon Anaviapik, Isaac Anaviapik, and Peterloosie (adopted). Now abandoned for a tent, a winter sod and skin house stands in the background. Photo: Joseph Idlout.

individuals must do everything on their own for their own self-gain and that failures are theirs to struggle through and solve alone. In contrast, based on the Inuit perspective, members of the community have shared responsibilities to do what they can to ensure that the community thrives. In the past, these

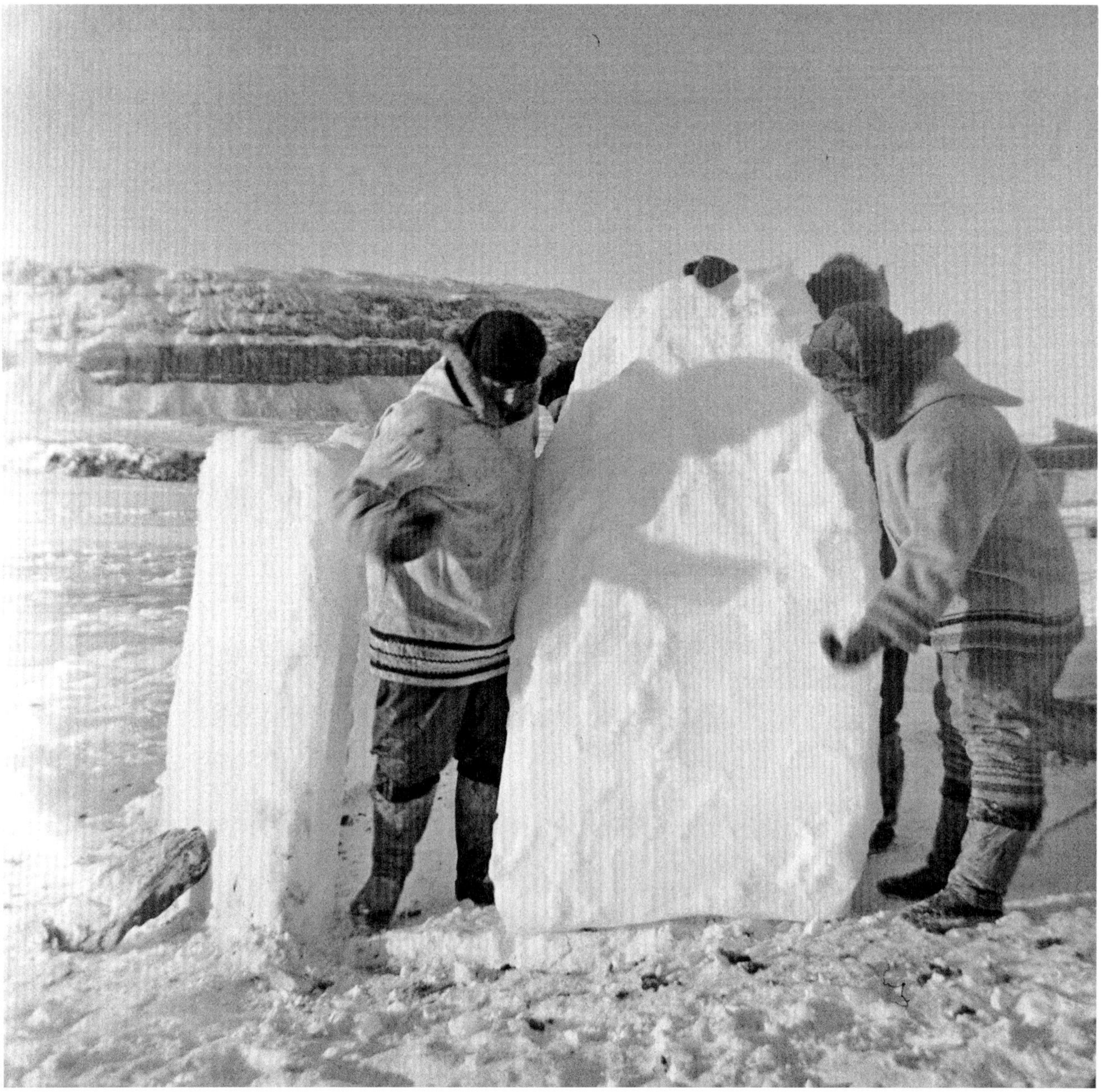

3.11 | Men, probably Gideon Qitsualik and Herodier Kadluk, erect an open-top ice house – or igluvigaq (snow shelter) – at Idlout's camp, Aulattivik, Eclipse Sound, North Baffin Island, October 1951. The blocks used in the construction will be frozen together. Photo: Joseph Idlout.

responsibilities included providing food and sharing labour, and they extended to individual behaviour, thus ensuring that everyone treated others in the community kindly and with respect while abstaining from actions that would cause harm to others. Through practices such as *pijitsirniq*, the contributions of everyone – whether hunters providing food or children fetching ice – ensure the well-being of the community. If you look at these photographs, you can see the ways that members of Idlout's camp provided for and served their community. Photographs such as the image of Paul Ullatitaq Idlout posing with a dead polar bear (see figure 7.7)[55] and the photograph of Herodier Kadluk preparing to harpoon a seal (see figure 3.9) depict men hunting for animals that would provide food for the camp, oil for lamps, and skins for clothing. Other photographs, including those of Kidlak and another woman at the camp, showcase skins that they prepared for use in making clothes for camp members. Ways of serving and providing for the community came in different forms, changing through time and with the introduction of different goods, as can be seen in a March 1952 photograph of Kidlak holding fox furs ready to be traded with the Hudson's Bay Company and in the photograph reproduced here of Kidlak and another woman with sealskins drying on a line (see figure 3.12).[56] Leah Idlout d'Argencourt Paulson reproduced the latter image in her 1975 article "First Inuit Picture on Canadian Money."[57] In these ways, burdens and struggles are solved through the help of the community. If one person lacks a skill set, there is always someone else available who can fill a needed role. And as burdens are shared, so is success.

The hunt and the related preparation of clothing and food require innovation and resourcefulness, characteristics of the IQ principle of *qanuqtuurniq*. Inuit have always had to be inventive and creative to survive in the Arctic environment. This resourcefulness is made apparent by ingenious Inuit inventions such as the *iglu* (igloo), snow goggles, the *amautik* (pl. *amautiit*, woman's parka), the *igluvigaq* (snow shelter), and the *qajaq* (kayak), as shown in Idlout's photographs (see figure 3.13). However, *qanuqtuurniq* is not limited to physical creations, as Inuit apply this principle to their lives as well. During hard times, such as the period of rapid change captured in Idlout's photographs, Inuit are encouraged to meet challenges with innovation and to adapt when necessary. Idlout's photographs illustrate a variety of ways that Inuit used what resources were available to them not only to survive but also to thrive in the Arctic. As southerners began to arrive in the Arctic, Inuit did not simply abandon their traditions and tools but often adapted traditional technology to incorporate new materials that became available to them. For example, photographs taken inside Idlout's sod house show how Inuit incorporated newspapers into the structure of their dwellings not only to serve as decoration but also to insulate and to keep dirt from falling inside.[58] Likewise, in many of the portrait photographs shot in Aulattivik and in Nuvurulua, the viewer can also see variations in the choices of material used to create clothing. Inuit had begun using fabric brought by southerners decades earlier to sew traditional patterns for *amautiit* and men's parkas, often putting their own twist on designs as well. This practice continued to the 1950s, when these photographs were made, and is still prevalent in Inuit sewing today. It is seen, for example, in the rickrack and bias designs on men's parkas (see figure 3.11). This design is still common today. And, finally, the very use of

3.12 | Kidlak (Idlout's wife) and another woman pose by a canvas tent used as a dwelling at the summer camp on the northwest tip of Aulattivik, Eclipse Sound, North Baffin Island, July 1952. Sealskins dry on a line, and the west coast of Cape Hatt is visible in the background – the same backdrop as that pictured on the old two-dollar bill. Photo: Joseph Idlout.

3.13 | Idlout's father, Akumalik, makes a wood *qajaq* frame for Doug Wilkinson at the summer camp on the northwest tip of Aulattivik, Eclipse Sound, North Baffin Island, September 1952. Photo: Joseph Idlout.

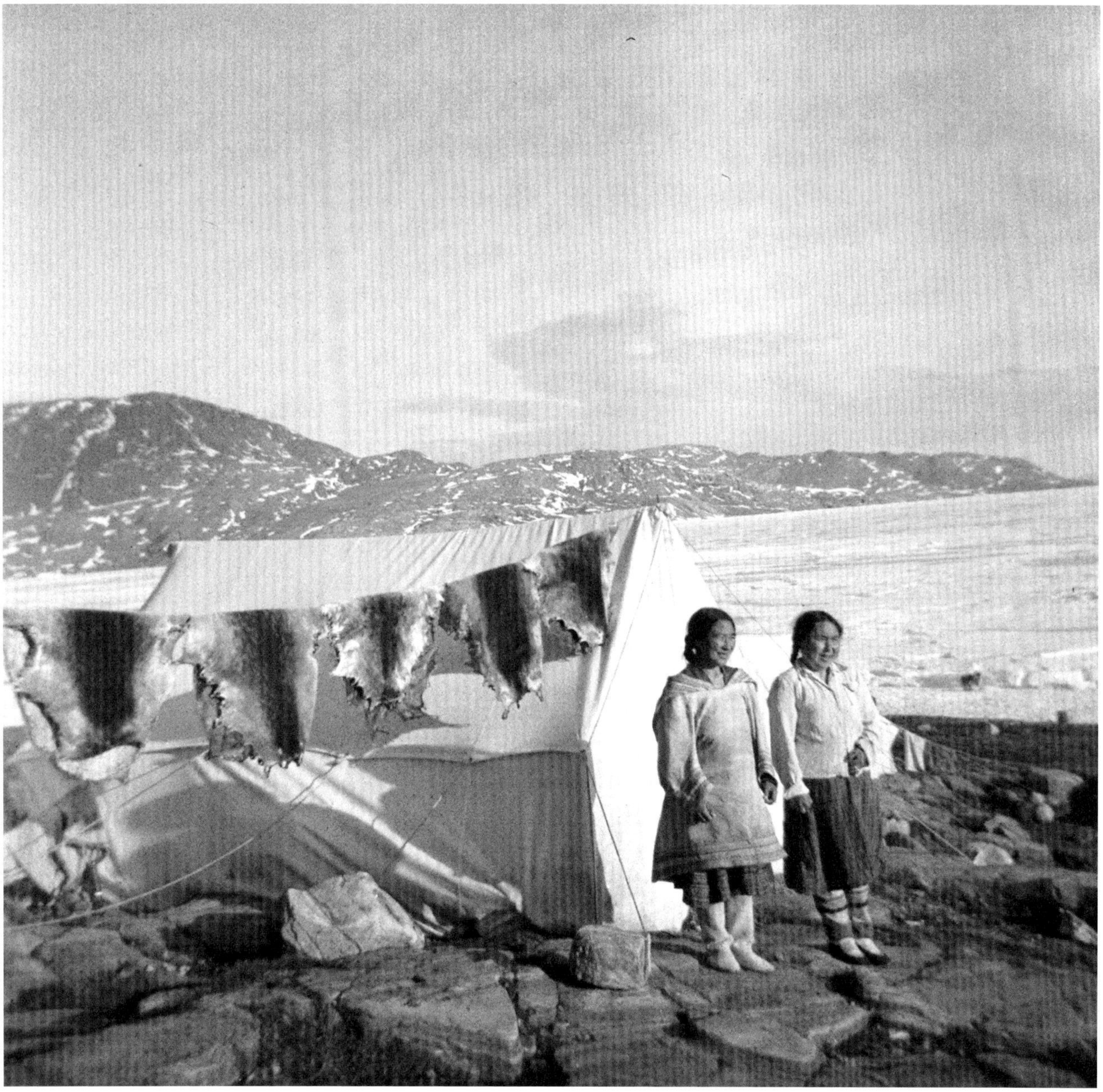

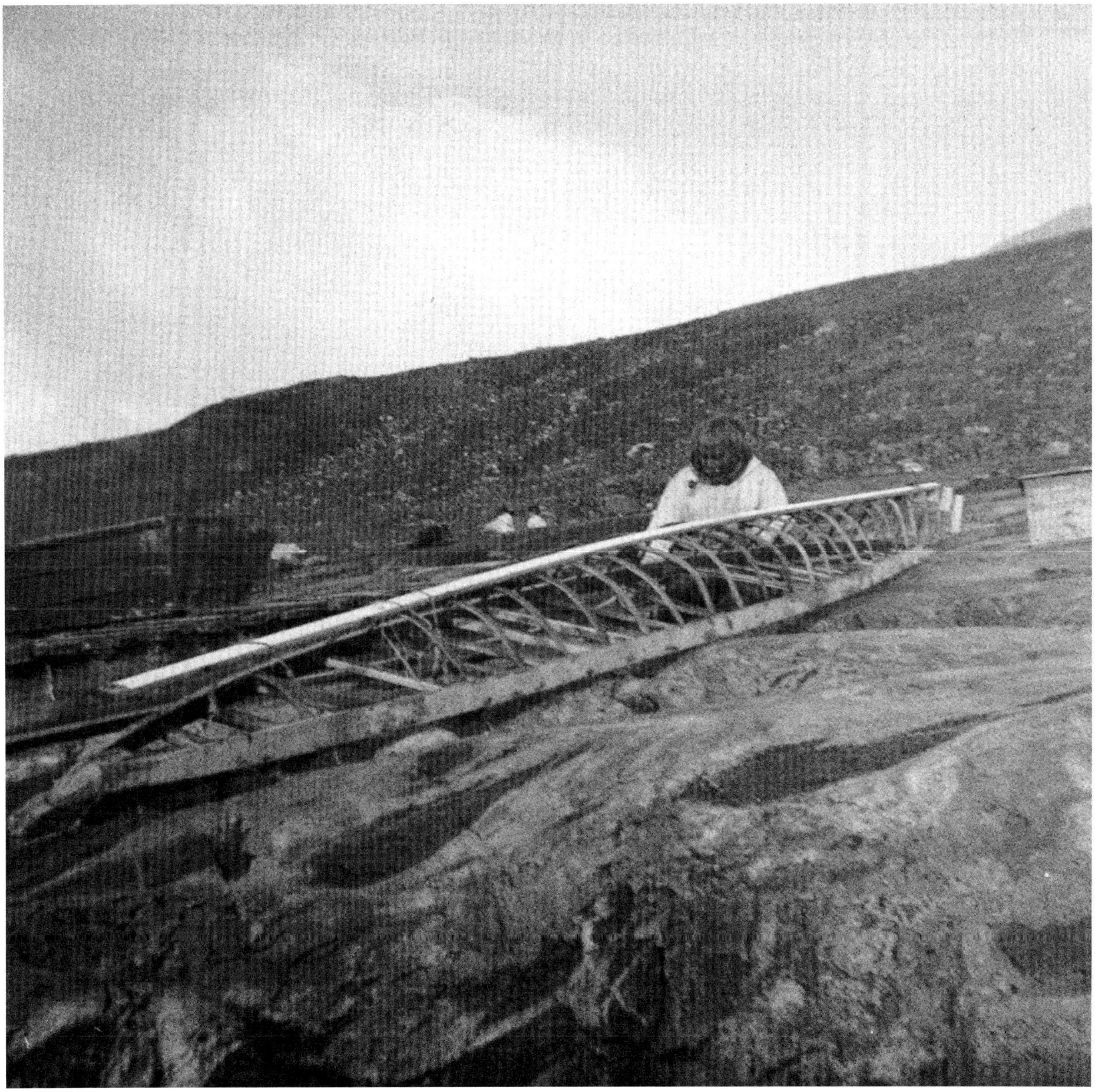

the camera itself in all of these images is a constant reminder of the principle of *qanuqtuurniq*; Idlout and his community were resourceful in adapting the technology of the camera and using it in Inuit ways. Inuit believe that change and struggle are a part of life. They cannot be avoided, but it is possible to thrive by adhering to principles such as *qanuqtuurniq*.

A close look at Idlout's photographs also demonstrates Inuit methods and beliefs surrounding the passing of knowledge and skills onto the next generation. This approach is characterized by the IQ principle of *pilimmaksarniq/pijariuqsarniq*, which represents the development and mastering of skills through observation, mentorship, practice, and effort. Traditionally, Inuit children were encouraged to observe skilled adults and Elders as they completed tasks in order to learn. As children became familiar with the steps involved, they began to practise on smaller versions, or they were given the responsibility of completing smaller tasks as they worked their way up to mastering the skill at hand from beginning to end. Children were also encouraged to learn by using all of their senses – that is, by listening, observing, and practising – as well as to learn through play. Practice, repetition, and progression ensured that the younger generations would be able to accomplish, and one day pass on, the skills necessary to become a contributing member of the camp. Idlout's camera captured many images of children observing mentors. These children closely attend to adults who are often stooped over, busily demonstrating how to properly skin and butcher different animals so that they can be used for food and clothing. In other photographs, children learn by observation how to cut snow blocks to be used for shelter, or they practise carrying babies in their *amautiit*. These photographs depict children as active and contributing members of the community and reflect the importance of passing on tradition (see figure 3.14). *Pilimmaksarniq/pijariuqsarniq* not only builds the confidence of children through the responsibilities that they are given but also fosters their sense of belonging and curiosity. All of these qualities contribute to what Inuit believe creates capable adults.

The final IQ principle, *avatittinnik kamatsiarniq*, extends beyond the community of Inuit to call for respect and care for the land, animals, and environment. Here, Idlout's photographs illustrate how members of the camp practised *avatittinnik kamatsiarniq* through their land use and relations to living things. The Inuit worldview sees humans as part of the natural world and as neither superior to nor less than our animal counterparts. In contrast to southern thought, Inuit believe that humans do not have the right to take as much as they want or do what they please with the natural world. Instead, Inuit believe that we share the responsibility of caring for and respecting our environment and the rights of all other living things that share the planet with us. It is believed that if people follow *avatittinnik kamatsiarniq* and take care of the land, the land will take care of them by providing plentiful game and the resources necessary for survival. On the contrary, mistreating animals or being wasteful will result in negative consequences. Important practices under this principle include leaving the *nuna* better than it was found, taking only as much as is needed to provide for one's family, showing respect to animals even after their death, and using every part of the catch. Idlout's photographs illustrate camp members showing respect and care for the animals and land by utilizing every part of the animal,

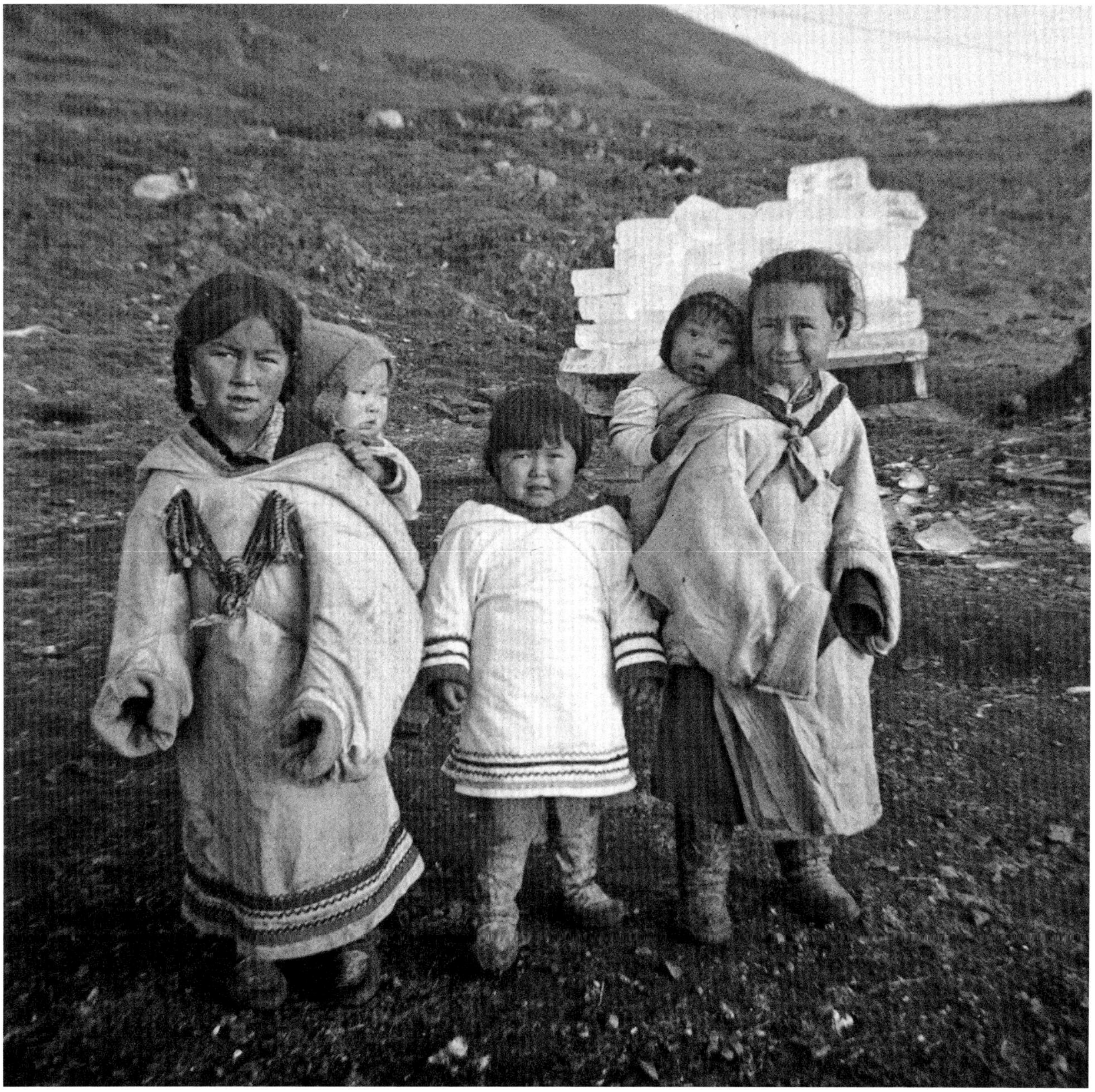

3.14 | Unidentified children at another camp on Eclipse Sound, North Baffin Island, c. 1953. Photo: Joseph Idlout.

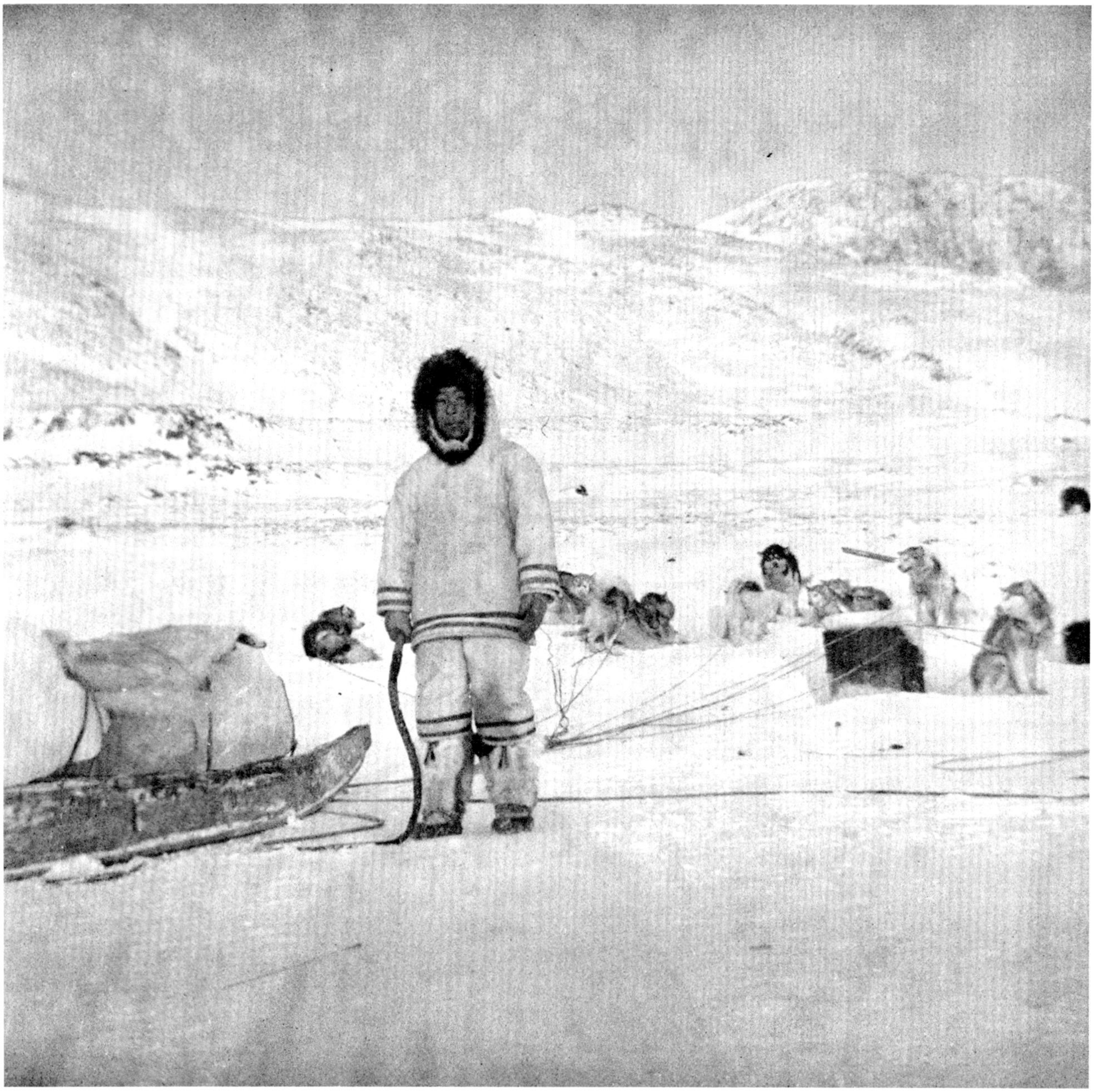

3.15 | Paul Ullatitaq Idlout brings an ice block by sled from a nearby frozen-in berg for water at Idlout's camp, Aulattivik, Eclipse Sound, North Baffin Island, late October 1951. Photo: Joseph Idlout.

including the intestines.[59] But perhaps the best depiction of the close relationship between Inuit and the natural world is seen in their relationships with *qimmiit* (sled dogs) (see figure 3.15). The dogs allowed Inuit to travel long distances to hunt and could guide a hunter home even in the worst *piqsiq* (blizzard).

They also ensured hunters' safety by alerting them to an approaching predator through the dogs' keen senses and loyalty.

Idlout's photographs in Aulattivik and in Nuvurulua were made just as an accelerated southern presence was wielding life-altering changes among Inuit. The images of sled dogs as integral to camp life and representative of the value of *avatittinnik kamatsiarniq*, for example, were made just as the Royal Canadian Mounted Police began to slaughter Inuit sled dogs across Inuit Nunangat. This slaughter of Inuit dog teams from the 1950s until well into the 1960s marks a point of devastating disruption of the relationship between Inuit and the environment. The killing of sled dogs confined Inuit to government settlements, curtailing their ability to freely travel the land and hunt, which in turn impacted the transfer of land-based knowledge and skills to younger generations.

Conclusion

In this co-written chapter, we argue that looking at Idlout's photographs of camp life through the lens of Inuit Qaujimajatuqangit provides a deeper understanding of the relationships between camp members and the *nuna*. Doug Wilkinson introduced Idlout to the southern technology of the camera, supplying him with the Kodak Duaflex camera with which the snapshots were made and instructing him in its use as well as the use of other cameras. But in Aulattivik, the camera became a tool for depicting and reflecting Inuit values. Drawing on the work of Inuk art historian Heather Igloliorte, we examine how the eight IQ principles are evident throughout Idlout's photographs. As a whole, Idlout's photographs demonstrate what it meant to be an Inuit community at the time and the cultural values that underscored every aspect of life. As noted, IQ principles also informed both our organization of the online exhibition *Ajjiliurlagit* and our writing of this chapter. In particular, the principle of *aajiiqatigiinniq* (decision making through discussion and consensus) guided our work together.

The Idlout family and other Inuit saw IQ principles within the photographs too. Leah Idlout d'Argencourt Paulson's November 1976 *Inuit Today* article "Merry Christmas!" – which follows this chapter – includes snapshots, some clearly taken with Idlout's camera.[60] Leah has captioned the photos "at the camp," identifying an image of Idlout, Kidlak, and children as "mom & dad" and another depicting three of her siblings as "brothers." These and the other photographs in the article show the family gathered together and travelling by sled. Leah describes preparations during the month leading up to Christmas: "Even we youngsters would help to skin the foxes and clean them so they would be ready a few days before Christmas. The grandparents would have more fox skins than usual to dry and clean. This was really fun and it was enjoyable for everyone to be so busy. It was the first signal of the happy Christmas we were going to have." In photographs, words, and memories, the Idlout family followed the principles of Inuit Qaujimajatuqangit to live in harmony together and with the *nuna*.

In the Idlout Family's Words 3

Leah Idlout d'Argencourt, "Merry Christmas!" *Inuit Today* 5, no. 10 (November 1976): 38–40, with photographs attributed to Joseph Idlout

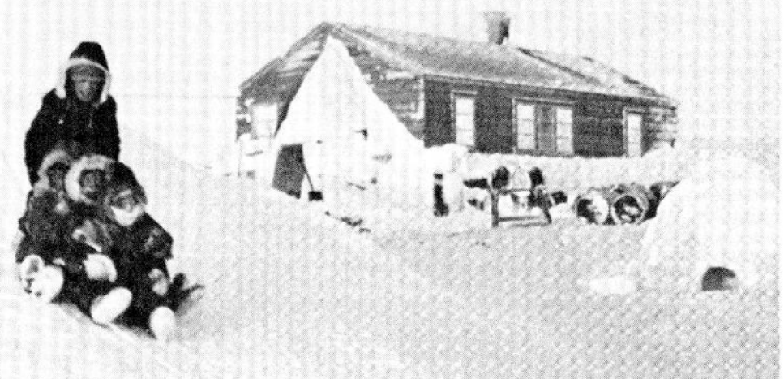

ᒥᐊᓕ ᑲᓚᓯᒪᓯ!

ᓕᐊ ᐃᑦᓚᕐᒥᑦ

ᕐᑯᕕᐊᓱᒃᕕᐅᐸ ᑕᕐᒃᑭᓇᓕᕐ ᑕᖕᒪᓂ ᐊᐅᓚᕐᑎᕕᖕᒥᐅᑕ ᐅᐤᓗᑕ ᒥᕐᑎᒪᑕᓕᐅᐸ ᕐᑲᓂᒥᔭᓂ ᐅᑮᕕᕐᑎᕐᓂ ᓄᑕᕋᐅ ᑎᐤᓗᖕᒪ ᓄᓇᕐᑲᓚᐅᕐᓯᒪᒪᑦᑕ, ᐊᖕᒍᑎᑦ ᑎᓇᒪᓂᐊᕋᓯ ᒃᑐᑦ ᐊᑯᓂᒃᑲᑦᓂᐊᓗᒃ ᐊᐅᐤᓚᕐᓯᒪᕙᓕᓚᐅᕐᓯᒪᔪᑦ. ᐊᒥᐅᑎᑳᒃᑲᑦᓂᕋᓯᐊᕐᓗᑎᒃ ᑎᓇᒪᓂᐊᓂᒃ ᓂᐅᕐᐳᑎᒃᓴᒥ ᖕᓂᒃ ᑲᒪᐸᓂᒃᑯᑦᓄᑦ. ᐃᓚᖕᒥᑦᓗ ᐃᕐᑲᐤᓕᐊᕐᑎᑕᐅ ᐤᓗᑎᒃ, ᓇᑦᑎᕋᓯᒥᐊᕐᑐᐤᓗ, ᕐᑭᖕᓂᕐᓯᓇᐊᕐᑐᐤᓗ ᒪᒃᑖᓂᒃ, ᐊᒪᓗ ᑐᒃᑐᐃᓯᕐᑐᑦ.

ᐅᕙᒍᐤᓘᑦᓃᑦ ᓯᐳ ᑦᑎᑎᒍᑦ ᐄᒃᑐᕐᑲᑕᐅᕙᓕᕐᓗᑕ ᑎ ᓇᒪᓂᐊᓂ ᓴᓗᒪᕐᓴᕐᓗᒥᑦᓗ ᐱᔮᕐᑎᓇᓇᓯᐊᕐᑎᐤᓗᒥᑦ ᕐᑯᕕᐊᓱᒃᕕᐅᐸ ᓯᕗᓂᑦᑎᐊᑯᓗᐊᒍᑦ. ᓂᖕᒥᐅᒃᑯᒃᑲ ᐃᑦᑐᒃᑯᒃᑲ ᐊᒥᕐᑯᓯᔭᕐᓂᕐᐸᐅᕐᑲᑦᑕᓚᐅᕐᑐᑦ ᐸᓂᕐᑎ ᓇᓇᓯᒃᑐᑦ ᐅᕐᓯᐃᔭᐃᐤᓗᑎᒃᓗ ᕐᑯᐃᓂᓂᐊᓗᖕᒥᑦᓂᒃ. ᑕᒪᑦᓇ ᕐᑯᕕᐊᕙᕐᐸᓚᐅᕐᑐᕐᒃ ᑐᐊᕕᕈᔭᓕᕐᓗᑕᓗ ᑕᒪᑦ ᑕᑦᑎᐊᕐᒃ. ᕐᑯᕕᐊᓱᒃᕕᐅᑦᑎᐊᕐᓂᐊᕐ ᑐᐊᑦᓅᓕᕐᒥᖕᒪᑦ ᑲᑦᔮᕐᓇᕐᓯᑦᓴᑎᒥᕐ ᑳᓚᐅᕐᓯᒪᖕᒪᒍ.

ᓄᓇᑦᑎᑦᓂ ᓂᐅᕕᓇᐊᕐᐸᓚᐅᖕᒥᒪᒪᑕᓕ ᐊᑐᓂᑦ ᕐᑯ ᕕᐊᔫᑎᒃᓴᓂᒪᔪᐊᕐᓗᑎᒃ. ᐊᖕᒍᑏᑦᓇᐃᑦ ᑕᐃᒪ ᕐᑲᐤ ᒍᓇᑦᔨᐊᕐᓂᐊᕐᓗᑎᒃ ᓂᐅᕕᕐᑎᒃᑯᑦᓄᑦ ᕐᑯᕕᐊᓱᒃᕕᒃᓯ ᐅᑎᓴᐃᔪᕐᑐᑦ ᓂᐅᕕᓇᐊᕐᓗᑎᒃ. ᐅᐊᑦᓇᕈᖕᒫ ᐅᑎᑦ ᓚᕐᒪᑕ ᐊᓕᐊᓇᐃᕐᕈᖕᒪ ᓇᒃᓴᑲᐤᓚᒃᑐᐊᓗᐃᑦ ᑕᑯᓕᒪᓇ ᖕᒥᑦᑐᓂᒃ ᕐᑲᐤᓗᓈᐤᓗ ᓂᕐᑭᖕᒥᑦᓂᒃ ᐊᑭᓄᕐᕋᓂᒃᓗ ᓴᓇᓯᒪᕙᒦᕐ ᑐᐊᑦᓄᖕᓂᒃ ᓇᒃᓴᑲᐤᓚᒃᓗᑎᒃ.

ᓇᐹᕐ ᑐᕐ ᑲᕐᒃᐸᓚᐅᖕᒥᑦᓇᑦᑕᓕ ᕐᑯᕕᐊᓱᒃᕕᒃᓯᐅᑎᓂᒃ ᓄᓇᑦᑎᑦᓂ ᕐᑲᐤᓗᓈᕐᑲᖕᒥᑦᑐᕐᒥᐅᖕᒎᐤᓗᑕ, ᑕᒪᒃᑯ ᓂᖕᒫᓗᑦᓃᑦ ᓈᕐᑐᖕᒍᐊᓂᒃ ᐱᑕᕐᑲᕐᒃᐸᓚᐅᖕᒥᒪᒪᑦ ᐊᒃᓗᓂᕐ ᒎᖕᒥᑦᔫᒪᓗᐊᕐᒃ, ᐱᑕᕐ ᑲᕐᒃᐸᓚᐅᖕᒥᔪᑦ ᓂᐅ ᕕᐊᒃᓴᓂᒃ, ᑭᖕᒍᕐᐸᓚᐅᖕᒥᑕᕗᐤᓘᑦᓃᑦ ᓱᖕᒥᐅᖕ ᒪᒪᑦᑕ. ᐅᐊᑦᓇᕕᓂᕐᖕ ᒫᕐ ᑯᕕᐊᓱᒻᕕᐅᓕᖅᒪᑦ ᕐᑲᐤᓗ ᓈᑦ ᓄᓇᖕᒪᑦᓂ ᓵᓇᑕ ᑲᓚᐅᓯᕐ ᑲᒡᒍᒡᒪᑕ ᑕᐃᒪᒎᕐᒃ ᐅ ᑭᐅᕐᑕᕐᔫᐸ ᕐᑭᑎᐊᓗᐊᓂᑦ ᓯᑯᐃᕐᐸᖕᒥᑦᑐᒥᑦ ᐱᐤᓗ ᓂ. ᓇᐅᒃᑰᕐᐸᖕᓂᕋᒥᓕᑭᐊᕐᒃ ᕐᑲᐤᓗᓈᑦ ᓄᓇᖕᒪᑦᓄᐊᕐ ᕐᓗᓂ! ᑕᑯᓚᐅᕐᓯᒪᖕᒥᑦᑎᐊᕋᑦᑎᒍᑦ ᓄᑕᕋᐅᑎᐤᓗᖕᒪ ᕐᑲᐅᓯᒪᔭᐅᖕᒥᑦᓗᓂᓗ ᓄᑕᕐᒃᑲᓄᑦ ᐃᓄᖕᓄᑦ.

38

Merry Christmas!

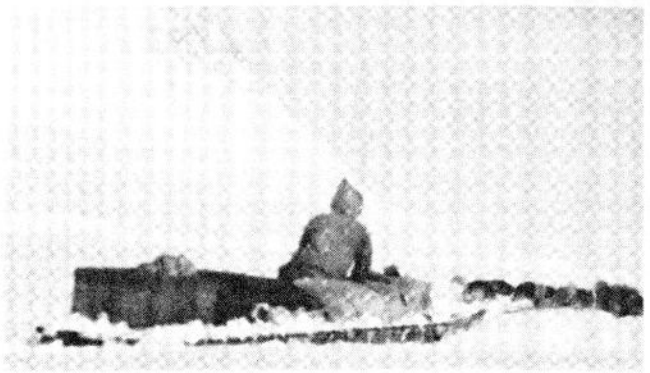

by Leah d'Argencourt

During the month before Christmas at Aulatsivik near Pond Inlet where our camp was situated when I was a child, the men would stay out trapping much longer than any other time of year. Their purpose was to get enough white fox pelts to trade with the Hudson's Bay store. Also some of the men would be sent out by the camp leader to get enough fresh Arctic char, seal meat, muktuk (narwhal skin) from the cache, and caribou meat.

Even we youngsters would help to skin the foxes and clean them so they would be ready a few days before Christmas. The grandparents would have more fox skins than usual to dry and clean. This was really fun and it was enjoyable for everyone to be so busy. It was the first signal of the happy Christmas we were going to have.

In our camp it was not possible for all the members of the family to go Christmas shopping for gifts. This was done only by the men, who would go to the Hudson's Bay store in the settlement. It was always surprising to see the things they brought back with them: unusual gifts that included special Qadlunaat food and machine-made clothing.

We had no Christmas trees in the camp, not even artificial ones. This was not because we were poor, it was just that there were none to be had at the Hudson's Bay store, and we didn't miss them.

A funny part of Christmas down South is that Santa Claus is supposed to come from the North Pole. I don't know which way he took on his way down south! We never saw him during my childhood, nor was he known by many Inuit children.

The night before Christmas, like children everywhere, we always had to go to bed before our parents so we would be bright and early getting up. The most important part was to rejoice and celebrate the birthday of our Lord Jesus Christ.

There is one Christmas I will never forget. That particular Christmas morning I woke up happy and feeling good to be with my loving parents. To my surprise they had hidden a Christmas gift between my duffle parka and the

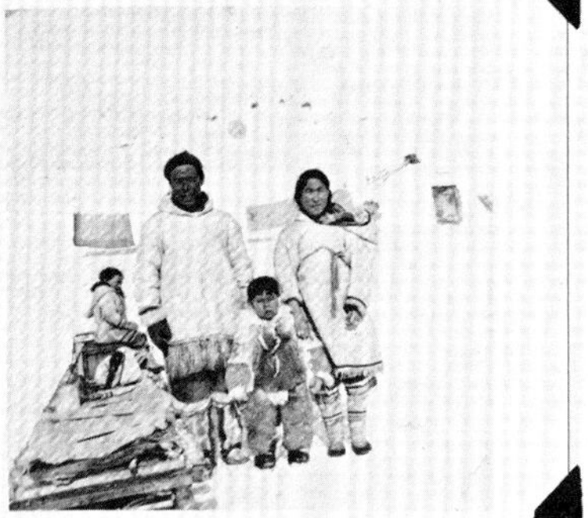

ᐊᑕᑕᒪ ᐊᓇᓇᒪᓗ
mom & dad

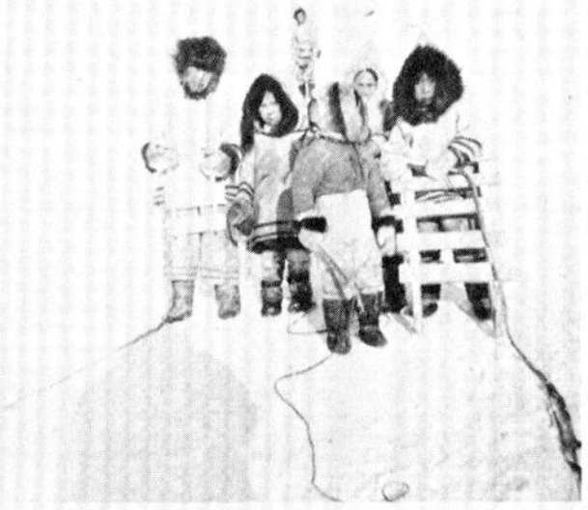

at the camp

ᐊᓂᑲ

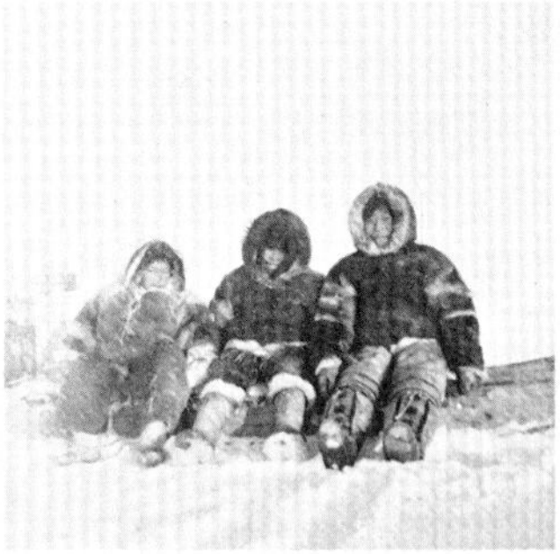

brothers

ᑲᐊ ᐃᓚᐅ

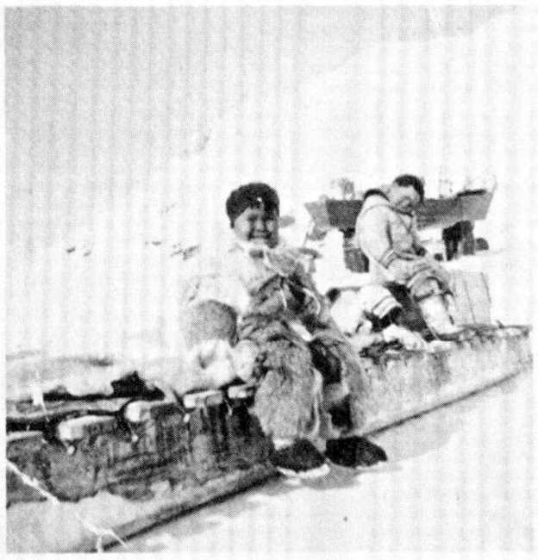

ᑲᓇᑎᓂ
ᐊᐅᓚᑎᕕᒥ

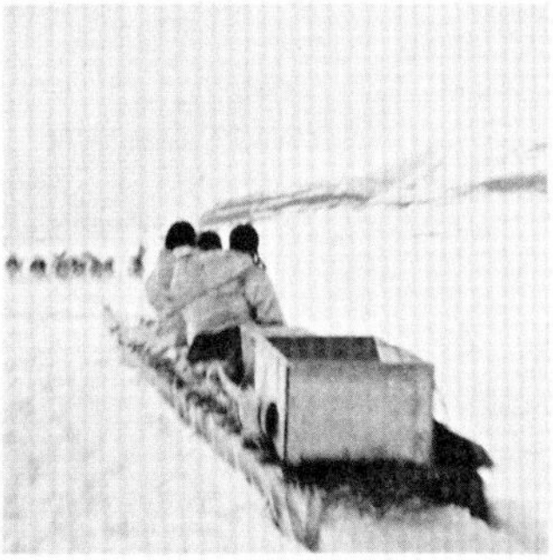

ᐅᑦᓄᐊᓂ ᕿᐱᐊᓱᒃᐱᐅᓂᐊᖏᖦᑎᓐᓗᒍ ᖃᐅᒃᐸᑦ, ᓄᑦᖅᑲᑎᒍᑦ ᑕᐃᒪᓐᓇᑦᑕᐅᖅ ᓇᓂᒥᐅᓚᒫᑎᑐᑦ, ᓯᓂᒐᓱ ᒥᐊᕐ ᑲᓕᕐᐸᓗᐅᕐᓯᒪᒐᑦᑕ ᐋᓐ ᒐᔪᖅᑳᕗᑦ ᒪᑭᑕᑎᓐᓗᒥᑦ ᓱᓕ ᐅᓐᓛᕈᕐᓂᐊᕋᑦᑕ ᒪᑭᖅᑳᕐᖕ ᒐᐅᑎᐅᓂᐊᕋᑦᑕ. ᕿᐱᐊᓱᒃᐱᒃᓯᐅᕈᑎᕐ ᑲᓗᐊᐸᓗᐅᕋᑦᑕᓕ ᐳᓱᓯᐅᐸ ᐃᓅᐱ ᐊ ᓇᓐᓕᐅᑎᖕᒪᑦ.

ᑕᐃᒪ ᐸᐃᒍᕈ ᓐᓇᖕᒋᓗᐊᕐ ᑕᕋ ᕿᐱᐊᓱᒐᐱᖕᒥᒃᓗ ᐃᖅᑲᐅᒪᓕᓐᐊᕐᖕ ᒐᐅᑎᒥᔫᔮᕐᓗᒍ. ᐅᓛᖕ ᒐᒍᑦ ᕿᐱᐊ ᓱᒐᐱᐅᐸ ᐃᖅᑯᒪᓚᓐᓇᒪ ᕿᐱᐊᓱᒃᑐᐊᑦᓅᓐᓗᖕᒐ ᐊᒻ ᒪᓗ ᐋᑦᑕᒃ ᑯᑎᑦᓃᑦᑐᐋᑦᓗᖕᒐ. ᕿᐱᐋᓱᓯᐊᕐᑐᐊᑦ ᓅᓚᐅᕐᓯᒪᒐᒪ ᕿᑯᓪᑕᐅᔭᒪ ᑲᒥᖕᒪᓗ ᐊᑭᓯᓐᔭᒪ ᐃᒻ ᒧᐋᓃᑦᓗᓂ ᑲᒪᓇᓚᐅᕐᓯᒪᕗᖅ. ᖃᓄᐊᓗᑭᐊᖅ ᐋᑕᒪ ᐋᓈᒪᓘᑦᓃᑦ ᑐᐸᓚᐅᕐᓂᖕᒥᑦᑎᐊᕐᓗᖕᒐ ᐊᑭᓯᓐᔭᒪ ᐃᒻᒧᐋᕐ ᑕᐱᓂᖕᒐ.

ᒥᐊᓕ ᑲᓖᓯᒪᓯ! ᒥᐊᓕ ᑲᓖᓯᒪᓯ! ᒥᐊᓕ ᑲᓖᓯᒪᓯ! ᑎᓴᒪᐅᔪᕐ ᔫᔪᒃᓴᐅᔪᐱᓂᐅᔪᒍᑦ ᓯᐊᒃᓗᑕ ᓯᓂᒃᑐᒍᑦ ᐃ ᒐᓕᕐᒥ ᓯᓂᒃᐱᑐᐃᑦᓇᕐᒥᒃ ᓯᓂᒃᐱᕐᑲᕐᑲᑦᑕᖕᒥᓱᖕᒐᕐ ᓗᑕ. ᓂᒐᓚᓱᒃᑐᑭᓐᓗᓂ ᑖᕋᓗᒃᓗᓂᓗ ᕿᐱᐊᓱᒃᐱᒃᑯᑦ ᐅᓛᖕᒍᔪᖅ ᓯᕗᓐᓕᕐᐸᓗᖕᒐ ᒪᑭᑦᑐᒪᔪᑦᑏᕐᑐᖕᒐ. ᕿᐱᐊᓱᒃᐱᒃᓯᐅᕐᑐᐊᑦᓄᒐᑦᑕ ᑭᓯᐊᓂ ᓱᕐᑯᑕᐅᔪᑦᓂᓐ ᓐᓗᓂ ᒪᑭᖅᑳᕐᓱᒃᐸᓗᐅᕐᓯᒪᒐᑦᑕ ᐸᓚᕋᑦᓂᐊᕋᑦᑕ ᑕ ᓯᐅᕐᑲᑦᑖᓇᐊᕐᑐᕐᓗᑕ ᓯᓚᖅᑲᑎᑦᑎᓄᑦ.....

ᐋᐃᑦᑖ! ᑲᒥᒍᑦᓇᖕᒥᒃᑯᓚᒃᓗᖕᒐᓕ ᑕᕝᕙ, ᒥᕐᓱ ᕐᓯᒪᔪᐋᓗᖕᒪᑎᒃ ᑲᓈᖕᒐᒍᑦ ᐊᓕᕐᓱᒃᑲᒃ. ᑕᕝᕙᐃᑦᓇ ᐊᓂᕈᓗᒃᑲᖕᒐᓯ ᐱᓕᕆᔪᐱᓂᒃ! ᐅᐊᑦᓈᖕᒥᓛᒃ, ᒪᑭᖅᑳ ᕐᓂᕐᐸᐅᔭᓇᐊᕐᑲᕋᒪ ᐱᒥᐊᖖᕋᓱᑐᐃᑦᓇᓕᕐᓚᖕᒐ! ᓂᖕ ᒐᒃᐱᒃᓴᐅᖕᒥᓯᒪᕗᖅ, ᕿᐱᐊᓱᒐᐱᐊᑦᓅᖕᒪᑦ. ᐊᓱᐃ ᓛᕋᑦᓄᒃ! ᐊᓱᐃᓛᕋᑦᓄᒃ ᓯᕗᓐᓕᐅᓐᓯᕈᓘᕗᖕᒐ! ᐅᐊ ᑦᓈ! ᑕᐃᒪᑦᑕᐅᖅ ᑭᓱᑕᕐ ᑲᓕᕋᓗᐊᓇᕙ, ᓂᒃᓕᓇᑲᓐᓚᒃ ᓗᓂ, ᐸᑐᒍᒃᑯᑦ. ᕿᔭᓇᕈᓗᒃ, ᑭᓱᐋᓗᒐᓗᐊᑭᐊᖅ ᑕ ᐃᒪᐅᑦᓚ-ᕋᓗᐊᓴᕙᖅ? ᐅᖅᑯᒻᒥᐊᒐᐃᑦ ᑎᓯᔪᑦ ᐊᒻᒪ ᓗ ᐸᐅᕐᖕ ᒑᓗᐃᑦ ᕿᑭᕐᓂᕐᑕᐃᑦ ᐱᓗᕐᓂᒃ ᓂᐱᔪᒪᐅᑲᓐ ᓚᒃᓗᑎᒃ ᐃᑭᕐᖕᒍᐊᑦᓃᑦᑐᑦ.

ᑕᕝᕙ ᐊᓂᔪᑦᓇᕐᓯᑕᐃᑦᓇᕋᒪ, ᐃᓚᓕᕐᑐᐋᑦᓗᑕ. ᓂᖕᒥᐅᒃᑯᑎᑦᓄᐊᖅᑳᕐᓂᐊᕐᓗᖕᒐ ᑕᐃᒪ. ᐱᓐᓚᑦᑎᖁᑦ ᓱᓕ ᒪᑯᐊ. , ᑐᓐᖕᒐᓇᕐᑐᐊᑦᓄᐃᑦ ᕿᐱᐊᓱᕈᔫᔭᕐᑐ ᐅᕙᒃᐸᕗᑦ. ᒥᐊᓕ ᑲᓖᓯᒪᓯ! ᑕᓯᐅᕐᑲᑦᑖᕐᓗᑕ. ᑕᐃ ᒪ ᓱᓕ ᐊᓂᐊᐱᒃ ᑯᑎᑦᓄᑦ.

ᐃᓐᖕᒥᓇᐊᕐ ᑐᓕᕐᓗᑕ ᕿᐱᐊᓱᒃᐱᒃᓯᐅᑎᓄᑦ ᐅᓛᒃ ᑯᑦ ᑲᑉᐳᔪᐊᑦᓅᔪᒍᑦ ᕿᐱᐊᐹᑦ. ᑕᐃᒪ ᐱᖕᒍᐊᕐ ᓂᐊ ᓕᕐᓗᑕ, ᐊᒻᒪᓗ ᓂᕆᔪᐋᓕᕐᓗᑕ ᐆᓚᑦᓴᒐᓕᕐᑐᓐᓗ ᒪᑯᐊ, ᓂᕐᑭᑯᓗᔭᐃᑦ ᐱᖕᒪᑕ ᐆᔪᓚᐅᕐᓯᒪᐅᕐᑐᑦ, ᐊ ᒻᒪᓗ ᐋᑦᓂᓯᑕᕐ ᑲᐅᕐᓗᓂ ᐆᑦᑎᓴᐅᕌᕐ ᑐᓂᒃ ᐋᓯᓂᒃᓗ ᐸᐅᕐᖕ ᒐᐅᓴᕐ ᑲᐅᕐᓗᑎᒃ ᐊᒻᒪᓗ ᐸᓂᕐᑐᒥᒃ ᐃᒻᒧᓚᐅᕐ ᓯᒪᔪᒥᒃ ᐃᒻᒧᓕᕐᓗᒥᑦ.

ᒫᑦᓇᒃᑯᓐᓘᑦᓃᑦ ᐃᓱᒪᒋᕙᒃᐸᕋ ᕿᐱᐊᓱᒐᐱᒃ ᖃ ᓐᓕᔮᕋᖕᒐᑦ, ᓇᑭᑦᑎᐊᕌᑦᓄᒐᓕᑭᐊᖅ ᑕᑯᓕᒪᓐᖕᒥᑦ ᑐᓂᒃ ᐋᑦᑕᒪ ᕿᐱᐊᓲᑎᒃᓴᓂᕐ ᑲᑦᑕᕐ ᑕᐱᓂᕆᔮᑎᒍᑦ.

ᒥᐊᓕ ᑲᓖᓯᒪᓐᓗᒃ ᑕᒪᑦᓯ ᐅᕐ ᑲᓚᒫᕐ ᑐᓯᒍᑦ.

seal skin boots that I was sleeping on as a pillow. I don't know how my father or mother ever managed to hide it there without waking me up.

Merry Christmas! Merry Christmas! Merry Christmas! There must have been about eight of us sleeping on the sleeping platform. It was a cold dark Christmas morning and I didn't want to be the first one to get up. But it was such a special morning and each child always tried to be the first one to be up and ready to go to the neighbours to shake hands with them.....

Oops! I can't get my seal skin boots on, there is something sewn up in the middle of the sank of my duffle socks. It must be one of my darn brothers again! Oh, I just have to be the first one to be up and ready! What is the use of getting mad? It is such a special day. I made it! I made it before them! Oops! There is something else, very cold, in the tip of my toe. Oh heck, what is it this time? The hard candies and the dried prunes stuck to the caribou hair inside the skin feet of my duffle socks.

When I was finally ready, everybody was full of laughter. The next thing was to go to our grandparents' house. They were still so sleepy, they could hardly open their eyes, but their faces were warm and smiling. Merry Christmas! We shook hands on this very special day. Then we moved on to my second-cousin's house.

The day began with Christmas hymns at a morning gathering. Then on to playing games, and finally eating different kinds of cooked meat, and home-made beans and rice with raisins and powdered milk.

Even now, when it is getting close to Christmas time, I still often wonder where my father managed to find such unusual gifts for me and my brothers.

A very merry Christmas to everyone.

4 Exchanged Gazes and Oversight

Joseph Idlout and Doug Wilkinson (1953–55)

By 1953, when Joseph Idlout and his camp members were visualizing the values of Inuit Qaujimajatuqangit (IQ) through the southern technology of the camera, Doug Wilkinson began contemplating how southerners could become more attuned to Inuit culture. Wilkinson proposed to spend a year at Idlout's camp. He saw this immersive experience as a way to arrive at solutions for what Wilkinson considered a contemporary crisis in Inuit life brought about by an increased southern presence in the Arctic and by the collapse of the fur trade. He argued that southerners working in government administration in the region needed to gain greater knowledge of Inuit culture while also involving Inuit in governance more actively. Wilkinson's year-long sojourn would constitute an "experiment" in immersive learning. Through this trip, as Wilkinson wrote at the time, he would be "bridging" Inuit and southern cultures.[1] In a disturbing assertion of cultural appropriation, Wilkinson stated that he wanted to "go North for the period of one year to live as an Eskimo with an Eskimo group ... I wanted to be accepted as an Eskimo."[2] Wilkinson's approach was both paternalistic and culturally appropriative. But paradoxically, in the early 1950s, such formulations were considered progressive. In privileging Inuit culture, Wilkinson challenged then prevalent assimilationist policies that normalized the south and set expectations for Inuit to adapt to its values. Yet it is crucial to recognize that Wilkinson's "experiment" would be in the service of the south and of the social welfare state's assimilation of Inuit.

One of Wilkinson's chief strategies for being accepted by Inuit was to live among them *without* the constant presence of a camera. By the early 1950s, Wilkinson had already travelled to the Arctic four times to shoot films and still images, and he had participated in the post-production of Arctic films shot by others.[3] As Wilkinson wrote later, his interest in Inuit culture throughout 1951 "was related directly to film."[4] But during the 1953–54 trip, he proposed to "take only my rifle and ammunition, personal clothing, sleeping bag, and my small still camera and film. I had a reputation as a picture taker to play down so I planned to use the camera only rarely for the first few months, and thereafter only when necessary to record important aspects of the trip. I wanted the people with whom I would be living to have no doubts as to why I was in their country."[5]

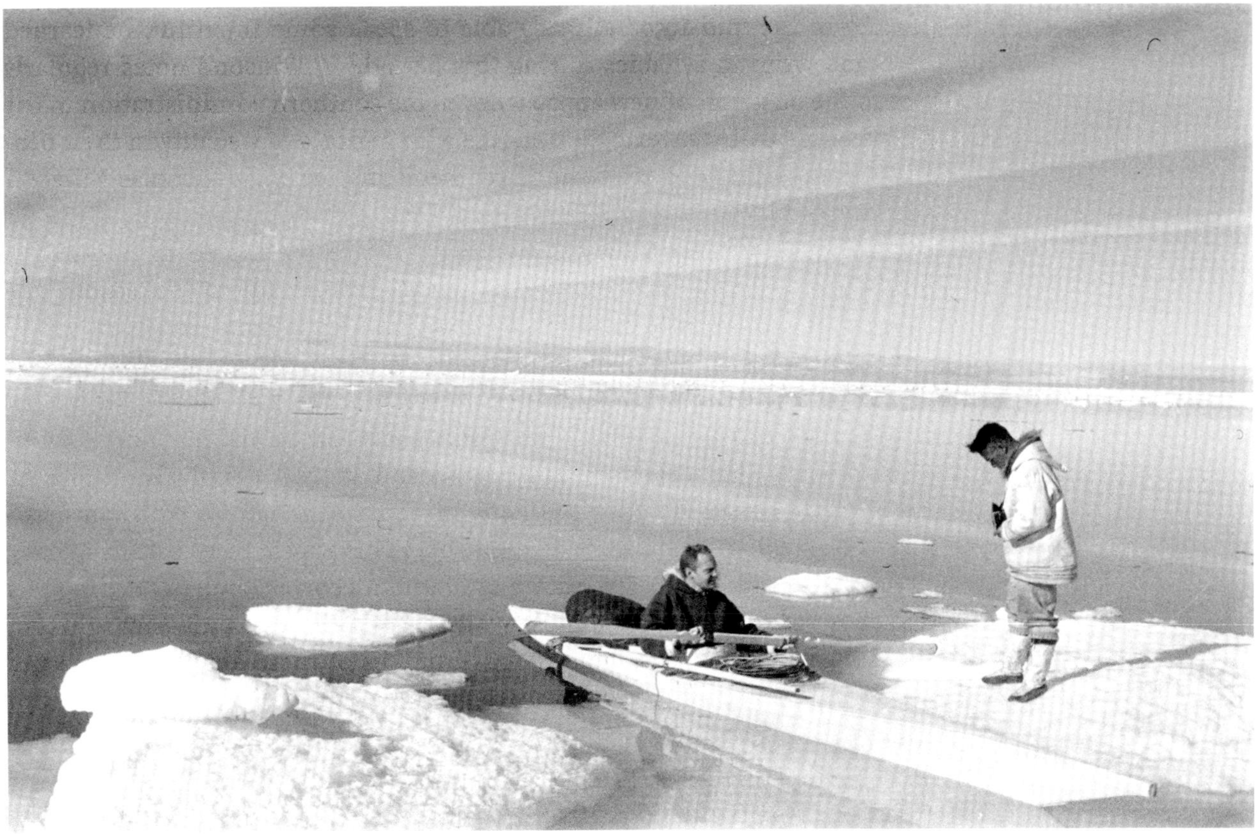

4.1 | Idlout photographing Doug Wilkinson, c. 25 July 1953. Uncredited photo.

What does it mean for Wilkinson to "play down" his "reputation as a picture taker"? What does this assertion suggest about visuality in the Qikiqtani region of the 1950s? Wilkinson seems to have grown aware that Inuit experienced the southern camera as an intrusion. Excessive filming or shooting still photographs, he believed, would inhibit community trust and implicitly distance him from the Inuit community. When Wilkinson states, "I wanted the people with whom I would be living to have no doubts as to why I was in their country," he acknowledges that his earlier presence at Idlout's camp and in other communities was motivated largely by making films and still images for southerners.[6]

With his cameras set aside temporarily, Wilkinson's record of the 1953–54 trip is largely textual and strategic: he was focused on developing policy and protocols for the administration of Inuit life. Although Wilkinson produced some images – including still photographs and four short newsreels – by all accounts, he did "use the camera only rarely for the first few months," or at least more rarely than he had during his previous stays in the north. Instead, Wilkinson wrote. He kept a detailed, daily journal, or field notes, during the thirteen-month sojourn, excerpting and adapting it for publication in a 1955 book and in articles appearing in the mid-1950s. Already able to speak some Inuktitut, he learned to read and write in syllabics during this period.[7] Wilkinson's notes regularly return to the question of new approaches to the southern administration of the region. As a result, these texts, too, engage with regimes of visuality in their proposals for the social management of Inuit life and for what Nicholas Mirzoeff terms "oversight."[8]

As Wilkinson became immersed in Inuit culture, attempted to adapt to it, and reflected on potential governmental interventions, Idlout looked on. The hunter watched the southerner learning to live off the land. To instruct Wilkinson, he employed the IQ principle of *pilimmaksarniq/pijariuqsarniq* (development of skills through observation, mentoring, practice, and effort). The hunter also observed Wilkinson – and other Qallunaat living or visiting North Baffin Island – through the lens of his own camera and, more occasionally, in texts of his own (see figure 4.1). Idlout's perceptions of and negotiations with southerners are embedded in the hunter's own images, in his appearances within Wilkinson's field notes, and in the few examples of Idlout's correspondence during this period. Whereas Wilkinson narrated cultural encounter mainly through text, Idlout did so in images. But Idlout's observations of these foreign visitors and tensions between Inuit and Qallunaat can also be gleaned in the archival record and through the disruptions and silences exercised by Idlout and the camp that Wilkinson recorded in his own notes.

This chapter looks closely at the 1953–54 period when Doug Wilkinson cohabitated with Idlout and his family at their spring and summer camp in Nuvurulua and at their winter camp in Aulattivik.[9] The story of this excursion – including textual and pictorial representations, some appearing in 1954 and 1955 – provides a key episode in the microhistory of Idlout and Wilkinson's relationship, one that stands as an example of Inuit-Qallunaat entanglements during the Sangussaqtauliqtilluta period. To unearth how the two interacted at the time, my examination pairs Wilkinson's perceptions of Inuit life from a southern perspective – articulated in field notes (or diary entries), films, and publications – with Idlout's photographs of southerners, including Wilkinson, as well as with Idlout's texts or interventions in texts. Although I propose that Wilkinson's writing and Idlout's images answered back to one another, we can also see interventions by Idlout, particularly in Wilkinson's field notes. In their immediacy, openness, and sporadic nature, the field notes allow for greater multivocality than more polished texts. That is to say that they not only reveal Wilkinson's perceptions but, between the lines, also make legible Idlout's and his other Inuit hosts' reactions and interventions.

In addressing this thirteen-month period in which Idlout and Wilkinson lived together, my overarching concern in this chapter – as in this book as a whole – is with transcultural encounter and the role of visuality (including textual narrations of the gaze and Nicholas Mirzoeff's concept of "oversight") within these encounters. Whereas the two preceding chapters each concentrate on one of the book's key protagonists, Joseph Idlout and Doug Wilkinson, this chapter presents them together as they exchange gazes. At the same time, this chapter moves from the examination of visual representations (in films and photography) to regimes of visuality, enacted through policy.

Policy and Oversight

After leaving Pond Inlet/Mittimatalik in the fall of 1951, Doug Wilkinson continued to ponder conditions of life for Inuit in the midst of an increasing southern presence.[10] As he later wrote, "The Eskimo was going through a difficult period because of the coming of the white man and his goods. He was now spending five months each year trapping the white fox and using the pelts to buy white man's food and supplies. This dependency on the trading post had robbed him of much of his initiative to hunt food."[11] Wilkinson believed that remedying the situation was a responsibility of the federal government and would spend the next few years devising what he thought would be the best action. These ongoing concerns shaped his 1953–54 trip.

In 1952, Wilkinson submitted a thirty-six-page report on the subject to the Northern Affairs Program,[12] with recommendations that encouraged Inuit traditional hunting patterns, along with a system of governmental intervention. Wilkinson proposed a decentralized system of Canadian governance in the Arctic. Field personnel (initially southerners but later Inuit) would be stationed in various areas across the north and would augment the present efforts of Royal Canadian Mounted Police (RCMP) officers and medical personnel.[13] The *Toronto Star* described his proposal as a "system of colonial government," quoting Wilkinson, who described each administrator as "a governor for his district, responsible only to the head of the administration in Ottawa. He would be the ultimate authority in his district (a very important point). His authority would be based first on law, and second on mutual confidence and esteem of all the whites and Eskimos in the district. He would be a stabilizing force, something sadly lacking at present."[14] Wilkinson's initial comments were aimed at interventions that would stabilize life in the Arctic while responding to Inuit needs as well as southern concerns.

Based on this report, Wilkinson was invited to join the inaugural meeting of the Eskimo Affairs Committee in May 1952.[15] The position of Northern Service officer, established by the committee in 1954 under its new Arctic Division, resembles Wilkinson's initial proposal.[16] Others on the committee shared his interest in "a policy of self-reliance" that would maintain Inuit life based on self-sufficient hunting, with minimal southerner trade.[17] Many scholars, including Alan Marcus, have argued that Inuit self-reliance may have been a key governmental motivation.[18] As the historian Richard Diumbaldo characterizes it, the members of the committee sought to "keep the native native despite the wholesale intrusion of the modern world."[19]

Although Wilkinson believed that southern interventions could provide solutions to the "Eskimo problem," he also argued that such actions were stymied by southerners' ignorance of Inuit life:[20]

> I felt we [southerners] were not helping the Eskimo to help himself, but rather letting him drift with the times; I felt, too, that our lack of initiative stemmed from the fact that we had all too little knowledge of the Eskimo himself, and his daily life on the land as it is lived today.
>
> Before we could do much to help the Eskimo, we should have to know how much of his old culture still remained and what had happened to his personality as an Eskimo. The only way to do so was to go into the country and live in close contact with the Eskimos.[21]

In correspondence of the time, Wilkinson also argued that it was only through such immersion "that we are going to find the solutions to the overall 'Eskimo Problem' of today. Any scheme for the future benefit of the Eskimo must collapse and die of it's [*sic*] own accord unless it is planned and operated by personnel who have a thorough understanding of Eskimo concepts of life (and death for that matter) in his land. More than anything else, the Eskimo needs guidance, guidance which he will only accept from someone he understands and who understands him."[22]

For Wilkinson, then, the first step in addressing the "Eskimo Problem" was to educate governmental representatives in the north about Inuit culture through immersion. His proposal, in a sense, envisioned a reversal of assimilationist policies through the establishment of Inuit culture as the norm to which the south should adapt. Yet, of course, Wilkinson's end goal remained "guidance" in how to adapt to the south and its market economies. He believed in paternalistic governance led by southerners. In short, Wilkinson's proposal remained assimilationist, even if he was more knowledgeable about and respectful toward Inuit culture than many of his contemporaries.

Planning the Trip

Wilkinson proposed himself as a case study for this intensive Inuit education of southerners. He suggested living for at least a year within an Inuit community in order to gain a fuller understanding of Inuit life. This undertaking, he believed, would allow him to make more valuable proposals "to help the Eskimo."

The lengthy trip would be expensive; Wilkinson budgeted fully $3,000 for travel and all related expenses.[23] He received funding for travel from the Arctic Institute of North America (AINA),[24] which had been established in 1945 with a mandate to promote research, amass collections, and disseminate interdisciplinary information about the Arctic.[25] Wilkinson said that he initially requested support from the National Film Board of Canada (NFB), explaining that when this appeal was denied, he resigned. Later, he stated that he left the NFB because there were no funds for films on Indigenous peoples.[26] Yet Wilkinson did not sever his connections with the NFB completely. He supplemented his income during the last month of the trip by shooting footage for four NFB newsreels, with a camera and film stock sent to him by ship in the spring of 1954.[27] Wilkinson also received support from the Department of Northern Affairs and National Resources, where staff endorsed his approach and were interested in his findings. The department put him on salary from 1 July to 1 September 1954 in order to facilitate the completion of his report.[28]

In his grant application to the AINA, Wilkinson adopted an academic tone, calling his project "An Experiment in Social Science among the Tununermiut Eskimos of North Baffin Island." Wilkinson's use of the word "experiment" echoes governmental language and attitudes toward Inuit at this time. Most infamously, as discussed in chapter 1, the relocations of Inuit to the High Arctic, for example, were characterized as "experiments."[29] The research was clearly intended to extend his thinking beyond the 1952 proposal, which Wilkinson considered "an interim document, that may well undergo much change and modification after my return from the next project."[30] As articulated in his grant proposal, Wilkinson's aim during the 1953–54 trip was as follows:

> To live among the Tununermiut Eskimos for a continuous period of eighteen months in order to study their material and social culture with emphasis on four main objectives:
>
> - To study the impact of recent developments on traditional Eskimo practices.
> - Where possible to assist the Eskimo in his adaptation to the changing conditions brought about by recent developments.
> - To propose policies for the more efficient local administration of the Eskimo especially in relation to the increasing pace of northern development.
> - To illustrate and interpret, particularly to the Canadian people, the position of the Eskimo as a Canadian citizen through films and other means.[31]

Throughout his proposal, Wilkinson maintained an interest in the "formulation of a policy for the successful development of the Canadian Eskimo as a full member of the ever growing community of Canada."[32] With this, his fifth trip to the Arctic, Wilkinson was focused on developing Inuit policy for the federal government.

For the 1953–54 trip, Wilkinson chose to live at Idlout's camp on North Baffin Island. He met some resistance in the choice of North Baffin for this research. H.A. Young, deputy minister of resources and development, writing to P.D. Baird of the AINA in 1952, described the people of North Baffin as "healthy, happy, and well adapted to their environment ... I do not think that there would be any really practical purpose served by Mr. Wilkinson's further sojourn among the Eskimos of Pond Inlet."[33] But Wilkinson persisted, telling Baird that he would learn more quickly by living in an environment that was relatively harmonious:

> I am not ready to go to a tough part of the Arctic. I am not ready to go to any part of the Arctic except as a student ... No, I am not ready to teach the Eskimo much of anything as yet. I must first learn, in the best school I can find, and in the shortest time possible. Perhaps I can sum up the position l find myself in, this way. I want to work for the Government, for reasons mentioned here and in my report, and others that must be self evident. However I am not interested in having a job, but rather in doing a job. And to do this job I must have certain qualifications I do not now possess. I want to attain these qualifications as qu[i]ckly as possible and then go on from there.[34]

For Wilkinson, the perception that Idlout and his camp were functioning well made them "the best school" for his "experiment."

Wilkinson envisioned a full immersion in Inuit culture at Idlout's camp. Indeed, his plans to some degree resembled cultural appropriation. In the most striking example, Wilkinson asked Idlout to take him on as "an adopted son."[35] The southerner imagined himself as an Inuk.

Although Wilkinson's cultural appropriation is troubling, there is no question that he and Idlout were close. The two had retained contact since the Wilkinsons' 1951 trip to North Baffin Island. Idlout's second daughter, Leah, spent the spring and summer of 1952 with the Wilkinsons in Gatineau, Quebec, across the Ottawa River from the national capital, following her treatment for tuberculosis in Quebec City.[36] Idlout and his father, Akumalik, were enlisted to prepare equipment for Wilkinson. In a letter reproduced in the 1954 *Photography* article discussed in the preceding chapter, for example, Idlout discusses a *qajaq* (kayak) that Akumalik built for Wilkinson's use during the 1953–54 trip.[37] Yet both men were apparently pragmatic and somewhat guarded about their relationship. For example, the Eastern Arctic Patrol report for 1952, as quoted by historian Shelagh D. Grant, conveys that Idlout was willing to have Wilkinson join his camp "provided he was self-sustaining and was prepared to pay the usual rates for any services that Idlout or other Eskimos may be asked to perform."[38] For his part, Wilkinson initially proposed paying the hunter $250 and stated in a publication that "Idlouk was not to get the money until after I had left the camp, lest it affect life in the camp."[39] However, Wilkinson's financial records from the trip itemize a total of $550 in fees paid out to Idlout in monthly increments plus a $25 gratuity to his wife, Kidlak, among other Inuit.[40]

At camp, while living on the land, Wilkinson would share accommodation with Idlout's immediate family, either in a sod house, tent, or *iglu* (igloo), depending on the time of year.[41] The household included Idlout; his wife, Kidlak; and six of their children, Paniloo (age sixteen), Leah (fourteen), Moses (nine), Pauloosee (seven), Noah (five), and toddler Ruth. The camp also included four other family groups. Idlout's parents, Akumalik and Arnaujaq, formed one family with their adopted sons, Elijah and Danielee. Kadloo and Leetia's family, including five children, formed a third family group. Also at the camp were Idlout's eldest daughter, Rebecca, along with her husband, Qitsualik, and his daughter from a previous marriage. The fifth family group comprised Idlout's eldest son, Paul Ullatitaq, and Ishoogituk. In total, twenty-nine people lived at the camp when Wilkinson arrived.[42]

Idlout and Wilkinson both altered their plans and made what seemed to them at the time to be professional and financial sacrifices to enable the experiment. By 1953, Idlout had agreed to resettle his family to Resolute/Qausuittuq in the High Arctic, as discussed in chapter 6, but he postponed these plans in order to spend the year with Wilkinson on North Baffin.[43] Wilkinson had deferred a job offer from the newly founded Department of Northern Affairs and National Resources, which established six initial Northern Service officer positions. By 1955, however, he would take a position with the Northern Service as an officer.[44]

Wilkinson departed from Toronto, where his family was then living, on 4 April 1953. Initially, Vivian Wilkinson had intended to join her husband in the spring of 1954, but the birth of their daughter, Beverley, in March 1953 prohibited this plan.[45] Doug Wilkinson would go alone. He travelled to North Baffin by train, several military aircraft that were delayed by weather, and two hair-raising dog team trips complete with a polar bear hunt.[46] In the end, the journey took fully ten weeks. It was only on 11 June that Wilkinson finally arrived at the camp with Idlout and his son Paniloo[47] and began trying to live as an Inuk. Wilkinson would remain on North Baffin conducting his "experiment" of living as an Inuk, with only periodic visits to the settlement of Pond Inlet/Mittimatalik.[48]

Field Notes

Wilkinson's diaries or field notes, now in the collection of the Nunavut Archives, provide a rich sense of his daily experiences at camp and his transcultural interactions with Idlout. As Wilkinson wrote to P.D. Baird of the AINA on 25 August 1953, two months after his arrival at camp, "My diaries and notebooks are jam packed with notes and observations. I've made a habit of carrying the notebook with me wherever I go, making on the spot notes of anything that strike[s] me, and right at the time it strikes. This not only applies to the daily life, but to impressions and opinions as they are recorded, even though I may change an opinion later on. Even in the *qajaq* I have a special board rigged up in front of the cockpit to hold my book."[49]

The field notes are copious. Scribbled in ink or pencil, they fill a series of five steno pads, with text scrawled on one side of the paper until reaching the back cover and then continuing on the verso. Often his notes have the continuous flow of "stream of consciousness" writing; at other times, they are brief and episodic. Key insights or observations are underlined or written in upper case, with scrawled arrows indicating paragraph breaks. Reading these journals, the researcher experiences a visceral sense of Wilkinson's presence and fluctuating moods. He seems to have poured all of his immediate perceptions, research, and emotions onto the pages of these small notepads. With its apparently spontaneous and unfiltered comments, the diary reads as a more unmediated reflection of experience than Wilkinson's films and subsequent publications. I highlight the journals because their somewhat unguarded and sporadic nature provides a direct sense of the trip itself while also, I argue, rendering legible Inuit interventions between the lines. Yet these journal entries are, of course, selective textual representations filtered through Wilkinson's experiences and through an always present agenda to develop welfare state policy.

Although chronological, Wilkinson's entries are not systematic. He jumps from one topic to another, documenting events of the day or various thoughts. Yet three broad, often overlapping themes emerge within the notepads. First, reflecting the format of the diary, Wilkinson's notes are self-reflexive. He narrates his own experiences on the journey and adaptations to life on the land. Second, the diary functions as anthropological field notes in which camp life and the people with whom he lives are described in detail. Finally, Wilkinson mulls over and rehearses policy proposals as well as writing about Inuit-Qallunaat relations, all ostensibly for the final report that he had promised the AINA.

Within the pages of these notepads, Wilkinson continuously narrates his own experience during the trip. Across the first few weeks of the notes, for example, he moves from recounting the tedium of travel delays[50] to 1,400 breathless words describing the bear hunt in which he participated while en route from Clyde River.[51] By 15 September, the group had moved to the winter camp, and Wilkinson felt settled in Aulattivik. Camp life was hierarchical and divided rigidly along gender lines. As a "son," Wilkinson was expected to engage in the masculine aspects of daily life: the hunt, care of dogs, and other related duties. Ostensibly afforded little agency, Wilkinson was expected to follow Idlout's (his "father's") directives unquestioningly.[52] Yet Wilkinson's daily routine also indicates that he may have been more absorbed in the life of an observer than in the labours of a son:

> My day usually follows this pattern 1) Up and out for look at weather 2) short diary entry on same 3) ... coffee and bannock 4) ... relief 5) write on book ... 7) work on language 8) lunch 9) syllabics 10) tea ... 12) then reading either ... Book or Freud or some such work ... 15) to sleep. In between there are all sorts of odd jobs to do. Today it was get ice for water. Take pictures of komatik [dog sled], carry back in. Help cut up seal for food and [for] dogs. Oh yes also, one hour each day for school sometime between 3 and 5 o'clock.[53]

Throughout the notes, Wilkinson recounts his own stumbling successes in hunting, living without sunlight, teaching children, and learning to speak Inuktitut and to write in syllabics. But these self-reflexive notes also indicate his private world since Wilkinson includes notes on the books that he is reading, such as those by Vilhjalmur Stefansson and Sigmund Freud, and expresses his own homesickness.

Journal entries addressing Wilkinson's own experience overlap with his observations of camp life. These portions of the diary are closest to the conventions of anthropological field notes. Wilkinson provides the names, ages, appearance, and activities of all camp members, describes other Inuit encountered on hunting trips, and discusses their familial or community connections. Family and camp gatherings, including Sunday prayer meetings led by Idlout, are recounted in detail.

Idlout is the focus of more reflection than anyone other than Wilkinson himself. Indeed, Idlout's name appears in virtually every entry that the southerner made in his field notes. Wilkinson not only describes Idlout hunting, praying, eating, and smoking but also quotes the hunter and posits Idlout as a model Inuk in a new relationship with the south. For the most part, Wilkinson's notes lavish praise on the hunter. He is described as "a remarkable guy," as "head and shoulders and body above any of the other Eskimos around," and in the racialized language that often enters Wilkinson's notebooks, as "one of the people who would advance his race."[54] Although Wilkinson admired the hunter, the strict hierarchies of camp life and Idlout's often autocratic nature also troubled the southerner:

> There is never any doubt ... at all as to who [wins], even if a point is in doubt. It is Idlouk ... It seems that he *must* win and I don't think he is above cheating to accomplish this ... He is ... the big man ... He would make a good boss ... for he is ... resourceful. He knows how to plan. Unfortunately, he does not know how to handle men. He treats his old man and his mother-in-law like dirt. And rarely speaks to Oodlootituk [Ullatitaq]. He doesn't understand why Oodlootituk is so silent with him. But it is easy to see. Oodlootituk is a man but Idlouk refuses to approach him as one. He is still Idlouk's son. He is this way with all others. He does not guide through respect but through ability alone.[55]

Wilkinson's characterizations of interpersonal relationships, like the example above, are filled with judgments and perhaps misinterpretations of relations.

Wilkinson also recounts the elements of daily life: tasks, leisure, interactions. Hunting excursions and techniques fill many pages, and food appears as a fixation across the journals. In all of these entries, Wilkinson absorbs the sights and sounds with a kind of raw amazement. He expresses genuine fondness for most members of the camp, particularly for Idlout's family, yet he complains frequently about hygiene, childrearing, noise, and tedium.

At times, Wilkinson's observations of camp life and of his own experiences expose colonialist attitudes while underscoring the difficulty of his adjustment to camp life.

> I like the people I am with. I am even fond of the land and the sea ... But to be here for a lifetime ... I am trying to get pictures into my head that seem to express the endlessness of this way of life and the lack of progression. Why, why are we alive when our race has been doing the same things for the past 1,000, perhaps ten-thousand years? Panyloo sharpening his knife. My "mother" scraping a skin ... everlasting talk about seals and komatiks, fish and dogs.[56]

Although Wilkinson gained knowledge of Inuit culture, he came away committed to his southern identity and yearning, in his often repeated phrase, to "go outside" (return to the south).[57] Wilkinson left North Baffin Island earlier than he had originally planned. After a final month in Pond Inlet/Mittimatalik shooting newsreels, he hitched a ride to Churchill on the "ski-equipped Dakota aircraft" on which the writer Katharine Scherman and a group of scientists had arrived at Pond Inlet/Mittimatalik.[58]

The experience of living at camp also confirmed Wilkinson's belief that the Inuit needed assistance from the south, although he remained firm that the assistance needed to be attuned to Inuit culture. This paternalistic belief informed the final theme appearing in the field notes. Wilkinson addressed these concerns in lengthy polemics, sometimes written in the relative comfort of the Hudson's Bay Company (HBC) post during his periodic stays in the settlement of Pond Inlet/Mittimatalik. Wilkinson argued that Inuit needed southern assistance "on humanitarian grounds." In making this point, he filled his journals with characterizations of his Inuit hosts that echo the language of social Darwinism, with value placed on modern Western conceptualizations of "progress." The notes are often troubling to read. Wilkinson wrote that the Inuit were "primitive," as they had "stagnated," and he noted, "Here is a group of ... intelligent people who ... [remain] in a state of stagnation while we have gone ahead to our present state of development." He added, "Centuries of stagnation have bred the thought of progress out of the race. Only we can help him put it back again."[59]

As with his 1952 report, Wilkinson's field notes argue for southern governmental intervention and, more specifically, for local settlements to be overseen by government administrators, or Northern Service officers, as they would shortly be known: "All efforts must be concentrated on development of regional headquarters ... Each HQ would have its own regional supervisor appointed by the government."[60] To support this proposal, Wilkinson reflects, often disparagingly, on Qallunaat presently stationed in the region, including personnel of the military,[61] Department of Transport, RCMP, and Hudson's Bay Company, as well as missionaries and bureaucrats in Ottawa. When an HBC staff member at Clyde River, for example, announces that he likes Inuit who "know their place, they act like Eskimos should, they never presume on an acquaintance with the white man," Wilkinson angrily dismisses him as a "bloody ignorant beggar … not intelligent [enough] to see any side of an argument but their own."[62] Wilkinson sees shortcomings across the Qallunaat community in the north: "Even the best of the whites in the country do not do the Eskimo any long term good. Only one who intends to spend life working with them can do this."[63] Six months into the trip, Wilkinson's frustrations extended to the Eskimo Affairs Committee: "And for goodness sake let's not form any more committees with well-intentioned but entirely incompetent panels of members."[64] Many of Wilkinson's rebukes are specifically directed at the RCMP: he charges that the police do not know the very laws that they are enforcing, have too much local authority, and hand out money too freely.[65] In Wilkinson's view, the establishment of regional government officers would rectify these problems. As he pronounced on 25 November 1953, "And of course I believe that there should be administrators to replace police."[66]

Yet Wilkinson also proposes an increase in Inuit involvement in governance. Although Wilkinson's language is often inflected with social Darwinism, he expresses respect for the Inuit he knows and advocates that they should have greater authority. For example, Wilkinson argues for "settlement council[s] – one white council, one Eskimo. Eskimo must come together into small productive units if they are to survive and prosper."[67] Four years later, in 1957, as a Northern Service officer posted at Baker Lake/Qamani'tuaq, Wilkinson would enact this proposal when he established an Inuit-led community council for the hamlet that proved to be a model for other communities.[68] But, again, even such Inuit-involved councils replaced pre-existing Inuit systems of governance with southern models.

Wilkinson's policy notes often focus on an Inuit economy. He outlines the unfairness of the present debt system and proposes the establishment of small industries to stabilize the Inuit economy in the wake of the collapse of the fur trade.[69] In his notes, Wilkinson ponders various possibilities, including handicrafts, but for the Pond Inlet/Mittimatalik region, he focuses on coal mining.[70] These proposals were probably made in response to calls by the Department of Northern Affairs and National Resources for economic projects. As Wilkinson intones, "One of the basic problems of this country is how to develop an internal economy of sorts. For there is only external trade, foxes go out, goods come in. This is no domestic market. Yet I think one could be developed. A domestic market does exist on a primitive scale. You have muktuk [narwhal fat] … This could be expanded to include the White Establishments. An Eskimo fishery to fill need[s] of establishments here rather than present system … The Government can help by assisting purchase power."[71] Throughout the notes, Wilkinson advocates for a southern intervention yet also insists that it be built on a knowledge of Inuit culture and directly engage Inuit in governance. He saw himself – and his model of an administrator – as "bridging" the gap between Inuit and the south and his relationship with Idlout as exemplary of this bridging.[72]

Disrupting the Narrative: Idlout Looks Back

Apart from providing raw accounts of Wilkinson's own experiences and thoughts, his field notes reveal that his Inuit hosts were neither completely accessible to him nor fully contained within the representational space of his notes. Wilkinson's limited comprehension of Inuktitut and his socially reduced status as a "son" (particularly in comparison to Idlout's singular authority at camp) often left him outside the loop of decisions and discussions. Finally, Idlout's ability to represent Wilkinson (and other Qallunaat) in images, negotiations, and some texts challenged presumed hierarchies between them. These dynamics characterized incidences of what Mary Louise Pratt terms "transculturation" in her classic text *Imperial Eyes* (1992).[73] Asserting their own presence, Idlout and the other camp members disrupt Wilkinson's written accounts of the trip.

At times, Wilkinson's rudimentary understanding of Inuktitut left him outside family dynamics. Although the southerner spent his days observing his hosts, he often does not appear to understand fully what he sees and hears. On 18 October 1953, for example, Wilkinson – quietly writing in his journal – narrates an argument he overhears between Kidlak and Idlout:

> A rather interesting thing is taking place. Kulluk [Kidlak] is talking to Idlouk. Her voice is shaky with emotion. I know she is talking about her own life because I can catch many of the references but I can't get the drift of what she is driving at. Idlouk is silent. She is talking a blue streak. I think it is about all the work she has to do around the house and it must be some form of complaint. Now she has stopped and Idlouk is talking. He is much quieter. It is a small crisis of some kind. Wish I knew just what it was all about. I heard lots of references to sewing ... Now Idlouk is referring to bible. He is quoting from same ... Idlouk's father took up the same theme. Something about women ... Sounds as though there is some sort of controversy raging in the camp.[74]

This excerpt is remarkable for underscoring how invasive Wilkinson's position was at the camp. Like any field researcher – including a historical researcher, like me, engaged in reading and analyzing another's private papers – Wilkinson operated, in effect, as a spy, surreptitiously observing and recording.[75] But it also shows that despite his extended proximity to camp members, Wilkinson remained apart from many aspects of their intimate lives. Instances such as this anecdote read like silences or voids in the journals, underscoring the limits of Wilkinson's engagement with his hosts.

Camp members also regularly reversed presumed colonial hierarchies and underscored Wilkinson's otherness in small, routine interactions. Since his 1951 sojourn at the camp – and throughout his subsequent relationship with Idlout, his family, and other Inuit – Wilkinson was known as "Kimmuk," "Qimmiq," or "Kingmik" (dog in Inuktitut). The nickname was a pun derived from the sound of Wilkinson's first name, Doug. According to Inuk Elder David Serkoak, Inuit of the period often gave visitors nicknames.[76] Wilkinson seems to have been good-natured about the teasing. Yet it also must have been a constant reminder of his lowly status at the camp. At other times, camp members teased Wilkinson about his absorption in what he termed the "white man's activities" of writing and photographing.[77] In his later book-length narrative of the trip, for example, Wilkinson recounts an anecdote in which he was so busy photographing a camp feast of *aluk* (animal fat) that no food was left for him. "For many days afterward, this provided humour for all at the camp."[78]

But perhaps the most striking – if subtle – disruptions to Wilkinson's narrative of a southerner taking on an Inuit identity appear in Idlout's photographs and film footage of Qallunaat. Among depictions of family and camp members, Idlout's camera also recorded images of the Qallunaat he and his camp members encountered. These photographs depict southerners stationed at Pond Inlet/Mittimatalik with whom Idlout interacted during visits to the settlement to trade furs, attend church, and participate in community events. The Anglican minister Donald Whitbread, HBC staff, and RCMP officers appear posing for Idlout's camera (see figure 4.2). Idlout's photographs, for example, include a sequence of seven photographs of an HBC clerk – known among Inuit, according to Wilkinson, by the name Angiyuqaaq – testing an outboard motor on a canoe.[79] In some respects, these photographs of Qallunaat reflect the IQ principle of *tunnganarniq* (fostering good spirits by being open, welcoming, and inclusive), as Augatnaaq Eccles and I discuss in chapter 3. These photographs depict southerners being included and welcomed by Idlout family members.

Wilkinson was, of course, among those welcomed with and through the camera. He and Idlout photographed together at camp, with Wilkinson attempting to develop film there.[80] The southerner also taught Idlout to operate a 16 mm camera. The hunter is credited as the cameraman on the troublingly titled five-minute newsreel *The White Eskimo* (1954).[81] The footage, later edited, shows Wilkinson driving a dog team in order to cut and haul ice for camp and helping to feed the dogs. The camera captures the action dynamically from behind, beside, or in front of the *qamutik* (sled).[82] Idlout also shot still photographs of Wilkinson. The southerner is depicted reading to Idlout's children and eating. In July 1953, Wilkinson orchestrated a shoot, later used in the 1954 issue of *Photography* magazine. One of the images, shot with Wilkinson's 35 mm camera by an unidentified figure, shows Idlout photographing Wilkinson (see figure 4.1). The southerner poses in the *qajaq* that Idlout's father, Akumalik, made for him, which Idlout had photographed earlier.[83] Wilkinson is also seen in a photograph with cinematographer Jean Roy and Vivian Wilkinson taken by Idlout aboard the CGS *C.D. Howe* as his daughter Leah was leaving for tuberculosis treatment in the south. This photograph appears in Leah's series of articles for *Inuit Today* magazine about her experience as a patient. An excerpt from the first article in

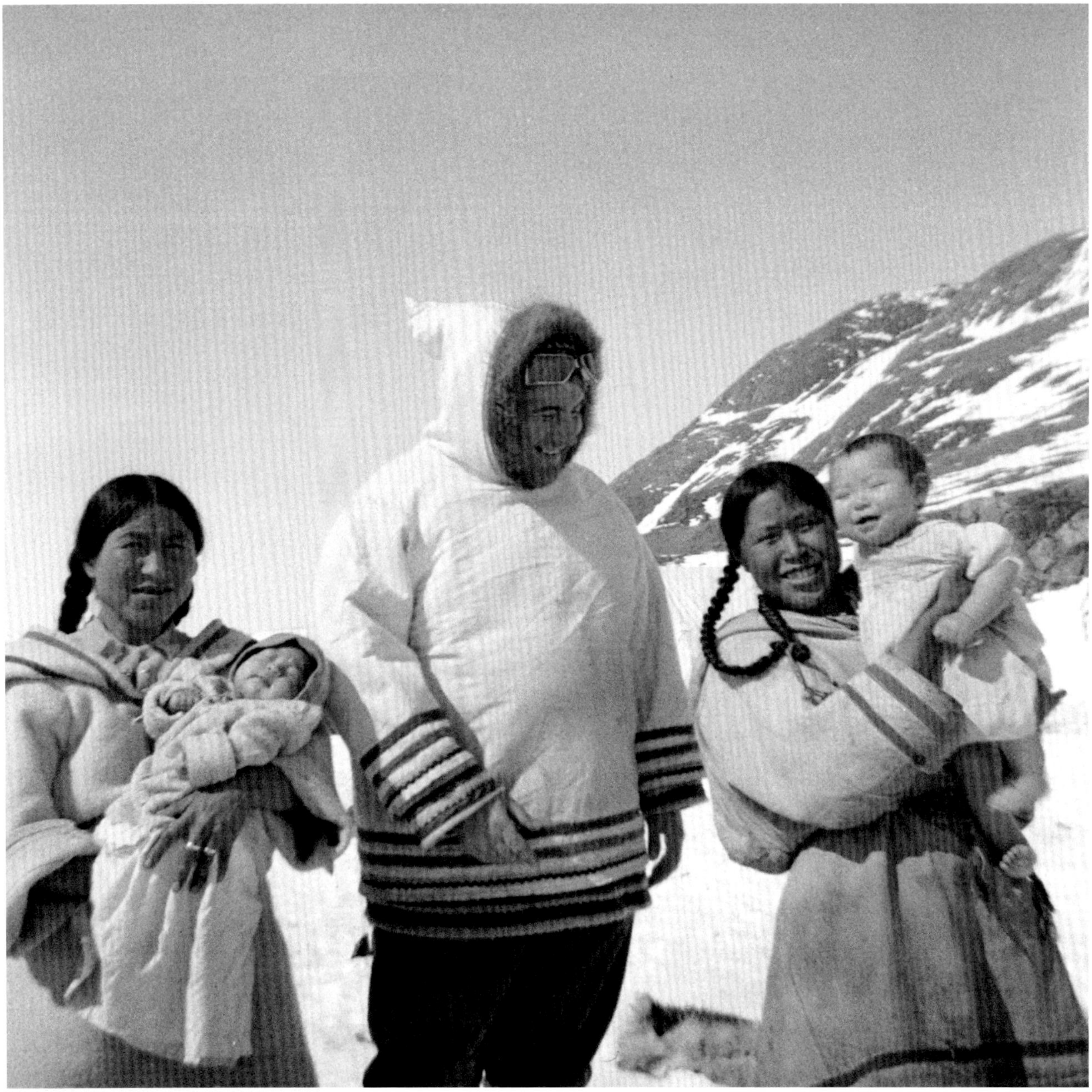

4.2 | Anglican minister Rev. Don Whitbread on a dogsled visit to camp, with Kidlak (Idlout's wife) and baby (*left*), south coast of Aulattivik, Eclipse Sound, North Baffin Island, March 1955. Photo: Joseph Idlout.

4.3 | Breaking summer camp in Nuvurulua, west of Pond Inlet/Mittimatalik, and loading all gear into Idlout's big boat for trip to the main camp in Aulattivik, August 1953. Pictured are Doug Wilkinson by his *qajaq* (*front left*) and Gideon Qitsualik, Herodier Kadluk, and other camp members in the background. Photo: Joseph Idlout.

this series is reproduced following chapter 1, and the final instalment is reproduced following chapter 4.[84]

In another image made with Idlout's camera, dated August 1953, Wilkinson is seen among members of the camp (see figure 4.3). The image shows most members preparing to move from Nuvurulua at the end of summer to their winter camp in Aulattivik. Gideon Qitsualik and Herodier Kadluk are in the foreground on the right passing goods to be placed in Idlout's large boat. Wilkinson is seen

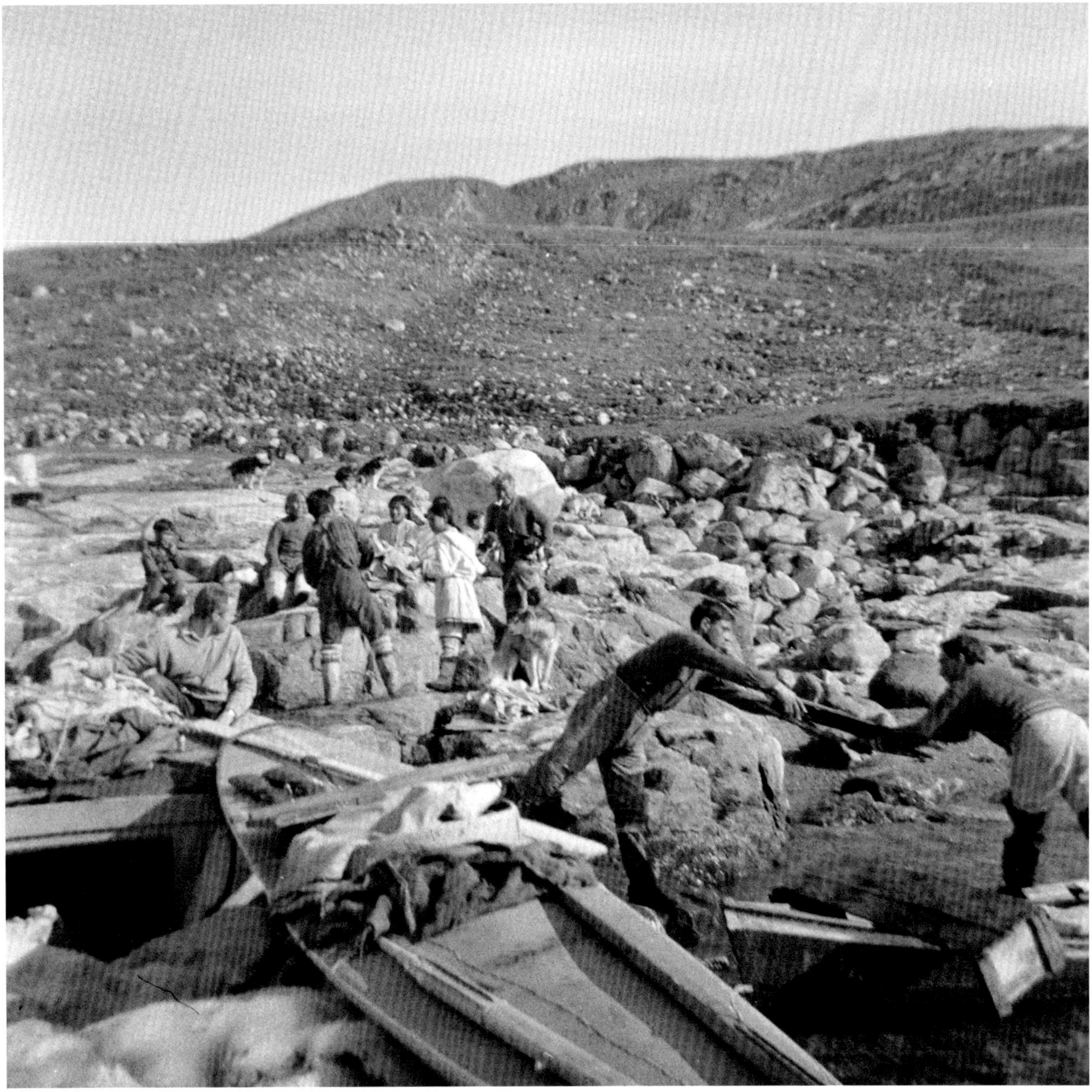

to the left crouched next to the *qajaq* that Akumalik built for him. This photograph, a document of a seasonal transition in camp life, portrays Wilkinson as a member of the camp. The IQ principle of *tunnganarniq* is performed with and for the camera.

Following Wilkinson's departure from camp, Idlout also shot a group of sixteen images depicting the American journalist Katharine Scherman and a team of scientists.[85] As noted, Wilkinson left North Baffin Island earlier than originally planned, catching a ride to Churchill on the aircraft that had brought the American scientists to the area.[86] Idlout and his family, after seeing Wilkinson off, served as guides for six weeks during the spring of 1954 for the American group. It was not uncommon for Inuit to act as guides for visitors, and the work helped to augment their living. In this case, they led the scientists to Bylot Island, across Eclipse Bay from Pond Inlet/Mittimatalik, where the eight southerners – including four biologists and a student – studied water fowl.[87] Idlout's family guided and fed them. Scherman, like Wilkinson, wrote about her experiences in the Arctic. Her 1956 book *Spring on an Arctic Island* describes the Arctic topography and, even more vividly, her reflections about Idlout and his family.[88]

Idlout's photographs of the expedition on Bylot Island feature the visiting biologists, sometimes shown with members of the hunter's family. One posed portrait depicts Kidlak with expedition participant Mary Drury (see figure 4.4). The two lean amiably toward each other, smiling for the camera. Other images show the southerners being introduced to Arctic life. Members of the expedition are seen dressed in Inuit clothing in one photograph. Another image depicts Kidlak showing an unidentified expedition member how to scrape fat from sealskin (see figure 4.5).

What does it mean when the Inuk subject of a southern gaze – represented literally in images as well as in text – turns the camera back on the observer? Many of Idlout's photographs of Qallunaat, including those of the Bylot Island expedition by visiting biologists, seem to feature Inuit culture. Again, following the IQ principle of *tunnganarniq*, they seem to welcome the outsiders. In Idlout's photographs during the Bylot Island expedition, for example, he did not highlight the scientists' own work so much as he put them in contexts that privilege Inuit ways of living. Other photographs by Idlout follow the conventions that Wilkinson would have modelled for the hunter. The portrait of Kidlak with Mary Drury, for example, exemplifies a formally posed portrait. Yet it – and other photographs – pointedly put Inuit and visiting Qallunaat on equal footing. But perhaps above all, the *act* itself of Idlout photographing was highly significant. In taking up the camera, at once a status symbol and indicator of the esteem with which southerners held him, and in subjecting southerners to *his* gaze, Idlout was clearly enacting the assertion of authority over them or claiming reciprocity, even as he welcomed them. Although posing or performing for photographs certainly involves the active agency of sitters, the person behind the lens – directing and framing their performance – possesses a high level of control and

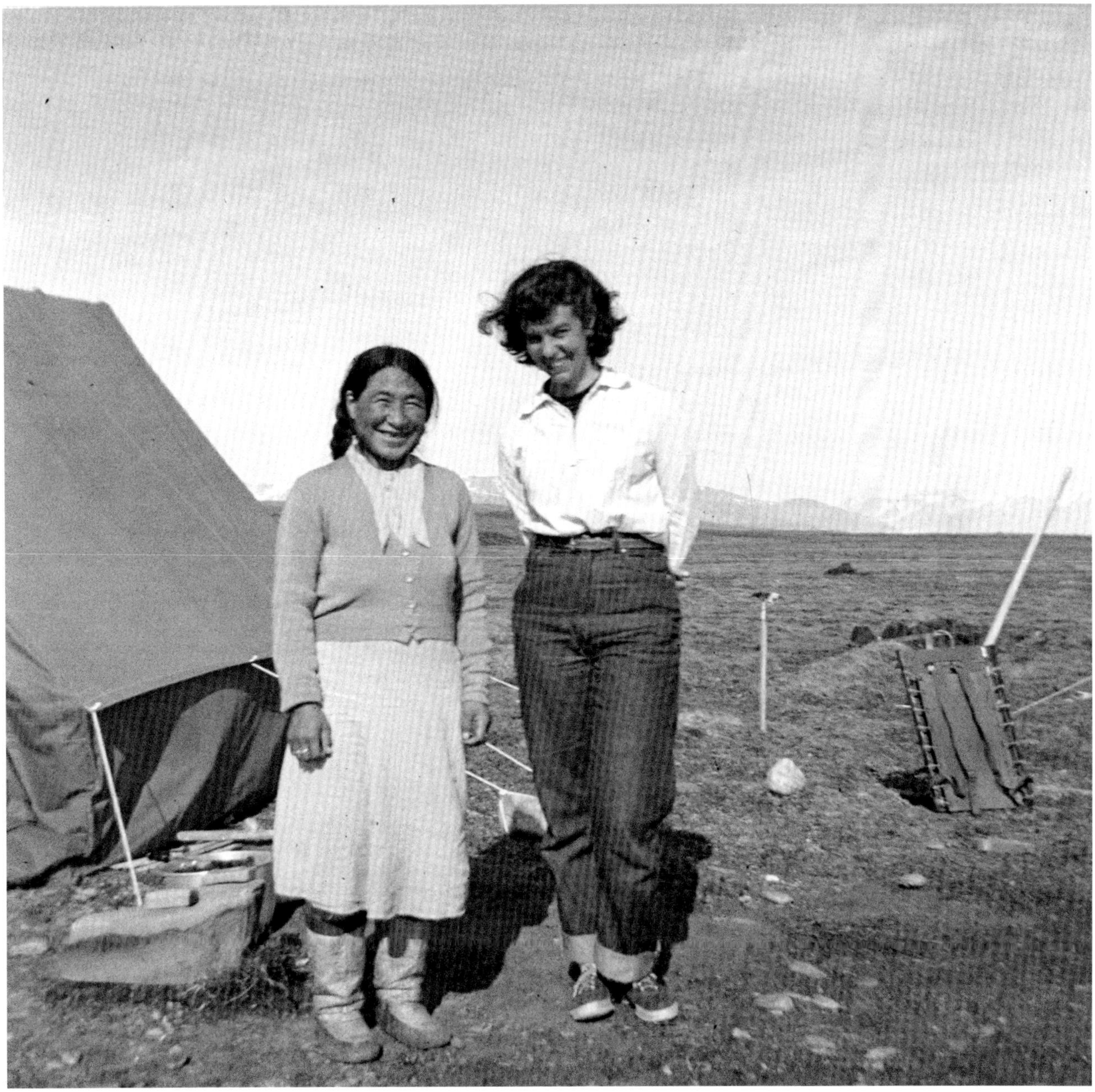

4.4 | Kidlak (Idlout's wife) and Mary Drury (wife of expedition biologist William Drury) pose outside of the Mazzeo Arctic Expedition tent, south coast of Bylot Island, July 1954. Photo: Joseph Idlout.

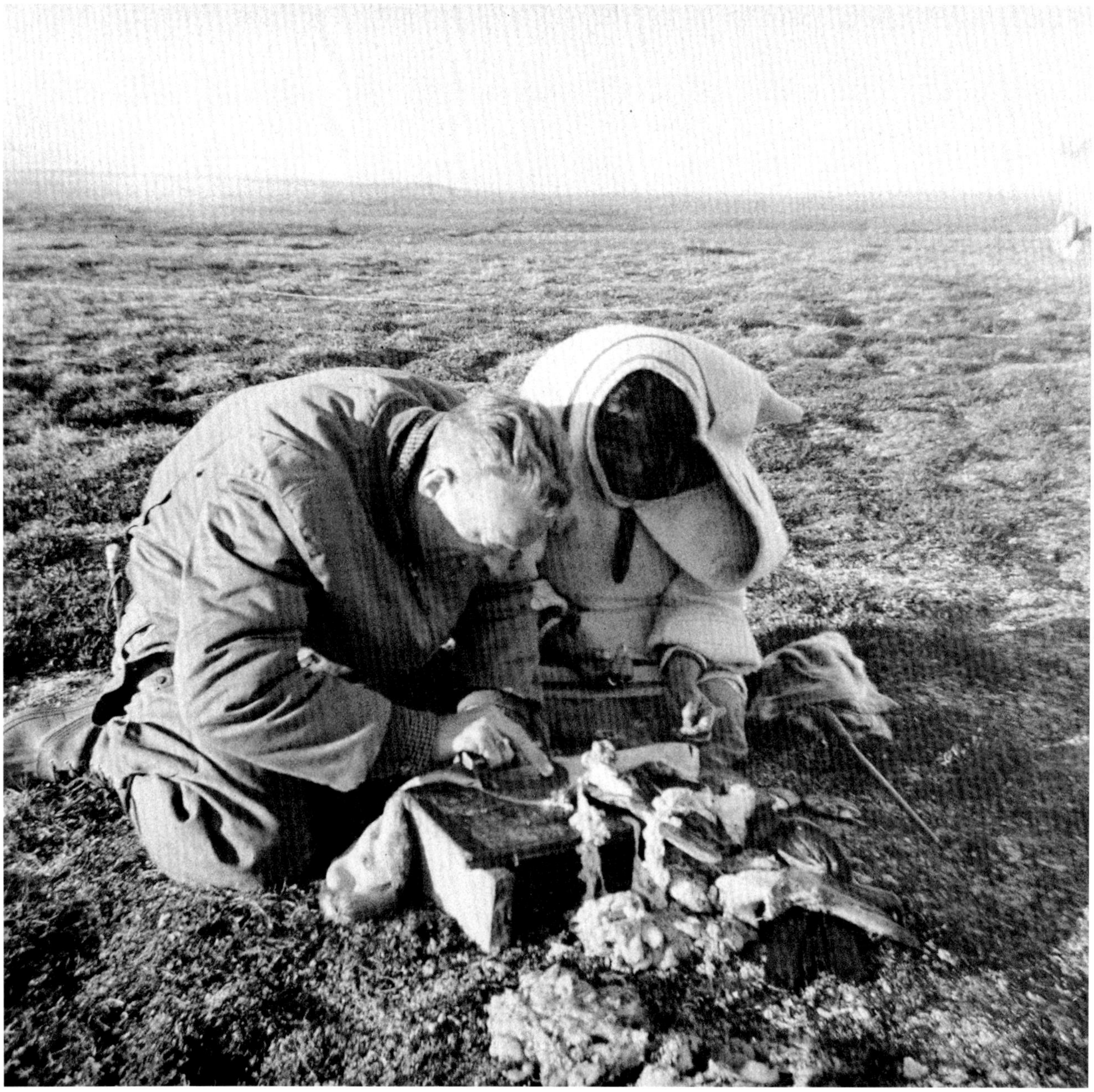

4.5 | Unknown expedition member attempts to scrape fat from sealskin under Kidlak's watchful eye on the inland tundra of the south coast of Bylot Island, July 1954. Photo: Joseph Idlout.

perceived authority. Indeed, the photographer is performing a role too, one that enacts hierarchical control. In claiming this status, Idlout seems to mimic colonial authority itself. In Homi K. Bhabha's familiar phrasing, the hunter quite literally "turn[s] the gaze of the discriminated back upon the eye of power."[89]

To "Go Outside": Wilkinson's 1953–54 Trip in the Southern Imagination

Southern Canadian and international audiences travelled vicariously with Wilkinson on the 1953–54 trip through publications and newsreels. These records included the four short newsreels that Wilkinson made with the crucial aid of Idlout and other camp members during his last month in the north: *Eskimos Mine Their Own Coal* (1954);[90] *Easter in Canadian Arctic* (1955);[91] *Eskimo Gets Medal from the Queen* (1954), on the ceremony at which Idlout was awarded a Coronation Medal;[92] and *The White Eskimo* (1954), recounting Wilkinson's experiences at Idlout's camp.[93] But Wilkinson seems to have focused most fully on published texts. Drawing on the themes that he had loosely articulated in the field notes, these publications are more highly choreographed representations of Wilkinson's own positions. In short, they replace the openness and ambiguities of the field notes with polish and univocality. Wilkinson's publications include some of the same culturally appropriative language that he used in his films. These writings include the sensationally titled 1954 *Maclean's* magazine essay "How I Became an Eskimo" and the 1954 *Photography* magazine article "Idlouk – Arctic Amateur," discussed in chapter 3. But Wilkinson's most substantial production about the trip was a 255-page book published by Clarke, Irwin and Company in 1955.

Wilkinson's monograph capitalized on widespread recent interest in the north as well as the popularity of his own filmmaking. The book itself was titled after his successful 1952 film, *Land of the Long Day*. Like the film, the 1955 monograph is also structured around the cycle of seasons and, periodically, echoes the film's narrative.[94] It was also likely modelled after and benefited from the popularity of Farley Mowat's 1951 book *People of the Deer*, about the Kivilaq region to the west of Hudson Bay. *People of the Deer* drew southern attention to starvations among the Ahiarmiut and criticized churches, the Hudson's Bay Company, and government inaction.[95] *Land of the Long Day*, like Mowat's book, combined aspects of a travelogue and popular ethnography with a polemic on Inuit welfare.[96]

Land of the Long Day reads like an adventure tale, with Wilkinson as its singular hero. Across eighteen chapters written in the first person, the narrative follows the southerner in his attempts to adapt to life at camp and to succeed as a hunter. After setting the stage with a description of life at the camp in winter, the book devotes fully four chapters to Wilkinson's arduous trip to Pond Inlet/Mittimatalik during the spring of 1953. Once at camp, hunting, fishing, and trapping – to obtain seals, foxes, caribou, narwhals, rabbits, geese, and char – dominate Wilkinson's life. The tension builds with each episode of his stumbling attempts to emulate Idlout's hunting prowess. "I had not yet learned patience, the patience that comes only after generations of such a life. Idlouk was hungry, but calm. I was hungry and short tempered. I cursed the seals, the rain, the dogs, the Arctic. None of this helped; I still got no seals."[97] After several weeks and more setbacks, Wilkinson at last earns Idlout's praise when he kills a seal and transports it back to camp without assistance: "Pride overcame fear. To call the other Eskimos for help would not do. With a silent prayer I shoved down on the seal and tilted the *qajaq* over to the right. Up came the seal and I jerked it across the rear deck. I straightened the *qajaq* so quickly that I very nearly rolled it over to the left. But I had made it safely and that was the end of my fear."[98] In excerpts like this, *Land of the Long Day* takes the form of a masculinized travelogue and quest narrative.

The book's final chapter shifts to a more polemic tone. But whereas Wilkinson's journals – and, in fact, his entire 1953–54 trip – suggest models for privileging Inuit culture and engaging Inuit in governance, *Land of the Long Day* concludes with an endorsement of assimilation. Wilkinson pleads for Inuit assistance "as they search for a new way of life in the face of violent change in old patterns of living."[99] And while acknowledging "a small number of understanding persons who have done much to ease the shocks of transition,"[100] he berates others who treat Inuit as "second-class citizens,"[101] unwittingly create misunderstandings, and refuse to engage with their culture. Yet ultimately, Wilkinson argues that assimilation is "inevitable":

> Our contact with the Eskimo has largely destroyed his old concepts of life, his culture. For many Eskimo groups, life has lost much of its meaning, for the meaning was closely tied in with a system of beliefs which we have held to be largely untenable. This has been inevitable. I know of no way in which many of the old beliefs of the Eskimo can exist alongside the new ones he must inevitably pick up from the white. But we must be sure we recognize that if we destroy old beliefs we must do all we can to replace them with new ones, ideas the Eskimo can grasp and either weave into the framework of his quasi-primitive existence or build on top of it.[102]

The book concludes with references to nation building, the role of an Inuit presence in securing Canadian sovereignty in the Arctic, and the paternalistic role of government. "As a Canadian citizen the Eskimo helps immeasurably to maintain our sovereignty over this tremendous land mass to the north … We must guide him forward to the day when he will be a full contributing member in the community of Canada. The Eskimos are proud, intelligent people. Canada is made up of a great diversity of proud, intelligent people. From this we gain our strength."[103] Published just as Wilkinson was about to enter the federal government's workforce as a Northern Service officer, *Land of the Long Day* moves from adventure tale to an endorsement of current government policies.

Land of the Long Day

DOUG WILKINSON

Illustrated with 26 photographs, 8 in full colour, by the author.

"MORE AND MORE you are getting to be like an Eskimo, and like my son," said Idlouk, chief man of the Aulatseevikmiut, to his friend Doug Wilkinson. "There are not many white men who live with the Eskimos as you are doing. When you go back to your land, I will write a note for you. It will be to the big chief of all the white men who come to our land on the boat in the summer."

Later on Idlouk did write that note; and here in syllabic characters, written on a scrap of paper torn from a small notebook, is what he had to say about his adopted son and friend:

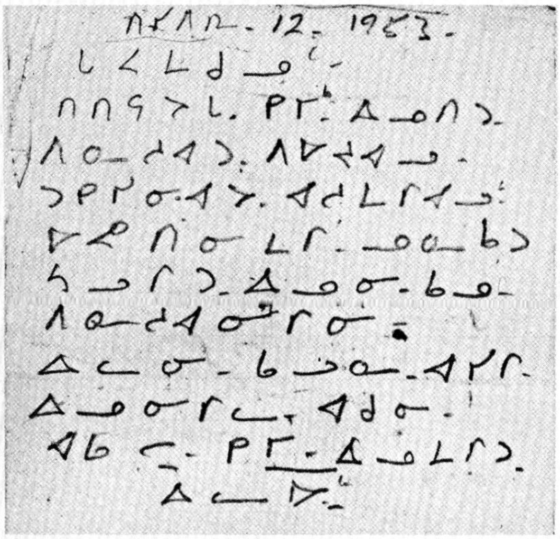

Translated, Idlouk's letter reads:

I write that Kingmik is doing things exactly as Eskimos do. He is a good man. He will understand very well about us when he is through. He lives right with us. He does not tell false things about the way the Eskimos live and do things.

4.6 | Promotional bookmark with text written by Idlout that accompanied Wilkinson's book *Land of the Long Day* (1955).

Interspersed throughout *Land of the Long Day* are photographs. In total, Wilkinson included eighteen black and white and eight colour photographs, apparently all shot by him with his 35 mm camera. Placed to illustrate key scenes in the narrative, the images depict the polar bear hunt, travel by dog team, Sunday prayers, chores, the Arctic landscape, and hunting scenes. Photographs of camp members, including Idlout, and other Inuit Wilkinson met on the trip also appear in the book. These portraits are presented and arranged in grids as though ethnographic representations of racialized types.[104] But, ironically, the book's own protagonist, Wilkinson, is absent from its visual content. Whereas the book's first-person narrative envelopes the reader in Wilkinson's own thoughts and experiences, he is rendered invisible in the photographic illustrations. Instead, all of the published photographs were shot by Wilkinson himself and, as a result, invite the reader to participate in this simulacrum of the author's own vision. In this way, the images themselves function as an extension of the first-person narrative yet without the self-reflexivity characterizing Wilkinson's text. However, paradoxically, Wilkinson's invisibility underscores his authority. In not picturing himself, Wilkinson implicitly refuses to racialize his own whiteness and signals the book as a work of white imagining. As Richard Dyer has influentially argued, "as long as white people are not racially seen and named they/we function as a human norm."[105]

Although the book *Land of the Long Day* presents an indelibly southern and white view, it includes one final assertion of Inuit agency in relation to the south. With the printing of the book, Clarke, Irwin and Company included a bookmark-sized insertion that reproduced a testimonial that Idlout wrote in syllabics about Wilkinson dated 12 September 1953 (see figure 4.6).[106] The inclusion of a syllabics text in this insert, of course, functions here as an index of both Inuit otherness and the authenticity of Wilkinson's journey. But the note itself holds one small subversive surprise. Wilkinson translates it as saying: "I write that Kingmik is doing things exactly as Eskimos do. He is a good man. He will understand very well about us when he is through. He lives right with us. He does not tell false things about the way the Eskimos live and do things." But this translation omits the name of the addressee to whom Idlout has ostensibly written. According to Inuktitut-English translator Rhoda Kayakjuak, Idlout's note is addressed "To the Government."[107] In this small gesture, Idlout insists on his own equity and authority in the face of an increasingly present south. Idlout's family, too, asserted themselves during this time of change. This chapter is followed by the final instalment of Leah Idlout d'Argencourt Paulson's five-part article on her experiences as a tuberculosis patient.[108] Here, Leah recounts her return to Inuit Nunangat and her family after her long stay in hospital and a sojourn near Ottawa with Doug and Vivian Wilkinson.

In the Idlout Family's Words 4

Leah Idlout d'Argencourt, "C.D. Howe V: Trip Back Home," *Inuit Today* 6, no. 10 (December 1977): 22–9, with photographs by Joseph Idlout and Doug Wilkinson

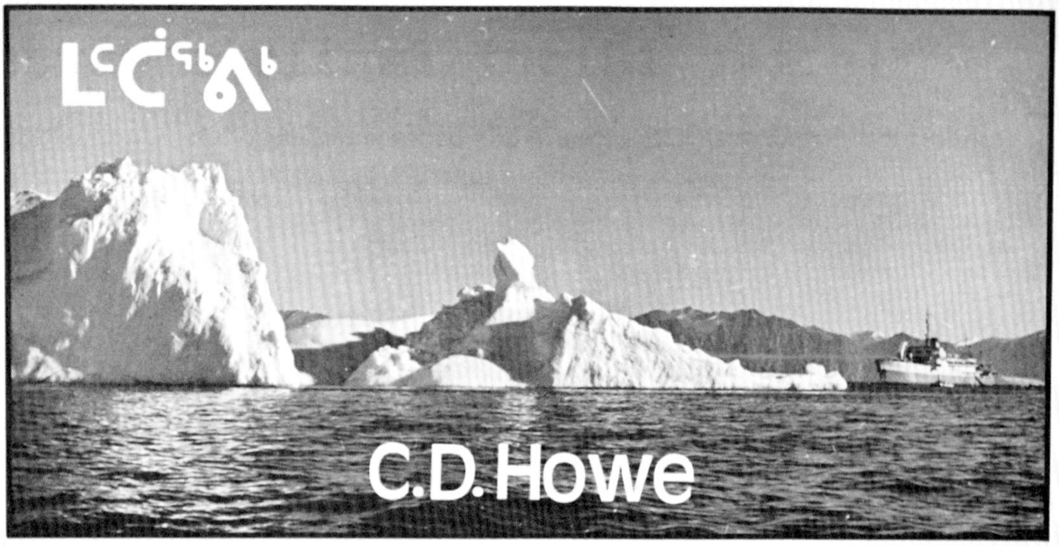

ᑕᓐᓂᒍᖕᒥᑦ ᓕᐊ ᐃᓐᓗᐅᑉ ᑎᕆᕐᑕᖕᒥᑦ

Part V *by LEAH IDLOUT d'ARGENCOURT*

ᐊᖕᒋᕐᕋᐅᓖᖅᑯᓂᕋ

ᑕᒪᕐᓇᐅᓕᕐᑎᓐᓄᒍ ᑕᖅᑭᖕᒐ ᔪᓚᐃ 1952 ᐅᓪᓗ ᓗᐅᕐᓯᒪᒍᑦ ᕐᑳᓐᓄᓈᑦ ᓄᓇᖕᒐᑦᓂᑦ ᒪᓐᑐᕆᐊᒥᑦ ᐅᑎᕆᐊᕐ ᑐᓕᕐᓗᖕᒐ ᒥᑦᑎᒪᑕᓕᖕᒍᑦ. ᑕᒪᑐᒪᓂ ᕐᑲᐅᓯᒪᑦᑎᐊᖅ ᒍᐊᐱᓕᕐᒪ ᓇᒎᖕ ᒐᐅᔭᕆᐊᒃᓴᑦᓂᒃ, ᓱᖕᒪᓐᓄ ᐅᓪᓚᕆᐊᒃᓴᖅ. ᐱᕐ ᑯᑎᒃᑲ ᐸᖕᓇᕐᓯᒪᔪᑐᕐ ᑲᐅᓕᕐᓄᑎᒃ ᐅᓪᓚᓗᐅᖕᖕ ᒋᑦᓂᑦᓂ ᐋᑐᐋᒥᑦ.

ᐅᒥᐊᕐᔪᐊᒐᓴᐃᑦ ᐄᒐᕐᐱᖕᒦᓗᐅᕐᓯᒪᔪᑦ ᒪᓐᑐᕆᐊᒥ, ᑭᓯᐊᓂᓕ ᐃᓕᓴᕆᑦᓗᐅᑎᒥᓗᐅᕐᓯᒪᔭᕐ ᒪᑦᑖᕐᐱᒃ. ᐃᓅᒍᖕᒐ ᓇᓂᓂᐊᕐᓚᐅᕐᓯᒪᖕᒥᒪᒥᔭᕐᒍᐊᕐ. ᕐᑭᒪᒥ ᐅᐸ ᐊᒪᐅᓕᒐᐅᓐᓄ ᕐᑲᐅᓯᒃ ᑲᑦᑎᐊᖅ ᒥᑦᓇᕐ ᑲᑦᑕᓗᐅᕐᓯᒪᖕᒪᖕᒐ ᓇᒎᖕ ᒐᕐᓂᐊᕆᐊᒃᓴᑦᑎᑦᓂᒃ, ᓇᔪᕐᑎᒦᑦᓇᑦ ᑎᐊᕐ ᑲᑦᑕᓗᐅᕐᓯᒪᓐᓄᒥᑦᓄ. ᑕᒪᑐᒪᓂ ᐃᑭᑎᑕᐅᓪᓚᕐ ᓅᐊᕐᒪ ᐅᒥᐊᕐᔪᐊᒧᑦ ᐋᓐᓗᐅᓄᐊᖑᓐᖕᒥᑕᐃᑦᓇᕐᓄᖕᒐ ᓵᕐᓄ ᐊᔪᐅᔪᑯᓅᕐ ᑐᖕ ᒐᐅᔪᑦᓇᐃᑕᐃᑦᓇᕐᓄᓂᓄ. ᕐᑯᐱᐊᓱᓗᐅᕐᓯᒪᖕᒥᑦᑐᖕᒐ ᑭᓯᐊᓂ ᕐᑭᒪᐃᓕᕆᐊᒃᓴᓐᓂᒃ ᕐᑭᒪᒥᒃᑯᑦᓂᒃ, ᓇᔪᐃᑦᓇᕈᒪᓕᕐᓄᐊᕐᓄᒥᑦ. ᐊᒃ ᓱᐊᓄᒃ ᐃᓄᐊᕈ ᑦᓃᓗᐅᕐᓯᒪᒐᒪ ᐅᓪᓚᕈᒪᔪᑦᓃᕐᓄᐊᕐᓄᖕᒐᓄ ᐊᖕᒥᕐᕐᕈᒪᓐᓄᖕᒐᓄ ᐃᓚᑦᓄᑦ.

ᐃᓱᒪᒥᔭᒃᑲ ᐊᓐᓯᒥᖕᒥᑦᑎᐊᒻᒪᓂᓕᓗᐅᕐᓯᒪᖕᒪᒥᑦ ᐃᓚᒃᑲ ᓱᓕ ᐅᖕᒐᒥᔭᓐᓘᒥᒐᓄᐊᕐᓄᒥᑦ, ᐊᒻᒪᓄᑦᑕᐅᖅ ᐊᓂᓕᒫᒃᑲ ᓇᒡᓕᒋᔭᓐᓘᒥᒐᓄᐊᕐᓱᒥᑦ ᓱᓕ ᐊᔪᓕᒫᓂᑦ ᓇᒡᓕᒋᓂᕐᐸᐅᖕᒥᑦᓇᕐᓄᒥᑦ. ᑭᓯᐊᓂᓕ, ᑕᐃᑦᓱᒪᓂᐅ ᑎᓐᓄᒥᑦ ᐊᕐᕿᑐᑦ ᐅᑭᐊᒃᓵᖕᒐᓂᑦ 1951 ᐅᐱᕐᖕᒑᖕ ᒐᓄᑦ 1952 ᑎᑭᓐᓄᒍ ᐅᖕ ᒐᐅᔮᓯᓐᓃᓗᐅᕐᓯᒪᒐᒪ ᐅᓐᓯᓐᑎᐊᕐᓄᐊᕐᓄᖕᒐ. ᓇᕈᓇᕈᔫᔭᕐᑎᑕᐅᖕᒥᑦᓇᕐᓄᖕᒐ ᐃᓄᐃᑦ ᓄᓇᖕᒐᑦᓂᑦ ᕐᑳᓐᓄᓈᑦ ᓄᓇᖕᒐᑦᓄᑦ, ᐊᓐᓯᕆᐸᓄᐊᕐᔪᑯᓄᖕᒥᑦᑎᐊᕐ ᑐᓄᑦ ᐃᓅᓯᖕᒥᑦᓄᑦ.

Trip back home

It was in July of 1952 that I left the South from Montreal to return to my family in Pond Inlet. This time I knew where I was going, and why. I had all my belongings already packed two days before I was to leave Ottawa.

There were many ships docked in the harbour at Montreal, but I recognized the C.D. Howe right away. Of course, if I had been on my own, I wouldn't have been able to find it. Doug and Vivian always informed me well ahead of time about what we were going to do, and they were always with me. This time, as I boarded the ship, I didn't feel like a stranger, or a lost kid. But I was not happy to be leaving the Wilkinsons, and part of me wanted very badly to stay with them. I felt really torn between wanting to stay and wanting to return home to my family.

My feelings had changed so much as a result of all that had happened to me, although love for my family hadn't, and of course I loved all my brothers more than anything in the world. But, during that year, from late 1951 up to the spring of 1952, everything had changed

ᐊᒻᒪᓗᑦᑕᐅᕐᒃ ᓇᓗᓇᓗᐊᕐᒃᑰᔨᓕᕐ ᑐᒥᒃ ᐊᑐᓕᕐᓗᖕᒪ ᐊᕐᕌᒍᒃᑲ 12-ᒨᑦ ᑎᑭᑎᓐᓗᒥᑦ 13-ᖑᕐᔪᕐᓗᒍ.

ᑭᖕᒍᓐᓕᐅᓕᕐ ᑐᒥᒃ ᐅᒥᐊᕐᔪᐊᒃᑰᕐᓂᕐ ᒪᑦᑖᕐᕙᒃᑯᑦ ᓯᕗᓐᓕᕐ ᕚᓚᐅᓐᖏᑦᑎᐊᕐᑐᖅ. ᑕᒪᑐᒪᓂᓗ ᑭᖕᒍᓐᓕᕐ ᒥ ᑲᒪᒋᔨᕐᑲᓚᐅᕐᓯᒪᓐᓗᖕᒪ ᓴᓂᕐᑎᒥᒃ, ᒪᒃᑯᒃᑐᑯᖕᒥᒃ, ᐆᔭᐅᓂᖕ ᒪᓂ ᐱᓇᓱᒪᓄᓚᐅᐱᓐᓚᑐᐃᑦᓇᕐᓗᓂᐅᒃ ᑮᓇᐅᓐᔭᒃᓴᓈᑎᒥᓐᓗᓂᐅᒃ ᐃᓕᑦᓂᐊᕐᕕᒡᔪᐊᕐᕕᖕᒨᑦ ᐃᓕᑦᓂᐊᕈᑎᒃᓴᒥᓂᒃ. ᔮᓐ ᑯᕆᑦᑕᖕᔪᓚᐅᕐᓯᒪᔪᖅ, ᐋ ᑐᕞᒥᐅᑕᐅᓐᓗᓂ. ᔮᓂᓗ ᐱᕐᑲᓐᓂᒃᑐᓐᓃᓗᖕᓕᓚᐅᕐᓯᒪᓪᓚ ᑦᓄᒃ, ᑕᐃᑦᓱᒪᓂ ᐅᑎᓕᕐᑎᓐᓗᖕᒪ ᐅᒥᐊᕐᔪᐊᒃᑯᑦ. ᕐᑯᕕᐋᓇᕐᓂᕐᓴᐅᓕᓚᐅᕐᓯᒪᔪᕐᓕ ᑲᒥᓴᐅᑦᑎᐊᓕᕐᓚ.

ᓄᕐᑲᕐᕕᒋᒋᐊᕐᖕᒪᓚᐅᕐᓯᒪᓴᕗᑦ ᑭᓐᖕᒪᕐᓂ ᐊᒻᒪᓗ ᑭᖕᒥᕈᒪᒥ, ᓘᒃ ᑖᕐ, ᓄᓕᐋᖕᒪᓗ ᐊᒻᒪᓗ ᐃᓄᑯᓗᖕᒥᒃ ᑎᒍᐋᖕᒪᑦ ᐱᖕᒪᓯᓂᒃ ᐊᕐᖀᒍᓕᑯᕝᓕᕐᑐᖅ ᐃᑭᓚᐅᕐᓯᒪᖕᒪᑕ ᐅᒥᐊᕐᔪᐊᒧᑦ. ᑭᖕᒥᕈᒪᒥᑦᑕᐅᖅ ᒥᐊᓚᒃᑯᒃ ᑕᐃᕕᑎᒃᑯᒃ ᑕᑯᔭᓐᓚᓚᐅᕐᓯᒪᓂᒪᒃᑭᒃ, ᒦᑦᓇᓕ ᓯᓕ ᑕ ᐃᒃᑯᐊᒃ ᐃᒃᓗᖕᓂᒥᐅᑕᐅᔪᒃ. ᑕᐃᕕᑎᐅᑉ ᒥᐊᓚᐅᓐᓗ ᐊᐱᕐᓱᒐᒍᑕᐅᔪᒥᒃ ᐊᐱᕐᓱᓚᐅᕐᓯᒪᖕᒪᖕᒪᒃ: "ᑕᑯᐊᐱ ᐃᓄᐃᐱᒃ! ᑭᓈᐱᐅᕕᑦ? ᓇᓂᒥᐅᑕᐅᕕᑦ?" ᑕᐃᒪᑦᓇᓱ ᓕ ᑭᐅᓐᓚᐱᖅᓕᕐᒥᒪᓚ: "ᓕᐊᕐ ᔪᕐᖕᒪ, ᒥᑦᑎᒪᑕᓕᖕᒥ ᐅᑕᐅᔪᖕᒪ." ᑕᐃᒪᓐᖕᒪᑎᐊᕐ ᑭᓇᓕᒫᑦ ᒥᑦᑎᒪᑕ ᓕᒃ ᓇᓃᒃᑲᓗᐊᕐᒪᖕᒫᑦ ᕐᑲᐅᔨᒪᔭᐅᓚᐅᕐᓯᒪᑦᓚᕐᓂ. ᑭᓯᐊᓂᓕ, ᒥᐊᕐ ᑕᐃᕕᑕ ᕐᑲᐅᔨᒪᓚᐅᕐᓯᒪᖕᒪᑎᒃ ᒥ ᑎᒪᑕᓕᒃ ᓈᓃᕐᑲᓐᓂᐊᒃᓴᖕᒪᒃᑲᓂᒃ. ᒥᐊᕐ ᑕᐃᕕᑐ ᕐᑲᐅᔨᒪᓚᐅᕐᓯᒪᖕᒪᑎᒃ ᒥ ᑎᒪᑕᓕᖕᕖᓚᐅᕐᓯᒪᖕᒥᒥᒍᕐ ᓯᕗᓪ ᓕᕐᒥᒡᓗ ᐅᐃᕕᓂᖕᒪ ᓴᓐᑎ ᐊᕕᓐᓯᕐ ᑐᐃᕆᐅᓚᐅᕐᓯᑐᕕᓂᖕ, ᒥᑦᑎᒪᑕᖕᒥᐅᓄᑦ ᐊᕕᓐᓯᕐ ᑐᐃᕆᒥᐅᖕᔪᔭᕐ ᑐᓚᐅᕐᓯᒪᔪᕕ ᓃᑦ. ᑕᐃᑦᓱᒪᓂᓕᑦᑕᐅᕐ ᐃᑦᑐᒃᑯᒃᑲ ᒥᑦᑎᒪᑕᖕᒥ ᐅᑕᐅᓗᐊᕐᑎᓐᓗᒥᑦ. ᕐᑲᐅᔨᒪᔭᒻᒪᓐᒋᓚᐅᕐᓯᒪᖕᒪᒋᑦ ᓂᖕᒋᐅᒃᑯᒃᑲ ᐊᑖᑕᓗ ᐃᓅᓂᐅᔭᕐᒃᑳᕐᑎᑦᓇᖕᒪ ᓕᓕ ᓯᓕ, ᐱᓇᓱᒃᑎᒌᓚᐅᕐᓯᒪᑦᓂᕋᒥᒃ.

ᑕᐃᒪᓕ, ᑕᐃᕕᑎ ᐅᕐᑲᓕᓚᐅᕐᓯᒪᖕᒪᑦ: "ᓄᓕᐊᒪ ᒥᐊᕐᐅᐸ ᓴᑦᓇᑎᓚᐅᕐᓯᒪᖕᒪᒍ ᐊᑦᑕᐃᑦ ᐃᓐᓚᐅᕐᒃ ᑲᒦᖕᓂᒃ, ᕐᑲᓐᓄᓈᑦ ᓄᓇᖕᒪᑦᓂᓐᖕᒪᑭᑎᔭᕐᓂᒃ ᐱᑦᓯᑎᑦ ᓕᕈᒃ" ᕐᑲᓄᐃᓕᔭᓐᐊᒃᓴᕐᒃ ᓇᓗᓕᓚᐅᕐᓯᒪᑉᐸᑉ, ᑕᕝᕙᑐ ᐊᓪᓚᒃᑭᑦ ᐊᓐᓄᕌᒃᑲ ᓈᒻᒪᒋᔭᑐᐃᑦᓇᒃᑲ, ᕐᑭᑐᕐᖕᒪ ᐅᔭᒃᑲᓗ, ᐊᒻᒪᓗ ᐅᕐᑲᓖᒪᕐᑯᑎᒃᑲ ᑭᓇᑐᐃᑦᓇᕐᓗᑦ ᐱᒃᑯᒥᐅᓗᒃᓴᑦᑐᖕᒪᕐᓯᕐᑐᕐ. ᕐᑯᐱᐊᓱᒃᑑᕐᒥᔫᒃ ᓄᐅ ᕐᓯᒪᓪᓚ ᑲᓪᓗᖕᒪᓗ ᐅᖕᒪᓱᒃᑐᕐᒥᐅᓂᒃ ᒥᑦᑎᒪᑕᖕᒥᒃ ᕐᑲᐅᔨᒪᔪᓂᒃ ᓂᖕᒋᐅᒃᑯᒃᑲᓂᒃ. ᐊᖏᕐᕋᕕᖕᒥᐅᓪᓚᒪᓐᓚᕐᓯᒪᓪᓚ ᐃᓅᕐᑳᖕᒪᓗᓐᓇᓗ ᓄᓕᐊᖕᒥᐅᑦ.

ᑕᐃᒪᓕ, ᐃᕗᔨᕕᖕᒥᐅᑦ ᑯᐱᐊᒃ ᑕᕐᕋᖕᒪᓂ, ᓄᒃ ᐸᐱᐊᑯᓗᒃ ᕐᑯᓕᓂᒃ ᐊᕐᕿᔪᕐᑲᓕᕐᑐᖅ ᓇᑲᓯᒪᔪᖕ ᓂᐅᖕᒪ ᐃᑭᓕᓚᐅᕐᓯᒪᖕᒥᖕᒪᓕᑦ. ᐊᑎᕐᑲᐅᓯᒪᔪᖕᒥᖕᒪᕐᑦ ᓇ ᒨᓯᓯᒥᒃ. ᕐᑯᐱᐊᓱᒃᑑᒥᓪᓚᓇᓚᐅᕐᓯᒪᓪᓚ ᐃᓅᕐᑳᑦᑕᐅᑦᓇᕐᓂᒥᓪᓚ ᐊᑯᓂᐅᑦᓯᓂᑉ ᐃᓄᖕᒋᑦᓕᓚᐅᕐᓯᒪᖕᒪᕐᓕᒪᓐᓗᒃᑲ ᐊᑎᕐ ᑲᑕᐅᕐᑎᐋᓇᕐᒪᑐᒪ. ᐊᐱᕐᓱᕈᕐᔭᕐ ᑲᑦᑕᐅᕐᓯᒪᒃᑯ ᐅᕐᑲᐅᓯᑎᓐᓇᕐᒪᐅᑦᓇᕐᓗᓇᐅᓐᓗᐅᕐᓯᒪᖕᒪᕐᓂᖕᒥᒃ.

ᑕᐃᒪᓕ, ᒨᓯᓯᐅᑉ ᐅᓂᒃ ᑲᐅᑎᓕᓚᐅᕐᓯᒪᖕᒪᖕᒪ ᕐᑲᓐ ᓂᐅᖕᒪ ᓇᐱᔪᕕᓂᐅᔭᓐᐊᒃᓴᖕᒪᓂᒃ. ᐅᕐᔪᓇᓱᒥᐊ ᕐᑲᑕᐅᑦᓂᕐᓗᓂᔫᕐ ᐅᒥᐊᒃᑯᑦ ᐊᑦᑕᒥᓄᑦ ᐃᓚᐅᑦᓂᕐᓗᓂ, ᐅᕐᑲᕐᓗᓂ — ᐋᓇᕐᑲᕐᑳᖕᒥᑦᓇᒥᔫᕐ— ᑕᐃᒪ ᐃᓄᒃ ᐅᔪᑦ ᐅᐃᒪᔭᓗᐊᕐ ᑐᐋᓕᕐᓂᕐᒥ ᑐᐊᕕᓗᐊᓐᓕᒥ ᐊᕐᓗᓂ ᕐᑭᒡᒋᕐᕕᐊᓕᐅᕐᓯᒪᑦᓂᕐᒪᔪ ᕐᑯᒃᑐᕐᖕᒪᔪᑦ. ᐃᓱᒪᒋᓕᐅᕐᓯᒪᖕᒥᒐᒃᑯᑦᑕᐅᕐᒃ ᐋᔪᑦ ᑕᑦᓇ ᐅᔪᓇᓱ ᒃᑎᐸᑦᓯᐅᕈᓗᒃ ᐅᓐᓕᕐᓴᕐᔫᓕᐊᒃᓴᐅᓗᐊᕐᓂᕐᐸᕐ ᑖᑦ ᓇ ᕐᑲᓄᐃᓕᐅᖕᒪᕐᑐᒃᑯᓗᒃ, ᐋᓇᕐᑲᕐᓂᓗ ᐱᕐᕈᓗᐊᕐ

so completely for me. In moving from the North to the South, I had entered a totally new and different world. At the same time, I had reached the difficult age of 12, just going on 13.

My second trip on the C.D. Howe was not at all like the first. This time, I was looked after by the ship's janitor, a really young lad, who had taken the job to make enough money to go back to university, whatever that was. His name was John Creighton, and he was from Ottawa. John and I soon became good friends, and my return trip on the C.D. Howe turned out to be more fun.

Our first stop was at Cape Dorset and Lake Harbour, where a doctor, his wife and their adopted three-year-old Inuk daughter boarded the ship. It was here also that I met Mary and Davidie, who are still living in Frobisher Bay today. Davidie and his wife asked me the typical Inuit questions: "Look at this dear little Inuk! What is your name? Where is your home?" As usual, I answered: "My name is Leah. My home is Pond Inlet." Most of the time, no-one knew where Pond Inlet was. But this time, Mary Davidie did know. So she asked: "What is your father's name? What is the name of your father's parents?" When I answered, she told me that, one time, when she was with her first husband Sandy who was a priest, they were with the Anglican service in Pond Inlet. This was at the same time my grandparents were in Pond Inlet. So she knew my grandparents and my father long before I was ever born, and they had worked together.

Then, Davidie said: "My wife Mary made your father Idlout a pair of kamiks (seal-skin boots), so have you got anything from the South for her?" I didn't know what to answer, as I only had clothes my own size, my dolls, and a few books that no one would be really interested in. I was really surprised to meet somebody so far away from Pond Inlet who actually knew my grandparents. It made me feel good to meet this couple.

Then, at Ivujivik in Northern Quebec, a young ten-year-old boy with a broken leg joined us on board. His name was Mosusie. I was really happy to have a companion, although he spoke a different dialect from me. I used to ask him all kinds of questions to encourage him to speak in his own dialect.

One time, Mosusie told me the story

of how his leg had been broken. He had gone out hunting in a boat with his father, he said - he had no mother - when one Inuk hunter got all excited and accidentally jumped straight onto his right thigh. I thought that stupid old hunter should have been more careful around this innocent, motherless boy. He was very shy and quiet, and I didn't blame him for this, just coming out of an isolated, unspoiled place, as he did. He was going to the hospital in Montreal to be treated - so John told me.

I know that I was not as innocent as Mosusie was. One time the poor boy couldn't get out of his bed for days and days, and he had absolutely nothing to do. He really looked bored, although he had the friendliest face. There was a buzzer to the janitor's room on the wall right by his bed. I told him to just keep pushing it and see what happened. Of course, I didn't tell him what it was. John came right away. He told me to explain to Mosusie what the button was for and to tell him not to touch it again. After John had left, I really had a good laugh, and I told Mosusie that he had made the Qadlunaaq helper come to our room when we didn't need him. He got shy and very scared.

Our third stop was at Fort Churchill, Manitoba, where Mosusie was taken out by airplane to the white man's land. The doctor and his wife from Lake Harbour bought me a pair of brown corduroy slacks and a pair of rubber boots from the store there. When I saw this family leaving for the South, their adopted Inuk daughter was all dressed up in a pink woolen suit, and her hair was all cut short and curled. They all said goodbye to me and I never heard of them again. I never even got to know their names.

Our next stop was at Coral Harbour on Southampton Island. Here, many Inuit visited me on board the ship. One middle-aged Inuk man came to tell me that his wife, sister, and some of his relatives had all died from the same sickness, and he said he was all alone. It all came out sounding so funny to me, because of the particular dialect he was speaking. He was all dressed in brown army clothing, although I don't think he was with the army. In those days, there were quite a few Inuit dressed in many different kinds of European clothing. You could see

24

ᕐᑯᐊᕐ ᑕᓕᐊᓛᕐᓯᒪᖕᒥᑲᑦᑕ ᐳᕕᕐᓂᑐᒧᓐᓄ. ᕐᑯᐊ ᕐᑕᒥᐅᖅᑰᓚᐅᕐᓯᒪᔪᕐᖕᒥᑦᓇ ᐃᒃᓯᕋᕐᔪᐊᒥᒃ ᐊᓐᓅᕋᕐ ᓯᒪᑯᑖᒎᒃᑯᓂ ᑕᐃᒪᑦᓇ ᐊᑕᔪᑯᑖᒃᓰᒎᕐ ᑲᑦᑕᓗᐅᕐᓯ ᒪᖕᒪᑕ ᑕᐃᒪ ᑕᐃᑦᓯᒪᓂᒃ ᑲᑦᓂᐅᑎᓐᑯᒍ ᐃᓯᒐᖕᒥᑦᓄᑦ ᑎᑭᐅᒪᔪᓂᒃ. ᐃᓄᒃᑎᑐᑦᑎᐊᖅ ᐅᕐ ᑲᕈ ᑦᓇᕐᑯᓂ ᑕᐅᑐ ᓐᖕᒥᑦᑯᒍ ᐃᓅᕙᓕᑦᑎᖅᑰᓯᑦᑎᐊᕐ ᑯᓂᒎᑦᓃᑦ ᐃᒐᓕᕐᓂᖕ ᒎᑦᓃᑦ, ᐃᓄᖕᓄᑦ ᒪᓕᑲᑉ ᑕᐅᔪᓐᓘᑯᓚᐅᕐᓯᒪᖕᒪᑦ ᑕᑎᒥᔭᓐᓘᒃ ᓇᑯᓇᕐᓂ ᑐᕐᓴᐅᑲᑉᑯᓂᑯ ᐃᓄᖕᓄᑦ.

ᐊᔪᕋᒎᔭᖕᒥᑦᓄᑦ ᓄᓇᓕᒐᖕᓄᑦ ᓄᖅᑲᕐᑲᑦᑕᓗᐅᕐᓯ ᒪᒐᑦᑕ ᓇᒍᕋᒎᔭᖅ ᑕᐸᐅᖕᒐ ᕐᑲᐅᓯᐃᑦᑐᓕᐊᕐᐸᓐᓕᐊ ᓐᑯᑕ, ᐃᑭᔪᕐᑲᑦᑎᐊᓛᕐᓯᒪᖖᒥᑦᑐᖅ ᑕᐃᑦᓯᒪᓂᐅᑎ ᓐᑯᒍ ᐋᓐᓂᐊᕕᓕᐊᕐᑐᓄᑦ. ᑭᓯᐊᓂᓕ, ᐃᓅᕐᑲᑎᓕᐊᑦ ᓅᓚᐅᕐᓯᒪᒐᒪ ᐃᑐᒃᒥᒃ ᐃᒃᐱᐊᕐᔪᖕᒥᐅᑕᕐᒥᒃ ᐃᑦᑐᕋ ᑯᑦᓂᒃ, ᐊᖕᒥᕐᕋᐅᓕᕐᑎᓐᑯᒍ ᐋᓐᓂᐊᕕᖕᒥᖕ ᑰᕐᑯᓂ Hᐊᐦᒥᑕᒥᑦ. ᒪᑦᑖᕐᕕᖕᒧᑦ ᐃᑭᑎᑕᐅᓚᐅᕐᓯᒪᖕᒪᑦ ᑰᓐᔪᐊᕐᑯᖕᒥ.

ᐃᑐᒃᓕ ᐃᓐᓇᑐᕐ ᑲᐅᓕᕐᑯᓂ. ᐊᓂᔪᒪᑲᔪᒃ ᑐᓐᑖᓗ ᐅᕐᓯᒪᖕᒪᑦ ᑭᓯᐊᓂᑯ ᐊᓂᕐ ᑲᑎᒥᑯᓂᖕᑲ ᐱᔪᕋᔭᕐ ᑲᑎᒥ ᓂᐊᕋᒃᑯ, ᐊᓂᔭᓐᓇᐊᒃᓴᖅ ᐃᕐᑭᐊᔪᕐ ᑲᑦᑕᕐᑎᓐᑯᖕᑲ. ᔪᖕᒥᐅᖕᑲ ᑲᑐᐃᑦᓇᓕᕋᒪ ᐃᓯᕐᓯᒪᓕᑲᔪᓕᕐ ᑯᖕᑲ, ᐊᓪᓚᒍ ᐃᒪᕐᔪᐊᕐᓯᐅᕐ ᑐᐋᒍᕐ ᑲᑦᑕᕐᑯᑕ ᐱᑲᑦᑕ ᓄᓇᓕᖕᓄᑦ ᑎ ᑭᓗᐅᖅᑳᕋᑕ. ᑕᑯᔭᒃᓴᕐᑕᕐᑲᕐᑲᑦᑕᓗᐅᕐᓯᒪᖕᖕᒥᓪᓚᑦ ᐃᒪᕐᐱᐊᒍᒃ ᑕᒪᑦᓴᔾᑎᓐᑯᒍ. ᐃᑐᒃ ᐅᕐᑲᕐᑲᑦᑕᓗ ᕐᓯᒪᖕᒪᑦ ᐃᓯᕐᓯᒪᐃᑦᓇᖖᑐᕐ ᑐᐊᒍᑲᒥᔫᖅ ᐋᓐᓂᐊᕕᖕ ᒦᑦᑐᓂ ᐃᕐᑭᐊᖖᑐᕐ ᑐᐊᒍᓚᐅᕐᓯᒥ ᐊᓂᑕᓗᓚᐅᕐᓯᒪᖖ ᒥᑦᓇᒥᔫᖅ. ᐊᖅᑐᓐᓚᓇᐅᑲᒥᔫᖅ, ᓯᓚᑐᓚᕐᑲᑦᑕᕐᑐ ᐋᒍᑲᒥ ᓯᖕᒥᐅᖖᑲᒍᕚᐳᑲᒥᐅᒃ. ᒪᓕᒃ ᑕᐅᔪᒪᐃᑦᓇ ᑦᑎᐊᕐᐸᒃᑯᓂᒍ ᐊᓂᔭᓇᐊᑕᓖᑦ ᑐᓴᕆᕐᑲᑦᑕᕐᓂᐊᕋᒥᖅ ᑲᔫᖅ. ᐃᓅᔾᑯᓂᔫᖅ ᓯᓕ ᕐᑲᓐᑯᓈᓂᒃ ᑲᐸᐃᐊᔪᒃ ᑲᒥ ᐊᓂᔫᔭᓇᐊᒃᓴᖅ.

ᐃᑐᒃ ᐋᓐᓂᐊᕕᖕᒥᒃ ᐅᓂᒃ ᑳᑦᓲᔭᕐᑲᑦᑕᕐᑎᓐᑯᒍ, ᐊᓐᓯᕆᖕᒥᑖᑦᓄᖕᑲᓂᒃ ᓇᔪᓚᐅᕐᑕᒪ ᐅᕐᑲᓐᓚᖅᑰᓯᕐᑲ ᑦᑕᓗᐅᕐᓯᒪᔪᖅ. ᐅᕐᑲᕐᑲᑦᑕᕐᑐᓂᑐ ᑲᐃᓐᑐᐊᕋᑎᐊᓗ ᖕᒥᔫᖅ ᐊᑐᕐᑐᓂᒃ, ᓂᓇᓂᐊᕐ ᑰᑐᖕᒥᑦᓂᒃ ᕐᑲᐃᑎᕐᑲᑦ ᑕᓗᐅᕐᓚᑕ ᐋᓐᓂᐊᕕᖕᒦᑦᑐᑦ ᓂᓇᓂᐊᕐᑕᖕᒥᑦᓂᒃ, ᑲᐃ ᓐᑐᐊᕐᑐᒍ ᐃᓚᑐᕋᓯᖕᒥᑦᓄᑦ ᑕᒪᐅᖕ ᑲᐃᑎᓇᐸᒃᑐᑎᒃ; ᐋᓐᓂᐊᖅᓯᐅᑎᑯᑐᖕᒥᑦᑐ ᐊᕐᓇᑯᑐᐃᑦ ᐱᓇᓯᐊᕐ ᑐᓐᑖᓗ ᕐᐸᒃᑐᑎᒃ ᓂᓇᑦᓇᕐᓯᔭᖅᖕᑲᑦ ᐊᓐᓕᕋᕐᔪᑦ ᑐᑦᓂᕐᓴᐃ ᕐᑲᑦᑕᕐᓚᑕ. ᐅᕐᑲᐅᔭᐃᑦᓇᑦᑎᐊᕐ ᑐᓂᑐ ᐱᑦᑎᐊᕐᑕᐅ ᔪᓐᓘᑐᕐᒥᔫᖅ. ᑭᒍᓯᓇᔾᓕᐊᖖᒪᑕᔫᖅ ᑕᐃᑲᓂ ᑭ ᒍᑎᖕᒍᐊᓗᐅᕐᑕᐅᓪᒪᓇᒃᑐᓂᔫᖅ, ᐃᑐᓵᖕᒥᑰᑐᒥᑲᑐ ᐊᕐ ᑐᓂᒥᑲᔫᖅ ᐊᑐᕐᓯᕐᑲᑦᑕᕐᑕᖕᒥᑦ ᐱᑖᕐᑎᑖᑦᓅᓚᐅᕐ ᒥ, ᐊᒥᐊᕐ ᑐᓂᒥᑦ ᐲᑦᑎᐊᓪᒪᓇᒃᐸᒃᑐᓂᒥᑦ ᐊᐃᕕᐅᐸ ᔫᖖᑲᑎᑐᑲᔫᖅ ᓴᓇᖕᔪᐊᑲᒃᓴᐅᖖᒪᑕ. ᑲᖕᔪᓯᕆᔪ ᖕᒥᑦᑎᐊᕐ ᑐᓂ ᐲᓚᐅᕐᐸᒃᑐᓂᑦ ᑕᑯᖅᑯᑎᓐᑐᓂᖅᑲ.

ᐃᑐᒃ ᑕᐃᒪᖕᑲᑐᐃᑦᓇᑦᑎᐊᖅ ᐋᓐᓂᐊᕕᓕᕐᓂᕐᑲᑦᑕ ᐅᕐᓯᒪᖕᒪᑦ. ᐅᕐᑲᖅᑐᓂ ᕐᑯᕕᐊᔪᑲᕕᐊᓘᓕᕐᑎᓅᔪᔫᖅ ᐋᓐᓂᐊᕕᖕᒥᐅᑦ ᓂᓇᕋᔫᔭᕐᑎᑕᐅᔪᓐᑰᓗᐅᕐᓂᕐᒥᒃ ᒪᒪᕐᑐ ᕋᔪᖕᓂᒃ ᐱᕋᕐᑐᓂᒃᑯ ᕐᑲᓄᐃᑦᑐᕋᔫᔭᕐᓂᒃ ᐸᐅᕐᖕᑳᒍ ᖕᓂᒃᑯ, ᑕᑦᑦᑐᐋᓐᓄᓂ ᑲᐃᓐᑐᐊᕋᑎᐊᒍᖕᒧᑦ ᐊᒧᑦᔪ ᑎᐊᒍᒧᖕᑦ ᕐᑲᐃᑕᐅᑉᐸᒃᑐᓂᒃ. ᑕᐅᑐᖕᒍᐊᕐᓇᕐᓯᓪᓚ ᓇᒃᐸᒍᓂᒥᑦ ᕐᑯᕕᐊᓇᕐᓯᑎᑐᐃᑦᓇᕐᑲᑦᑕᓗᐅᕐᓯᒪᖕᒪᒍ.

ᐃᑐᒃ ᕐᑯᕕᐊᔪᓚᐅᕐᓯᒪᖕᒪᑦ ᐃᓅᕐᑲᑎᒥᔭᓇᐊᒃᓴᑦ ᓂᒃ ᒪᑦᑖᕐᕕᒃᑯᑦ, ᐃᕐᖕᒍᑦᕐᑲᖅᓂᕐᕐ ᑐᓂᑐ ᐅᕙᑦᓂᒃ ᐃᓛᒃ, ᓂᖕᒥᐅᑦᓂᔫᖅ ᐃᓚᕐᑲᕐᒥ ᐅᕐᑲᓐᓚᑦᑎᐊᓚᐅᕐ ᓯᒪᔫᒐᒍᐊᖅ, ᐅᓐᓂᕐᓴᑦᓇᓐᓄᐊᕐᑎᑦᓇᒍ ᑕᒪᒃ ᑯᓂᖕᒐ ᑕᐃᑦᓯᒪᓂᐅᑎᓐᑯᒍ. ᐊᓪᓚᒍ ᕐᑲᐅᓯᒪᐃᑦᓇᖕᒥᑦᑕ ᓂᒃ ᐃᓕᕆᔭᐅᓇᓯᐊᓂᐊᒃᓴᖅ ᐋᓐᓅᖕᓄᑦ ᑕᑯᕐᑲᑦᑕᐃ ᑦᓇᖕᒥᑕᑐᑦ ᕐᑯᕕᐊᓇᐅᔪᖅᑰᓯᐅᓯᒪᓇᓂ. ᓯᖅᑯᐃᒥ

them at all the stops along the route of the C.D. Howe wearing a whole variety of military caps and articles of clothing. Once in awhile, some Inuit would ask me to give them something coming from the South. But I had nothing to spare out of the few things I had, for I was only 12.

We also stopped at Koartak and Povungnituk. I think it was in Koartak where I saw a Roman Catholic priest covered in a long black dress from head to feet, like they used to wear in those days. He spoke fluent Inuktitut, and the Inuit there sure were following him around as he was explaining things and interpreting for them.

We stopped at many more settlements on our way up to the Eastern Arctic, but hardly anyone got on the ship to be taken out to the hospital. By now, I was sharing my cabin with Etuk, who was returning from a stay in the hospital in Hamilton, Ontario. He had boarded the C.D. Howe at Fort Churchill.

Etuk was around his middle age. He often wanted to go out with me for a walk on the deck, but I was not much interested in going outside. I had already become used to staying indoors, especially when we were out on the sea for long periods of time between settlements. There was nothing interesting to see but the open water. Etuk told me he got so tired of staying inside at the hospital and never being allowed outdoors. He was an Inuk hunter, he said, an outdoor man. He wanted me to accompany him whenever he went out so I could interpret for him. He told me he was still scared to go out alone among the Qadlunaats.

When Etuk spoke of the hospital in Hamilton, it sounded so different from the Parc Savard in Quebec. He said they had a big cart there, carrying all the food for the patients, which they pushed along the corridors into the rooms; and the hospital nurses were all busy at mealtime serving the patients with their meals on trays. He said they treated him very well. The dentist there even made him a partial denture, although it was not too comfortable, so he filed it down himself to adjust it to fit, and it was just like carving a walrus tusk. He was not at all shy to take it out to show me.

Etuk never stopped talking about the hospital. He said during Christmas time

25

ᕐᓚᒃ ᑲᓗᐊᓴᐤᓗᒍᓗ ᓄᓇᕐ ᑲᑎᒥᓚᐅᕐᓯᒪᒐᑦᑎᒍᑦ ᑖᒃᑯ ᐊ ᐃᓚᒦᓕᒫᑦ ᐅᓯᐱᑦᑎᑦᓂ. ᐊᒻᒪᑦᑕᐅᖅ ᐃᕐᓂᖕ ᓚ ᓴᖕᒍᔭ ᐅᒥᐊᕐᔪᐊᒃ ᑰᕐ ᑲᑎᒥᓚᐅᓴᐤᓗᒍ ᕐᑲᐤᓗᓈᑦ ᓄᓇᖕ ᓚᑦᓄᐊᓕᕐᓗᑕ ᒪᑦᑖᕐᐱᒃᑯᑦ.

ᐊᒻᒪᑦᑕᐅᖅ ᑲᒪᑎᑕᐅᓚᐅᕐᓯᒪᖕᒥᒐᒪ ᑕᕙᕙ ᐅᕙᓂ ᒪᓇᓐᖕᒥᑦᑐᓄᐊᕐ ᑲᑦᑕᕋᑦᑕ ᓄᓇᓕᖕᓄᑦ ᐅᖕᓚᔪᒃᑐᒥᐅ ᕌᓗᖕᓄᑦ ᑕᐃᑦᓯᒪᓂᐅᑎᐤᓗᒍ ᐃᓄᐃᑦ ᓄᓇᓄᑦ ᐊᔪᐊᓄᑦ ᓇᕆᓗᐊᕐᐸᙵ ᒥᓯᖕ ᓚᖅᑎᐤᓗᒥᑦ. ᐸᖕᓂᕐ ᔫᓕᐊᕋᑦᑕ ᑕᐃᑲᓂᒥᐅᑦ ᐃᓚᖕᒥᑦ ᕐᑲᐅᓯᒪᔭᕐ ᑲᖅᓂᕋᓚᐅᕐᓯᒪᖕᒪᑕ ᐊᑖᑕᑦᓂᒃ. ᕐᑭᖕᑲᓯᕐᓗᓂᒎᖅ ᑕᐅᕗᖕ ᓛᓗᒃ ᑎᑭᓚᐅ ᕐᓯᒪᑦᓂᕐᒪᑦ ᒥᑦᑎᒪᑕᓕᖕᒥᑦ ᐊᔪᓇᕐᓱᐃᓯᒥᒃ ᒥᑭᑦᓂ ᕐᓴᒥᒃ ᐱᕐ ᑲᑎᕐᑲᖅᓗᓂ. ᐊᒻᒪᑦᑕᐅᖅ ᐊᖕ ᓚᔪᑯᓗᓚ ᓇᐱᑲ ᐸᖕᓂᕐ ᔫᒦᓚᐅᕐᓂᓇᐤᓗᓂ ᒥᑭᑦᓂᕐᓴᐅᐸ ᐊᖕ ᓚᔪ ᖕᓚᓂᒃ ᓇᔪᕐᑎᕐ ᑲᖅᓗᓂ ᐄᙵ ᓚᓕᒥᑦ ᓚᓐᑕᓐᒥᑦ, ᑯ ᐃᐸ ᓄᓇᖕ ᓚᑦᓂᙵ ᓛᓚᐅᕐᓗᓂ. ᑖᒃᑯᐊ ᒥᑭᑦᓂᕐᓴᕐᓗ ᐊᖕᒥᓂᕐᓴᕐᓘᖅᑯᕐ ᑐᕐᖕᒥᒃᑯᐊ ᓯᕗᐤᓕᕐᐸᐅᐤᓗᑎᒃ ᐃᓄ ᐃᑦ ᓄᓇᖕ ᓚᑦᓂ ᕐᑲᐅᓯᐃᑦᑐᕐᒥᐅᓂᕐᓴᖅ ᐊᔪᓇᕐ ᑐᐃᓯᐅ ᕐᖕ ᓚᓇᐊᓚᐅᕐᓂᕐᒪᑎᒃ.

ᑲᖕᒥᕐᓗᒑᐱᖕᒥᑦᑕᐅᖅ ᐃᓄᖕᒥᑦ ᐅᕐᑲᕐᑲᑦᑕᓚᐅᕐᓯ ᒪᖕᒥᖕᒪᑕ ᕐᑲᐅᓯᒪᔭᕐ ᑲᖅᓂᕋᕐᓗᑎᒃ ᐃᓚᑦᓂᒃ ᑲᒪᓇᕐ ᐸᓚᐅᕐᑐᑦ ᓛᓂᑐᕐ ᑳᓗᒃ ᓄᓇᓖᑦ ᐃᓚᕐᑲᖅᓂᕋᐅᕐᓗᑎᒃᓗ ᓂᖕᒥᐅᑦᓂᒃ. 1940 ᐊᕐᕌᒍᖕᒥᑕ ᐃᓚᖕᒥᑦᓂ ᐊᖕᓚ ᔪᑯᓗᓚ ᐅᕙᑦᑎᑦᓄᙵ ᓚᐅᓕᕐᓗᓂ ᐊᑖᑕᒃᑯᑎᑦᓄᑦ ᐊᐃᔭ ᐅᓚᐅᕐᓯᒪᖕᒥᖕᒪᑦ ᑲᖕᒥᕐᓗᒑᐱᖕᒥᑦ ᕐᑭᒧᒃᓯᖕᑯᑦ. ᐅᕐᑲᐅᓯᑯᓗᖕᒥᑦ ᑕᐃᒪ ᑖᒃᑯᖕᓇᖕᓂ ᐸᖕᓂᕐᔫᒥᓗ ᑲᖕ ᒥᕐᓗᒑᐱᖕᒥᓗ ᑐᓴᕐᓂᓇᓚᐅᕐᓯᒪᓖᑭᑦ ᐊᕐᓇᕐᓯᐅᑎᑯᓘᖅ ᑰᔨᔪᒥᒃ ᐅᕐᑲᐤᓚᕐᑲᑦᑕᕐᒪᑕ. ᐊᑯᓂᑐᕐ ᑲᐅᓕᕐ ᔫᓚᓗ ᐊᖅ ᑐᓵᙵ ᒍᐊᕐᔫᒥᔭᕐ ᑲᑦᑕᓚᐅᕐᓯᒪᒐᒃᑭᑦ ᐊᓂᒍᕐᓯᒪ ᔭᑐᕐ ᑲᓇᓕᕋᓗᐊᕐ ᓗᑎᒍᑦ.

ᑕᐃᑦᓯᒪᓂᐅᑎᐤᓗᒍ, ᐃᓄᓕᒫᑦᑎᐊᑲᓴᐃᑦ ᐊᐤᓄᕌᕐᓯ ᒪᐅᓯᕐ ᑲᖅᐸᓚᐅᕐᓯᒪᖕᒪᑕ ᕐᑯᓕᑦᑕᐅᔭᕐ ᑲᐅᕐ ᑐᐃᑦᓇᐅᐤ ᓗᑎᒃ ᕐᑲᓕᐹᓕᖕᓂᒃ ᕐᑲᐅᐤᓗᕐᑐᓂᒃ ᑭᓯᐊᓂᓗᐊᖅ ᐊᒻ ᒪᓗ ᓇᑦᑎᕋᕕᓂᕐᓂᒃ ᑲᒥᒃᓯᒪᐅᕐᑐᐊᑦᓅᐤᓗᑎᒃ (ᒫᐤᓇ ᓕ ᑕᑯᓇᕐᐸᓕᕐᑐᓂᒃ ᑲᒥᐊᓗᒃᓯᒪᐅᕐᑐᓂᒃ ᑭᓯᐊᓂ ᓄᓇ ᓂ ᓇᓂᑐᐃᑦᓇᕐᓯᐊᖅ) ᓰᕐ ᑲᐃᒻᒪ ᑲᒪᓇᕆᔪᒻᒪᓇᓰᖕᒍᓕ ᕐᑐᕐᓘᑦᓅᑦ ᑲᒥᒃᓯᒪᔪᐊᑦᓄᖕᓂᒃ ᑕᑯᔪᕐᑲᑕᐃᑦᓇᕋᒥ. ᐃᓕᓴᕐᓇᕐᑐᐊᑦᓅᕐᑲᑦᑕᓚᐅᕐᓯᒪᖕᒪᑕ ᑕᒪᒃᑯᓂᖕᓚ ᐊᑐ ᕆᓯᑐᕐ ᑲᖅᒥᖕᓂᒃ ᐅᑎᕐᐸᐤᓕᐊᓕᕐᓗᑕ ᑕᑯᕐᑲᑦᑕᓕᓇᐤᓗ ᒥᑦ ᐅᐊᒃ, ᐃᓕᓴᕐᓇᒦᒃ, ᐊᕐᓇᐃᐤᓗ ᒪᑯᐊ ᐊᒫᕐᑐᑦ ᓄᓇᖕᓂ ᓇᓂᑐᐃᑦᓇᑦᑎᐊᖅ ᒥᑭᑦᑐᕐ ᑲᓵᖕᓚᒥᒃ.

ᐊᖅᑯᓵᕐᐸᐤᓕᐊᔭᓕᒫᑦᑎᑦᓂ, ᑕᐃᒪᙵ ᓚᑦ ᑖᒃᑯᓂᖕ ᓚᑦᑕᐃᑦᓇᖅ ᑕᒪᑦᓯ ᐊᐱᕐᓯᕐᑐᑦ: "ᑭᓈᐱᐅᕕᑦ? ᓇᓂ ᒥᐅᕌᐱᐅᕕᑦ? ᕐᑲᓄᐃᑦᓂᕋᕕᑦ? ᑮᓇᐅᓚᕕᑦ? ᓇᓂᒥᐅᑕ ᐅᓚᕕᑦ?" ᑕᐃᒪᙵ ᓚᑦ ᐊᑎᑦᓂᒃ ᐅᕐᑲᐅᑎᒐᒃᑭᑦ ᐊᕐ ᕌᒍᑦᓂᒃᓗ, ᕐᑲᐤᓗᓈᑦ ᓄᓇᖕ ᓚᑦᓂᙵ ᓛᓇᐊᒃᓴᑦᓂᒃᓗ, ᐋᐤᓂᐊᕕᖕᒥ. ᐱᔨᑎᑯᓘᓂᕋᕐ ᑕᐅᕐ ᑲᑦᑕᓚᐅᕐᓯᒪᒐᒪ ᐃᓄ ᑐᐊᑯᓘᐤᓗᑎᑦ ᑕᐅᓇᙵ ᓛᓘᕐᐱᑦ ᐅᐊᑲᐤᓚᖕᓛ.

ᐅᑎᓕᕐᓗᑕ, ᑕᒪᐃᑦᓂᑦᑎᐊᑭᓗᒃ ᑲᑎᓯᕐ ᑲᑦᑕᓕᓚᐅᕐ ᓯᒪᒐᒪ ᒪᑦᑖᓇᐊᕐ ᑐᕐ ᑐᓕᒫᑦᑎᐊᓂᒃ. ᓯᕗᐤᓕᕐᑎᔫᙵ ᒥᑦᑎᐊᕐᑐᖅ ᐅᒥᐊᕐᔪᐊᒃ ᑰᕆᓯᓇᓚᐅᕐᑕᑦᑐᑦ, ᑕᒫᓂ ᐊ ᕐᑯᐊᓂ ᓯᓂᒃᕕᕐᑲᕋᒪ ᕐᑲᓄᐃᓕᐅᕆᔫᔭᕐᑐᑦ ᓇᔪᓚᖕᒥᑦ ᓂ ᐳᓛᕐ ᑕᐅᑦ ᑕᐃᓕᓇᖕ ᓚᓗ ᐳᕙᒃᓗᙵᒥᑦᓇᒪ. ᑎᓴᒪᓂᒃ ᓯᓂᒃᕕᓕᖕᒦᑦᓗᖕᓚ ᐊᓇᓇᐊᕐ ᑐᕐᕕᕐᑲᒻᒪᓇᒃᓗᓂ ᐅᐊᓴᕐ ᕕᑯᓗᕐᑲᖅᓗᓂᓗ ᐊᒻᓚᓄᑦ.

ᕐᑯᕕᐊᔪᕆᔫᔭᕐᑎᑕᐅᕐᑲᑦᑕᓚᐅᕐᓯᒪᒐᒪ ᑕᑯᕆᔫᔭᕐᑲ ᑦᑕᕐᓗᖕᓚ ᑭᓇᒃᑯᑦᓂᕆᔫᔭᖅ ᐃᓄᖕᓂᒃ; ᐅᖕᓚᔪᒃᑐᕐᒥ ᐅᑖᓘᐤᓗᖕᓚ ᒥᑦᑎᒪᑕᓕᖕᒥᑦ. ᐊᑭᐊᓂᒥᐅᑦ ᑯᐱᐊᒃ ᑕᕐᕋᕐᓚᓂᒥᐅᑦ ᐅᕐᑲᐅᓯᕐᑕᕐᑲᖅᒥᖕᒪᑕ ᓄᓇᑦᑕ ᒥᒃᓵ ᓂᒥᐅᓂᒃ ᕐᑲᐅᓯᐃᑦᑐᕐᒥᐅᑕᐅᓂᕋᐃᐤᓗᑎᒃ. ᕐᑲᐅᔪᑦ

the patients had been given all kinds of fresh fruit, piled so high on a cart that they had to bring it up by the elevator. He said they had so much to eat on that special day.

Etuk was very happy I was with him on the C.D. Howe trip, and he called me his grandchild. Actually, he was related to my grandmother. I remembered him very slightly from the time long before when he and his family had lived with us in our camp. His son Sanguja had made the trip down with me on the C.D. Howe.

Another surprise was in store for me when we stopped at Pangnirtung. I learned that the people there also knew of my father. It turned out that one time he had made a trip by dogteam there all the way from Pond Inlet with the Anglican Archdeacon John Turner. Also, my eldest sister Rebecca had stayed for awhile in Pangnirtung once, after she had returned from her trip to London, England. She had lived there in Pangnirtung for about a year with John Turner's brother and his family. John Turner and his brother were two of the first Anglican priests to go up to the Eastern Arctic.

Clyde River was yet another place where I met Inuit who said that they knew my family, and some were even related to my grandmother. In the late 1940's, my sister Rebecca had been taken there by my parents by dogteam. The dialect in those two communities - Pangnirtung and Clyde River - sounded so musical and feminine that I kept hearing it over and over again in my mind, long after the ship had pulled away.

At that time, most Inuit were dressed in parka covers made of white duck material and brand new sealskin boots (since replaced by the rubber boots and shoes of today). It was really good to see my people again, dressed this way, and to watch the women carrying the babies on their backs.

All along the way, the same old questions kept coming up: "What is your name? Where is your home? Where are you returning from? What was wrong with you? What is your name, and how old are you?" Each time I would tell them my name and my age, and that I had been in the white man's land, in a place where sick people went. And they told me how brave I was to have travelled all alone like that.

On the trip back, I met just about

ᓇᓐᒥᑦᑐᒥᒃ ᐊᑎᕐ ᑲᖅᑎᑕᐅᓐᒪᑦ, ᑐᓴᓐᓇᐊᕐᓐ ᓚᓕᔩᕐᓗ ᒍ ᐃᔪᓐᔭᖕᑰᓗᒥᓕᐅᕐᓯᒪᔭᕐᓗᐊᕐ ᐅᕐ ᑲᐅᑕᐅᒥᐊᕐᓐ ᓚᕐ ᒍᔭᓕᕐᑎᖕᓗᒍ. ᕐᑲᐅᓲᓐ ᒍᓚᓗᐊᕐᒥᓚᑦᑕᓕ, ᓲᕐ ᑲᐃᒻ ᒪ ᐅᐱᕐᓐ ᓚᒻᒪᓐᑐᐊᕐᓐ ᓚᑦ ᑖᕐᓯᔪᑦᓇᐃᖕᓕᓲᓐ ᒍᖕᓗᑕ. ᑭᓯᐊᓂᓕ ᐊᐃᕙᕐ ᑲᑎᕐ ᑲᕐᓱᐊᓚᐅᕐᓯᒪᓐᒥᑦᑐᓐ ᓚᓗ ᐱᓚ ᐅᕐᑐᓐᓚ, ᑕᐃᒪᓐᓇ ᐅᕐᑲᕐᑲᑦᑕᓕᕐᒪ ᕐᑲᐅᓯᐃᑐᒥᐅᓂ ᕐᕐᓗᒍ ᓄᓇᓚ ᕐᑲᐅᓯᔭᐅᖕᓚᐅᑎᒥᓂᓴᐅᕐᑲᑦᑕᓕᓚᐅᕐᓯᒪ ᓐᒪᑦ, ᒥᕐᑎᒪᑕᓕᓐᒦᑐᐃᑦᓇᕐᑲᑦᑕᕆᑦᓃᕐᓗᓐᓚ. ᑕᐃᒪ ᕐᑲᐅᓯᐃᑦᑐᒥ ᓄᓇᕐᑲᖅᑐᓐᓚ ᐅᕐᑲᕐᑲᑦᑕᓕᕐᒪ, ᐊᒻᒪ ᓗ ᕐᑲᓂᒥᓂᕐᕐᓗᒍ ᐊᑯᑭᑦᑐᒥᐅᓄᑦ ᓄᓇᓐᒍᐊᑎᒍᑦ.

ᑲᑎᔨᕆᓗᔭᕐ ᑲᑦᑕᓗᐅᕐᓯᒪᓚᓗᐊᕐᓗᓐᓚ ᐅᕐ ᑲᐅᔨᕐ ᑲᑎ ᒦᓐᒥᕆᓲᔭᕐ ᑐᓂᒃ ᓄᓇᓂ ᐊᑐᓂ, ᐊᐱᕐ ᓯᕆᑎᒥᕐ ᑲᑦᑕᕐ ᑕᓐᒥᑦ ᐃᓕᑦᓇᒃᑭᑦ ᐅᕐ ᑲᕆᑦᓇᑦᑎᐊᕐ ᑲᑦᑕᓚᐅᕐᓯᒪᔫᓐ ᓚ. ᑕᐃᒪᓗ, ᐃᓕᑦᑎᑦᔫᒦᓯᒪᕐ ᑲᑦᑕᓕᓚᐅᕐᓯᒪᓚᓚ ᐃ ᓄᓐᓂᒃ ᐋᖕᓂᐊᕕᓐᒦᑦᑐᓂᒃ ᑲᑎᒪᒃᓕᕐ ᑲᑦᑕᐅᕐ ᑲᑦᑕᐅ ᕐᓗᓐᓚ ᐅᕐ ᑲᐅᔨᕐ ᑲᑎᒦᓐᒥᕆᓲᔭᕐ ᑐᓂᒃ.

ᑕᖅᑭᓂᒃ ᑎᓴᒪᓂᒃ ᕐᑭᒪᒥᒃ ᑯᑦᓃᓕᐅᕐᓗᓐᓚ ᑎᓴᒪᐃ ᑦᓇᐅᓚᓗᐊᕐᑎᖕᓗᒥᑦ, ᐃᓄᓐᓂᒃ ᑲᑎᔨᕐ ᑲᑦᑕᓕᑕᐃᑦᓇᕐ ᒥᓚᓚ, ᑲᓐᒍᓯᓕᐅᖅᑲᕐ ᑲᑦᑕᓕᐅᐱᖕᓕᓕᐅᕐᑐᓐᓚ ᐃᓄᒃ ᑎᑐᑦ ᐅᕐ ᑲᖕᓕᒥᐊᒃᓴᖅ. ᐅᕐ ᑲᐅᔨᕐ ᑲᕐ ᑲᑎᐅᓐᒥᖕᓖ ᓗᒃᓗᓐᓚᓗ ᐊᔾᔪᓕᒫᓂᑦ ᐃᓅᕐ ᑲᑎᒥᐊᒃ ᑕᑦᓂᑦ. ᑭᓯᐊᓂᓕ ᐅᕐ ᑲᐅᑎᔭᐅᕐ ᑲᑦᑕᓕᓚᐅᕐᓯᒪᓚᓚ ᑐᑭᓯᒃᓴᐅᑦᑎᐊᕐ ᑐᖕᑰᑦ ᓂᕐᕐ ᑕᐅᖕᓗᓂ ᕐᑲᐅᓯᐃᑦᑐᕐᒥᐅᑎᒍᑦ ᐅᕐ ᑲᐅᔨᕐ ᐳᑦ ᐊ ᔨᓂᑦ ᐅᕐ ᑲᐅᔨᕐᓂᑦ.

ᑕᐃᒃ ᑯᐊᑦᑕᐅᖅ ᐃᓄᐃᑦ ᒪᑯᐊ ᐊᑭᐊᓂᒥᐅᓐ ᒍᓂᕐᕐᑕ ᐳ ᑭᓐ ᒪᐱᒥᐅᑦᓗ — ᓲᕐ ᑲᐃᒻᒪ ᐊᖕᒍᑎᓐᒥᑦ ᐱᓗᐊᕐ ᑐᒥᒃ — ᐅᖕᓵᓇᓕᐅᕐᓯᒪᓚᒃᑭᑦ ᐃᓕᕐᓱᕐ ᑲᓐᒥᑦᑎᐊᕐ ᑐᖕᓕ ᐃᓅᓚᓗᐊᕐᓗᑎᒃ. ᒪᑦᑖᕐᕕᓕᐊᑐᐊᕐᒥᒃ, ᑲᓐ ᒍᓯᕆᔪᓐᒥᑦᑎᐊᕐ ᑲᑦᑕᓕᐅᕐᓕᑕ ᐅᒥᐊᕐᔪᐊᖓ ᓇᓘᕆᓗ ᔭᖅ ᐊᐃᓚᓗᐊᓐᓇᐊᒃᓴᖅ ᐃᓕᕐᓯᕆᔪᓐᒥᑦᑎᐊᕐᓗᑎᒃᓗ ᑕ ᓗᕆᒃ ᑯᑎᓐᒥᑦᑎᐊᕐᓗᑎᒃ. ᐃᓚᓐᒥᑦᓘᑦᓃᑦ ᐅᒥᐊᒃ ᑕᕐ ᑲᖅᕕᓐᓚᓄᑦ ᐳᓕᕐᕆᔫᔭᑐᐃᑦᓇᕆᒪᖕᓗᑎᒃ. ᑭᔅᒥᔭᕐ ᑲᓐᒥᑦᑎᐊᕐᒥᒃ ᓴᓇᓐᒍᐊᓚᕐᒥᓐᓂᒃ ᓂᐅᕐᕆᑎᕐᑲᕆᒫ ᖕᓕᓕᔩᓐᓚᒥᒃ ᓂᐅᕕᕐᕆᒪᖕᓗᑎᒃᓗ ᐅᒥᐊᕐᔪᐊᐸ ᓂᐅᕕᕐ ᕕᑯᓗᐊᓂ ᐃᒥᓚᕐᓂᒃ ᐅᕐᑯᒻᒥᐊᓚᕆᔫᓐᓂᒃᓗ ᐅᐃᒪᔭᕆᔪ ᑦᑎᐊᕐᓗᑎᒃ ᓇᕆᑦᑕᐃᓕᓐᒥᑦᑎᐊᒻᒪᓐᕐ ᑲᑦᑕᓕᐅᕐᓯᒪᓐ ᒪᑕᓕ.

ᐊᓕᐊᓇᐃᕆᔫᕐ ᑐᖕᑰᕐ ᑲᑦᑕᓕᓚᐅᕐᓯᒪᓐᒪᑦ ᑕᒪᒃᑯ ᐊ ᐃᓄᐃᑦ ᐊᔪᐊᓂᒥᐅᑦ ᑲᑎᕆᔪᓐᓇᐊᓐᒥᑦᓂᒃ ᓱᓐᒥᐅᑎ ᒐᒪ ᓇᓂᑐᐃᑦᓈᓐᓇᐊᖅ ᓄᓇᓕᓐᓂ ᐊᔪᓂᒥᐅᑦ. ᐃᒪᑦᓇ ᑲ ᓐ ᒍᓯᒃ ᑐᖕᑰᖕᓗᓐᓚ ᐋᖕᓕᔪᐊᒍᔭᐃᓐᓗᓐᓚᓗ ᐱᕙᓕᐅᕐ ᓗᐊᕐᓗᓐᓚ ᐃᓄᓐᓂ ᒫᓂᕆᓗᑐᐃᑦᓈᓕᒪᓐᒥᑦᓂᑯᒥᒃ ᐅᕐ ᑲᖕᓕᕐ ᑲᑎᕐ ᑲᑦᑎᐊᕐ ᑲᑦᑕᓕᕐᓗᓐᓚ, ᐃᒪᑦᓇ ᓄᒫᓲᔭᑐᐃ ᑦᓇᕆᖕᓃᕐᓗᓐᓚ ᐊᔪᐅᒪᔪᑎᑐᑦ, ᓂᖕᓕᕆᑦᓇᓐᒥᑦᑐᐊᓗ ᒃᑎᑐᖕᓗ. ᑕᐃᒪᓕ, ᓇᓂᑐᐃᑦᓇᖅ ᐃᓅᕐ ᑲᑎᑦᓂᒃ ᑲᑎ ᓯᔭᕿᓐ ᓚᓚ ᓄᓇᓕᓐᓂ ᐅᒥᐊᕐᔪᐊᒃᑰᕐᓗᓐᓚ, ᐃᓄᓐᓂᒃ ᑲᑎᔨᓂᐊᕐ ᑐᐊᑦᓅᓕᕐᓂᐊᕐᒥᒥᐊᒃᓴᖅ ᑲᔪᒥᓇᔭᕐ ᑲᕐ ᑲᑦᑕ ᓕᓚᐅᕐᓯᒪᓚᓚ, "ᐊᓂᑦᑎᑐᑦ ᕐ ᑲᑕᓐᒍᑎᑐᑦ ᐱᒥᐊᓚ ᐅᕐᓯᒪᔫᓐᓚ" ᐃᓅᕐ ᑲᑎᑦᓂᐊᑐᐃᑦᓇᓐᒥᖕᓗᓐᓚ. ᐋᖕᓚ ᑕᕐ ᑲᕐ ᑲᑦᑕᕆᑦᓃᓚᐅᕐᓯᒪᔫᖅ, ᑕᒪᒃᑯᐊᓖᑦ ᑕᑯᔭᓐᓚᐅ ᑦᑎᐊᒻᒪᓐᒃ ᑕᕐᓗᐊᒃᑲ.

ᐃᓅᔨᕐ ᐊᖕᔾᔨᔪᑦᑑᐅᕐᓯᒪᓐᒪᒍ ᐃᓗᓐᒥᕐᓱᓇᓗᐊᕆᑦ ᓅᓚᐅᕐᓯᒪᔪᖅ ᐃᓕᕐ ᑲᐅᕆᔫᔭᑐᐃᑦᓇᓐᓇᐊᒃᓴᖅ ᐊᔪᓂᒃ. ᑕᐃᑦᓯᒪᓂᓂᐅᖅᑰᕐᑐᖅ ᕐᑯᕕᐊᓇᕆᔫᕐᓗᓐᒃ ᐱᓐ ᒍᐊᕐ ᑐᐊᓗᓐ ᓅᓚᐅᕐᓯᒪᓚᓚ ᐃᓄᒥᐊᔫᓗᓐᓂ ᓂᕐᔪᑎᑦᕐ ᑲᐅᖅᑐᓂ ᓱᓐ ᒥᐅᑎᑎᑕᐅᓚᐅᕐᓯᒪᖅᑰᕐᓚ ᐊᓕᐊᓇᐃᒥᕆᔫᕐᓗᒥᑦ ᐃ ᓄᒥᐊᓖᓗᓚᓗᐊᓂᒃ ᕐ ᑲᓄᐃᒃᓴᕆᑦᓅᓚᐅᕐᓯᒪᓚᓚ ᑲᐸᐃᐊᔪ ᕆᔪᒍᑦᓃᕐᓚ ᕐ ᑯᓐ ᒥᐊᕐᕕᐊᓗᓐᒥ. ᐊᑯᓂᕆᓗᒃ ᑲᐸ ᐊᔨᐃᑦᓇᕆᔪᑐᕐ ᑲᓚᐅᕐᓯᒪᓚᓚ ᕐ ᑲᓄᐃᓕᓂᐊᓴᓗᐊᓐᓇᐊᒃᓴᖅ

every single person who boarded the C.D. Howe for a medical examination. Unlike my first experience onboard the ship, I was right in the middle of all the activity, as I was staying in a cabin at the stern of the boat. It was a four-bed room and was even equipped with its own toilet and sink.

I really enjoyed meeting so many Inuit along the way; and most of them were interested to meet an Inuk, like myself, who came from a place so far away in the North, such as Pond Inlet. Northern Quebec Inuit even had a name for the High Arctic which meant: "A place that never has daylight". Of course, it sounded rather funny to me when somebody first mentioned it. After all, we had daylight there too. But I didn't argue about it, and it turned out that describing my home in that way made it a lot easier to explain where I was from, rather than just saying Pond Inlet. So, I began to say simply that I was from a place that had never seen daylight, and that it was close to Greenland, according to the map.

Although I was meeting people speaking so many different dialects, I quickly got used to their questions. Too, I had already been prepared by the many dialects spoken by the Inuit patients at the hospital.

After spending just four months with the Wilkinsons, when it came time for my first meeting with my fellow Inuit, I felt shy speaking Inuktitut again. I was especially afraid to speak my own dialect at first, because it was so different from the others. But then, many people told me it was much easier to understand than any other dialect.

I found the Inuit from Northern Quebec and Cape Dorset - especially the men - to be outspoken for Arctic people. When they got on the C.D. Howe, they did not hesitate to tour around the ship. Some of them were even eager to go up to the captain's cabin. They seemed to be very bold, especially when it came to selling their carvings and going to the canteen to buy soft drinks and sweets.

It was very exciting for me to meet all these people as we stopped at the different settlements. They encouraged me to be brave and speak out, instead of being a lost, tongue-tied kid all the time. Now, whenever I met my fellow Inuit,

ᓇᓗᓇᖅᑰᕆᐤᓗᓂ — ᒪᑦᑖᕐᕖᒃ ᑰᓯᒥᐊᕐᖕ ᑲᑦᓚᕋᒪ, ᐊᒻᒪᓗ ᐋᐤᓂᐊᕕᐊᓗᖕ ᔫᑦᓚᕋᒪ. ᑕᐃᒃ ᑯᐊᓕ, ᕐᑭᒻᒥᒃ ᑯᑦ ᐊᒻᒪᓗ ᓴᓐ ᑯᐱᑕᓐ ᑕᐃᕐᓇ ᐅᒥᐊᕐᔪᐊᒥ ᑲᒪᔨᒥᓚᐅᕐᓯᒪᔭᕋ, ᐊᒻᒪᓗ ᑕᒪᒃ ᑯᐊ ᐃᓅᕐ ᑲᑎᒃᑲ ᐱᑦᑎᐊᕐᑎᒥᕐ ᑲᑦᑕᓚᐅᕐᓯᒪᔭᒃᑲ ᐃᑲᔪᕐ ᑐᒻᒪᓇᐋᓗᓚᐅᕐᓯᒪᖕᒪᑕ ᐅᖓᑦᓂᒃ ᕐᑯᕕᐊᔪᒐᔾᔨᒥᔪᕈᕐᑎᑕᐅᐤᓗᖕᒐ ᕐᑭᒃᓴᖕᒐᑐᐃᑦᓇᕐᑐᒥᒃ ᐃᓅᓯᕐ ᑲᓕᕐᓂᐊᕐ ᑐᒃᓴᐅᓚᐅᕐᓯᒪᒐᓗᐊᕐ ᑐᖕᒐ ᓄᑖᒥᒃ ᐊᑐᒐᕐ ᑲᓕᕐᑎᐤᓗᖕᒐ ᐊᐤᔨᐅᓐᖕᒥᑦᑎᐊᒻᒪᓐᒃ ᑐᒥᒃ ᐃᓅᓯᓐᕙᒃ ᑕᑦᑕᑦ ᑕᐃᑦᓯᒪᓂᐅᑎᐤᓗᒍ. ᕐᑯᔭᒥᔭᒻᒪᓐᐊᓗᒥᒐᓗᐊᕐᐸᒃ ᑲ ᑭᓇᒃᑯᑐᐃᑦᓇᐃᑦ ᐅᕙᑦᓂᒃ ᐃᑲᔪᕐᓯᕐᓯᒪᓚᐅᕐᑐᑦ ᑐᑭᓯᒪᑦᑎᐊᓚᐅᕐᑐᐤᓗ ᓂᕕᐊᕐᓵᖕ ᔪᑎᐤᓗᖕᒐ ᓃᕐᓗ ᐊᔪᐅᓯᒪᑦᑎᐊᓕᕐᑎᐤᓗᖕᒐ ᐊᖕᒐᔪᖅᑳᑦᓂᒃ ᓇᔫᑎᔪᓐᓃᕐᑎᐤᓗᖕᒐ ᐅᖕᒐᔨᒥᔅᓗᒥᔭᓐᐅᕐᓗᒥᑦ ᓯᕗᐤᓚᕐᐹᑦᑎᐊᒻᒪᓐᖕᒥᒃ.

ᕐᑲᐅᔨᒪᑦᑎᐊᓚᐅᕐᓯᒪᔪᖕᒐ ᑎᑭᓐᓂᐅᔭᓕᕈᑎᑦᑎᑦᓂᒥᑦᑎᒪᑕᓕᖕᔫᑦ. ᕐᑯᓐᖕᒥᐊᔫᔅᔪᓚᐅᕐᓯᒪᒐᒪ ᐅᒥᐊᕐᔪᐊᒃᑯᑦ ᓯᒐᔭᕐᐸᓯᒃᑰᕐᓗᑕ ᐃᓛᒃ ᓴᓕᐊᒃᓗᑕ ᓄᓇᖕᒐᔪᑦ ᕐᑭᖅᕐᑭᑖᓗᐸ, ᐃᑦᑐᕐᑯᑦᓂᕐ ᑐᒥᒃᓗ ᐃᓅᕐ ᑲᑎᕐᑲᓚᐅᕐᓯᒪᒐᒪ, ᐃᑐᖕᒥᒃ ᐃᒃᐱᐊᕐᔪᖕᒥᐅᑕᕐᒥᒃ, ᐅᕐᑲᐅᑎᕙᐤᓕᐊᔫᔅᔪᓚᐅᕐᓯᒪᖕᒪᖕᒐ ᑕᒪᒃᑯᐊ ᓄᓇᐃᑦ ᓴᕐᐸᑦᑕᑦ ᐊᑎᖕᒥᑦᓂᒃ ᐅᐊᒃ ᐃᓕᑦᕐᓯᔪᖅ ᐅᐊᔪᓈᕐᐤᓚᒃᐸᒃᓗᓂ.

ᑕᑯᒥᐊᐤᓚᓕᑕᐃᕐᓇᕐᑲᕿ ᐊᑖᑕᒃᑯᒃᑲ ᐅᐊᒃᑲᐤᓚᖕᑳ ᐃᓕᓴᕐᓇᒦᒃ ᐊᓕᐊᓇᐃᕿᓗᖕᑳ ᐊᒃᓯᐊᓗᒃ ᕐᑯᓚᓇᕐᓯᕐᑎᐊᖅᑰᕆᓚᐅᕐᑎᐤᓗᒍ. ᕐᑭᐅᖕᒐ, ᕐᑯᕕᐊᓯᐊᖕᒥᕐᑎᕐᔫᐊᖕᒥᑦᑐᖅ ᕐᑭᒃᓵᕐᓂᕐᔫᐊᖕᒥᑦᑐᖅ, ᑭᓯᐊᓂᓕ ᕐᑯᕕᐊᓯᓗᐊᓚᐅᕐᒪ ᑕᐃᒪᕐᓇ ᕐᑯᕕᐊᓯᒃᑎᒥᓗᐊᓚᐅᕐᓯᒪᑎᒥᓐᖕᒥᓚᖕᒐ ᐊᐤᔨᕐᑲᖕᒥᑦᑐᒥᒃ ᐊᑖᑕᒐ ᐅᖕᒐᒥᔭᕿ ᐊᔪᑎᒻᒪᓐᐋᓗᓚᐅᕐᓯᒪᖕᒪᑦ ᕐᑯᓄᓇᓂᓗ ᑕᑯᑦᓚᓕᑕᐃᕐᓇᕐᒥᒐᒃᑯ.

ᑕᐃᒪᓕ ᐅᑎᕐᓗᖕᒐ ᐊᔾᖕᔪᖅᑲᖅᑐᕕᓃᑦ ᐃᓚᒃᑲ ᐅᑎᕐᕕᒥᐸᒃᑲ. ᐊᓂᕐᓇᕆᓂᕐᐹᕐ, ᐸᐅᓪ ᐅᐤᓚᑎᑦᖅ, ᓄᓕᐊᕐ ᑲᓕᖅᑐᖅ ᓂᕕᐊᕐᓴᐅᕐ ᑲᑎᑐᐊᕆᕐ ᑲᑦᑕᕐ ᑕᕕᓂᕐᓄᑦ ᐱᕐ ᑲᕐᓇᕆᔭᐅᕐᓛᓗᐤᓂᒃ ᓱᕈᓯᐅᓂᓕᒫᕐᓂ. ᐅᐊᕐᓇᐅᔭᕈᓗᖕᒌ ᓄᒃᕐ ᑲᓕᕐᓗᖕᒐᓗ ᓅᑎᒥᒃ ᑎᑭᑦᑐᖕᒐ. ᓱᓇᐅᕙᕙ ᐅᓇ 7—ᓂᒃ ᑕᖅᑭᕐ ᑲᓕᓈᕐᑐᕕᓂᖅ ᑐᓴᓚᐅᕐᓯᒪᐤᓚᖕᒥᑕᕐ ᓄᒃᖅᑳᓇᐅᕈᑎᒥᐤᓗᒍ ᐊᕐᓇᐅᐤᓗᓂ. ᑕᐃᕐᓱᒪᓂᐅᑎᐤᓗᒍ ᐊᓂᒐ ᓄᒃᖅᓯᕐ ᕚᓇᓚᐅᕐᓯᒪᔭᕙᑦ, ᓄᐊ ᐃᐤᓚᐅᖅ ᐱᕈᕐ ᑐᕕᓂᑯᓗᒃ ᑕᐅᖅ ᐅᕐ ᑲᒃᑲᑰᓕᕐᓗᓂᓗ. ᕐᑭᑐᕐᖕᒐᑐᐃᕐᓇᓇᓚᐅᕐᓯᒪᒐᒃᑯ ᐆᐤᓚᓚᐅᖅᑳᕐᓇᖕᒐ ᕐᑲᐤᓗᓈᑦᓄᓇᖕᒐᑦᓄ. ᐋᓇᒪ ᐅᕐ ᑲᐅᑎᓚᐅᕐᓯᒪᔫᖕᒐ ᕐᑭᓄᐤᓚᕐᑐᐤᓘᓗᓚᐅᕐᓂᕐᕐᓗᓂᐅᒃ ᕐᑭᐊᕐ ᑲᑦᑕᓚᐅᕐᓂᕐᕐᓗᓂᐅᒃ.

ᓄᓇᓖᐤᓘᑦᓃᑦ ᐊᐤᔨᒥᔫᔭᕈᑦᓃᕐ ᑕᖅᑎᑦ ᐃᖅᑲᐅᓛᔭᑦᑎᑐᑦ, ᑕᐃᒪᑦᓇᐅᑦᑎᐊᖅᑰᕆᔪᑦᓃᕐ ᑐᑦ. ᓂᖅᑎᐅᒃᑯᒻᒪᓗ ᐃᓪᓗᑯᓗᖕᒐᑦ ᒥᑦᑎᒪᑕᖕᒦᑦᑐᖅ, ᐅᕐᑎᔪᐋᖅᑰᕆᐊᓚᐅᕐᓯᒪᔪᖅ ᓂᐅᕐᕈᒐᑦᑕ ᕐᑲᐤᓗᓇᑦᕆᐊᕐᓗᑕ, ᒥᑭᑦᑐᑰᖅᑰᕆᓕᕐᓗᓂ, ᑕᒪᒃᑯᐊᓗ ᐃᒡᓗᑯᓗᖕᒥᑦ ᒥᑭᒐᓕᐅᖅᑲᖅᑐᑰᐤᓗᑎᒃ ᓄᓇᓕᖕᓂ ᕐᑲᐤᓗᓈᓄᑦ ᐃᒡᓗᕐᑯᑎᒥ ᓴᐅᔩᒐᓗᐊᑦ.

ᒥᑦᑎᒪᑕᓕᖕᒥ ᒪᑦᑖᕐᕖᒃ ᑭᓴᕐᓯᒪᓂᖕᒐᓂ ᓱᓕ, ᐊᓈᓇᒪ ᓴᕐᓇᑎᐤᓗᓂᐅᒃ ᓴᓐ ᕐᑯᓕᑦᑕᐅᔭᒃᓴᖕᒐᓂᒃ, ᕐᑯᔭᕐᓇᒦᕈᑎᐅᐤᓗᓂᓗ ᐊᑖᑦᑎᖕᓄᑦ ᑲᒪᔨᒥᑕᐅᕐᓂᓇᔭᕐᓂᒃ ᐊᑭᓕᐅᑕᐅᑕᐅᕐᓯᒪᔪᑦ ᐊᐤᔨᒥᐤᓚᖕᒪ ᓯᒐᓕᐊᒃᓴᖕᒥᕐᓂᒃ ᔫᒃ ᐊᐤᒥᔪᒃ ᒪᕐᑭᒃ ᐋᓇᒪ ᕐᑯᓕᑦᑕᐅᔭᓕᐊᐤᒐᓄᑦ. ᐊᑖᑕᒪ ᓯᐊᒃᑯᓗᒥᑎᐤᓗᓂᐅᒃ ᐅᕙᑦᓄᑦ.

ᒪᑦᑖᕐᕖᒃ ᐆᐤᓚᕐᒪᑦ ᒥᑦᑎᒪᑕᓕᖕᒥᑦ, ᑕᐸᕙ ᑕᐃᒫᖅᑳᖅ ᓃᕐᓗ ᐃᓚᒃᑲ ᐆᐤᓚᕐᑐᑦ ᐊᔪᐅᒪᔪᑎᑐᑦ ᐱᖅᑰᕆᖅ ᑳᓕᓐᐅᐤᓗᖕᒐ ᐃᓚᐤᓚᑦᑖᓂᓕᕐᓗᐊᕐᓗᖕᒐᓕ.

no matter at which settlement the C.D. Howe was anchored, I felt good to see my own "brothers and sisters" again. They were no longer strangers to me, even if I had never met them before.

The changes that had taken place in my life made it easier for me to mingle in crowds of people. I think that being in that happy circus crowd helped in this way. It had taken me a long time to get over my fear of not knowing what was going to happen to me - first on my trip down on the C.D. Howe, and then at the hospital. Of course, the Wilkinsons and John Creighton, and my own fellow Inuit helped me a lot to become a happier person in new and different situations. I am very grateful to all those people who accepted and understood me when I was a lost kid without my parents so far away from home for the first time.

I knew when we were about to arrive in Pond Inlet. I had been watching from the ship's deck as the long coast glided by, and I had a fatherly companion, Etuk from Arctic Bay, to tell me the names of the various camps as we passed.

My reunion with my parents was the happiest moment in my entire life. I cried, not because I was sad, but because I was so happy to be back with my brave wise proud father again.

I learned that many changes had taken place in my family while I had been away. My favourite brother, Paul Idlout, was now married to a girl who I had only known well in my childhood. I also had a new younger sister called Ruth. She was already seven months old, and I had never even heard any news about her in the months I had been gone. My youngest brother at that time, Noah Idlout, had grown into a big boy and he was speaking so well. He had been my baby before I had left for the South. My mother told me that he had cried so much for me.

The settlement, too, seemed different from what I had remembered. My grandparent's house at Pond Inlet, that used to seem so large when we visited from the camp, looked so small now, as did all the other buildings in the community.

While the C.D. Howe was at Pond Inlet, my mother made my friend John a duffle parka. In return, he gave my parents two cartons of cigarettes. My father referred to him as my "servant".

When the C.D. Howe left Pond Inlet, I

ᑭᓱᑐᐃᑦᓇᓕᒫᑦ ᐊᓐᓯᕆᑎᐋᖅᑰᓯᔪᑦᓃᕐᒪᕆᑦ ᐊᐅᓐᓚᐅ ᕐᓇᖅᒐ ᐊᑐᕐᑕᐅᕙᓚᐅᕐᑐᑦ ᓱᕐᕋᓐᖅᕆᒃᑲᔪᐊᕐᔪᑎᒃ ᐃᒻᒪᕐᑳ ᐅᕙᖅᒐᖅᑳᖅ ᕐᑲᓐᔪᓈᑦ ᓄᓇᖅᒐᑦᓄᐊᕐᓯᒪᓕᕐᔪᖅᒐ. ᑕᒪᕐᒥᑦᑎᐋᖅ ᓲᕐᑲᐃᒻᒪ ᐃᓚᓕᒫᒃᑲ ᕐᐱᐊᓱᖅᒪᑕ ᐅᑎᕐᒪ ᐱᑦᑎᐊᕐ ᑐᐃᑦᓈᓗᓐᔪᑎᒃ, ᐊᒻᒪᓗ ᓱᓕ ᐊᑖᑕᒪ ᐸᓂᓐᓇᓐᔪᓂᖅᒐ. ᑭᓯᐋᓂᑦᑕᐅᖅ ᑕᕙᕙ ᓄᑲᕐᑲ ᕐᑲᓕᕐᒥᕆᓐᔪᖅᒐ ᐃᓚᕆᓕᐅᑎᔪᕝᕕᓂᕐᒥᒃ ᐊᐅᓐᓚᕐᓯᒪᔭᕝᕕᓂᐅᑎᓐᔪᖅᒐ, ᕐᑯᕕᐊᕆᔭᕐᔪᐊᕐᓕ ᓄᑲᖅᑳᕿᒪᐅᔭᐃᑦᓇᕐᒪ ᐋᓃᓐᓇᕐᓃᑦᓇᒪ.

ᕐᑲᓐᔪᓈᓕᖅᓃᑦᔪᑕ ᓱᓕ, ᐃᓄᒐᓴᖅᓄᑦ ᐊᐱᕐᓱᕐᑕᐅᕐᑲᑦᑕᓚᐅᕐᓯᒪᒐᒪ ᐅᕐᑲᓐᓚᒃᑲᑦᓂᕐᑯᔭᐅᓐᔪᖅᒐ ᓕᐊᕐ ᑰᑎᒃ ᐅᕐᑲᓐᓚᑯᔪᓚᐅᕐᒥᑮᓚᔭᐅᕐᑲᑦᑕᕐᔪᖅᒐ. ᐅᕐᑲᐅᓯᓕᑰᓕᕐᒪᒎᖅ ᐊᓐᓯᐅᓐᖅᕆᑦᑐᕆᒃ. ᐅᓐᓯᖏᓐᖅᕆᑦᑎᐊᕐᔪᐊᕐ ᔪᖅᒐᓕ — ᑲᑎᓯᔪᐊᕐᑲᑦᑕᕐ ᑐᕕᓂᐅᔪᑦ ᐅᕐᑲᐅᓯᕐᑲᑎᕆᓐᖅᕆᑦᑐᓂᒃ ᓱᓇᐅᕙᕙᑦᑕᐅᖅ ᐊᓐᓯᐅᓐᖅᕆᑦᑐᕆᒃ ᐅᕐᑲᐅᓯᕐᑲᕐᑲᑕᐅᓕᕐᒥᔪᖅᒐ — ᑲᒪᕆᔭᐅᕐᐤᑦᑕᓕᕐᒪ ᒥᑦᑎᒪᑕᓕᖅᒥᐅᖅᔪᕐᑲᑎᑦᓄᑦ ᐅᕐᑲᐅᓯᓕᑰᔪᖅᒐ ᐃᔪ ᓇᔭᐅᓕᕐᓂᕐᒪᓗᑭᐋᖅ ᐃᓂᕐᑯᒥᔭᐅᓐᔪᖅᒐᓗ ᑐᓴᕐᓂᓇᓂ ᕐᕐᑕᐅᓐᔪᓂ ᐃᑲᓚᕐᑎᑦᑎᕐᑲᑦᑕᓕᓚᐅᕐᓯᒪᒐᒪ.

ᑕᐃᒪᓕ, ᐊᑖᑕᒪ ᓂᐅᕕᕐᕕᓕᐊᕿᑎᖅᒪᖅᒐ ᑮᓇᐅᔭᐤ ᓚᑦᑖᓂᒃ ᓴᕕᕐᔭᖅᓂᒃ ᕐᑲᓐᔪᓈᑦ ᓄᓇᖅᒐᑦᓃᑦᓂᑦᓂ ᓄᐊᑕᕕᓂᑦᓂᒃ ᓂᐅᕐᕿᑎᕐᑲᓇᐊᕐ ᑐᕐᔪᖅᒐ $3.00−ᓚᓂᒃ, ᐊᒃᓚᒃᑎ ᐲᑦ ᒪᕐᑳᒃ, ᓂᐅᕕᕐᑎᒃᑯᑦ ᐊᖏᔪᖅᑳᖅᒐᑦ, ᕐᑲᓐᔪᓇᐅᔭᐃᑦᓇᑦᑎᐊᕐᔪᓂ ᐅᕙᑦᓄᑦ. ᐃᓅᔭᕿ ᕐᓇᕐ ᑐᐤᑦᑑᓐᔪᓂ. ᐅᕐᑲᓚᐅᕐᓯᒪᖅᒪᑦ ᓄᑲ ᐸᐱᐊ ᑯᖅᑰᓯᓂᕐᕐᔪᓂᖅᒐ, ᕐᑲᖅᓕᑯᑖᒃᓯᒪᒐᒪ ᑲᒥᐊᓗᒃᓯ ᒪᓐᔪᖅᒐᓗ ᔭᐃᑲᒃᓯᒪᓐᔪᖅᒐᓗ ᐱᒐᒪ ᔭᐃᑲᒐ ᐊᒪᐅᓕ ᒐᐅᐸ ᐋᓇᖅᒐᑕ ᓴᓇᓚᐅᕐᓯᒪᔭᖅᒐ. ᑲᓐᖅᑯᓯᒃᑎᑕᐤ ᓐᓅᒥᓕᓚᐅᕐᓯᒪᖅᒪᖅᒐ ᐊᒃᓚᒃᑎᕿᓘᐸ ᓄᑲ ᐸᐱᐊᑯᓘᖅᑰ ᓯᓂᕐᕐᔪᓂᖅᒐ ᐸᓂᕆᔭᐅᔪᐊᑦᓚᕐᑎᐤᔪᖅᒐ ᐊᑖᑕᓄᑦ!

ᐄᓛᒃ, ᑕᒪᐃᑕ ᓄᓇᓕᖅᓂ ᐊᕔᕿᕐ ᑑᔮᓚᐅᕐᓯᒪᖅᒪᑕ ᐋᓐᓚᔪᐊᕐᓇᓕᕐᔪᑎᒃ. ᑭᓯᐋᓂᑦᑕᐅᖅ, ᐆᓯᕕᑦᑎᑦᓂ ᐋᓐᓚᕿᕐ ᓅᔭᔪᐊᓚᐅᕐᓯᒪᕆᕗᑦ.

by Doug Wilkinson

felt a little like a stranger in my own family. I mean by this that things were not the same as they had been before I left to go down South. All the members of my family were very good to me, and I was still my father's favourite daughter. But there was that other girl in the family now too!

While we were in the settlement, many Inuit kept asking me to speak to them in my new "cute" dialect. Without even realizing it - as a result of my meeting so many Inuit from other places - I had taken on a different dialect that amused the people of Pond Inlet.

Then, when my father took me to the Hudson's Bay store with my $3.00 savings from my year in the South, Pete Murdock, the Hudson's Bay manager, kept speaking English to me. This was despite the fact that he also spoke fluent Inuktitut. He told me that I looked like a little boy, with my slacks and rubber boots and the jacket that Vivian Wilkinson's mother had made for me. He made me feel so shy!

. Yes, everything in the settlement seemed so strange and different to me now. But, back in the camp, it was to seem even stranger still.

by Joseph Idlout

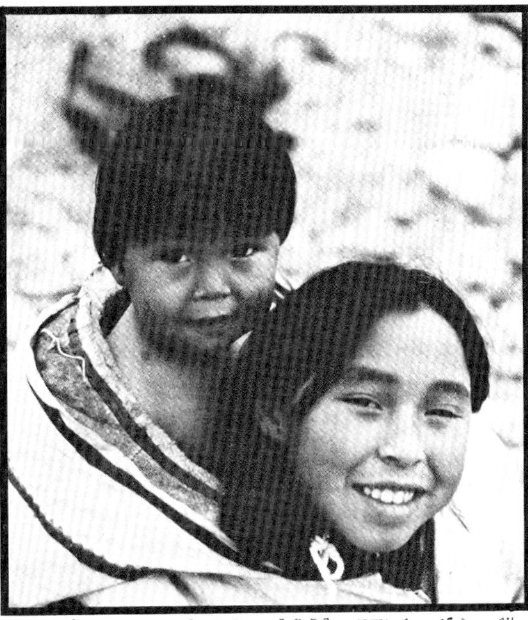

Noah Idlout and Leah d'Argencourt 1951

ᓄᐊ ᐃᓛᐅᖅ ᓕᐊ ᐃᑦᓚᐅᖅᑯ 1951 ᕿᒥᐅᑉ ᐊᑦᓯᓕᐊᖕ

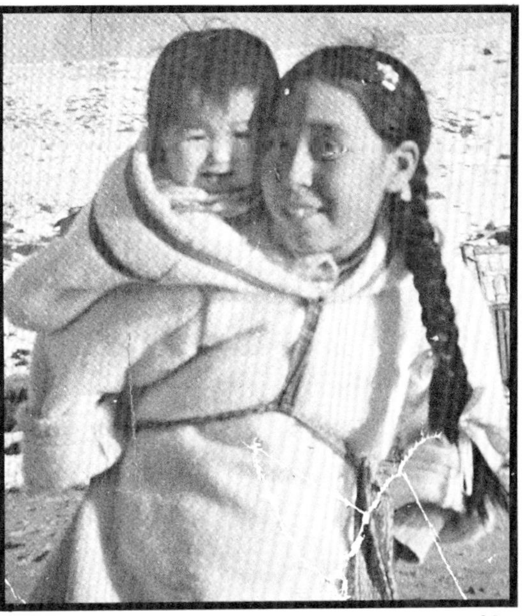

Ruth Cookie and Leah d'Argencourt 1952

ᕈᑎ ᑯᑭ ᓕᐊ ᐃᑦᓚᐅᖅᑯ 1952-ᒥ

29

5 The Crown

Connections, Disconnections, and Racialized Visuality in Governor General Vincent Massey's Tour of the North (1956)

Following his family's relocation to Resolute/Qausuittuq in the High Arctic, his daughter Leah's return from the south, and the publication of Doug Wilkinson's book *Land of the Long Day* (1955), Joseph Idlout continued to photograph (see figure 5.1). Unfortunately, to my knowledge and that of Idlout's family, no known images credited to Idlout from Resolute/Qausuittuq survive. Nonetheless, it is clear that the hunter took photographs, exchanged photographs,[1] and taught his children to use a camera while in Resolute/Qausuittuq.[2] Other Inuit in the community also photographed.[3] As his granddaughter Madeleine d'Argencourt states in the foreword to this book, Idlout was "so proud of his camera."

On 23 March 1956, Idlout posed with fellow High Arctic exiles Daniel Salluviniq and Zebeddie Amarualik, each man holding a camera and apparently poised to take snapshots (see figure 5.1).[4] Like most photographers, they appear absorbed in the task of excising a fragment of time and space in order to render a direct encounter in visual form.

The subject of their concentrated attention, just beyond the frame of the photograph, holds a prominent place in the history of Canadian nationalism and in Canada's relationship to the British Crown. Cataloguing records at Library and Archives Canada, where the photograph of Idlout, Salluviniq, and Amarualik is now housed, describe the three photographers as awaiting the arrival of Governor General Vincent Massey, the representative of the Crown in Canada, at Resolute/Qausuittuq.[5] Massey was undertaking a historic tour of the north as a public gesture intended to assert Canadian sovereignty in the Arctic. Resolute/Qausuittuq was the northern-most settled community that Massey visited and the tour's most politically significant stop. It was there that the Canadian government had laid claim to sovereignty over the High Arctic in part by establishing a hamlet at Resolute/Qausuittuq and populating it with Inuit coerced to move far from their homes.[6] Idlout, Salluviniq, and Amarualik were among those High Arctic exiles.

Posed as members of a greeting committee, Idlout, Salluviniq, and Amarualik appear to be ready to capture an image of this illustrious visitor even as they

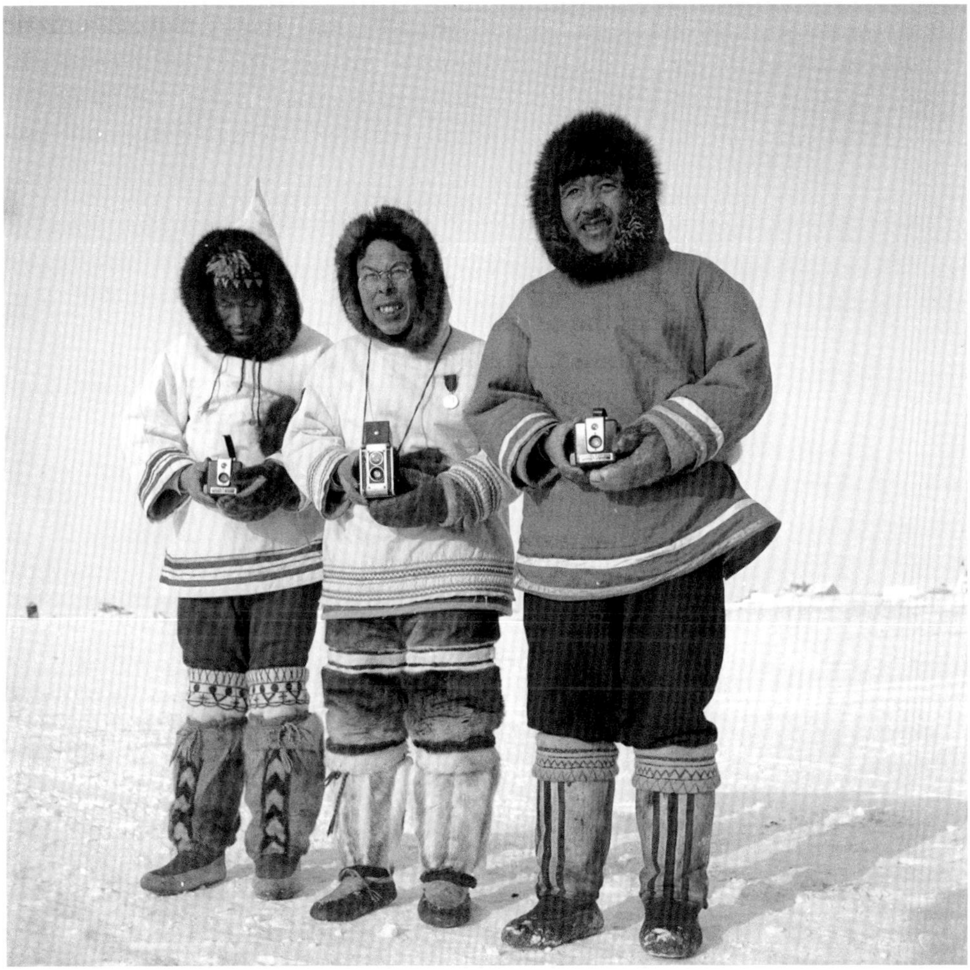

5.1 | Daniel Salluviniq, Joseph Idlout, and Zebeddie Amarualik, holding Brownie cameras, await the arrival of Governor General Vincent Massey at Resolute/Qausuittuq, March 1956. Photo: Gar Lunney.

themselves are framed by a camera. Indeed, the image of the three photographers is also the product of a photographic gaze that frames and seems to fix an encounter from a specific bodily and cultural perspective. Gar Lunney, a southern Canadian staff photographer with the National Film Board of Canada's Still Photography Division, shot this negative. At the time, Lunney was on assignment following the governor general's historic 1956 tour of the north. Over the course of seventeen days, Lunney made dozens of negatives featuring Massey, the dramatic scenery of the north, and the people encountered at each stop on the tour: Inuit, other Indigenous people, and settlers. Staged photographs shot in Resolute/Qausuittuq, like this example, provided visual evidence of a Canadian presence in the High Arctic.

Massey's 1956 northern tour, spanning some 16,000 kilometres from northern Quebec to Aklavik in the western Arctic, was a highly choreographed performance of nationalism, a series of gestures that enacted Canada's claim to sovereignty over the Arctic in the midst of the Cold War.[7] Undertaken with the aid of the Royal Canadian Air Force (RCAF), the tour mapped Canada's Arctic regions as an interconnected network, unified under Crown and country. In effect, the tour was performed for southern Canadians and international audiences, announcing Canada's claims to Arctic sovereignty. Each stop featured elaborate displays of an idealized north constructed specifically for the tour and visited by the governor general. National and international audiences of the time viewed this elaborate performance through a series of news reports, photographs, and films depicting the people and locales visited on the excursion, with Massey himself as the central actor throughout. Above all, audiences *looked* at Massey *looking* – at the Arctic terrain and sea but, especially, at the many Inuit and other Indigenous peoples he encountered. The tour was primarily a visual performance in which southerners were shown the north and, particularly, shown the Indigenous people living there as subjects of the Dominion of Canada and objects of a racialized settler-colonial gaze. The 1956 tour performed national sovereignty in part through visuality.

In this chapter, I explore *The Hunter, the Crown, and the Camera*'s overarching theme of visuality in Inuit-Qallunaat interactions in the Qikiqtani region during the 1950s through the specific case study of Massey's 1956 tour. In cartographic records and specially designed displays as well as in photographs, news accounts, and films, the tour projected Canadian claims to Arctic sovereignty in visualized forms. Indeed, as I argue here, visuality became a theme of the tour as a whole. In news accounts and in image after image, there is an emphasis on the gaze. But unlike Idlout's photographs and Wilkinson's cinematic and still images, the visual record of the 1956 tour highlights the idealized gaze of the visiting governor general. Its projection declares settler-colonial authority through claims of visual mastery that are often highly racialized. As photo studies scholar Shawn Michelle Smith writes, "Looking and seeing [are] racialized practices ... Subjects are produced through practices of looking ... Looking is learned, and ... seeing is culturally coded in terms of race."[8] These racialized "practices of looking" produced subjectivities of nationhood in relation to the north. But they were always returned by Indigenous gazes.

Massey and his entourage spent just over five days, from 20 to 26 March 1956, in the Qikiqtani region, where the governor general encountered both Joseph Idlout and Doug Wilkinson. Although the following pages provide a detailed discussion of Massey's 1956 tour as another example of Inuit-Qallunaat visual entanglement, I take two long detours in this account of the trip to examine the key protagonists in this multiple-chapter microhistory of the Inuit-Qallunaat encounter between Joseph Idlout and Doug Wilkinson. Wilkinson is encountered as the designated host and coordinator of the sojourn at Iqaluit/Frobisher Bay, where his plans for building a settlement – with their emphasis on forms of assimilation – are analyzed. Idlout is seen as a newly arrived exile to Resolute/Qausuittuq in the High Arctic and is one of the subjects of the tour's racialized gaze. How Idlout and his community's lived experience at Resolute/Qausuittuq contrasts with the official nationalist discourse of Massey's tour provides one of the focal points of the chapter. Although this chapter chiefly examines the perspectives of the Crown and the federal government, I argue that their gazes were always returned both by Inuit and by other Indigenous people encountered and always undermined by contingencies and excesses – visual information beyond the control of the organizers. The image of Joseph Idlout, Daniel Salluviniq, and Zebeddie Amarualik – focusing their cameras back at the governor general and his entourage – exemplifies the returned gazes of Inuit throughout the tour and indeed interactions with the south more broadly. Inuit agency and authority were always already visible.

Massey and the North

Charles Vincent Massey (1887–1967) served from 1952 to 1959 as the country's first Canadian-born governor general (see figure 5.2). He arrived at Rideau Hall, the governor general's official residence, under the Liberal government of Louis St-Laurent (1948–57) but would remain in the role during the first two years of the Conservative government of John Diefenbaker (1957–63). For many people in Canada, the appointment of a Canadian as governor general in 1952 signified the dominion's newly established place on the world stage as a now mature state with a measure of independence within the Commonwealth.

Yet Massey was hardly a populist advocate of Canadian independence. A staunch royalist, wealthy heir to the Massey-Harris fortune,[9] and anglophile, he had spent almost a decade as the high commissioner for Canada in the United Kingdom (1935–46).[10] Massey was, in short, ideally suited to represent and promote the Crown in Canada during a period of growing US influence. As he stated in a 1961 speech, "The Crown-in-Parliament is the supreme symbol of our nationhood and our greatest defence against absorption into a continental state. Our feeling for the Monarchy is marked everywhere by warmth and devotion."[11]

The governor general had enjoyed a remarkably diverse and privileged career before entering Rideau Hall. In addition to his posting as high commissioner in London, Massey variously worked as a lecturer at the University of Toronto, an actor, the head of his family corporation, a minister without portfolio under Prime Minister William Lyon Mackenzie King, a representative to the United States (1926–30), and the chancellor of the University of Toronto (1948–52).[12] Above all, Massey was a cultural nationalist.[13] Today, he is perhaps best remembered for chairing the influential Royal Commission on National Development in the Arts, Letters and Sciences from 1949 to 1951[14] and for advocating the arts as a means to aid, in historian Karen Finlay's words, "the construction of a national community."[15]

Massey's term as governor general coincided with the Canadian government's northern focus under both the St-Laurent and Diefenbaker governments. Reflecting this geopolitical orientation, Massey undertook two official trips to the

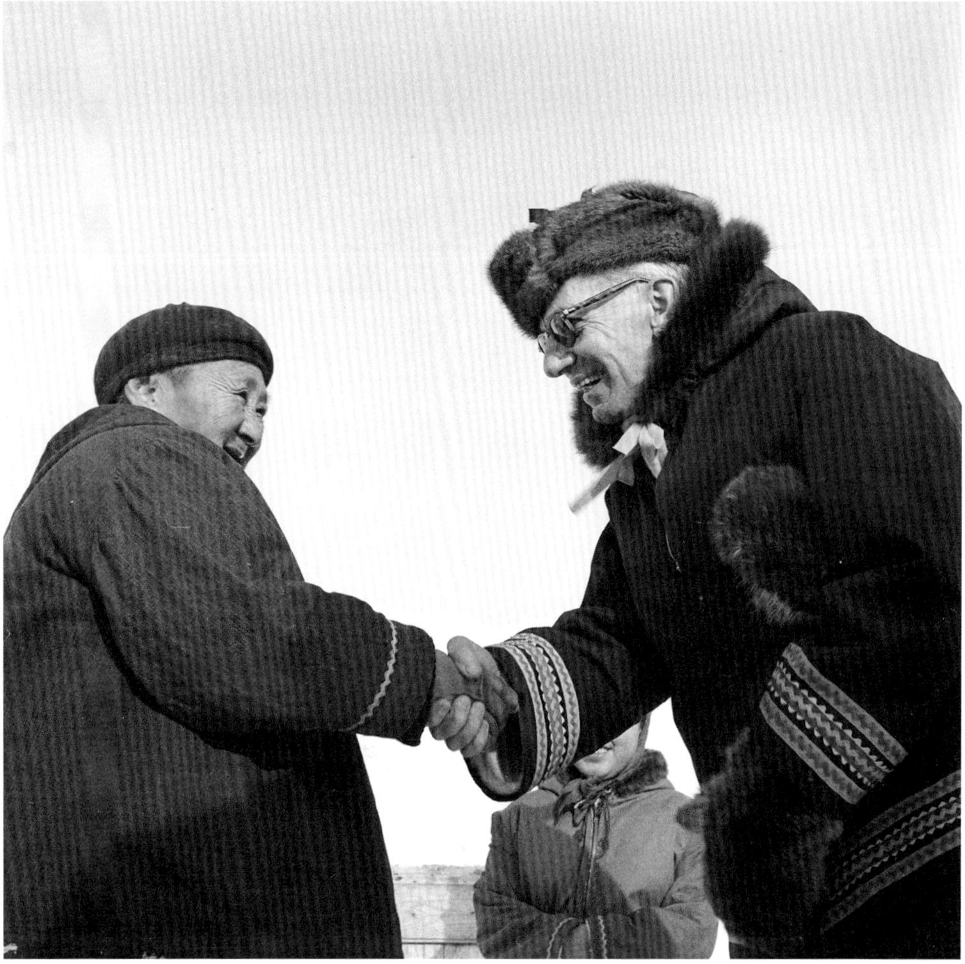

5.2 | Governor General Vincent Massey shakes hands with Nellic, an eighty-five-year-old Inuk woman, March 1956. Photo: Gar Lunney.

far north. He was not, however, the first governor general to travel to the far north. John Buchan (Lord Tweedsmuir of Elsfield), who served as Canada's governor general from 1935 to 1940, holds this distinction. Tweedsmuir travelled up the Mackenzie River to the western Arctic during the summer of 1937.[16] But Massey's trips, coinciding with a historic moment when the Canadian government promoted the country's "centre of gravity ... being moved north,"[17] were of greater political significance.

The initial voyage to the Arctic by Massey as governor general was relatively brief. In 1953, just a few months after assuming the office, he travelled to the western Arctic, where he visited Yellowknife and Fort Smith in the Northwest Territories before stopping at Churchill in Manitoba.[18] During this tour, in an address delivered to the Yellowknife Board of Trade and the Yellowknife Branch of the Canadian Institute of Mining and Metallurgy, Massey described the contemporary significance of the north for Canada:

When we observe that it lies adjacent to the Arctic area of the only other great Arctic power in the world; and when we recall also that our relations with that power are of the first importance to ourselves and to our allies, there is no need to explain why the eyes of every Canadian with any understanding of international affairs, turn constantly northward.

I am happy to think, however, that we are not exclusively, or even principally, concerned with matters of strategy and defense, important though these may be. Increasingly we of the southern fringes are being invited, and compelled, to realize the infinite economic and social possibilities of this land.[19]

Massey's speech reflects emerging policy in Ottawa under the St-Laurent government. With a nod to strategic Cold War defence, he suggests that Canada has gained new prominence in the global community.[20] But, like many officials in Ottawa, Massey also envisioned Arctic and Subarctic regions as holding great economic potential for southerners to reap.

Although Massey would later describe himself as a "mere tripper" in the north,[21] official journeys by governors general are, of course, performances of nationalist symbolism. As Renée Hulan has stated, "When the figurehead of the Canadian government visits a region, the trip designates the place as Canadian sovereign territory."[22] Through his physical presence in the Arctic, Massey claimed these vast regions for the Canadian nation. As summarized by Tania Long, co-bureau chief of *The New York Times* in Ottawa and a member of the press corps accompanying Massey's 1956 tour, "The chief purpose of the seventeen-day trip to the isolated communities scattered through the snowy barren lands of the North … is to visit the people there, and by so doing, to make them feel a part of Canada. The part of the country Mr. Massey will see for the first time is developing rapidly, as a result of measures being taken to defend this continent's northern approaches, and is becoming a vitally strategic zone."[23] The practice of touring the Arctic has become a mainstay of recent governor generals. Tours of the far north by Governors General Adrienne Clarkson, Michaëlle Jean, David Johnston, and Julie Payette have continued the tradition of staging the region to project national values and Canadian sovereignty over the Arctic.[24] With the installation of Inuk journalist and Inuit rights activist Mary Simon as Canada's first Indigenous governor general in 2021, official tours of the north have made Inuit presence and political agency more visible than under her predecessors.

Mapping the North: The 1956 Tour

The governor general's 1956 tour was far more extensive than the one that he had undertaken three years earlier.[25] Over seventeen days from 20 March to 5 April 1956, Massey and his entourage travelled from northern Quebec to Tuktoyaktuk on the Beaufort Sea. The journey covered about 16,000 kilometres over five time zones and the Arctic Circle in its mission to project a Canadian presence in the far north.[26]

In total, twenty-nine people accompanied Massey. Thirteen crew members with the No. 412 Transport Squadron of the RCAF flew and maintained the Canadair C-5. Massey's personal party of eight included his eldest son, Lionel, in his capacity as secretary to the governor general and Lionel's wife, Lilias. Because Vincent Massey's wife, Alice Massey (née Parkin), had died in 1950, Lilias and Lionel often accompanied and assisted the governor general. In turn, Lionel was accompanied by his own assistant, Esmond Butler. The rest of the personal party comprised representatives of the military, government, and Royal Canadian Mounted Police (RCMP): Captain Guy Robillard of the RCMP, Superintendent Douglas Forrest of the RCMP, Graham Rowley of the Department of Northern Affairs and National Resources, and Wing Commander Keith Greenaway of the RCAF.

Notably, reflecting the tour's emphasis on promoting Canada's sovereignty, fully ten members of the media accompanied Massey. They included representatives of the National Film Board of Canada (NFB), the Canadian Broadcasting Corporation (CBC), the Associated Screen News, the Canadian Press, the British United Press, the North American Newspaper Alliance, Federal News Photographs, *Time-Life Magazine, The Globe and Mail,*[27] and a French-language correspondent for various presses. Also accompanying the tour, although not listed in the trip personnel, was Tania Long, quoted above, who filed stories about the tour for *The New York Times.*

The Department of Northern Affairs and National Resources (DNANR) organized the tour and published its official guide. Reflecting the elaborate protocols used by the governor general's office and apparently prepared largely for the accompanying media personnel, the guide provides a detailed, hour-by-hour itinerary, a program of activities arranged at the ten communities visited, and twenty-six "notes on points of interest." Each note, of one to three typed pages, recounts information about the history, geography, and significance of key sites. They are decidedly colonial in tone. European explorers, the Hudson's Bay Company, and mining and military operations are given precedence over Inuit experiences in the various locales. They provided members of the media on the tour with a ready settler-colonial narrative of the regions visited. Indeed, news accounts closely follow the itinerary established by the DNANR.[28]

The guide closes with a large political map, which has been folded twice and affixed to the back cover. Stretching from Kalaallit Nunaat/Greenland in the east to Alaska and Siberia in the west, the map is centred on the Canadian Arctic. A precise red line traces the tour's meandering route from Great Whale River in Quebec to six stops in the Northwest Territories – Iqaluit/Frobisher Bay, Sanirajak/Hall Beach, Resolute/Qausuittuq, Cambridge Bay/Iqaluktuuttiaq, Tuktoyaktuk, and Aklavik – before continuing to Whitehorse in the Yukon and then to The Pas in Manitoba.[29] At Resolute/Qausuittuq, the most northerly point on the tour, the line extends upward, indicating a planned flight over the North Pole. Rather than a mere afterthought, the map forms an appendix, an authoritative document suggesting empirical evidence that supports the text inside and the nationalist mission of the tour as a whole. Whereas the various "notes on points of interest" narrate distinct and specific regional histories from a settler-colonial perspective, the map proposes a unified vision. In one glance, it renders the whole of the tour visible and contained within national boundaries. Here, the map serves as a visualized technique of authority, what Nicholas Mirzoeff terms "oversight." He argues, "As a technique of governance, visualized domination was both represented by and encapsulated in the ... technology of mapping."[30] In short, this map of the 1956 tour signals the authority of both the Crown and the government enacted through visuality to project a unified Canadian Arctic.

Each stop on the 1956 tour provided spectacles and opportunities for the governor general to be seen in the territory and for the accompanying media to record his presence. Like the guide's map, these events visualized the Arctic as sovereign Canadian territory. The governor general's office arranged displays, performances, and opportunities for Massey to address constituents. The DNANR organized meetings between Massey and residents of the north, including Inuit, RCMP officers, Hudson's Bay Company staff, scientists, and mining company personnel.[31] Designated hosts at each settlement introduced the party to life in the Arctic and Subarctic.

Iqaluit/Frobisher Bay: Doug Wilkinson and the Display of Culture and Assimilationist Policies

In Iqaluit/Frobisher Bay, Doug Wilkinson served as the governor general's designated host (see figure 5.3).[32] After returning to Ottawa from his second sojourn with Idlout's camp, Wilkinson joined the DNANR as a Northern Service officer (NSO), working initially in the national capital and then moving to Iqaluit/Frobisher Bay, which was formally established as a town in 1955. Wilkinson was one of the first two officers appointed. He would next be posted at Baker Lake/Qamani'tuaq from 1957 to 1958.[33] As a Northern Service officer, Wilkinson implemented some of the policy proposals that he had mulled over during his 1953–54 sojourn at Idlout's camp on North Baffin Island. But, above all, he and other officers were agents of the federal government in the region. As Prime Minister Louis St-Laurent stated in announcing the establishment of the DNANR, the government believed that it "would be desirable to have on the statute books a department of northern affairs and to have representatives of the department of northern affairs present in various parts of these territories and symbolic of the actuality of the exercise of Canadian sovereignty over them."[34] Wilkinson's specific responsibilities included liaising between the federal government, various

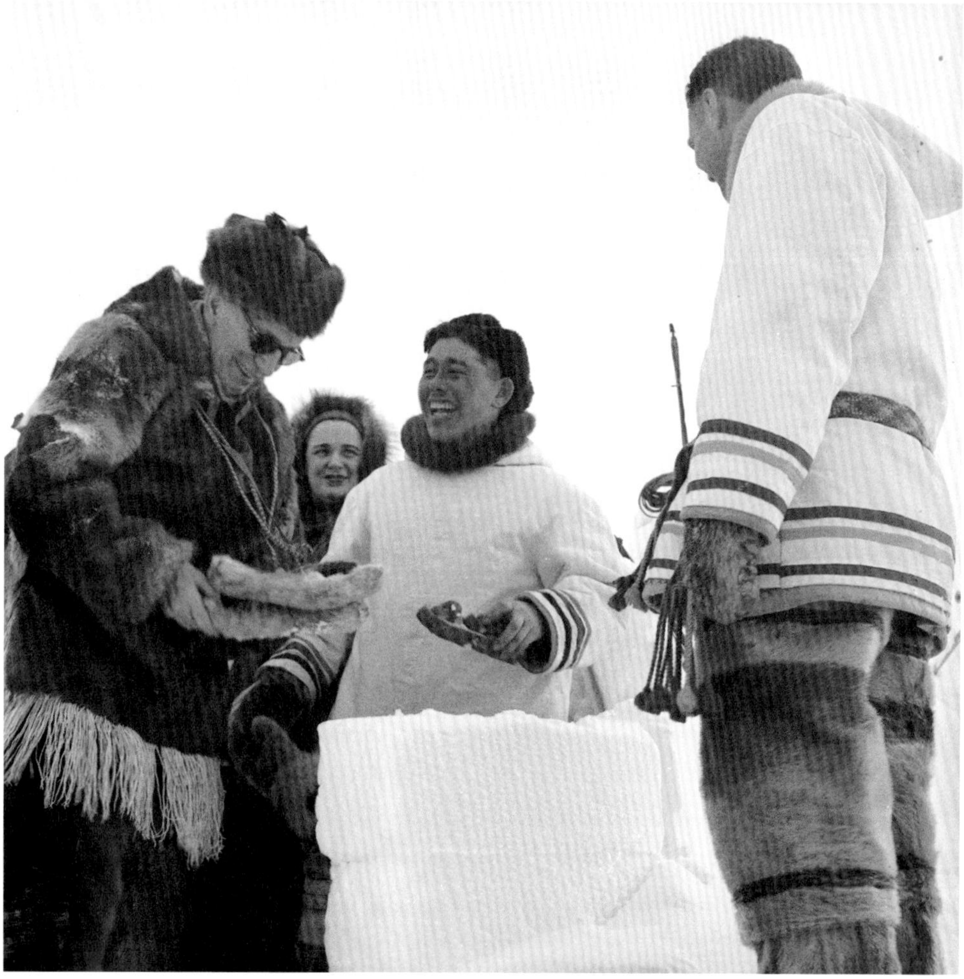

5.3 | Governor General Vincent Massey enjoys a joke with an English-speaking Inuit man, Special Constable Etouloupiac, at Iqaluit/Frobisher Bay, March 1956. Photo: Gar Lunney.

settlers stationed in the region, and Inuit. He would, later, for example, participate in the DNANR's October 1957 Arctic Conference, the first gathering of its kind, and would therefore play a role in the debates that formed future policies.[35]

While serving as a Northern Service officer in Iqaluit/Frobisher Bay, Wilkinson wrote a detailed portrait of the community that presented the DNANR's impact in glowing terms, thus providing a semblance of what Massey may have encountered there as a result of the careful orchestration of government agents like Wilkinson. Entitled "The Eskimos of Frobisher Bay,"[36] the paper was probably given as a talk by Wilkinson to a meeting of the Arctic Circle in Ottawa on 13 November 1956.[37] In the paper, Wilkinson largely promotes the work of the DNANR in assimilating Inuit in the Iqaluit/Frobisher Bay region through town planning and specially constructed housing. The paper opens with a look back at how the establishment of a military base in the area in 1942 impacted Inuit lives. Wilkinson describes these changes in starkly primitivizing terms: "Until the summer of 1942, the Eskimos of the Frobisher Bay remained semi-nomadic hunters, their physical lives and modes of behaviour and thought little changed from those of their ancestors of five hundred years ago. Overnight they were catapulted from the Stone Age into the 20th Century. In 1941 the hand of the hunter held a harpoon: in 1942 it held a hammer. The man who had driven only a dog team found himself driving a truck. Eskimo hunters dug ditches, erected telephone poles, manhandled oil drums up the sloping sandy beach." Wilkinson goes on to narrate how Inuit engaging in wage labour at the base built temporary housing nearby. As Wilkinson disparages, "Quickly the little shack town beside the base began to look like a slum."[38]

As an aside, it is worth noting that about the same time that Wilkinson met with Massey and wrote his speech about the town of Iqaluit/Frobisher Bay, DNANR officials and architects in Ottawa also turned their attention to housing in the area. As architectural historian Rhodri Windsor Liscombe has shown, the DNANR's chief architect at the time, E.A. Gardner, proposed a utopian modernist town plan for Iqaluit/Frobisher Bay. The plan featured thirty-six futuristic apartment towers arranged as a circle around administrative buildings. The unrealized plan calls to mind Michel Foucault's discussion of the panopticon.[39] And, indeed, as Liscombe notes, "The northern recipients seldom figure in the intercourse of planning beyond being subjects of investigation and objects of reconstruction ... The projection of distant power ... is the manifest logic of the Frobisher scheme."[40]

Gardner's modernist architectonic fantasy of surveillance and power in Iqaluit/Frobisher Bay was, of course, never realized; instead, Doug Wilkinson oversaw the building of a "new town" of more modest proportions (see figure 5.4). It would, nonetheless, be constructed under the surveillance of the DNANR and administered by the local Northern Service officer, Wilkinson himself. As he wrote in his 1956 paper,

> In this town Eskimos who have left their hunting trapping way of life will be able to build a new kind of social existence based on their status as wage earners in a monied economy. They will live in properly equipped, serviced houses, paid for out of their own earnings at their jobs. They will live as neighbours to departmental employees from the south. They receive hospital and nursing care from the Department of National Health and Welfare personnel living in the town. Their children attend a school during the day (and the adults at night) which is operated and staffed by the Education Division of the Department of Northern Affairs. They receive vocational training under the watchful eye of the Technical Officer. A rehabilitation centre will provide means for Eskimos from many areas in the Eastern Arctic, who may be unable or unsuited to return to the hunting-trapping life, to seek new means of livelihood. Co-ordinating the growth of the town and the integration of the indigenous Eskimo into its growth, is the Northern Service Officer.[41]

5.4 | Row of houses with hydro lines, Iqaluit/Frobisher Bay, c. 1956–60. Photo: Rosemary Gilliat Eaton.

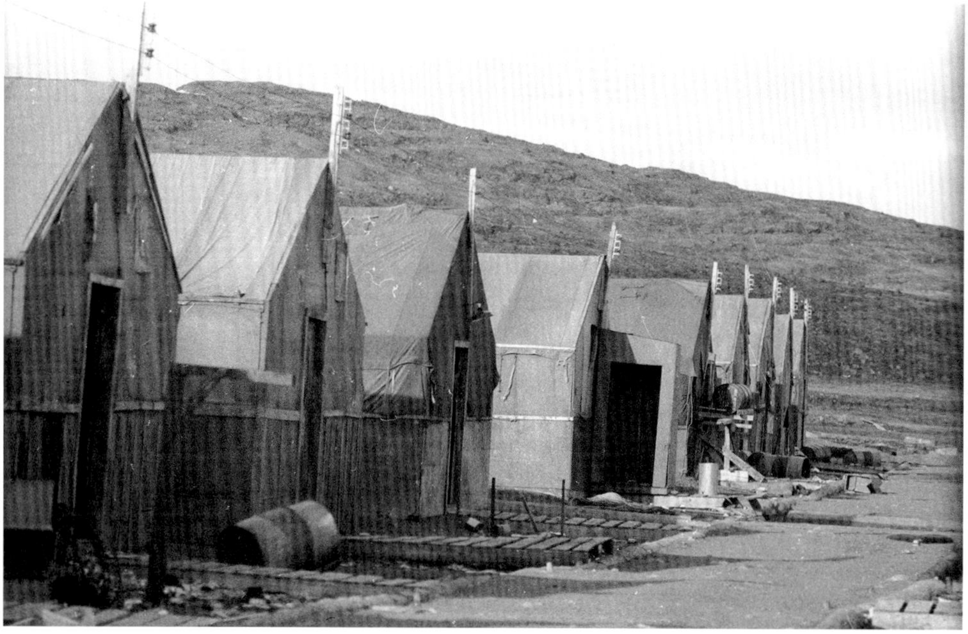

The "new town" of Iqaluit/Frobisher Bay would become, in Wilkinson's words, "a showplace in the Canadian Eastern Arctic":

> Each year will grow the hopes and ambitions of its Eskimo residents. For better or for worse, they are moving swiftly along a path over which there can be no return, carried along by events they neither instigated nor perhaps even desired. In one generation the Frobisher Bay group of Eskimos is making the jump from a stone age existence to that of 20th Century civilized man. The present status of the members of the group is uncertain for they belong to neither the old order nor to the new. But already patterns of conduct are changing and the long slow process of change has begun. With proper guidance and understanding, the Frobisher Bay Eskimo is building in his harsh land a new place for himself and his children.[42]

Wilkinson is ambivalent about how the town will transform Inuit lives ("for better or for worse"), yet he also offers an optimistic – if paternalizing – picture of the future for Inuit ("with proper guidance and understanding"). This optimistic paternalism, with its endorsement of assimilation, shaped Massey's encounter in Iqaluit/Frobisher Bay and throughout his 1956 tour.

As the official tour host in Iqaluit/Frobisher Bay, Wilkinson coordinated the Massey party's stay from 20 to 22 March, presenting the region simultaneously through assimilationist and primitivizing lenses. At their arrival, Wilkinson introduced the visiting dignitaries and accompanying media to a greeting party comprised of three unidentified Inuit, members of the RCAF, the RCMP, and the US Air Force, and a representative of the construction firm the Foundation Company of Canada.[43] *The Globe and Mail* even termed Wilkinson the "mayor of Frobisher Bay";[44] of course, the community did not have a mayor until the 1970s, but for a time, visiting southerners saw Wilkinson as the de facto community leader and guide.[45] That was in part because he oversaw the government's development of the "new town" in Iqaluit/Frobisher Bay. Wilkinson was at once the impresario of events arranged for Massey's party at Iqaluit/Frobisher Bay and himself a performer in the spectacle.

Wilkinson arranged for Massey and his entourage to see the various vestiges of southern influence in Iqaluit/Frobisher Bay. Massey and his party stayed in one of the seven houses initially constructed in the "new town" and visited a private Inuit home there. The DNANR's official guide to the tour touted the building program in Iqaluit/Frobisher Bay.[46] Wilkinson also organized tours to the Hudson's Bay Company (HBC) post, the nursing station, and the school, where the governor general addressed a group of children.[47] Southern commercial businesses also actively engaged with the tour. For example, the Foundation Company of Canada hosted a lavish dinner of imported food in Iqaluit/Frobisher Bay on 21 March, and the HBC post manager hosted a lunch on 22 March.[48] On Massey's final evening in the town, a dance was held in Apex, just outside of Iqaluit/Frobisher Bay, at the RCAF's garage workshop, another facility that Wilkinson later lauded in his 1956 paper.[49] At these tours and, notably, at a dinner hosted by Wilkinson and his wife, Vivian, a southern presence and the integration of Inuit into southern life was put on display. (Other stops across the north on Massey's ambitious tour also featured institutions brought to the north by southerners, including health facilities in Cambridge Bay/Iqaluktuuttiaq and The Pas, federal day schools in Tuktoyaktuk and Aklavik, the Catholic parish in Sanirajak/Hall Beach, the Anglican cathedral in Aklavik, and various RCMP detachments throughout.)

In Iqaluit/Frobisher Bay, Wilkinson paired the promotion of southern interventions in the north with highly choreographed displays of Inuit culture, often presented in a primitivizing manner. For the tour, Wilkinson arranged for the construction of a series of temporary displays on the beach near the HBC post. There, the governor general visited a specially built *iglu* (igloo) and examined hunting equipment. A highlight of the experience took place when the elderly Massey and his daughter-in-law rode across the beach on a *qamutik* (sled).[50] And, again, this pattern of presenting primitivizing displays of Inuit culture would be repeated at other stops along the ambitious tour. For example, Massey searched for muskox during a flight around Resolute/Qausuittuq,[51] fished at Cambridge Bay/Iqaluktuuttiaq,[52] and studied other vestiges of Inuit life. Representations of how Inuit had adapted southern technologies were not included.

Such fascinations with traditional Inuit life at Iqaluit/Frobisher Bay and elsewhere on the tour were often presented within a colonial frame. The tour's official guide, for example, included a historical portrait of the Iqaluit/Frobisher Bay region that, as with all of the short regional profiles, emphasizes a British colonial presence. The reader is told that when the American explorer Charles Francis Hall passed through the area in the mid-nineteenth century, "he was surprised to meet an Eskimo woman who spoke excellent English. It transpired that she and her husband had been to England on board a whaling vessel. The Prince Consort had met them and invited them to Buckingham Palace, where they had spent some time with Queen Victoria and the little princes and princesses."[53] The inclusion of this curious anecdote seems aimed to present a close and amicable relationship between the Crown and Inuit.

Years later, Massey remembered his visit to Iqaluit/Frobisher Bay in fond – if condescending – tones: "I had my first contact with Eskimo life at Frobisher. To visit Eskimos in their huts or igloos was always a pleasant experience – they are delightful people, as all who know the North seem to agree, and the children have charming manners."[54] At Iqaluit/Frobisher Bay, Massey encountered a highly choreographed performance of "Eskimo life" that paired depictions of compliant Indigeneity with markers of assimilation, all arranged by Wilkinson.

Inventing Resolute/Qausuittuq: Idlout and the High Arctic Relocations

Late in the afternoon on Friday, 23 March 1956, Massey's party arrived at Resolute/Qausuittuq on Cornwallis Island in the High Arctic. The governor general's arrival was witnessed by Joseph Idlout, newly relocated to Resolute/Qausuittuq with his family the previous year, as well as by other Inuit, including Daniel Salluviniq and Zebeddie Amarualik (see figure 5.1). But Massey's presentation of Resolute/Qausuittuq starkly contrasted with the lived experience of these High Arctic exiles.

Resolute/Qausuittuq marked the most northernly and symbolically loaded stop on the tour. Throughout the 1950s, it held great political significance for federal officials in Ottawa. Indeed, the Canadian government invented Resolute/Qausuittuq.

Located on Cornwallis Island at 75 degrees latitude, Resolute/Qausuittuq is a place with no known previous history of long-term habitation by present-day Inuit or their ancestors. As the Qikiqtani Truth Commission reports, archaeological evidence indicates that Tuniit and Thule peoples periodically lived in the region between 1500 BCE and 1000 CE. But Inuit had never settled in this area of the High Arctic.[55]

Southerners established both a physical and a toponymic presence in the region in the postwar period. The settlement was named for the British ship HMS *Resolute*, which had been lost in the vicinity in 1850 while searching for the Franklin Expedition. The region remained remote and unpopulated until after the Second World War. In 1947, the US and Canadian governments launched a joint ionospheric (weather) station at Resolute/Qausuittuq, just a few years before they began collaborating on the Distant Early Warning Line, located at various stations across the Arctic but far south of Resolute/Qausuittuq. By 1949, the Royal Canadian Air Force had established a base at Resolute/Qausuittuq, serving as an alternative to the US air base in Thule, Kalaallit Nunaat/Greenland.

A sustained Inuit presence at Resolute/Qausuittuq dates from only 1953 and was orchestrated entirely by the federal government as part of the High Arctic relocations, which also included relocations to Grise Fiord/Ausuittuq.[56] Previous attempts to relocate Inuit to the High Arctic date from as early as the 1920s,[57] but it was only in the early 1950s that extensive plans were undertaken.[58] The archival record confirms that the federal government undertook the High Arctic relocations as an "experiment" or series of "experiments."[59] Although there remains some debate among historians over the government's prime motive for the relocations, it is clear that the "experiments," at least ostensibly, were aimed both at humanitarian relief and at securing Canadian sovereignty in the High Arctic.[60] Historian Shelagh D. Grant argues that "sovereignty-related concerns were primary influences on the choice of sites and probably the timing; economic concerns were primary influences on the selection of Inukjuak Inuit as 'volunteers' and the overall design of the projects."[61] Frank Tester and Peter Kulchyski similarly suggest that welfare and Canadian sovereignty became "entangled in the minds of some officials within the Department of Resources and Development and the RCMP."[62] Indeed, asserting Canadian sovereignty in the High Arctic was a prominent concern. Although Cold War rhetoric about threats from the Soviet Union were prominent in the media, the Canadian government was perhaps equally concerned about the potential of US claims to the North American Arctic and about the periodic presence of Greenlanders in the area. As Prime Minister St-Laurent intoned in 1953, "It is clearly indicated that the government and parliament want further attention given to the development of our north country, and I may say that that was further impressed upon us by the fact that there have to be quite a number of non-Canadians going into that territory. We felt that it was very important to have the situation such that whenever they went there they realized they were in Canadian territory and in territory that was administered by Canadian authorities."[63]

The creation of permanent settlements populated by Inuit in Resolute/Qausuittuq and Grise Fiord/Ausuittuq marked the High Arctic as "Canadian territory." The Canadian government's rhetoric about Arctic sovereignty in the 1950s is remarkably resonant today with international tensions over the region in the 2020s.

Government officials in Ottawa and their representatives in the field orchestrated all aspects of the High Arctic relocations. They identified Inukjuak/Port Harrison Inuit, who lived on the coast of Hudson Bay, to be relocated, ostensibly as a humanitarian effort because of southern claims that their home region was overcrowded.[64] Located about 2,000 kilometres north of their home, Resolute/Qausuittuq and Grise Fiord/Ausuittuq represented utterly foreign conditions for Inuit from Inukjuak/Port Harrison. To address this issue, the government also identified Inuit from Pond Inlet/Mittimatalik to help acquaint Inukjuak/Port Harrison Inuit with conditions in the High Arctic, particularly as regarded hunting.[65] RCMP officers at Inukjuak/Port Harrison and Pond Inlet/Mittimatalik were charged with recruiting Inuit for relocations.

Notably, Inuit had no say in these decisions. Although the High Arctic relocations would alter their lives and the lives of their descendants irrevocably, no Inuit were ever present at meetings where the relocations were discussed and designed.[66] And in testimony after testimony, the exiles repeated that they felt coerced and powerless when faced with Qallunaat authorities.

Yet the experiment proceeded. In the late summer of 1953, seven families from the area around Inukjuak/Port Harrison were sent on a meandering voyage aboard the CGS *C.D. Howe*, an Eastern Arctic Patrol vessel. As recalled by John Amagoalik, on the ship as a young child, the group transferred to an icebreaker, the CCGS *D'Iberville*, at Pond Inlet/Mittimatalik, with three families from this area joining them.[67] With ten families now aboard, four disembarked at Resolute/Qausuittuq, and the remaining six families went on to Grise Fiord/Ausuittuq in September 1953.[68] Testimonies from this first group of exiles recount severe deprivation and hardship, including a lack of housing; many pleaded to return to their home regions.[69] In less than two years, despite these grave situations, the government relocated yet more Inuit to the High Arctic. In 1955, four families from Inukjuak/Port Harrison were relocated to the High Arctic, with one family sent to Grise Fiord/Ausuittuq and the others to Resolute/Qausuittuq.[70] As part of the same 1955 transport, Joseph Idlout and his extended family of fourteen arrived in Resolute/Qausuittuq.

Idlout's 1955 relocation to Resolute/Qausuittuq had been long anticipated and delayed. With the collapse of fur prices, Idlout likely saw the move as one that would provide new hunting opportunities. As noted earlier, Idlout had agreed to move with the first group of exiles in 1953, but he deferred these plans in order to work with Doug Wilkinson during the southerner's thirteen-month stay in 1953–54 in Aulattivik, Idlout's winter camp on North Baffin Island.[71] As Frank Tester and Peter Kulchyski report, HBC officials were also reluctant to see the most successful hunter and trapper leave the Pond Inlet/Mittimatalik area. His absence would be felt economically by the company.[72]

The Idlout family's relocation was marked by tragedy even before leaving North Baffin. The family travelled to Arctic Bay/Ikpiarjuk in the summer of 1955 to board the *C.D. Howe* for Resolute/Qausuittuq. According to research conducted by Kenn Harper and by Frank Tester and Peter Kulchyski, Idlout's father, Akumalik, was resistant to the idea of relocating and took his own life rather than move to Resolute/Qausuittuq.[73] Without Akumalik, both a spiritual leader and a seasoned hunter, the family was diminished.

In August 1955, Idlout and his remaining extended family boarded the *C.D. Howe*, the same vessel that had carried his daughter Leah south for tuberculosis treatment. In addition to the hunter, the group included his wife, Kidlak, and their younger children Leah, Moses, Paul, Noah, Ruth, and Susan; Idlout's mother, Arnaujaq, with her adopted sons, Ilksoo (Elijah) and Daniel; and Idlout's son, Paul Ullatitaq, his wife, Ishoogituk, and their young son Philiposie.[74] Four families from the area around Inukjuak/Port Harrison were also on the ship, three of which would also be relocated to Resolute/Qausuittuq.[75] In total, thirty-four Inuit were transported to Resolute/Qausuittuq in 1955, where they would live with the eighteen Inuit who had been moved in 1953, including Jaybeddie Amagoalik's family from Pond Inlet/Mittimatalik and three other families from Inukjuak/Port Harrison.

Idlout's family immediately found themselves in unfamiliar territory both geographically and socially. The exiled families had no housing and had to resort to building their own dwellings from materials found at the military dump (see figure 5.5). Southern officials stated that they had enlisted the Pond Inlet/Mittimatalik families – Idlout's as well as Amagoalik's – for relocation to

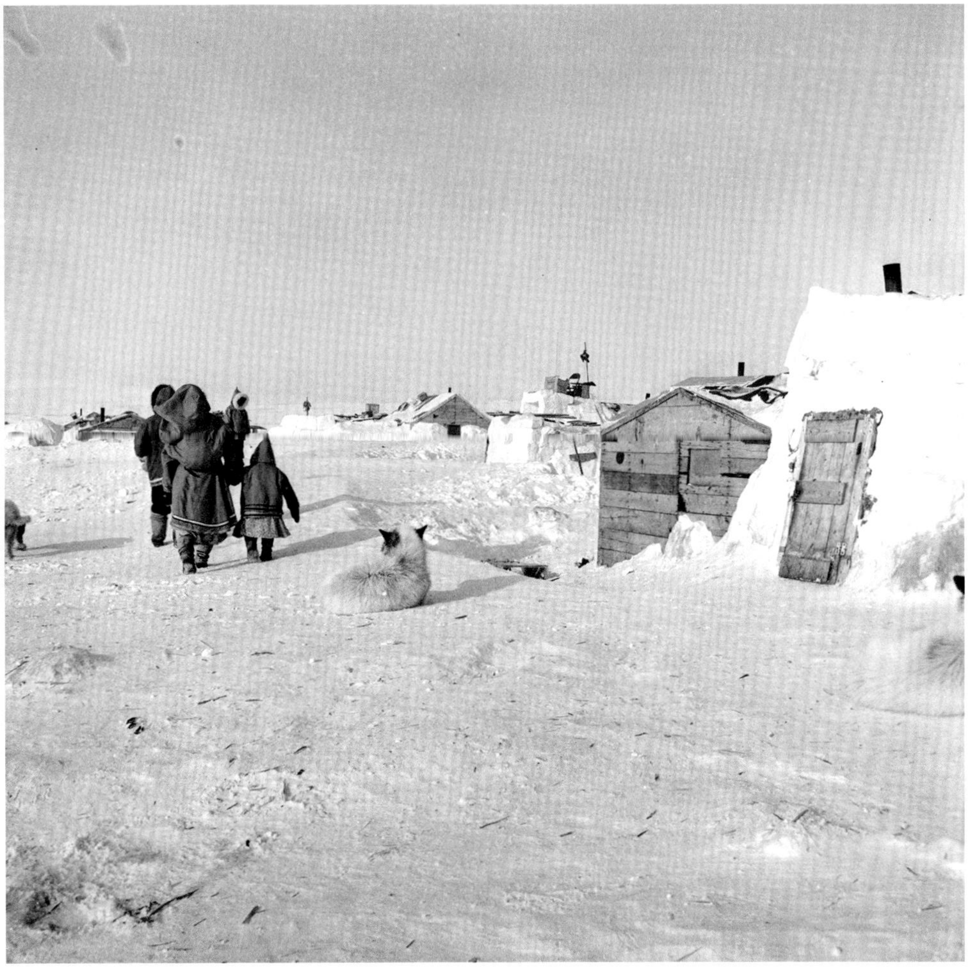

5.5 | Inuit community at Resolute/Qausuittuq as seen during Governor General Vincent Massey's northern tour, March 1956. Photo: Gar Lunney.

Resolute/Qausuittuq in order to help the Inukjuak/Port Harrison Inuit adjust to the conditions in the High Arctic.[76] This decision was predicated on the belief that the living – and particularly, hunting – conditions were similar. But Pond Inlet/Mittimatalik is located about 570 kilometres southeast of Resolute/Qausuittuq and is sheltered from the harsher conditions of the High Arctic.[77] Arriving at Resolute/Qausuittuq, Idlout's family members were taken aback. As quoted at more length in chapter 1, Idlout's son Moses, speaking to the *Iqqaumavara* project, provides a vivid account of his perceptions of Resolute/Qausuittuq upon disembarking from the ship: "When we arrived there, Qausuittuq is … very different from Mittimatalik … When one grows up in a place, that land becomes a part of that person. The land is a part of that person. When these people left their very own blood relatives and the land they're connected to, to never return, that had a big impact."[78] In a testimony also made to the *Iqqaumavara* project, Idlout and Kidlak's daughter Susan (later Susan Salluviniq) discussed how difficult it was for the family to hunt game in the Resolute/Qausuittuq area: "They were craving for things that they were used to, like snow geese and other, ducks or whatever, because there was hardly anything around here. There was no vegetation, no char, big chars that they were used to. There were no geese around in the spring time, some native food that they were used to, or even things like berries, there was nothing here."[79] Idlout's family experienced a rupture from their own land and encountered a harsh and unfamiliar terrain.

The social dynamics of the move were equally difficult. As Moses Idlout recalled when interviewed for the *Iqqaumavara* project, "We left many, many relatives in Mittimatalik. Now, they are scattered. When a family that grew together is broken, they scatter. That's what happened to our relatives. There's no doubt there was hardship."[80] Living among families from Inukjuak/Port Harrison also posed difficulties. The two groups spoke different dialects and had to learn to communicate with one another. Tensions arose. Idlout had expected to be the head of camp and to hold a privileged position among Inuit and with Qallunaat. Idlout began working for the RCAF at Resolute/Qausuittuq, but he was denied the position that he had expected.

Massey at Resolute/Qausuittuq: Performing National Sovereignty

In contrast to Idlout's and the other exiles' lived experiences, the Massey tour paints a jarringly rosy picture of their lives. The tour's official guide states that the exiles were "voluntarily moved to Resolute" and that the move "is proving very successful." Out of a total population of fifty-four, the only Inuk mentioned by name is Idlout, whom the guide identifies as "the central figure in the film *Land of the Long Day*."[81] The record of the governor general's tour does not acknowledge how Idlout and the other exiles struggled to survive at Resolute/Qausuittuq. These hardships are masked beneath the glossy smiles of Cold War soft diplomacy.

Instead, during Massey's short visit to Resolute/Qausuittuq, Canadian sovereignty over the Arctic would be the dominant narrative. On his second day there, Massey was taken on a remarkable 1,700-kilometre detour over the North Pole. As recounted in his 1963 memoir, "The North Pole lives in our imagination as something remote, inaccessible, and awe-inspiring – to think of flying over it and looking down on it was more than one could resist ... The Air Force had provided me with a canister in which were put the obvious documents about the expedition and one of the little blue Governor-General's flags. This container had the essential facts inscribed on it in several languages and was dropped over the Pole ... Inside there were instructions asking whoever found it, if it were ever found to communicate with Ottawa."[82] To record this event for posterity, Massey posed nervously before movie and still cameras with the 9-kilogram canister[83] and made a national radio broadcast while flying over the North Pole,[84] in addition to being cited by the press.[85] Indicating the reach of the Commonwealth, one of Massey's radio transmissions was scheduled to be aired in London, along

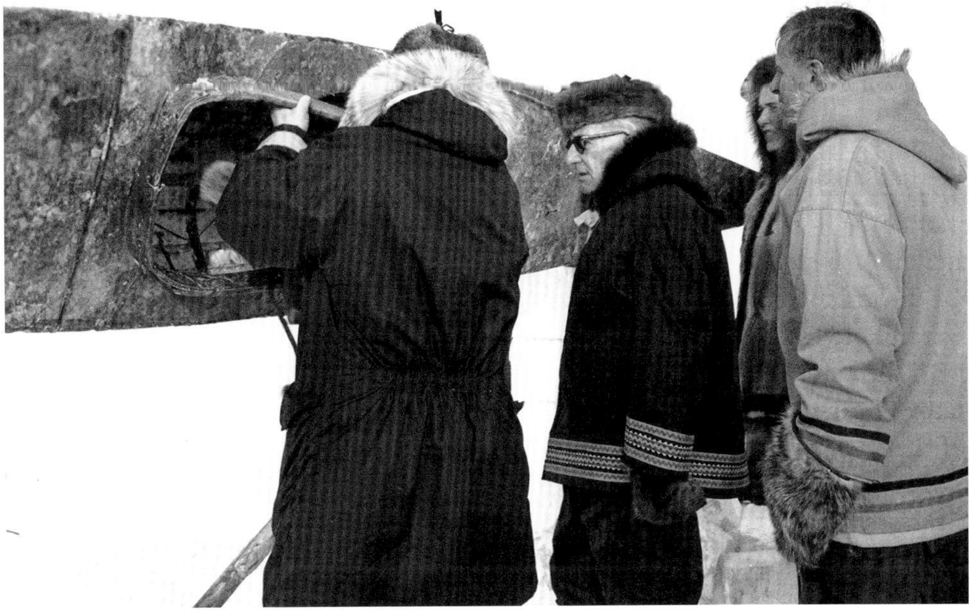

5.6 | Governor General Vincent Massey looks at a *qajaq*, Resolute/Qausuittuq, March 1956. Photo: Gar Lunney.

with a broadcast made by the commander of the base of the Royal Society's expedition in the Antarctic.[86] The act of dropping a flag representing Canada and the Crown over the North Pole and thereby designating it as "Canadian sovereign territory,"[87] captured the attention of the world.[88]

Back on the ground, Massey was introduced to both the scientific and Inuit communities at Resolute/Qausuittuq by the designated site host, Flight Lieutenant J. Forrest, commanding officer of the local RCAF base. He toured the ionospheric station and spoke with a number of scientists there. In addition, and as in the tour organized in Iqaluit/Frobisher Bay by Wilkinson, Forrest also arranged for Massey and members of his party to speak with Inuit relocated to Resolute/Qausuittuq and to inspect a *qajaq* (kayak) (see figure 5.6) and pose with a *komatik* (dog sled) (see figure 5.8). In effect, Inuit in Resolute/Qausuittuq, like those at other points on the tour, were part of a human display. These displays and the resulting press reports were aimed to demonstrate the success of the High Arctic resettlements, purportedly showing Inuit both successfully living off the land and sea as well as integrating into the values of settler Canadian life. Even Massey noted the disconnect between settler rhetoric and Inuit experience when he remarked, in his 1963 memoir, that the "contrast between these scientific activities and the primitive Eskimo life in the native settlements near at hand was dramatic."[89]

Picturing the Encounter: Racialized Visuality

Massey's 1956 northern tour was above all visual. In their meticulous organization of the tour and in orchestrated displays and activities like those at Iqaluit/Frobisher Bay and Resolute/Qausuittuq, the governor general's office and the DNANR presented the north as a stage on which to enact a performance of nationhood and the Crown. But, as I argue throughout this chapter, this performance was largely *visual* – not only in its attention to visual spectacle but also in its dissemination through carefully arranged images and descriptive texts in the popular press.

Indeed, the organizers seem to have recognized the value of visual documentation – still photographs and motion pictures – that provided captivating emblems of Canada and the federal government's presence in the region. Of the ten media personnel officially listed as members of the expedition, four were photographers or cameramen: Wilfred Doucette, a television cameraman with the CBC;[90] Roy Tash, a newsreel cameraman with Associated Screen News; James Lynch, a still photographer with Federal News Photos; and Gar Lunney of the NFB.[91]

The film *Arctic Journey: A Photographic Record of His Excellency the Governor General's Visit to the Canadian Arctic* and a related newsreel provide telling examples of the tour's visual representation.[92] Roy Tash shot the footage for both (see figure 5.7). The newsreel was distributed to English-speaking audiences

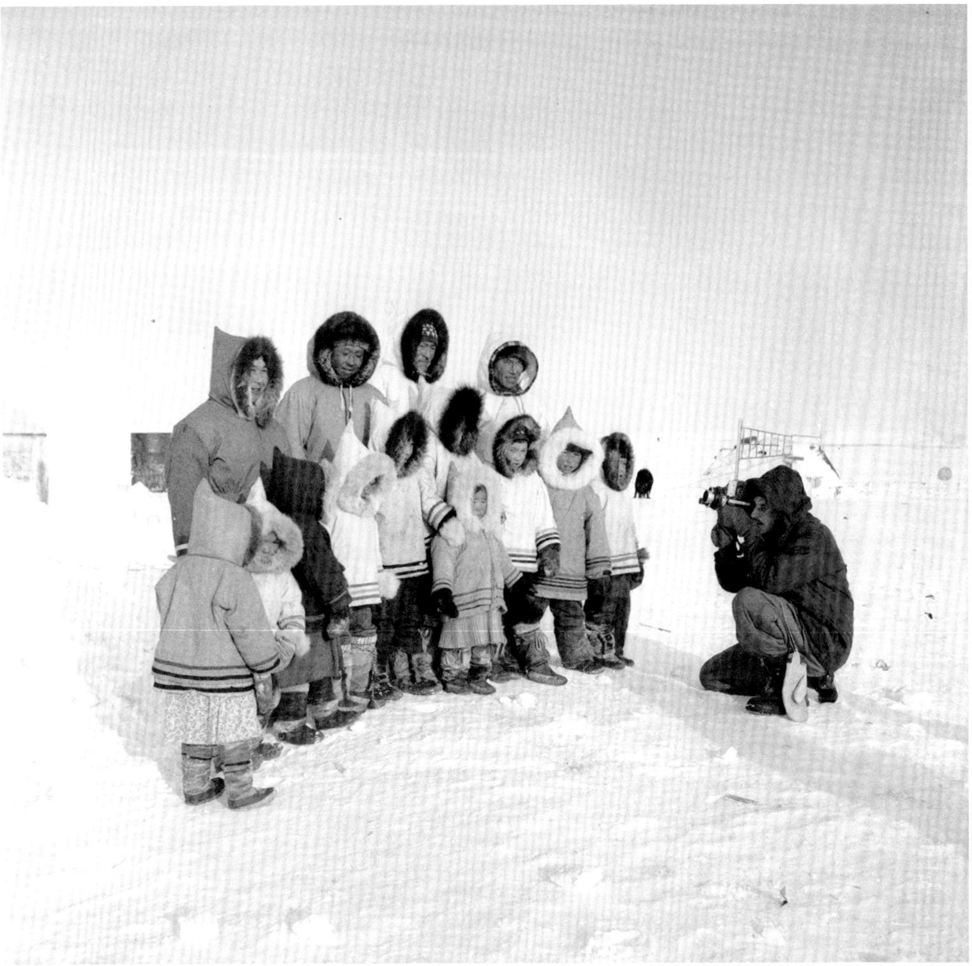

5.7 | Inuit children in Resolute/Qausuittuq line up to be filmed by Associated Screen News cinematographer Roy Tash during Governor General Vincent Massey's northern tour, March 1956. Photo: Gar Lunney.

worldwide through British Movietone News.[93] The 16 mm film, edited by Arnold Hogue for Associated Screen News, exists in different versions. Library and Archives Canada holds a thirty-one-minute black and white print as well as a fifty-six-minute colour print, both silent.[94] The newsreel distributed by British Movietone News ran to a pithy fifty-two seconds, with voice-over.[95] Editing the footage in different versions enabled wider distribution. In all versions, the emphasis is on Massey himself. He becomes the intended audiences' guide to the north. In the twenty-four-minute black and white print, for example, Massey is almost never absent from view. The film follows the tour's itinerary closely, with intertitles signalling the different locations visited. Footage of each stop opens and closes with Massey at the RCAF aircraft waving to well wishes, as though greeting the film's audience too. The flight over the North Pole, displays of traditional Inuit life, and southern institutional interventions are all seen through Massey's experiences. Massey, the official representative of the Crown in Canada, is the star of the film. As he waves, shakes hands, rides in a *komatik*, and studies new construction in the Arctic, Massey embodies governmental authority and its contemporary concern over the question of Canadian sovereignty in the region. Indeed, Massey's own gaze became a surrogate for southern viewers taking in the north at a distance and viewing the Inuit (and other Indigenous peoples) as racialized subjects of the Dominion of Canada.

A closer examination of still photographs made by the NFB's Gar Lunney exemplifies how the north and, particularly, the Indigenous people living there were seen as subjects of the Dominion of Canada and objects of a settler-colonial gaze. In short, these images crystallize how the tour's racialized visuality took form.[96] Whereas the filmic records of the tour shot by Tash presents the governor general as an animated presence, the still photographic holdings freeze the intercultural encounters in ways that distill the effect of the gaze. In total, Lunney produced 158 photographs depicting each stop along the winding trip, although he depicted some communities more thoroughly than others. Aklavik, in the Mackenzie Delta of the western Arctic, where the party stayed from 30 March to 2 April, for example, is the subject of fully forty-four images, whereas The Pas, Manitoba, where they had a brief and final stopover before returning to Ontario, is depicted in only three. Of the other extant negatives, there are seven of Great Whale River in Quebec, eight of Sanirajak/Hall Beach, sixteen of Iqaluit/Frobisher Bay, twenty of Resolute/Qausuittuq, twenty-five of Tuktoyaktuk, ten of Cambridge Bay/Iqaluktuuttiaq, and thirteen of Whitehorse. In addition, Lunney shot eight negatives on board the RCAF plane during the flight over the North Pole, one image of a northern defence station, and three at an undisclosed location along the Distant Early Warning Line.[97]

As I have discussed elsewhere, the NFB's Still Photography Division, where Lunney had been a staff photographer of long standing, was mandated to promote Canadian nationhood pictorially.[98] His work – like that of the division generally during the 1950s – was largely promotional. Rarely diverging from the tightly scheduled itinerary organized by the governor general's office and the DNANR,[99] the photographs cast the people and institutions of the nine communities visited in cheerful hues. Massey's dutiful smile spreads across the shoot.

Although several images show the governor general with southern scientists and industrial officials, most feature Inuit and other Indigenous people. In images shot by Lunney in Iqaluit/Frobisher Bay at the specially prepared displays, Massey is seen examining a *qajaq* and a bear hide, visiting an *iglu* specially constructed for his visit, and riding a *komatik*, as well as examining hunting equipment, sampling country food (or wild game), visiting the school, and attending a dance.[100]

Many of these photographs reflect a long and well-documented history of the ethnographic gaze and a salvage paradigm (see figures 5.8 and 5.9). Their pictorial fascination with "traditional" culture can be seen as primitivizing, contributing to what Johannes Fabian has familiarly termed "allochronism." That is, these

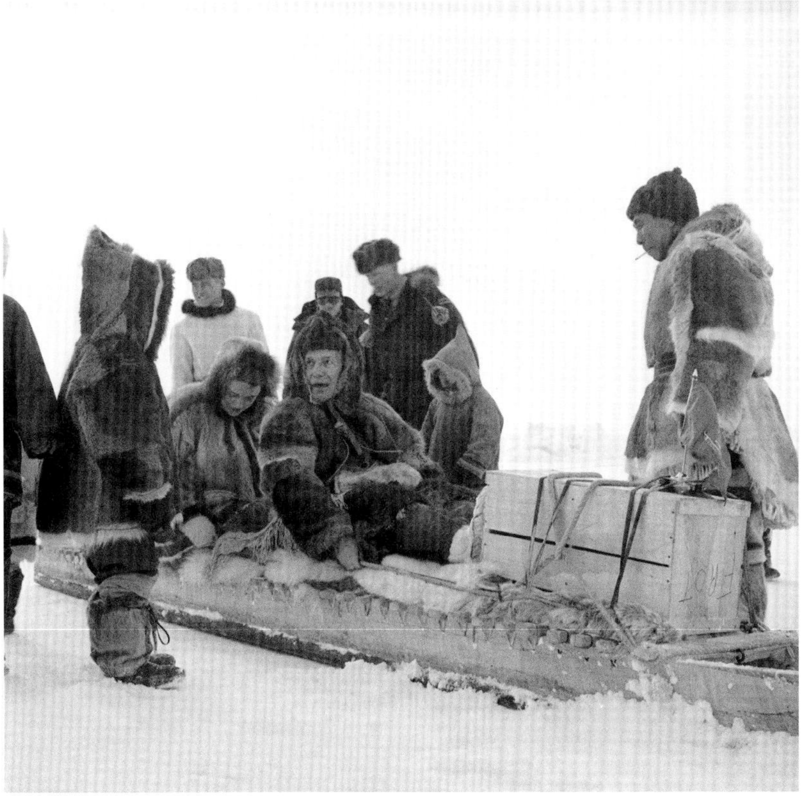

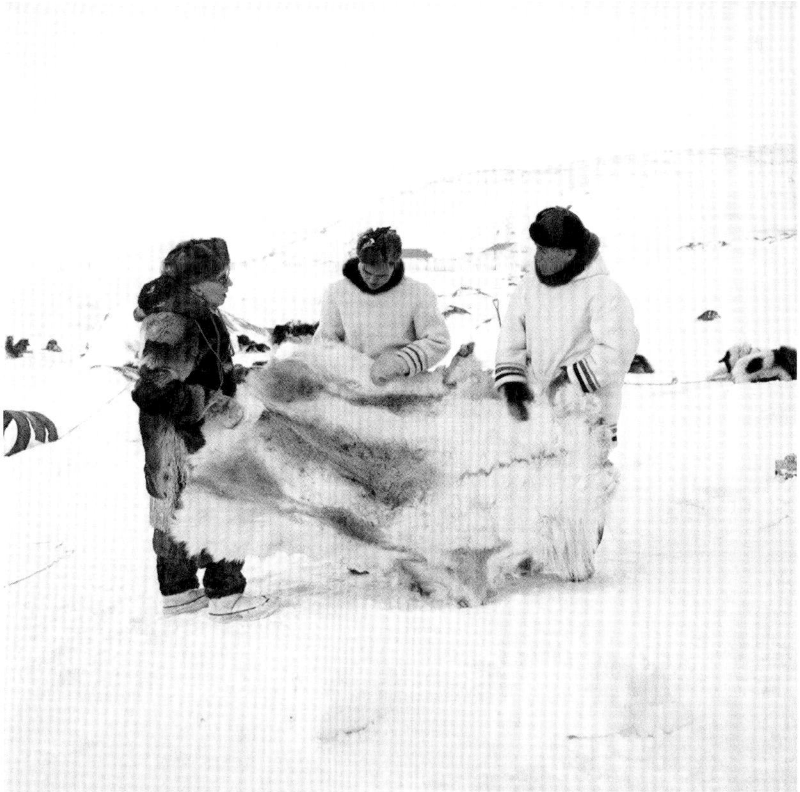

5.8 | Governor General Massey chats with a young Inuit boy, Iqaluit/Frobisher Bay, March 1956. Photo: Gar Lunney.

5.9 | Governor General Vincent Massey examines a bear hide at Iqaluit/Frobisher Bay, March 1956. Photo: Gar Lunney.

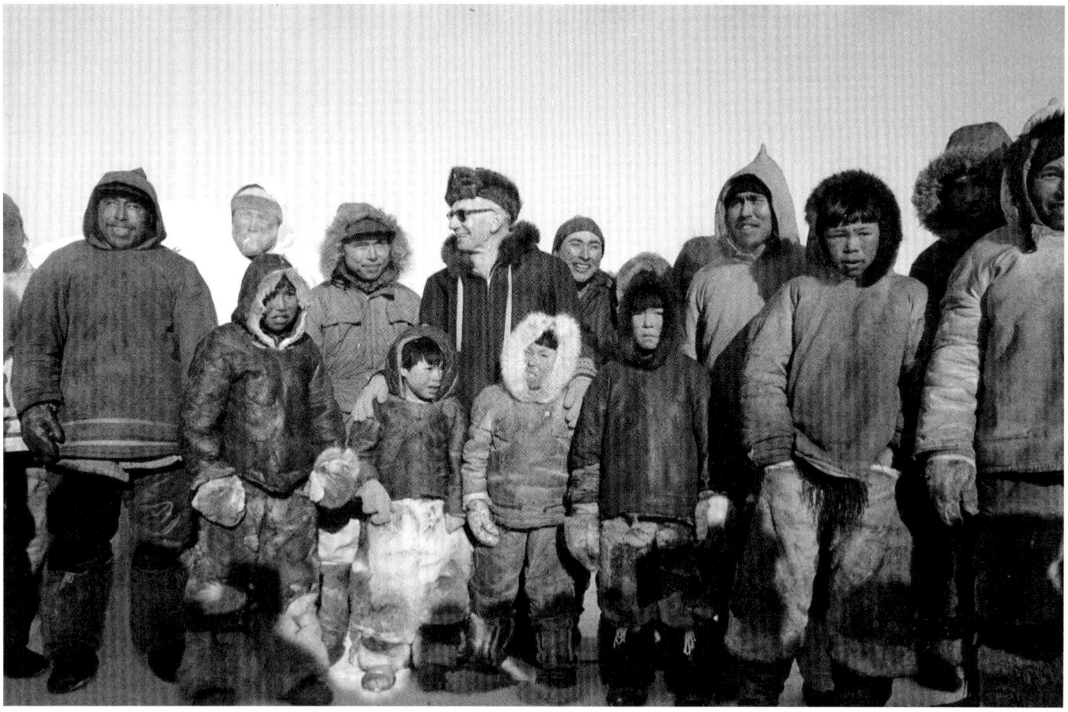

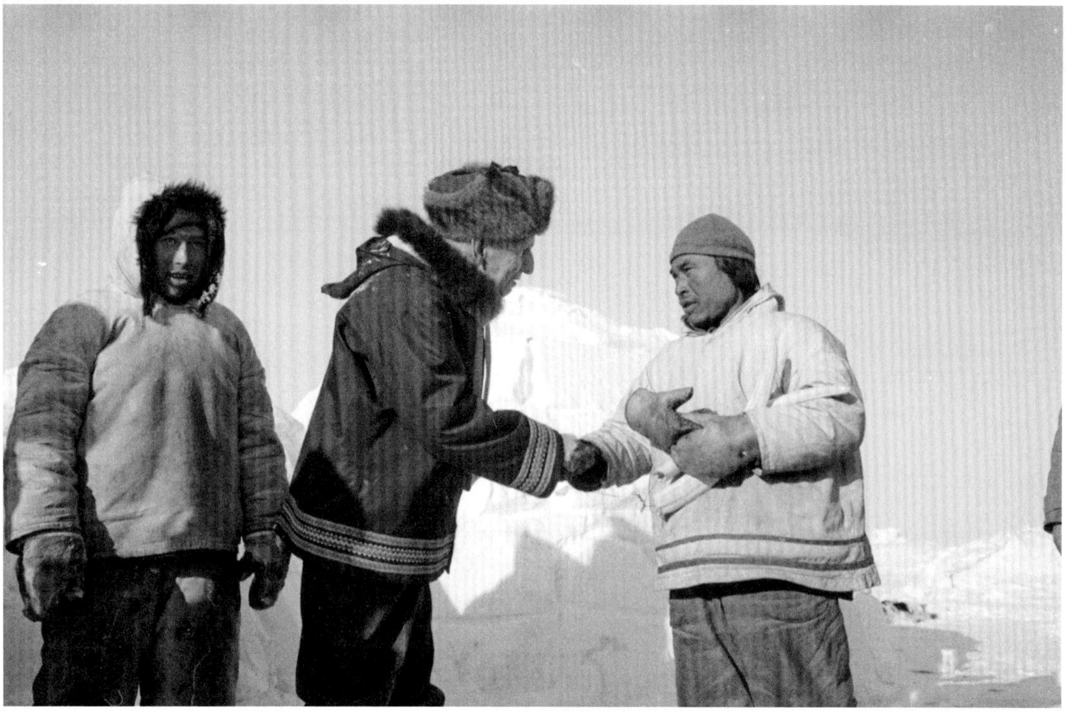

5.10 | Governor General Vincent Massey surrounded by a group of Inuit at Sanirajak/Hall Beach, March 1956. Photo: Gar Lunney.

5.11 | Governor General Vincent Massey shakes hands with Akomali, who presents him with walrus tusks at Sanirajak/Hall Beach, March 1956. Photo: Gar Lunney.

photographs seem to fix their subjects temporally outside of the modern.[101] Typical of much ethnographic photography, these images are often posed frontally. Sitters are more often than not presented without names, or the spellings of their names appear to be improvised. The Inuit subjects here seem reduced by the camera to interchangeable ethnographic types – a population to be managed rather than individuals to be known.

Such now conventional critiques of the colonial photograph are certainly applicable to Lunney's images of the 1956 tour, but this body of photographs also racializes its subjects – and its viewers – through a recurrent emphasis on vision and the gaze, particularly in the numerous images depicting Massey posing with the Inuit he encountered.[102] Here, to quote Shawn Michelle Smith again, "looking itself constitutes a performance of race."[103]

In many of the photographs, Massey greets Indigenous members of the communities visited (see figures 5.10, 5.11, and 5.12, along with figures 5.2 and 5.3). As familiar representations of the encounter between constituents and a visiting dignitary, they follow a fairly consistent visual format, framing the scene as a shallow stage set focused on the lead actor. The images usually position Massey

5.12 | Governor General Vincent Massey visits the Department of National Health and Welfare hospital, where he talks to an Inuit woman, Mary, who holds her ten-hour-old daughter, Solamin, Iqaluit/Frobisher Bay, March 1956. Photo: Gar Lunney.

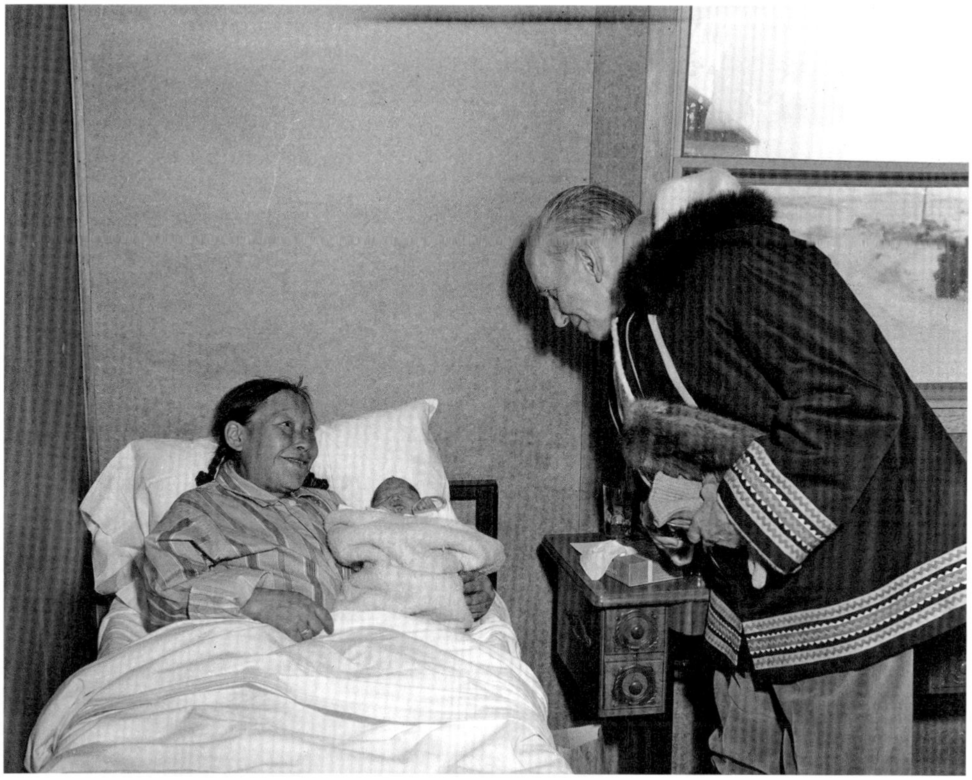

prominently in the centre of the frame, to one side, or near the foreground. In this way, the images reproduce a common trope in official promotional images – the photograph of greeting as an emblem of accord – representing the literal reach of government, with the governor general playing the role of benevolent benefactor.

In all of these images, Massey presents himself in a relatively active pose – as though caught in motion – in contradistinction to the somewhat frontal and inert positioning of the often unnamed Inuit in the frame. Massey typically appears to be looking at the people with whom he poses just as the eventual intended viewer of the image would gaze at them too. In effect, Massey seems at times to be viewing an imagined future image even while he himself is standing before the camera.

With his face turned away from the camera and gazing at those beside him, just as the eventual viewer of the image would gaze at them, these posed photographs have the effect of virtually absenting Massey from the image. They render him an active agent and possessor of the gaze, *not* its object. They call to mind bell hooks's assertion that controlling the gaze is a marker of racial privilege and Richard Dyer's contention that, paradoxically, white absence marks white privilege.[104] Here, Massey serves not only as an embodiment of the Crown and of the Canadian state but also as an idealized surrogate for an intended southern viewer's vicarious visual encounter with the north. As a result, these images teach an intended southern Qallunaat viewer *how* to look.

Disrupting the Colonial Gaze: Excesses and Contingencies

Although such readings expose Massey's gaze as a performance of white privilege, attention to visuality is not merely a circular argument so intent on examining the visual assertions of power that it unwittingly reinforces the very authority it critiques.[105] Instead, visual culture studies enable a more dialogic reading, recognizing the agency of those in the image. As Margaret Olin has written, "There must be someone to gaze and there must be someone to gaze back."[106]

And, many people – many Inuit – do gaze back from Gar Lunney's photographs of the 1956 tour and from the tour's visualization of the Arctic more broadly. Their returned gazes disrupt assertions of settler-colonial authority. The photograph of Idlout, Daniel Salluviniq, and Zebeddie Amarualik focusing their cameras, with which I opened this chapter, exemplifies this dynamic.

The returned gaze is also evident in other photographs, including one that Lunney shot on 21 March 1956, the first full day of Massey's sojourn in Iqaluit. The governor general was scheduled to visit the display that Doug Wilkinson had organized on the beach outside the Hudson's Bay Company post. The centrepiece of the display was an *iglu*. It had been staged as the home of the Kaulowou family.[107] A family identified as the "Kaulowous" pose in the *iglu* with Massey (see figure 5.13). The parents and an infant sit on a platform next to

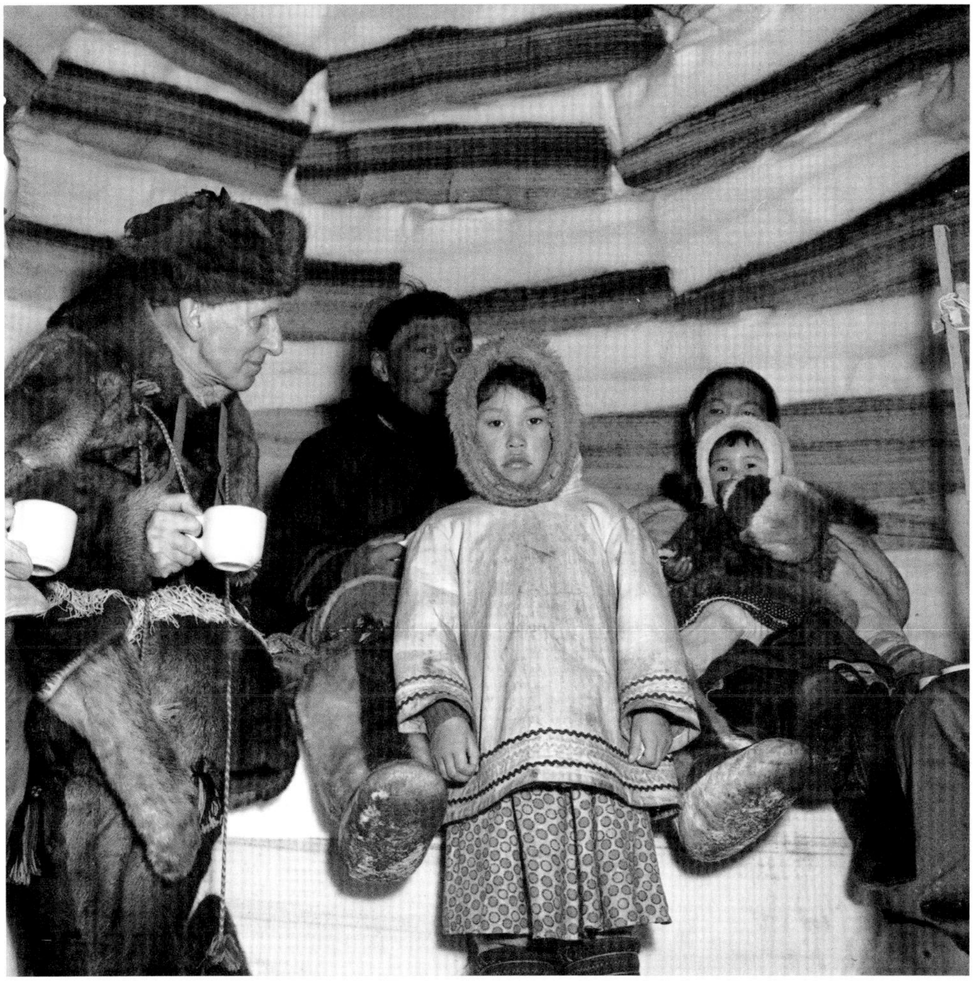

5.13 | Governor General Vincent Massey enjoys a cup of tea in the *iglu* home of the Kaulowou family at Iqaluit/Frobisher Bay, March 1956. Photo: Gar Lunney.

Massey while their young daughter stands leaning against her father's legs in the near foreground. The most storied of all colonial refreshments, tea, was offered to the governor general and his daughter-in-law, Lilias, whose hand is visible holding a mug at the left of the frame. The staging is apparently meant to resemble an afternoon visit in the family's home, although it is notable that none of the family members are drinking tea. In the image, Massey adopts what is now a familiar pose: he is pictured to one side of the frame looking toward the family's young daughter. In this way, the photograph is arranged as a conventional image of greeting or encounter between Massey and his Inuit hosts. But it is not Massey's polite interest in the family that captures the viewer's attention. Instead, the conventional narrative staged for the tour is broken by the wary gaze of the young daughter, standing awkwardly in the centre of the frame, and by those of her family in the background.

The visual record of Massey's tour is filled with such disruptions or breaks. They are seen in what anthropologist Deborah Poole terms "the excessive detail and the temporal contingencies" of the photograph.[108] As Poole has argued, photographs are characterized by these excesses, details that seep into the image beyond the control of the photographer or the commissioning agency.[109] In turn, the disruptive nature of excesses, or uncontained appearances, is underscored temporally by the notion of photographic contingency. As articulated by Walter Benjamin, the photograph always possesses a "spark of contingency" that speaks of the "here and now."[110] Photographic contingencies draw attention to a photograph's sitters as contemporaries with their viewers and therefore not a people frozen in a remote past.[111] Globally, excesses and contingencies create spaces where other meanings reside.[112] Even the meticulous staging of Massey's 1956 northern tour and the work of skilled photographers and filmmakers could not suppress visual excesses and contingencies. They disrupt the prescribed colonial narrative of the tour through sitters whose poses do not conform to the desired protocol and in visual evidence of individual lives and stories. Above all, the many gazes back at the camera indicate lives outside of the frame; those depicted in the photographs gaze knowingly, assessing the scene as active agents. The young girl in Iqaluit/Frobisher Bay, along with the image of Idlout, Daniel Salluviniq, and Zebeddie Amarualik with their cameras in Resolute/Qausuittuq, among many others, suggest other points of view, ones that reverse the presumed colonial gaze. They look upon Massey and his party themselves as foreign curiosities.

At other times, contingencies and "visual excesses" – evidence of life lived beyond the tidy narrative of Massey's tour – do not directly involve the gaze. A closer look at Lunney's photographic record of the brief stop at Resolute/Qausuittuq, for example, reveals additional contingencies and excesses that counter the official discourse about scientific achievement and Canadian sovereignty in the High Arctic. As the party walked through the Inuit encampment at Resolute/Qausuittuq to the organized displays, Lunney took two negatives of Inuit housing (see figure 5.5).[113] With a dog sleeping in the foreground, the focus is on a dwelling at the right of the frame. It has been built from wood scraps found at the Resolute/Qausuittuq military dump and then packed with snow using the skills of *iglu* construction, with more building materials added to stabilize the structure. This dwelling is indicative of how Inuit lived at Resolute/Qausuittuq at a time when their increasing calls for adequate housing were met with little action. As Massey paraded national sovereignty and touted the government's claims about the success of the relocations, such images revealed the lived hardships of Inuit exiles.

The photographic record of Governor General Vincent Massey's historic 1956 tour of Inuit Nunangat provides a telling case study of the assertion of settler-colonial racialized visuality. Specifically examining a body of photographs shot during the tour by photographer Gar Lunney for the NFB, I have argued that these images thematize visuality and reveal how "seeing is culturally coded in terms of race."[114] In examining the moment of the tour in 1956, I provide close readings of a few images within their specific historical context, attempting to show how these images present Massey as an idealized surrogate for an intended southern, settler viewer. The images imply Massey as an active agent with the Inuit he encounters as anonymized objects of a settler-colonial gaze. Wilkinson's efforts to build an assimilated "new town" in Iqaluit/Frobisher Bay reinforces the government vision of the tour. In stark contrast, the grim realities of life in Resolute/Qausuittuq for Idlout and the other High Arctic exiles expose the official colonizing vision as a fabrication masking the exploitation of Inuit. In examining images from the tour, I have paid attention to "visual excesses" and the returned gaze to reveal the agency of the Indigenous sitters and to counter the official narrative of the tour.

Idlout continued to look back at racialized visuality through his own camera and through language. The hunter wrote about his own experiences in a small number of publications and in his regular correspondence with Wilkinson and with other southerner government officials. Indeed, during Massey's sojourn

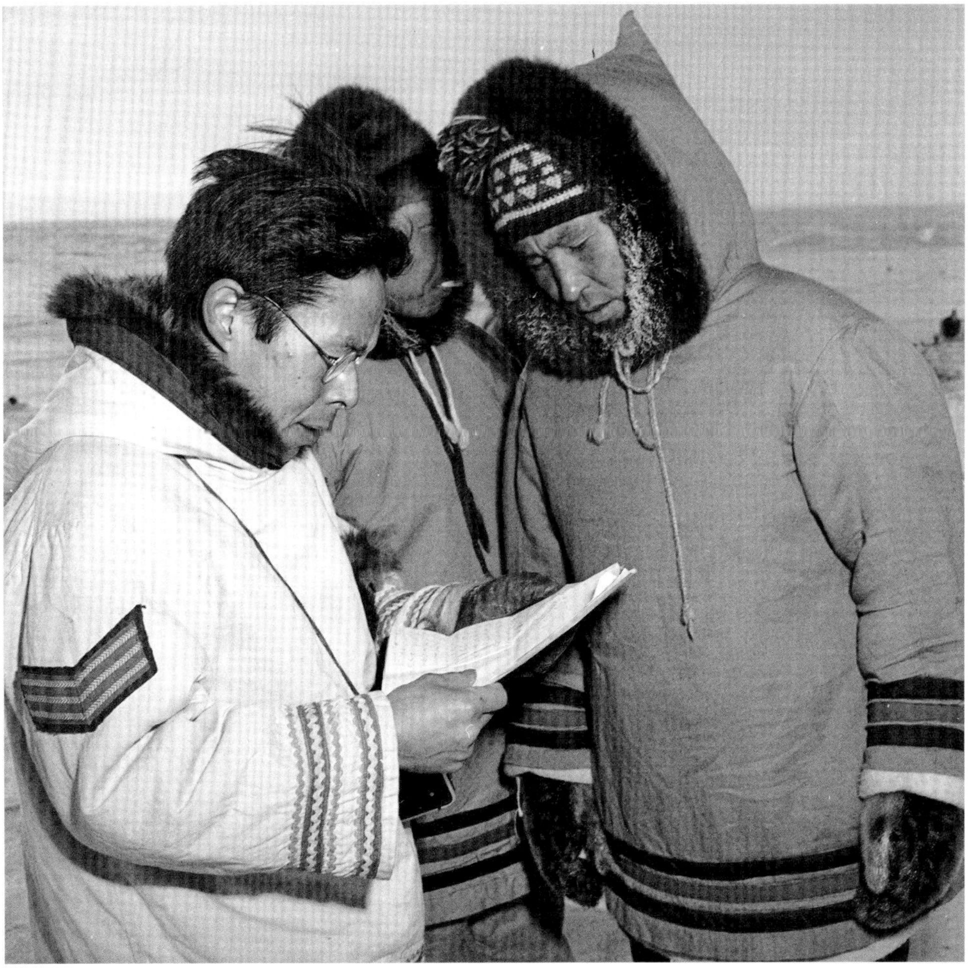

5.14 | Idlout, adoptive father of Northern Service officer Douglas Wilkinson, reads a letter written in Inuit syllabics by Wilkinson, presented to him by Governor General Vincent Massey at Resolute/Qausuittuq, March 1956. Photo: Gar Lunney.

at Resolute/Qausuittuq, Lunney photographed the hunter reading a letter from Wilkinson in Inuktitut syllabics (see figure 5.14).[115] Like the camera, syllabic writing has a long history of Indigenous-settler cultural contact and assertions of Inuit agency. Until contact with outsiders, Inuktitut – in its various dialects – was an oral language. European missionaries developed syllabic script for Inuit in the eastern Arctic beginning in the nineteenth century, basing it on a syllabic system designed earlier for the Cree.[116] For Idlout, writing – like the camera – was a way to express his own perspectives and agency. That is seen, for example, in the 1959 article that he wrote about his sojourn in Kalaallit Nunaat/Greenland for *Inuktitut Magazine*, which is accompanied by his own photographs from the trip. That article follows this chapter.[117] In chapter 6, I propose that these photographs and the article – as well as Idlout's correspondence with the south – constituted forms of resistance.

In the Idlout Family's Words 5

Joseph Idlout, "Resolute Bay Man Visiting Greenland," *Inuktitut Magazine*, May 1959, 11–21, with translation by Rhoda Kayakjuak

ᑲᐅᓯᐃᑐᒥᐅ ᐊᑯᑭᑐᓄᑦ ᓂᐅᕈᓯᒪᔪᓂ ᐅᓂᑲᕕᓂᖏᑦ

ᐃᓚᐅ ᑎᒥᓯᑯᑦ ᐊᐅᓚᓂᔪᓂ ᑲᔪᓇᑦ ᓄᓐᒐᓄᑦ ᐊᑐᐊᒍᑦ ᐅᐱᓐᒐᒪᑎᑯᑦ. ᐊᐱᑎᔭᐅᒐᒥ ᑕᑯᔭᑐᓕᒪᔭᑎᐊᒃᓴᓐᒐᓂᒃ ᐊᑯᑭᑐᓄᑦ ᑲᔪᔪ ᐱᐅᓯᑲᒪᓐᒐᑕ, ᐊᒐᓯ 29ᒥᒃ ᐊᐅᓚᔪᑎᒃ ᐊᑯᑭᑐᓄᑦ. ᐃᓄᐃᑦ ᑲᓇᑕᒥᐅᑦ ᐊᕗᕆᓐᕆᑐᓂᒃ ᓄᓇᓕᑦ ᑯᓕᐊᔪᑎᒃ ᐊᐅᓚᑐᕕᓂᑦ ᑕᑯᔭᑐᔪᑎᒃ ᐊᑯᑭᑐᒥᐅᓂᒃ. ᑕᑯᐊ ᐃᓚᐅᑉ ᐅᓂᑲᕕᓂᖏᑦ ᐊᑯᑭᑐᓂᔪᓂ.

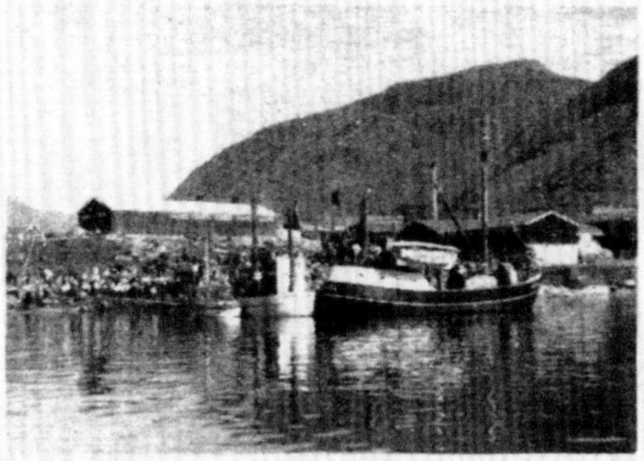

ᓯᑎᐱᑎ 1, 1958. ᓄᕗᓄᑦ 8ᒍᐊᑎᔪᒍ ᐅᓚᑯᑦ ᐊᑯᑭᑐᓄᑦ ᑎᑭᐳᒍᑦ ᓴᓐᒐᓄᑦ ᓄᑲᕋᑕ ᐅᑕᑭᔪᑕ. 1 ᑕᕗᓐᒐᑎᔪᒍ ᐅᒥᐊᒥᒃ ᑲᐃᔭᑲᐳ ᐸᕆᐊᑐᒥᒃ, ᐱᓐᒐᓯᑦ ᐃᑭᔪᑎᒃ ᐅᐸᑎᓄᑦ. 2ᒥ ᑎᑭᓕᐳᒍᑦ ᑯᑭᓴᑐᐊᔪᕗᑦ ᓴᓂᑯᑕᕗᔪ ᓄᓇᓕᐊᐱᑦ, ᑯᑭᐅᔭᐊᕋᔪᒍᑦᔪ ᑯᑭᓴᑐᐊᔪᕗᑦ ᐱᓐᒐᓯᐊᑎᔪᑎᒃ. ᑭᓴᔪᑕ ᒪᔭᐊᓕᕋᑕ ᑭᓯᐊᓂ ᐃᓄᐃᑦ ᐊᒃᔪᓇᒍᑦ ᓴᐳᑎᔭᐅᔪᑎᒃ, ᐅᐊᑲᓕᓐᒐ ᑕᑯᔭᒪᔭᑦ. ᒪᕈᓂᒃ ᐊᓐᒐᔭᑲᓕᑦ ᐃᓄᓂᒃ ᑲᔪᓇᓂᒃ ᒪᕈᓂᒃᑕᐅ. ᐃᓄᐃᑦ ᐊᓐᒐᔭᑲᑦ ᑲᑯᑕᒥᒃ ᐊᑐᐳᑦ, ᐃᓄᐃᑦ ᐊᓐᒐᔭᑲᓕᑦ ᓇᒥᓂ ᑭᓯᐊᓂ ᐃᓄᒥᒃ ᑲᔪᓇᑦᓕ ᑲᔪᓇᒥᒃ. ᐃᒪᒍ ᐃᓄᐃᑦ ᐊᒥᓯᑎᕆᔭᑦ 2400 ᑲᔪᓇᓕᒍ 400. ᐅᑲᔪᕕᐊᓄᐊᔪᑕ ᐅᑲᓚᐳᒍᑦ ᐃᓚᕆᓂᒥᒃ ᑯᔭᓕᓂᒥᒃᔪ ᐅᐸᓐᒐᔪ ᐃᓚᐃᔭᔪ ᐊᓐᒐᔭᑲᕕᒃᐳᔪ ᐅᑲᔪᐳᒍᑦ ᓯᓚᒥ ᑐᓂᔪᑕ ᓴᓇᐅᒐᒥᒃ ᐅᔭᕋᒃᒥᒃ ᒥᓯᒐᒥᒃᔪ ᐊᓄᕋᒥᒃ. ᑐᓂᔭᐅᔪᑕᑕᐅ ᐊᓇᐅᑉ ᐊᓄᕋᓐᕆᓂᒃ ᐸᓐᒍᑎᐳᔪ ᐊᓄᕋᓐᕆᓂᒃ, ᑐᓂᔭᐅᔪᑕᔪ ᐅᑲᓕᒪᑲᓂᒃ ᐊᕗᑕᑲᐅᑐᓂᒃ. ᐊᑯᑭᑐᒥᐅᔪ ᐊᓐᒐᔭᑲᓐᒐᑦ ᐅᑲᔪᐳ ᑯᕕᐊᓯᑲᑎᕆᑯᕗᓂᒥᒃ ᐃᓚᕆᓯᒪᓂᒥᒃᔪ. ᐃᒃᔪᑯᑎᓐᒐᓄᑦ ᐊᓐᒐᔭᑲᐸ ᑲᑎᒪᕕᓐᒐᓄᐊᐳᒍᑦ ᐃᒥᑎᑕᐅᔪᑕ ᑕᒪᑕ ᓯᐳᑐᔪᑕᔪ. ᐃᒥᔪᒥᒃ ᐊᑐᑐᐹᔪᐃᑦ ᐅᐸᓐᒐᔪᓂᑦ ᐊᑐᐳᓐᒐ, ᐊᓇᑕᐅ ᐊᓐᒐᔭᑲᓐᒍᑲᑕᐅᔭ ᐅᐸᓐᒐᔪ ᐃᓚᐃᔭᔪ ᑲᑲᓯᔪ ᓂᐱᓕᐅᑕᐅᔪᑕ ᐯᐸᓂᒃᔪ, ᐅᐱᑯᕕᐳᓕᒥᔪ ᐱᑎᑕᐅᕆᔪᑕ. ᐅᒥᐊᔭᐊᑎᓄᐊᑎᕗᒍᑦ ᐃᒐᐱᐸᔪᒍᑦ ᐃᒐᕗᒍᑦ.

Page 11:

The people of Resolute Bay visiting Greenland Stories

Idlout had left on an airplane to Qallunaat Nunaat (Southern Canada) to Ottawa during an early Spring season. He was asked if he would like to see and go to Greenland; and learn about their lifestyle. On August 29th, he left for Greenland. The ten Inuit of Canada from different communities to visit Greenland. These are Idlout's stories during his stay in Greenland.

September 1, 1958. To Nuuk at 8:00 AM we arrived, to Greenland. In front of the communities, we docked, and we waited. 1:00 PM, a boat arrived to welcome us, and three of them boarded our boat. At 2:00, when we arrived, the weapons went off; and while we sailed by a beautiful land with a community, with big weapons, which were shot three times. When we docked, and while we were getting off the ramp, the Inuit were separated from the crowd with a rope. There were too many people who wanted to see us. They had two leaders who were Inuit and the other two were Qallunaat (Caucasions). The Inuit leaders wore white shirts, Inuit had their own leader; and the Qallunaat consult with Qallunaat leaders. I heard Inuit that participated were 2400 and Qallunaat participants were 400. We were taken to a podium, and we spoke about relationship, and gratitude. So me, Elijah and our leader spoke outside. We gave gifts of soapstone and handmade Inuit clothes. We were also given a gift of a book with lots of photographs. The leader of Greenland spoke to us about making sure we have fun and appreciate this new relationship. At a big house, we met with the leaders at the chambers and we were given drinks and were smoking. We all drank alcohol including me, and the leaders too. Me and Elijah were taped and were given papers and environment we were at was very gratifying. We boarded back to a boat, and then cooked at their kitchen.

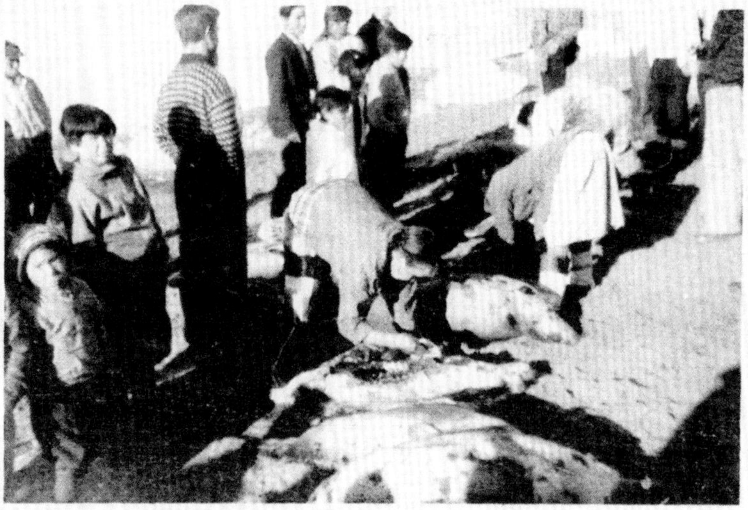

ᐊᑯᑭᑐᒥᐅᑕ ᐋᓇ ᓇᑎᒥᒃ ᐱᓚᑐ.

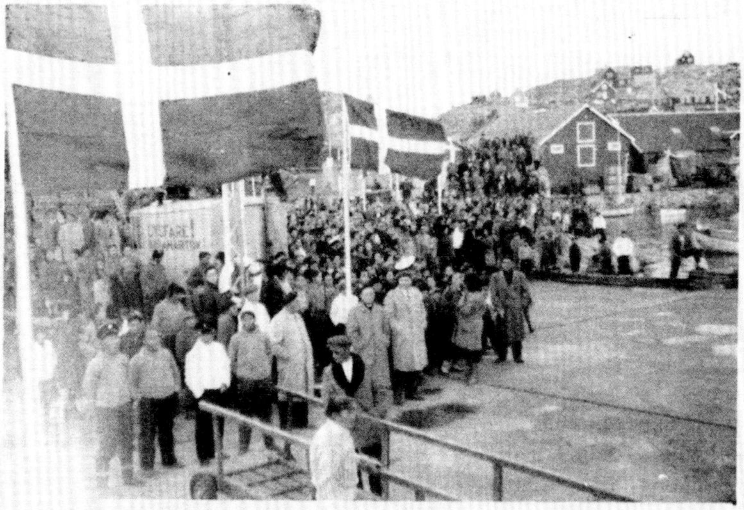

ᐊᑯᑭᑐᒥᐅᑦ ᑲᓇᑕᒥᐅᓂᒃ ᑕᑯᔫᑐᓯᒪᔪᑦ.

Page 12 (captions):

The Greenlandic women butchering on the floor.

The Greenlandic people came to see the Canadians.

ᓄᓇᑯᐊᒧᑦ ᐊᐃᔭᐅᓗᑕ ᕿᓯᒧᑦ ᐸᐅᓐᒐᐅᔭᐅᓗᑕ ᓯᕗᓕᒥᒃ ᐃᒡᓗᑯᑎᓐᒋᑦ ᑕᑯᓗᒋᑦ ᐃᓕᓂᐊᐱᐊᓗᓗ, ᑭᓯᒐᓚᓐᒋᓂᒃ ᑭᒥᕈᐊᑎᑕᐅᓗᑕ ᐃᓕᓂᐊᕕᑯᓗᑕ ᑕᒪᐱᓄᑦ ᐊᑐᑐᓄᑦ ᐅᒪᔪᓄᑦᓗᓂᑦ ᐃᓕᓂᐊᕕᒃ ᑕᓇᒍ ᐃᓕᓂᐊᕕᒃᔭᐊ ᑕᒪᐃᓂᑦ ᓄᓇᓂᑦ ᐊᓐᒐᔪᑲᓐᒍᒪᑦ,, ᐊᓂᐊᑯᕕᓐᒐᓗ ᑕᒪᐃᓂᑦ ᐱᓚᑐᕕᐅᔪ ᐳᕙᓂᓗᓂᑦ ᐳᕙᒃᓗᑐᓗ ᑕᕗᓐᒐ ᐊᐃᐸᒃᑐᒍ. ᐃᓕᓂᐊᐱᔪᐊᕈᒪᓕᑐᑦᓗ ᑕᕗᓐᒐ ᐊᐃᐸᒃᑐᑦ ᓇᑭᑐᐃᓇ ᓄᓇᓂᑦ ᐊᓯᐊᓂ ᑕᒪᐃᓂ ᐃᓕᓂᐊᕕᑲᕋᓗᐊᑎᑦᓗᒍ, ᐊᓂᐊᕕᑲᕋᓗᐊᑎᑦᓗᒍᓗᓂᑦ, ᓯᑫᒪ ᐃᒡᓗᑲᓕᓂᒪᑦ ᑲᓗᓇᓂᑦ ᐅᓇ ᐊᕈᒍᑎᑦᓗᒍ 1721 ᐊᔪᑎᑐᐃᐳᑕᓗᑎᒃᓗ ᐃᓄᓐᒍᐊᕋᓗᒃ ᓴᓇᓯᒪᔪ ᐊᔪᑎᑐᐃᐳᕕᓂᓐᒐᒍ ᓯᕗᓕᐸ ᐃᒪᐃᑐᑦ ᐊᔪᑎᑐᐃᐳᓐᒋᑦ LUTHERAN MISSION ᑐᒃᓯᐊᑎᐊᓂ ᐊᓂᐊᕕᒃᒥ ᑕᒪᐃᑕ ᐃᓄᐱᑦ ᐊᑭᓕᕙᓐᒋᑐᒍ ᑭᓯᐊᓂ ᐊᓐᒐᔪᑲᓐᒋᑕ ᑭᓇᐅᔭᓐᒋᓄᑦ ᐊᑐᐸᒃᑐᒍ. ᑐᒃᓯᐊᐱᐊᓗᒃ ᐃᓄᐱᑦ ᓇᒥᓂ ᐱᒋᒪᑦᔪᒃ, ᓯᕗᓕᒥᒃ ᓂᐅᕕᓕᕋᒥᒃ ᑲᑐᐳᓗᑎᒃ ᑭᓇᐅᔭᑯᑎᒥᒃᓂᒃ ᐊᑐᐸᒃᒪᑕᒍ. ᓯᕈᓯᑯᕕᕆᑦᓗ ᐃᒡᓗᐃᑦ ᓯᕈᓯᑦᒍ ᐱᓇᓯᐊᕈᓯ ᐊᑕᐅᓯ ᓇᑎᑦᓗᒍ ᐃᒣᑐᒥᒃ ᐊᑕᑕᑯᓐᒋᑦ ᑭᓇᐅᔭᒥᒃ ᑐᓂᐸᒃᑐᑦ 30¢. ᐃᑐᑯᕕᒃᓗ ᐃᓚᓐᒋᑦ ᐃᓄᐃᑦ ᓇᒥᓂ ᐱᒋᔪᓂᔪᒃ ᐃᓚᓐᒋᑦ. ᐅᓄᒪᑦ ᓂᑎᓕᐳᒍᑦ ᓂᑎᔭᑐᕕᑯᑎᐊᓗᐊᓄᑦ ᐃᓄᐃᑦ ᑲᓗᓇᑦᓗ ᑲᓯᐅᒪᓚᑕ ᓇᓴᓐᒋᓇᑭᑦ ᐊᒥᓯᐊᓗᐃᑦ ᐊᑐᓂᑦ ᐃᓄᑎᒍᑦ ᓴᓂᓕᑲᐅᓗᑕ ᐊᑯᑭᑐᒥᐅᓂᒃ ᐊᒃᓯᐊᓗᒃ ᐊᐱᓯᑐᑦ ᑲᓇᑕᒥᐅᓂᒃ ᑲᓇᑕᒥ ᐃᓄᐃᑦ ᑕᐃᒪᐃᑐᓂᒃ. ᐱᑲᒋᕙ ᐅᑲᐅᓯᓐᒋᑦ ᑐᑭᓯᓇᑐᒪᑎᐅᒍᓗᐊᑦ ᑭᓯᐊᓂ ᐃᓚᓐᒋᑦ ᓯᑲᓗᐊᒪᑕ. ᑫᒥ ᐊᓂᓕᐳᒍᑦ. ᐅᒥᐊᔭᐊᑎᓄᐊᓗᑕ ᐊᒃᓯᐊᓗᒃ ᐃᒥᓗᒥᒃ ᐊᑐᑐᑦ ᐊᒃᓯᐊᓗᒃ. ᐊᓇᐃᑦ ᐅᒥᐊᔭᐊᑕ ᓯᓚᑕᓂᐳᑦ.

ᓯᑎᐱᑎ 2,1958. <u>ᑲᑲᒥ</u> 2ᒥ ᐊᐅᓚᓗᑕ ᐅᓚᑯᑦ ᐃᓄᓂᒃ ᒪᕈᓂᒃ ᑐᓴᕗᓴᑎᓂᒃ ᐃᓚᐅᔭᒃᑲᓕᓗᓂ ᐊᓇᒥᒃᓗ. ᑲᑲᒥᐅᓄᑦ ᐊᑯᓴᐳᒍᑦ, ᐃᒪᒃᓕ ᐊᒥᓯᑎᒋᔪᑦ 250 ᐊᒃᓯᐊᓗᒃ ᑯᕕᐊᓯᒃᑐᑕᐅ ᐃᓚᓕᐅᓚᒥᒃᓗ ᑎᑐᓗᑕᓗ, ᐅᓐᒐᓯᒃᑐᐊᓗᐃᑦᒍ ᐊᒥᓯᐊᓗᒃᓂᒃ ᐱᕙᑐᑦᒍ ᐅᑭᐅᓐᒋᓇ 4000 ᐊᒥᐊᓕᑲᓄᑦᓗ ᑲᓗᓇᓄᑦ ᐱᔭᐅᕙᒃᑐᒍ ᐳᑫᔭᑦ ᐊᓇᐃᑦ ᐅᒐ ᐊᑕᐅᓯ ᐊᑭᑲᑐᒍ 30 ᓂᐅᕕᐊᒃᓴᑯᑎᓐᒋᓂᓗ ᑭᒥᕈᐊᓗᑕ ᑲᓇᑕᒥᐅᓂᑦ ᐊᑭᑐᓂᓴᐅᑯᑐᑦ. ᑭᓇᐅᔭᑯᑎᓐᒋᓗ ᓴᓐᒋᑐᐊᓗᐃᑦ. ᐊᐅᓚᓕᕋᑕ ᑎᑭᓕᕋᑕᓗ ᑯᑭᓴᑐᐊᓗᕙᒃᑐᑦ. ᑭᒥᑲᓐᒋᑐᑦ.

<u>ᐅᓗ ᓯᓚ ᐃᓚᓐᒐᒍᑦ ᑲᕕᓯᓕᒃᒥᐅᓄᑦ</u> 1 ᑕᕗᓐᒐᑎᓗᒍ ᐊᓇᒥᒃ ᐊᓐᒐᔪᑲᓕᑦ ᐃᒡᓗᐊᓂ ᐃᒥᓗᑕ ᑲᐱᑐᓗᑕᓗ, ᑭᓐᒍᐊᓂᑐᑦ ᑐᑐᑲᑐᑦᒍ ᓄᓇᓐᒐ ᐃᑲᓗᑲᓗᓂᓗ ᐊᒐᓂᒃᓗ ᐅᑭᐅᓐᒋᓇ ᐅᒐᐸᒃᑐᒍ ᐃᒪᒃ ᐊᒥᓯᑎᒋᔪᓂᒃ 4000 ᐊᒥᓯᐸᓗᒃᓂᒃ. ᑕᑯᓇᓂ ᐊᓐᒍᑦ ᓴᑲᒥᑲᑐ ᐅᒪᔪᓂᐊᑎᕕᓂ ᐊᕋᒍᓕᒍ 73ᓂᒃ.

Page 13:

A vehicle arrived and picked us up; and the bus took us for tour. First stop was to their homes; then we saw the school, they showed us their different things around the town. We went through a school and that was used for different thing (such as; learning about animals), and we went into a university, the leaders' headquarters, and their regional hospital. It is a place where they perform surgeries, place TB patients here too. The people working on the doctorate degree attends there from anywhere outside of Greenland; although they also have everything at their own universities, and hospitals, it is because they have building from Qallunaat since the era of 1721; they finally have a priest now and the statue of the late priest whom was the first preacher at LUTHERAN MISSION that is in the hospital and is still standing. All of us Inuit didn't pay, only the leader used his money to pay for us. The big mission is owned by the people, first time, they purchased it together with their money. They were financed from the bank. There is a residence for children and these children given by their father of 30 cents once a week. The senior homes whom are relatives residence are owned by their Inuit. Later that evening, we ate at a huge feast building. I did not count how many Inuit and Qallunaat were participating. Each Inuk had a companion from Greenland and they were asking a lot of questions about Canadians, and about the Canadian Inuit and stuff like that. Their language is understandable, but some spoke very fast. 9:00, we are getting ready to leave. We went back to our boat and everyone drank a lot of alcohol, and women are around our boat for invitation.

September 2, 1958. We left Kangaamiut at 2:00 in the morning and two Inuit interpreters were now aboard and a woman. People from (KAKA?), we stopped in, and about 250 aboard the boat, and were in very good mood and we had tea with them. They caught cods and they fish lots of them. In just one year was 4000 and they are market to American Qallunaat and the women packed the fish. One cod cost 30 in their market, and we calculated that they were more expensive than Canadians but their money has less value. Everytime we depart or arrive they would shoot their weapons. They did not have dogs.

That same day to Kapisiliit town 1:00 At a woman leader's home, we ate and we drank coffee. Later on they told us that they have caribou and fish and cod. In just one year they caught 4000 and that was plenty. There was a man here who used to be a renewable resource officer and he is now 73 years old.

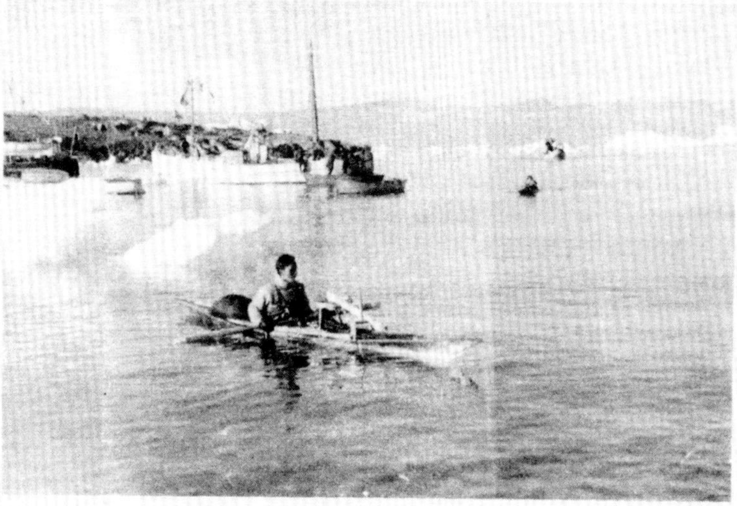

ᐊᑯᑭᑐᒥᐅ ᐃᓄᒃ ᑭᔭᑐᑐ.

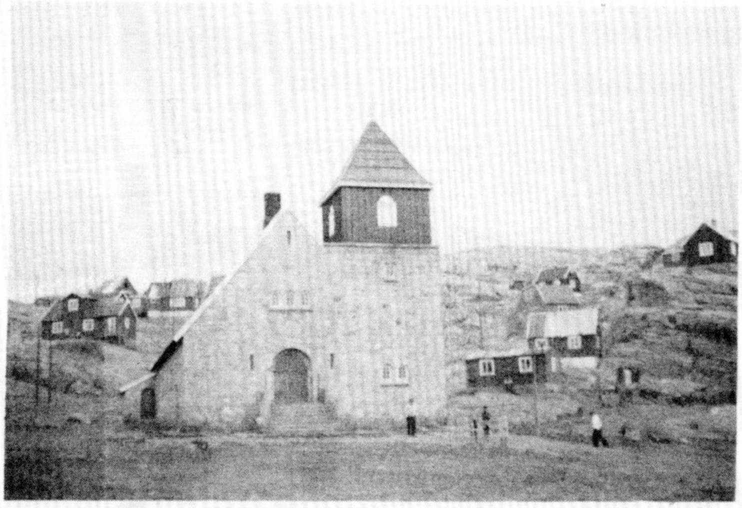

ᐅᒪᓇᒥᐅᓂ ᑕᓇ ᐅᔫᕆᒃ ᑐᒃᓯᐊᕕᒃ.

Page 14 Captions:

A Greenlandic Inuk riding his *qajaq* (kayak).

Ulummannaq town's stone church.

ᑦᓭ ᐃᑎᓂᖓ ᓄᓇᓕᑯᓗᓄᑦ ᐃᓄᐃᑦ ᐊᖑᑎᑦ ᑕᓕᒪᐃᓇᐅᑯᑐᑦ ᑐᑐᓂᒃ ᐅᒪᔪᑯᑎᑲᑐᑦ ᓇᒥᓂ ᐱᕆᔭᖕᒋᑦᒍ, ᑲᓗᓇᒥᐅᑕᑦ ᐃᒪᒃ ᐊᒥᓯᑎᕆᔪᑦᒍ 1,700 ᑕᒪᑐᒪ ᑐᑐᖕᒋᑦᓗ ᑲᑎᒪᕝᕕᒃᑐᒍ, ᐃᓕᓂᑦ ᐊᐅᓕᓯᒪᕝᕕᒃᑐᒍ. ᑲᓗᓇᑦ ᑭᒥᖕᒋᓂᒃ ᑭᒥᑲᑐᑦ, ᐊᑯᓂᓂᓴᓂᒃᓗ ᑐᓴᐅᒪᑎᐊᑐᑦ ᐊᖑᑦ ᐱᐅᔪᐊᓗᑯᑐ ᑕᕝᓂ ᓯᓂᓗᑕ. ᒋᓯᓯᑉ ᐃᓄᓂᖕᒪᑕ ᑭᖑᒪᓂ ᐅᔭᑲᑦ ᑲᓗᓇᓂ ᐊᕙᒍ ᑭᓯᐊᓂ 800 ᓇᑎᑦᓗᒋᑦ ᓴᓇᔭᕕᓂᖁ ᑲᐅᔨᒪᔭᖕᒋᑦ, ᐊᒥᓯᓂᒃ ᑐᓴᐅᒪᑎᐊᑐ ᑐᓄᓂᖁᓯᒥᖕᒪᓂᕕᓂᓗ ᑲᖕᒪᒪᑎᐅᒪᖕᒪᑦ ᐊᐱᓯᖕᒋᓇᑯ ᑐᐊᕕᕙᒪ ᐃᑐᓴᔪᐊᑯᑦ ᒥᑯᓴᑯᑦ ᑐᓴᐅᒪᔭᖕᒋᑦ.

ᓯᑎᐱᑎ 5, 1958. ᒪᓕᑐᒥᐅᓄᑦ ᐅᓗ 12 ᑕᕗᖕᒪᑎᓗᒍ 1ᒥ ᒪᔪᐊᐳᒍᑦ ᐊᒥᔪᐊᓗᒥᔪᑦ ᐊᖕᒪᔪᑲᓕᑦ ᒪᖁᓂᒃ ᐱᐅᔪᐊᓗᓂᒃ ᑕᒪᒥᒃᓗ ᐊᔪᑎᓯᐃᕗᐅᓗᑎᒃ ᐅᐱᑐᒃ ᑕᒪᒥᒃ. ᓄᓇᖕᒪᑦ ᐊᒃᓯᒪᑎᐊᓗᒃ ᐅᔭᕙᒃ, ᓴᓇᓯᒪᔪᑦ ᐊᑯᑎᖕᒋᑦᓗ ᐅᖕᒪᑕᓂᑕᐅ ᐊᒥᓯᐊᓗᓂᒃ ᓴᓇᔪᑦ ᓇᑕᓇᓂᒃᓗ ᑲᓗᓇᑦᓗ ᓄᓇᖕᒪᓄᑦ ᓂᑭᓴᓕᐅᐳᑦ ᐊᒥᐊᓕᑲᓄᑦᓗ. ᓂᖕᒋᐅᕙᓗᒃᒥᓗ ᑕᑯᓗᖕᒪ ᐊᕙᒍᑲᑐ 89ᓂᒃ ᐊᕙᒍᑲᑐ ᓯᓕ ᐱᓯᐸᒃᑐ 8 ᐅᑐᑦ ᐅᖕᒪᓯᑎᕆᔪ ᑐᒃᓯᐊᕕᒃ ᐅᐸᐸᑕᖕᒪᒍ ᐱᓯᒃᓗᓂ ᓄᑭᑲᑎᐊᐳ ᓯᓕ. ᐃᓄᐃᑦ ᐊᒥᓯᓂᖕᒋᑦ 1,700 ᑕᒪᐃᓂᒃ ᓂᑭᓴᓂᒃ ᐱᑕᑲᐳᑦ ᓇᒪᑐᓂᒃ ᐊᖕᒋᓗᐊᑐᓂᒍ ᑕᑯᓄᖕᒪ. ᐃᓄᓗ ᑕᓇ ᑐᒃᓯᐊᕕᖕᒪ ᐱᕆᔭᖕᒪ ᓇᒥᓂ ᐊᑭᓕᓯᒪᑦᓗᒍ ᐯᐸᑯᑎᑕᑎᑕᐅᓗᖕᒪ ᐃᒪᐃᑐᓂ "ᒋᓯᓯᐅᑉ ᐅᑲᐅᓯᖕᒋᑦ" ᑲᑎᒪᕕᐊᓗᖕᒪᑦᓗ ᑕᑯᓗᒍ. ᐅᓄᒪᑦ ᒧᒥᑐᐊᐱᐅᓕᓗᑎᒃ ᐃᓄᒃᑎᑐᑦᓗ ᑕᒪᓂᒥᐅᑦ ᐃᓄᐃᑦ ᒧᒥᐅᓯᖕᒋᓂᒃ ᐊᓇᖕᒋᑦ ᒧᒥᑐᑦ ᑲᒥᓯᒪᑦᓗᑎᒃ.

ᓯᑎᐱᑎ 6,1958. ᑲᑲᒥᐅᓄᑦ ᑲᑲᒥᐅᓄᑦ ᑎᑭᐳᒍᑦ 8ᒥ ᐅᓕᑯᑦ ᐃᓄᖕᒋᑦ ᐊᒥᓯᓗᐊᖕᒋᑐᑦ 500, ᐊᖕᒪᔪᑲᖕᒋᑦ ᐅᒃᐱᑐᑦᑕᐅ ᒪᖁ. ᑐᑐᓂᒃ ᓂᑭᓕᐊᓗᐃᑦ ᓂᑯᓂᒃᓗ ᐅᒪᓂᒃᓗ ᐊᒥᓯᐊᓗᒃᓂᒃ ᓇᒧᑐᐃᓇᖁ ᓄᓇᓕᒃᓄᑦ ᑐᑐᓂᒃ ᓂᑭᓴᓂᒃ ᑐᓂᕝᕕᒃᑐᑦ, ᓄᓇᖕᒪᒍ ᑐᑐᓕᒪᑎᐊᓗᕗ ᐅᐊᑲᓕᖕᒪ ᐊᑯᑭᑐᓂ ᓄᓇᓯᐊᕙᓗᒃ ᓇᓂᔭᐅᓯᒪᔪ ᓂᑭᓴᓗᑲᐳ ᑐᓄᓂᒥᐅᓄᑦ ᓇᐅᑯᑎᓂᒃ ᐅᓇᓂᒃ ᑐᓂᔭᐅᓗᑕ ᐊᕗᖕᒋᓂᒃ ᐊᖑᕕᖕᒪᓗ ᑲᑎᓕᓗ ᐊᖑᓇᓯᑎᖕᒋᑦ ᐊᕕᒥᒃᓗ.

ᓯᑎᐱᑎ 8, 1958. ᑦᓭ ᑯᓕᓴᒥᐅᓄᑦ ᐅᓕᑯᑦ ᑎᑭᐳᒍᑦ ᑯᓕᓴᓄᑦ ᐃᓄᐃᑦ 1,100 ᑭᔪᒃᓴᓕᑎᔪᐊᓗᐃᑦ. ᐊᓄᕙᓂᒃ ᐊᑎᑦᓗᑕ ᐳᓕᑲᑕᒃᐳᒍᑦ ᑕᑐᐊᓗᑯᑦ ᑕᑲᓇᑐᐊᓗᒃ ᓯᕿᒪ ᐃᒪᒃ ᐳᑐᓂᖕᒪ ᐃᓯᒪᒃ 3 ᐊᕙᒍᓂᒍ 35ᓂᒃ ᐳᓕᓯᒪᓕᑐᑦ ᐅᖕᒪᓯᒃᑐᒧᑦ ᑎᑭᑐᐊᓗᐃᑦ. ᐊᑯᑭᑐᓄᑦ ᑕᒪᐃᓄᑦ ᑕᒪᖕᒪᒍ ᑭᔪᒃᓴᑕᐸᒃᑐᑦ, ᐃᑲᕙ ᐊᑕᐅᓯ ᐃᒪᒍ ᐱᕝᕕᒃᑐᑦ 40 ᒥᑭᓗᐊᑐᒥᒃ

Page 15:

Still in Itilleq. The small town with only maybe about 5 men and they farm their caribou. The Qallunaat population was about 1,700 and the caribou are gathered in one spot, some usually are out on the land. They use Qallunaat dogs, they know their traditions quite well, I think this is a perfect spot for men to sleep in. Before Jesus was born, I think they are still using the same rocks around after 800 AD he knew these were built around that era. He knows everything and he's been to Arctic Bay but I did not ask him when that was. I was in a rush, but Ittuksaaqjuat and Mikushak know about it.

September 5, 1958. Maniitsoq on day 12, the time is 1:00. We followed and they have big leader and they are two of them and are preachers too and both are very religious. Their land has a lot of rocks, they had built their roads. Many people are working on the other side too. He is working with fish, halibut that will be eaten by southern cities and to the Americans. I saw a very old lady and she is 89 years old and she still walks on her own. The Inuit owned the church, they had purchased it. They gifted me a bible, title "Jesus' words". I saw the huge gathering place. In the evening, they had a fun dance, they all square dance which is an Inuit dance, and the women dance with their boots.

September 6, 1958. Kangaamiut. We arrive Kangaamiut at 8:00 AM and the population is 500, Their two leaders are religous too. Their diet is caribou meat. They have many cod and much dried meat. They gather caribou meat for anyone who needs it. They said their land has plenty of caribou. Greenland is such an stunning land. They had settled here for the wealth of country food. They gave us two identical *unaaq* (harpoons). They brought us to see whale hunters too.

September 8, 1958. Kulisamuit. Still we arrive in the morning to (Kulusuk?) and their population is 1,100 and they are all working with birch. We had to put on special coveralls and visit them. It is very hard and exhausting, it is because the water is 3 feet. He said he's been here 35 years whom arrived here from far distance. The Greenland waters have plenty of wood, they keep them in water for an hour and they retrieved about 40 logs which was not enough.

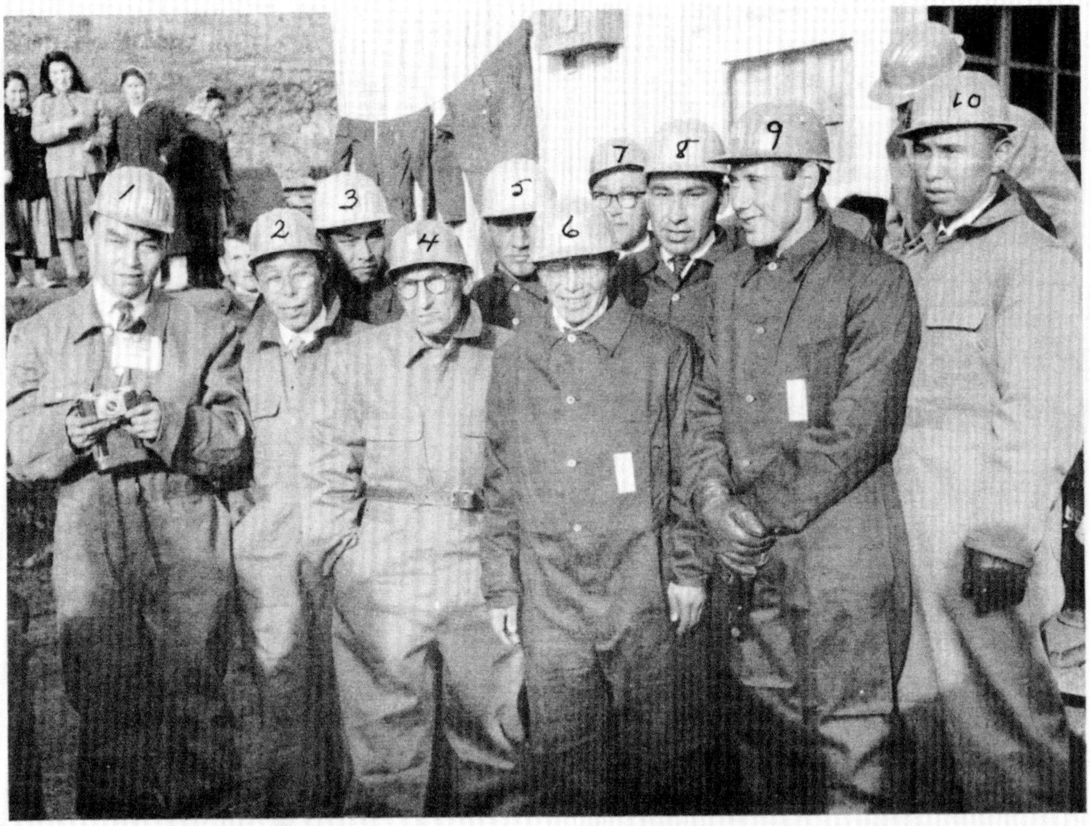

ᑕᑯᐊ ᐃᓄᐃᑦ ᑲᓇᑕᒥᐅᑦ ᐊᑯᑭᑐᓂ ᑯᓕᓴᓕᒥ ᑭᔭᓴᓕᑎᔭᓂᒃ ᑕᑯᔪᑐᓯᒪᔭᑦ, 1. ᐃᓚᐱᔪ ᒪᓂᑰᔪᒃ ᒪᐃᓇᓯᑯᒥᐅ, 2. ᐃᓚᐅ ᒥᑎᒪᑕᓕᒃᓕᐅ, 3. ᑲᓐᒋᓇ ᑭᓐᒐᒥᐅ, 4. ᓴᓕ ᓯᒥᑎ ᐊᒃᓚᐱᐅᑉ ᑲᓂᒋᔪᓂ ᑐᑐᑯᐱᒃᒥᐅ, 5. ᐊᑕᒥ ᑐᑕᓕᒃ ᐸᓕᐊᔭᒃᒥᐅ, 6. ᔪᐃᒥᓯ ᑲᑉᓇ ᐃᑲᓗᑐᓯᐊᒥᐅ, 7. ᐊᑯᑭᑐᒥᐅ ᐊᓐᒐᔭᑲ, 8. ᑲᑲᓯ ᐸᓂᑐᒥᐅ, 9. ᔭᐊᐳ ᑯᓂᐊ ᐊᑭᒋ ᑯᔭᐊᒥᐅ, 10. ᑎᑭᐱᒃ ᐃᑲᓗᒥᐅ, ᓴᓕ ᒍᐊᑕᓐ ᐊᒃᓚᐱᒃᒥᐅ ᑯᐃᓂᓗᐊᒪᑦ ᑭᔭᓴᓕᑎᐱᒃᓘᑦ ᐳᓚᔭᓇᓐᒋᒪᑦ ᐃᓯᕈᓇᓂᓐᒋᒪᑦ ᑕᑉᓂ ᐊᐳᑲᓐᒋᓚ.

Page 16: Caption

These are Inuit from Canada. They are in Greenland touring the logging facility. 1. Elijah Menarik, from Mailasikut, 2. Idlout from Pond Inlet, 3. Kanaaginaq from Kinngait (Cape Dorset), 4. Charlie Smith, who lives around Aklavik around Tuktoyaktuk, 5. Adamie Tootalik from Paliaqjuk, 6. Jamesie Evanna from Iqaluktuuttiaq (Cambridge Bay), 7. The leader of Greenland, 8. Qaqqasiq from Pangnirtung, 9. George Koneak from Kuujjuaq, 10. Tikivik from Iqaluit. Charlie Gordon is from an office but he is too fat and didn't fit to go inside the log factory so he is not in the picture.

ᐱᕙᒃᑐᑦ ᐊᑯᑭᑐᒥᐅᓄᑦ ᑕᑯᐊ ᐃᓄᐃᑦ ᑲᑐᓇᒥᒃ ᐊᓐᓚᔭᑲᓂᑦ. ᑭᔭᓴᓂᐊᑎᑦ ᐃᒥᓗᒃᒥᒃ ᐊᑐᓗᐊᓐᒋᑐᑦ ᐃᓗᓇᓐᒋᑦ ᐃᒥᒪᒥᒃ ᑭᓯᐊᓂ. ᑭᒥᑲᑐᑦ ᑲᔭᑲᓗᑎᓗ.

ᓯᑎᐱᑎ 9,1958. <u>ᐅᒪᓇ</u> ᐅᒪᓇᒥᐅᓄᑦ ᑎᑭᐳᒍᑦ ᐅᓚᑯᑦ ᐃᓄᐃᑦ ᐃᒣᑐᑦᒍ 700, ᑐᒃᓯᐊᕕᑲᑐᑦ ᐅᔭᕋᓗᒃᒥᒃ ᐃᓯᑕᕈᑦ ᓯᕈᓕᐸᐅᓗᒍ ᐃᒡᓗᐊᓗᒃ ᐅᔭᕋᓗᒃ ᓴᓇᓯᒪᑎᐊᑐ ᐃᓄᐃᑦ ᓄᓇᓐᓚᑕ ᐅᔭᕋᓐᓚ ᓴᓇᔪᕕᓂ 1936 ᑕᓯᒥᓐᓚ. ᐊᓐᒍᓇᓯᐊᑐᑦ ᑕᒪᐃᓂᒃ ᐸᐃᐹᓂᒃᓗ ᒪᑎᑕᐅᑎᓄᑦᓗ. ᐅᑭᐅᒥ ᐅᓗᑯᑦ ᓇᑎᕋᓯᐊᑐᒍ ᑲᔭᑲᐅᑐᑦ. ᐊᒃᓴᑲᔪᓂᒃ ᒪᕿᓂᒃ ᑕᑯᓇᓗᑕ ᐃᓄᓂᒃ ᐱᓐᓚᓯᓂᒃ ᐊᓐᓚᔭᑲᓂᑦ. ᑕᓇ ᑐᒃᓯᐊᕕᐊᓗᒃ ᑲᓗᓇᑦᒍ ᐱᕆᔭᓐᓚᑦ, ᓯᓂᒍ ᑐᑐᑲᑐ ᓄᓇᓯᐊᕋᓗᔭᑐ.

ᓯᑎᐱᑎ 10,1958. <u>ᐃᓗᓕᓴ</u> ᐅᓚᑯᑦ ᑎᑭᐳᒍᑦ ᐃᓗᓕᓴᓄᑦ, ᑲᐱᑐᓗᑕ ᐃᓄᐃᑦᓕ ᐃᒣᑐᑦᒍ 1,400 ᑐᒃᓯᐊᕕᐊᓗᑲᐳᑦ ᐊᑯᓂᓂᓴᓗᒃ 1779 ᓴᓇᔪᕕᓂ. ᓯᓕᒥ ᒍᒥᓗᑕ, ᓴᒃᑲᒥᕆᒃ ᐊᐅᔭ ᐊᑕᐅᓯ ᓇᑎᕙᒃᑐᒍ 100, ᐃᒪᒃ ᓇᑎᐅᑉ ᓂᑭᓐᓚ ᐊᑭᑲᕙᒃᑐᒍ $2.84 ᒥᑭᓗᐊᑐᒥᐅᔭᑐ ᑕᒪᓂᓗ ᑯᓄᑦ ᐃᓄᒍᓯᒪᓂᐸ ᐃᑐᓕᑐᒥᑦ ᐅᑲᐅᔭᐅᓚᒪ ᑲᓗᓇᑲᑎᓇᒍᒍ ᐃᓄᐃᑦ ᐊᒥᓯᓕᐅᓐᒋᑐᑦ ᑭᓯᐊᓂᒍ ᑲᓗᓇᑲᓕᑎᑦᓗᒍ ᐊᒥᓯᓕᐸᑦ. ᑲᓗᓇᓂᒃ ᐊᑕᑕᑲᑐᑦ ᐊᒥᓯᐊᓗᒃᒪᑕᒍ ᓯᑫᒪ ᐃᓄᒃᒥ ᐊᑕᑕᑲᑐᑦ ᐊᒥᓯᓐᒋᑐᑯᓗᒪᑕ ᐊᑯᑭᑐᓂ ᒪᓇᒍ ᓇᓕᐊᓄᑦ ᑲᓗᓈᑦᓗ ᐃᓄᐃᑦᓗ ᑲᑎᒪᕙᒃᒪᑕ ᑎᑭᑉᑐᓂᒍ ᐅᒥᐊᔭᐊᓂᑦ ᓇᐹᑎᑕᐅᔭᑦ ᐊᒥᓯᕙᒃᒪᑕ. ᑲᓇᑕᒥᓕ ᑕᐃᒪᐃᓐᒋᓕᑦ ᓯᑫᒪ ᐃᓄᐃᑦ ᐅᐃᑲᕋᑎᒃ ᐊᑯᓂᐊᓗᒃ ᐃᓕᓐᒋᑦ ᑭᑐᓐᓚᑕᐸᓐᒋᒪᑕ ᐱᑯᔭᐅᕙᓐᒋᓇᒥᒃ ᐊᓐᒍᑎᒍᑦ, ᐊᑯᑭᑐᓂᓕ ᑕᐃᒪᐃᓐᒋᓕᑦ ᓯᑫᒪ ᐊᒥᓯᓕᐸᑦ ᐃᓄᐃᑦ.

<u>ᓯᓂᒃᑐᒍᑦ ᑕᕙᓂ</u> ᑲᑲᒥᐅᓄᑦ ᓯᓕ ᓄᓇᓕᒃᓄᑦ ᑲᑲᒥᐅᑦ ᑭᒥᔭᐊᑯᑎᓕᑦ ᐱᓐᓚᓯᓂᒃ ᓴᐅᕋᑯᑎᑲᑐᑦᒍ 500 ᓇᒥᓂ ᐱᕆᔭᓐᒋᑦᒍ ᐃᓄᑕᐅ, ᐃᓄᑭᑐᐊᐱᐅᓗᑎ ᐊᐱᓯᓗᐊᓐᒋᑐᑦ. ᑲᓗᓇᓂᑦ ᓴᓇᔪᕕᓂᒥᒃ ᐃᑲᓗᓂ ᐸᔭᒧᑦ ᐅᑎᕕᑲᑐᑦ ᐊᕋᒍᑲᑐᒍ ᑕᓇ ᐃᓗᐱᓂ ᐅᔭᕋᒃ ᓴᓇᓯᒪᔭ 100 ᑕᐃᒪᓇᐅᓂᕋᑕᓐᒋᓕᑦ ᐊᑯᑭᑐᑦ ᓄᓇᓐᓚᑕ ᑭᑭᑕ ᓴᓂᐊᓂᒍ ᑲᓗᓇᑦ ᐱᔭᕕᓂᑦ ᑕᓇ ᓄᓇ ᑐᑐᑲᑐᕈ ᐃᑲᓗᑲᓗᓂᓗ ᓇᑎᑲᑕᓐᒋᑐᒍ ᑭᒥᑲᓐᒋᑐᑕᐅ.

<u>ᓯᓕ ᓄᕈᓂ ᐅᑎᒧᑦ</u> 1 ᑕᕈᓐᓚᑎᑦᓗᒍ ᐸᓕᓕᑎᕈᒍᑦ ᑲᓗᓈᑐᒪᑎᒃ ᐃᓕᑯᓯᑲᕋᓯᐊᑐᑦ ᐃᓄᒃᒥᓗ ᓇᒥᓂ ᓂᐅᕕᕕᑲᑐᑦ ᐊᓇᑦ ᓂᑭᓂᒃ ᓂᐅᕕᐊᒃᓴᑲᒥᔭᑦ, ᑕᒪᓂ ᑲᓗᓇᓂᒃ

Page 17:

September 9, 1958. Uummannaq. We arrive Uumana in the morning. The population is 700. They have a stone church. That was our first visit and the building is made of stone and that stone is from Inuit land and it was built in 1936. They hunt everything including marine mammals with nets. During winter they hunt during the day and they have many *qajait* (kayaks). We saw two people from (Aksakayuk?) and they have three Inuit leaders. They said the stone church belongs to Qallunaat (Caucasions). They have rich land that also has caribou.

September 10, 1958. Ilulissat. We arrive in the morning to Ilulissat. We drank coffee and the population there is 1,400 and they have big cathedral and very old building was built in 1779. We had a dance outside, In (Sakamilik?) in one summer they catch 100 seals, and in fact the seal meat cost $2.84 and it's cheap; and here, I was asked how we survive by an elder since there are no white people and there were few Inuit but since white people arrived, they have bigger population. There are many children fathered by white men and the ones who are fathered by Inuit are fewer in Greenland, but now White people and Inuit live in harmony and these people arrived by ships and the pregnated women are many in numbers. It is not the same in Canada, the fact the Inuit are single and don't have children for a long time. It is forbidden by men, but it is different in Greenland so they now have more population because of it.

We spent the night here Kangaamiut is small town and they own their land and there are 500 and they are all Inuit. They are not over populated and they don't ask too many questions. The white people made smoked fish and the tombs made of stone of 100 he said and it's in the Greenland island that white people owned. Their community has caribou and fish, but they don't catch seal and no dogs.

Now to Nuuk, heading back at 1:00 we arrived and visited and they are living like the white men and the store is run by an Inuk and woman also sells fish. There are many white people.

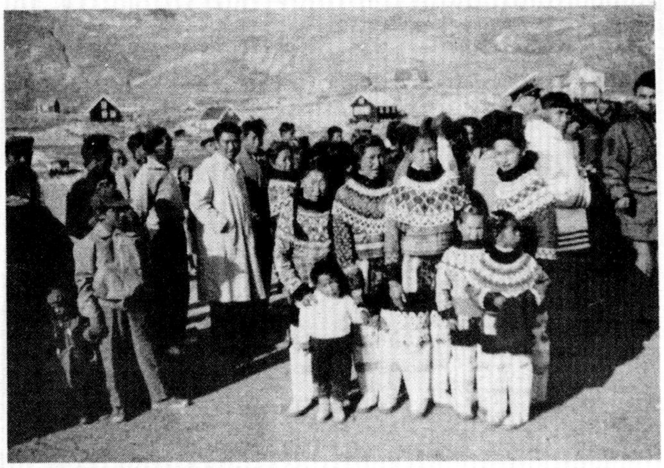

ᐊᓇᐃᑦ ᐊᑯᑭᑐᒥᐅᑦ, ᑕᓕᐱᒐᒐᓂ ᑕᐸ ᑕᑯᐊ
ᐊᓐᒍᑎᑦ ᑲᓇᑕᒥᐅᑦ ᑲᐅᓗᑕᒥᒃ ᓯᓚᐸᓕᒃ
ᑲᓕᐸᓕᒃ ᑲᑲᓯ ᐸᓂᑐᒥᐅ, ᐃᓚᐃᔪᓗ
ᒪᓂᕋᔫᒃ ᓴᓂᐊᓂᑐ.

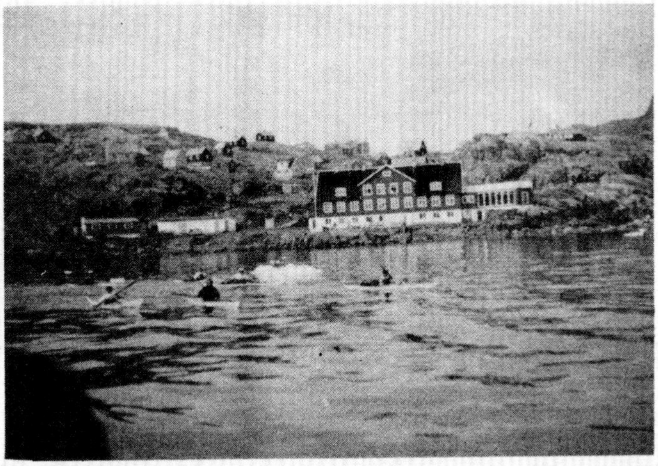

ᐅᒪᓇᒥ ᑕᓇ ᐃᒡᓗ ᐊᓂᐊᒋᒃ.

Page 18 Captions:

Inuit of Greenland, from left there are men from Canada. The one with white parka is Qaqasiq from Pangnirtung, Elijah Manirajak is next to him.

In Uummannaq, that building is a hospital.

ᐊᑕᑕᒃᑐᑦ ᐊᒥᓱᐊᓗᕗᑦ ᐃᓄᐃᑦᑐ ᐃᓚᖏᑦ ᑲᑐᓇᒥᒃ ᓄᓕᐊᒃᑐᑦ. ᓇᓕᑎᓐᒐᑦᑐ ᐃᓄᒃ ᑲᑐᓇᒥᒃ ᓄᓕᐊᒃᒥᔭ. ᐊᒃᓱᐊᓗᒃ ᐃᒥᓗᒥᒃ ᐊᑐᑦ ᐃᒥᓗᑯᕚᓗᑎᒃᑐ ᐃᓄᐃᑦᑐ ᓇᒥᓂ ᐊᑭᕆᐊᓗᓂᒃ ᐱᑲᑦ ᓴᐅᕋᓂᒃᑐ. ᑭᓱᐊᓂᒍ ᑕᓇ ᐁᕕᑲᐸᓐᕆᑐ ᓇᓄᕆᑦᑐ ᓯᓇᓐᒪ ᑲᓂᑐᑯᓗᒪᑦ ᑕᑯᐊ' ᑲᔭᒥᒃ ᐊᑐᐸᓐᕆᓕᑐᑦᒍ ᐊᕙᒪᓯᐊᑐᑦᑐ. ᑕᕙᓂ ᓂᓐᕆᐅᓐᒍᓂᐸ 79ᓂᒃ ᐅᑭᐅᓕᒃ ᓯᓕ ᐱᓯᒍᓇᑎᐊᑐ, ᐃᐸᓴᒍ ᐊᕙᑐᑲᓂᐳ ᑎᑲᒍᓕᒃᒥ ᐊᓐᕆᔪᓐᕆᑐᒥᒃ.

ᓯᑎᐱᑎ 11,1958. ᑲᓯᕆᐊᓐᒍᐊᓂ ᑲᓯᕆᐊᓐᒍᐊᓄᑦ ᑎᑭᐳᒍᑦ ᐃᓄᑭᑦᑐᑦ 500, ᒍᒥᓗᑕᓗ ᑕᑯᔭᒃᓴᑯᑎᓐᕆᓂᒃ ᑕᑯᑯᔭᐅᓐᕆᓗᑕ, ᑲᓄᐃᕆᔭᐅᒪᓐᒪᑕ ᑐᓴᓐᕆᓴᒃ, ᓯᓂᓗᑕ ᑕᑯᓇᓂ.

ᓯᑎᐱᑎ 12,1958. ᐊᓯᐊᒥᐅᓂ ᑎᑭᐳᒍᑦ ᐅᓄᒃ ᑐᓂᔭᐅᓗᑕ ᑲᔭᓐᒍᐊᒥᒃ ᒪᕿᓂᒃ ᓂᒍᒥᐊᒪᓗ, ᑲᑎᒪᕕᓐᒪᑦᓂᓗ ᐃᒥᓗᑐᐸᓗᕙᒃᑐᑦ, ᐃᓄᑎᐊᕙᓗᔭᒥᔭᑦ ᐊᓐᒪᔭᒃᑲᓕᑦ ᐱᐅᔭᐊᓗᒃᒥᑕᐅ ᐅᑲᓗᒃᕕᓐᒪᓂᓗ ᐅᑲᓗᓐᒪ ᐃᒪᒃ "ᑕᒪᓂ ᑎᑭᓂᕐᓂ ᑲᓇᑕᒥᐅᑎᒍᑦ ᑎᑭᐳᒍᑦ ᐊᓐᒪᔭᑲᑎᓄᑦ ᐃᑲᔭᑕᐅᓗᑕ ᒪᕙᒪᑯᓄᑦ" ᐃᓄᒃᑎᒍᑦ ᑯᓕᐅᓗᑕ ᑕᒪᐅᓐᒪᑐᒍᑦ ᑕᒣᓂᒃ ᑯᔭᓕᓗᑕ ᑕᒪᓂᓗ ᓂᑎᑎᑕᐅᕙᓂᑎᓂᒃ ᐊᑭᑲᓐᕆᑐᒥᒃ ᐃᓕᕆᓂᑎᓂᓗ ᐊᑕᐅᓯᐅᓂᑎᓂᒃ ᑕᒪᐃᑕ ᐅᑲᐅᓯᒃ ᑐᑭᓯᐅᑎᐊᒪᑕᒍ ᑯᔭᓇᐳ.

ᓯᑎᐱᑎ 14,1958. ᓯᓯᒥᐅᓄᑦ ᑎᑭᐳᒍᑦ ᑲᓄᐃᑐᒪᓐᒪᑕ ᑐᑭᓯᓐᕆᓕᑲ, ᓄᕙᓂᒍᑦ ᓄᓇᓕᐊᓐᕆᓇᒪ, ᐃᓄᐃᑦ ᐃᒪᒃ ᐊᒥᓱᑎᕆᔭᑦᒍ 1,700 ᑲᓄᐃᑐᒪᓐᒪᑕ ᑐᑭᓯᓐᕆᓕᑲ.

ᓯᑎᐱᑎ 17,1958. ᐸᒥᐅᓄᑦ ᑎᑭᐳᒍᑦ ᓯᓕ ᓄᓇᒍᑦ ᓯᓕᒍᑦᑐ ᐊᔭᒐᒪ ᑕᑯᓐᕆᓴᑲᓗᓂᑦ, ᐃᓄᐃᑦᒍ 900 ᐅᓐᒪᓯᒃᑐᐊᓗᐃᑦᒍ ᐊᒥᓱᐃᑦ, ᐊᐃᑕ ᐊᒃᓱᐊᓗᒃ ᓄᕙᑲᒪ ᑕᑯᓐᕆᓴᑲ ᑭᐱᓐᒍᓗᓐᒪᓗ.

ᓯᑎᐱᑎ 19,1958. ᓇᓴᒥᐅᓄᑦ ᐅᓕᑯᑦ ᑎᑭᐳᒍᑦ ᐃᓄᐃᑦ 900, ᒪᔭᐊᒐᑕ ᓯᐱᑯᓗᐃᑦ ᑐᑯᒐᑕᐅᔭᑦ ᐃᒪᓇᒍ ᑐᑯᑕᐅᔭᑦ ᐅᓗᒥ 350 ᒣ ᑕᑭᓐᒪᓂ ᐃᓄᔭᕕᓂᑦᒍ, ᓂᑭᑕᑎᑕᐅᓗᑕᓗ ᓴᓇᔭᒃᓴᐅᔭᑐᓂᒃ ᑲᓐᒪᑕᔭᓂᒃ, ᐊᓇᑦ ᐊᓐᒍᑎᓂᑦ ᐊᒥᓱᓂᓴᓗᐃᑦ ᓴᓇᔭᑦ ᐱᓐᒪᓯᑦ ᐊᓐᒪᔭᑲᓐᕆᕐ ᐱᓐᒪᔭᐊᑦ ᐊᓇ, ᐳᓕᐸᕗᑦ ᑲᑐᓇᒥᒃ ᐅᐃᑲᑐ ᐃᒍᓯᐅᒪᓂᒃ ᑕᓕᒪᓂᒃ ᐱᑲᑐ. ᐃᓐᒪᓕᒥᒍ

Page 19:

There are many Inuit who are fathered by white people and women are married to them. The *Naalakti* (communicator) is an Inuk married to white woman. They drink a lot of alcohol and they want us to drink as much as they do. The Inuit has many ptarmigans and Red phalarope. They don't have walrus and not much polar bear. But the floe is very close, so they don't use *qajait* anymore for walrus hunting. The eldest woman is 79 years old and able to walk just fine. Yesterday someone caughts whale and Minke whale and not that big.

September 11, 1958. Qasigiannguit We arrive Qasigiannguit. They are not over populated of 500 and we danced with them. They did not show us around and I didn't understand how they felt about us. We spent the night here.

September 12, 1958. Aasiaat. We arrived at night, and they gifted us toy *qajait* and two purses, they drink alcohol in the meeting place. They appear to be a very friendly people and their leader is very good to us. I went on a radio saying, "We are from Canada just arrived and our leader from government helped us to make an announcement." We the Inuit there were 10 of us who arrived there and we thank the people that they fed us well for free. We are all related and that we are united were spoke about and that I am thankful they understood us.

September 14, 1958. Sisimiut. We arrive here. I didn't know what went on because I have a bad cold and I didn't get off the boat and go to the land. The population there is 1,700 but I don't know what kind of community it is.

September 17, 1958. Paamiut we arrived but I still didn't go outside and did not see anyone. The population I heard was 900 and they live far apart from what I was told. I am very disappointed with myself being sick and it was extremely boring.

September 18, 1958. Narsaq. We arrived in the morning and population is 900. When we embarked the ship we saw sheep being killed and they said. They killed 350 today. They were born in the month of May, they provided us food that we will cook, There were more women than men who are working and there were three leaders and one of them is female. We visited the one who is married to a whiteman and they have five cows from England.

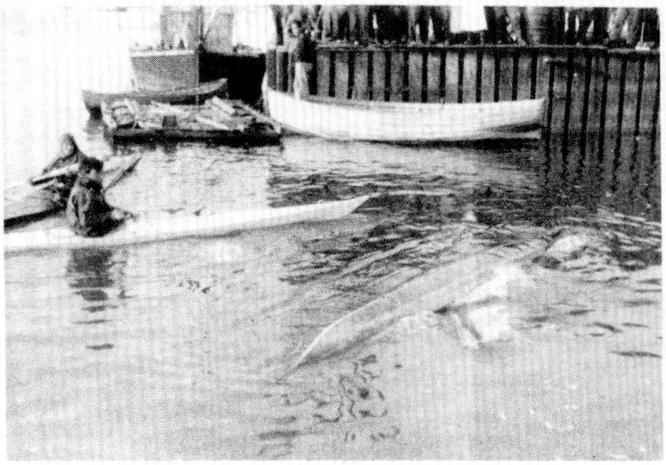

ᑕᑯᐸ ᑕᒐ ᑲᔭᑐᑦ ᐅᐃᔭᓗᑎᒃ.

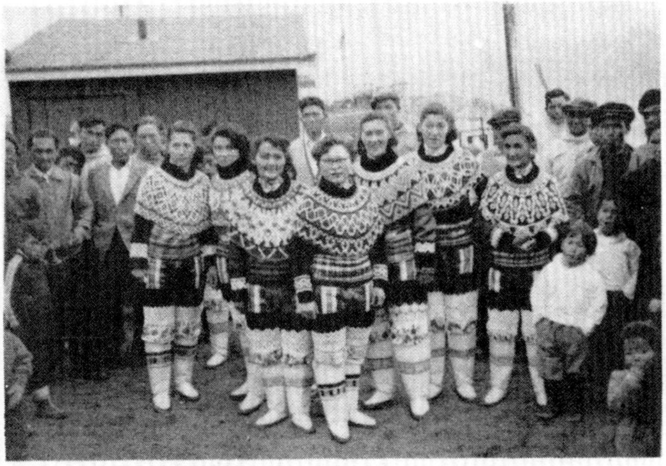

ᐊᓇᐃᑦ ᐊᒌᑭᑐᒥᐅᑦ ᐊᓄᕋᑐᑲᒥᓂᒃ ᐊᓄᕋᓯᒪᔪᑦ
ᓴᐸᖕᒐᓂᒃ ᐊᑐᑦ.

Page 20 – Captions:

These are demonstrating *qajaqing* and they can flip their *qajait*.

The women of Greenland wearing their traditional clothing with beads.

ᓂᐅᕕᑕᕕᓂᖕᒥᑦ ᓴᐅᕋᓂᒃᓗ 6ᓂᒃ, ᐊᑭᒋᐊᓗᓂᓗ 5ᓂᒃ, ᑯᑯᓯᓂᒃᓗ ᑭᑐᓐᒪᑎᑦ 6, ᑲᓐᑐᐃᓗ ᑭᑐᓐᒪᑎᑦ 8ᓐᑐᕗᑦ, ᐱᕈᓯᕕᑲᑐᑦᓗ ᐊᓐᒋᕗᒥᒃ ᓇᒥᓂᕈ ᐱᓐᒋᑦ ᐊᒃᓯᐊᓗᒃ ᐱᐅᕗᑦᑕᐅ ᐃᓄᐃᑦ ᑕᑯᐊ.

ᓯᑎᐱᑎ 20,1958. ᑲᑯᑐᓄᑦ · ᐅᓄᑯᑦ 7ᒥ ᑲᑯᑐᓄᑦ, ᐅᐊᑲᓚᓐᒪ ᐊᓕᐊᓇᐃᐳ ᐃᓄᐃᑦ ᐊᒥᓯᐊᓗᐃᑦ 1,900 ᒫᑯᑐᐃᑦ ᐅᓇᑕᑐᓴᐅᔭᑐᐊᓗᐃᑦ ᑲᓗᓇᒥᒃ ᐊᓐᒪᕙᑲᑲᓗᑎᒃ, ᑯᕕᐊᓇᐳ ᓯᓚᒥ ᐅᑲᓗᒃᐳ ᑕᓇ ᐊᓐᒪᕙᑲᓐᒪᑦ ᑕᒪᐅᓐᒪ ᑎᑭᓇᑕᑐ ᑲᓇᑕᒥᐅᓂᒃ ᐊᑯᓂᑦ ᐅᑕᑭᒪᒥᒃ ᐊᑭᑲᓐᒋᑐᒥᒃ ᑐᓂᓂᐊᐳᑐᑦ ᓂᑎᓂᑎᓂᒃᓗ ᑯᕕᐊᓯᑲᑎᒋᑯᓗᑕ ᑐᓂᔭᐅᓗᑕ, ᐅᒥᐊᓐᑐᐊᒥᒃ ᐃᒡᓗᑲᑐᒥᒃ, ᑎᒥᐊᓗ ᒥᓯᒪ ᐊᓗᓗᔭᐅᑦ, ᓴᒪᑎᐊᐱᒃᒥᓗ, ᐱᔭᑎᒪᑦ ᐅᑲᓚᓗᓐᒪᑕᐅ ᑕᒪᐅᓐᒪ ᑎᑭᓂᑎᓂᒃ ᐃᒪᒃ ᑯᔭᓕᕗᑐᑦ ᑕᒣᑕ ᐃᓄᐃᑦ ᑯᔭᒋᕙᕗᑦ ᑯᕕᐊᓯᑲᑎᒋᕙᕗᑦᓗ ᑲᓗᓇᕗᑦ ᑯᔭᓕᓗᑎᒃᑕᐅ. ᐅᑎᕈᑕᓗ ᑲᓇᑕᑐᑦ ᐅᓂᑲᓴᑲᓂᐊᓂᑎᓂᒃ ᐱᑎᐊᕕᐅᓂᑎᓂᒃᓗ ᓂᑎᑎᑕᐅᓂᑎᓂᒃᓗ, ᐱᕚᒃᑕᕗᑦᓗ ᑕᑯᔭᒃᓴᐅᑎᑕᐅᑯᓗᒥᑦ ᑲᓘᓈᓄᑦᓗ ᐃᓄᓄᑦᓗ. ᐃᓪᓗᐊᓗᒃᒧᑦ ᐃᓯᕋᑕ ᐊᒃᓯᐊᓗᒃ ᐱᒥᓗᑕ ᐊᒃᓯᐊᓗᒃ ᐅᑲᑐᐊᓗᐃᑦ ᓯᓗ ᑎᓐᒥᐊᑎᑐᑦ ᓂᐱᑲᐳᑦ ᓯᓗ ᑲᐅᕈᒪᑎᐊᓐᒋᑐᔭᐳ. ᒧᒥᓗᑕᓗ ᑯᕕᐊᓇᐳ ᐊᒃᓯᐊᓗᒃ, ᑕᕝ ᓄᓐᑐᐳ ᐃᓄᐃᑦᑐ ᐊᑯᑭᑐᒥᐅᑦ ᑕᒣᑕ ᐃᒣᑐᕗᑦ 24,000.

ᐃᓚᐅᑉ ᑎᑎᕋᑕᓐᒋᑦ.

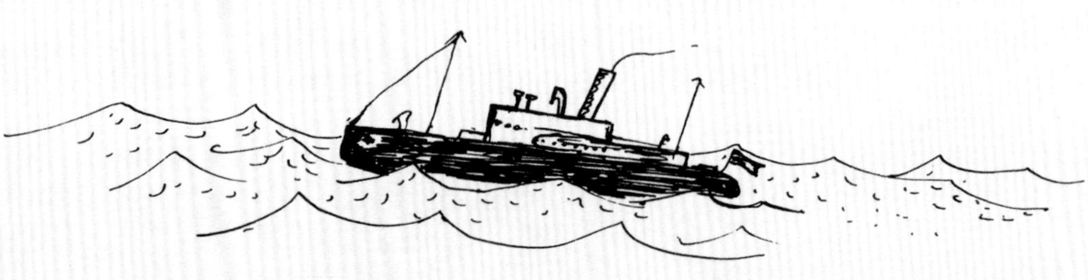

Page 21:

They bought Red phalarope and five ptarmigan, six pigs; they also got eight geese, they have a big farm and they own it. The people there are so nice to us there.

September 20, 1958 (Qeqertat?) At evening 7:00 we arrive Qeqertat. Oh my goodness, it was so much fun, and there were so many Inuit, at a population of 1,900, and they had youth dressed like the army and they had a Qallunaaq leader. It is so much fun here, and the leader made a speech outdoors and announced our arrival and said that they had waited a long time for Canadians to arrive. We gave gifts and we ate together, and we were also gifted a toy boat with fish and feather mats. We were also given a beautiful flag. We were very thankful. All of us Inuit we thanked them and were celebrating, and our Qallunaat were very grateful. The gifts we received will be for all Inuit and Qallunaat. When we entered a huge building, we had plenty to drink, and everyone was talking at the same time, and they sounded like a flock of birds; like the Greenlandic language because we had a hard time understanding their language. We danced and celebrated. This is the end and the Greenlandic population is 24,000.

Written by Idlout.
(Translation: Rhoda Kayakjuak)

6 The Hunter in Exile

A View from Kalaallit Nunaat/Greenland and Resolute/Qausuittuq (1958–68)

In the article for *Inuktitut Magazine*, reproduced preceding this chapter, Idlout recounts his 1958 trip to Kalaallit Nunaat/Greenland. The hunter was one of ten Inuit leaders as well as five southern officials participating in a voyage sponsored by the Canadian federal government. Ten uncredited snapshots illustrate the article. These photographs were probably taken with Idlout's Kodak Duaflex camera, as were a group of seventy-seven photographs shot during the trip and credited to the hunter that are now in the Nunavut Archives.[1]

Among that larger group of photographs is a snapshot taken on the deck of the Canadian Department of Transport's icebreaker the CCGS *Ernest Lapointe* during the voyage from Iqaluit/Frobisher Bay to the west coast of Kalaallit Nunaat/Greenland (see figure 6.1).[2] The photograph depicts two of Idlout's fellow Inuit delegates, possibly George Koneak of Kujjuaq/Fort Chimo in the foreground and Charlie Smith of Aklavik in the background. Idlout has composed the image from behind, depicting the two men as they gaze out at sea toward an iceberg in the distance. And from this perspective, Idlout the photographer – and future viewers of the image – join their gaze. The image focuses on the act of viewing itself, representing curiosity and anticipation as features of the gaze. And, indeed, the Kalaallit Nunaat/Greenland trip provided Idlout and the other Inuit delegates an opportunity to look outward and to encounter other regions of the circumpolar north and the Greenlandic Inughuit, Tunumiit, and Kalaallit residing there. In turn, Idlout and the other delegates would turn that outward gaze on their own lives during Sangussaqtauliqtilluta, the period of disruption.

This chapter examines the last years of Idlout's life and his growing resistance to assimilationist policies at that time. Here, I look closely at the 1958 trip to Kalaallit Nunaat/Greenland by Idlout and the other delegates as an incident of emerging resistance. I outline government documents about the trip in order to contextualize it as a mission with an assimilationist agenda. But my attention is particularly on images shot either by Idlout or by fellow passengers using his camera during the voyage. Although this body of images does not depict Resolute/Qausuittuq or the Qikiqtani region, when studied in tandem

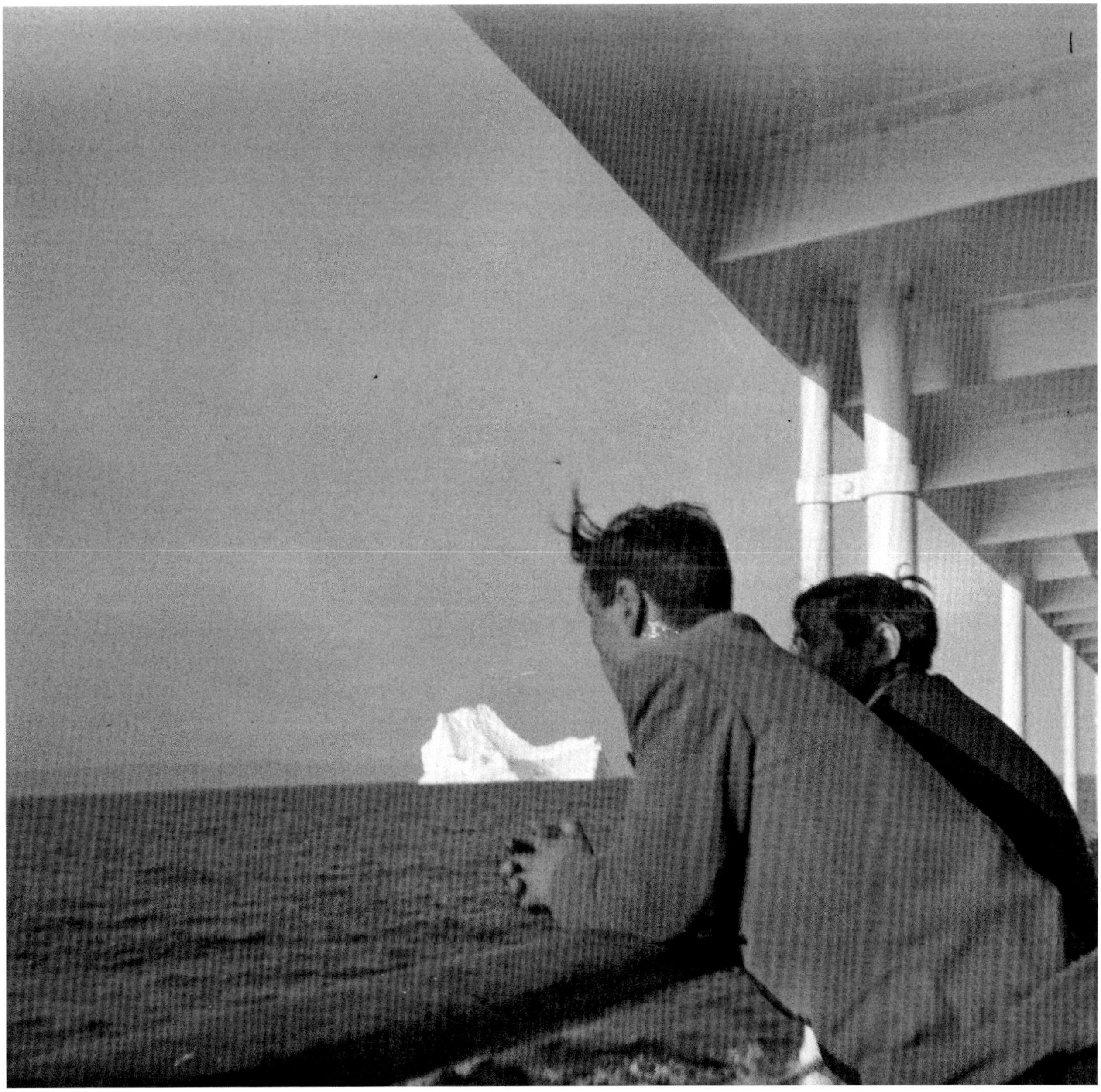

6.1 | Passengers on the deck of the Canadian Department of Transport's icebreaker the CCGS *Ernest Lapointe* during the voyage taken by Idlout and nine other Canadian Inuit from Iqaluit/Frobisher Bay to settlements on the west coast of Kalaallit Nunaat/Greenland, September 1958. The men in the photograph are possibly George Koneak of Kujjuaq in the foreground and Charlie Smith of Aklavik. Photo: Joseph Idlout.

with contemporary Inuit correspondence, they reveal much about emergent Inuit reflections, cultural assertions, and refusals in the wake of the High Arctic relocations. Idlout's *Inuktitut Magazine* article provides important contexts for his photographs. In this chapter, I argue that a close reading of these photographs and words, as well as other archival documents, reveals Inuit reactions against assimilationist policies.[3] The Kalaallit Nunaat/Greenland trip provided Idlout and the other Inuit travellers an opportunity to meet Inuit from another region of the circumpolar north. They absorbed how Greenlandic Inughuit, Tunumiit, and Kalaallit lived and with that information reflected on their own situations and experiences in Inuit Nunangat. The trip to Kalaallit Nunaat/Greenland occurred during a period when Inuit, particularly the High Arctic exiles, were subject to assimilationist policies. Indeed, the trip was developed by government officials to model what they perceived to be Greenlanders' assimilation into southern, European culture. Yet at this time, Idlout and the other Inuit delegates were also beginning to challenge southern authority and seeking to move forward in a way that centred their own people and culture. As I argue in this chapter, Idlout and the other Inuit delegates encountered Greenlandic Inughuit, Tunumiit, and Kalaallit who were also resisting colonization in their relationship with Denmark. I contend that Idlout's images and words were part of these circumpolar challenges and refusals.

The final section of the chapter returns to Resolute/Qausuittuq where continuing hardships suffered by the exiles prompted resistance to government officials. Idlout and his fellow High Arctic exiles, increasingly corresponded with southern officials whose "experiment" had brought them to the High Arctic.[4] They used language to make demands and express their needs. The enhanced contact with southerners experienced in Resolute/Qausuittuq was often negotiated through words. And words written at the time by High Arctic exiles, including Idlout, provide notable records of their protests and resistance. These interactions between exiles and the south were also experienced visually. Idlout and Kidlak, along with their family and community, continued to be the subjects of the camera's gaze. They were featured in yet another newsreel made by Doug Wilkinson under the auspices of the National Film Board of Canada (NFB), *Eskimo Village, Resolute* (1963). Although Idlout's relationship with the south would continue to be mediated through camera images, the field of vision expanded in Resolute/Qausuittuq. The intimate exchange of gazes between Idlout and Wilkinson was now more explicitly part of a broader network of colonial and bureaucratic oversight.[5]

In making Idlout's photographs and narration of the Kalaallit Nunaat/Greenland trip the centrepiece of this chapter, my goal is to frame Idlout's experiences as a High Arctic exile in terms of Inuit agency and resistance. In this way, I attempt to follow Unangax scholar Eve Tuck's advice to avoid "damage-centered research."[6] Here, although I acknowledge the historical fact of transgenerational trauma caused by the High Arctic relocations, I try to show how these harms do not completely define the lives of Idlout and the other exiles. Specifically, I try to show how what Tuck terms the "complexity, contradiction, and the self-determination" of Inuit lives can be gleaned by emphasizing Inuit agency.[7] This agency is seen in the words of Idlout and other exiles located throughout various archival sources and particularly in Idlout's photographs of Kalaallit Nunaat/Greenland. These photographs, including the image at sea discussed above, provide a counterpoint to the hunter's experiences in Resolute/Qausuittuq, one that he would continue to reflect upon during his final years. Accordingly, rather than focusing solely on the traumas of the High Arctic relocations, the Kalaallit Nunaat/Greenland trip – an episode that throws into high relief assimilationist efforts and Inuit agency – develops a path for agency and resistance.

The material presented in this chapter remains timely – indeed, urgent. In the mid-2020s as this book went into production, the US government threatened to annex Kalaallit Nunaat/Greenland. Inuit across the circumpolar north and much of the international community expressed solidarity with Kalaallit Nunaat/Greenland and its sovereignty. Indeed, more than sixty Inuit from Nunavik travelled to Nuuk to show their support for Greenlanders in February 2026.[8] At the same time, greater national and international attention has turned to Inuit Nunangat's strategic location and resources. The resistance to the assimilation of the Greenlandic Inughuit, Tunumiit, Kalaallit, and Inuit during the 1950s is a crucial model for defying imperialism today.

"To see something of the culture and way of life": Canadian Officials Plan the Trip to Kalaallit Nunaat/Greenland

Working with External Affairs and the Danish government, the Department of Northern Affairs and National Resources (DNANR) sponsored the September 1958 Kalaallit Nunaat/Greenland trip as a form of exchange between Inuit. Coordinated under the direction of R.A.J. Phillips, head of the DNANR's Arctic Division, the trip was seen as a reciprocation of a 1956 trip by a group of Greenlanders to Inuit Nunangat.[9] The archival record describes it as an opportunity to expose Inuit from Inuit Nunagat to Greenlanders while providing an opportunity for southern officials to gather information about various policies active in Kalaallit Nunaat/Greenland, including economic and educational.[10]

But the archival record also indicates that assimilationist motivations were central to the Kalaallit Nunaat/Greenland exchange. As an internal report summarized, "The trip will enable a group of carefully selected Canadian Eskimo to see something of the culture and way of life of the Greenland people, and to observe the effects of their transition from primitive living to a modern wage economy. The same sort of transition is taking place in the Canadian Arctic today, but in Greenland the change has gone on longer. Furthermore, the trip will enable Ottawa officials to learn more of how the Danish Government is handling its Arctic business."[11] In a July 1958 letter to the Treasury Board, the deputy minister of the DNANR, R.G. Robertson, expressed assimilationist motivations for the Kalaallit Nunaat/Greenland trip even more explicitly:

> The principal purpose is to assist in the very rapid adjustment that Canadian Eskimo are having to undergo. Most of our Eskimo are in a very primitive state and in many cases there are signs of a developing sense of inferiority and inadequacy coming, largely, from the feeling that it is the white man who is able to do the things that have to be done to get along, and that the Eskimo is in a sense a "second-class" citizen. In Greenland the native people have undergone a much greater transition. They publish newspapers in the Eskimo language, sit on the legislative and municipal councils, have university degrees, and occupy positions at all levels. We think that there would be a very important psychological advantage in having a group of Eskimo, drawn from various parts of the Canadian Arctic, see what Eskimo can do with the white man's way of life. We think that if they came back to their settlements and told the local people about such things, it would do a great deal to avoid the possible sense of inferiority that has been a persistent problem with so many of the Indians.[12]

In contemporary internal documents like these ones – as well as in speeches, press releases, and internal governmental correspondence – it is clear that DNANR officials wanted to encourage Inuit in Canada to see Greenlanders as models in what they perceived to be assimilation into southern society.

A number of Canadian officials had long looked to Kalaallit Nunaat/Greenland's approach to the administration of the Arctic and Inuit lives. As Peter Clancy and P. Whitney Lackenbauer have shown, Kalaallit Nunaat/Greenland was touted as a model for Arctic administration in the influential Cantley Report of 1950 and subsequently discussed by members of the Eskimo Affairs Committee.[13] Indeed, in organizing the 1958 trip, DNANR officials lauded Kalaallit Nunaat/Greenland as "years ahead in social and economic development."[14]

The Inuit Delegates En Route to Kalaallit Nunaat/Greenland

The Arctic Division of the DNANR spent several months during the first half of 1958 identifying and recruiting Inuit participants for the trip. At pains to enlist Inuit throughout Inuit Nunangat, from Aklavik in the west to Kuujjuarapik in the east, government officials enlisted individual Northern Service officers to recommend candidates and recruit them. Doug Wilkinson, by this time the Northern Service officer at Baker Lake/Qamani'tuaq, was among those enlisted to recruit Inuit.[15] Wilkinson and James Houston were also called upon to secure small carvings as gifts for the Kalaallit Nunaat/Greenland hosts, and a sealskin coat was commissioned as another gift.[16] Phillips and his staff in the Arctic Division provided officers with detailed instructions for their recommendations:[17]

"To take full advantage of this opportunity the men or Eskimo selected should be intelligent, observant, and well regarded in the communities they represent to assure that their experience will be relayed to others when they return."[18] According to *Inuktitut Magazine*, Idlout was recruited during a trip to Ottawa.[19]

Organizers hoped that Inuit participants would convey the information – that is, Inuit integration into European, or southern, society – that they anticipated the visitors would witness in Kalaallit Nunaat/Greenland. DNANR correspondence shows that recruits were expected to absorb any cost of lost employment; beyond supplying meals and transportation, there is no mention of renumeration. However, in a stark demonstration of the trip's assimilationist motives, the DNANR requested $1,200 from the Treasury Board to clothe the Inuit participants in southern-style business suits.[20] Although the division initially hoped to include a few Inuit women among the group, this plan had been abandoned by May 1958, and only men were considered.[21] The DNANR's Northern Service officers responded to Phillips with dozens of potential participants.[22] But there are also hints in their correspondence of reluctance on the part of Inuit recruits; the officers enumerate those who declined the offer or were unavailable due to family commitments or other government work, including on the Distance Early Warning Line.[23]

In the end, ten Inuit men travelled on the voyage. As planned, they represented regions from across most of Inuit Nunangat and, indeed, would go on to become illustrious Inuit leaders. In addition to Idlout, they included James Evanna of Cambridge Bay/Iqaluktuuttiaq, Charlie Gordon of Aklavik, Charlie Smith of Aklavik, George Koneak of Kujjuaq/Fort Chimo, Elijah Menarik of Inukjuak/Port Harrison, Qaqqasiq of Pangnirtung, Kananginak of Kinngait/Cape Dorset, Adam Tootalik of Taloyoak/Spence Bay, and Joe Tikivik of Iqaluit/Frobisher Bay.[24] Most of the Inuit delegates are identified in a photo taken at a lumber yard and reproduced on page sixteen of the 1959 *Inuktitut Magazine* article written by Idlout, reproduced preceding this chapter.[25] The Inuit delegates were transported to Iqaluit, where they waited to embark on the voyage. By 11 August, Idlout was already in Iqaluit. Indeed, Phillips suggests that Idlout was included on the trip in part to enable him to visit his daughter Leah, where she was convalescing at the rehabilitation hospital.[26]

Five southern Qallunaat officials were also approved to travel on the voyage. Phillips personally led the delegation. In addition, the voyage included J.V. Jacobson, chief of the Education Division in the Department of Northern Affairs;[27] Robert A. Jenness, acting chief of the Industrial Division in the DNANR;[28] W. Winston Mair, chief of the Canadian Wildlife Service; and a DNANR official identified as "Mr. Findlay."[29] They were later joined on the voyage by Captain C. Pederson of the Royal Greenland Trading Company and his wife.[30]

After several delays, members of the delegation departed for the journey in late August 1958. They sailed on the Canadian Department of Transport's icebreaker the CCGS *Ernest Lapointe* from Iqaluit/Frobisher Bay to the west coast of Kalaallit Nunaat/Greenland.[31] As guests of the Greenland National Council, the delegates followed a fifteen-day itinerary, stopping at several ports of call along the island's west coast. As outlined in the schedule, they spent the first three days at the capital, Nuuk (known at the time as Godthaab), and over the next twelve days visited settlements around Disko Bay, Egedesminde, Kangamiut, Maniitsoq (then known as Sukkertoppen), and Hosteinsborg. The Greenland National Council also arranged for them to see the Qullissat mine on Disko Island and to visit scenic sites.[32] Phillips later recounted the range of visits and what he perceived to be the culture shock for the Inuit delegates. They saw "schools and hospitals, the orphanages and the churches, the generating stations and the water works, the modern factories for the processing of the fish which gives Greenland its living. Most of these things were entirely new to Canadian Eskimo still living close to a land which can no longer support them. A home for the aged, a newspaper office, even a community hall were ideas as new to the Eskimo as were the animals on the farms of southern Greenland."[33] In Phillips's narration of the tour, southern-style industry and institutions were showcased. Kalaallit Nunaat/Greenland was intended as a model of assimilation into the south and a wage economy.

Kalaallit Nunaat/Greenland as Seen by Idlout

Throughout the trip, Idlout kept his eyes open and his camera lens focused on the new environment and on the strangers he encountered. He shot dozens of images, occasionally handing his Kodak to another delegate so that the hunter himself could be seen in the frame. Idlout's photographs of Kalaallit Nunaat/Greenland visually narrate the voyage and the ports of call visited. Yet they differ from the official itinerary and from Phillips's retrospective account of the trip. The photographs taken with Idlout's prized Kodak record the hunter's own perceptions and reflect his values. Like his photographs of camp life from earlier in the 1950s, the Kalaallit Nunaat/Greenland photographs reflect on relationality. And they visualize some of the principles of Inuit Qaujimajatuqangit (IQ).

The hunter's photographs are illuminated by his own contemporaneous words. Idlout authored an eleven-page article about the trip for the May 1959 issue of *Inuktitut Magazine*, a publication written entirely in syllabics, as reproduced preceding this chapter.[34] As Zebedee Nungak wrote in 2012, "When the first issue of *Inuktitut* appeared in 1959, it was quite a sensation among Inuit. Previously, the only written material widely available in Inuktitut had been the Bible and prayer books. Now, here was a publication devoted to Inuit life and culture, which also started serving as a documentary venue for different aspects of 'progress' then stirring for the first time across the Arctic. Here was potential to bridge the great distances separating people and places in the Arctic!"[35] Although funded by the DNANR, the magazine features Inuit authors and editors and, as Nungak suggests, has contributed to Inuit assertions of Inuit identity.[36] The Kalaallit Nunaat/Greenland article includes statistics supplied in the itinerary, but the recollections are specific to Idlout. Ten uncredited photographs illustrate the *Inuktitut* article. They show the same sights seen in Idlout's Kalaallit Nunaat/Greenland photographs held in the Nunavut Archives or, in some cases, are close variants. These ten published images were likely also by Idlout or made with his camera.[37] The *Inuktitut* article records Idlout's own perceptions of Kalaallit Nunaat/Greenland and of the events attended, and it identifies the people with whom he travelled as well as those he encountered on the west coast of Kalaallit Nunaat/Greenland. In effect, the *Inuktitut* article provides a key to the collection of seventy-seven Kalaallit Nunaat/Greenland photographs credited to Idlout in the Nunavut Archives. Reading Idlout's photographs in the Nunavut Archives alongside his article augments the hunter's outward gaze. I am grateful to Rhoda Kayakjuak for translations of the *Inuktitut* article.

Idlout was not alone in photographically documenting the trip, as a group portrait taken with Idlout's camera reveals (see figure 6.2). This image – one of seven shot on board the *Ernest Lapointe* as it sailed toward Kalaallit Nunaat/

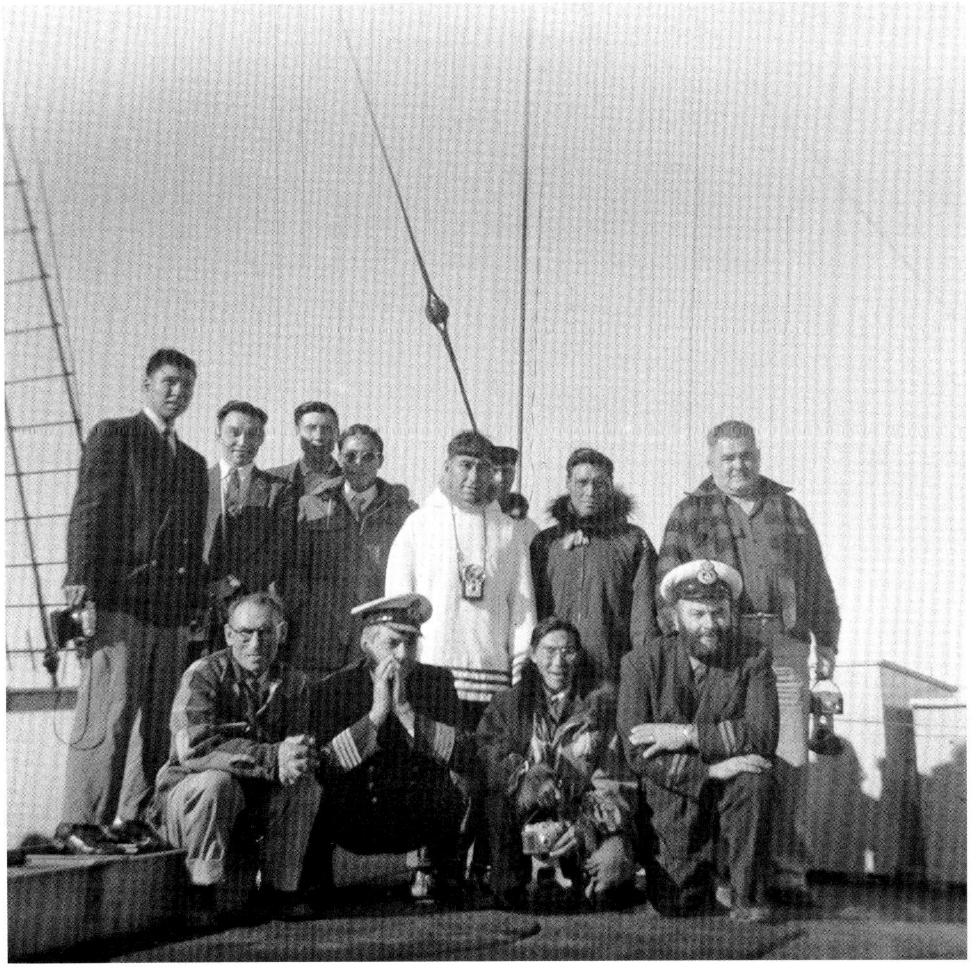

6.2 | Delegates and crew on the deck of the CCGS *Ernest Lapointe*, September 1958. Idlout is in the top row, fourth from the left. Uncredited photo taken with Idlout's camera.

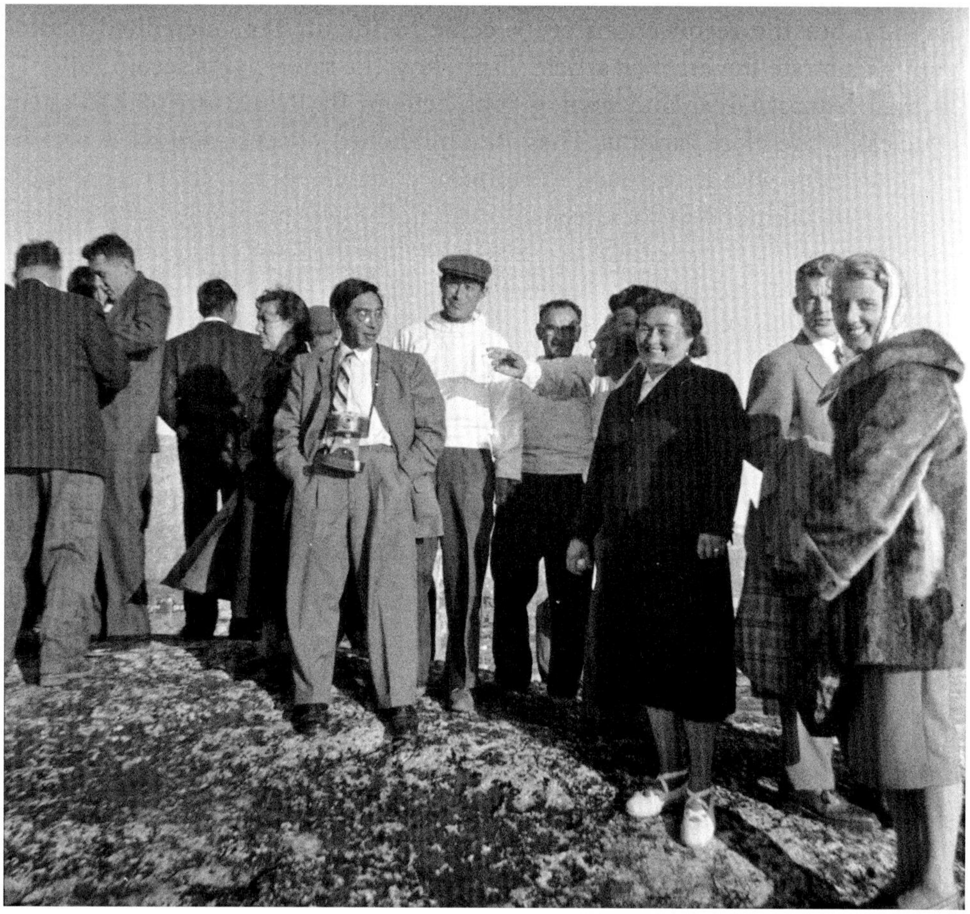

6.3 | Group of people in Kalaallit Nunaat/Greenland, September 1958. Charlie Smith of Aklavik (centre) carries a camera with its case slung around his neck. Photo: Joseph Idlout.

Greenland from Iqaluit/Frobisher Bay – depicts several delegates and crew posing to mark the beginning of the voyage. Idlout himself can be seen standing in the top row, fourth to the left in sunglasses; apparently, the hunter loaned his Kodak Duaflex to the unseen photographer to record his own membership in this group. Studied more closely, this snapshot reveals a notable detail: three of the Inuit and the Qallunaat man to the far right carry cameras themselves.

In another photograph taken after arriving in Kalaallit Nunaat/Greenland, Idlout pictures Inuk delegate Charlie Smith of Aklavik at the centre of the frame, his camera with its case slung around his neck (see figure 6.3). As noted earlier, by the 1950s, it was becoming more common for Inuit men to own a camera.[38] Like Idlout, Daniel Salluviniq, and Zebeddie Amarualik, the three photographers seen greeting Governor General Vincent Massey in figure 5.1, some of the Inuit delegates to Kalaallit Nunaat/Greenland had adapted the southern technology of the camera to their own ends.[39]

Idlout's text in *Inuktitut Magazine* closely follows his own experience of the itinerary established by the Kalaallit Nunaat/Greenland hosts, and his images both in the text and among the larger group in the Nunavut Archives illustrate many of these key sites and events. The delegates arrived in Nuuk to a large celebration. Afterward, they toured schools, a university, a hospital, and the Lutheran mission. Each stop along the way provides similar greetings and tours of facilities.[40] However, Idlout missed the festivities held between 14 and 17 September, when he stayed on the ship with a bad cold, feeling bored.[41] Among the Kalaallit Nunaat/Greenland sites on the itinerary that Idlout's photographs capture are a visit to a lumber yard[42] and to a Lutheran church, the latter image conveying a missionary presence.[43] In the midst of these vestiges of European impact stand the Inuit delegates carefully clad in their business suits in a performance of supposed assimilation. Idlout's photographs also record the Kalaallit Nunaat/Greenland scenery, including the various ports of call, fiords, and townscapes. Yet Idlout's words and images tell stories that do not adhere strictly to the tour's assimilationist itinerary but instead reveal a fascination with Greenlanders and their way of life rather than with the institutions emphasized by the DNANR organizers of the trip.

As with Idlout's photographs of his camps, Aulattivik and Nuvurulua, Inuit Qaujimajatuqangit infuses his images and narration of Kalaallit Nunaat/Greenland during the trip. Idlout's photographs attest to many of the principles of IQ that he experienced and witnessed among Greenlandic Inughuit, Tunumiit, and Kalaallit. He was continually impressed by how welcoming the hosts were in every community, encapsulating the principle of *tunnganarniq* (fostering good spirits by being open, welcoming, and inclusive) (see figure 6.4). Throughout, by watching his hosts, Idlout learned new skills related to hunting and to self-determination, reflecting *pilimmaksarniq/pijariuqsarniq* (development of skills through observation, mentoring, practice, and effort). He noted the collaboration, resourcefulness, and care for the *nuna* (land) and animals practised by the Inughuit, Tunumiit, and Kalaallit he encountered, along with indications of *qanuqtuurniq* (being innovative and resourceful), *piliriqatigiinniq/ikajuqtigiinniq* (working together for a common cause), and *avatittinnik kamatsiarniq* (respect and care for the land, animals, and environment). These principles are seen across Idlout's Kalaallit Nunaat/Greenland images and in his *Inuktitut Magazine* article.

Idlout's knowledge of hunting, for example, forms a key theme throughout the *Inuktitut* article and is grounded in observing his Inughuit, Tunumiit, and Kalaallit hosts and their care for community and environment. Idlout references hunting and fishing at each stop. When a large crowd boarded the ship on 2 September, he learned about their experience fishing for cod and marketing them to "American Qallunaat." At stops along the way, he notes in the article information about the Greenlanders harvesting caribou and cod at Kapisiliit on 2 September and halibut at Maniitsoq on 5 September, their use of nets to catch marine mammals at Uummannaq on 9 September, and the availability of ptarmigans and red phalarope at Nuuk on 19 September. Idlout reports on a conversation on 6 September with a Kangaamiut Greenlander: "Their diet is caribou

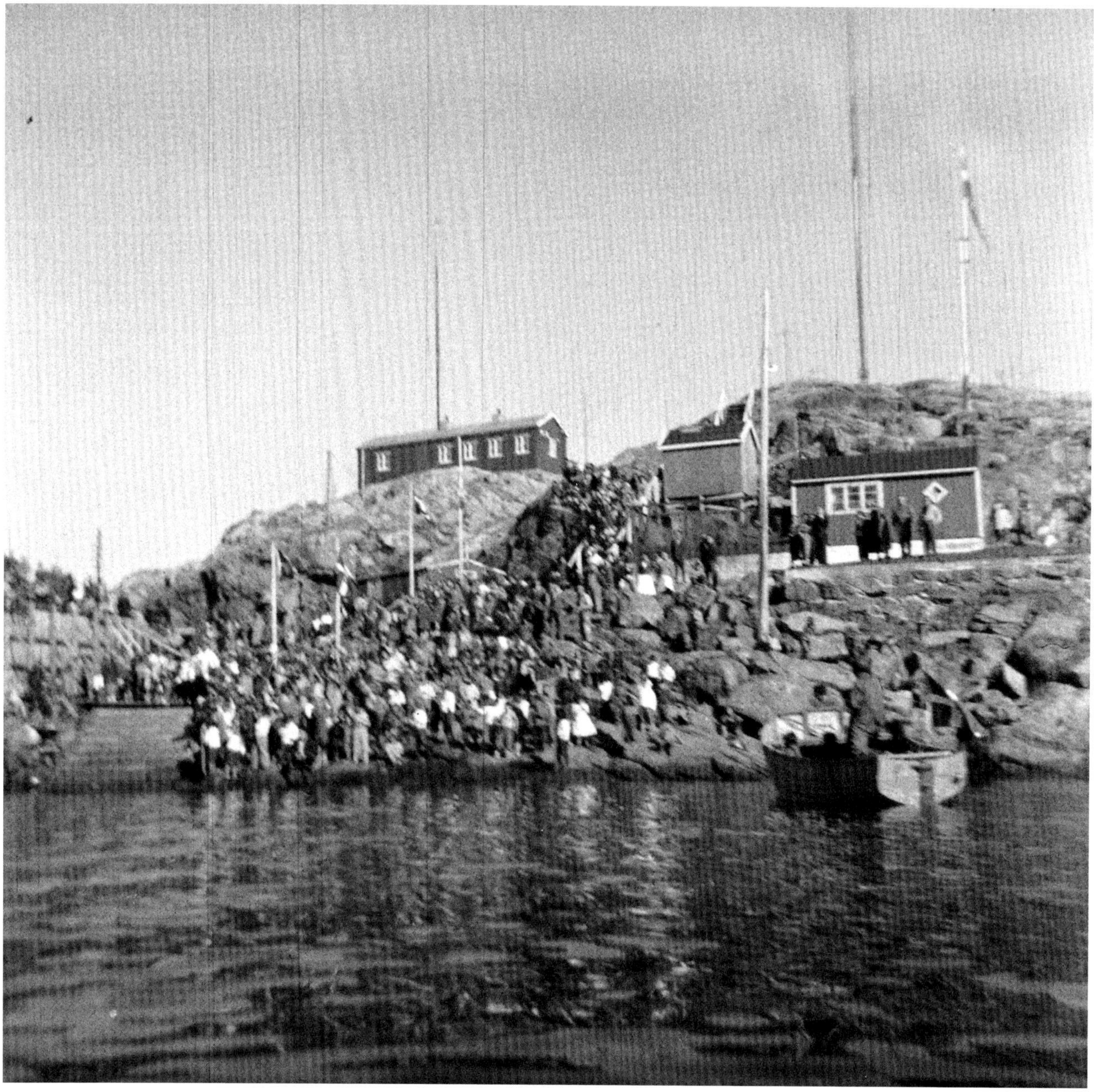

meat. They have many cod and much dried meat. They gather caribou meat for anyone who needs it. They said their land has plenty of caribou. Greenland is such a stunning land. They had settled here for the wealth of country food. They gave us two identical *unaaq* (harpoons). They brought us to see whale hunters too."[44] Idlout also records differences between his experiences and those of his hosts. Writing in Nuuk, for example, he notes, "They don't have walrus and not much polar bear. But the floe is very close, so they don't use *qayait* (kayaks)

6.4 | A Kalaallit Nunaat/Greenland community viewed from the water, September 1958. Photo: Joseph Idlout.

6.5 | A man in a *qajaq* watched by people on a dock, Kalaallit Nunaat/Greenland, September 1958. Photo: Joseph Idlout.

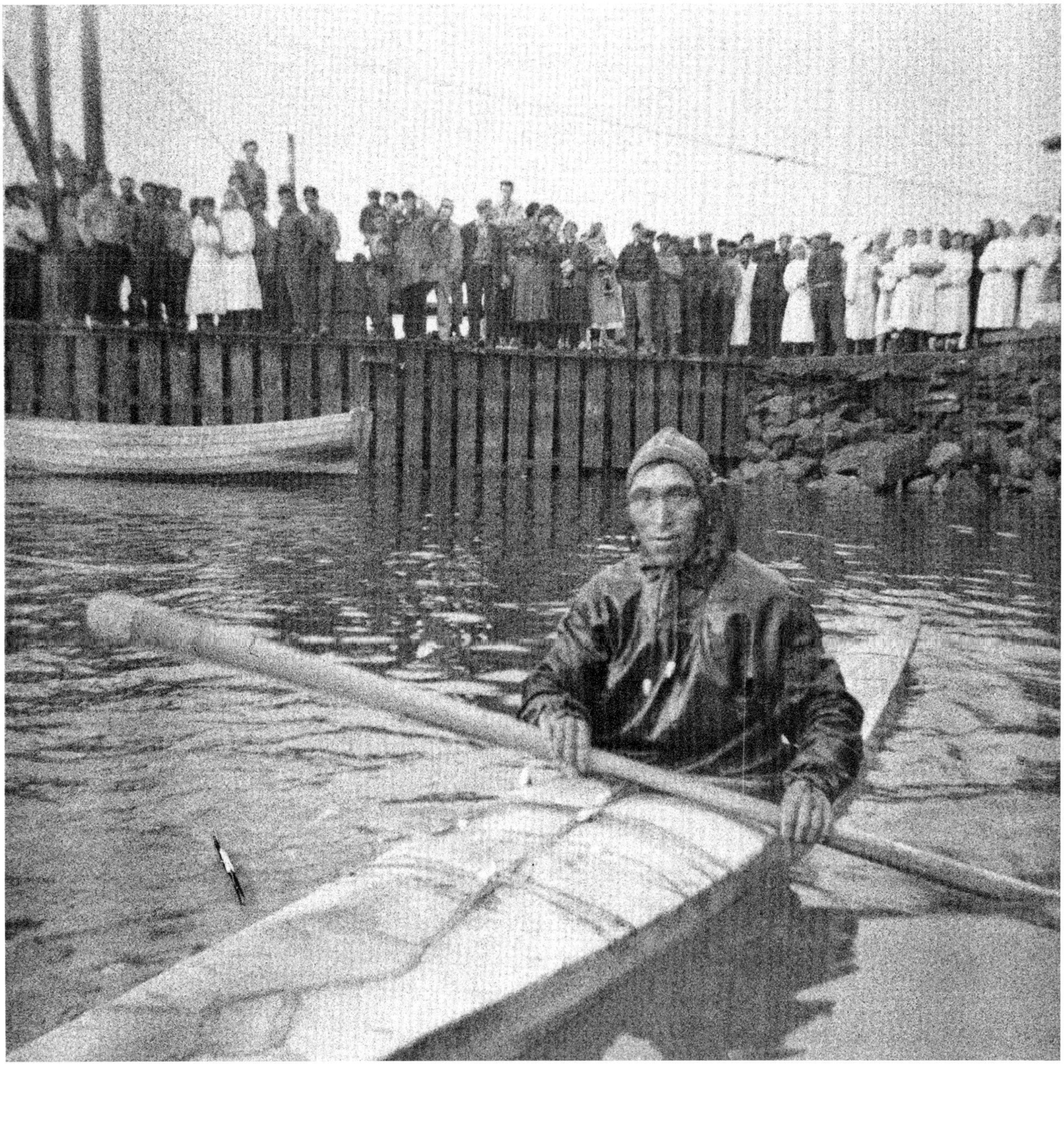

anymore."[45] He notes that the people either did not have dogs or used "Qallunaat dogs" for herding.[46] In contrast to the information that he could garner in conversation, Idlout's photographs are restricted to sites available on the itinerary. Yet the experienced hunter captured vestiges of life on the land, including the butchering of meat and fully six images of unidentified Greenlanders in *qajait*, as he learned new skills through observation and by respecting the skills and innovation of his hosts (see figure 6.5).[47]

Above all, Idlout's attention was drawn to the people – especially the Greenlanders – he encountered. Visually and textually, Idlout was impressed by the crowds and the attention granted to the visiting delegation. Of their arrival at Nuuk on 1 September, the hunter writes, "At 2:00, when we arrived, the weapons went off; and while we sailed by a beautiful land with a community, with big weapons, which were shot three times. When we docked, and while we were getting off the ramp, the Inuit were separated from the crowd with a rope. There were too many people who wanted to see us."[48] Idlout regularly depicted the excited crowds on docks and in towns that came to greet the visitors (see figure 6.6).

Taken from his own perspective, these photographs represent the excitement of being welcomed as honoured visitors. The IQ principle of *tunnganarniq* is palpable. Inuit from Inuit Nunangat and Greenlanders greeted one another with great enthusiasm. At Nuuk, Idlout recalled, "Later that evening, we ate at a huge feast building. I did not count how many Inuit and Qallunaat were participating. Each Inuk had a companion from Kalaallit Nunaat/Greenland, and they were asking a lot of questions about Canadians and about the Canadian Inuit and stuff like that. Their language is understandable, but some spoke very fast."[49] At Qeqertat on 20 September, one of the last days of the trip, Idlout enthused,

> Oh my goodness, it was so much fun, and there were so many Inuit, at a population of 1,900, and they had youth dressed like the army, and they had a Qallunaaq leader. It is so much fun here, and the leader made a speech outdoors and announced our arrival and said that they had waited a long time for Canadians to arrive. We gave gifts and we ate together, and we were also gifted a toy boat with fish and feather mats. We were also given a beautiful flag. We were very thankful. All of us Inuit, we thanked them and were celebrating, and our Qallunaat were very grateful. The gifts we received will be for all Inuit and Qallunaat. When we entered a huge building, we had plenty to drink, and everyone was talking at the same time, and they sounded like a flock of birds ... because we had a hard time understanding their language. We danced and celebrated.[50]

Idlout's photographs also demonstrate this captivation with his hosts.[51] His snapshots depict burgeoning crowds as they gather on docks to meet the visitors[52] or walk along the shore.[53] He records the delegates meeting their hosts

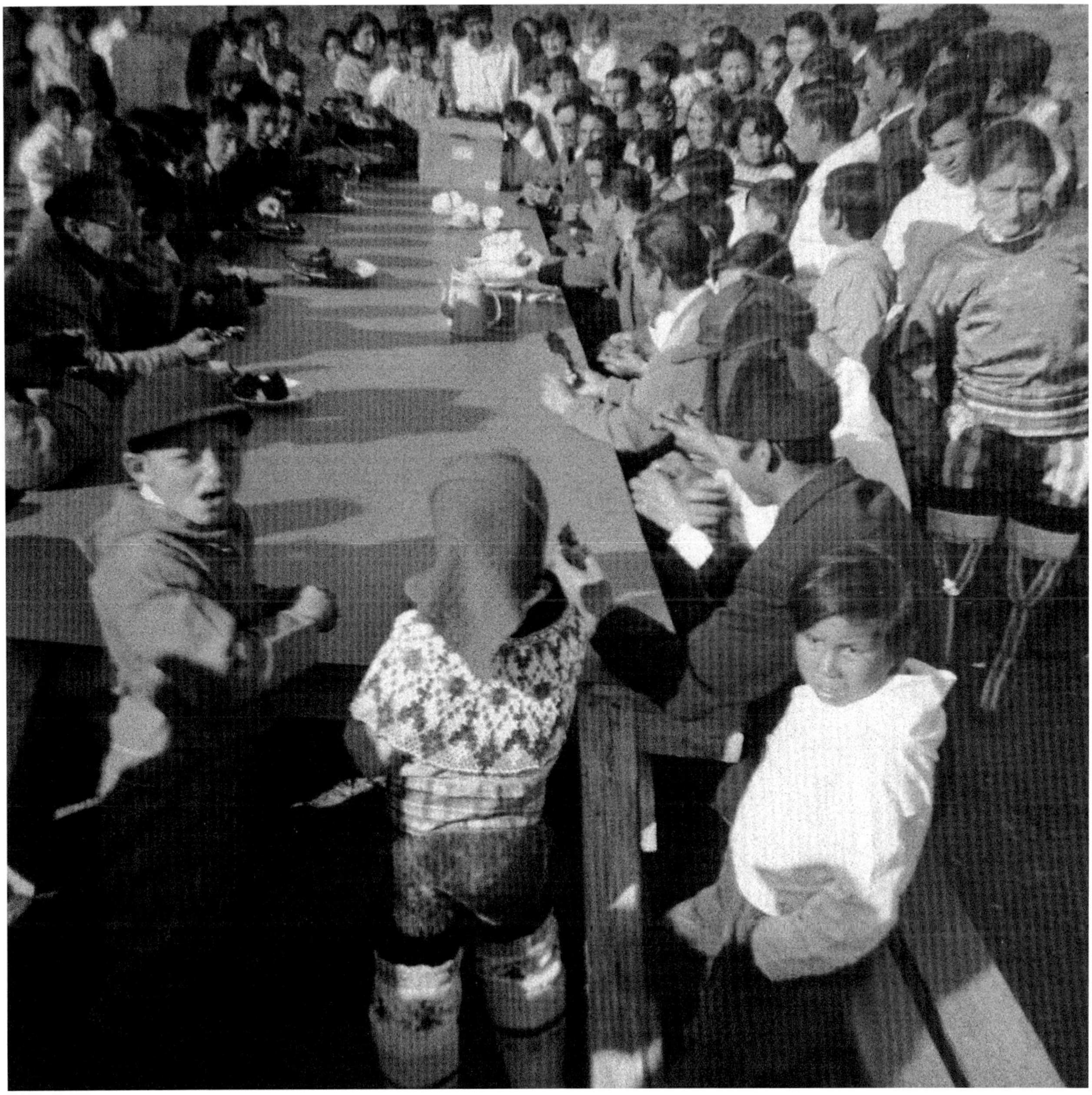

6.6 | A large group of people around a table, Kalaallit Nunaat/Greenland, September 1958. Photo: Joseph Idlout.

across a table set up out of doors with dozens of Greenlanders looking on at the spectacle.[54] Throngs of children wave Danish flags in exuberant greeting.[55] And Idlout pictures a Greenlander official standing apart from the crowd to address the visitors.[56] The photographs of crowds follow the conventions of tourist snapshots. Taken quickly and, at times, without any apparent attempt to compose the scene, they capture the excitement and energy of the visits.

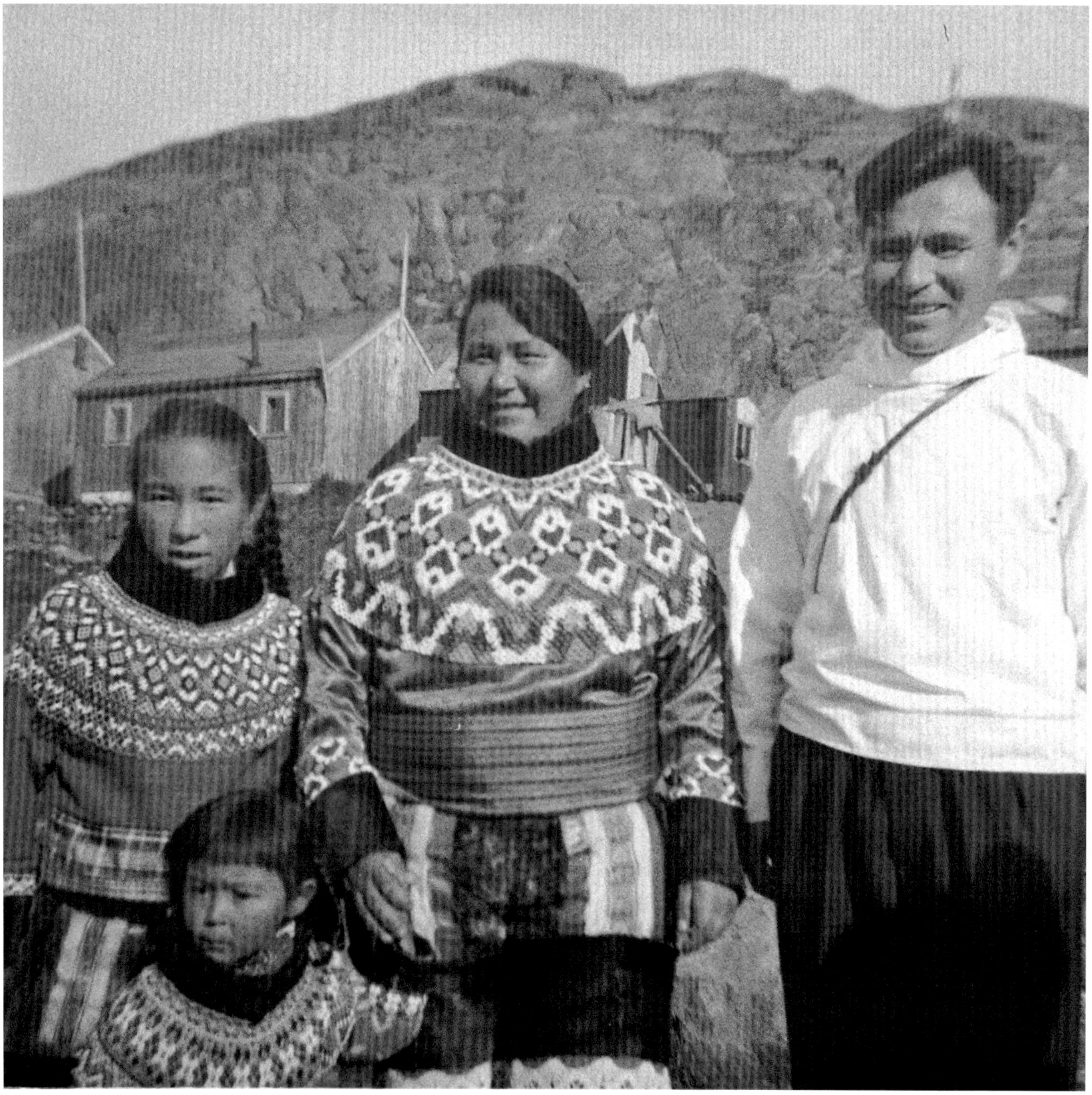

6.7 | Greenlandic Inuit pose in traditional clothes, September 1958. Photo: Joseph Idlout.

6.8 | Joseph Idlout (*second from the left*) and three Greenlandic Inuit men pose at a lumber yard in Kalaallit Nunaat/Greenland, September 1958. Uncredited photo taken with Idlout's camera.

Several of these photographs seem to focus particularly on the distinctive dress of West Greenlanders (see figure 6.7). According to the Nunatta Katersugaasivia Allagaateqarfialu (Greenland National Museum and Archives), Greenlanders from the region today (as during the 1950s) wear traditional dress to mark an important occasion. It is clear that the visit was a major event in the communities visited on the west coast of Kalaallit Nunaat/Greenland. The men wore anoraks made of unbleached (white) linen over black trousers. The women's traditional dress was more elaborate, comprising short sealskin pants, a stocking,

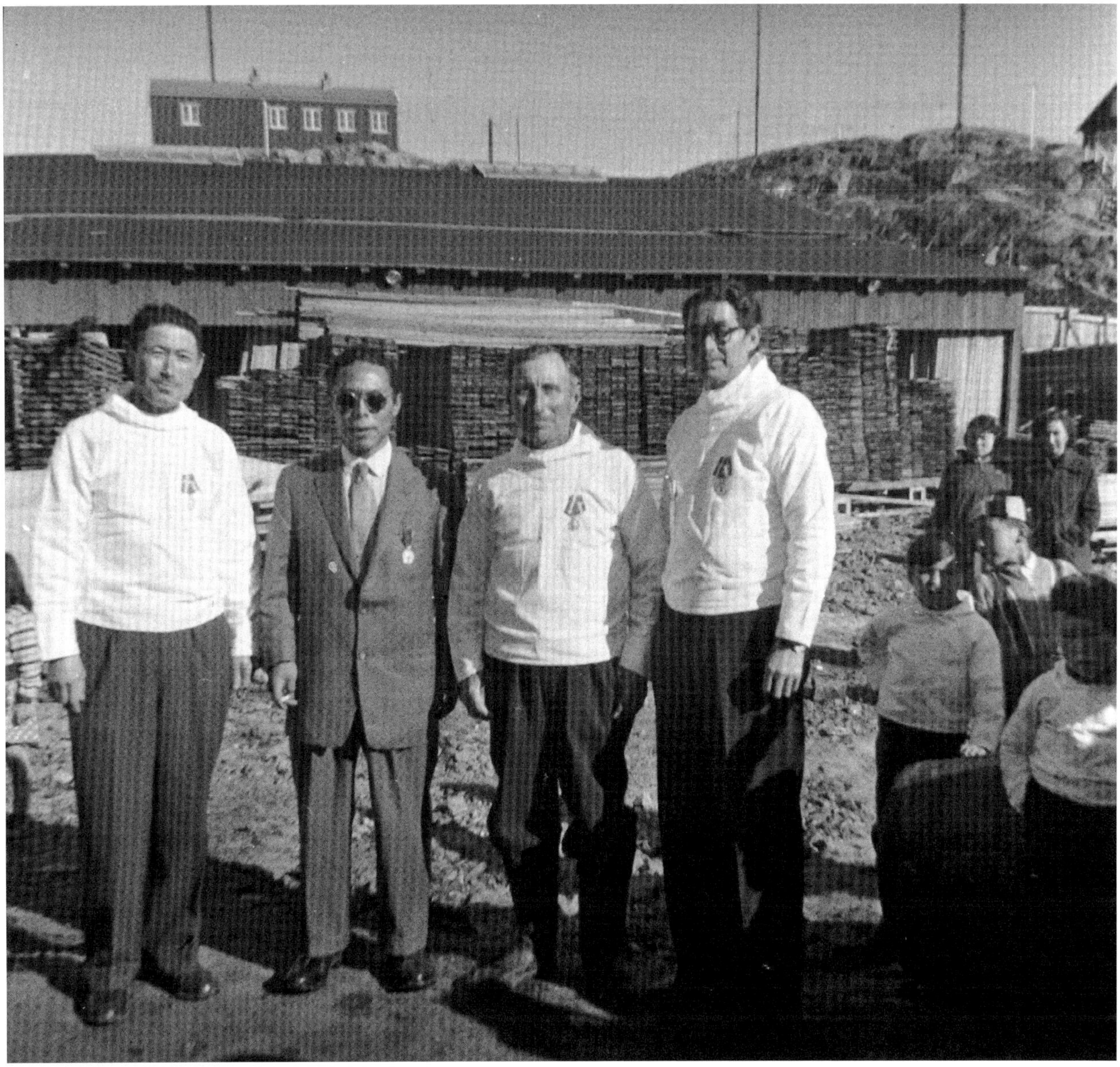

and *kamiik* (boots), all topped by an anorak with an inner layer. Over the anorak, the women donned elaborate beaded collars, inner collars, and wristlets.[57]

In some of Idlout's photographs, Inuit delegates are pictured with their Greenlandic Inughuit, Tunumiit, and Kalaallit hosts. The delegates' southern-style business suits, that constant vestige of governmental assimilation initiatives meant to symbolically present delegates as fully adapted to southern culture, were in stark contrast to the more practical and historically rich Greenlanders' traditional garb. On several occasions, Idlout handed his camera to someone else to record his own interaction with Greenlanders (see figure 6.8).[58] Like precursors to today's selfie, these photographs attest to the photographer's own presence in these new environments and connections with others.

The Inuit groups were fascinated by one another and, despite their different dialects, were able to communicate.[59] As R.A.J. Phillips later noted, "the talking never ceased" between the Inuit delegates and Greenlanders.[60] Indeed, Idlout's *Inuktitut Magazine* article is filled with remnants of conversations between the two groups. As noted above, writing about the last day of the trip, 20 September, Idlout recalls entering a huge building, where "everyone was talking at the same time, and they sounded like a flock of birds."[61] Despite the difficulties communicating, the conversations continued. Idlout and Elijah Menarik spoke to the crowds at Nuuk, and on 12 September, Idlout was interviewed on radio, telling his Greenlander audience, "We are all related, and we are united."[62] And Idlout recorded what he learned from his hosts through observation and respect, reflecting the IQ principles of *pilimmaksarniq/pijariuqsarniq* and *inuuqatigiitsiarniq* (respecting others, relationships, and caring for people), however halting the communication may have been.

Through these sometimes-disjointed conversations, Idlout took note of the agency – political and financial – that Inuit seemed to hold in Kalaallit Nunaat/Greenland. Throughout the photographs, Kalaallit Nunaat/Greenland's Inuit leaders appear welcoming the guests and speaking. Idlout and the other Inuit delegates registered how much authority their hosts appeared to have. In Nuuk, Idlout remarked during a hospital visit that tuberculosis treatments were available; patients did not have to be sent away as in Inuit Nunangat. The mission and the seniors' homes were owned by Inuit. He noted that they had been financed by the bank.[63] In Maniitsoq on 5 September, Idlout noted that the local church had been purchased by Inuit.[64] And in conversations mentioned by Idlout, Inuit Greenlanders share their experiences of a Qallunaat presence.[65] Although Canadian governmental officials designed the tour in order to present what they perceived to be Greenlanders' assimilation into southern Danish society, that was not what Idlout and the other delegates saw and heard. Instead, they witnessed what they perceived to be Inuit with greater agency and control of their own affairs and their use of this agency to serve and work together for common causes – consistent with the IQ principles of *piliriqatigiinniq/ikajuqtigiinniq* and *pijitsirniq* (serving and providing for family and/or community).

Idlout's photographs of Greenlanders, illuminated by his words, reveal the relational character of photography and deeper cultural connections. These images demonstrate how the act of photographing and the photograph itself mark encounters and social practice.[66] Like Idlout's photographs from the earlier 1950s at his camp (discussed in chapter 3), the Kalaallit Nunaat/Greenland photographs contemplate the notions of connection and encounter. As I have argued here, these images – like Idlout's words – are informed by the principles of Inuit Qaujimajatuqangit.

Governmental Perspectives

If Idlout connected with and contemplated Greenlanders through his camera, government officials saw a different view of the 1958 trip. Upon returning from Kalaallit Nunaat/Greenland, R.A.J. Phillips of the Arctic Division reflected on the trip in a radio program aired by the Canadian Broadcasting Corporation (CBC). His comments on Kalaallit Nunaat/Greenland were also covered by *The Globe and Mail*.[67] In the transcript of the CBC broadcast, he recounts the official sites visited and reactions from a few of the Inuit delegates. Throughout, the Arctic Division chief presents the Inuit delegates as inferior to their Kalaallit Nunaat/Greenland counterparts. As Phillips summarizes, "We went to learn from an Arctic country more advanced than ours, and to let Canadian Eskimo see the kind of future they might have."[68] Elsewhere in the speech, he intones, "In the Canadian visitors, the Greenlanders found a race of equals, a people who seemed just a little backward."[69] But Phillips closes his CBC address by noting a new loyalty to Canada that he perceived among the participating Inuit delegates: "Our people were no longer thinking of themselves only as Eskimo, the inhabitants of a northern wilderness. They were Canadians and loyal to their hopes for Canada."[70] In Phillips's view, the voyage to Kalaallit Nunaat/Greenland was a success. He suggests that the Department of Northern Affairs and National Resources had achieved its goal of promoting the assimilation of Inuit into European, or southern, Canadian values.

However, Phillips's perceptions may not have reflected contemporary Inuit experience in either Inuit Nunangat or Kalaallit Nunaat/Greenland. Questions of Inuit loyalty to the settler state and national belonging were being hotly debated at the time in Kalaallit Nunaat/Greenland. Greenlandic Inughuit, Tunumiit, and Kalaallit were asserting their own authority against European colonialism. Mads Lidesgaard, rector of a seminary in Kalaallit Nunaat/Greenland whom the delegates had met, wrote to J.V. Jacobson, a member of the Canadian delegation, about the impact of the 1958 trip: "We also remarked that your Eskimo clearly have shown that they wanted to be Canadian and not in any case Eskimo. In this country where a rather romantic national feeling is very strong, such things may make a deep impression. I really hope that your Eskimo shall learn [i.e., teach] ours something in that direction – and that ours will not learn [i.e., teach] yours a special Eskimo national feeling. As the situation stands, I really fear that a strong national feeling may be a very dangerous thing [in] a country as Greenland."[71] Explorations of Inuit sovereignty were appearing beneath the surface of the trip's carefully choreographed emphasis on southern or European assimilation.

Indeed, despite Phillips's and Lidesgaard's perceptions, by the late 1950s, an Inuit "national feeling" – one centred on self-determination or sovereignty – was indeed growing among Inuit in Inuit Nunangat too. The Sangussaqtauliqtilluta period traumatized many Inuit, but it also fuelled resistance. Seeds for the establishment of Nunavut, for example, were being sown in the years before the 1970s. Inuit were speaking back to southern authority.

In the years following the 1958 trip, Inuit members of the delegation to Kalaallit Nunaat/Greenland did, indeed, take leadership roles; but if Phillips and the other organizers at the DNANR imagined these men as compliant supporters of the Canadian government's assimilation policies for Inuit, they were mistaken. They increasingly asserted Inuit autonomy and challenged the authority of the Crown and its governmental agents. George Koneak, for example, participated in the government's first meeting of the Eskimo Affairs Committee in 1959, demanding clearer explanations of federal finances to Inuit.[72] Koneak later became a strong political leader in Nunivik, serving as governor of the Makivik Corporation and as a chief negotiator in the James Bay and Northern Quebec Agreement of 1975, the first major land claims agreement in Canada.[73] Joe Tikivik would go on to become mayor of Iqaluit/Frobisher Bay in the 1970s as Inuit were demanding greater authority in government.[74] After working as a translator for the government, Elijah Menarik became an influential radio and television host using media to connect Inuit.[75] Kananginak Pootoogook became one of the most prominent Inuit artists of his generation and a leader at the renowned West Baffin Eskimo Cooperative in Kinngait/Cape Dorset.[76] The trip to Kalaallit Nunaat/Greenland seems to have had a sustained impact on the delegates.[77]

The Return to Resolute/Qausuittuq

Joseph Idlout, too, remembered the trip to Kalaallit Nunaat/Greenland and the models of Inuit autonomy and authority that he witnessed there. As C.N. Bolger of the Arctic Division noted to Constable T. Jenkins of the Royal Canadian Mounted Police (RCMP), who was stationed in Resolute/Qausuittuq in 1960, "Idlout went to Greenland in 1956 [*sic*: 1958] and saw much there that made a deep impression on him. He explained to the Director [Bent Sivertz] in Ottawa on his return that wherever he went in Greenland, he saw men in offices just like the Director's and these men were, as a general rule, Eskimos; whereas this was never the case in Canada. He said also that he was much interested in seeing Inuit as teachers. Even the principals of big schools, the directors of the radio station, administrators of communities, etc., were Inuit [in Greenland]."[78]

Like the other Inuit delegates to Kalaallit Nunaat/Greenland, Idlout – and his fellow High Arctic exiles – increasingly demanded greater authority for Inuit and changes to their new home in Resolute/Qausuittuq, as evidenced in their correspondence with government officials.[79]

The Resolute/Qausuittuq that Idlout returned to was largely segregated, with Inuit living 6 to 8 kilometres from the Royal Canadian Air Force (RCAF) base and the weather station, with their peripatetic groups of southerners. The community of about sixty-one Inuit – from fifteen families[80] – who lived in Resolute/Qausuittuq during the late 1950s comprised exiles from both Inukjuak/Port Harrison and Pond Inlet/Mittimatalik, including Idlout's extended family.[81] Social dynamics among the two Inuit groups were at times challenging. They spoke different dialects and had to learn to communicate and collaborate with one another.[82] Inuit were initially prohibited from visiting the base. Indeed, the military had been opposed to the relocation of Inuit to Cornwallis Island.[83]

Despite the segregation, a southern presence in the form of heightened bureaucracy administered by southern officials and the influence of the RCAF base strongly impacted Inuit life at Resolute/Qausuittuq. The exiles were both reliant on and restricted by southern institutions. An RCMP officer was assigned to oversee the Resolute/Qausuittuq exiles. This position was initially held by Ross Gibson beginning in 1953, by Corporal Douglas S. Moodie beginning in 1958, by Constable T. Jenkins beginning in 1960, and by Corporal Ron Gordon beginning in 1962. The base, although off limits, provided the only regular medical services available nearby for Inuit, and in a reflection of the severe hardships that Inuit endured, they at times resorted to scavenging for food and building scraps discarded by the military. The base also provided seasonal wage employment for ten Inuit men.[84] Idlout, for example, was among the Inuit men hired by the RCAF to provide training in Arctic survival.[85] In correspondence of the time, the hunter describes teaching air force personnel how to build an *iglu* (igloo).[86] For Idlout and other exiles, the introduction of a wage economy marked a dramatic change in their lives. Indeed, Doug Wilkinson published a contemporaneous indictment of southern economic and governmental expansion to the Arctic, including the introduction of a wage economy, in which he noted the negative impact on Inuit life.[87]

Yet Inuit at Resolute/Qausuittuq had little of the authority and autonomy that Idlout had witnessed in Kalaallit Nunaat/Greenland. Idlout had expected to be the head of camp and to hold a privileged position among Inuit and with Qallunaat alike. Alan Rudolph Marcus reports that Ross Gibson, the RCMP officer during the settlement of exiles in Resolute/Qausuittuq, firmly told Idlout that the hunter was *not* the "boss" there; Gibson was.[88] Indeed, the RCMP officers assumed authority over Inuit, managing the only store available and acting as liaisons between them and the military and weather station staffs.[89] When Idlout was denied permission to visit the RCAF base, he wrote sarcastically to Doug Wilkinson that "Resolute is very good country only to[o] bad we are Eskimos."[90]

Wilkinson followed up by forwarding Idlout's letter and his own concerns to Bent Sivertz in Ottawa: "The phrase in the second para 'only to bad we are Eskimos' is a poignant one. Obviously Idlouk has been made to feel inferior in being told he is not to visit the base ... If Idlouk does not find the satisfactions he seeks at a place like Resolute, then his talents are being wasted."[91] Idlout was clearly frustrated by this lack of authority, and Wilkinson shared this frustration.

Housing, one of the gravest issues facing the exiles at Resolute/Qausuittuq, was a key subject of their complaints to southern authorities, as discussed by the Qikiqtani Truth Commission (see chapter 1); the question of housing also illustrates the tensions with southern management of life in the High Arctic. The first group of exiles arrived at Cornwallis Island in 1953 with supplies that were inadequate for their survival. As the Qikiqtani Truth Commission reports, "They had no water transportation with the exception of two small one-man kayaks, no storage space, and no stores, and their tents were in very poor condition."[92] Indeed, the exiles lived in tents that had been constructed for conditions in Nunivik, hundreds of kilometres south. This was not adequate for High Arctic winds and temperatures. Gibson sought out support from the RCAF and southern officials. Yet the exiles spent the long winter of 1953–54 in tents. In the spring of 1954, the Inukjuak/Port Harrison exiles' pleas to return to Nunivik were denied. Resigned to staying at Resolute/Qausuittuq, all of the exiles began building homes out of materials scavenged from the RCAF dump.[93] When Idlout and his family arrived in 1955, the government also sent materials for three houses. But these items were deemed to be unusable, and the exiles continued to build from scavenged materials, constructing fourteen by 1960 (see figure 5.5).[94] In March 1962, Daniel Salluviniq,[95] whose family had arrived from Inukjuak/Port Harrison nine years earlier, wrote with a detailed complaint about the inadequate state of housing: "I want to know from the government why, we must live in shacks built from scrap when Resolute is one of the coldest places. If at all possible it would be best if we have a proper house to live in. And I want to hear what the governments have to say to this and as soon as possible because I'm going to keep writing to you."[96] Although living conditions for the exiles were clearly unhealthy, southern authorities assured themselves and the south that the exiles were adequately housed. Earlier, on 10 March 1957, a series of six photographs of Resolute/Qausuittuq houses taken by Corporal Douglas S. Moodie were sent to Ottawa as apparent proof that the exiles were well sheltered.[97] And in response to Salluviniq's 1962 plea, the department said that the present housing was warm and that anyone wanting a house would have to purchase it, an expense beyond the means of the Resolute/Qausuittuq exiles.[98]

Doug Wilkinson, although a vocal critic of southern treatment of Inuit, also contributed to the government's visual staging of conditions at Resolute/Qausuittuq. Now working as an independent filmmaker, Wilkinson made a short film about Inuit life in Resolute/Qausuittuq in 1963 under the auspices of the NFB.[99] Entitled *Eskimo Village, Resolute*, the six-minute newsreel reframes the settlement as a successful community with the trappings of the south's middle-class suburban life.[100] Shot in the summer, the film evades the harshest conditions of life in the High Arctic. The newsreel opens with a scanning shot of housing along the shore. The first half of the film is devoted to the new co-op. The opening of its doors brings out Inuit adults and children, who study and select products, including pablum, tobacco, baking powder, and various canned goods. Corporal Ron Gordon notes each purchase in a small ledger.[101] With smiles on their faces, the community members carry home boxes of goods, and the store is tidied. The accompanying narrative reinforces the southern governmental framing of the scene: "The staples rarely run out and the Eskimo housewives now shop for their groceries much as do their counterparts in southern Canada."[102] The last few minutes of the film take place at Idlout and Kidlak's home. Corporal Gordon, after dropping off their store-bought goods, is invited in for coffee.[103] The camera lingers on signs of middle-class comfort: a transistor radio, stove, and a china tea set. Kidlak pours milk for the youngest children while she, Idlout, the officer, and one of their older sons sit down to coffee. Their daughter Susan is seen briefly playing with a stuffed animal.[104]

But the film's cheerful tone masked severe difficulties in Resolute/Qausuittuq. Inuit, for example, remembered the store as a source of exploitation, although it is presented in the film as a bounty of accessible goods. As the Qikiqtani Truth Commission has shown, "Qausuitturmiut were not always paid their wages directly, but rather received 'credits' from the government via the RCMP. Qausuitturmiut could then spend their credits at the RCMP-run store, although the credit system appears to have been poorly managed, and many Qausuitturmiut allege that they often worked without remuneration."[105] And the seemingly tranquil scene at Idlout and Kidlak's home belied growing frustrations and difficulties.

Idlout and the other exiles increasingly voiced their complaints to southern authorities in an effort to assert their power.[106] They did so in person with the RCMP and visiting southerners[107] as well as through their correspondence with officials in Ottawa.[108] Idlout, for his part, regularly corresponded with Wilkinson, with Leo Manning, an Inuktitut translator at the DNANR, and with Bent Sivertz, director of the Northern Administration Branch of the DNANR.[109] As Frank Tester, Paule McNicoll, and Piita Irniq have argued, within the context of the Inuit tuberculosis crisis, writing letters "gave Inuit an opportunity to ask questions and raise concerns they had as patients and relatives."[110] Idlout and the other Inuit exiles complained about welfare, supplies, and management. In a 1965 letter to the Advisory Commission on the Development of Government in the Northwest Territories, Idlout alerted authorities that "here in the settlement we have not enough electricity, or it is too weak. They had put in the generator in 1957. Even sometimes our electricity equipment stops."[111] Other correspondence addressed schooling. Idlout's daughter Leah had established a makeshift school at Resolute/Qausuittuq in 1957.[112] Her actions may have been a catalyst in establishing a day school in the community.[113] Parents kept a close eye on the school, complaining periodically to officials in the south about the school teachers who had been sent to Resolute/Qausuittuq.[114]

An incident in May 1963 particularly angered the exiles, leaving them disillusioned with the RCMP and with southerners more broadly. Salluviniq, Kadloo, and Idlout all wrote separately about the incident and about their complaints regarding Constable Jenkins.[115] As Idlout explained in his undated letter:

> I'm writing to find out if the law with respect to helping Inuit has changed. Because three men came to Resolute Bay nearly starving, and many dogs died of starvation coming in from Kuuganajuk near Creaswell Bay on Somerset Island to Resolute Bay three more men came in March. They weren't starving one of them is Daneillie who did some work for the air force base and bought a few things with the money he earned the other guy bought some groceries with the polar bear hide, but the third guy left with nothing from the store not even ammunition. When we approached the police about the situation he just says that he is the boss of Resolute.[116]

The hunter further complained in the letter about the RCMP officer's unwillingness to help during a flu outbreak and remarked that the current teacher was not liked. Idlout, an Inuk who had worked so closely with Qallunaat for many years, tellingly closed his letter by saying, "I must admit that we still don't understand the white peoples' way of thinking and their customs."[117] In the midst of growing hardships and frustrations, Idlout did not forget the models of greater Inuit autonomy and authority that he had witnessed in Kalaallit Nunaat/Greenland. In 1965, the hunter wrote to the Advisory Commission on the Development of Government in the Northwest Territories reminding them that "in 1958, I and several people went to visit Greenland Eskimo. They had Eskimo bosses there. Their people and the land was well controlled, better than what we are today."[118] Embedded in Idlout's images and words, as well as in the gazes of the other Inuit participants and Greenlanders, was a look back at policies of assimilation and efforts toward cultural autonomy. Rather than integrating into colonial standards, Inuit participants from Inuit Nunangat – including Idlout – witnessed assertions of Inuit autonomy. Certainly, the brief trip to Kalaallit Nunaat/Greenland was not a direct catalyst or causal agent, but it took place during a time when demands for Inuit political agency were beginning to grow – demands that would reap autonomy for the Inuit in the decades to come.

The resistance against government policies and officials seen in letters from the Inuit of Resolute/Qausuittuq was growing across Inuit Nunangat – and it continued to grow in Kalaallit Nunaat/Greenland. Writing in 2012 about the early years of *Inuktitut Magazine*, Zebedee Nungak sees Inuit "asserting their identity and being very proud of their language and culture."[119] John Amagoalik, who was relocated with his family to Resolute/Qausuittuq in 1953, was a child when these letters of resistance were being written. He would go on to become a leader in the Inuit fight for self-governance, pivotal in the 1994 Nunavut Land Claims Agreement and in the 1999 formation of Nunavut. Decades later, Zacharias Kunuk's acclaimed 2019 film *One Day in the Life of Noah Piugattuk* deployed camera vision to look back at the Sangussaqtauliqtilluta period and Inuit resistance. The film stages a tense 1961 confrontation between the title character and a Qallunaaq government official known only as "boss." Words pass between them in Inuktitut and English, translated with varying accuracy and nervous diplomacy by a third figure, a younger Inuk man. "Boss" has travelled to Noah Piugattuk's camp in an effort to convince the Inuk man to move his family to a settlement and enrol his children in government schools. Kunuk's camera captures Inuit refusal in Noah Piugattuk's unflinching returned gaze – an assertion of authority shared by Joseph Idlout and Inuit throughout Sangussaqtauliqtilluta.

The remaining years of the 1960s brought sadness to Idlout's family. Kidlak passed away in 1965.[120] By this point, with increasing access to alcohol, Resolute/Qausuittuq had become what Idlout's daughter Susan termed a "sick community."[121] Speaking of this period in Resolute/Qausuittuq, John Amagoalik recalled, "Alcohol had a devastating effect on our community life."[122] Idlout, too, was gravely impacted by access to alcohol. On 2 June 1968, the hunter died in a snowmobile accident.

But Idlout's life – and images – would be remembered and continue to inspire Inuit for generations, as seen in another article written in 1975 by Idlout's daughter Leah for the journal *Inuit Today*, reproduced following this chapter. As seen in Leah Idlout d'Argencourt Paulson's words and in continuing dialogue with Idlout's family in the 1990s and more recently, the hunter became a model of the Inuit cultural survivance discussed in chapter 7.

In the Idlout Family's Words 6

Leah Idlout d'Argencourt, "First Inuit Picture on Canadian Money," *Inuit Today* 1, no. 9 (October 1975): 32–3, 43, with photographs by Joseph Idlout

FIRST INUIT PICTURE ON CANADIAN MONEY

ᓯᖁᕐᓇᕐᐸᒥᒃ ᕿᓇᐅᔭᖅ ᐃᓄᖕᖑᐊᕐᑕᓕᒃ

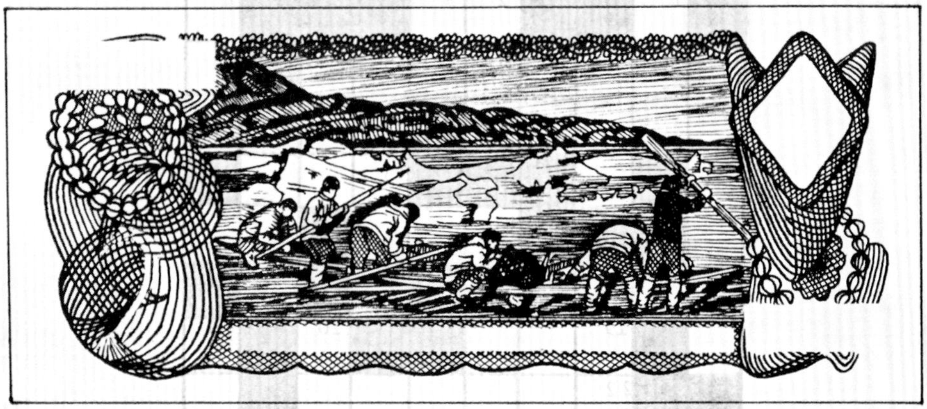

ᒫᓇ 1975ᒥ $2.00 ᓄᓵᖅ ᕿᓇᐅᔭ ᑲᓇᑕᒥ ᐃᓄᖕᖑᐊᕐ ᑕᖅᑲᐅᕐᑐᖅ ᑐᓄᐊᓂ.

ᓵᑯᐊ ᐃᓄᖕᖑᐊᑦ ᕐᑲᐅᔨᒪᔭᒃᑲ ᑭᓇᒃᑰᒪᖕᓛᑕ ᐃᓚ ᒥᔭᐅᓚᐅᕐᔨᒪᓚᒪ ᑌᑦᓯᒪᓂ ᑕᕝᕙ ᐊᑦᔨᓕᐅᕐ ᑕᐅᑎᑦᑐᒥᑦ ᐅᐱᕐᖕᕆᕕᑦᑎᓐᓂ ᓄᕗᕈᓗᐊᓂ. ᐊᑦᔨᖕᖑᐊᖕᖑᕗᑦ: ᓴᐅᒥᖕᒥᑦ ᑕᓕᕐᐱᖕᔪᑦ ᓴᐅᒥᒃᓕᕐᐹᖅ, ᐊᖕ ᓄᑲᖕᒪ ᐅᐃᖕᑲ ᕿᑎᐅᓂ ᕐᑭᑦᓯᐊᓕᒃ, ᐱᑕ ᐸᓂᓗᒃ ᐊᓂᑲ, ᓱᓗᓂ Hᐃᕈᑎᐊ ᑲᒡᓗᒃ ᐊᓂᐊᐱᑲ, ᐸᐅᓪ ᐃᒡᓗᐅᖅ ᐊᓂᑯᓗᑲ, ᐊᑖᑕᑲ ᔫᓯᐱ ᐃᒡᓗᐅᖅ, ᐃᓗᔭ ᐃᖅᓗ ᐊᓂᒡᓗᐊᕐ.

ᕐᑭᑭᕐᓵᓗᐸ ᒥᑦᑎᒪᑕᓕᐅᐸ ᕐᑲᓂᒦᔭᓂ ᓄᕗᕈᓗᐊᓂ ᑐᓄᓂᕐᒥ ᕐᑭᑭᕐᑕᒥᑦᑕᐅᖅ ᐅᐱᕐᖕᕆᕕᕕᓂᑦᑎᓐᓃᑦᑐᑦ ᑌᒪ 1951ᖕ ᔪᑎᑦᑐᔪ ᕐᑭᓚᓗᑲᕐᓱᒃᑐᑦ, ᐸᕐᓇᒃᑐᐋᑦᑐᑎᒃ ᕐᑲᔭᕐᑐᕐᑲᑦᑕᓚᐅᕐᒪᑎᒃ ᐊᓵᑕᒐ ᐃᑦᓚᐅᖅ ᐊᒻᒪᓗ ᑲᑦᓗᒃ, ᑐᐱᒃᓴᒥᒃ ᐊᕐᑲᕐᑎᑦᑐᔪ ᐊᐊᕐᓯᒪᑦᑐᓂ ᕐᑲᔭᖕᑲ, ᐊᕙᑕᕐᑲᕐᑐᑎᒃ ᓇᑦᑎᕐᒥᒃ ᓇᓱᒃᓯᒪᓱᒥᒃ, ᐅᓈᕐᑲᕐᑐᑎᒃ ᕐᑭᓚᓗᑲᕐᓯᐅᒪᒥᒃ ᐊᖕᔪᕕᑲᕐᑲᕐᑐᑎᒃᑐ, ᕐᑯᑭᐅᑎᕐᑲᕐᑐᑎᒃᑐ. ᐸᐅᓪ ᐃᑦᓚᐅᖅ ᒥᑎᐅᓂ ᕐᑭᑦᓯᐊᒃᑐ ᐳᕕᕐᓯᖕᖑᐊᕐᑐᒃ ᐊᕙᑕᕐᒥᒃ ᐊᑦᓴᔪᐊᒃ ᑕᕝᕙᓂ, ᐃᓚᖕᒥᑦ ᕐᑲᔭᕐᒥᒃ ᐸᕐᓇᒃᑎᑦᑐᒥᑦ, ᐅᒥᐊᕐᑐᕐᑐᑦ ᐊᓯᖕᒥᑦ ᑭᖕᑯᓂᖕᑲᓂ ᒪᓕᖕᓂᐊᕐᑐᑎᒃ. ᑐᐊᕕᕐᑐᐋᕐᑲᑕᓚᐅᕐᒪᑕ ᑲᑐᑦᓯᑦᑐᑎᒃ ᐸᕐᓇᒃᐸᓚᐅᕐᑐᑦ ᐃᑲᔪᕈᓐᓇᕐᑐᓕᒫᑦ ᐃᑲᔪᕐᑐᑎᒃ ᐊᖕᔪᑎᑦ ᓄᑲᐸᐃᐊᑦᑐ ᕐᑭᓚᓗᑲᑦᑕ ᕐᑲᓕᕖᕐᑎᑦᑐᔪ ᐱᓗᐊᕐᑐᑎᒃ.

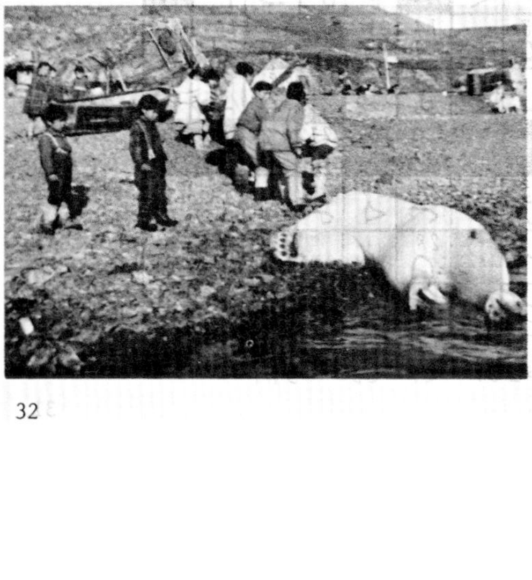

by LEAH IDLOUT d'ARGENCOURT

This story is about the new 1975 Canadian two dollar bill with the Inuit picture on the back.

I know the Inuit in this picture. I was with them when they were filmed. This picture was taken in our spring camp at Nuvurulua on Curry Island. From left to right my brother-in-law Gideon Qitsualik, Peter Paniloo my brother. Herodia Kadluk second cousin,Paul Idlout brother, Joseph Idlout my late father, and Elijah Erkloo my cousin.

About 20 miles from Pond Inlet,Baffin Island, is Curry Island, which was our family spring camp. It was in 1951 in the Narwhal hunting season. The men were rushing to prepare themselves for hunting the Narwhal. My father and Kadluk used to go out to hunt by kayak. The kayaks were covered with painted canvas. Avataq Seal float, two different types of Narwhal harpoons, and rifles were taken as weapons in the kayaks. Paul Idlout and Gideon Qitsualik are blowing the air into the seal floats in this picture, while the others are preparing the kayaks. The rest of the men and boys will follow behind with the boats. The men used to hurry, working together, and any boys who were old enough would help, especially at the first Narwhal hunting season.

The picture was taken by Doug Wilkinson. It is called "Land of the Long Day". The title is only in English. All the family of Idlouts are in the picture.

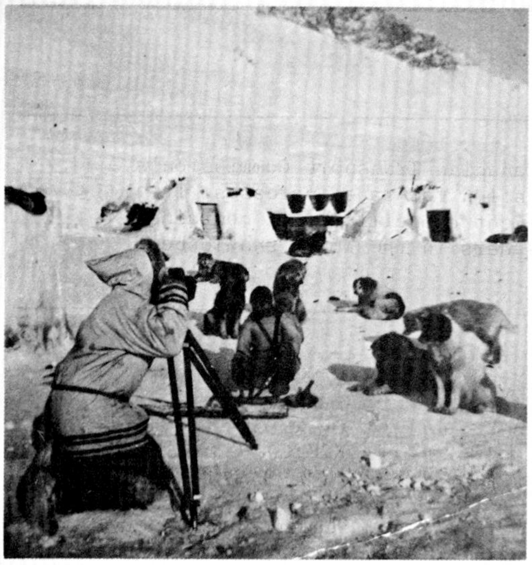

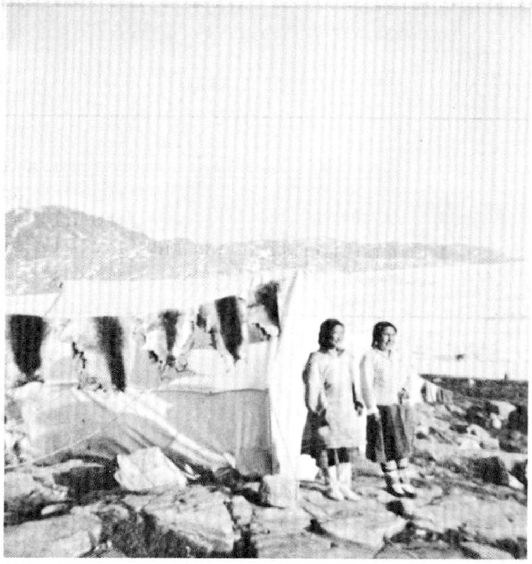

ᑕᓇᔭᐅᓯᐊᖅ ᑐᓚᐅᕐᓯᒪᔪᑦ ᕐᑭᒪᒥᕐᔪᑦ ᕿᓐᓇ ᐊᖅᑐᑦ ᕐᑲᑦᑐᓈᑎᑦ ᐊᑎᕐᑲᕐᑐᖅ Doug Wilkinson ᑕᕐᓇᔭᖅ ᐊᑎᕐᑲᕐᑐᖅ ᕐᑲᑦᑐᓈᑎᑦ ᑭᓯᐊᓂ Land of the Long Day ᕿᒃᑯᐊᓗ ᐃᑦᓚᐅᐸ ᓄᓕᐊᖅᑲᓗ, ᕐᑭᑐᕐᖅᑲᒥᑦᓗ, ᐃᑦᑐᒃᑲᓗ ᓂᖅᒥᐅᒃᑯᒃᑲ ᓄᓇᑦᑎᑦᓂᒥᐅᓕᒫ ᑲᓴᑦ ᐊᑦᓯᕐᑲᕐᑲᑕᐅᔪᑦ. ᐅᐱᕐᖅ ᑲᒃᓵᖅ ᑐᕙᑦᓕᐊᓕᕐᑎᑦᓗᑐ ᐊᐅᓚᑦᑎᕕᖅᒥᑦ ᐅᑮᕕᑦᑎᓐᓂᑦ ᐱᒥᐊᕐᓗᑎᒃ ᓅᐸᕈᓗᐊᓂᓗ ᐅᐱᕐᖅᒥᕕᑦᑎᓐᓂ ᐅᑦᓛᕐᑎᑦᓗᑕᓗ, ᐅᑦᓛᕐᐸᒃᑎᑦᓗᒥᑦ ᕐᑭᒧᒃᓯᒃᑯᑦ ᐅᒥᐊᒃ ᐅᓯᑦᓗᑎᒃ.

ᐊᑦᓯᕐᑲᕐᑲᑕᐅᔪᓕᒫᑦ ᐊᑐᓂᑦ ᐱᓇᓱᑲᕐᒥᖅᓂᒃ ᐱᓇᓱᒃᑎᑦᓗᒥᑦ ᕐᑲᑦᓈᕐᑲᓐᖅᒥᑦᑐᕐᒥᐅᖅᑐᑦᓗᑎᒃ, ᓄᑕᖅᑲᑦ ᐃᓕᓐᓂᐊᕐᐸᒃᑎᓐᓇᒥᑦ, ᐊᖅᑐᓇᓯᖅᓃᓐᓇᕐᔪᑦ ᑎᓴᑲᓂ ᐊᕐᓯᖅᓂᕐᔪᑦᓗ ᐃᓅᓯᖅᑲᕐᑎᑦᓗᑕ, ᕐᑲᑦᓗᓇᑦᓯᐊᕐᐸᒃᑲᓗᐊᕐ ᓗᑎᒃ ᓰᕐᑲᐃᒪᒪ ᕐᑲᑦᓘᓈᕐᑕᓂᒃ ᐊᓐᓅᕐᑲᕐᐳᑦ, ᑲᒥᕐᑲᐅᕐ ᓗᑎᒃᓗ ᓇᑦᑎᕐᔭᓂᒃ ᐃᐸᕐᐅᓯᕐᒥᖅᓂᒃ ᐅᔭᕐᓯᐅᑎᒥᖅᓂᒃ ᐊᑦᓴᓐᖅᑐᐊᒥ ᕐᑯᓕᑦᑕᐅᔭᕐᓯᒪᐅᕐᓗᑎᒃᓗ ᕐᑯᓕᑦᑕᐅᔭᒃᓴᓂᒃ.

ᑌᑦᓯᒪᓂᐅᑎᑦᓗᑐ ᐊᖅᑐᑎᑦ ᕐᑲᑯᕐᑌᓐᓇᕐᓂᒃ ᕐᑲᓖᕐᑲᕐᐸᓚᐅᕐᒪᑕᓕ ᐊᕐᓇᑦᓘᓐᓃᑦ ᕐᑯᓕᑦᑕᐅᔭᒃᓴᓂᒃᓗᑕᐅ ᐊᕐᓯᕐᑲᐅᕐᓗᑎᒃ. ᑕᕙ ᑌᒫᑦᑐᓂᒃ ᐊᑐᓐᖅᑐᐊᕐᑐᑦ ᑕᒃᓴᐅᕚᑦ ᐊᑦᓯᖅᒥᓐᓂ. ᒫᓐᓇᐅᔪᒃᑯᑦᓚ ᐊᑦᓯᕌᓐᖅᒥᑦᑐᓂᒃ ᑕᕐᓴᖅᒥᑦ ᑕᒪᕐᒥᒃ ᐊᖅᑐᑎᑦ ᐊᕐᓄᑦᓗ ᓯᓖᕐᑲᕐᐸᓚᕐᐳᑦ, ᐃᓄᖅᓅᕐᑐᕐᑲᑐᐊᕐᒥ ᑕᒃᓴᐅᕙᓚᕐᑐᑦ, ᑕᕐᓴᕐᑲᐅᐳᔪᔭᕐᑐᓂᒃ ᕐᑲᓖᕐᑲᐅᕐᑐᑦ.

ᕐᑲᐅᓯᔪᒪᔪᕐᑲᕐᓂᐊᕐᑐᒃᓴᐅᖅᒥᖅᒪᑦ ᕐᑲᓄᐃᒻᒪᑎᒃ ᕐᑲᓃᒃ ᑐᐱᒃᓴᒥᒃ ᐊᒥᕐᓯᒪᑦᓗᑎᒃ ᐊᒥᐊᕐᓯᒪᓐᓂᕐᒪᓛᑎᒃ. ᐋᓇᓇ ᕐᑭᑐᕐᖅᑲᕐᑲᓚᐅᕐᒪᑦ ᐅᓄᕐᑐᓂᒃ ᕿᓐᓇᓗ ᑲᓲᓗᐸ ᓄᓕᐊᖅᑲ ᒥᕐᓰᑎᑐᑦ ᒥᕐᓯᑐᐃᓐᓇᓴᐊᑭᓐᓂᕐᓴᐅᖅᒪᑦ ᐊᒻᒪᓗ ᐅᕐᑭᓐᓂᕐᓴᐅᑦᓗᓂ ᐊᐅᔭᑲᑦᑕᒃᑕᐅᔭᓇ ᐊᖅᑲᓂᒃ ᐅᓯᔭᐅᔭᓇᐊᖅᑲᓘᓃᑦ ᐅᒥᐊᒻᒪᓇᒃᑯᑦ ᐅᑦᓛᕐᑲᑦᑕᕐᓗᓂ. ᐊᒥᐊᖅᑲᓕ ᑐᖅᑐᔪᕈᔪᑐᐃᓐᓇᔫᕙᓚᐅᕐᑐᖅ ᓯᑯᓄᑦ ᐃᓚᒥᓕᐅᓯᒪᓖᔮᕐᓗᓂ, ᓴᐅᓂᖅᒥᑦ ᑐᓄᓂᕐᒥᐅᑎᑐ ᓴᓇᔭᐅᓯᒪᑲᓗᐊᕐᓗᑎᒃ ᓰᕐᑫᒪᒪ. ᐃᓛᒃᑲ ᐊᖅᑐᑎᑦ ᓴᓇᐅᓯᕐᒥᖅᓂᒃ ᐱᐅᒥᔭᒥᖅᓂᒃ ᐃᓗᐊᕐᓂᕐᐸᐅᔪᓇᔭᒥᖅᓂᒃᓗ ᓴᓇᐅᓯᕐᑲᓚᐅᕐᒥᔪᑦ ᕐᑲᓗᑎᑲᐅᕐᓂᕐᒥᒃ ᕐᑲᔭᑲᐅᕐᓂᕐᒥᒃᓗ ᑭᓲᑦᔪᓯᖅᑲ ᑌᒃᑲᖅ ᑲᔪᐃᓐᓇᐅᔭᕐᓗᐊᕐ ᓗᑎᒃ ᐃᓚᖅᒥ ᐊᑦᓯᕌᖅᒥᓐᓂᕐ ᑲᐅᕿᕐᔪᑯᕐ ᑲᑦᑕᓚᐅᕐᑐᑦ.

During the early spring, we used to start from Aulattivik, our winter camp, and travel by dog team with a small boat on the Qamutik (sled), moving to the spring camp. In those days we used to travel by dog team before the ice broke up.

At the camp, my mother, the children, and the aged grandparents, all had work to do before the long night. We were living only on hunting and trapping where there were no white people. Of course, the children were not going to school. From time to time, the men would go to the settlement to trade their skins.

As you can see in this picture, all of the men and the boys are dressed in European clothing with duffle parkas and socks, only wearing waterproof seal skin spring boots. In those days, the men and women used to wear only duck white material as their parka cover. But, today, you can see colourful Inuit parkas on both men and women when you go up to the North.

You may wonder why the kayak was covered with painted canvas material. It was easier for my mother, with many children, and for Kadluk's wife, to use the sewing machine to sew it together, and then it was painted by the men. Also it was lighter to move around, or to attach to the motor boat when travelling. The paint color was light blue to match the ice, but the frame was built like any other type made in Pond Inlet.

Cont. P. 43

ᐃᓄᐃᑦ ᐱᔪᒪᔪᒥᑦ ᑭᒍᓕᐅᑎᒐᒃᑐᒥᑦ ᑕᒪᓇ ᑭᓇᐅᔭᒃ ᐃᒥᓂᒃ ᐊᒃᑭᒍᓇᑎᓗᒍ ᐊᑲᐅᒋᓂᒋᑦ ᐊᒥᒌᒋᓗᐊᑲᑕᕋᓗᐊᒃᑐᑎᒃ ᓇᒪᑲᑎᒃ. ᐃᓄᐃᑦ ᐱᔪᒪᔪᒥᑦ, ᐃᓗᓇᑕ ᑲᐅᔾᒪᑲᑕ, ᑲᒪᒋᔭᐅ ᓂᐸᒍᑲᑕᑎᐊᑲᑎᐊᒋᑦ ᐃᓄᓂᒃᒥ ᐊᒪᓗ ᐊᑐᑕᐅ ᒋᐸᑕ ᐱᔪᒪᔪᒥᑦ ᐊᑲᐅᒋᓕᑎᔩᐸᑐᑎᒃ ᑲᓄᑐᐃ ᓇᒃ ᐅᓗᐃᑦ ᓈᓕᐊᑎᓗᒋᑦ.

ᑭᓇᐅᔭᑦ ᐊᒋᓂᓕᑦ ᒥᓕᔭᓂ ᐊᑐᑕᐅᐹᐸᑦ ᓇᒪᑐᓂᒃ ᑕᑯᓇᑲᒃᓂᒃ ᐊᒃᑭᑕᐅᔪᑎᓂᒃ ᑲᓗᓇ ᑦ ᓄᓇᑲᓐᓂ ᐊᒪᓗ ᒌᓕ ᒥᓕᔭᑦ ᐊᑐᑕᐅᐹᑭᐳ ᑦ ᑯᕕᐊᒌᑯᓗᒋᑦ ᑲᓗᓇᑦ ᑕᓕᕕᓴᑦ ᑕᑯᓇᑐ ᒋᑦ.

ᐃᓄᐃᑦᓕ ᑭᓯᐊᓂ ᐱᑎᑕᐅᔪᒪᒋᓚᑦ ᒥᑭᔪ ᑲᓗᐊᒥᒃ ᑭᓇᐅᔭᒥᒃ ᑕᐹᑲᑦ ᒥᓕᔭᓂᒃ ᑲᓗ ᓇᓄᑦ ᐊᑐᑕᐅᐹᑐᓄᑦ ᐃᑲᔪᑎᓂᒃ ᐊᒃᑭᒍᑕᓂ ᒃ ᐃᓄᑎᑐᑐᓂᒃ ᑕᓕᕕᓴᑯᑐᓂᒃ ᐃᑲᔪᒪᑎᑲᔭ ᑐᓂᒃ ᐃᓄᓂᒃ ᐊᒋᔪᒥᒃ. ᐊᒌᒪᑎᑦᓕ ᐊᒃᑭ ᐊᑐᓇᒋᓚᒃ ᑐᓂᓯᔭᐅᓗᓂ ᓯᑲᓕᓂᑯᓂᒃ.

ᒌᓕᔪᑎᕕᓯ, ᓯᐱᓯ, ᐃᑲᔪᓂᕋᒃᑐᓯ ᐃᓄ ᐃᑦ ᓄᓇᑲᓐᓂᒃ ᑐᓂᓯᑐᐃᓇᒃᑐᓯ ᐃᓄᓂᒃ ᐃ ᓕᑉᓯ ᓯᑲᓕᓂᑯᒋᓂᒃ?

ᔪᓐᓇᕐᓂᕐᓴᐅᓕᕐᒪᑕ ᓄᓇᓕᖕᓂ ᐱᕖᓕᑦ ᐃᑲᔪᕐᑲᑎᒦᑦ ᑎᐊᕐᓂᐊᕐᑐᒃᓴᐅᒐᓗᐊᕐᐳᑦ ᓇᖏᓂᕐᓗ ᓄᓇᒋᒐᒥᑦᔪᒃ ᐱᔪᓐᓇᕐᓯᔪᓇᕐ ᕿᓯᓕᕐᐸᓪᓕᐊᓗᑎᒃ ᐃᑲᔪᕐᓯᔪᓂᐊᕐ ᑯᔪ ᒥᓇᕐ ᔫᒐᓗᐊᑦ ᖄᑯᐊ ᑎᑎᕋᕐᓯᒪᔪᑦ, ᐅᕐᑲᐅᓯᑦᓚ ᖅᒥᒃᑎᑐᑦ ᐊᑐᕐᐸᓪᓕᐊᕐᓂᕐᓴᐅᓂᐊᕐᒪᑕ.

Two dollar bill

All men have their own taste in making their own wooden sleds or kayak frames. Even if they have the same form, little odds and ends make each one different from the other.

Our View

Yet the Inuit are not even allowed to pinch a part of these millions to help produce some Inutituut programs that will undoubtedly benefit them in a big way. It is pretty hard to satisfy your stomach when you are being offered crumbs.

Really now, CBC, do you really think you are serving the north by giving the Inuit your crumbs?

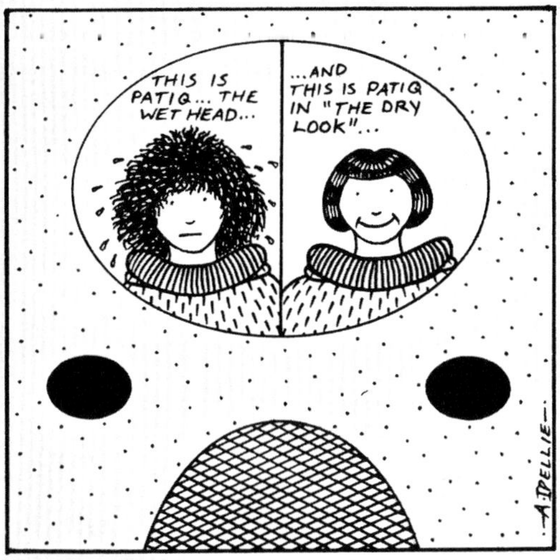

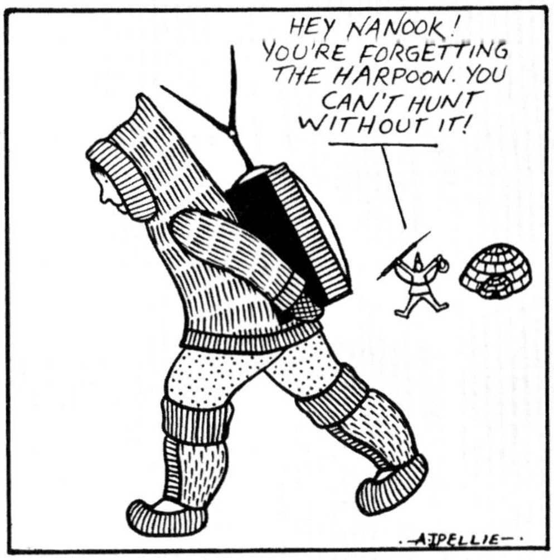

7 The Hunter Returns

1975 · 1990 · 2018–23

Carol Payne with Leah Idlout d'Argencourt Paulson, Lucie Idlout, Paul Ullatitaq Idlout, Susan Salluviniq, Ludy Pudluk, Jacob Anaviapik, Elisapee Ootoova, Ruth Sangoya, Joshua Idlout, and Solomon Awa, as well as contributions by Alexandra Anaviapik, Christina Williamson, and Augatnaaq Eccles

By 1975, seven years after Joseph Idlout's death, the hunter's image was suddenly everywhere. That year, the Bank of Canada issued a new two-dollar bill featuring Idlout and other members of his camp on its verso (see figure 7.1).[1] The bill circulated widely across the country, its image of the Inuit hunters a visual emblem of Canada's claim to sovereignty over the Arctic.[2] But within Inuit communities, the bill held divergent meanings. In October 1975, not long after the bill was printed, Idlout's daughter, Leah Idlout d'Argencourt Paulson, published the article "First Inuit Picture on Canadian Money" in *Inuit Today* magazine, reproduced preceding this chapter. In this article, sparked in part by photographs and by the engraving on the two-dollar bill, she drew on her own knowledge and memory – what is termed *unikkaat* in Inuktitut – to write in loving detail about camp life and her extended family.

Like the photo-based reminiscences by her siblings Paul Ullatitaq Idlout and Susan Salluviniq recounted in the introductory chapter (and revisited later in this chapter), Leah's article is an example of Indigenous relationality. Leah's, Paul's, and Susan's discussions call to mind Opaskwayak Cree scholar Shawn Wilson's argument that Indigenous relationality – with people, the land, cosmology, and epistemology – is central to Indigenous identity.[3] Within Inuit culture more specifically, as Rachel Qitsualik has argued movingly, an Inummarik (lit. "true human") lives in harmonious relation with *imaq* (water), *nuna* (land), *sila* (sky), animals, and people.[4] These harmonious relationships with the environment, seasons, and people are also key components of Inuit Qaujimajatuqangit.[5] Through relationality, Leah Idlout d'Argencourt Paulson's story breathes new life into the banknote image. Whereas in the south the two-dollar bill circulated as a static and colonial rendering of Indigeneity in the service of the settler state, her words and emphasis on relationality transform it into a nuanced and specific portrait of extended family and place, celebrated for their distinctive skills, creativity, and connections.

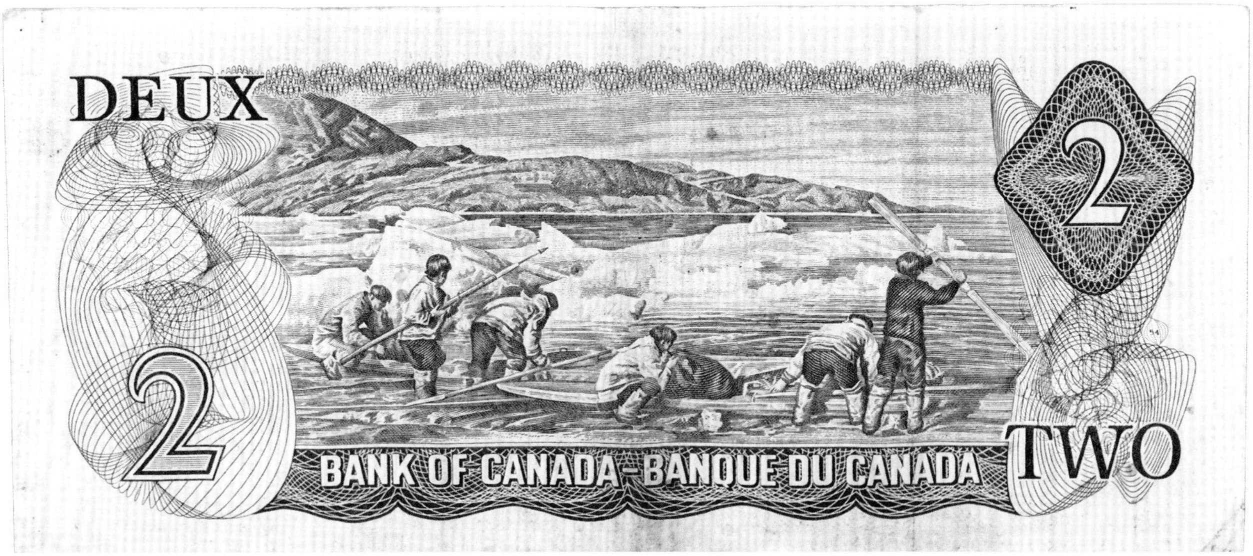

7.1 | Canadian two-dollar bill, 1975. Image courtesy of Mitchell Frank.

Leah's 1975 article "First Inuit Picture on Canadian Money" and recent photo-based encounters by Paul Ullatitaq Idlout and Susan Salluviniq, among others, also confirm scholar Elizabeth Edwards's contention that photographs – and reproductions based on photographs, like the engraving on the 1975 two-dollar bill – themselves are "relational objects."[6] Within this conceptualization, photographs are understood to be not only visual representations with indexical connections to lived experience but also material objects and social actors in a dynamic network of connections and interactions.[7] As Edwards and Martha Langford, among other scholars, have shown in different ways, sensory experience, particularly orality, activates images and shapes meaning.[8] But the images themselves charge this process. Photographs "extend time and space through sets of multiple relationships, their piled-up significances, an aggregate of relationships ... [and] the ways in which photographs exist with their viewers are always, like relationships, dynamic."[9] Through these dynamic relationships, "photographs have divergent, nonlinear, social biographies spread over divergent multiple material originals and multiple, dispersed, and atomized performances."[10]

This chapter traces the "divergent, nonlinear, social biographies" of images depicting Idlout, as well as those credited to him, with an emphasis on photographs and other visual media as sentient, "relational objects" and potential components of Inuit relationality and the Inuit worldview. Specifically, I follow the social biographies of these images through three case studies. The first examines the 1975 Canadian two-dollar bill, with its engraving after a Wilkinson photograph depicting Idlout and members of his camp, as well as the subsequent reception of this image, particularly by Idlout's daughter Leah Idlout d'Argencourt Paulson in her article reproduced before this chapter. The second case study also examines southern-made images of Idlout and members of his camp, here in their remediation for the 1990 documentary *Between Two Worlds*, which exposes governmental policy impacting Inuit in part through archival images. In these two case studies, the meanings of images depicting Idlout shifted dramatically from markers of Canadian settler authority to focal points for a critique of this authority and its role in Sangussaqtauliqtillut, or disruption. The chapter culminates with its third and final case study, a discussion of how Idlout's descendants (including Paul Ullatitaq Idlout and Susan Salluviniq) and other community members are reactivating photographs credited to Idlout today. This reactivation also includes the online exhibition *Ajjiliurlagit ("Let me take your picture"): The Photographs of Joseph Idlout*, co-curated by Inuk historian, curator, and educator Augatnaaq Eccles and me, which is introduced in chapter 3. Reflecting a resurgence of interest today in Inuit history as told by Inuit themselves, Idlout's images have great significance for the hunter's descendants, community members, and others across the Qikiqtani region. As relational objects, they represent reclaimed histories and confirm Inuit survivance. However, this Inuit account of the Sangussaqtauliqtilluta period remains entangled with the south through Qallunaat researchers like me. It is a collaborative retelling.

With this chapter, *The Hunter, The Crown, and The Cameras* returns to recent history. As explained in the introductory chapter, the book's circular narrative structure is intended to honour and learn from nonlinear or cyclical modes of representing the past that are often a feature of Inuit culture. Privileging present readings also effectively demotes official governmental narratives of the 1950s; they are no longer the central authoritative statements in this story. Instead, in returning to the present – and, more specifically, in featuring contemporary Inuit reframings of historical images – I want to privilege Inuit voices and their tellings of history. As I have argued before, photographs and films exist not only in a past tense but are also relational objects that continue to engage in the dynamics of historical consciousness and thus potentially play roles in Inuit relationality. This chapter – and the book as a whole – closes with Elders' and family members' relational experiences with Idlout's photographs. Rather than offering a conventional conclusion, this chapter signals that both the story of the Inuit and the family history in these photographs will continue to be told.

Circulation and Currency: Idlout's Image on the 1975 Canadian Two-Dollar Bill

Leah Idlout d'Argencourt Paulson wrote her 1975 *Inuit Today* article "First Inuit Picture on Canadian Money" in response to the federal Canadian government issuing a two-dollar bill depicting Idlout and some of the men and boys of his camp preparing for the hunt. The image on the 1975 two-dollar bill was based on one of dozens of photographs that Wilkinson and cameraman Jean Roy shot in 1951 during the filming of *Land of the Long Day* (1952). These photographs included production stills, images of re-enactments made on set to depict an actual scene in the motion picture and a crucial part of film promotion.[11] The

NFB circulated production stills during Idlout's lifetime and in the years following his death in order to promote *Land of the Long Day* and other films (see figures 2.1 and 2.11). They also circulated in a range of publications by the Still Photography Division of the National Film Board of Canada (NFB), demonstrating the inherent mobility of the photographic image.[12]

The source image for the 1975 two-dollar bill, now in the collection of the Bank of Canada Museum, appears to have been a more spontaneous image, one not initially used for subsequent NFB publications (see figure 7.2).[13] Originally a colour transparency, it was among the images that Wilkinson maintained in his own collection. He used transparencies to illustrate public talks and perhaps projected this one during an address that he gave to members of the Arctic Circle club in Ottawa in April 1952.[14]

This specific photograph pictures six male members of the camp, boys and men, preparing for the hunt. The filmmaker shot numerous images of the collective work associated with the hunt, reflecting a narrative emphasis on seasonal labours throughout the film *Land of the Long Day*. The scene depicted in this photograph resembles preparations for the film's climactic second hunting

7.2 | Inuit hunters, c. 1952. Photo: Doug Wilkinson.

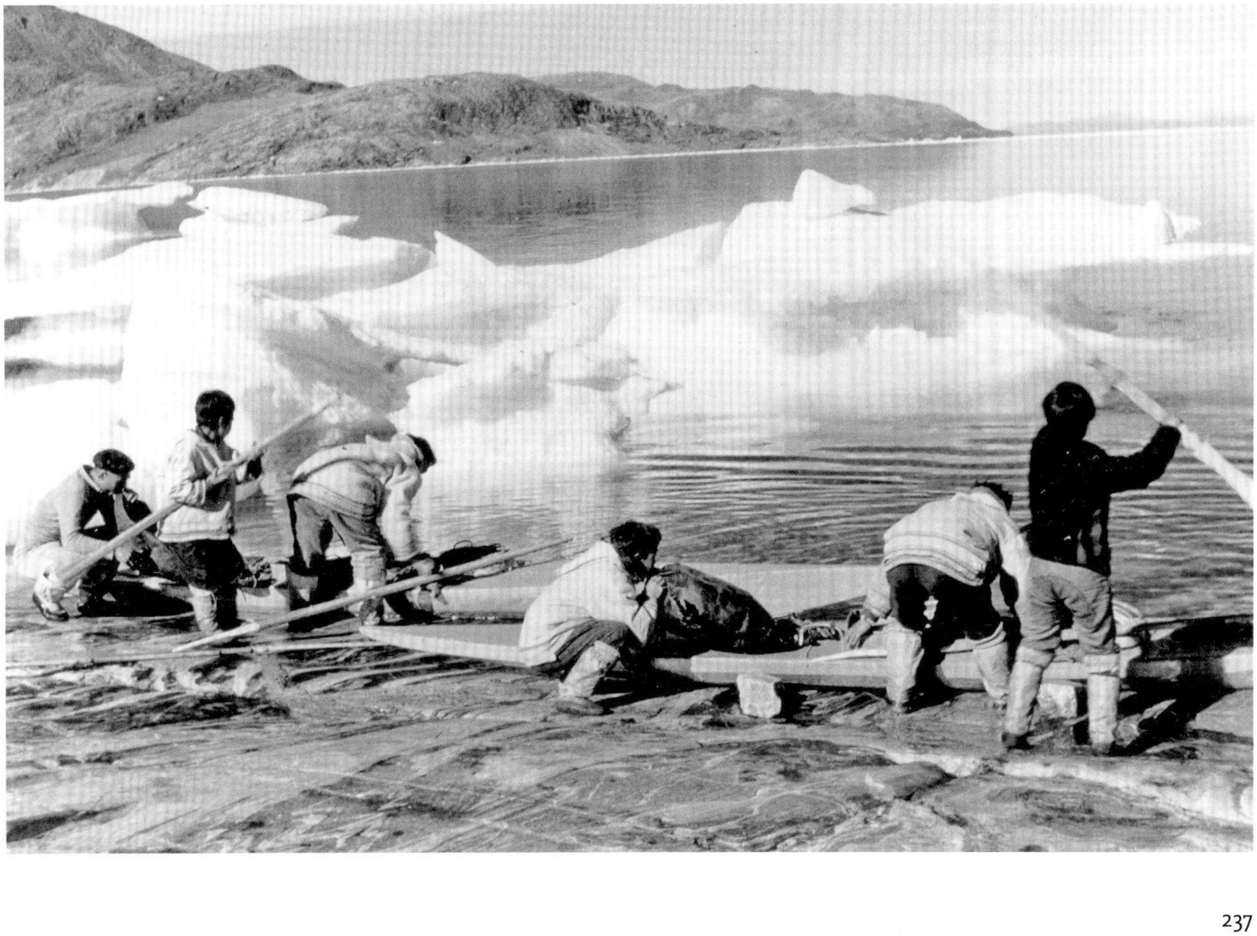

scene, in which Idlout and Kadloo hunt white whales and narwhals from their *qajait* (kayaks). Here, most of the figures wear duffel coats with *kamiik* (boots) protecting their feet from the wet. They crouch or stand at the shore before a pair of *qajait*. Two of the figures have paddles, one hoists a harpoon, two others each inflate an *avataq* (sealskin float), and the final figure grasps the edge of a *qajaq*. The men and boys are fully engaged in this demanding work. Indeed, their faces are averted from the gaze of the camera; instead, focusing on their tasks or looking toward an iceberg in the mid distance, they seem to anticipate the hunt to follow.

With its wide horizontal axis, Wilkinson's composition is at once expansive and intimate. The figures fill the near foreground in a loose line from the near lower right to the far left, where they extend farther into the picture plane. A harpoon and a paddle raised by figures at left and right respectively frame the view and focus our attention toward the sea ice.

Wilkinson shot this photograph on shore, positioned behind the six men. Limited depth of field and the positioning of the figures across the foreground have the effect of collapsing space and creating a sense of the sea ice bearing down on the figures. By adopting a vantage point relatively close to the hunters, Wilkinson constructs the drama of the scene while enhancing the intimacy of shared labour. In effect, the photographer/filmmaker – and the eventual viewer of the image – seem to look upon the scene from the same crouching posture adopted by some of the men and boys pictured. And, like them, we seem to look out toward the looming sea ice preparing for the drama of the hunt.

Notably, unlike in many images credited to Idlout, all of the figures pictured are turned away from the camera. Initially, this seems to deny the productive possibilities of the returned gaze, which – as argued throughout this book – disrupts and contests colonial claims to authority through visuality. Instead, this specific photograph – like many of the promotional images that Wilkinson shot – is composed so that the intended southern viewer's consumption of "traditional" Inuit life is uncontested. In this way, conceived through the lens of colonial and ethnographic distance, the photograph constructs a visual narrative of Inuit resourcefulness, cooperation, and masculinity in a demanding natural environment. And, of course, none of these men and boys were identified on the iconic piece of currency; turned away from the camera, they could be consumed as types, not historic individuals.

As a tableau appearing on a federal banknote, this image was framed by Canadian national and settler-colonial identity. Wilkinson sold all copies of this colour transparency and its rights to the Bank of Canada in the mid-1960s, years before it was issued on the banknote.[15] The 1975 two-dollar bill was part of a series of new banknotes called Scenes of Canada issued between 1969 and 1970.[16] The Bank of Canada innovated with this series by printing in multicoloured tints (the two-dollar bill, for example, was printed in terracotta) and by exclusively using photographs as source material for the engravings. The bank argued

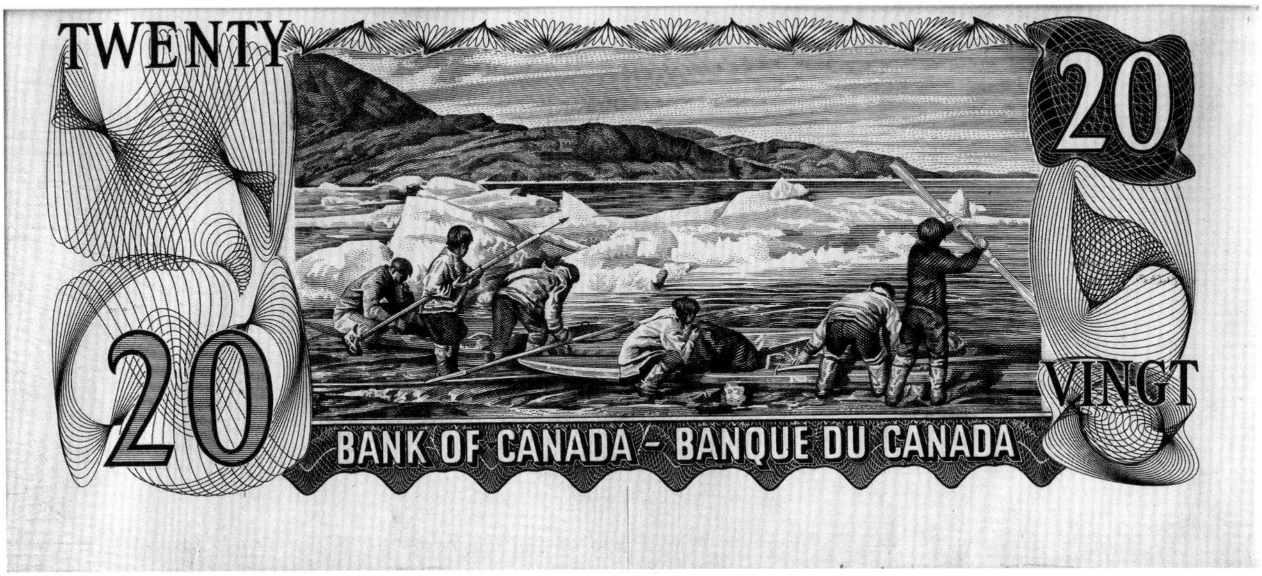

7.3 | Bank of Canada printing proof, twenty dollars, 1971.

that photographic verisimilitude would render counterfeit reproductions easier to detect.[17] Artists translated the source photographic images into engravings, modifying them. Here, artist C. Gordon Yorke recrafted Wilkinson's photograph (see figure 7.3).[18] In order to align with the particular format of the banknote, Yorke elevated the vantage point slightly and diminished the open sea. But the figures were reproduced faithfully after the photograph.[19]

Each illustration in the Scenes of Canada series featured a scenic vignette of activity from across the country. Bank guidelines mandated that images adhere to the "wide shallow proportions" of the notes, have substantial detail and contrast in order to translate well to an engraving, possess a "pleasant, essentially pictorial character" without being "pictorial 'cliches,'" and depict subjects that are "as widely distributed across the country as possible."[20] The resulting illustrations ranged from views of lumbering on the Ottawa River ($1 bill) and the Polymer Corporation in Sarnia, Ontario ($10 bill), to the musical ride of the Royal Canadian Mounted Police (RCMP) ($50 bill) and Lunenburg Harbour ($100 bill).[21] The scenes reproduced predominant conceptualizations of the Canadian settler state as simultaneously bucolic, prosperous, and ordered. The routine repetition of these visual tropes on currency reinforced the values to which they alluded.[22] In this way, they visually replicated the values extolled by the federal government during the 1970s, which had been voiced decades earlier by prominent figures like Prime Minister Louis St-Laurent and Governor General Vincent Massey, as discussed earlier in this book.[23]

The 1975 two-dollar bill was ubiquitous. In southern Canada of the mid-1970s, two dollars was enough to buy a large meal at a fast-food restaurant or 14 litres of gas. Millions of southern Canadians habitually pulled a two-dollar bill from their purses, wallets, or pockets, exchanging it for small purchases while they glanced absent-mindedly over the Arctic scene depicted. But in the Qikiqtani region, where two dollars had notably less buying power than it did in the south, the image of Idlout's camp on the new bill was the subject of more focused attention.

In October 1975, the hunter's daughter Leah, then an editor at *Inuit Today* magazine, published the essay about the two-dollar bill reproduced preceding this chapter.[24] "First Inuit Picture on Canadian Money" appeared in both syllabics and English. The article's opening page contains an illustration of the banknote by Inuk artist Alootook Ipellie and a photograph taken with Idlout's camera of a hunted polar bear.[25] The next page includes a photograph of Kidlak and an unidentified woman credited to Idlout and a second image apparently showing the cinematographer Jean Roy filming.

Leah reframes the photograph of the six figures used on the two-dollar bill in terms of the distinct tradition of Inuit story work. Indeed, she opens the essay by announcing, "This is a story." What follows is a narrative prompted by the image and drawing on her own personal memory of events. In short, the essay is an example of photo-based *unikkaat,* or *inuusirmingnik unikkaat,* defined by Keavy Martin as Inuit life stories based on personal experiences.[26] In recent writing, Beth Greenhorn, Deborah Kigjugalik Webster, Christina Williamson, and I have employed the term photo-based *unikkaat* to understand the ways that Inuit renarrate southern photographs, translating colonial visuality into Inuit story work.[27] Photo-based *unikkaat* is characterized by specificity and the ability to develop a story prompted by, but not limited to, the representational form of the photograph. Importantly, it is also rooted in Inuit understandings of Indigenous relationality. This rootedness is seen in Rachel Qitsualik's discussion of how an Inummarik (lit. "true human") lives in relational harmony with *imaq* (water), *nuna* (land), and *sila* (sky).[28] It also reflects Opaskwayak Cree scholar Shawn Wilson's description of relationality: "Identity for Indigenous peoples is grounded in their relationships with the land, with their ancestors who have returned to the land and with future generations who will come into being on the land. Rather than viewing ourselves as being in relationship with other people or things, we are the relationships that we hold and are part of."[29] Leah's story exemplifies Inuit relationality and the holistic Inuit worldview defined by her niece, Rachel Qitsualik. Speaking directly to the reader, Leah engages in a conversation that is precise in its details and reflects her deep relationships to the land and to the people depicted. Writing from personal experience, she recounts events and activities during her childhood at the camps in Aulattivik and in Nuvurulua. She identifies all of the figures in the banknote image and how they are related to her: "my brother-in-law Gideon Qitsualik, Peter Paniloo my brother. Herodier Kadluk second cousin, Paul Idlout brother, Joseph Idlout my late father, and Elijah Erkloo my cousin." Although faced away from the camera, the figures were readily identifiable to her, as they were to members of their extended family and others in the area.[30] Indeed, Leah Idlout d'Argencourt

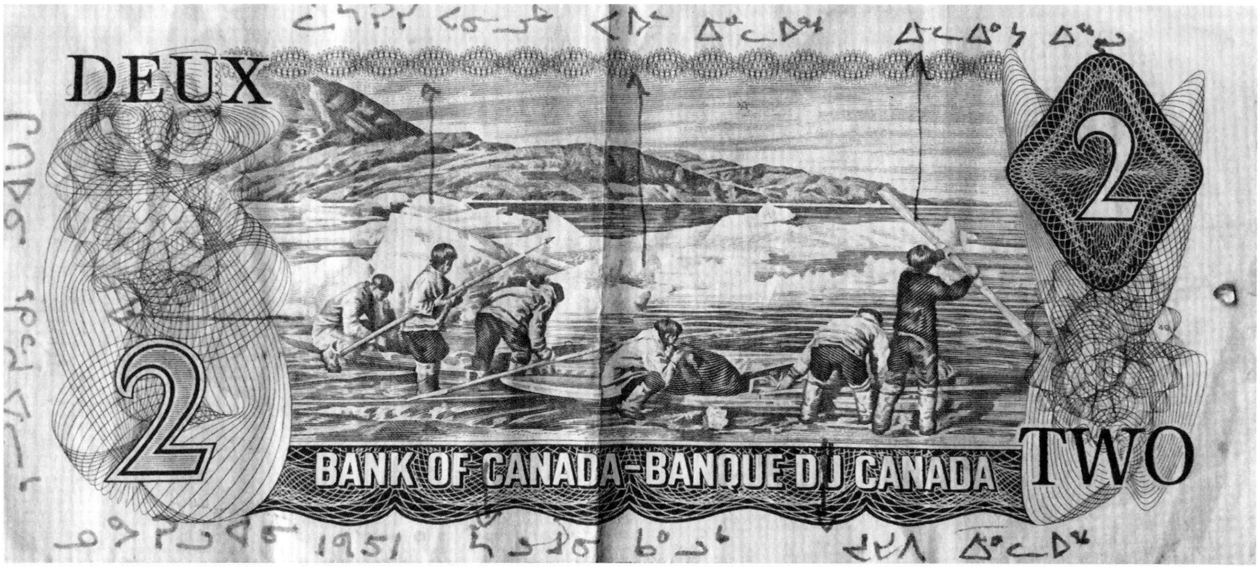

Paulson had identified all the figures directly on a bill, now in the collection of John MacDonald (see figure 7.4).[31]

7.4 | Canadian two-dollar bill annotated by Leah Idlout d'Argencourt Paulson with identifications of the figures depicted. From left to right: Gideon Qitsualik, Lazarus Paniluk Peter Paniloo, Solomon Kalluk, Paul Ullattitaq Idlout, Joseph Idlout, and Elijah Erkloo.

The article also reframes the two-dollar bill visually. As she did periodically in her publications for *Inuit Today*, Leah reproduces some of her father's own photographs. We see camp members hauling a polar bear carcass to shore (see figure 3.1), Kidlak and another woman standing before drying sealskins (see figure 3.12), and an image possibly of Doug Wilkinson looking through the viewfinder of his own camera. The three photographs are not explicitly credited, but like the illustration of the banknote by Alootook Ipellie, they emphasize Inuit vision.

Idlout d'Argencourt Paulson describes the skin *kamiik* worn by all of the figures, while also clarifying that although the photograph would have been perceived as a pre-contact scene in the south, all are in fact wearing "European clothing," apart from the *kamiik*. She engages with relations to the land, framing her story geographically and temporally. For example, she explains that the scene took place in 1951 at their spring camp in Nuvurulua on North Baffin Island, about 50 kilometres west of Pond Inlet/Mittimatalik, in the midst of narwhal-hunting season. Leah explains details of the hunt. Her father and Kadluk would go hunting by *qajaq*, with the other men and boys following in other boats. She tells of the work required before the hunt, including Paul Ullatitaq Idlout and Gideon Qitsualik inflating the two *avataaq*. Leah looks beyond the frame of the photograph to describe broader contexts for the scene. We learn, for example, how the family travelled from their winter camp in Aulattivik by *qamutik* (sled) to the spring camp and how they lived by hunting and trapping, only rarely visiting settlements.

Idlout d'Argencourt Paulson also infuses her story with the contributions of unseen women and girls (like her) to the labours of camp life and the hunt by including the photograph of Kidlak and another woman (see figure 3.12). Leah also highlights less visible work by women: "You may wonder why the *qajaq* was covered with painted canvas material. It was easier for my mother, with many children, and for Kadluk's wife, to use the sewing machine to sew it together, and then it was painted by the men. Also it was lighter to move around or to attach to the motor boat when travelling. The paint color was light blue to match the ice, but the frame was built like any other type made in Pond Inlet."[32] The story closes with Leah insisting on the specificity of the scene and Inuit hunting skills: "All men have their own taste in making their own wooden sleds or *qajaq* frames. Even if they have the same form, little odds and ends make each one different from the other."[33]

This 1975 article, published during the same year that the two-dollar bill first circulated, reframes the meaning of the image that it reproduced. What the federal government presented to southerners as a classic settler-colonial rendering of Indigenous life meant to stand as a marker of national sovereignty became – through Leah's story work – a loving remembrance of family, culture, and community.

With the circulation of the two-dollar bill, Gideon Qitsualik, Peter Paniloo, Herodier Kadluk, Paul Ullatitaq Idlout, Joseph Idlout, and Elijah Erkloo became celebrities. Some of the surviving boys and men enjoyed their new-found renown.[34] Kadluk recounted to journalist Nellie Erkloo, daughter of Elijah Erkloo, "It was our chance to show other Canadians something of our life here. I'm very happy they did it ... When I saw the two-dollar bill later on, I sort of jumped from shock. Holy smoke, I was on the picture. I had no idea and it never crossed my mind that a part of the film would be depicted on the two-dollar bill. When I saw it, I was just happy about it. The sudden realization and nostalgia – when I recognized the picture – of that day that we were filmed out near Aulatseevik [Aulattivik], all came back to me."[35] They autographed banknotes for friends and strangers alike. Peter Paniloo, for example, recalled to Nellie Erkloo that he was flown to southern Canada by the Nunasi Corporation to sign bills as part of a promotional event.[36] The men in the photograph and others collected the two-dollar bill as souvenirs.[37]

But the two-dollar bill also became the subject of contestation. By 1982, some of the people depicted and their descendants noted with irony that although their likeness had been imprinted on countless financial transactions, they themselves had never been compensated.[38] As Maudie Qitsualik, daughter of Gideon Qitsualik and granddaughter of Joseph Idlout, told reporter Peter Howell, "The Canadian government used it without anybody's permission and no one was paid a thing."[39] Elijah Erkloo recounted to his daughter, the journalist Nellie Erkloo, "Although our picture was on the two-dollar note, when one has no money or when one does not have a two-dollar bill, being depicted on a banknote had absolutely no use for us."[40] (Wilkinson, who had not been informed when the banknote was published, appears to be the only person paid, having sold the transparency and rights to the Bank of Canada in the 1960s.[41]) John Crust of the *Winnipeg Sun* quoted an anonymous official with the Bank of Canada claiming that because "you couldn't identify any individual unless you had the original photograph," there was "no case for financial compensation."[42] Clearly, Leah Idlout d'Argencourt Paulson's story demonstrates how wrong this argument was; even with their backs turned to the camera, all of the figures were recognizable, identifiable, known.

The two-dollar bill would continue to be a focal point of discussion for years to come.[43] In 2014, the musician Lucie Idlout – a daughter of Leah and granddaughter of Idlout – discussed the 1975 two-dollar bill in a radio program aired by the Canadian Broadcasting Corporation (CBC).[44] Almost forty years had passed since the Bank of Canada had issued the note, which was subsequently replaced by other designs and eventually by a series of coins (the toonie) issued through the Royal Canadian Mint.[45] But the image still prompted a vivid story of Inuit struggles and resilience. Lucie addressed the image on the two-dollar bill in terms of her forebears coerced relocation to Resolute/Qausuittuq only four years after Wilkinson's initial photograph was shot. She told the CBC, "I don't think there's any coincidence the photograph was shot in the 50s, just before the relocation ... It is another example of how Inuit were part of asserting sovereignty over different parts – so Canada could claim it as their own." Lucie's account of the two-dollar bill ends with a note of what Indigenous scholar Gerald Vizenor terms "survivance."[46] She states that the image on the bill "became less of a photo and more of a piece of our history – that involved important people from my family and people I love very much."[47]

Between Two Worlds

If tracing the history of the two-dollar bill revealed a "social biography" that comprised ethnographic imaging, nationalist discourse, and Inuit restorying, other images of Joseph Idlout became more explicit catalysts in colonial critique. In 1990, Idlout was the subject of the Investigative Productions documentary *Between Two Worlds* (see figure 7.5).[48] Told in part through archival film footage and still photographs, the film circulated the hunter's image internationally. Screened at film festivals from New York to Hawaii and Leningrad, it reached even larger audiences through broadcasts in the United Kingdom, Australia, Japan, Sweden, and Germany as well as across Canada.[49] But rather than standing as a nationalist emblem, Idlout's life story and likeness are deployed in *Between Two Worlds* in an effort to expose the events of Sangussaqtauliqtilluta. Indeed, at the time, the film was one of the most trenchant southern public history critiques of Canadian settler colonialist treatment of Inuit and specifically of the High Arctic relocations; in many respects, *Between Two Worlds* is a model

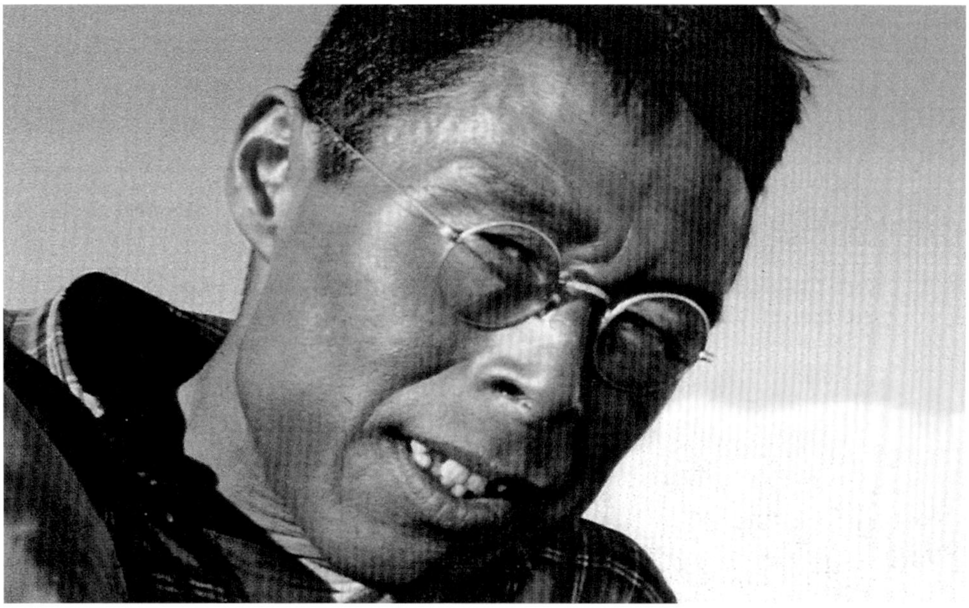

7.5 | Portrait of Idlout on the case of the DVD release of *Between Two Worlds* (1990). Photo: Doug Wilkinson.

for reaching large audiences while privileging Inuit perspectives and restorying the southern record.

Between Two Worlds is ostensibly a cinematic biography of Joseph Idlout. Director Barry Greenwald, producer Peter Raymont, and writer/co-producer Barbara Sears recreate the hunter's life from the early 1950s until his death through a dynamic mix of archival film stock and still photographs, contemporary footage, and voice-over narration. Along the way, they also introduce the viewer to contemporary life in Pond Inlet/Mittimatalik and Resolute/Qausuittuq. Clips from contemporary interviews are interspersed throughout the film, providing more instances of relationality. The most prominent is commentary by Idlout's son Peter Paniloo filmed in Pond Inlet/Mittimatalik; but the filmmakers also interviewed residents Elijah Erkloo, who grew up at Idlout's camp, and Elder Elisapee Ootoova. All three speak in Inuktitut, accompanied by English subtitles. Finally, in a fourth interview, Doug Wilkinson recounts his memories of Idlout.

Archival photographs and film clips are integral to the film's critical reexamination of history.[50] Raymont had earlier explored this theme in his 1981 documentary *Magic in the Sky*, which also provided a history of how Inuit have been photographed and filmed by Qallunaat.[51] In the 1990 film *Between Two Worlds*, the filmmakers include a brief history of how popular imaging of Inuit has long perpetuated stereotypes, featuring footage from a 1901 Thomas Edison film and clips from Robert Flaherty's *Nanook of the North* (1922).[52] Other contextual footage was gathered from Library and Archives Canada (then known as the National Archives), including footage of the Northwest Passage and a 1954 newsreel of Idlout receiving a Coronation Medal.[53] In addition, the filmmakers secured private film footage shot by Doug Wilkinson, now in the Nunavut Archives, that depicted Idlout's home in Resolute/Qausuittuq, including a scene of Kidlak pouring tea; these scenes were clearly shot for the NFB newsreel *Eskimo Village, Resolute* (1963). Similarly, a number of Wilkinson's still photographs are reproduced in *Between Two Worlds*. The NFB was the key source for the remaining archival film footage,[54] which included contextual material such as the 1901 Edison footage, 1922 footage from the RCMP's Eastern Arctic Expedition, and 1922 footage of Joseph-Elzéar Bernier's expedition, as well as footage from films made contemporaneously to Idlout's life.[55] The filmmakers mainly used footage of Idlout and his camp, most shot by Wilkinson, including the newsreels *Easter in Canadian Arctic* (1955) and *Resolute: Eskimo Village* (1960).[56] But above all, the film featured footage from Wilkinson's *Land of the Long Day*. In total, almost seven minutes from the 1952 feature film appear in *Between Two Worlds*;[57] indeed, in addition to a retelling of Idlout's life, the film is a reconsideration of *Land of the Long Day*.

Supported by this archival footage, the film's focus on Inuit experience reflects cultural approaches of the 1980s and 1990s to represent greater cultural diversity, including an emphasis on Indigenous cultures.[58] Its critique of governmental interventions in Inuit lives situates *Between Two Worlds* in a broader current of anti-institutional advocacy in documentary cinema.[59]

Between Two Worlds employs some of the familiar devices of expository documentary cinema to tell Idlout's story. The film guides viewers and creates cohesion with the aid of a seemingly authoritative and anonymized male voice-of-God narration. Spoken by the writer, actor, and filmmaker William Whitehead, the narration provides links between the components of the film and regularly reiterates the film's central argument. Early in the film, for example, we are told of Idlout and other men at his camp that "during their lifetime, they would see one way of life disappear and another replace it. They are men who have lived in two worlds."[60] References to being caught "between two worlds" become a refrain, repeated throughout the film and linking the action. Evidentiary editing further creates cohesion in the film, compressing temporal duration and organizing the brief clips of archival film stock, still photographs, contemporary film footage, and interviews to advance the overall argument of cultural disconnection. The sounds of Inuktitut conversation, snowmobile engines, dogs barking, and newsreel soundtracks provide auditory texture and a sense of immersion for the viewer. The visual and audio sources are consistently marshalled in support of the film's didactic intention to expose the impact that southern interactions and specifically the High Arctic relocations had on Inuit lives. The majority of the archival film clips and stills were made under the auspices of the NFB.

The narrative arc of *Between Two Worlds* follows the structure of tragic drama. The film begins with Idlout's death. The opening title sequence features a snowmobile racing across the ice directly toward the static camera. As the approaching vehicle fills the screen and the volume of its engine reaches a crescendo, the narrator intones, "Joseph Idlout, an Inuk living in Resolute Bay, was last seen alive shortly after 1 a.m. June the 2nd, 1968. At 4 a.m. Idlout's daughter called the Royal Canadian Mounted Police to say her father had not come home. The police began a search and Idlout was found dead late that afternoon. His skidoo had gone over a 35 foot cliff. An investigation was conducted and the coroner decided that an inquest was not required. Idlout was buried on the 5th of June at 10 p.m. What the coroner could not say was what lay behind the death of Joseph Idlout."[61] This opening sequence coaches the viewer to experience Idlout's life story as tragedy.

The following scenes establish the hunter as a heroic figure and then, with slowly building tension, narrate his fall. The film presents Idlout's acumen as a hunter through clips from *Land of the Long Day* and newsreels dating from the early 1950s, interspersed with footage from present-day Pond Inlet/Mittimatalik. Recollections of the camp by Paniloo, Wilkinson, and Erkloo animate the archival source material while establishing Idlout's skill and intelligence. With footage and still images from *Land of the Long Day* on screen, the hunter's son Paniloo recalls, "My father used to say that when you were trying to catch an animal you had to take it seriously. If you saw an animal you were not supposed to rush or panic. When you panic, the animal can sense it too. And when you do it calmly, the animal is calm too. My father had the ability to do it very well because he was aware of what had to be done properly. He knew how to hunt well because he did it carefully. That's why he was a great hunter." Doug Wilkinson commends Idlout: "I really don't remember ever seeing a more confident, a more, a more successful appearing human being in all my life."

Increasingly, the film's narrative turns bleak. The collapse of the fox fur trade, the arrival of southern bureaucracy, and the establishment of mandatory schooling are recounted by Elisapee Ootoova, Elijah Erkloo, and Peter Paniloo. Ironically, the filmmakers pair their recollections of hardship with archival governmental footage extolling changes in Inuit lives. The disconnect between these southern views and memory of Inuit lived experience underscores the film's overall theme. Inuit life has been altered irrevocably and Idlout's confidence shaken. The final twenty minutes of *Between Two Worlds*, culminating in the film's dramatic climax, are set in Resolute/Qausuittuq. In footage that Wilkinson shot there for newsreels, we see Idlout at first adapt to life at the margins of the High Arctic military base, where we are told, "What amounts to a policy of apartheid is maintained."[62] The film concludes as it began, with Idlout's death in 1968. The narrator notes that officially it was considered an accident, although Paniloo, after examining the snowmobile tracks, asserted that it was a suicide. The film's final words are spoken by Paniloo, who hums a song that they used to sing at camp called "I Want to Go Back to the Way We Were." He laments, "I know we can't go back to those times, and I know we can't go back to our younger days. We can't help growing old even though we want to stay young.

It seemed as if everything around us was good, and everyone was happy. But you can't be like that forever."

Between Two Worlds struck a powerful affective chord with viewers. It won several awards and largely glowing reviews.[63] Many of the film's intended viewers, southern and international audiences, likely would have learned for the first time about the impact of the relocations and other government policies on Inuit through the film. In this regard, *Between Two Worlds* effectively restoried the southern record and created broad awareness. The filmmakers' decision to structure *Between Two Worlds* as a tragedy, framed by Joseph Idlout's death, reflected approaches in the 1990s. Doing so allowed them to transmit a message about the relocations in powerful and affecting ways. With *Between Two Worlds*, Idlout became associated with the injustice of the relocations and the power of protest.

Yet, despite the film's emphasis on a tragic framing, what Unangax scholar Eve Tuck terms the "complexity, contradiction, and the self-determination of lived lives" is evident throughout *Between Two Worlds*.[64] Self-determination is heard in the words of Paniloo, Erkloo, and Ootoova. For example, before the film's action turns to Resolute/Qausuittuq, Paniloo reflects on the sharing of Inuit knowledge: "Some Inuit had great knowledge too. The person with the gift of a certain knowledge would be the one to deal with whatever needed to be done. If this person had knowledge about life, he would be followed in his instructions. If this person had knowledge about the land, people would follow his instructions. This is the same as a person with a doctor's degree. Even today there are some Inuit like that."[65] Interventions like Paniloo's remind the viewer of the agency of Inuit and that their lives are not defined by concepts of harm. Paniloo's comments relate to "survivance," the well-known concept coined by Gerald Vizenor. As Vizenor writes,

> The character of survivance creates a sense of native presence over absence, nihility, and victimry. Native survivance is an active sense of presence over absence, deracination, and oblivion; survivance is the continuance of stories, not a mere reaction, however pertinent. Survivance is greater than the right of a survivable name. Survivance stories are renunciations of dominance, detractions, obtrusions, the unbearable sentiments of tragedy and the legacy of victimry. Survivance is the heritable right of succession or reversion of an estate and, in the course of international declarations of human rights, is a narrative estate of native survivance.[66]

I argue that Inuit agency and survivance are also embedded within the archival footage and still images that appear in *Between Two Worlds*, just as they are embedded within the featured interviews. They are seen through "visual excesses," images that point toward experiences and meanings beyond the control of the photographer or filmmaker.[67] When Idlout gazes back at the camera, the fullness of his life disrupts ethnographic film's othering and reaches out to the viewers across the history of *Between Two Worlds'* reception.

Between Two Worlds, like the archival images that it remediates, had its own social biography. After the film's production and world premieres, the NFB obtained nonexclusive Canadian educational distribution rights to *Between Two Worlds*.[68] In 2011, it was selected as one of sixty films to be made widely accessible when the NFB launched the collection *Unikkausivut: Sharing Our Stories*.[69] Schools across Nunavut, for example, were given free access to the films, and the Government of Nunavut's Department of Education – working in collaboration with the NFB and the Inuit Relations Directorate of Aboriginal Affairs and Northern Development Canada – developed an educational resource guide to accompany them. The guide reframes the selected NFB films in terms of the eight principles of Inuit Qaujimajatuqangit (IQ).[70] The guide and films are also organized around the themes of Inuit history, Inuit culture, Arctic geography and environment, and changes and challenges in the north. Discussions of each theme include suggestions of NFB films, guiding questions, media literacy approaches, classroom activities, and activities beyond the classroom. *Between Two Worlds* is a suggested film for the theme of changes and challenges in the north. An understanding of the history of cultural conflict – including the High Arctic relocations – is presented as knowledge that will aid cultural revitalization efforts.[71] Educators developing the curriculum guide directed discussion toward a balance between IQ and southern-based knowledges as well as a discussion on Inuit representation in decision making.[72] Subsequent viewings of and discussions about *Between Two Worlds* – including the educational curriculum developed for *Unikkausivut* – demonstrate the power of reception to reframe meanings.

The Hunter's Photographs Return

There is a brief episode twenty-three minutes into *Between Two Worlds* with another hint at Idlout's own returned gaze. As the film slowly zooms in on a still colour image of Idlout removing supplies from his motorboat, the narrator recites a litany of Idlout's material acquisitions: "He has a thirty-five foot motor boat, the only one in the region. He has two *qajait*, one rowboat, three tents, three hundred traps, four sleds, thirty dogs, nine rifles and a camera."[73]

"A camera" – the final, culminating item on this list of material wealth – signals Idlout's success both as a hunter and in terms of southern material accumulation. But, as this book has shown, the hunter's Kodak Duaflex was not merely a consumer product but also a tool through which Idlout represented his own family, community, and Inuit culture while returning the gaze of southerners. And like the images used on the two-dollar bill and in *Between Two Worlds*, Idlout's own photographs continue to exist and touch viewers, particularly Inuit viewers, today. For the hunter's son Paul Ullatitaq Idlout and daughter Susan

Salluviniq, and for several other family members and Elders, seeing Idlout's photographs brought them back to life at camp in the 1950s, and their recollections have in turn reanimated the photographs. These conversations will continue through the online exhibition *Ajjiliurlagit ("Let me take your picture"): The Photographs of Joseph Idlout*, co-curated by Augatnaaq Eccles and me, with the collaboration Idlout family members and the Nunavut Archives.

Most of the interviews about Idlout's photographs were conducted in 2018 in Nunavut at Pond Inlet/Mittimatalik and at Iqaluit by Alexandra Anaviapik (a biological great-granddaughter of Idlout), historian Christina Williamson, and me. Pond Inlet/Mittimatalik is a thriving community of about 1,500. Prized for its breathtaking scenery, it has become a popular stop for cruise ships and ever-increasing numbers of tourists, phones and cameras in hand. The hamlet's *Community Guidelines* advise visitors, "We invite you to take pictures of our beautiful scenery and our community, but please ask permission before taking pictures of us, our children or our homes."[74] The photograph remains a space of contestation in the community.

In Pond Inlet/Mittimatalik, we spoke with Ludy Pudluk (now deceased), a son of Kadloo and Leetia who had grown up at Idlout's camp; Joshua Idlout, one of Idlout's grandsons; and the Elders and knowledge keepers Elisapee Ootoova (now deceased), Jacob Anaviapik, and Ruth Sangoya. We also spoke at the Nattinak Visitors Centre in Pond Inlet/Mittimatalik with a group of Elders that included Elijah Erkloo and Daniel Komangapik, both of whom had been adopted by Idlout's parents and, like Ludy Pudluk, had grown up at Idlout's camp. In Iqaluit, also in 2018, Christina Williamson and I interviewed Paul Ullatitaq Idlout as well as Solomon Awa, an Elder and knowledge keeper in Pond Inlet/Mittimatalik. After a long pause precipitated by Covid-19 restrictions and personal circumstances, Eccles and I conducted the final interview in 2023 with Susan Salluviniq in Ottawa at my home.

All of the participants responded to photographs in the interviews, most by viewing photo albums, although we also projected images in the group gathering and used individual photographs. The albums that Elders and family members viewed were modest, being mass-produced binders fitted with plastic sleeves into which we had inserted dozens of photographs (see figures 7.6 and 7.7). They had been printed from digital files in the Douglas E. Wilkinson fonds with permission of the Nunavut Archives. During our meetings and interviews, many of the photographs' subjects were identified. Brightly coloured sticky notes covered the plastic sleeves with the names of sitters in English and Inuktitut syllabics. We prepared copies of all the photographs for Elders, who were also paid as participants.[75] With great generosity, they shared their ideas with us and with viewers of the online exhibition.

The participating Elders and descendants saw themselves, family, and friends as children and young adults decades before. Throughout the interviews, they recalled life on the land and, to a lesser extent, the changes that occurred in

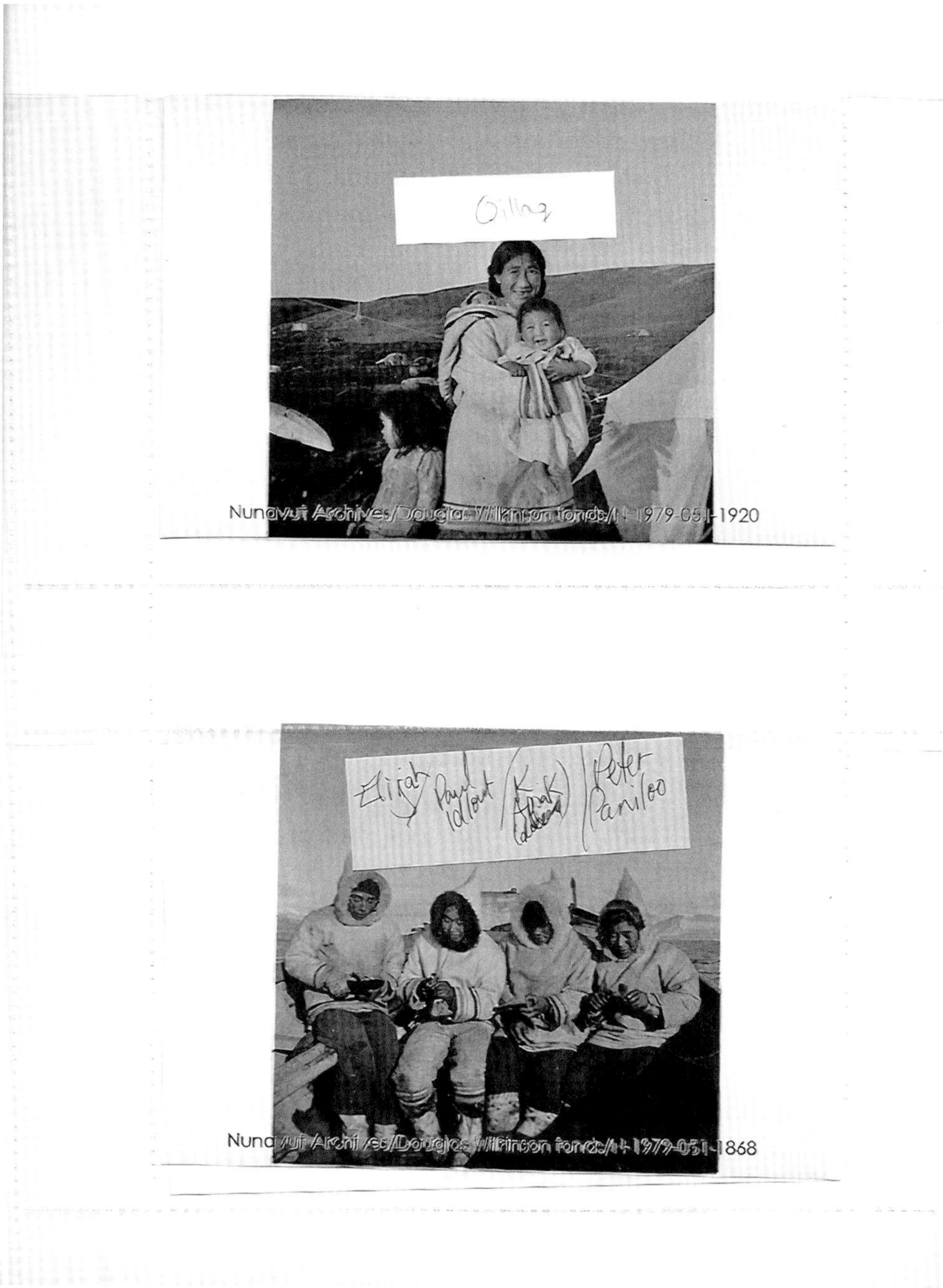

7.6 | Two pages from the album of Idlout's photographs used in the 2018 interviews.

the 1950s and entanglements with the south. Of course, it was not lost on them that, as southern researchers involved in these interviews, we were also part of this entanglement.

The interviews and recollections were infused with a sense of holistic unity and care for others that is foundational to Inuit Qaujimajatuqangit and is also at

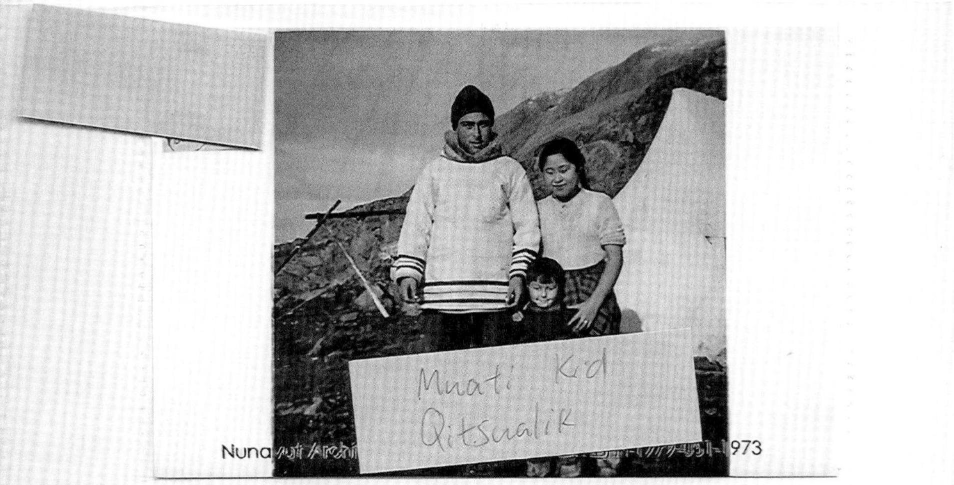

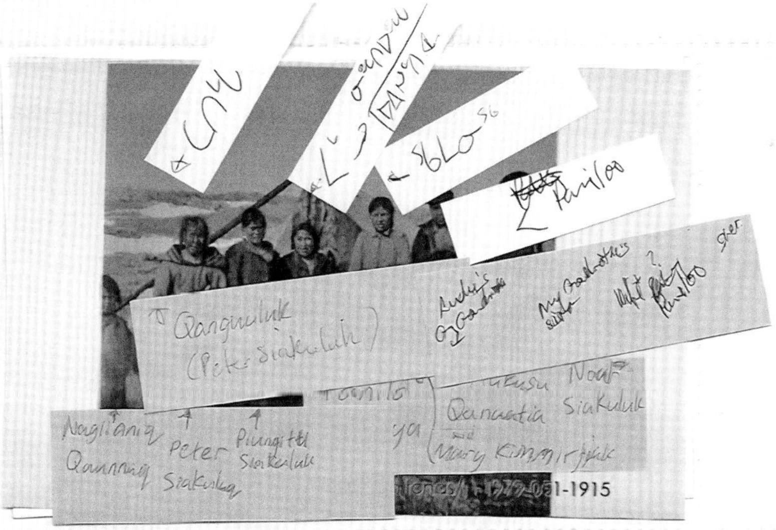

the core of Rachel Qitsualik's discussion of Inuit sovereignty and the concept of an Inummarik (lit. "true human").[76]

Idlout's eldest son, Paul Ullatitaq (1935–2025), spoke with Christina Williamson and me in Apex, just outside of Iqaluit (see figure I.1). Retired from his careers as an RCMP special constable and as the first Inuk and first Nunavut-born

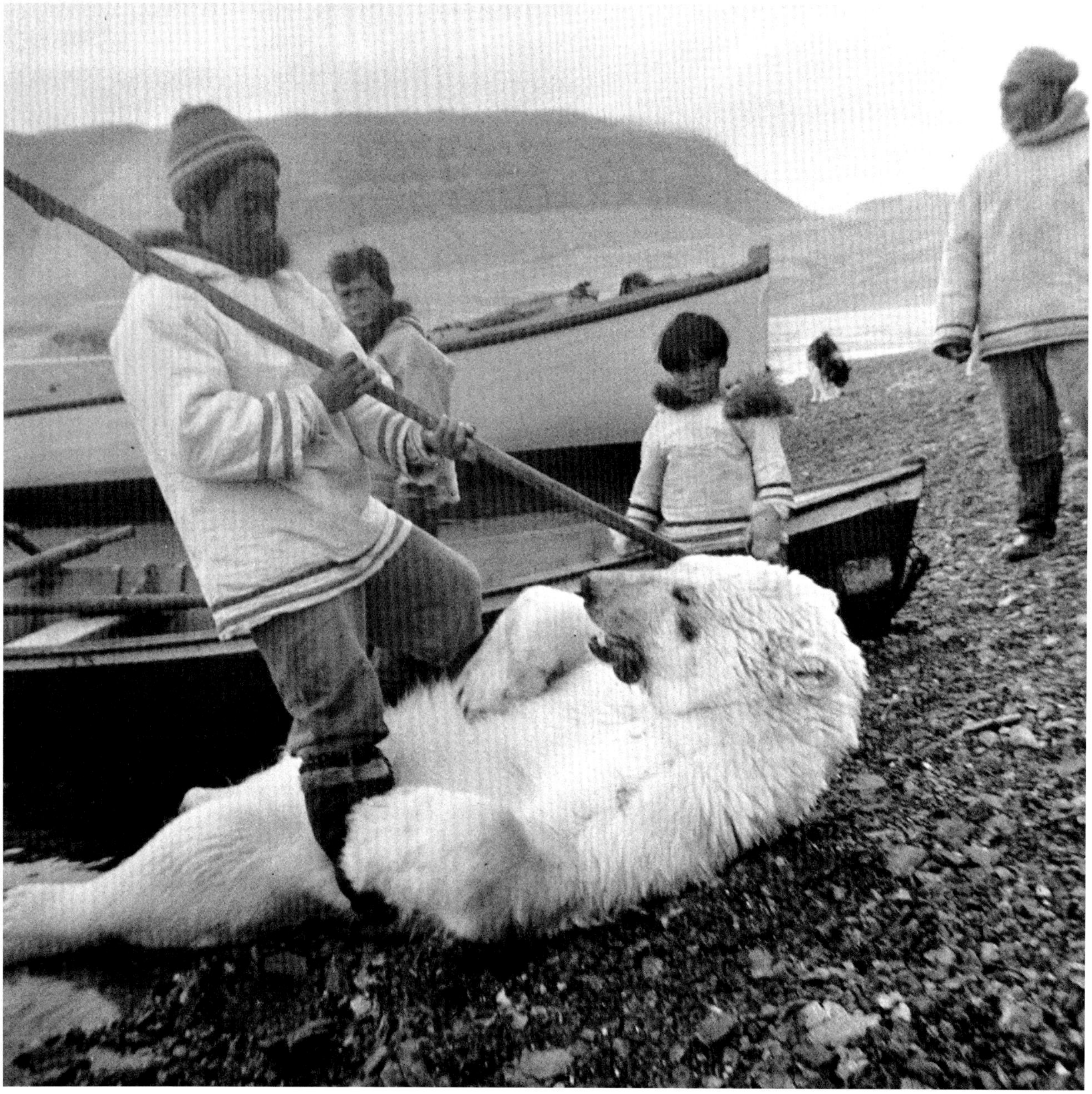

7.7 | Paul Ullatitaq Idlout, observed by Pauloosee Idlout and Herodier Kadluk, poses with a dead polar bear prior to skinning at Idlout's camp, Aulattivik, Eclipse Sound, North Baffin Island, August 1952. Idlout's big boat and row boat are in the background. Photo: Joseph Idlout.

Anglican bishop of the Diocese of the Arctic, Paul Ullatitaq was eighty-four years old at the time. He enthusiastically studied the photo album while speaking to us about the images. Paul Ullatitaq's son Eric had introduced us to his father and helped to arrange our meeting. The three of us sat talking in the kitchen of Bishop Idlout's home in Apex, the album resting in front of him.

Bishop Idlout had not seen most of the photographs in the album before, yet they held a deep and immediate sense of familiarity for him. As he told us, "This land is still in my head. I was there many days when I went outside. The hill is in my head."[77] As I noted in the introductory chapter, Paul Ullatitaq Idlout is visible on almost every page of the photo album. He appears as a young man posed with family and camp members. In one sequence of images, he and his first wife, Ishoogituk, one of Ludy Pudluk's sisters, walk toward the Anglican church in Pond Inlet/Mittimatalik on their wedding day and greet well-wishers. In others, he is pictured participating in the hunt. Perhaps the most spectacular of these images is a photograph of him standing astride a dead polar bear (see figure 7.7). Paul Ullatitaq raises the enormous creature's head with a hook. The image culminates the long hunt captured in other photographs by Idlout (see also figures 3.1, 3.6, 3.7, and 3.8). During the meetings and interviews conducted by Christina, Alexandra, and me in Pond Inlet/Mittimatalik the week before, this image had been the most popular of the photographs. Young boys, in particular, were drawn to it, gasping in awe at the sight of the triumphant hunter, not much older than themselves; they snapped up the extra copies of this photograph that we had printed. And back in Apex, at his kitchen table, Paul Ullatitaq, too, smiled broadly and laughed when he turned the page to see the dramatic image.

In Pond Inlet/Mittimatalik, Ludy Pudluk (1943–2019) studied the album with great interest and ready laughter, speaking to Alexandra, Christina, and me. Ludy Pudluk, a son of Kadloo and Leetia, grew up at Idlout's camp near Pond Inlet/Mittimatalik. In 1958, his family joined Idlout in Resolute/Qausuittuq, where Pudluk spent most of the rest of his life. He became a revered leader, receiving the Order of Nunavut in 2018. Pudluk served five terms between 1975 and 1995 as the representative for the High Arctic in the legislative assembly of the Northwest Territories and later served as the mayor of Resolute/Qausuittuq. He was remembered as a climate change activist and, in the words of Nunavut senator Dennis Patterson, as "one of the driving forces behind the creation of Nunavut."[78]

When we entered Ludy Pudluk's home in Pond Inlet/Mittimatalik, we immediately saw that he valued images as relational objects that signalled familial and cultural connections.[79] There, hanging in pride of place, were framed copies of the 1975 two-dollar bill. His father, Herodier Kadluk, was among the figures featured on the bill. But Ludy had surrounded the bills and a reproduction of the original image with more recent portraits of family members. As with Leah Idlout d'Argencourt Paulson's article, Ludy Pudluk had reframed the governmental image through a form of visual story work that mapped family connections.

In leafing through the album, Ludy Pudluk – like Paul Ullattitaq Idlout – saw himself. He appears as a young boy in the early 1950s, including in a group portrait of his family as well as in images made by Wilkinson. Pudluk remembered Wilkinson teaching Idlout to use the camera and seeing him photograph. He identified many people in Idlout's photographs, and the images also sparked memories of hunting and life on the land. Looking at photographs of men and boys building an *igluvigaq* (snow shelter) (see figures 3.11 and 7.8), Pudluk recalled, "Idlout and my father were relatives. I think that's why they camped and [were] helping to get supplies. At the end of the year, we take the seals and animals we caught and bury them. That gets really rough. They start around this time of year so they will have enough supply all winter in the cold season because there's not much hunting in the cold season."[80]

Memories of life on the land animated all of the interviews. In a group identification session with Elders in Pond Inlet/Mittimatalik, brothers Elijah Erkloo and Daniel Komangapik saw themselves appear often in Idlout's photographs (see figure 7.9).[81] The identification session took place at the Nattinak Visitors Centre, Pond Inlet/Mittimatalik. Elijah and Daniel had been adopted by Idlout's parents, Akumalik and Arnaujaq. At the 2018 identification session, they recalled Akumalik as a strict parent, even as they delighted in seeing his and Arnaujaq's image. Other photographs transported them to the life of hunting and fishing, including a portrait of Elijah posing with frozen char alongside Paul Ullatitaq Idlout and Peter Paniloo (see figure 7.10).

Ruth Sangoya, also adopted by Idlout's mother, Arnaujaq, had lived at their camp as a child and had maintained contact with the family. Ruth was able to identify many people in the photographs. When she encountered an image of the wedding between Paul Ullatitaq Idlout and his first wife, Ishoogituk, Ruth paused. Ishoogituk had been a good friend of hers, and she had not seen the image in years (see figure 7.11).

Elders and knowledge keepers Elisapee Ootoova (1931–2021), Jacob Anaviapik, and Solomon Awa generously shared their time to view the photographs and shared their experiences of life on the land and connections with the Idlout family. Elisapee spoke about Idlout's family, women sewing and her own experience of learning to sew, and relations with southerners. An important advocate of Inuit culture and the Inuktitut language, she spoke in her own language for most of the interview.[82] While looking at the photographs, Jacob, Alexandra Anaviapik's father, spoke eloquently about hunting and living at camp. He described the many responsibilities at camp and on the hunt. In looking at the images of ice shelters (see figures 3.11 and 7.8), he recalled the preparation of *igunaq* (fermented meat).[83] Solomon, mayor of Iqaluit and a knowledge keeper originally from North Baffin Island, was prompted by Idlout's photographs to share his own stories of the hunt and the importance of hunting for Inuit.[84]

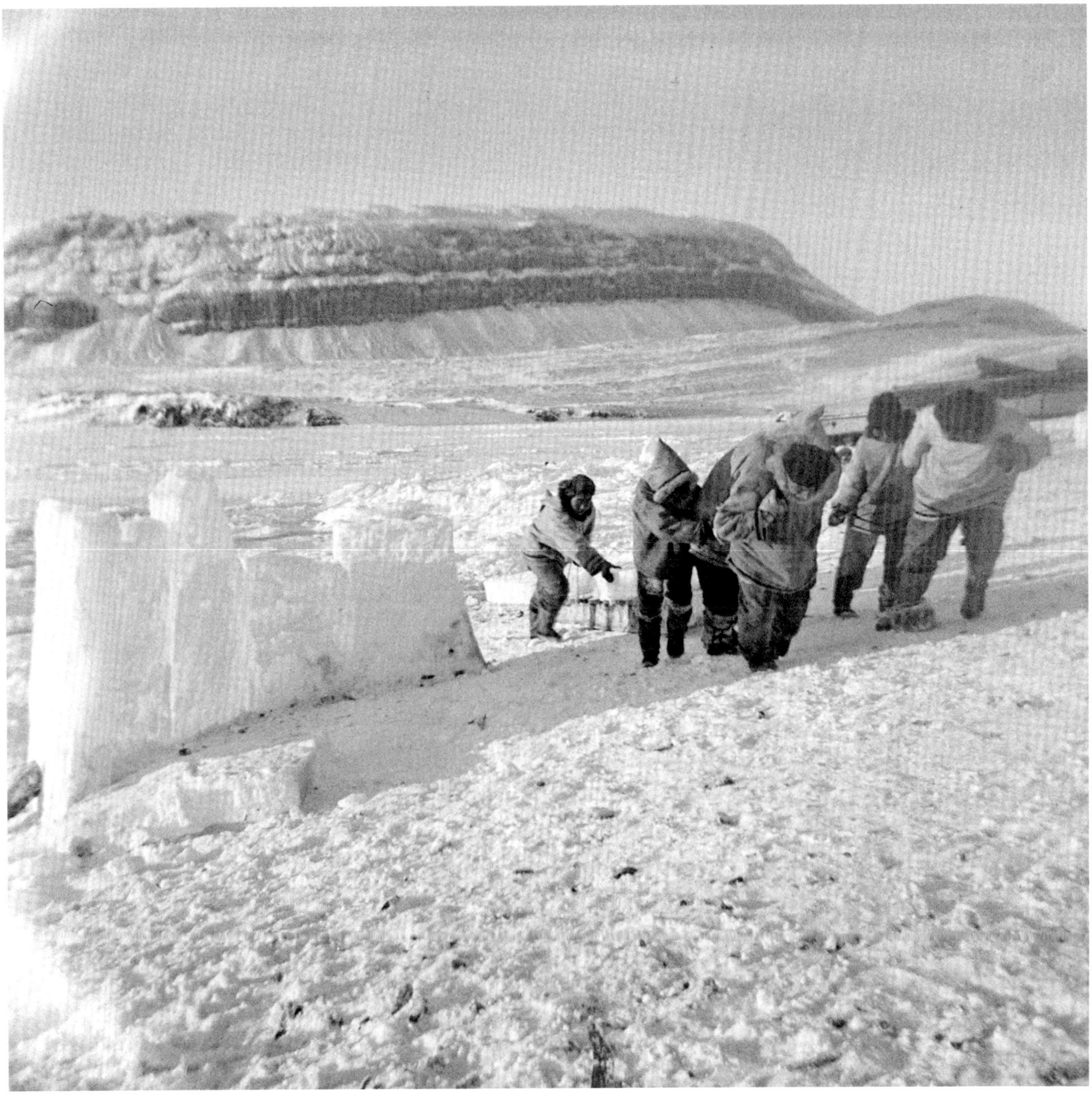

7.8 | Men and boys draft blocks of sea ice on a sled for a partially erected open-top ice house – or igluvigaq (snow shelter) – at Idlout's camp, Aulattivik, Eclipse Sound, North Baffin Island, October 1951. Photo: Joseph Idlout.

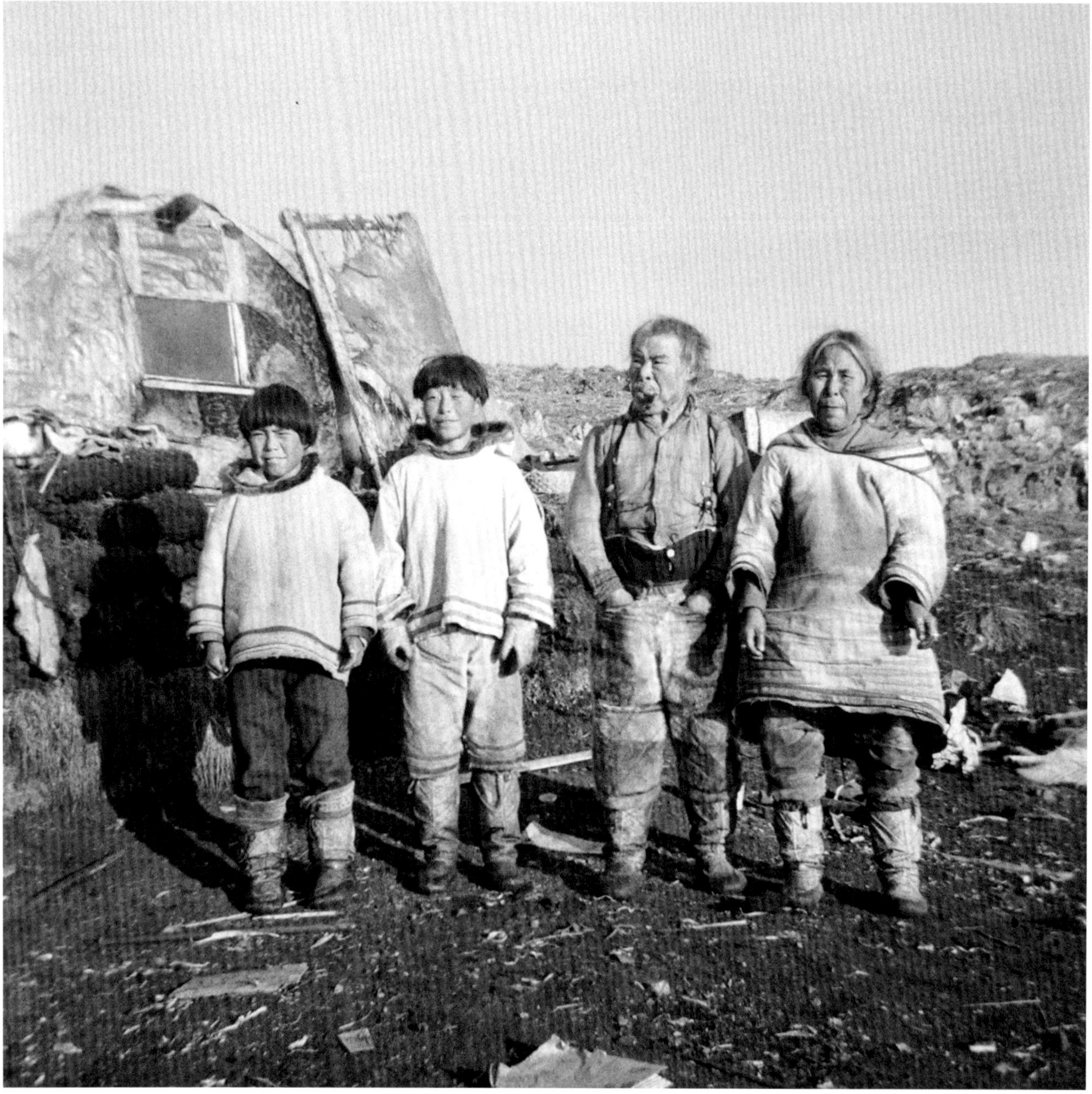

7.9 | Family portrait: Danielee (Dan) Komangapik and Elijah Erkloo, Idlout's brother's children, raised by their grandparents after his death, and Akumalik and Arnaujaq, Idlout's parents, in front of their sod and wood winter house at Idlout's camp, Aulattivik, Eclipse Sound, North Baffin Island, September 1951. Photo: Joseph Idlout.

7.10 | Paul Ullatitaq Idlout, Peter Paniloo, and Elijah Erkloo pose with frozen char brought to camp from Sapotit, Aulattivik, Eclipse Sound, North Baffin Island, October 1951. Photo: Joseph Idlout.

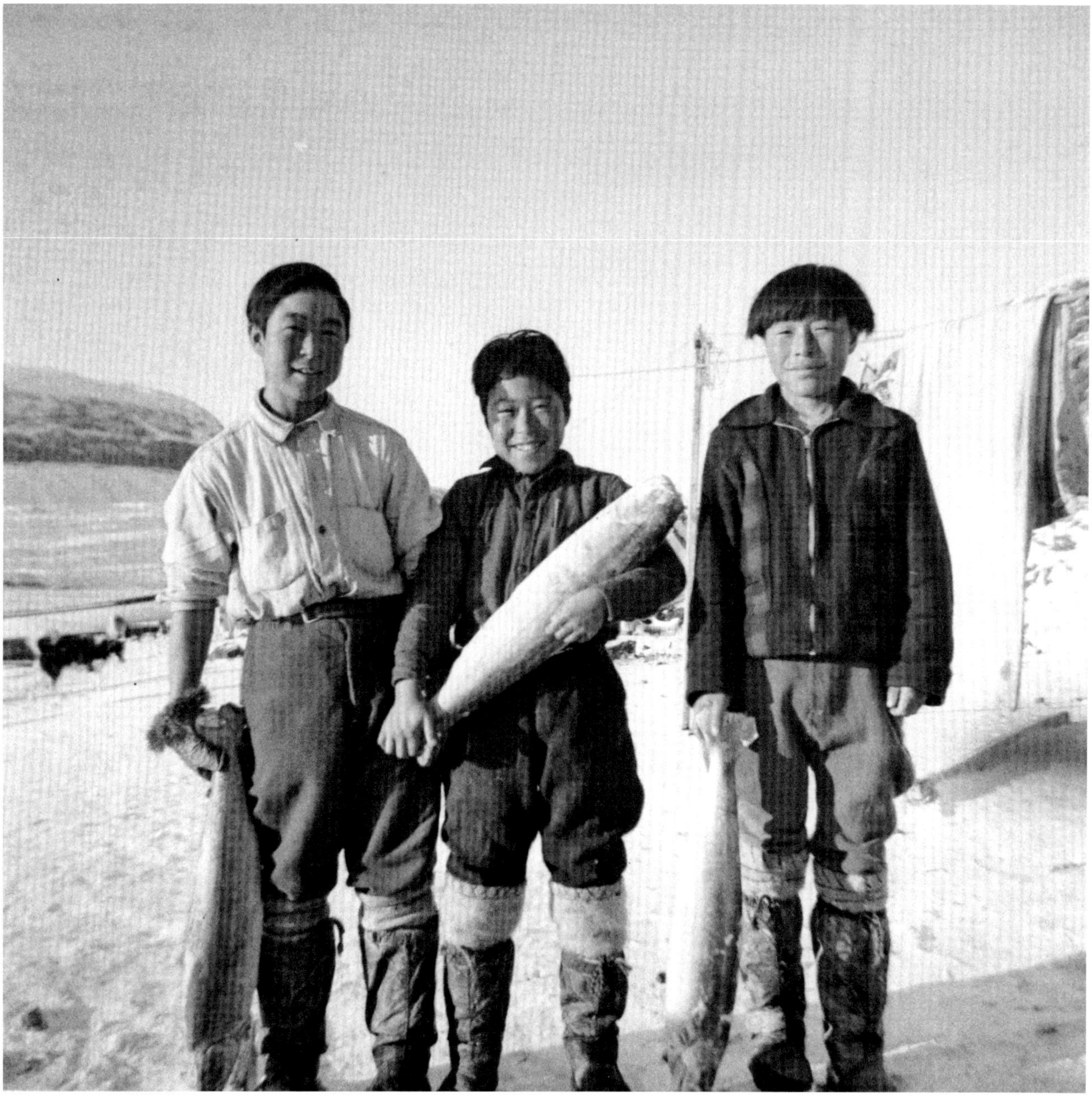

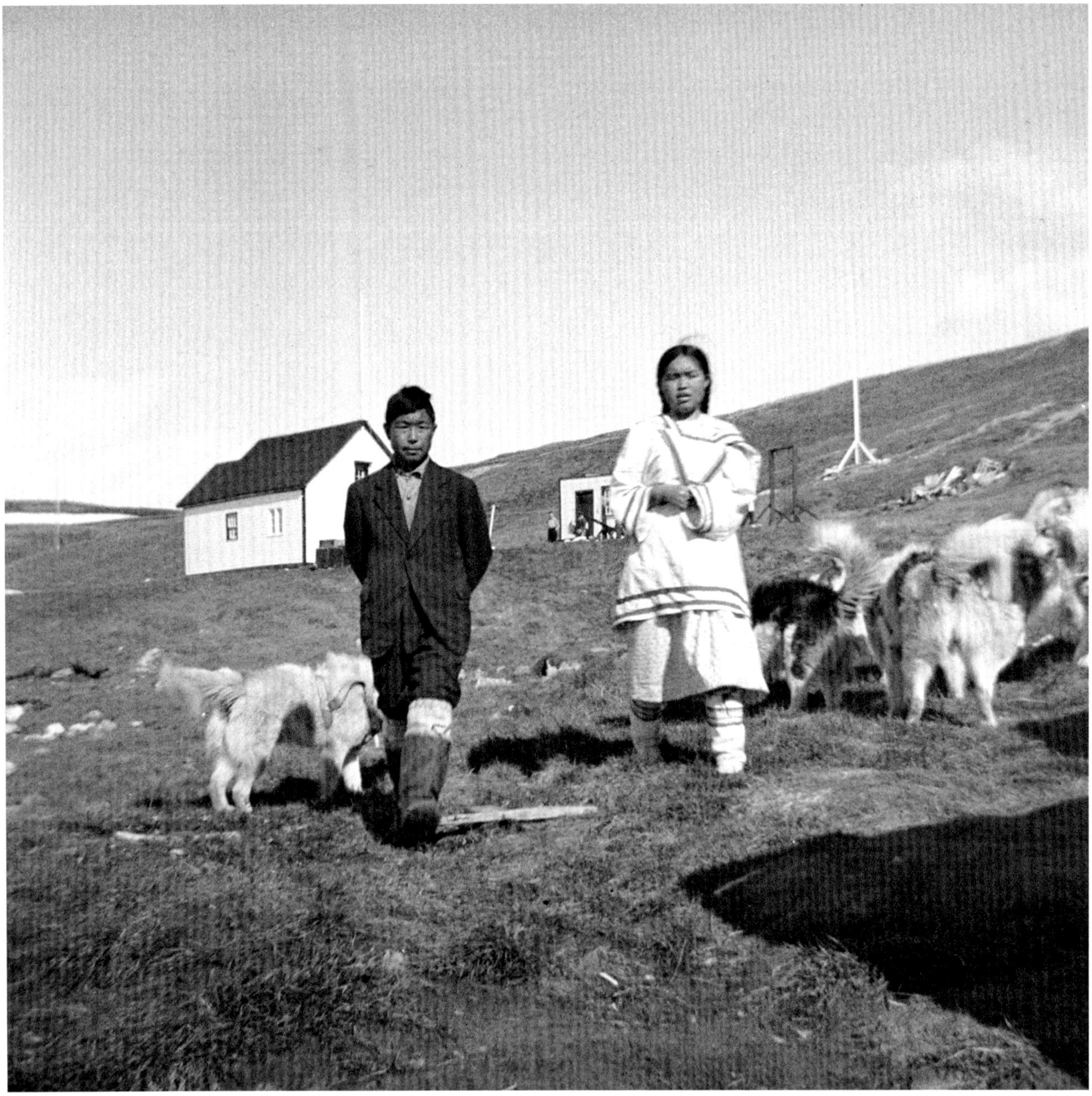

7.11 | Bride and groom Paul Ullatitaq Idlout and Ishoogituk, Paul's first wife, walk away from Anglican mission church after their wedding ceremony as RCMP dogs run loose, Pond Inlet/ Mittimatalik, North Baffin Island, August 1952. Photo: Joseph Idlout.

7.12 | Narwhal head with double tusk, Koluktoo Bay, Milne Inlet, Eclipse Sound, North Baffin Island, August 1952. Photo: Joseph Idlout.

For younger generations of the Idlout family, the photographs were equally vivid. Joshua Idlout, Paul Ullatitaq's son, spoke with Alexandra, Christina, and me in Pond Inlet/Mittimatalik. Through the images, he considered not only what his father had taught him about hunting but also the model that his grandfather, Idlout, and great-grandfather, Akumalik, had provided. Joshua told us about his first narwhal hunt (see figure 7.12). Narwhal were plentiful in the waters around Aulattivik, but Joshua and interviewees noted that a double-tusked

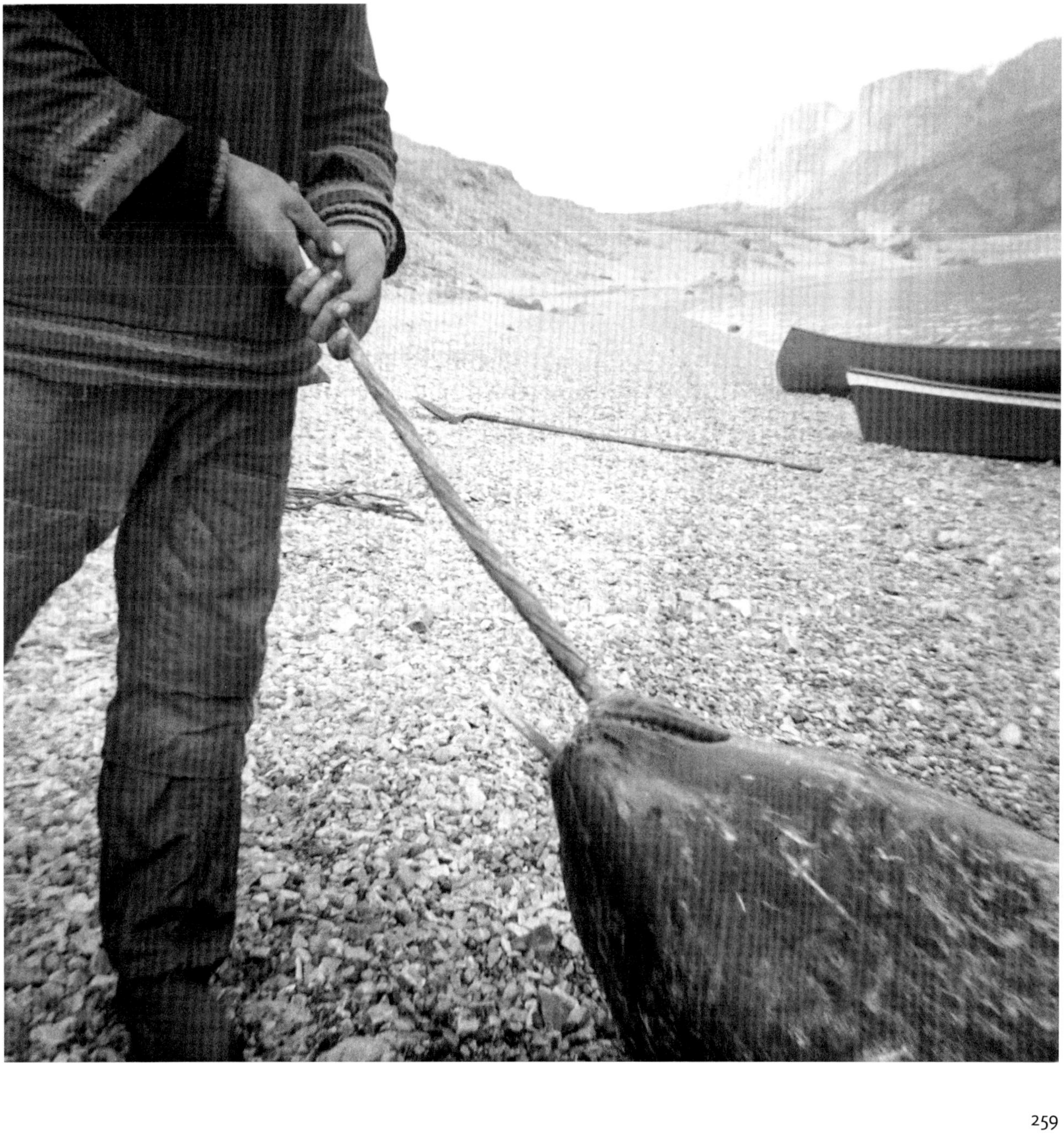

narwhal was unusual. He started the story by saying, "We foremost respect the animals that are around us. You can't waste what you caught, [and must] share what you caught with the families that are hungry." Then Joshua narrated a riveting story about the hunt and familial connections with the land:

> We start hearing narwhals ... There was my dad, myself, and my cousin. We were up most of the night. The first lead I came to, there was about a part of seven young males [narwhals] with tusks. He was just about to shoot the one in the front, but he thought the others in the back would get him. The ones in the back were shot, but we didn't know there was one in the middle. When I shot him, I knew I had him. He was dying, and two other narwhals came up beside him and hugged him and they took him down. They tend to do that with their own. Protect each other and maybe in a way find out if they'll be okay. Like I said, I didn't see him again.
>
> But during another time that same day, another pod came, my first time hunting a narwhal with my dad. My first hunt with him and my first kill. I actually harpooned him myself while dad was a good maybe half a mile from us. My cousin on the other side was yelling out, asking for help too 'cause he caught one too. So dad had to decide which one to go to. My narwhal went to the other side of the lead, so I had to find another way to cross it. So I went across it and harpooned it and came back.
>
> When we butchered our meat, dad said that was enough, we got enough. He just wanted one young one, one black yearling or two because it's nicer meat for the ladies, softer, tender. Just when we were going home, crossing another lead, a big full whale came up right in front of us. He was a lot bigger than us, so we let him pass through and crossed and went home. It's hard work coming home in this area in the spring; the ice has really thin areas. My grandfather taught us how to get around this area, especially the area he was born. That was my dad's hunting ground. That's where we did most of our hunting.[85]

For Joshua Idlout, the photographs invoked deep experience of Inuit cultural values and relationality with family and with the land, particularly through hunting.

More recently, in Ottawa, Susan Salluviniq, Idlout's youngest daughter, sat down with Augatnaaq and me over some of her father's photographs, as discussed in the introductory chapter. She, too, revisited family and experiences through the photographs (see figure I.2). Susan has lived in Resolute/Qausuittuq since her family's relocation in 1955. She is a former mayor of the hamlet and an advocate for the High Arctic relocatees. This interview was not the first time that Susan had seen her father's photographs, and the camera provided a bond between the two. As she told us, "I remember looking through pictures that my father had taken. He gave me a camera for my birthday. I guess he wanted this to

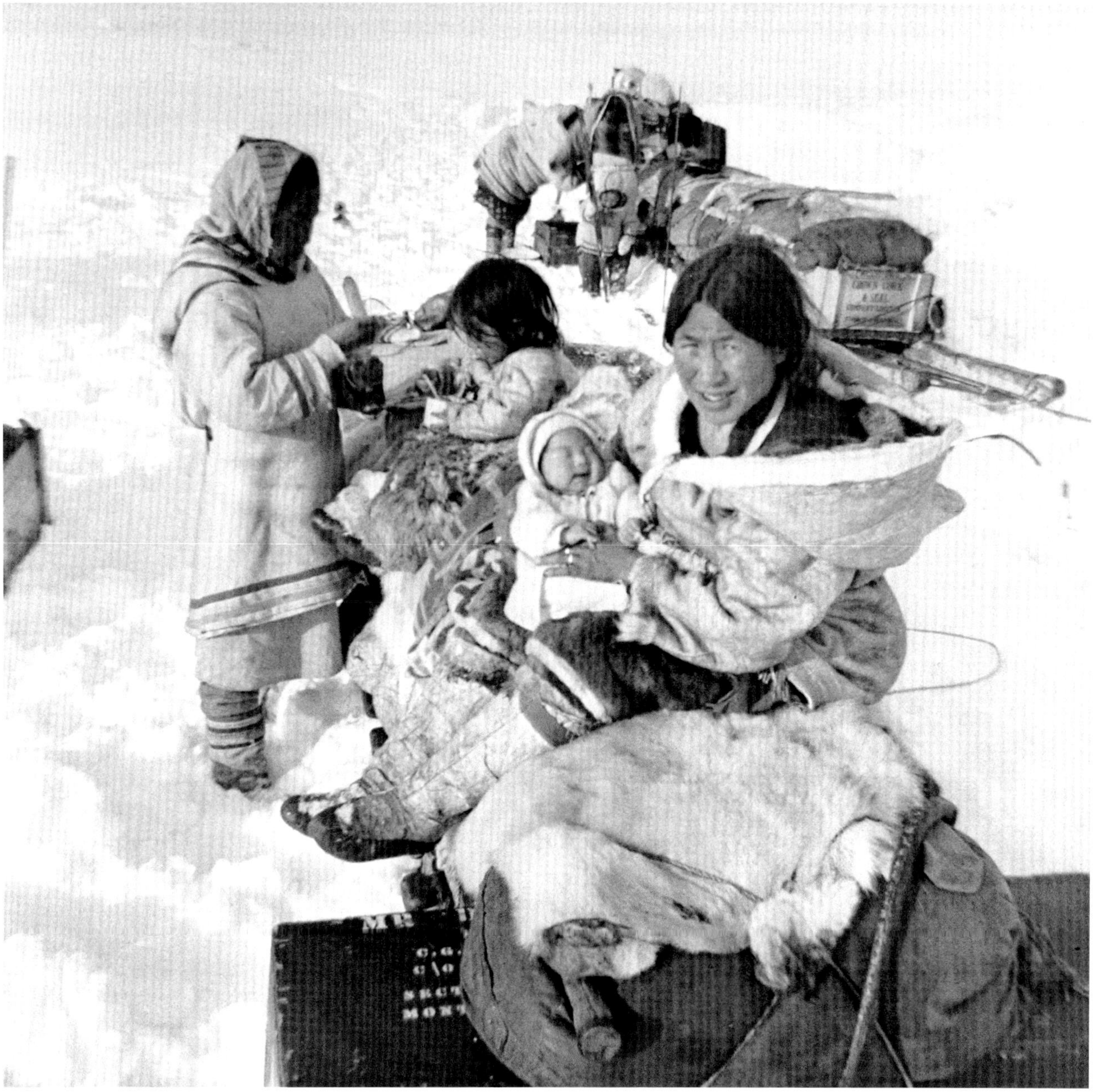

7.13 | Sleds stop for "mug-up" on sea ice at Eclipse Sound between Pond Inlet/Mittimatalik and Aulattivik, North Baffin Island, May 1954. From left to right: Leah Idlout, Ruth Idlout, and Kidlak (Idlout's wife) with Susana Idlout.

continue of him taking pictures."[86] Susan was a young child, still being carried by her mother, Kidlak, in the hood of her *amautik* (woman's parka) when the family was relocated to the High Arctic. As a result, she does not have personal memories of the winter camp in Aulattivik or of the spring camp in Nuvurulua, where most of the photographs were shot; nonetheless, they brought back memories of her father's hunting prowess and of travelling with him to hunt seals as a young child. When she saw pictures of her mother, Susan smiled deeply and recalled how much sewing she had needed to do and how beautiful their clothes had been (see figure 7.13). Above all, the photographs represented a deep familial bond: "They were living in very peaceful surroundings. Caring. They were so at peace. Looking at the pictures, [I see] a total different way of life from how we are living today. You know we are working at home or in the community. We'll go camping to get closer to the family, and you can tell that they were close."[87] She recalled how Idlout and Kidlak welcomed and cared for relatives, including Kadloo's family and relatives visiting from Pond Inlet/Mittimatalik. She wanted extra photographs to distribute to extended family in Resolute/Qausuittuq.

Although Idlout's photographs do not explicitly depict Resolute/Qausuittuq, they provided Susan with an opportunity to reflect on life in the High Arctic. She talked about the hardships experienced by the High Arctic relocatees in Resolute/Qausuittuq, explaining that people lived without adequate housing and had to find food and fire wood at the military base's dump. Years of anger and substance abuse followed. As Susan recalled,

> When we were children, we would get into fights. There would be a separation between the people who were relocated from northern Quebec and the Baffin region. We would call each other names and throw rocks and be angry at each other. But when there was a hearing about the relocation, we found out that we weren't angry at each other; we were angry at what the government had done to the relocatees. My husband and I never used to like Resolute Bay. When my husband's father was talking about returning to Inukjuak, my husband and I agreed that we would follow him because we didn't like Resolute. It was desolate. Such a terrible place. But my husband's father, my father-in-law, did not return to Inukjuak. So we stayed in Resolute. After the relocation hearing, we found out that we live in a very beautiful community where there is plenty of wildlife. We didn't know that Resolute was nice until after the hearing.[88]

Susan herself played an important role in this healing process. She was one of the leaders who advocated for the relocatees. As mayor, she had met with Prime Minister Stephen Harper and pressed him for an apology, something that the relocatees had long been demanding. That apology eventually came in 2010 from John Duncan, minister of Indian Affairs and Northern Development.[89]

As in all relational experiences over photographs, viewers engaged beyond the literal subject of the images; the photographs provided an impetus for reviewing relationships.

Conversations over Joseph Idlout's photographs will continue through the online exhibition *Ajjiliurlagit ("Let me take your picture"): The Photographs of Joseph Idlout*, curated by Augatnaaq Eccles, working with me. The exhibition, organized with the collaboration of the Nunavut Archives and designed by the Inuit-owned, Iqaluit-based design firm Atiigo, is intended to bring the photographs to members of the Idlout family, to Inuit across Inuit Nunangat, and to broader communities. As Augatnaaq and I discuss in detail in chapter 3, the exhibition is organized around Inuit Qaujimajatuqangit principles. To reach across generations, Augatnaaq has designed a teacher's guide so that younger generations can continue to learn from these photographic assertions of Inuit agency and culture.[90]

Returning Rather Than Concluding

Discussions about Joseph Idlout's photographs reinforce the stories that the images always already told about intergenerational interdependence and Inuit culture. In these ways, the stories shared about Idlout's photographs offer an Inuit worldview. They are not merely "counter-stories" to southern colonial sources.[91] In short, the interviews based on Idlout's photographs constitute decolonial actions by privileging Inuit cultural values – including the principles of Inuit Qaujimajatuqangit and the holistic worldview discussed by Rachel Qitsualik[92] – over southern ones and by underscoring an Inuit vision always already in the images.

But Inuit oral tradition also values the telling of the past in the present, a cyclical worldview in which ancestors are inextricably linked to their descendants through cultural tradition and through story. In this way, photo-based oral histories challenge conventional linear historical narratives, which tend to be dominated by narrations of colonial officials. Using photographs to link past and present – to make the past appear in vivid, and affective, forms today – ruptures a colonial narrative that typically privileges contact with southerners as an originating moment and that frames Indigenous cultures *within* a colonial temporality. Here, this conceptualization of time – based on Western progress, with one event leading directly to another – is shattered: time collapses as generations encounter one another. Rather than Inuit being plugged into a Western linear narrative, Western technologies (like the camera) are reimagined as tools of intergenerational connection – like naming practices and oral traditions.

Joseph Idlout's photographs and their reactivation by his descendants and community principally speak of Inuit cultural values and histories while also talking back to colonial history. They reimagine the camera as an Inuit tool that can tell stories of Inuit cultural values and community connections. And, in turn, the recent conversations recounted here create nonlinear historical narratives that privilege the present, embodied experience through which the past has been reactivated.

Following the "biographies" of images in this chapter underscores a central argument of this book: that a transhistorical framing and an emphasis on visual representations and the concept of visuality, when combined with oral tradition, provide means to acknowledge Inuit agency. This book has attempted to privilege the Inuit visual and oral history record, while also showing that archival research can unearth valuable Inuit records and institutional contexts without privileging colonialist perspectives. The visual achieves this openness because, as W.J.T. Mitchell has argued, "vision is never a one-way street, but a multiple intersection teeming with dialectical images."[93] Always available to multiple readings, meanings, and interpretations, the visual remains open to historical discourse's multiple voices and experiences. Paired with oral historical records, the visual speaks of Inuit culture.

This book – and the research project that it grows from, including the online exhibition *Ajjiliurlagit ("Let me take your picture"): The Photographs of Joseph Idlout* – honours Idlout's presence and that of his family. It is also an attempt to *listen* from the south to Inuit experience of this period of disruption while *looking* not only for signs of visuality as settler-colonial authority but also for multidirectional lines of the gaze and for Inuit disruptions of colonial authority that have always asserted and continue to assert Inuit presence.

Figures

Notes

Note on Language, Spelling, and Names

1 Harper, "Inuktut or Inuktitut?"

Introduction

1 Idlout d'Argencourt, "First Inuit Picture."
2 My thanks to Madeleine d'Argencourt and Lucie Idlout for advice on spelling their grandmother's name. Elsewhere, the spelling varies. Find a Grave, "Kidla Rebecca Idlout (1916–1965)."
3 Goldring, "Historians and Inuit," 498, 514.
4 Leah's articles from the 1970s are signed with her name at the time, Leah Idlout d'Argencourt. However, throughout this book, I use her name later in life, Leah Idlout d'Argencourt Paulson.
5 Wilson, "Relationality"; Nunavut Department of Education, Curriculum and School Services Division, *Inuit Qaujimajatuqangit*, 22–4.
6 Elsewhere, she uses the term "social objects." Edwards, "Photographs and the Sound," 27.
7 As discussed in chapter 2, little is known about Idlout's early life. In a 1954 *Maclean's* article, Doug Wilkinson stated that Idlout was thirty-eight years old in 1953–54, but this age is not confirmed. Further, his first name – Joseph – was the product of Christian missionaries' efforts to baptize Inuit and give them Biblical names. Before contact, Inuit used single names, and indeed he was often known simply as Idlout. A broader history of contact between the people of the region and outsiders is better known. According to the Qikiqtani Truth Commission, the Tununirmiut people of North Baffin Island experienced gradually increasing contact beginning in 1903 with the establishment of a shore station at present-day Pond Inlet/Mittimatalik, although it was only episodically visited by whalers and others, including the sea captain Joseph-Elzéar Bernier (1852–1934). When the Hudson's Bay Company established a post at Pond Inlet/Mittimatalik in 1921, followed the next year by an RCMP post and in 1929 by the arrival of Catholic and Anglican missionaries, the Tununirmiut, who still lived on the land, became valued as guides for visitors from the south. By the 1950s, contact had accelerated. Idlout's daughter Susan Salluviniq and his granddaughter Lucie Idlout have suggested that Idlout was the only son of Bernier. H.A. Larson, RCMP, teletype to RCMP post, Pond Inlet, 14 April 1953, reproduced in Grant, *"Errors Exposed,"* 245; Roberts, *Eskimo Identification*; Susan Salluviniq, interview by Augatnaaq Eccles and Carol Payne, Ottawa, 22 March 2023; Lucie Idlout, "Le prix du relogement"; Wilkinson, "How I Became an Eskimo," 29.
8 For writing on Pitseolak, see Pitseolak and Eber, *People from Our Side*; Racette, "Returning Fire," 75–6; Adams, "Arctic and Inuit Photography, Part Two"; Wise, "Photographic Memory"; Norman, "Control Mapping"; and Sangster, *Iconic North*, 282–7.
9 Pitseolak and Eber, *People from Our Side*, 12–13.
10 However, Inuit women at times photographed. Pitseolak's second wife, Aggeok, and Paulette Anerodluk are two examples. Sangster, *Iconic North*, 282–7.
11 The text describes the average Inuk as "the gentleman who asks you politely when you leave the plane if he might take your picture with his new Leica with the soft focus lens." Phillips and Parsons, *This Is the Arctic*, 42.

12 Elder Ann Meekitjuk Hanson, a writer and former commissioner of Nunavut (2005–10), told me that this gifting of cameras was common. Ann Meekitjuk Hanson, interview by Carol Payne, Apex, Baffin Island, 10 May 2018. In further examples of Inuit photographers, Idlout and a few other Inuit delegates on a trip to Kalaallit Nunaat/Greenland in 1958 also carried cameras, as discussed in chapter 6. A 1958 guide for southerners moving to Inuit Nunangat, written by DNANR officials R.A.J. Phillips and George Franklin Parsons, references Inuit photographers. Phillips and Parsons, *This Is the Arctic*, cover illustration, 42. In addition, as Sandra Dyck writes, Dorothy Eber found that by 1950 it was "not unusual" to see Inuit with cameras. Dyck mentions, for example, that Pauta Saila (1916–2009), Paulassie Pootoogook (1927–2006), Sakiassie Ragee (1924–2003), and Salomonie Pootoogook (1913–1958) were photographers at this time. Eber, "Peter Pitseolak, an Historian for Seekooseelak," 13–15, 20, cited in Dyck, "Looking for Kenojuak Ashevak," 189–92.

13 Wilkinson also wrote extensively about Idlout, most notably in a 1955 book that shares its name with the earlier film. Wilkinson, *Land of the Long Day*.

14 For a discussion of the limitations of counter-narratives, see Cameron, *Far Off Metal River*, 173. See also Tuck and Yang, "Decolonization Is Not a Metaphor."

15 Payne, "'You hear it in their voice'"; Payne and Ellison, "Views from the North"; Payne, Taylor, and Hayes, *Views from the North*.

16 Payne et al., eds, *Atiqput*. For an important Inuit critique of archival practice, see Campbell and Bishop-Stall, "Inuit Approach to Archival Work."

17 See Payne et al., eds, *Atiqput*; and Payne, "Culture, Memory."

18 Webster and Payne, "'Onwards.'" Deborah Kigjugalik Webster and I, along with Inuit knowledge keeper Bernadette Dean and University of Cambridge professor Michael Bravo, also lead the research program Inuit Re-envisioning Arctic Photography: International Collaboration and Colonial Critique.

19 Payne and Thomas, "Aboriginal Interventions."

20 Payne, "Lessons with Leah"; Payne, *Official Picture*, 165–88.

21 Located at https://www.josephidloutphotographs.ca/en and https://www.josephidloutphotographs.ca/iu/home.

22 "Idlout Family Reflections."

23 Igloliorte, "Curating Inuit Qaujimajatuqangit."

24 Moran, director, Centre for Truth and Reconciliation, "Keynote Address."

25 Nickels, Shirley, and Laidler, eds, *Negotiating Research Relationships*; Qikiqtani Truth Commission, "Thematic Reports and Special Studies 1950–1975"; Qikiqtani Truth Commission, *Analysis of the RCMP Sled Dog Report*. See also Secretariat on Responsible Conduct of Research, "Research Involving the First Nations"; and Inuit Tapiriit Kanatami, *National Inuit Strategy on Research Roundtable*.

26 Qitsualik, "Inummarik."

27 Campt, *Listening to Images*.

28 In several of the chapters, governmental records from Library and Archives Canada have been crucial. I have studied these records closely in Ottawa. In sifting through this material (and other collections), the Social History of the Eastern Arctic Database has been very helpful. I gratefully acknowledge Frank Tester, Peter Kulchyski, Paule McNicoll, and the University of British Columbia for making the database public and widely accessible at https://nunavutsocialhistory.arts.ubc.ca/.

29 As Davis argues of her own influential work, "'local storytelling' may serve a global program by my own move toward decentering." Davis, "Decentering History," 192.

30 For a fascinating study of related issues drawing on conceptualizations of settler-colonial "ways of seeing," see Mamers, "Settler Colonial Ways."

31 Amagoalik, "Reconciliation or Conciliation?" 36, also referenced in Igloliorte, "'We Were So Far Away.'" Amagoalik quotes the civil servant H.A. Proctor's report of 28 March 1952 titled "The Future of the Canadian Eskimo." Meren, "'Commend Me the Yak,'" 356.

32 Cook, "Canada's Arctic Islands," 4.

33 St-Laurent, in Government of Canada, *House of Commons Debates*, First Session, Twenty-Second Parliament, vol. 1, 8 December 1953, 697, also quoted in Cook, "Canada's Arctic Islands," 4. Cook's article is reprinted in *The Arctic Circular* 28, nos 1–2 (1980): 32–4.

34 Goldring, "Historians and Inuit," 498.

35 Wolfe, "Settler Colonialism," 388.

36 Tester and Kulchyski, *Tammarniit (Mistakes)*, 9–10, passim.

37 In this way, the eastern Arctic provides a fascinating case study of what Sumathi Ramaswamy describes as colonialist (and settler-colonialist) struggles occurring "at the level of the image." The inhospitable and remote geography of the region was settled remotely through bureaucratic technologies that, I believe, can be understood as forms of visuality. Ramaswamy, "Introduction," 3, quoting Pinney, *Photos of the Gods*, 8. This study is also informed by scholar Damian Skinner's call for a settler-colonial art history, although the material in this book does not fit comfortably within conventional art history. In particular, I agree with his suggestions that Indigenous and settler practices should not be separated, that the study of settler colonialism should be transhistorical, and that conventional media hierarchies should be upended. Skinner, "Settler Colonial Art History." For an important transhistorical and transdisciplinary study of settler colonialism through art and archives, see Mamers, *Settler Colonial Ways*, and for an important discussion of truth and reconciliation from a settler perspective, see Regan, *Unsettling the Settler Within*.

38 R.A.J. Phillips, Chief of the Arctic Division, Canada, to Bishop (Anglican) Donald Marsh, 16 December 1957, Northwest Territories Archives, Alexander Stevenson fonds, N-1992-023, box 17, file 7, Policy – Inuit 1935–59, quoted in Qikiqtani Truth Commission, *QTC Final Report*, 22.

39 Thanks to Carol Williams for her insights and discussions on this material.

40 Qikiqtani Truth Commission, *QTC Final Report*, 17:

> By 1975, all but a few Inuit families lived in government-created permanent settlements, and many of them felt that their lives had become worse, not better. The decision to give up the traditional way of life was almost never an easy one, and once made, it proved to be irreversible. Inuit made enormous sacrifices by moving into settlements, living in permanent housing, giving up their *qimmiit* [sled dogs], sending their children to school, or accepting wage employment. Once they had made their decision, they discovered that government assurances of a sufficient number of jobs and better living conditions were illusory in many cases. Looking around, Inuit often felt and saw despair as they, their family members, and their neighbours struggled to adjust to circumstances beyond their control, even though some received benefits from living in settlements, such as less risk in daily life, better health care, and options to work for wages rather than hunt. Settlement life often imposed a new form of poverty, and hindered access to the land and the country food that nourished them.

41 I am grateful to Brenda Vellino for discussions about Tuck's essay. Tuck, "Suspending Damage." Tuck's comments also call to mind ethical concerns about treatments of historical violence, as discussed by Monica Patterson (see chapter 1). Patterson, "Ethical Murk," 213–14.

42 Tuck, "Suspending Damage," 413.

43 Tuck, "Suspending Damage," 414.

44 Tuck, "Suspending Damage," 415, original emphasis.

45 Tuck, "Suspending Damage," 415–16.

46 Tuck, "Suspending Damage," 416.

47 St-Laurent, in Government of Canada, *House of Commons Debates*, First Session, Twenty-Second Parliament, vol. 1, 8 December 1953, 697, also quoted in Cook, "Canada's Arctic Islands," 4. Cook's article is reprinted in *The Arctic Circular* 28, nos 1–2 (1980): 32–4.

48 St-Laurent, in Government of Canada, *House of Commons Debates*, First Session, Twenty-Second Parliament, vol. 1, 8 December 1953, 700.

49 For a discussion of oral histories, see Payne and Ellison, "Views from the North."

50 Bennett and Rowley, eds, *Uqalurait*; Kublu, Laugrand, and Oosten, "Listening to Our Past"; Nakasuk et al., *Inuit Worldviews*, vol. 1; McGrath, "*Isumaksaqsiurutigijakka*"; Collignon, Therrien, and Duchemin-Pelletier, eds, *Orality/Oralité*; Dorais, *Language of the Inuit*; Laugrand and Oosten, *Inuit Shamanism and Christianity*; Nakasuk et al., *Inuit Worldviews*, vol. 1; Wachowich et al., *Saqiyuq*.

51 Igloliorte, "Arctic Culture/Global Indigeneity"; Tester and Irniq, "Inuit Qaujimajatuqangit"; Laugrand, "Écrire Pour Prendre"; Martin, "'Are We Also Here for That?'"

52 Cruikshank, *Social Life of Stories*; Cruikshank, *Do Glaciers Listen?*.

53 Cameron, *Far Off Metal River*.

54 Martin, *Stories in a New Skin*, 98–120, 139.

55 Inuit Literatures/Littératures inuites, https://inuit.uqam.ca/en.

56 Payne et al., eds, *Atiqput*.

57 Qikiqtani Truth Commission, *QTC Final Report*; Qikiqtani Truth Commission, *Nuutauniq: Moves in Inuit Life*; Goldring, "Historians and Inuit," 498.

58 Tester and Kulchyski, *Tammarniit (Mistakes)*; Tester and Kulchyski, *Kiumajut (Talking Back)*.

59 Marcus, *Relocating Eden*; Marcus, *Inuit Relocation Policies*; Grant, "Case of Compounded Error"; Grant, *"Errors Exposed"*; Grant, *Arctic Justice*; Lackenbauer and Shackleton, *When the Skies*; Stern, *Historical Dictionary*.

60 See, for example, Harper, "Akumalik"; Harper, "'Our Picture Was Once."

61 Stern and Stevenson, eds, *Critical Inuit Studies*; Krupnik, *Early Inuit Studies*. In addition, the journal *Études Inuit Studies*, the key vehicle for scholarship in the field, has yielded important insights for this study.

62 Bravo, *North Pole*; Cheetham, "Monumental Ephemera."

63 McMaster, ed., *Inuit Modern*; Dyck, *Sanattiaqsimajut*; Lalonde, *Pitseolak Ashoona*; Vorano, "Creators"; Igloliorte, "Arctic Culture/Global Indigeneity."

64 Igloliorte, "Curating Inuit Qaujimajatuqangit"; Lalonde, *Pitseolak Ashoona*; Vorano, "Cape Dorset Cosmopolitans"; Hudson, Igloliorte, and Lundström, *Qummut Qukiria!* Among the many curatorial initiatives are Qaumajuq, the Inuit museum affiliated with the Winnipeg Art Gallery (https://www.wag.ca/about/qaumajuq/) and *Uummaqutik: essence de la vie* at the Musée des beaux-arts de Montréal (http://www.museesmontreal.org/fr/expositions-et-evenements/expositions/uummaqutik-essence-de-la-vie).

65 Condon, "History and Development"; King and Lidchi, eds, *Imaging the Arctic*; Geller, *Northern Exposures*; Adams, "Arctic and Inuit Photography, Part One"; Stern, "History of Canadian Arctic Photography"; Langford, "Richard Harrington's Guide"; Langford, "Richard Harrington's Indigenous Madonnas"; Racette, "Returning Fire"; Tippett, *Between Two Cultures*; Ross, "Use and Misuse."

66 Geller, *Northern Exposures*; Sangster, *Iconic North*; Boas, "Eskimo of Baffin Land"; Flaherty and Hubbard Flaherty, *My Eskimo Friends*; Close, *Framing Identity*; Birnie-Danzker and Partridge, "Qikiqtaaluk," 35.

67 Clifford, "On Ethnographic Allegory," 112–13.

68 Edwards, "Objects of Affect"; Edwards, "Photographs and the Sound"; Harney and Phillips, eds, *Mapping Modernisms*; Lien and Nielssen, eds, *Adjusting the Lens*; Lydon, ed., *Calling the Shots*; Lydon, *Eye Contact*; Pinney, *Photography and Anthropology*; Pinney and Peterson, *Photography's Other Histories*; Phillips, *Trading Identities*; Poole, "Excess of Description"; Ruby, *Picturing Culture*; Strassler, *Refracted Visions*; Wright, *Echo of Things*; Moser, *Projecting Citizenship*.

69 Tsinhnahjinnie, "When Is a Photograph?"; Passalacqua and Tsinhnahjinnie, *Our People*; Lonetree, "Heritage of Resilience"; Pedri-Spade, "'But They Were Never'"; Raheja, "Reading Nanook's Smile"; Thomas, "At the Kitchen Table"; Vizenor, "Fugitive Poses." See also Williams, "Indigenous Uses of Photography."

70 As the anthropologists Aaron Glass and Brad Evans have discussed, such analyses constitute "a refocusing of attention away from 'ethnographic authority' … and toward an acknowledgment of collaborative production, even if under strained and unstable political conditions." Glass and Evans, "Edward Curtis Meets the Kwakwa̲ka̲'wakw," 10. See also Lydon,

ed., *Calling the Shots*; Geismar and Herle, *Moving Images*; Wright, *Echo of Things*; Strassler, *Refracted Visions*; and the influential theory of Azoulay, *Civil Contract of Photography*.

71 Racette, "Returning Fire"; Harlan, "Indigenous Photographies."

72 For important discussions of Inuit and cameras, see a special issue edited by Jason Fox and Heather Igloliorte of *Inuit Art Quarterly* 37, no. 1 (2024).

73 Pitseolak and Eber, *People from Our Side*; Eber, "Peter Pitseolak and the Photographic Template."

74 Sangster, *Iconic North*, 282–7.

75 The *Inuit Art Quarterly*, a publication of the Inuit Art Foundation, features profiles of these artists and many others. See "Robert Kautuk"; Fredericks de Araujo, "Jimmy Manning"; "Barry Pottle"; and "Katherine Takpannie."

76 Raheja, *Reservation Reelism*; Evans, *Isuma*; Brady and Kelly, *We Interrupt This Program*; National Film Board of Canada, "Alethea Arnaquq-Baril"; Tripp, "Asinnajaq." For examples of asinnajaq's recent work, see National Gallery of Canada, "New Generation Photography Award."

77 Sturken and Cartwright, eds, *Practices of Looking*, 22.

78 Mitchell, "Showing Seeing," 175.

79 McMaster, Lum, and McCormick, "Entangled Gaze." This article's use of the "entangled gaze" is in turn indebted to Thomas, *Entangled Objects*.

80 In relatively early writing, for example, Mirzoeff defines visuality as "the intersection of power with visual representation." Mirzoeff, "Subject of Visual Culture," 4.

81 Mirzoeff, *Right to Look*, 196.

82 Mirzoeff, "On Visuality"; Mirzoeff, *Right to Look*, 123–54.

83 Mirzoeff, *Right to Look*, 6.

84 Mitchell, "Showing Seeing," 175.

85 Poole, "An Excess of Description."

86 Mirzoeff, *Right to Look*, 25.

87 Throughout his book *The Right to Look* and in other writing, Mirzoeff terms such resistance "countervisuality." I have eschewed this terminology because it suggests that "the right to look" is reduced to a response to authority. As in Cameron's critique of counternarratives, cited above, it is important to recognize and acknowledge that Indigenous agency is not solely a response to colonial authority. Cameron, *Far Off Metal River*, 173.

88 Smith, "Introduction," 2.

89 Phillips, *On Historical Distance*.

90 For a broader discussion of temporality and Indigenous cultures in the United States, see Rifkin, *Beyond Settler Time*.

91 First popularized in Italy during the 1970s, microhistory's best-known proponents are Carlo Ginzburg and Natalie Zemon Davis. See Ginzburg, "Microhistory"; and Davis, "Decentering History."

92 Idlout's later surviving photographs, dating from 1958 and depicting a trip to Kalaallit Nunaat/Greenland, are the centrepiece of chapter 6.

93 They were relocated to two sites: Grise Fiord/Ausuittuq and Resolute/Qausuittuq.

94 For a survey of *Inuktitut Magazine*, see Nungak, "Five Decades."

95 Kopytoff, "Cultural Biography of Things"; Edwards, "Exchanging Photographs."

Chapter One

1 *Iqqaumavara*, "Moses Idlout."

2 *Iqqaumavara* is a project undertaken by Productions du Cerf-Volant with the collaboration of the Makivik Corporation and the National Film Board of Canada. The producers are Marquise Lepage, Jean-François Arteau, François Dorval, and Johanne Bergerson. The website is based on an original idea developed by Marquise Lepage and Martha Flaherty, following the production of Lepage's film *Martha of the North* (2008). *Iqqaumavara*, "Team."

3 *Iqqaumavara*, "Moses Idlout."

4 For a discussion of *unikkaat* in Inuit literature, see Martin, *Stories in a New Skin*.

5 Payne et al., eds, *Atiqput*. A selective survey of this literature includes McGrath, "*Isumaksaqsiurutigijakka*"; Collignon, Therrien, and Duchemin-Pelletier, *Orality/Oralité*; Dorais, *Language of the Inuit*; Laugrand and Oosten,

Inuit Shamanism and Christianity; Nakasuk et al., *Inuit Worldviews*, vol. 1; Bennett and Rowley, eds, *Uqalurait*; Kublu, Laugrand, and Oosten, "Listening to Our Past"; and Igloolik Oral History Centre, "Igloolik Oral History Project."

6 See Qikiqtani Truth Commission, https://www.qtcommission.ca/en/; and *Iqqaumavara*, http://www.iqqaumavara.com/.

7 Eekgeesiak, "Foreword," 8.

8 Goldring, "Historians and Inuit," 495.

9 Royal Canadian Mounted Police, *Final Report*, 10–13, 22. Also cited in Qikiqtani Truth Commission, "Commission."

10 Royal Canadian Mounted Police, *Final Report*, 23.

11 For the Qikiqtani Truth Commission's detailed response to the RCMP report, see Qikiqtani Truth Commission, *Analysis of the RCMP Sled Dog Report*.

12 In the same press release, Pita Aatami, president of Makivik Corporation at the time, stated that "the RCMP report worsens the cultural divide and bitterness caused by the killing of the Inuit sled dogs." Qikiqtani Truth Commission, "RCMP Self-Investigation."

13 Truth and Reconciliation Commission of Canada, *Final Report*; Truth and Reconciliation Commission of Canada, *Truth and Reconciliation Commission of Canada: Calls to Action*.

14 Qikiqtani Truth Commission, *QTC Final Report*, 11.

15 Qikiqtani Truth Commission, "Thematic Reports and Special Studies 1950–1975."

16 The Indigenization of judicial process has been addressed by several scholars recently. Brieg Capitaine and Karine Vanthuyne, for example, draw on the work of Tanya Goodman and others regarding "symbolic action" to argue that testimony for the Truth and Reconciliation Commission of Canada uses "the power of actors' stories and discourses … [to] transform social relations." Miranda Brady, in similar analyses, has demonstrated that witness statements for the commission speak through layers of meta-narrative, in this way subverting potential colonial appropriations of the restorative justice process. Capitaine and Vanthuyne, *Power through Testimony*, 8; Brady, "Media Practices," 128–38.

17 Qikiqtani Truth Commission, *QTC Final Report*, 14.

18 Qikiqtani Truth Commission, "Hearings & Interviews."

19 Qikiqtani Truth Commission, "Hearings & Interviews."

20 Qikiqtani Truth Commission, *QTC Final Report*, 14.

21 Goldring, "Historians and Inuit," 495.

22 Goldring, "Historians and Inuit," 514.

23 Qikiqtani Truth Commission, *QTC Final Report*, 15.

24 Qikiqtani Truth Commission, "Thematic Reports and Special Studies 1950–1975."

25 Qikiqtani Truth Commission, "Key Findings."

26 Qikiqtani Truth Commission, *QTC Final Report*, 54. These four broad rubrics are, in turn, discussed in more detail in the report under the themes: "Acknowledging and Healing Past Wrongs," 55–60; "Strengthening Inuit Governance," 60–7; "Strengthening Inuit Culture," 67–73; and "Creating Healthy Communities," 74–81. The report provides specific recommendations for each.

27 *Iqqaumavara*, "Larry Audlaluk." See also Audlaluk, *What I Remember*.

28 *Iqqaumavara*, http://www.iqqaumavara.com/.

29 Marquise Lepage, email correspondence with author, 9 January 2022.

30 *Iqqaumavara*, "Team."

31 Lepage, dir., *Martha of the North*.

32 Marquise Lepage, email correspondence with author, 9 January 2022.

33 *Iqqaumavara*, "About."

34 The timeline itself is not presently available on the site.

35 The five communities are the two High Arctic hamlets of Resolute/Qausuittuq and Grise Fiord/Ausuittuq, the exiles' home communities of Inukjuak/Port Harrison and Pond Inlet/Mittimatalik, and Iqaluit/Frobisher Bay, the capital of Nunavut.

36 *Iqqaumavara*, "Home."

37 Thomasie Alikatuktuk, quoted in Qikiqtani Truth Commission, "RCMP Self-Investigation."

See also Qikiqtani Truth Commission, "Commission."

38 John Amagoalik, interview by Qikiqtani Truth Commission, Iqaluit/Frobisher Bay, 17–19 June 2008, https://www.qtcommission.ca/en/qtiq31.

39 Qikiqtani Truth Commission, "Key Findings."

40 Regan, *Unsettling the Settler Within.*

41 Million, "Felt Theory."

42 Cook, "Politics of Indigenous Voice," 75, original emphasis.

43 Patterson, "Ethical Murk," 213–14, original emphasis.

44 High, "Going Beyond," 119.

45 Tuck, "Suspending Damage."

46 According to the QTC, "The interconnectedness of kinship and place is central to the Inuit worldview ... Qallunaat often mistook and continue to mistake the semi-nomadic history of Inuit as evidence of a lack of attachment to place. In fact, the ability to move to follow game while also maintaining connections with kin who live over a wide geographic area is the result of an intimate experience of place." Qikiqtani Truth Commission, *Nuutauniq: Moves in Inuit Life*, 13.

47 Elisapee Ootoova, interview by Qikiqtani Truth Commission, Pond Inlet/Mittimatalik, 9–11 December 2008, https://www.qtcommission.ca/en/qtpi05.

48 Qikiqtani Truth Commission, *Nuutauniq: Moves in Inuit Life*, 13.

49 For a detailed discussion of the concept of consent and its intercultural complexity in this situation, see Qikiqtani Truth Commission, *Nuutauniq: Moves in Inuit Life*, 10–12.

50 Apphia Killiktee, interview by Qikiqtani Truth Commission, Pond Inlet/Mittimatalik, 9–11 December 2008, https://www.qtcommission.ca/en/qtpi01.

51 Isaac Qiyuapik, interview by Qikiqtani Truth Commission, Pond Inlet/Mittimatalik, 9–11 December 2008, https://www.qtcommission.ca/en/qtpi08.

52 Chapters 5 and 6 include discussions of the Idlout family's experiences during the relocations.

53 Grant, *"Errors Exposed,"* 12–16.

54 Tester and Kulchyski, *Tammarniit (Mistakes)*; Marcus, *Relocating Eden.*

55 Friesen, "'Human Flagpoles.'"

56 The phrase is also repeated by several scholars, including Tester and Kulchyski, *Tammarniit (Mistakes)*; Wright, *Our Ice Is Vanishing*, 142–73; and Stern, *Historical Dictionary*, 165.

57 *Iqqaumavara*, "Markoosie Patsauq." For discussions and archival records that quote government officials discussing the locations as an "experiment," see Grant, *"Errors Exposed"*; Marcus, *Relocating Eden*, 67–123; and Tester and Kulchyski, *Tammarniit (Mistakes)*, 102–204.

58 *Iqqaumavara*, "John Amagoalik."

59 *Iqqaumavara*, "Moses Idlout."

60 Qikiqtani Truth Commission, *Aaniajurliriniq: Health Care in the Qikiqtani Region*, 23–7.

61 For example, Cornelius Kadloo remembered the death of his sister after a visit to the ship at Pond Inlet/Mittimatalik. Cornelius Kadloo, interview by Qikiqtani Truth Commission, Pond Inlet/Mittimatalik, 9–11 December 2008, https://www.qtcommission.ca/en/qtpi03.

62 Inuit Tapiriit Kanatami, "Nanilavut." The Nanilavut (Let's find them) initiative was launched in 2019. A collaboration between Inuit Tapiriit Kanatami, the federal government, and the four regional Inuit associations, Nanilavut established a database of 4,500 Inuit tuberculosis patients sent to the south, including approximately 850 who died there.

63 Dora Padluk, interview by Qikiqtani Truth Commission, Resolute/Qausuittuq, 14–16 April 2008, https://www.qtcommission.ca/en/qtrb02.

64 Lepage, dir., *Martha of the North*; Marquise Lepage, email correspondence with author, 9 January 2022.

65 Ham Kudloo, interview by Qikiqtani Truth Commission, Pond Inlet/Mittimatalik, 9–11 December 2008, https://www.qtcommission.ca/en/qtpi07.

66 Jaykolasie Killiktee, interview by Qikiqtani Truth Commission, Pond Inlet/Mittimatalik, 9–11 December 2008, https://www.qtcommission.ca/en/qtpi10.

67 Idlout d'Argencourt, "C.D. Howe I–V."

68 Qikiqtani Truth Commission, *Paliisikkut: Policing in the Qikiqtani Region*, 11.

69 Elisapee Ootoova, interview by Qikiqtani Truth Commission, Pond Inlet/Mittimatalik, 9–11 December 2008, https://www.qtcommission.ca/en/qtpi05.

70 Elizabeth Kyak, interview by Qikiqtani Truth Commission, Pond Inlet/Mittimatalik, 9–11 December 2008, https://www.qtcommission.ca/en/qtpi06.

71 For information, see Legacy of Hope Foundation, "We Were So Far Away."

72 John Amagoalik, interview by Qikiqtani Truth Commission, Iqaluit/Frobisher Bay, 17–19 June 2008, https://www.qtcommission.ca/en/qtiq31.

73 Joshua Idlout, interview by Qikiqtani Truth Commission, Pond Inlet/Mittimatalik, 9–11 December 2008, https://www.qtcommission.ca/en/qtpi12.

74 Malachi Arreak, interview by Qikiqtani Truth Commission, Pond Inlet/Mittimatalik, 9–11 December 2008, https://www.qtcommission.ca/en/qtpi15.

75 See also Elizabeth Kyak, interview by Qikiqtani Truth Commission, Pond Inlet/Mittimatalik, 9–11 December 2008, https://www.qtcommission.ca/en/qtpi06; and Paomee Komangapik, interview by Qikiqtani Truth Commission, Pond Inlet/Mittimatalik, 9–11 December 2008, https://www.qtcommission.ca/en/qtpi17.

76 Jaykolasie Killiktee, interview by Qikiqtani Truth Commission, Pond Inlet/Mittimatalik, 9–11 December 2008, https://www.qtcommission.ca/en/qtpi10.

77 Apphia Killiktee, interview by Qikiqtani Truth Commission, Pond Inlet/Mittimatalik, 9–11 December 2008, https://www.qtcommission.ca/en/qtpi01.

78 Dora Padluk, interview by Qikiqtani Truth Commission, Resolute/Qausuittuq, 14–16 April 2008, https://www.qtcommission.ca/en/qtrb02.

79 Elisapee Ootoova, interview by Qikiqtani Truth Commission, 9–11 December 2008, https://www.qtcommission.ca/en/qtpi05.

80 Ham Kudloo, interview by Qikiqtani Truth Commission, Pond Inlet/Mittimatalik, 9–11 December 2008, https://www.qtcommission.ca/en/qtpi07.

81 Qikiqtani Truth Commission, *Paliisikkut: Policing in the Qikiqtani Region*, 21.

82 Qikiqtani Truth Commission, *Paliisikkut: Policing in the Qikiqtani Region*, 11.

83 As Elizabeth Kyak stated, "RCMP were treated like children. They had no idea what was up here but they wanted to run everything to their satisfaction. My grandparents used to talk about RCMP when they were new coming up north, they had no idea about the weather or climate. Treated like little kids because they didn't know how to function outside of their house." Elizabeth Kyak, interview by Qikiqtani Truth Commission, Pond Inlet/Mittimatalik, 9–11 December 2008, https://www.qtcommission.ca/en/qtpi06.

84 Elijah Panipakoocho, interview by Qikiqtani Truth Commission, Pond Inlet/Mittimatalik, 9–11 December 2008, https://www.qtcommission.ca/en/qtpi04. Also quoted in part in Qikiqtani Truth Commission, *Paliisikkut: Policing in the Qikiqtani Region*, 10–11.

85 Qikiqtani Truth Commission, *Paliisikkut: Policing in the Qikiqtani Region*, 22–4. For more on Inuit special constables, see Webster, "Unrecognized"; and Zelniker, "Northern Researcher Digs."

86 Elizabeth Kyak, interview by Qikiqtani Truth Commission, Pond Inlet/Mittimatalik, 9–11 December 2008, https://www.qtcommission.ca/en/qtpi06.

87 Ham Kudloo, interview by Qikiqtani Truth Commission, Pond Inlet/Mittimatalik, 9–11 December 2008, https://www.qtcommission.ca/en/qtpi07.

88 Ordinance Respecting Dogs, 1949 revisions, quoted in Qikiqtani Truth Commission, *Qimmiliriniq: Inuit Sled Dogs in the Qikiqtani Region*, 17.

89 Jaykolasie Killiktee, interview by Qikiqtani Truth Commission, Pond Inlet/Mittimatalik, 9–11 December 2008, https://www.qtcommission.ca/en/qtpi10.

90 Ham Kudloo, interview by Qikiqtani Truth Commission, Pond Inlet/Mittimatalik, 9–11 December 2008, https://www.qtcommission.ca/en/qtpi07.

91 Jaykolasie Killiktee, interview by Qikiqtani Truth Commission, Pond Inlet/Mittimatalik, 9–11 December 2008, https://www.qtcommission.ca/en/qtpi10.

92 Malachi Arreak, interview by Qikiqtani Truth Commission, Pond Inlet/Mittimatalik, 9–11 December 2008, https://www.qtcommission.ca/en/qtpi15.

93 Qikiqtani Truth Commission, *QTC Final Report*, 19.

94 On 14 August 2019, the Canadian government acknowledged the grave impact of Sangussaqtauliqtilluta in the Qikiqtani region in a public apology. The minister of Crown-Indigenous relations at the time, Carolyn Bennett, issued the apology. Government of Canada, "Minister of Crown-Indigenous Relations." See also Qikiqtani Truth Commission, "Statement of Apology."

95 Qikiqtani Truth Commission, "About the Photographs," 6–7.

96 John Amagoalik's quote is used in director Peter Raymont's NFB film *Magic in the Sky* (1981), quoted in Geller, *Northern Exposures*, 14; and in Dyck, "Looking for Kenojuak," 188.

97 Pratt, *Imperial Eyes*.

98 Pratt, *Imperial Eyes*, 7.

99 The preface also cites a specific experience witnessed by John Amagoalik in 1956, which I reference in chapter 5.

100 Qikiqtani Truth Commission, "About the Photographs," 6–7.

101 Here, Gerald Vizenor's familiar concept of "survivance" comes to mind. As Vizenor states, "The character of survivance creates a sense of native presence over absence, nihility, and victimry. Native survivance is an active sense of presence over absence, deracination, and oblivion; survivance is the continuance of stories, not a mere reaction, however pertinent. Survivance is greater than the right of a survivable name. Survivance stories are renunciations of dominance, detractions, obtrusions, the unbearable sentiments of tragedy and the legacy of victimry. Survivance is the heritable right of succession or reversion of an estate and, in the course of international declarations of human rights, is a narrative estate of native survivance." Vizenor, "Aesthetics of Survivance," 1.

102 Eekgeesiak, "Foreword," 8.

103 Idlout d'Argencourt, "C.D. Howe I."

Chapter Two

1 Wilkinson, *Land of the Long Day*, 20.

2 Flaherty, "Preface"; Marcus, *Relocating Eden*, 14–15.

3 "Toronto Film Society – Members' Evaluation form," [1951], National Film Board of Canada Archives (hereafter NFB Archives), 51-410, *Land of the Long Day* production files.

4 As noted in the book's introduction, my thinking about Indigenous agency before the camera is informed by a wealth of work by Indigenous scholars and critical anthropology. See, for example, Tsinhnahjinnie, "When Is a Photograph?"; Lonetree, "Heritage of Resilience"; Pedri-Spade, "'But They Were Never'"; Raheja, "Reading Nanook's Smile"; and Thomas, "At the Kitchen Table." See also Williams, "Indigenous Uses of Photography."

5 Find a Grave, "Kidla Rebecca Idlout (1916–1965)." My thanks to Madeleine d'Argencourt and Lucie Idlout for information about their grandmother.

6 Qikiqtani Truth Commission, *Community Histories 1950–1975: Pond Inlet (Mittimatalik)*, 3. For a history of the region, see also Grant, *Arctic Justice*, 9.

7 Harper, "Akumalik." For Doug Wilkinson's photograph of Akumalik showing his tattoos, see Nunavut Archives, Douglas E. Wilkinson fonds, GN-1991-059-0116. My thanks to Deborah Kigjugalik Webster for this information.

8 Susan Salluviniq, interview by Augatnaaq Eccles and Carol Payne, 22 March 2023.

9 For a detailed history of the region, see Grant, *Arctic Justice*, 7–23.

10 Grant, *Arctic Justice*, 7–23.

11 The Qikiqtani Truth Commission dates the whaling station to 1903, whereas Grant says that it was established in 1904 after Captain James Mutch had wintered at Erik Harbour in 1903–04. Grant, *Arctic Justice*, 21; Qikiqtani

Truth Commission, *Community Histories 1950–1975: Pond Inlet (Mittimatalik)*, 4.

12 Qikiqtani Truth Commission, *Community Histories 1950–1975: Pond Inlet (Mittimatalik)*, 4.

13 "Akoomalik and Nanora left today for Button Point only," 10 July 1922, HBC Ledger, 1922–23, Hudson's Bay Company Archives, b.465.a.2 Pond's Inlet 1922–23.

14 The next most successful hunters were Angnaweeapik with 78 foxes and Jobie with 76. "Journal of Events," 31 May 1946, Hudson's Bay Company Archives, item 3. In January of the same year, the HBC recorded Idlout as trapping 71 foxes, the second-best rate after the hunter Eenooagak with 78. "Journal of Events," 31 January 1946, Hudson's Bay Company Archives, item 2.

15 Anglican Church of Canada, "General Synod Archives."

16 Harper, "Akumalik."

17 Harper, "Akumalik."

18 Anglican Church of Canada Archives, M96-7, Diocese of the Arctic, series 1, Archibald Lang Fleming Records, subseries 1-1, Clergy files 1927–72, box 1, boxes 17 1a–d, 2, 3; Anglican Church of Canada Archives, M96-7, Diocese of the Arctic, series 1, Turner, John Hudspith, Rev. (Pond Inlet; Moffet Inlet), 1 of 4 files, 1929–47; Flint, *Operation Canon.*

19 Anglican Church of Canada Archives, M96-7, Diocese of the Arctic, series 1, Archibald Lang Fleming Records, subseries 1-1, Clergy files 1927–72, box 1, box 17 1d; Anglican Church of Canada Archives, M96-7, Diocese of the Arctic, series 1, Turner, John Hudspith, Rev. (Pond Inlet, Moffet Inlet), 4 of 4 files, 1946–48.

20 Akumalik seemed to serve as a handyman for the missionaries but also did Bible reading with them and led services himself when out on the land. "Towards the end of January Akoomalik went away to the floe edge hunting … on the Sundays he is away, he holds service for the people in that camp." Harold Duncan, journal, 24 July 1932, Scott Polar Research Institute, Thomas H. Manning Polar Archive, Harold Duncan Papers, MS1576/2.

21 Other ministers at Pond Inlet/Mittimatalik included Rev. Harold Duncan (1929–33), Rev. Maurice Sidney Flint (1937–40), Rev. Thomas Daulby (1944–53), and Rev. Donald Whitbread (1926–78). Anglican Church of Canada Archives, M96-7, Diocese of the Arctic, series 1, Archibald Lang Fleming Records, subseries 1-1, Clergy files 1927–72, box 1, boxes 17 1a–d, 2, 3; Anglican Church of Canada Archives, M96-7, Diocese of the Arctic, series 1, Turner, John Hudspith, Rev. (Pond Inlet, Moffet Inlet), 1 of 4 files, 1929–47; box 2, item 1; Anglican Church of Canada Archives, M96-7, Diocese of the Arctic, series 1, Daulby, Thomas, Rev. (Pond Inlet) 1944–61, box 2; Anglican Church of Canada Archives, M96-7, Diocese of the Arctic, series 1, Flint, Maurice Sidney, Rev. (Pond Inlet) 1937–56, box 2, file 2; Scott Polar Research Institute, Thomas H. Manning Polar Archive, Harold Duncan Papers, MS1576.

22 "Got the purchase slip for the rifle Akoomalik surreptitiously bought last week … Spoke to Akoomalik for 50 minutes about his deceitfulness. Had a time of prayer about it." Harold Duncan, journal, 3 October 1932, Scott Polar Research Institute, Thomas H. Manning Polar Archive, Harold Duncan Papers, MS1576/1/3; "hypocrisy of these people – anything to get material things," Harold Duncan, journal, 19 September 1932, Scott Polar Research Institute, Thomas H. Manning Polar Archive, Harold Duncan Papers, MS1576/2/2.

23 Thomas Daulby, form letter to supporters, 15 August 1950, Anglican Church of Canada Archives, M96-7, Diocese of the Arctic, series 1, Archibald Lang Fleming Records, subseries 1-1, clergy files 1927–72, box 1, item 4.

24 The Tununirmiut negotiation with missionaries, of course, calls to mind Homi K. Bhabha's discussion of the rejection of British missionaries on the Indian subcontinent in his classic essay "Signs Taken for Wonders."

25 Among discussions of the history of ethnographic photography of Inuit in the eastern Arctic, see Stern, "History of Canadian Arctic Photography"; Condon, "History and Development"; and Geller, *Northern Exposures.*

26 According to Jim Burant, on board the chartered whaling vessel the *Neptune*, members of Low's expedition, which was charged with

asserting Canadian sovereignty in the Arctic islands, photographed the scenery and people they met. Burant, "Using Photography"; Grant, *Arctic Justice*, 26–8.

27 Grant, *Arctic Justice*, 130–40; Geller, *Northern Exposures*, 19–20.

28 Geller, *Northern Exposures*, 24–37.

29 Yet, as Geller eloquently states, "despite the sense in which these images are merely pale ghosts, stand-ins for the people portrayed, they continue to convey something more 'real': hints of past lives lived, paths crossed – the North that is more than that which can be mapped and measured and counted in the quest for knowledge and control." Geller, *Northern Exposures*, 36.

30 For more on Project Naming and other reidentification projects, see chapter 7.

31 For an insightful discussion of Wilkinson's life, particularly his experience as a Northern Service officer in Baker Lake/Qamani'tuaq, where he established an "Eskimo Council," see Kulchyski and Tester, *Kiumajut (Talking Back)*, 204–38; and Brum and Pennington, N92-012 *Douglas E. Wilkinson Fonds*. The Douglas E. Wilkinson fonds now reside in the Nunavut Archives. In 1954, Wilkinson recounted, "There was nothing in my background to suggest a predilection for Eskimo life." Wilkinson, "How I Became an Eskimo," 28–9. See chapter 4 for a discussion of this provocative article and other publications by Wilkinson.

32 More than twenty years after his first journey north, Wilkinson was still publishing about the region. Wilkinson, *Arctic Coast*; Wilkinson, *Arctic Fever*.

33 Wilkinson, *Land of the Long Day*, 18.

34 A production worksheet and other archival documents credit Wilkinson as the director, although the actual film credits list him as the arranger and editor. "Master Card Index, Work Sheet," 3 April 1947, NFB Archives, 07-035, Exercise Musk-Ox, vol. 1 (1946); Wilkinson, dir., *Exercise Musk-Ox*. The credits read, "Photography – Roger Racine; Arranged and edited by – Doug Wilkinson; Maps and animation – Allan Ackman; Commentator – Robert Anderson; Music and effects – Joan Edward, Nina Finn; Production – Robert Anderson, E.W. Scythes." See also Holloway, "Exercise Musk-Ox"; and Thrasher, "Exercise Musk Ox," 27.

35 Lauder, *Tracks North*; Thrasher, "Exercise Musk Ox."

36 Wilkinson, dir., *Exercise Musk-Ox*; "NFB Information Sheet," December 1946, NFB Archives, 07-035, Exercise Musk-Ox, vol. 1 (1946). Released in December 1946, the film proved popular. It was screened almost 1,800 times across Canada and further circulated through some sixty-three national and international loans and forty-one sales.

37 Robert Anderson, who wrote the script for *Exercise Musk-Ox*, is listed as the producer of *Going North*. "Production Request," 28 November 1947, NFB Archives, 12-112, "Going North."

38 Doug Wilkinson, section on prior Arctic experience, in "Application for Grant-in-Aid," Library and Archives Canada (LAC), Arctic Institute of North America fonds, MG28-179, vol. 83, file 8, 2.

39 "NFB Information Sheet," 1948, NFB Archives, 12-112 "Going North."

40 Nichols, *Introduction to Documentary*, 121–5; Nichols, *Representing Reality*.

41 "Reel 2 and Typescript," 1948, 8–9, NFB Archives, 12-112 "Going North." The narration reads,

> The Arctic barrenland is the home of the Eskimo. He never leaves it. His environment supplies all his simple requirements and dictates the whole manner of his living. He dresses first in a light caribou skin – fur turned in. Then another skin – fur turned out. The skins are soft and light and these two layers are better than one heavy garment. The Eskimo may not know it, but his dress is scientifically efficient in its use of still-air insulation. The hairs on the furs trap layers of still air – one outside, and another next to the body. Many pockets of air between the two skins form still another layer. Dead enclosed air is a good insulator. Dressed like this, the Eskimo can keep warm in the Arctic winds he faces on the move. Mud frozen on his sled runners and covered

later with water to form a layer of smooth ice, eases the burden for his dogs, and he can carry all his worldly goods on his sled as he wanders in search of good hunting. He is a skilled hunter, for his life and his family's depend on his certain hand and eye. The caribous is a principal source of meat, and provides the best skins for winter clothing.

42 Doug Wilkinson, section on prior Arctic experience, in "Application for Grant-in-Aid," LAC, Arctic Institute of North America fonds, MG28-179, vol. 83, file 8, 2. Although records credit S.J. Bailey, Wilkinson contributed photographs to Library and Archives Canada, "Album 37, Eastern Arctic Patrol," which contains 626 photos, and to Library and Archives Canada, "Album 66, Eastern Arctic Patrol," which contains 79 photos.

43 Ralph Foster, Memo, 3 May 1949, NFB Archives, 11-207, Classroom Films Project.

44 Michéa, dir., *Across Arctic Ungava*. See also Library and Archives Canada, "Across Arctic Ungava."

45 Rousseau, "Botany Report"; Aubert de la Rue, "Geology."

46 T.C. Daly to Chester Kissick, US Army Base, Churchill, 15 June 1949, NFB Archives, 11-207, Classroom Films Project. See also the *Arctic Circular* article "Arctic Note Book Series."

47 The two films elicited a complaint to the NFB from Donald Marshall, the Anglican bishop of the Arctic, that they were made "purely and simply" because of their "propaganda value for the Roman Church." Marshall's letter (11 January 1951) is quoted by Film Commissioner W. Arthur Irwin in his response to the bishop. W. Arthur Irwin to Donald Marsh (Bishop of Arctic – Anglican), 23 January 1951, NFB Archives, 11-207, Classroom Films Project.

48 See "Teaching Notes: How to Build an Igloo," NFB brochure distributed to schools, NFB Archives, 11-207, Classroom Films Project.

49 Wilkinson, dir., *How to Build an Igloo.*

50 Dubois, "'How to Build an Igloo.'"

51 National Film Board of Canada, "Arctic Dog Team."

52 "*Arctic Dog Team* Typescript," 1949, NFB Archives, 11-207, Classroom Films Project.

53 Wilkinson also later listed in his filmmaking activities research for director Nils Rasmussen's 1950 NFB film *Hunters of the North Pole.* Doug Wilkinson, section on filmmaking, in "Application for Grant-in-Aid," LAC, Arctic Institute of North America fonds, MG28-179, vol. 83, file 8, 2.

54 In a letter to Chester Kissick about the film *How to Build an Igloo*, Tom Daly of the NFB recounted, "The interior igloo stuff is being reserved for inclusion in Doug Wilkinson's larger opus on Eskimo life." T.C. Daly to Chester Kissick, US Army Base, Churchill, 15 June 1949, NFB Archives, 11-207, Classroom Films Project.

55 "Films of the Eastern Arctic." This short description of initial plans for the project appeared in a November 1950 issue of *The Arctic Circular*, the newsletter of the Arctic Circle, an informal organization of Arctic researchers and amateurs in Ottawa. Wilkinson, who periodically wrote for the journal and attended the Arctic Circle's meetings at this time, likely supplied the information himself, although it was published after he had departed for the north. *The Arctic Circular* was published from 1948 to 1984. The Arctic Circle, hosting monthly meetings in Ottawa, is still in existence. The Arctic Circle, "Welcome to the Arctic Circle."

56 "Films of the Eastern Arctic." Several amateur films were made in the region at this time. Wilkinson may be alluding to films such as one by Americans Lewis Rasmussen and Betty Rasmussen titled *Arctic Holiday*, which was shot in Churchill and Arviat/Eskimo Point in 1947. See "Arctic Holiday."

57 "Films of the Eastern Arctic," 56.

58 Of course, *Nanook of the North* was far from the only Arctic film of the silent era. For more on the history of early cinema in the North American Arctic, see Geller, *Northern Exposures.*

59 Wilkinson, *Land of the Long Day*, 20.

60 Grimshaw, "Who Has the Last Laugh?" 421.

61 Marcus, *Relocating Eden*, 11–14.

62 Flaherty and Hubbard Flaherty, *My Eskimo Friends*, 1, 119–70.

63 See, among others, Marcus, "Nanook of the North"; Winston, *Claiming the Real*; and Rony, *Third Eye*. For overviews of the extensive critical literature on *Nanook of the North*, see Grimshaw, "Who Has the Last Laugh?"; and Skare, *Nanook of the North*.

64 Raheja, "Reading Nanook's Smile." Inuk throat singer Tanya Tagaq's recent performances with screenings of *Nanook of the North* also constitute, in my view, an effort to re-engage with the agency of the performers in the film. See Gordon, "Inuk Throat Singer."

65 Wilkinson and Vivian Jean Latremouille (1919–2011) married in October 1941. The two would enjoy a close and sustaining marriage lasting sixty-five years until Doug Wilkinson's death. "Vivian Wilkinson: Obituary."

66 Wilkinson may have initially hoped to film around Arviat/Eskimo Point, but production was delayed due to epidemics (including poliomyelitis) in the Keewatin District. In a letter to Chester Kissick about the film *How to Build an Igloo*, Tom Daly of the NFB recounted, "The interior igloo stuff is being reserved for inclusion in Doug Wilkinson's larger opus on Eskimo life, which was to have been shot this year, but was postponed, as you are no doubt aware, till next year because of the epidemics." T.C. Daly to Chester Kissick, US Army Base, Churchill, 15 June 1949, NFB Archives, 11-207, Classroom Films Project. That year, a polio epidemic was reported in the Keewatin District, followed the next year by an influenza epidemic farther west in Cambridge Bay/Iqaluktuuttiaq. "Poliomyelitis in Keewatin District"; Porsild, "Biological Exploration," 2–3.

67 Wilkinson, "National Film Board Arctic Project," 37.

68 "Films of the Eastern Arctic," 57.

69 Wilkinson, "National Film Board Arctic Project," 37.

70 Wilkinson, "National Film Board Arctic Project," 37.

71 Desjardins, dir., *Making Movie History*.

72 Wilkinson proposed that the 16 mm stock could be blown up "quite satisfactorily." "Films of the Eastern Arctic," 57.

73 Flaherty wrote about screening rushes for the film's participants. See, for example, Flaherty and Hubbard Flaherty, *My Eskimo Friends*, 135–6. In the preface to his book about the film, Flaherty wrote, "I took with me not only cameras, but apparatus to print and project my results as they were being made so my character and his family could understand and appreciate what I was doing. As soon as I showed them some of the first results, Nanook and his crowd were completely won over." Flaherty, "Preface."

74 Wilkinson, "National Film Board Arctic Project," 38.

75 "Transcript," 2 October 1951, NFB Archives, 51-319, *Sister Pelagie* production files; Wilkinson, dir. *Sister Pelagie*. Wilkinson also shot a still photograph of Sister Pelagie during the ceremony: "Twenty year old Sister Naye Pelagie became Canada's first Inuit nun. Sister Pelagie is shown as she takes her vows on entering the Order of the Grey Nuns during a ceremony in the Roman Catholic Church at Chesterfield, N.W.T." Photo of Sister Pelagie, March 1951, Chesterfield, Northwest Territories, photographer Doug Wilkinson, LAC, National Film Board of Canada fonds, Still Photography Division fonds, acc. 1971-271, PA-184553. See also Laugrand and Oosten, "Case of Pelagie Inuk."

76 Wilkinson, dir., *Arctic Lifeline*; NFB Archives, 52-106, *Arctic Lifeline* production files; Wilkinson, "National Film Board Arctic Project," 38.

77 Wilkinson, "National Film Board Arctic Project," 37.

78 Although shot in colour, production files indicate that the two films were distributed in both colour and black and white. *Land of the Long Day* "Summary," 1952, NFB Archives, 51-410, *Land of the Long Day* production files; "NFB Angotee Information Sheet," 1952, NFB Archives, 51-405, *Angotee* production files.

79 Wintle, "Moving Image Technology," 36; Hickey, "First Movies Made."

80 "The name of Angotee was chosen, mainly because he was an old man who was very well respected in the Chesterfield community and he was the first man to die in the polio epidemic. And … it's a remembrance of old Angotee.

And his son-in-law is the man who plays the father in the film." Doug Wilkinson, interview by Shelagh Mackenzie and Mary Sparling, 29 March 1985, La Have, Nova Scotia, for Inuit Art Documentation and Film Research Project, 4, LAC, Department of Indian Affairs and Northern Development fonds, R216-3855-6-E, RG85-E-2.

81 Credits identify Singeetuk (Shineektuk) as the father, Ookpik as the mother, Maunee as the grandmother, Madelaine as the elder sister, and Tooga as the younger sister. The actors portraying the title character are John Ell (of a family descended from Nivissannaq) as the infant, Angotee at age two, Tooga at age seven, Celesteno at age twelve, and Aliuk at eighteen to twenty. The film also includes a number of other Inuit and settlers not identified by name in the credits or in archival records. "NFB Angotee Location Schedule and Titles," 1952, NFB Archives, 51-405, *Angotee* production files. For a later reference to Singeetuk's role in the film, see W.G. Kerr to R.A.J. Phillips, 15 January 1958, LAC, Department of Indian Affairs and Northern Development fonds, RG85, vol. 465, file 1005-1, 10, box 14.

82 Doug Wilkinson, interview by Shelagh Mackenzie and Mary Sparling, 29 March 1985, La Have, Nova Scotia, for Inuit Art Documentation and Film Research Project, 12, LAC, Department of Indian Affairs and Northern Development fonds, R216-3855-6-E, RG85-E-2.

83 Wilkinson, "National Film Board Arctic Project," 38

84 "Snow Baby Is Born."

85 "NFB Angotee Information Sheet," 1952, NFB Archives, 51-405, *Angotee* production files.

86 Arnaquq-Baril, *Indigenous Filmmaking*, 2.

87 This scene was not in Wilkinson's initial outline, which did not include southerners at all and was more fully primitivizing, including commentary on infanticide. "Arctic Film Project Story Outline #3," 30 June 1950, NFB Archives, 51-405, *Angotee* production files.

88 "Angotee Commentary (Narration Script)," 1952, NFB Archives, 51-405, *Angotee* production files.

89 Donald Marshall, bishop of the Arctic from 1950 to 1974, who complained that *Arctic Dog Team* and *How to Build an Igloo* were made because of their "propaganda value for the Roman Church" (see note 47), apparently did not protest to the NFB either about the Catholic marriage ceremony in *Angotee* or about the 1951 short *Sister Pelagie*.

90 Doug Wilkinson, *Land of the Long Day*, 21.

91 Doug Wilkinson, *Land of the Long Day*, 21.

92 Hudson's Bay Company Archives, "Herodier, Gaston."

93 David Kalluk, interview by Qikiqtani Truth Commission, Pond Inlet/Mittimatalik, 9–11 December 2008, https://www.qtcommission.ca/en/qtrb01.

94 Ludy Padluk (Pudluk), interview by Qikiqtani Truth Commission, Pond Inlet/Mittimatalik, 9–11 December 2008, https://www.qtcommission.ca/en/qtrb03.

95 Flaherty, "Preface"; Marcus, *Relocating Eden*, 14–15.

96 Raheja, "Reading Nanook's Smile," 1161–2.

97 Doug Wilkinson, interview by Shelagh Mackenzie and Mary Sparling, 29 March 1985, La Have, Nova Scotia, for Inuit Art Documentation and Film Research Project, 12, LAC, Department of Indian Affairs and Northern Development fonds, R216-3855-6-E, RG85-E-2.

98 "Qitsualik said the leader of the Eskimo group, whom he estimated to be between 45 and 50 at the time, was probably the only one paid anything for the film work." Quoted in "$2 Bill Has His Picture."

99 Remuneration was typical. For example, Idlout and his father, Akumalik, were paid by the missionary Harold Duncan for skins, game, and repairs. Scott Polar Research Institute, Thomas H. Manning Polar Archive, Harold Duncan Papers, MS1576, 1.1–1.3, 2.1–2.2.

100 Wilkinson, "National Film Board Arctic Project," 38.

101 "$2 Bill Has His Picture."

102 Desjardins, dir., *Making Movie History*.

103 Wilkinson had initially planned simply to film flora and fauna in the region. "Films of the Eastern Arctic," 57.

104 "Scripting and Research Request," 1 November 1951, NFB Archives, 51-410, *Land of the Long Day* production files.

105 The shorter version, *Arctic Saga*, was printed in 35 mm. "Information Sheet," 10 June 1952, NFB Archives, 51-341, *Arctic Saga* production files.

106 When their own stock libraries did not have adequate recordings, the NFB sought out material from research scientists. See, for example, Arthur A. Allen to Michael Spencer, 31 March 1952, NFB Archives, 51-410, *Land of the Long Day* production files.

107 In contrast, snapshots that Wilkinson took of Idlout's camp at this time and during a later trip reveal a number of purchased items. Further, Wilkinson talks in later publications about Idlout saving up to buy products. Wilkinson, "Idlouk – Arctic Amateur."

108 There is a link between Curtis's work and that of Wilkinson's model, Flaherty. According to Alan Rudolph Marcus, Curtis screened a print of *In the Land of the Head Hunters* for Flaherty in 1915. Marcus, "Nanook of the North," 202–3.

109 "Films of the Eastern Arctic," 20.

110 *Nanook of the North*'s opening intertitles read in full: "The mysterious Barren Lands – desolate, boulder strewn, wind-swept – illimitable spaces which top the world. The sterility of the soil and the rigor of the climate no other race could survive: yet here, utterly dependent upon animal life, which is their sole source of food, live the most cheerful people in all the world – the fearless, lovable, happy-go-lucky Eskimo. This picture concerns the life of one Nanook (The Bear), his family and the little band of followers, 'Itivimuits' of Hopewell Sound, Northern Ungava, through whose kindliness, faithfulness and patience this film was made."

111 One recorded song repeats the name Angotee several times. It was likely recorded for the earlier film of the same name but incorporated into *Land of the Long Day*. "Music Cue Sheet," July 1952, NFB Archives, 51-410, *Land of the Long Day* production files. Wilkinson himself was dissatisfied with the quality of the audio recordings, which he said were all made "as tests." Wilkinson played them for the anthropologist Marius Barbeau, who in turn wanted to use the recordings "on a disc of Canadian folksongs." Wilkinson noted in correspondence that he was "even less happy" about this prospect. Doug Wilkinson to Louis Applebaum, memorandum, 13 March 1952, NFB Archives, 51-341, *Arctic Saga* production files.

112 As Wilkinson stated, "For the recordings of *Land of the Long Day*, there's a lot of material in it in Eskimo, as the various Eskimo people speak, there's recording of birds and wildlife, none of that was recorded in the Arctic, none at all ... We could not get the recorder to work in the cold ... so, they had a number of people in the Immigration Hospital [*sic*] in Quebec City, and we knew some of them. So, we went down to Quebec City on two different occasions with the Film Board crew and recorded all the voices." Doug Wilkinson, interview by Shelagh Mackenzie and Mary Sparling, 29 March 1985, La Havre, Nova Scotia, for Inuit Art Documentation and Film Research Project, 1, LAC, Department of Indian Affairs and Northern Development fonds, R216-3855-6-E, RG85-E-2.

113 Idlout d'Argencourt, "C.D. Howe IV." A narrative posted by Canadian Geographic about Inuit tuberculosis patients states that Leah was moved to a hospital in Hamilton until 1955; however, her own recollections suggest that she returned to the Arctic in 1952. Canadian Geographic, "Roads to Reconciliation."

114 Idlout d'Argencourt, "C.D. Howe III," 31.

115 In the text for the second intertitle, Wilkinson hints at his authorship by carefully using the conditional tense: "This is their story ... told as Idlouk *would have* told it" (emphasis added).

116 Les McFarlane, "Notes re Baffin Island Commentary," memorandum, n.d., NFB Archives, 51-410, *Land of the Long Day* production files.

117 The brief scene of the young seal sliding down a hill featured a seal caught and kept for filming. "We'd catch a seal or have one brought to us. We usually caught them ourselves there because we were out all the time. Jean [Roy] kept it in his tent ... The sequence in Land of the Long Day where the young seal is in the water and you see it come up and out of the hole ... that was one of our captives and we found a place where there was that great big pool ... We finally found one [a hole in the ice] with a blocked-off opening and for photographs we

chucked him in and he could swim in and out, come in and out of his hole." Doug Wilkinson, interview by Shelagh Mackenzie and Mary Sparling, 29 March 1985, La Have, Nova Scotia, for Inuit Art Documentation and Film Research Project, 15, LAC, Department of Indian Affairs and Northern Development fonds, R216-3855-6-E, RG85-E-2.

118 "Baffin Island Shot List," [1951], NFB Archives, 51-410, *Land of the Long Day* production files.

119 McMahon, *Arctic Twilight*, 191.

120 "Toronto Film Society – Members' Evaluation form," [1951], NFB Archives, 51-410, *Land of the Long Day* production files.

121 *Land of the Long Day* was one of three Honourable Mentions at the Robert J. Flaherty Film Awards in 1952. Janet Scellen to Don Chatwin, telegram, 28 October 1952, NFB Archives, 51-410, *Land of the Long Day* production files. The other awards included the Grand Prize at the International Short Film Festival, La Spezia, Italy, 1957; the Gulf of Salerno Grand Trophy at the Annual Documentary Film Festival, Salerno, Italy, 1956; the Diploma of Honour at the International Sports Film Festival, Cortina d'Ampezzo, Italy, 1954; and the Golden Reel Award – First Prize – Category: Geography and Travel at the Annual Golden Reel Film Festival, Film Council of America, Chicago, 1954. National Film Board of Canada, "Land of the Long Day."

122 Pierre de Bellefeuille to Arthur Irwin et al., memorandum, 26 June 1953, NFB Archives, 51-410, *Land of the Long Day* production files. Although the *Picture Post* pictorial mainly addresses the birth scene from *Angotee*, the four-page spread also includes a portrait of Idlout shot during the filming of *Land of the Long Day*. "Snow Baby Is Born." World Wide Photos also requested images from the shoot. Anthony J. Wright to Len Chatwin et al., memo, 26 June 1953, NFB Archives, 51-410, *Land of the Long Day* production files.

123 "Toronto Film Society – Members' Evaluation Form," [1951], NFB Archives, 51-410, *Land of the Long Day* production files.

124 The screening was for the Women's Royal Canadian Naval Service, Vancouver Branch. The comment from the report is quoted in correspondence from producer Michael Spencer. Michael Spencer to Jim Patterson (NFB, Vancouver), 23 July 1953, NFB Archives, 51-410, *Land of the Long Day* production files.

125 Michael Spencer to Jim Patterson (NFB, Vancouver), 23 July 1953, NFB Archives, 51-410, *Land of the Long Day* production files.

126 The close-up appears during a brief scene of Idlout and Kadloo eating *muktuk* (narwhal fat). It appears at 27:52.

127 Arnaquq-Baril, *Indigenous Filmmaking*, 2; Fabian, *Time and the Other*, 31.

128 Doug Wilkinson, interview by Shelagh Mackenzie and Mary Sparling, 29 March 1985, La Havre, Nova Scotia, for Inuit Art Documentation and Film Research Project, 6–7, LAC, Department of Indian Affairs and Northern Development fonds, R216-3855-6-E, RG85-E-2.

129 Idlout, "Letter to an Administrator."

130 Idlout d'Argencourt, "Spring," 49.

Chapter Three

1 Idlout d'Argencourt, "Spring."

2 Idlout d'Argencourt, "Spring," 49.

3 Idlout, "Letter to an Administrator," my translation.

4 Government of Nunavut, *Incorporating Inuit Societal Values*, 21.

5 Tagalik, "*Inuit Qaujimajatuqangit*."

6 Government of Nunavut, "Our Guiding Principles."

7 Idlout d'Argencourt, "First Inuit Picture," 32.

8 Idlout's later surviving photographs, dating from 1958 and depicting a trip to Kalaallit Nunaat/Greenland, are the centrepiece of chapter 6.

9 Igloliorte, "Curating Inuit Qaujimajatuqangit."

10 Located at https://www.josephidloutphotographs.ca/en and https://www.josephidloutphotographs.ca/iu/home.

11 The photographs are housed in the Nunavut Archives within the Douglas E. Wilkinson fonds. Until 2017, the fonds was accessible online through the Northwest Territories Archives, located in the Prince of Wales Northern

Heritage Centre in Yellowknife, Northwest Territories, which then housed it.

12 Campbell and Bishop-Stall's proposal is organized around the original six IQ principles: *aajiiqatigiinniq, piliriqatigiinniq/ikajuqtigiinniq, tunnganarniq, inuuqatigiitsiarniq, pilimmaksarniq/pijariuqsarniq,* and *qanuqtuurniq*. Campbell and Bishop-Stall, "Inuit Approach to Archival Work."

13 We are grateful to the reader for this insight.

14 Karetak, Tester, and Tagalik, eds, *Inuit Qaujimajatuqangit.*

15 Among the literature are Karetak, Tester, and Tagalik, eds, *Inuit Qaujimajatuqangit*; Tester and Irniq, "Inuit Qaujimajatuqangit"; and Tagalik, "*Inuit Qaujimajatuqangit.*"

16 Igloliorte, "Curating Inuit Qaujimajatuqangit."

17 Igloliorte, "Curating Inuit Qaujimajatuqangit," 103.

18 Eccles, "Curatorial Essay."

19 Eccles, "Teacher's Guide."

20 For example, in interviews with Elders conducted in Pond Inlet/Mittimatalik and Iqaluit/Frobisher Bay in 2018, Idlout's son Paul and Ludy Pudluk as well as the brothers Elijah Erkloo and Daniel Komangapik, all members of Idlout's camp in the 1950s, recalled him photographing regularly. Paul Idlout, interview by Christina Williamson and Carol Payne, Apex, Baffin Island, 10 May 2018; Ludy Pudluk, interview by Alexandra Anaviapik, Carol Payne, and Christina Williamson, Pond Inlet/Mittimatalik, 7 May 2018; Elijah Erkloo and Daniel Komangapik, interview by Alexandra Anaviapik, Carol Payne, and Christina Williamson, Pond Inlet/Mittimatalik, 9 May 2018. See also Boudaud, "Les photos de famille," 81.

21 See, for example, photographic documents of Governor General Vincent Massey's sojourn in Resolute/Qausuittuq during his 1956 tour of the north, which include pictures of Idlout and his camera. Among these documents are "Governor General's Northern Tour: Three Inuit Men Holding Brownie Cameras Await the Arrival of the Governor General Vincent Massey at Resolute Bay, N.W.T.," March 1956, Resolute Bay, photographer, Gar Lunney, Library and Archives Canada (LAC), National Film Board of Canada fonds, e002265651. Director Barry Greenwald's 1990 documentary *Between Two Worlds* also shows images of Idlout's home in Resolute/Qausuittuq photographed in 1955 or later with his Duaflex camera.

22 These photographs include seven taken with Idlout's camera illustrating Idlout d'Argencourt, "Merry Christmas!"; an image of Jean Roy with Doug and Vivian Wilkinson on board the CGS *C.D. Howe* credited to Joseph Idlout that appears in Idlout d'Argencourt, "C.D. Howe I," 41; and a snapshot of Leah as a child carrying a younger sibling in her *amautik* (woman's parka) that is paired with a photograph taken by Doug Wilkinson of the two children, although not taken at the same time, that is reproduced in Idlout d'Argencourt, "C.D. Howe V," 29.

23 Philippa Ootoova, community archivist, Pond Inlet Archives, Pond Inlet/Mittimatalik, email correspondence with author, 13 September 2016.

24 Nunavut Archives, Douglas E. Wilkinson fonds; Wilkinson, "Idlouk – Arctic Amateur."

25 Wilkinson, "How I Became an Eskimo"; Wilkinson, *Land of the Long Day*; Wilkinson, dir., *White Eskimo*. Interestingly, although Idlout served as cameraman for the latter newsreel, his photography is not mentioned in either the 1954 article or the 1955 book cited here.

26 Fabian, *Time and the Other*, 31.

27 Wilkinson, "Idlouk – Arctic Amateur," 38.

28 Idlout d'Argencourt, "C.D. Howe I"; Idlout d'Argencourt, "C.D. Howe V."

29 Akumalik, Idlout's father, constructed the *qajaq*.

30 Rhoda Kayakjuak, translation of 1954 published letter, email correspondence with author, 26 November 2018; Nellie Erko, translation of 1954 published letter, email correspondence with author, 28 November 2018.

31 Wilkinson, "Idlouk – Arctic Amateur," 38–9.

32 Wilkinson, "Idlouk – Arctic Amateur," 39.

33 In the 1954 *Photography* article, Wilkinson says that he arranged for the camera and film to be sent to Idlout in Pond Inlet/Mittimatalik on a supply ship. However, archival records suggest

that the Duaflex had been used by Wilkinson's own family on the eve of the trip. It is more likely that Wilkinson brought the Kodak with him, along with his more professional film and still cameras. Wilkinson, "Idlouk – Arctic Amateur," 107.

34 Toronto Metropolitan University Archives and Special Collections, "Cameras"; Toronto Metropolitan University Archives and Special Collections, "Item 2005.006.05.58." As with much vintage photography equipment, hobbyists are often the best sources. On the Duaflex, see Munger, "Kodak Duaflex IV."

35 It remains unclear whether Wilkinson sent the processed images back to Idlout, but we do know that Leah Idlout d'Argencourt Paulson had access to these photographs. She later reproduced some of them in two *Inuit Today* articles reproduced in this volume: Idlout d'Argencourt, "Merry Christmas!"; and Idlout d'Argencourt, "First Inuit Picture."

36 Wilkinson, "Idlouk – Arctic Amateur," 107.

37 A press release for *The White Eskimo*, a newsreel about Wilkinson's 1953–54 stay on North Baffin Island, credits Idlout as "Eskimo hunter trained on camera especially for this newsreel." National Film Board of Canada, "The White Eskimo," press release, December 1954, prod. 54-321-13, Owlatseevik [Aulattivik], North Baffin Island, Nunavut Archives, Douglas E. Wilkinson fonds. The equipment was shipped to Pond Inlet/Mittimatalik by the NFB, enabling Wilkinson to make four short newsreels. In addition to this film on Wilkinson's experiences, they address the local coal mine, Easter services at the Anglican church, and the ceremony awarding Idlout a Coronation Medal. The NFB press release credits Idlout as the cameraman for *The White Eskimo*. Brum and Pennington, *N92-012 Douglas E. Wilkinson Fonds*.

38 According to the 1994 guide to the Northwest Territories Archives – compiled before the transfer of the Douglas E. Wilkinson fonds to the Nunavut Archives – the photographic component of the fonds includes 5,241 photographs, comprising 2,193 black and white negatives and 3,048 colour slides. The overall number for the black and white negatives includes Idlout's snapshots. Schiwy and Moir, *Northwest Territories Archives*. The still photographs appear to have been acquired in 1979 (N-1979-051) and have been inventoried separately from moving images and archival documents (N-1992-012). Brum and Pennington, *N92-012 Douglas E. Wilkinson Fonds*.

39 Wilkinson originally donated Idlout's negatives to the Northwest Territories Archives, where they were included in the Douglas E. Wilkinson Fonds (1945–72). See Schiwy and Moir, *Northwest Territories Archives*.

40 Toronto Metropolitan University Archives and Special Collections, "Cameras"; Toronto Metropolitan University Archives and Special Collections, "Item 2005.006.05.58."

41 Canadian Museum of History, "Peter Pitseolak."

42 Pitseolak and Eber, *People from Our Side*, 12–13.

43 Pitseolak with Eber, *People from Our Side*, 4.

44 Pitseolak with Eber, *People from Our Side*; Eber, "Peter Pitseolak and the Photographic Template."

45 Williamson, "Sewing in Arviat"; Zawadski, *Nuvisi*.

46 Hanson, "Story about Names," 125.

47 Arnakak, "Commentary," quoted in Igloliorte, "Curating Inuit Qaujimajatuqangit," 104; and in Tagalik, "*Inuit Qaujimajatuqangit*," 1. See also Tulugarjuk and Arnakak, eds, *Unikkaaqtuat Qikiqtaninngaaqtut*.

48 Quoted in Government of Nunavut, *Qaujimatait Report*, 2; and in Tagalik, "*Inuit Qaujimajatuqangit*," 2.

49 Qitsualik, "Inummarik," 32.

50 Qitsualik, "Inummarik," 31.

51 Igloliorte, "Curating Inuit Qaujimajatuqangit," 103.

52 Igloliorte, "Curating Inuit Qaujimajatuqangit," 108.

53 See Payne et al., eds, *Atiqput*.

54 In a 2018 interview with Ludy Pudluk, we discussed this photograph as depicting storage for food. My thanks also to Augatnaaq Eccles and Nancy Karetak-Lindell for terminology.

55 Augatnaaq Eccles notes that the hunters would not have gone near the bear, let alone on top of it, unless it was completely dead, as it would

still have been dangerous to do so. In the photo, Paul uses the hook end of a tool to lift the head.

56 The image of Kidlak holding furs is Nunavut Archives, Douglas E. Wilkinson fonds, N-1979-051-2082.

57 Idlout d'Argencourt, "First Inuit Picture," 33.

58 See, for example, Nunavut Archives, Douglas E. Wilkinson fonds, N-1979-051-1972.

59 See, for example, Nunavut Archives, Douglas E. Wilkinson fonds, N-1979-051-1935.

60 Idlout d'Argencourt, "Merry Christmas!"

Chapter Four

1 "I realized before coming up here that a great gap existed between the primitive and civilized man. I am now bridging that gap, putting a foot in each life as it were and this trip has some of each." Doug Wilkinson, diary entry, 12 August 1953, Nunavut Archives, Douglas E. Wilkinson fonds.

2 Wilkinson, *Land of the Long Day*, 21.

3 Doug Wilkinson, "Application for Grant-in-Aid," Library and Archives Canada (LAC), Arctic Institute of North America fonds, MG28-179, vol. 83, file 8, 2.

4 Wilkinson, *Land of the Long Day*, 20.

5 Wilkinson, *Land of the Long Day*, 21.

6 Wilkinson, *Land of the Long Day*, 20.

7 Doug Wilkinson to Colonel P. Baird, 23 August 1953, in "Application for Grant-in-Aid," LAC, Arctic Institute of North America fonds, MG28-179, vol. 83, file 8, 4.

8 Mirzoeff, *Right to Look*, 10.

9 Idlout d'Argencourt, "First Inuit Picture," 33, 32.

10 Wilkinson describes the report several times, but to date, I have not been able to locate a copy of it. Wilkinson may have had some reservations about the report, which he thought of as "an interim document," and therefore have limited its circulation. As he wrote to Colonel P.D. Baird of the Arctic Institute of North America, "I look upon it as an interim document, that may well undergo much change and modification after my return from the next project. For this reason I have been only showing it to my friends, and to those having a definite interest in the Eskimos." Doug Wilkinson to Colonel P. Baird, 2 March 1953, in "Application for Grant-in-Aid," LAC, Arctic Institute of North America fonds, MG28-179, vol. 83, file 8. See also Wilkinson's description of the report in Dempsey, "Young Torontonian."

11 Wilkinson, "How I Became an Eskimo," 30.

12 At the time, the administration of Inuit was handled by the Northern Affairs Program, which was under the Department of Resources and Development. From 1953 to 1966, it was known as the Department of Northern Affairs and National Resources (DNANR). Bonesteel, *Canada's Relationship with Inuit*, 11, 166.

13 In the report, Wilkinson also proposed having the RCMP identify areas with plentiful game where Inuit could be relocated. Royal Commission on Aboriginal Peoples, "Voices of Former Officials," 193.

14 Quoted in Dempsey, "Young Torontonian."

15 "Meeting on Eskimo Affairs, 19–20 May 1952," reproduced in Clancy and Lackenbauer, eds, *Shaping Inuit Policy*, 13–26; "Conference on Eskimo Affairs" (although Wilkinson is not mentioned by name in this 1952 *Arctic Circular* report); Royal Commission on Aboriginal Peoples, "Voices of Former Officials," 193; Clancy, "Making of Eskimo Policy"; Grant, *"Errors Exposed,"* 2–3.

16 Clancy, "Making of Eskimo Policy," 195; Qikiqtani Truth Commission, *Official Mind of Canadian Colonialism*, 27–8.

17 Royal Commission on Aboriginal Peoples, *High Arctic Relocation*, 60–1; Bonesteel, *Canada's Relationship with Inuit*, 166; Marcus, *Relocating Eden*.

18 Marcus, *Relocating Eden*.

19 Diumbaldo, *Government of Canada*, 110.

20 Elsewhere, Wilkinson stated, "The police, the doctors and nurses are directly interested in the health and welfare and security of the Eskimo, but they have no definite and continuing policy. Individuals manning the stations know next to nothing of the people or the country, and care even less. Very few can speak even basic Eskimo." Quoted in Dempsey, "Young Torontonian."

21 Wilkinson, *Land of the Long Day*, 20.

22 Doug Wilkinson to Colonel P. Baird, 22 October 1953, in "Application for Grant-in-Aid," LAC, Arctic Institute of North America fonds, MG28-179, vol. 83, file 8.

23 Doug Wilkinson, "Application for Grant-in-Aid," LAC, Arctic Institute of North America fonds, Research Grants, 1952–54, MG28-179, MIKAN no. 4788595. According to the Bank of Canada, $3,000 in 1952 would be equivalent to just over $33,000 in the 2020s. Bank of Canada, "Inflation Calculator."

24 Doug Wilkinson, "Application for Grant-in-Aid," LAC, Arctic Institute of North America fonds, Research Grants, 1952–54, MG28-179, MIKAN no. 4788595.

25 The AINA was initiated by Dr Charles Camsell (deputy minister of mines and resources), Walter Stowell Rogers (director, Institute of Current World Affairs), businessman George Raleigh Parkin, and Dr John Johnston O'Neill (Department of Geological Sciences, McGill University). A federally endorsed agency, the AINA was established by an act of Parliament. Senate of Canada, *Bill H: An Act to incorporate the Arctic Institute of North America as Passed by the Senate, 1 November 1945*, 1–2. The records of the AINA are now housed at the University of Calgary, although some materials are located at Library and Archives Canada. See University of Calgary, "Arctic Institute of North America."

26 Doug Wilkinson, interview by Shelagh Mackenzie and Mary Sparling, 29 March 1985, La Have, Nova Scotia, for Inuit Art Documentation and Film Research Project, 8, 20–21, LAC, Department of Indian Affairs and Northern Development fonds, R216-3855-6-E, RG85-E-2:

> The Film Board at this time was under very heavy pressure from the Government of Canada not to make films on Eskimos and Indians … Well this was right after the Second World War. Canada in the view of the rest of the world, was thought of as the home of the North American Indian and Eskimo hunters and that. And we had suddenly become an industrial nation, and External Affairs wanted films on our factories, and big cities that were growing up … As a matter of fact when we finished *Land of the Long Day* and *Angotee* we were told flatly, that's why I left the Film Board, we were told flatly, no more for at least two or three years, you know, there just isn't enough money to, we have to go now into other directions.

27 Doug Wilkinson to Alfred S. Galt, AINA, New York, 9 August 1954, in "Application for Grant-in-Aid," LAC, Arctic Institute of North America fonds, MG28-179, vol. 83, file 8: "On my last trip I did not make any films. I simply had a 35 m/m movie camera with me and shot four news-reel type stories for the NFB. One story was on myself, another on the coal mine at Pond Inlet, another on the Eskimo Idlouk receiving his Coronation Medal, and the fourth on the Easter at Pond Inlet. My only intent in making these films was to make money, so that I would be reasonably free to write the reports from the trip when I came outside." On the AINA grant application, Wilkinson wrote, "The National Film Board of Canada has expressed the desire to supply me with a motion picture camera and film stock, so that I can begin to gather film footage to be used in possible future films on the Eskimo. I would receive a contract fee for my services. No amount has been set, but the figure of $1000 has been suggested. I would propose to use this money to cover my living expenses during the fall and early winter of 1954 while the reports from the trip are being written." Douglas Wilkinson, "Application for Grant-in-Aid," LAC, Arctic Institute of North America fonds, MG28-179, vol. 83, file 8, item 26, 5.

28 F.J.G. Cunningham to A.C. Wemberley, 24 June 1954, LAC, Department of Indian Affairs and Northern Development fonds, RG85, vol. 425, file 3-1-6-4-1 [1].

29 For a discussion of the impact on Idlout and his family, see chapters 5 and 6. See also Tester and Kulchyski, *Tammarniit (Mistakes)*, 119–21; Marcus, *Relocating Eden*, chs 3, 4, and 8; Grant, *"Errors Exposed,"* 12–14; and Clancy and Lackenbauer, eds, *Shaping Inuit Policy*, vii.

30 Doug Wilkinson to P.D. Baird, 2 March 1953, in "Application for Grant-in-Aid," LAC, Arctic

Institute of North America fonds, MG28-179, vol. 83, file 8.

31 Doug Wilkinson, "Application for Grant-in-Aid," LAC, Arctic Institute of North America fonds, MG28-179, vol. 83, file 8.

32 Doug Wilkinson, "Application for Grant-in-Aid," LAC, Arctic Institute of North America fonds, MG28-179, vol. 83, file 8.

33 H.A. Young to Colonel P. Baird, 18 October 1952, in "Application for Grant-in-Aid," LAC, Arctic Institute of North America fonds, MG28-179, vol. 83, file 8; Doug Wilkinson, "Application for Grant-in-Aid," LAC, Arctic Institute of North America fonds, MG28-179, vol. 83, file 8.

34 Doug Wilkinson to Colonel P. Baird, 22 October 1952, in "Application for Grant-in-Aid," LAC, Arctic Institute of North America fonds, MG28-179, vol. 83, file 8, 3; Doug Wilkinson, "Application for Grant-in-Aid," LAC, Arctic Institute of North America fonds, MG28-179, vol. 83, file 8,

35 Wilkinson, "How I Became an Eskimo," 28–9; Wilkinson, *Land of the Long Day*, 45. Wilkinson initially approached Idlout's father, Akumalik, asking him to "adopt" the southerner for a year. That would have made Wilkinson the brother of Idlout, then head of camp. The change to associating more closely with Idlout was likely a reflection of the hunter's elevated status in camp. Dempsey, "Young Torontonian."

36 Hickey, "Eskimo Girl," 8; "Gift for Leah," 5. In April 1952, Wilkinson shot a "photostory" about Leah at his home under the aegis of the NFB. In *The Globe and Mail* article "A Gift for Leah," she is seen posed eating ice cream, playing with a dog, and brushing her hair, indicating that the text of the June article may also have been an NFB product. See, for example, "Leah Idlout sitting in front of a mirror and combing her hair, Kingsmere, Quebec," April 1952, photographer Doug Wilkinson, LAC, National Film Board of Canada fonds, Still Photography Division fonds, acc. 1971-271, e010692619.

37 The letter from Idlout to Wilkinson is reproduced – although, as discussed in chapter 3, mistranslated – in Wilkinson, "Idlouk – Arctic Amateur," 39–41. Rhoda Kayakjuak, translation of 1954 published letter, email correspondence with author, 26 November 2018; Nellie Erko, translation of 1954 published letter, email correspondence with author, 28 November 2018.

38 Eastern Arctic Patrol for 1952, LAC, Department of Indian Affairs and Northern Development fonds, RG22, vol. 176, file 40-2-20, part 3, 7, quoted in Grant, *"Errors Exposed,"* 185.

39 Wilkinson, "How I Became an Eskimo," 30.

40 Hudson's Bay Company Invoice itemizing wages, made out to D.E. Wilkinson, 4 May 1954, signed by Pete Murdoch, D.E. Wilkinson, Statement of Expenses and Receipts, 1953–54, in "Application for Grant-in-Aid," LAC, Arctic Institute of North America fonds, MG28-179, vol. 83, file 8.

41 Wilkinson, *Land of the Long Day*, 53.

42 Doug Wilkinson, diary entry, 9 December 1953, Nunavut Archives, Douglas E. Wilkinson fonds; Wilkinson, *Land of the Long Day*, 53–8.

43 Marcus, *Relocating Eden*, 83. See also Tester and Kulchyski, *Tammarniit (Mistakes)*, 184–92.

44 Doug Wilkinson to Colonel P. Baird, 22 October 1953, in "Application for Grant-in-Aid," LAC, Arctic Institute of North America fonds, MG28-179, vol. 83, file 8, 3: "I might say that it has not been easy for me to turn down (or at it's best postpone) a potential offer of employment, in favour of something in which of necessity I must utilize most of my rather meagre savings to carry on the incidental expenses that seem to accrue in this rather complicated world of ours." On the establishment of the DNANR and its Northern Service officers, see Clancy and Lackenbauer, eds, *Shaping Inuit Policy*, xii, 49–51, the latter pages containing "Minutes of the Fourth Meeting of the Eskimo Affairs Committee," 10 May 1954.

45 Doug Wilkinson, "Application for Grant-in-Aid," LAC, Arctic Institute of North America fonds, Research Grants, 1952–54, MG28-179, MIKAN no. 4788595.

46 Wilkinson and his Clyde River guides Simonee and Jacko hunted the polar bear on 21–22 May. Doug Wilkinson, diary entries, 18 April to 11 June 1953, Nunavut Archives, Douglas E. Wilkinson fonds. Wilkinson also narrates the bear hunt and reproduces a picture of the dog

teams circling the bear in *Long of the Long Day*, 38–42.

47 Doug Wilkinson, diary entry, 11 June 1953, Nunavut Archives, Douglas E. Wilkinson fonds; "RCMP Patrol Reports – Ponds Inlet Detachment," 1944–56, 496, LAC, Royal Canadian Mounted Police fonds, RG18, vol. 3668, file G. 567-69.

48 Doug Wilkinson, *Land of the Long Day*, 255. Wilkinson, usually travelling with Idlout, visited Pond Inlet/Mittimatalik periodically for extended periods. They were, for example, at the settlement from April to May 1954. Wilkinson stayed at the Hudson's Bay Company station, apparently using the typewriter there to correspond with P.D. Baird of the AINA.

49 Doug Wilkinson to Colonel P. Baird, 25 August 1953, in "Application for Grant-in-Aid," LAC, Arctic Institute of North America fonds, MG28-179, vol. 83, file 8.

50 Doug Wilkinson, diary entry, n.d. April 1953, Nunavut Archives, Douglas E. Wilkinson fonds: "Settled down to more waiting, five days to be exact before we finally flew to Frobisher Bay. Five days of trying to put in time."

51 Doug Wilkinson, diary entry, 22 May 1953, Nunavut Archives, Douglas E. Wilkinson fonds: "What a scramble was going on. One big white bear surrounded by some thirty yapping, snapping dogs. They had him cornered of course but they couldn't do much less than worry her. And she was no mean adversary. Already there was blood on the snow when some hapless dog had caught a clip from a paw or a nip of the teeth." The scene is also recounted in Wilkinson, *Land of the Long Day*, 38–42.

52 Wilkinson, *Land of the Long Day*, 57.

53 Doug Wilkinson, diary entry, 16 October 1953, Nunavut Archives, Douglas E. Wilkinson fonds.

54 Doug Wilkinson, diary entries, 3 June and 11 October 1953, 5 February 1954, Nunavut Archives, Douglas E. Wilkinson fonds.

55 Doug Wilkinson, diary entry, 12 August 1953, Nunavut Archives, Douglas E. Wilkinson fonds.

56 Doug Wilkinson, diary entry, 6 October 1953, Nunavut Archives, Douglas E. Wilkinson fonds.

57 See, for example, Doug Wilkinson, diary entries, 30 November and 7 December 1953, Nunavut Archives, Douglas E. Wilkinson fonds; Doug Wilkinson to Colonel P. Baird, 7 January 1954, in "Application for Grant-in-Aid," LAC, Arctic Institute of North America fonds, MG28-179, vol. 83, file 8.

58 Scherman, *Spring on an Arctic Island*, 11–16; Wilkinson, *Land of the Long Day*, 255.

59 Doug Wilkinson, diary entries, 1 December 1952 ("on humanitarian grounds"); 12 August 1953, 4 October 1953, 30 November 1953 ("primitive"); 12 August 1953, 4 October 1953, 1 December 1953, 5 February 1954 ("stagnated"); 1 December 1953 ("Here is a group"); 12 August 1953 ("Centuries of stagnation"), Nunavut Archives, Douglas E. Wilkinson fonds.

60 Doug Wilkinson, diary entry, 7 December 1952, Nunavut Archives, Douglas E. Wilkinson fonds.

61 During his long delay at Iqaluit/Frobisher Bay, for example, Wilkinson made observations of the Air Force base. Doug Wilkinson, diary entry, 31 May 1953, Nunavut Archives, Douglas E. Wilkinson fonds.

62 Doug Wilkinson, diary entry, 2 June 1953, Nunavut Archives, Douglas E. Wilkinson fonds.

63 Doug Wilkinson, diary entry, 18 August 1953, Nunavut Archives, Douglas E. Wilkinson fonds. Later, Wilkinson expands on this assessment: "The majority of whites who come north are incapable of helping the Eskimo except in the most elementary sense. They have neither the training nor the aptitude to understand the world in which they live." Doug Wilkinson, diary entry, 1 December 1953, Nunavut Archives, Douglas E. Wilkinson fonds.

64 Doug Wilkinson, diary entry, 4 October 1953, Nunavut Archives, Douglas E. Wilkinson fonds.

65 Doug Wilkinson, diary entries, 18 and 25 August 1953 (local authority), 4 October 1953 (money), Nunavut Archives, Douglas E. Wilkinson fonds.

66 Doug Wilkinson, diary entry, 25 November 1953, Nunavut Archives, Douglas E. Wilkinson fonds.

67 Doug Wilkinson, diary entry, 25 August 1953, Nunavut Archives, Douglas E. Wilkinson fonds.

68 For a detailed discussion of Wilkinson's posting at Baker Lake/Qamani'tuaq and the community's "Eskimo Council," see Kulchyski and Tester, *Kiumajut (Talking Back)*, 204–38;

"Minutes of the Eighth Meeting of the Committee on Eskimo Affairs Held in Ottawa, 13 May 1957," reproduced in Clancy and Lackenbauer, eds, *Shaping Inuit Policy*, 87–106.

69 Doug Wilkinson, diary entry, 25 August 1953, Nunavut Archives, Douglas E. Wilkinson fonds.

70 During his final month of the trip, while staying at Pond Inlet/Mittimatalik, Wilkinson shot a short newsreel on coal mining in the area for the NFB. National Film Board of Canada Archives (hereafter NFB Archives), 11-207, Classroom Films Project, production files 54-309. A version with a running time of one minute and twenty seconds was released by British Pathé. See Wilkinson, dir., *Eskimos Mine Their Own Coal*.

71 Doug Wilkinson, diary entry, 25 November 1953, Nunavut Archives, Douglas E. Wilkinson fonds.

72 Doug Wilkinson, diary entry, 12 August 1953, Nunavut Archives, Douglas E. Wilkinson fonds.

73 Pratt employs the term "transculturation" to describe "how subordinated or marginal groups select or invent from materials transmitted to them by a dominant or metropolitan culture." Pratt, *Imperial Eyes*, 6.

74 Doug Wilkinson, diary entry, 18 October 1953, Nunavut Archives, Douglas E. Wilkinson fonds.

75 Agee and Evans, *Let Us Now Praise*.

76 David Serkoak, interview by Deborah Kigjugalik Webster and Carol Payne, Ottawa, 3 July 2019.

77 As Wilkinson wrote to Baird at the AINA, "Always I am careful not to let these 'white man's activities' interfere with my life as an Eskimo. For I want all the people to accept me as an Eskimo, or as much so as is possible." Doug Wilkinson to Colonel P. Baird, 25 August 1953, in "Application for Grant-in-Aid," LAC, Arctic Institute of North America fonds, MG28-179, vol. 83, file 8, 5.

78 Wilkinson, *Land of the Long Day*, 216.

79 Photographs credited to Idlout, Nunavut Archives, Douglas E. Wilkinson fonds, N-1979-051-1901-1907.

80 Doug Wilkinson, diary entry, 11 October 1953, Nunavut Archives, Douglas E. Wilkinson fonds: "Have just finished developing a half roll of 35 mm film [details problems with developer]. Tried to do a roll of Idlouk's but couldn't get it in the spool. Have to use my parka as a changing bag and this is not so good."

81 NFB Archives, 54-321-13, *White Eskimo* production files.

82 Doug Wilkinson to Alfred S. Galt, AINA, New York, 9 August 1954, in "Application for Grant-in-Aid," LAC, Arctic Institute of North America fonds, MG28-179, vol. 83, file 8; National Film Board of Canada, "The White Eskimo," press release, December 1954, prod. 54-321-13, Owlatseevik [Aulattivik], North Baffin Island, Nunavut Archives, Douglas E. Wilkinson fonds. Brum and Pennington, *N92-012 Douglas E. Wilkinson Fonds*.

83 There is a related image of Wilkinson in the *qajaq*, clearly taken at the same time with the southerner's camera. It is uncredited but likely shot by whomever took the image of Idlout photographing Wilkinson but possibly by Idlout himself. Nunavut Archives, Douglas E. Wilkinson fonds, N-1979-051-0128.

84 Idlout d'Argencourt, "C.D. Howe I," 41. An excerpt from part 2 of the series also appears in Petrone, ed., *Northern Voices*, 225–35.

85 Nunavut Archives, Douglas E. Wilkinson fonds, N-1979-051, item nos 2001 to 2018. See also Scherman, *Spring on an Arctic Island*.

86 Scherman, *Spring on an Arctic Island*, 11–16; Wilkinson, *Land of the Long Day*, 255.

87 The group included Scherman's husband Axel Rosin, an amateur ornithologist and chairman of *The New York Times* and president of the Book of the Month Club; Dr Josselyn Van Type from the University of Michigan; and Professor William Drury, Dr Richard Miller, Dr Benjamin Ferris, and student Edward Ames, all from Harvard University. Katharine Scherman and Mary Drury, wife of William Drury, were the only women included. Scherman, *Spring on an Arctic Island*; "Geese Are Found."

88 Scherman, *Spring on an Arctic Island*, 11–16.

89 Bhabha, "Signs Taken for Wonders," 160. See also, Bhabha, "Of Mimicry and Man."

90 NFB Archives, 11-207, Classroom Films Project, production files 54-309. A version with

a running time of one minute and twenty seconds was released by British Pathé. See Wilkinson, dir., *Eskimos Mine Their Own Coal.*

91 NFB Archives, 11-207, Classroom Films Project, production files 54-321-21. The newsreel was released by British Pathé only outside of Canada. See Wilkinson, dir., *Easter in Canadian Arctic.*

92 Four versions of the newsreel were released under various titles, which are included among the entries for Wilkinson in the Bibliography. These versions are the Warner Pathé release *Eskimo Gets Medal from the Queen* (0:36) and three British Pathé releases: *Canada: Eskimos Award* (0:22), *Canada: Eskimo Medal* (0:49), and *Eskimo Receives Coronation Medal* (3:29). Clips from the newsreels are included in Greenwald, dir., *Between Two Worlds.* The ceremony took place during Doug Wilkinson's 1953–54 stay with Idlout's camp, and Wilkinson also photographed the event. See Nunavut Archives, Douglas E. Wilkinson fonds, N-1979-051-1979, 1980, 1981, 1982, 1983, 1984, 1985, 1986. Idlout also appears briefly in *Easter in Canadian Arctic* (1955), a British Pathé newsreel directed by Wilkinson.

93 Wilkinson, dir., *White Eskimo.*

94 Toward the end of the book, for example, Wilkinson quotes Idlout saying, "Tomorrow the sun will return to our land," phrasing similar to voice-over refrains on the film's soundtrack. Wilkinson, *Land of the Long Day,* 219. See chapter 2 for discussions of narrative in the film *Land of the Long Day* (1952).

95 Mowat, *People of the Deer.* For a discussion of Mowat's book, see Marcus, *Relocating Eden,* 16–18.

96 Baird, "Land of the Long Day."

97 Wilkinson, *Land of the Long Day,* 72.

98 Wilkinson, *Land of the Long Day,* 136.

99 Wilkinson, *Land of the Long Day,* 245.

100 Wilkinson, *Land of the Long Day,* 246.

101 Wilkinson, *Land of the Long Day,* 252.

102 Wilkinson, *Land of the Long Day,* 246.

103 Wilkinson, *Land of the Long Day,* 253–4.

104 See, for example, the six photograph layout in Wilkinson, *Land of the Long Day,* 56–7.

105 Dyer, *White,* 1–2. I make a similar argument in Payne, *Official Picture,* 195.

106 In the book, Wilkinson describes the context for Idlout's testimonial and, more briefly, its use as a promotional text on the bookmark, which he can carry "in my wallet so that it accompanies me wherever I go. Although the films I have made have won many awards and the plaques and certificates testifying to this are among my most prized possessions, not one of these honours occupies the same place in my heart as that note from Idliouk. Written in syllabic character writing on a scrap of paper torn from a small notebook, it is my graduation diploma from the school of the Arctic, the only school diploma I have ever had." Wilkinson, *Land of the Long Day,* 137.

107 Rhoda Kayakjuak, translation of note, email correspondence with author, 26 November 2018.

108 Idlout d'Argencourt, "C.D. Howe V."

Chapter Five

1 Idlout's correspondence shows that he kept multiple copies of photographs in his possession and apparently shared these prints, using photography as a form of exchange. On 15 February 1959, for example, he wrote to Leo Manning, an Inuktitut translator working for the Department of Northern Affairs and National Resources, mentioning that he had enclosed a photograph picturing the two of them. It is not clear from the letter whether the picture was taken with Idlout's own camera. Joseph Idlout to Leo Manning, 15 February 1959, Library and Archives Canada (LAC), Department of Indian Affairs and Northern Development fonds, RG85, vol. 93, file 250-14, part 2. For more on this collection of letters, see Tester, McNicoll, and Irniq, "Writing for Our Lives."

2 In conversation, his daughter Susan Salluviniq recalled that Idlout had photographed only occasionally, although she fondly remembered him giving her a camera at this time. Susan Salluviniq, interview by Augatnaaq Eccles and Carol Payne, Ottawa, 22 March 2023.

3 Extant photographs shot by other exiles at Resolute/Qausuittuq, including Minnie Allakariallak and Sarah and Simeonie Amagoalik,

provide a sense of life there from Inuit perspectives. See Amagoalik, *Changing the Face of Canada*, 21, 29, 30.

4 "Fall 2003 Cover Identification," *Inuit Art Quarterly* 20, no. 1 (2005).

5 The full caption reads, "Governor General's Northern Tour: Three Inuit Men [Daniel N. Salluviniq (Sudlovenick), Joseph Idlout, and Zebeddie Amarualik] holding Brownie cameras await the arrival of Governor General Vincent Massey at Resolute Bay, N.W.T., March 1956."

6 In addition to Resolute/Qausuittuq, Inuit were also relocated to Grise Fiord/Ausuittuq, which remains the northern-most settled community in Canada. Qikiqtani Truth Commission, *QTC Final Report*; Marcus, *Relocating Eden*.

7 As stated by Jean Lesage, then minister of northern affairs and national resources, in a letter of thanks to Massey, "Nothing I know of has done as much as Your Excellency's trip to draw the attention of Canadians to this almost forgotten part of Canada." Jean Lesage to Vincent Massey, 23 April 1956, University of Toronto Archives, Vincent Massey Papers, B1987-0082.

8 Smith, "Introduction," 2.

9 Following a 1953 merger with the British company Harry Ferguson, it became known as Massey Ferguson. Today, it is a subsidiary of the international conglomerate AGCO Corporation. Massey Ferguson, "About Us."

10 Bissell, *Young Vincent Massey*, 169–70; Lloyd, *Diplomacy with a Difference*, 40. Massey's 1939 Dominion Day message, delivered from London while serving as High Commissioner for Canada, provides keen evidence of his affinity with the United Kingdom during the early months of the Second World War. Massey, "Vincent Massey's Dominion."

11 Massey, *Canadians and Their Commonwealth*, 19.

12 Bissell, *Young Vincent Massey*; Bissell, *Imperial Canadian*; Carter, "His Excellency."

13 Cultural nationalism is the overarching theme of Massey's 1948 treatise *On Being Canadian*, as well as the driving force behind the so-called Massey commission. For a commentary on Massey's cultural nationalism, see Grace, *On the Art*.

14 Litt, *Muses, the Masses*.

15 Finlay, *Force of Culture*, 7. Paul Litt, like Finlay, notes that "the commissioners invariably presented the role of culture as that of cultivating the informed and responsible democratic citizen." Litt, *Muses, the Masses*, 302.

16 Galbraith, "Never Be off the Road." Thanks to Karla McManus for discussing Tweedsmuir with me.

17 St-Laurent, in Government of Canada, *House of Commons Debates*, First Session, Twenty-Second Parliament, vol. 1, 8 December 1953, 697, also quoted in Cook, "Canada's Arctic Islands," 4. Cook's article is reprinted in *The Arctic Circular* 28, nos 1–2 (1980): 32–4.

18 Rowley, *Cold Comfort*, 281.

19 Massey, "Southerner in the North," 14.

20 For a fascinating discussion of photography in the service of Canada's Cold War machinations, see Parsons, "Sovereign Territories."

21 Vincent Massey to Jean Lesage, 17 April 1956, University of Toronto Archives, Vincent Massey Papers, B1987-0082 386(36)b. See also Massey, "Report on the North," 45.

22 Hulan, *Northern Experience*, 179.

23 Long, "Massey to Tour Canadian Arctic."

24 In 2001, Adrienne Clarkson became the first governor general since Massey to undertake an official tour of the north. Since Clarkson's tour, it has become a staple of the governor general's term in office. Both Michaëlle Jean in 2009 and David Johnston in 2011 also garnered extensive press during their northern tours.

25 Massey, "Report on the North."

26 The five time zones covered were Eastern Standard Time, Central Standard Time, Mountain Standard Time, Pacific Standard Time, and Yukon Standard Time. The Yukon would adopt Pacific Standard Time in 1973.

27 Joe MacSween of *The Globe and Mail* was a member of the tour's press corps.

28 For example, missives published in *The Globe and Mail* and *The New York Times* held close to the itinerary.

29 Department of Northern Affairs and National Resources, "Visit of His Excellency the Right Honourable Vincent Massey, Governor General, to the Canadian Arctic, March 20 to

April 5, 1956," LAC, Department of Northern Affairs and National Resources fonds, R9167-12, file: Canadian Arctic Tour – The Right Honourable Vincent Massey 1956; Tash, dir., *Arctic Journey*.

30 Mirzoeff, *Right to Look*, 58.

31 Department of Northern Affairs and National Resources, "Visit of His Excellency the Right Honourable Vincent Massey, Governor General, to the Canadian Arctic, March 20 to April 5, 1956," LAC, Department of Northern Affairs and National Resources fonds, R9167-12, file: Canadian Arctic Tour – The Right Honourable Vincent Massey 1956.

32 Department of Northern Affairs and National Resources, "Visit of His Excellency the Right Honourable Vincent Massey, Governor General, to the Canadian Arctic, March 20 to April 5, 1956," 13–14, LAC, Department of Northern Affairs and National Resources fonds, R9167-12, file: Canadian Arctic Tour – The Right Honourable Vincent Massey 1956.

33 Doug Wilkinson, diary entries, 1953–68, Nunavut Archives, Douglas E. Wilkinson fonds, N92-012; Brum and Pennington, *N92-012 Douglas E. Wilkinson Fonds*.

34 St-Laurent, in Government of Canada, *House of Commons Debates*, First Session, Twenty-Second Parliament, vol. 1, 8 December 1953, 700.

35 Government of Canada, "First Arctic Conference."

36 Wilkinson, "Eskimos of Frobisher Bay."

37 The title listed by the Arctic Circle for a talk given by Wilkinson on 13 November 1956, "New Town of Frobisher Bay, the First Year 1955–6," differs from that of the transcript quoted here. Yet it is probable that Wilkinson wrote "Eskimos of Frobisher Bay" for this talk. Arctic Circle, *Meetings of the Arctic Circle*, 3.

38 Wilkinson, "Eskimos of Frobisher Bay," 3.

39 Foucault, *Discipline and Punish*, 195–228.

40 Liscombe, "Modernist Ultimate Thule," 71.

41 Wilkinson, "Eskimos of Frobisher Bay," 4–5.

42 Wilkinson, "Eskimos of Frobisher Bay," 5.

43 The three Inuit in the greeting party represented "inhabitants of the new town," "inhabitants of the village," and "natives on the land." None of the three are identified by name. Other named members of the party were Wing Commander C.D. Campbell-Rogers, commanding officer of the RCAF station; Major G. Dorman of the RCAF; Major Fox, commander of the 6650th US Air Force base; Chief Constable Arthur Deer of the RCMP; and R.F. Shaw of the construction firm Foundation Company of Canada. Department of Northern Affairs and National Resources, "Visit of His Excellency the Right Honourable Vincent Massey, Governor General, to the Canadian Arctic, March 20 to April 5, 1956," 12, LAC, Department of Northern Affairs and National Resources fonds, R9167-12, file: Canadian Arctic Tour – The Right Honourable Vincent Massey 1956.

44 The article states, "Doug Wilkinson, mayor of Frobisher Bay and an officer in the Canadian Government's Northern affairs division, is playing an important role in the tour." See "Eskimo Dress." Also cited in Bauldic, "Art and Mass Production."

45 Wilkinson also reported on the community to southerners. The Arctic Circle, a group of experts on Arctic affairs gathering in Ottawa, noted a report given by Wilkinson on 13 November 1956 titled "New Town of Frobisher Bay, the First Year 1955-6." Arctic Circle, *Meetings of the Arctic Circle*, 3. As noted, this report is likely the paper cited here as "Eskimos of Frobisher Bay."

46 Department of Northern Affairs and National Resources, "Visit of His Excellency the Right Honourable Vincent Massey, Governor General, to the Canadian Arctic, March 20 to April 5, 1956, LAC, Department of Northern Affairs and National Resources fonds, R9167-12, file: Canadian Arctic Tour – The Right Honourable Vincent Massey 1956, 40–1.

47 Department of Northern Affairs and National Resources, "Visit of His Excellency the Right Honourable Vincent Massey, Governor General, to the Canadian Arctic, March 20 to April 5, 1956," LAC, Department of Northern Affairs and National Resources fonds, R9167-12, file: Canadian Arctic Tour – The Right Honourable Vincent Massey 1956, 13.

48 Department of Northern Affairs and National Resources, "Visit of His Excellency the

Right Honourable Vincent Massey, Governor General, to the Canadian Arctic, March 20 to April 5, 1956," LAC, Department of Northern Affairs and National Resources fonds, R9167-12, file: Canadian Arctic Tour – The Right Honourable Vincent Massey 1956, 14.

49 Wilkinson, "Eskimos of Frobisher Bay," 5.

50 Department of Northern Affairs and National Resources, "Visit of His Excellency the Right Honourable Vincent Massey, Governor General, to the Canadian Arctic, March 20 to April 5, 1956," LAC, Department of Northern Affairs and National Resources fonds, R9167-12, file: Canadian Arctic Tour – The Right Honourable Vincent Massey 1956, 13–14.

51 MacSween, "No Muskox for Massey."

52 MacSween, "Massey Attends Eskimo Dances."

53 Department of Northern Affairs and National Resources, "Visit of His Excellency the Right Honourable Vincent Massey, Governor General, to the Canadian Arctic, March 20 to April 5, 1956," LAC, Department of Northern Affairs and National Resources fonds, R9167-12, file: Canadian Arctic Tour – The Right Honourable Vincent Massey 1956, 39–40.

54 Massey, *What's Past Is Prologue*, 486.

55 Qikiqtani Truth Commission, *Community Histories 1950–1975: Resolute (Qausuittuq)*, 11–12.

56 The history of the High Arctic relocations has been told through testimonies and historical accounts. In this brief contextual sketch, I am indebted to these important sources, which include testimonies from Inuit as well as government officials to the 1993 Royal Commission on Aboriginal Peoples, to the Qikiqtani Truth Commission, and to the *Iqqaumavara* project (conducted in collaboration with the Makivik Corporation of Nunavik), as well as published testimonies of exiles, such as John Amagoalik, Larry Audlaluk, and Markoosie Patsauq. Essential historical texts on the subject include Amagoalik, *Changing the Face of Canada*; Audlaluk, *What I Remember*; Patsauq, *Uumajursiutik unaatuinnamut*; Grant, *"Errors Exposed"*; Tester and Kulchyski, *Tammarniit (Mistakes)*, 102–204; Marcus, *Relocating Eden*, 65–123; and Lackenbauer, ed., *Human Flagpoles?*

57 Tester and Kulchyski, *Tammarniit (Mistakes)*, 104–13; Grant, *"Errors Exposed,"* 43–5.

58 Qikiqtani Truth Commission, "Thematic Reports and Special Studies 1950–1975"; Qikiqtani Truth Commission, *Nuutauniq: Moves in Inuit Life*, 20–4.

59 Tester and Kulchyski, *Tammarniit (Mistakes)*, 119–21; Grant, *"Errors Exposed,"* 12–14; Lackenbauer, ed., *Human Flagpoles?*, vii.

60 Grant, *"Errors Exposed,"* 12, 40; Tester and Kulchyski, *Tammarniit (Mistakes)*, 113–19; Lackenbauer, ed., *Human Flagpoles?*, i–xx; Loo, *Moved by the State*, 28–72.

61 Grant, *"Errors Exposed,"* 41.

62 Tester and Kulchyski, *Tammarniit (Mistakes)*, 119.

63 St-Laurent, in Government of Canada, *House of Commons Debates*, First Session, Twenty-Second Parliament, vol. 1, 8 December 1953, 697.

64 Grant, *"Errors Exposed,"* 3; "Minutes of First Meeting of Special Committee on Eskimo Affairs, 16 October 1952," reproduced in Clancy and Lackenbauer, eds, *Shaping Inuit Policy*, 27–32.

65 Tester and Kulchyski, *Tammarniit (Mistakes)*, 184.

66 The extensive archival record of meetings and the voluminous literature on the subject confirm that there were no Inuit involved in high-level discussions. Lackenbauer, ed., *Human Flagpoles?*, iv–v.

67 Amagoalik, *Changing the Face of Canada*, 20.

68 Families headed by Simeonie Amagoalik, Alex Patsauq, and Daniel Salluviniq, all from Inukjuak/Port Harrison, and a family headed by Zebeddie Amarualik, from Pond Inlet/Mittimatalik, were sent to Resolute/Qausuittuq. Families headed by Aquiatusuk, Joadamie Aqiatusuk, Philipusie Novalinga, and Thomasie Amagoalik, all from Inukjuak/Port Harrison, and families headed by Simon Akpaliapik and Samuel Anukudluk, all from Pond Inlet/Mittimatalik, were sent to Grise Fiord/Ausuittuq. Royal Commission on Aboriginal Peoples, *High Arctic Relocation*, 9–10; Marcus, *Relocating Eden*, 227–8; Qikiqtani Truth Commission, *Community Histories 1950–1975: Grise Fiord (Ausuittuq)*, 26–7.

69 Qikiqtani Truth Commission, *Community Histories 1950–1975: Resolute (Qausuittuq)*, 27–8; Royal Commission on Aboriginal Peoples, *High Arctic Relocation*, 17–116.

70 A family headed by Josephie Flaherty, from Inukjuak/Port Harrison, was sent to Grise Fiord/Ausuittuq. Inukjuak/Port Harrison families headed by Levi Nungak, Johnnie Echalook, and Mawa Iqaluk went to Resolute/Qausuittuq. Royal Commission on Aboriginal Peoples, *High Arctic Relocation*, 11–12; Marcus, *Relocating Eden*, 228–9.

71 See chapter 4 for a detailed discussion of this period. Marcus, *Relocating Eden*, 83; Tester and Kulchyski, *Tammarniit (Mistakes)*, 184–92. As described above, by 1955, when Idlout and his family moved to Resolute/Qausuittuq, Wilkinson had entered his own new life as a Northern Service officer in Iqaluit/Frobisher Bay, a position he also held later at Baker Lake/Qamani'tuaq.

72 Tester and Kulchyski, *Tammarniit (Mistakes)*, 186–7.

73 Tester and Kulchyski, *Tammarniit (Mistakes)*, 187; Harper, "Akumalik."

74 Marcus, *Relocating Eden*, 229.

75 A family headed by Josephie Flaherty, from Inukjuak/Port Harrison, was sent to Grise Fiord/Ausuittuq. Inukjuak/Port Harrison families headed by Levi Nungak, Johnnie Echalook, and Mawa Iqaluk went to Resolute/Qausuittuq. Royal Commission on Aboriginal Peoples, *High Arctic Relocation*, 11–12; Marcus, *Relocating Eden*, 228–9.

76 Marcus, *Relocating Eden*, 111.

77 The Qikiqtani Truth Commission notes that the people of the area – including Idlout's family – are known as Tununirmiut, "people of the shaded place." Qikiqtani Truth Commission, *Community Histories 1950–1975: Pond Inlet (Mittimatalik)*, 3.

78 *Iqqaumavara*, "Moses Idlout." See chapter 1 for a lengthier excerpt from Moses Idlout's interview.

79 *Iqqaumavara*, "Susan Salluviniq."

80 *Iqqaumavara*, "Moses Idlout."

81 Department of Northern Affairs and National Resources, "Visit of His Excellency the Right Honourable Vincent Massey, Governor General, to the Canadian Arctic, March 20 to April 5, 1956," LAC, Department of Northern Affairs and National Resources fonds, R9167-12, file: Canadian Arctic Tour – The Right Honourable Vincent Massey 1956, 45–6.

82 Massey, *What's Past Is Prologue*, 486–7.

83 The scene was documented by Gar Lunney in still photographs and by Roy Tash both for the film *Arctic Journey* and in a newsreel made from Tash's footage. British Movietone News, "Polar News."

84 See two photographs of Massey dated 24 March 1956 in LAC, National Film Board of Canada fonds, Still Photography Division fonds, acc. 1971-271, nos 76259 and 76263; "His Excellency the Governor General's Address over the North Pole, 24 March 1956," University of Toronto Archives, Vincent Massey Papers, B1987-0082.

85 "Massey Leaves a Message."

86 "His Excellency the Governor General's Address at Resolute Bay, 24 March 1956," University of Toronto Archives, Vincent Massey Papers, B1987-0082.

87 Hulan, *Northern Experience*, 179.

88 See, among many other news stories covering the tour, "Massey to Fly over North Pole."

89 Massey, *What's Past Is Prologue*, 486.

90 In the 1940s, Doucette had been a prolific still photographer employed by the NFB.

91 The other media personnel were J.B. MacSween of Canadian Press, Louis R. Sherman of British United Press, Eric Downton of the North American Newspaper Alliance, Charles D'Aoust as a French-language correspondent, and Byron Riggan of *Time-Life Magazine*. Department of Northern Affairs and National Resources, "Visit of His Excellency the Right Honourable Vincent Massey, Governor General, to the Canadian Arctic, March 20 to April 5, 1956," LAC, Department of Northern Affairs and National Resources fonds, R9167-12, file: Canadian Arctic Tour – The Right Honourable Vincent Massey 1956. Although not listed in the DNANR's official guide, the surviving photographic record also shows that Tania Long, one of the bureau chiefs of *The New York Times* in Ottawa, also travelled with the party.

92 Tash, dir., *Arctic Journey*. Thank you to archivist Caroline Forcier-Holloway, who screened a digital copy of this film with me at Library and Archives Canada on 24 April 2019. Her insights and exchanges about the film have informed my thinking.

93 British Movietone News, "Polar News."

94 The thirty-one-minute black and white version of *Arctic Journey* is in LAC, Roy Tash fonds, 1956.0059, where it is listed in the archival records as a twenty-four-minute film, although a screening indicated the longer length noted here. The colour version is in LAC, Government House fonds.

95 British Movietone News, "Polar News."

96 Library and Archives Canada has 158 negatives in its National Film Board of Canada fonds, Still Photography Division fonds; however, some are duplicates. Although Lunney undoubtedly made more exposures, this collection is the entire body of images known to survive.

97 "Finding Aid, Part Five," microfiche, LAC, National Film Board of Canada fonds, Still Photography Division fonds, acc. 1971-271.

98 Payne, *Official Picture.*

99 Among the exceptions, in Whitehorse, Lunney shot a playful group photograph of fellow members of the media corps. LAC, National Film Board of Canada fonds, Still Photography Division fonds, acc. 1971-271, no. 76187.

100 Department of Northern Affairs and National Resources, "Visit of His Excellency the Right Honourable Vincent Massey, Governor General, to the Canadian Arctic, March 20 to April 5, 1956," 13–14, LAC, Department of Northern Affairs and National Resources fonds, R9167-12, file: Canadian Arctic Tour – The Right Honourable Vincent Massey 1956.

101 Fabian, *Time and the Other*, 31. Fabian defines "allochronism" as "a persistent and systematic tendency to place the referent(s) of anthropology in a Time other than the present of the producer of anthropological discourse."

102 While several images show the governor general with southern scientists and industrial officials, most feature Inuit and Indigenous people. For the purposes of this chapter, I examine only images of Inuit.

103 Smith, "Introduction," 2; Smith, *Photography on the Color Line.*

104 See hooks, *Black Looks*; Dyer, *White.* Hooks is also cited in Smith, "Introduction," 1, 3, 9.

105 Payne, *Official Picture*, 180.

106 Olin, *Touching Photographs.*

107 Kaulowou was likely a made-up name, as it was not in use among Inuit.

108 Poole, "Excess of Description," 163.

109 Poole, "Excess of Description."

110 Benajmin, "Little History of Photography," 510.

111 Fabian, *Time and the Other.*

112 For a discussion of Australian Aboriginal rereadings of photographs, see Lydon, *Eye Contact*; and Lydon, *Calling the Shots.*

113 The second image of Resolute/Qausuittuq housing in 1956 depicts Inuit houses as they existed during Governor General Vincent Massey's 1956 northern tour, photographed by Gar Lunney. LAC, National Film Board of Canada fonds, Still Photography Division fonds, acc. PA-191424.

114 Smith, "Introduction," 2.

115 Unfortunately, little correspondence between them has survived in the Nunavut Archives or in Idlout family records. But, as discussed in chapter 6, other correspondence from Idlout to the government is extant.

116 Written Inuktitut now has a dual system of syllabics and Roman orthography. Palluq-Cloutier, "History of Inuktitut Writing Systems."

117 Idlout, "Resolute Bay Man."

Chapter Six

1 Photographs from the trip are now in the Douglas E. Wilkinson fonds of the Nunavut Archives. The photographs were catalogued by Doug Wilkinson, who was not a delegate. As a result, his cataloguing records are not detailed. In this book, I have added more information about sitters whom I have been able to identify.

2 R.J. Herman, Commanding Marine Division, to R.A.J. Phillips, 24 July 1958, Library

and Archives Canada (LAC), Department of Indian Affairs and Northern Development fonds, RG85, vol. 466, file 1005-7, 11, box 107 (2); R.A.J. Phillips to Donald Snowden, "Exchange to Greenland," memorandum, 31 May 1962, LAC, Department of Indian Affairs and Northern Development fonds, RG85, vol. 1380, file 1005-7, box 316 (1).

3 For help with archival research for this chapter, I am indebted to Evangeline Mann.

4 Grant, *"Errors Exposed,"* 12, 40; Tester and Kulchyski, *Tammarniit (Mistakes)*, 113–19; Marcus, *Relocating Eden*, ch. 3; Lackenbauer, ed., *Human Flagpoles?*, i–xx; Loo, *Moved by the State*, 28–72.

5 Meren, "'Commend Me the Yak,'" 349; Loo, *Moved by the State*, 11–16.

6 Tuck, "Suspending Damage," 409, passim. I am grateful to Brenda Vellino for discussions about Tuck's essay. Tuck's comments also call to mind ethical concerns about treatments of historical violence, as discussed by Monica Patterson and referenced in chapter 1. Patterson, "Ethical Murk."

7 Tuck, "Suspending Damage," 416.

8 Robertson, "Canadian Inuit Head to Greenland."

9 The 1956 trip by Greenlanders included visits to Iqaluit/Frobisher Bay and Pangnirtung. Doug Wilkson spoke to the delegates in Iqaluit/Frobisher Bay. Manning, "Visit of Greenlanders."

10 According DNANR official Bent Sivertz, "The trip arose through an informal invitation from a party of Greenlanders, visiting the Canadian Arctic in 1956." Following a formal invitation from the Danish government and acceptance by the Canadian Department of External Affairs, the DNANR took over all aspects of the trip. B.G. Sivertz to the Deputy Minister, "Trip to Greenland," memorandum, 1 August 1958, LAC, Department of Indian Affairs and Northern Development fonds, RG85, vol. 466, file 1005-7, 11, box 107 (2).

11 "Eskimo, Government Officers, to Visit Greenland," report, 26 August 1958, LAC, Department of Indian Affairs and Northern Development fonds, RG85, vol. 466, file 1005-7, 11, box 107.

12 R.G. Robertson, Deputy Minister of DNANR, to D.M. Watters, Secretary of Treasury Board, 29 July 1958, LAC, Department of Indian Affairs and Northern Development fonds, RG85, vol. 466, file 1005-7, 11, box 107 (2).

13 "Excerpts from 'Survey of Economic Conditions among the Eskimo of the Canadian Arctic' (Cantley Report)," reproduced in Clancy and Lackenbauer, eds, *Shaping Inuit Policy*, 1–12: "What most people have had in mind in putting forward this suggestion was that the Canadian trade and administration should be patterned on those of Greenland and the Arctic made a closed territory ... The approach is paternalistic and the Greenland administration is again held up as a pattern to be followed" (8).

14 "Canadian Eskimos Return from Greenland," DNANR press release, 27 September 1958, LAC, Department of Indian Affairs and Northern Development fonds, RG85, vol. 1380, file 1005-7, box 316 (2).

15 D.E. Wilkinson to R.A.J. Phillips, 5 February 1958, LAC, Department of Indian Affairs and Northern Development fonds, RG85, vol. 465, file 1005-1, 10, box 14; R.A.J. Phillips to D.E. Wilkinson, Baker Lake/Qamani'tuaq, 15 May 1958, LAC, Department of Indian Affairs and Northern Development fonds, RG85, vol. 465, file 1005-1, 10, box 14.

16 R.A.J. Phillips to Mr Stewart, memorandum, 31 July 1958, LAC, Department of Indian Affairs and Northern Development fonds, RG85, vol. 466, file 1005-7, 11, box 197 (2); R.A.J. Phillips to Bent Sivertz, "Greenland Visit," memorandum, 15 May 1958, LAC, Department of Indian Affairs and Northern Development fonds, RG85, vol. 465, file 1005-1, 10, box 14.

17 In addition to gauging each candidate's "suitability," Northern Service officers were instructed to them ask five questions:

1 Does he wish to make the trip?
2 If in wage employment, can he obtain leave of absence for a month or more?
3 Is he prepared, and can he afford, to lose a month's salary?
4 If married, does his wife wish to go and is she suitable? If women are included we

do not expect more than three wives will be selected.

5 If married, who will look after and provide for his dependents while he is away?

R.A.J. Phillips to Bent Sivertz, "Greenland Visit," memorandum, 15 May 1958, LAC, Department of Indian Affairs and Northern Development fonds, RG85, vol. 465, file 1005-1, 10, box 14.

18 A.J. Boxer references the memorandum sent to him by R.A.J. Phillips on 3 December 1957 requesting that he recruit candidates from the western Arctic. A.J. Boxer to R.A.J. Phillips, memorandum, 18 January 1958, LAC, Department of Indian Affairs and Northern Development fonds, RG85, vol. 465, file 1005-1, 10, box 14.

19 Editors' preface to Idlout, "Resolute Bay Man," 11: "Idlout had left on an airplane from Qallunaat Nunaat (southern Canada) to Ottawa during an early Spring season. He was asked whether he would like to see and go to Greenland and learn about their lifestyle. On 29 August, he left for Greenland" (trans. Rhoda Kayakjuak).

20 The bill for the suits totalled $1,200, a large enough sum in 1958 that Deputy Minister R.G. Robertson had to justify the expense to the Treasury Board. As Robertson wrote to the secretary of the board, "The $1200.00 for clothing is because most of the ESKIMO who will be going from Canada do not have anything but ragged and inadequate skin clothing, or things of that kind. Apart from the fact that it would not look too well for Canada if ESKIMO from here were badly clothed, the more important point is that they would again be likely to feel inferior, be self-conscious about mixing with the better dressed Greenland ESKIMO, and consequently not get the most important advantages that we see in the trip." R.G. Robertson, Deputy Minister of DNANR, to D.M. Watters, Secretary of Treasury Board, 29 July 1958, LAC, Department of Indian Affairs and Northern Development fonds, RG85, vol. 466, file 1005-7, 11, box 107 (2). See also the draft proposal and budget sent to the Treasury Board, 15 July 1958, LAC, Department of Indian Affairs and Northern Development fonds, RG85, vol. 466, file 1005-7, 11, box 107 (3); and R.A.J. Phillips to Mr Doyle, "Clothing Purchases for Eskimos Visiting Greenland," memorandum, 22 August 1958, LAC, Department of Indian Affairs and Northern Development fonds, RG85, vol. 466, file 1005-7, 11, box 107 (2).

21 R.A.J. Phillips to Bent Sivertz, "Greenland Visit," memorandum, 15 May 1958, LAC, Department of Indian Affairs and Northern Development fonds, RG85, vol. 465, file 1005-1, 10, box 14.

22 A.J. Boxer to R.A.J. Phillips, 18 January 1958; A.J. Boxer to R.A.J. Phillips, 15 February 1958; A.J. Boxer to R.A.J. Phillips, 27 February 1958; D.E. Wilkinson to R.A.J. Phillips, 5 February 1958; E.J. Saunders to R.A.J. Phillips, 25 March 1958; F.J. Neville to R.A.J. Phillips, 9 April 1958; J.R. Langin to R.A.J. Phillips, 21 March 1958; J.P. Richards to James Houston, 30 March 1958; Jameson Bond to R.A.J. Phillips, 26 March 1958; Jameson Bond to R.A.J. Phillips, 24 May 1958; P.B. Gorelick to R.A.J. Phillips, 5 March 1958; R.A.J. Phillips to W.G. Kerr, 29 January 1958; W.G. Kerr to R.A.J. Phillips, 28 January 1958, LAC, Department of Indian Affairs and Northern Development fonds, RG85, vol. 465, file 1005-1, 10, box 14.

23 Among potential recruits was another performer in Wilkinson's films: Singeetuk (Shineektuk) of Rankin Inlet/Kangiqtiniq, an actor in *Angotee: Story of an Eskimo Boy* (1953). Ultimately, Singeetuk did not join the voyage. W.G. Kerr to R.A.J. Phillips, 15 January 1958, LAC, Department of Indian Affairs and Northern Development fonds, RG85, vol. 465, file 1005-1, 10, box 14; National Film Board of Canada Archives (hereafter NFB Archives), 51-405, *Angotee* production files.

24 R.A.J. Phillips to Dr J.S. Willis, 19 August 1958, LAC, Department of Indian Affairs and Northern Development fonds, RG85, vol. 466, file 1005-7, 11, box 107. This letter lists all Inuit participants in the delegation. See also Crowe, *History of the Original Peoples*, 203.

25 "These are Inuit from Canada. They are in Greenland touring the logging facility. 1. Elijah Menarik, from Mailasikut, 2. Idlout from

Pond Inlet, 3. Kanaaginaq from Kinngait (Cape Dorset), 4. Charlie Smith, who lives around Aklavik around Tuktoyaktuk, 5. Adamie Tootalik from Paliaqjuk, 6. Jamesie Evanna from Iqaluktuuttiaq (Cambridge Bay), 7. The leader of Greenland, 8. Qaqqasiq from Pangnirtung, 9. George Koneak from Kuujjuaq, 10. Tikivik from Iqaluit. Charlie Gordon is from an office but he is too fat and didn't fit to go inside the log factory so he is not in the picture." Idlout, "Resolute Bay Man," 16, trans. Rhoda Kayakjuak.

26 R.A.J. Phillips to the Deputy Minister, memorandum, 11 August 1958, LAC, Department of Indian Affairs and Northern Development fonds, RG85, vol. 466, file 1005-7, 11, box 107 (1): "Idlout's inclusion on the list of ESKIMO selected to go to Greenland was partly due to the presence of his daughter Leah in Frobisher Bay. Leah, a resident of the Rehabilitation Centre, is in ill health and in a disturbed mental condition, and for this reason it was desirable, if at all possible, that her father be with her."

27 Trevor Lloyd to J.V. Jacobson, 3 March 1959, LAC, Department of Indian Affairs and Northern Development fonds, RG85, vol. 1231, file 1005-7-1, part 2, box 148. Jacobson authored the report "Education in Greenland 1958–59," 1959, LAC, Department of Indian Affairs and Northern Development fonds, RG85, vol. 1231, file 1005-7-1, part 2, box 148. Trevor Lloyd is also the author of "Changing Greenland," a 1959 article published in *The Beaver.*

28 Jenness held several positions with the DNANR, including head of community planning in the Development Section of the Northern Administration and Land Branch. See University of British Columbia, Social History of the Eastern Arctic Database.

29 In addition to the official identified as "Mr. Findlay," a woman identified as "Miss Findlay" did a survey of sheep farming in Kalaallit Nunaat/Greenland. Clancy and Lackenbauer, eds, *Shaping Inuit Policy*, 45.

30 R.A.J. Phillips to Captain C. Pederson, 19 September 1958, LAC, Department of Indian Affairs and Northern Development fonds, RG85, vol. 1380, file 1995-7, box 316 (2).

31 There were a number of delays and difficulties in arranging transport. See R.J. Herman to R.A.J. Phillips, 24 July 1958, LAC, Department of Indian Affairs and Northern Development fonds, RG85, vol. 466, file 1005-7, 11, box 107 (2); and R.A.J. Phillips to Donald Snowden, "Exchange to Greenland," memorandum, 31 May 1962, LAC, Department of Indian Affairs and Northern Development fonds, RG85, vol. 1380, file 1005-7, box 316 (1).

32 John Knox to Bent Sivertz, 8 May 1958, LAC, Department of Indian Affairs and Northern Development fonds, RG85, vol. 465, file 1005-1, 10, box 14. See also Bent Sivertz, "Itinerary for Greenland Visit," memorandum, n.d., LAC, Department of Indian Affairs and Northern Development fonds, RG85, vol. 466, file 1005-7, 11, box 107 (2).

33 R.A.J. Phillips, "The New Neighbour," transcript of radio address, CBC Radio, 3 November 1958, 2–3, LAC, Department of Indian Affairs and Northern Development fonds, RG85, vol. 1380, file 1005-7, box 316 (1).

34 Idlout, "Resolute Bay Man." Archival issues of *Inuktitut Magazine* are available through Inuit Tapiriit Kanatami. Thanks to Rhoda Kayakjuak for the translations.

35 Nungak, "Five Decades," 16.

36 Nungak, "Five Decades," 24.

37 It is highly possible that ten negatives from Idlout's camera were selected for the article and that, since these negatives remained with *Inuktitut Magazine*, they were not included in the Nunavut Archives. However, on such a carefully, orchestrated tour, many of the delegates would have photographed similar staged events, and as a DNANR publication, the magazine may have used another Inuk's or southern official's photographs. Still, it is likely that these images were also shot with Idlout's camera. It is notable that in the group photograph of Inuit delegates that appears on page sixteen of the article (see figure 6.2), Idlout appears without his camera; it is likely that he loaned it to whoever took the image.

38 Ann Meekitjuk Hanson, interview by Carol Payne, Apex, Baffin Island, 10 May 2018; Eber, "Peter Pitseolak, an Historian for Seekooseelak," 13–15, 20, cited in Dyck, "Looking for Kenojuak Ashevak," 189–92.
39 As noted in the introductory chapter, a 1958 guide for southerners moving to Inuit, written by DNANR officials R.A.J. Phillips and George Franklin Parsons, references the prevalence of Inuit photographers. Phillips and Parsons, *This Is the Arctic*, cover illustration, 42.
40 Idlout, "Resolute Bay Man," 11–13.
41 Idlout, "Resolute Bay Man," 19.
42 In addition to figure 6.8, with the Inuit delegates posing at the lumber yard, see a second view of the facility in Nunavut Archives, Douglas E. Wilkinson fonds, N-1979-051-2131.
43 For Idlout's image of a Lutheran church, see Idlout, "Resolute Bay Man," 14, and for his photograph of a missionary, see Nunavut Archives, Douglas E. Wilkinson fonds, N-1979-051-2146.
44 Idlout, "Resolute Bay Man," 15, trans. Rhoda Kayakjuak.
45 Idlout, "Resolute Bay Man," 19, trans. Rhoda Kayakjuak.
46 Idlout, "Resolute Bay Man," 15, trans. Rhoda Kayakjuak.
47 Idlout, "Resolute Bay Man," 12. See also the images on page 14 of this *Inuktitut Magazine* article. For Idlout's images of *qajaqing*, see Nunavut Archives, Douglas E. Wilkinson fonds, N-1979-051-2123, 2125, 2126, 2133, 2134, and 2135.
48 Idlout, "Resolute Bay Man," 11, trans. Rhoda Kayakjuak.
49 Idlout, "Resolute Bay Man," 13, trans. Rhoda Kayakjuak.
50 Idlout, "Resolute Bay Man," 21, trans. Rhoda Kayakjuak.
51 Unfortunately, the Greenlanders in the photographs were not identified.
52 Nunavut Archives, Douglas E. Wilkinson fonds, N-1979-051-2143 and 2148.
53 Nunavut Archives, Douglas E. Wilkinson fonds, N-1979-051-2144.
54 Nunavut Archives, Douglas E. Wilkinson fonds, N-1979-051-2142.
55 Nunavut Archives, Douglas E. Wilkinson fonds, N-1979-051-2178 and 2179.
56 Nunavut Archives, Douglas E. Wilkinson fonds, N-1979-051-2136.
57 Greenland National Museum and Archives, "Kalaallisuut."
58 In addition to the image reproduced here, see, among others, Nunavut Archives, Douglas E. Wilkinson fonds, N-1979-051-2121 and 2185.
59 Inuit in Canada and Kalaallit Nunaat/Greenland continued to write to each other. R.A.J. Phillips to Donald Snowden, "Exchange to Greenland," memorandum, 31 May 1962, LAC, Department of Indian Affairs and Northern Development fonds, RG85, vol. 1380, file 1005-7, box 316 (1), 2.
60 R.A.J. Phillips, "The New Neighbour," transcript of radio address, CBC Radio, 3 November 1958, LAC, Department of Indian Affairs and Northern Development fonds, RG85, vol. 1380, file 1005-7, box 316 (1).
61 Idlout, "Resolute Bay Man," 21, trans. Rhoda Kayakjuak.
62 Idlout, "Resolute Bay Man," 19, trans. Rhoda Kayakjuak.
63 Idlout, "Resolute Bay Man," 13.
64 Idlout, "Resolute Bay Man," 15.
65 Idlout, "Resolute Bay Man," 17.
66 Here, I allude not only to the influential conceptualizations of photography as an encounter engaging multiple participants, as developed by Azoulay, *Civil Contract of Photography*, but also to photography as a social practice characterized through affective engagement, as discussed in Edwards, "Objects of Affect"; and Edwards, "Photographs and the Sound."
67 "Wealthier, Too."
68 R.A.J. Phillips, "The New Neighbour," transcript of radio address, CBC Radio, 3 November 1958, 1, LAC, Department of Indian Affairs and Northern Development fonds, RG85, vol. 1380, file 1005-7, box 316 (1).
69 R.A.J. Phillips, "The New Neighbour," transcript of radio address, CBC Radio, 3 November 1958, 2, LAC, Department of Indian Affairs and Northern Development fonds, RG85, vol. 1380, file 1005-7, box 316 (1).
70 R.A.J. Phillips, "The New Neighbour," transcript of radio address, CBC Radio, 3 November 1958, 2, LAC, Department of Indian Affairs and

Northern Development fonds, RG85, vol. 1380, file 1005-7, box 316 (1).

71 Mads Lidesgaard to J.V. Jacobson, 28 January 1959, LAC, Department of Indian Affairs and Northern Development fonds, RG85, vol. 1380, file 1005-7, box 316.

72 Marcus, *Relocating Eden*, 196; Clancy and Lackenbauer, eds, *Shaping Inuit Policy*.

73 Crown-Indigenous Relations and Northern Affairs Canada, *James Bay and Northern Quebec*. See also Makivik Corporation, https://www.makivik.org/.

74 Pearson, "Remembering Iqaluit Leader"; R.A.J. Phillips to Dr J.S. Willis, 19 August 1958, LAC, Department of Indian Affairs and Northern Development fonds, RG85, vol. 466, file 1005-7, 11, box 107. This letter lists all Inuit participants in the delegation.

75 "Elijah Menarik"; "Vintage CBC North."

76 Lecocq-Lemieux, "Kananginak Pootoogook."

77 According to artist Jimmy Manning, Kananginak Pootoogook would later spend three months in Kalaallit Nunaat/Greenland "learning about the Greenlandic artist co-operative membership system." Jimmy Manning, quoted in Folger, "How Did Kananginak Pootoogook Help?"

78 Mr C.N. Bolger to T. Jenkins, 8 August 1960, LAC, Department of Indian Affairs and Northern Development fonds, RG85, vol. 1955, file A-1003-6.

79 Correspondence cited here is in the holdings of Library and Archives Canada. Some of this correspondence was also excerpted by official Gerard Kenney in his report to the Royal Commission on Aboriginal Peoples. Gerard Kenney, untitled report.

80 Bob Gould to Mr Lariviere, memorandum, 17 October 1958, LAC, Department of Indian Affairs and Northern Development fonds, RG85, vol. 1951, file A-1000 123, vol. 1.

81 By this point, Kadloo's family had joined Idlout's at Resolute/Qausuittuq. As Ludy Pudluk (Padluk) told the Qikiqtani Truth Commission, "My father and Joseph were related. They were at the same camp. The mail would go out once a year maybe. One time, my father had a hard time maintaining enough food for the winter. Joseph Idlout asked him if he wanted to come to Resolute. He would help him out. My father said, 'Yes, okay.'" Ludy Padluk (Pudluk), interview by Qikiqtani Truth Commission, Pond Inlet/Mittimatalik, 9–11 December 2008, https://www.qtcommission.ca/en/qtrb03. See also Marcus, *Relocating Eden*.

82 Tester and Kulchyski, *Tammarniit (Mistakes)*, 190–1.

83 Tester and Kulchyski, *Tammarniit (Mistakes)*, 176–7; Grant, *"Errors Exposed,"* 71.

84 Bob Gould to Mr Lariviere, memorandum, 17 October 1958, LAC, Department of Indian Affairs and Northern Development fonds, RG85, vol. 1951, file A-1000 123, vol. 1.

85 Idlout to Department of National Affairs and Northern Resources, 12 April 1960, LAC, Department of Indian Affairs and Northern Development fonds, RG85, vol. 93, file 250-14, part 1, A20170505 2018-07-19 09-53-26; Qikiqtani Truth Commission, *Community Histories 1950–1975: Resolute (Qausuittuq)*, 33.

86 Idlout to W.G. Brown, 25 April 1962, LAC, Department of Indian Affairs and Northern Development fonds, RG85, vol. 93, file 250-14, part 1, A20170505 2018-07-19 09-53-26.

87 Wilkinson, "Vanishing Canadian." Although this article in *The Beaver* is highly critical of southern interventions in the north, Wilkinson's adoption of the rhetoric of a salvage paradigm ("vanishing") reflects the colonial state's long-standing paternalistic and hierarchical treatment of the Inuit and other Indigenous peoples.

88 Marcus, *Relocating Eden*, 111. In a later letter to Idlout, Bent Sivertz presented the hunter with an egalitarian view and a rejection of the concept of a "boss": "I notice that you say that I am the Eskimo's boss. This is not quite right. We are all citizens of Canada, Eskimo people, white people, and many other races. Everyone is free in this whole country to make his own decisions and there are not any bosses over the Eskimo or other people." But clearly Idlout's and the other exiles' experiences demonstrated that there was a decided power imbalance in favour of southerners, who behaved as "bosses."

Bent Sivertz to Idlout, 10 January 1957, LAC, Department of Indian Affairs and Northern Development fonds, RG85, vol. 1951, file A-1000 123, vol. 1.

89 In his 1959 article in *The Beaver* – as he had done in his earlier field notes – Doug Wilkinson criticizes the power of RCMP officers over Inuit: "In effect the R.C.M. Police took over control of the cash economy of many areas of the Arctic. When Family Allowance issues of food were finally made to Eskimos through the R.C.M.P. detachments, they assumed a close control over the destiny and movement of every Eskimo. This reduced the role of the Hudson's Bay Company and also that of the missions. In the Arctic settlements the relationship between individuals changes. Instead of being jointly responsible for the well-being of the group, now the R.C.M.P. were clearly in a position of power." Wilkinson, "Vanishing Canadian," 27.

90 Idlout to Doug Wilkinson, 16 December 1955, LAC, Department of Indian Affairs and Northern Development fonds, RG85, vol. 1951, file A-1000 123, vol. 1.

91 Doug Wilkinson to Bent Sivertz, 2 January 1956, LAC, Department of Indian Affairs and Northern Development fonds, RG85, vol. 1951, file A-1000 123, vol. 1.

92 Qikiqtani Truth Commission, *Community Histories 1950–1975: Resolute (Qausuittuq)*, 26.

93 Qikiqtani Truth Commission, *Community Histories 1950–1975: Resolute (Qausuittuq)*, 27–8.

94 Qikiqtani Truth Commission, *Community Histories 1950–1975: Resolute (Qausuittuq)*, 30.

95 In federal archives, Daniel Salluviniq's name is spelled "Sadluvinik." I employ the spelling of the name used by his family, Salluviniq. Susan Salluviniq, Idlout's youngest daughter, was Daniel Salluviniq's daughter-in-law.

96 Sadluvinik [Daniel Salluviniq] (E9-1765) to DNANR, 5 March 1962, LAC, Department of Indian Affairs and Northern Development fonds, RG85, vol. 93, file 250-14, part 1, A20170505 2018-07-19 09-53-26.

97 W.J. Fitzsimmons to the Director, Indian and Northern Health Services, Department of National Health and Welfare, memorandum, 10 March 1957, LAC, Department of Indian Affairs and Northern Development fonds, RG85, vol. 1951, file A-1000 123, vol. 1.

98 A letter translated by Elijah Erkloo states, "The reason we were not shipping houses was because we knew that none of you were asking for a house. We also knew that the houses which were built by the Inuit are warm and bigger. Anybody who wants to buy a house in Resolute can inform the local police and they will let us know." DNANR to Sadluvinik [Daniel Salluviniq], trans. Elijah Erkloo, 1 May 1962, LAC, Department of Indian Affairs and Northern Development fonds, RG85, vol. 93, file 250-14, part 1, A20170505 2018-07-19 09-53-26. Salluviniq wrote back about the difficulty of affording a house and the needs of his wife, Sarah, a former tuberculosis patient. Sadluvinik [Daniel Salluviniq] (E9-1765) to DNANR, 20 May 1962, LAC, Department of Indian Affairs and Northern Development fonds, RG85, vol. 93, file 250-14, part 1, A20170505 2018-07-19 09-53-26.

99 Wilkinson had made an earlier film at Resolute/Qausuittuq in 1961 titled *Resolute – Hub of the Arctic*, a six-minute newsreel promoting the RCAF base and the joint weather station. It includes footage of a helicopter being unloaded, the release of a weather balloon, and several aircraft, as well as brief footage of a few Inuit men working at the base and driving a truck. NFB Archives, 61-323-28, *Resolute – Hub of the Arctic* production files and film.

100 NFB Archives, 62-323-20, *Eskimo Village, Resolute* production files and film.

101 Although the store was a co-op, the film indicates that the RCMP played a key role in its management at this time.

102 *Eskimo Village, Resolute* press release, NFB Archives, 62-323-20, *Eskimo Village, Resolute* production files and film.

103 Wilkinson had to receive approval from the RCMP to show Gordon in such a relaxed manner in the film. Tim Wilson of the RCMP responded after screening the film for RCMP division heads, "They don't want it thought that the mounties are involved in 'shopkeeping' but don't mind admitting that they help supervise the shops which are actually run by

the Eskimos themselves." Tim Wilson (RCMP) to K. Ferris (NFB), 18 June 1963, NFB Archives, 62-323-20, *Eskimo Village, Resolute* production files and film.

104 *Eskimo Village, Resolute* press release, NFB Archives, 62-323-20, *Eskimo Village, Resolute* production files and film: "Corporal Gordon relaxes with his friend, Joseph Idlout, in the latter's house following the evening at the store. Ten years ago, Joseph Idlout was a pure Eskimo hunter living at a small camp on the north shore of Baffin Island. Today he owns this small but comfortable house at Resolute and works at the nearby air base on a permanent basis. His wife serves coffee in dainty cups, with cream and sugar besides."

105 Qikiqtani Truth Commission, *Community Histories 1950–1975: Resolute (Qausuittuq)*, 34–5. Although the Qikiqtani Truth Commission reports that a co-op was established in 1960, the film indicates a high level of control by the RCMP, showing Constable Jenkins to be the person who opens the store and records purchases.

106 In his memoir, John Amagoalik details how Inuit in Resolute/Qausuittuq advocated for better conditions. Amagoalik, *Changing the Face of Canada*, 25–6.

107 Alan Rudolph Marcus, for example, reports on a 1956 meeting in Resolute/Qausuittuq with J.C. Jackson, the DNANR's head of the Eastern Arctic Patrol, noting that all of the Inuit men at the camp with Idlout and Johnnie Echalook were particularly vocal. Marcus, *Relocating Eden*, 118.

108 In 1960 correspondence to Constable Jenkins, C.N. Bolger of the Arctic Division noted, "There is, as I expect you know, a steady flow of letters [from Inuit to Ottawa], mostly related to welfare but by no means confined to this subject." He explained that Sivertz had encouraged the personal correspondence. C.N. Bolger to T. Jenkins, 8 August 1960, LAC, Department of Indian Affairs and Northern Development fonds, RG85, vol. 1955, file A-1003-6.

109 As early as December 1956, Idlout wrote a largely positive letter to Sivertz, yet he used the opportunity to complain about a lack of ammunition and boats. Idlout also insisted – against governmental advice – on travelling to Taloyoak/Spence Bay. Joseph Idlout to Bent Sivertz, 18 December 1956, LAC, Department of Indian Affairs and Northern Development fonds, RG85, vol. 93, file 250-14, part 1, A20170505 2018-07-19 09-53-26.

110 Tester, McNicoll, and Irniq, "Writing for Our Lives," 122.

111 Joseph Idlout to Advisory Commission on the Development of Government in the Northwest Territories, trans. P. Koolerk, 30 November 1965, LAC, Department of Indian Affairs and Northern Development fonds, RG22, vol. 687, AC35.

112 "Eskimo Girl Starts Own"; Payne, *Official Picture*, 165–7, 175–80, 187–8.

113 J.V. Jacobson, Chief of Education Division, to R.A.J. Phillips, 12 July 1957, LAC, Department of Indian Affairs and Northern Development fonds, RG85, vol. 461, file 630 123-1.

114 Sadluvinik [Daniel Salluviniq] (E9-1765) to DNANR, 6 May 1963, and Alex Kayuk (E9-723), 6 May 1963, LAC, Department of Indian Affairs and Northern Development fonds, RG85, vol. 93, file 250-14, part 1, A20170505 2018-07-19 09-53-26.

115 Salluviniq writes, "This is the first time I've known a policeman who just doesn't care about Inuit in need of help. I came here in 1953 and I know that the police normally cared for the society. But this one does not. He's okay with us. But we don't like his attitude towards people without money. But he should not exclude those in need of help." Sadluvinik [Daniel Salluviniq] (E9-1765) to DNANR, 6 May 1963, and Kadloo, Resolute, to DNANR, 8 May 1963, LAC, Department of Indian Affairs and Northern Development fonds, RG85, vol. 93, file 250-14, part 1, A20170505 2018-07-19 09-53-26.

116 Idlout to DNANR, [May 1963], LAC, Department of Indian Affairs and Northern Development fonds, RG85, vol. 93, file 250-14, part 1, A20170505 2018-07-19 09-53-26.

117 Idlout to DNANR, [May 1963], LAC, Department of Indian Affairs and Northern Development fonds, RG85, vol. 93, file 250-14, part 1, A20170505 2018-07-19 09-53-26.

118 Joseph Idlout to Advisory Commission on the Development of Government in the Northwest Territories, trans. P. Koolerk, 30 November 1965, LAC, Department of Indian Affairs and Northern Development fonds, RG22, vol. 687, AC35.
119 Nungak, "Five Decades," 24.
120 Kidlak passed away in Edmonton while travelling for health care. Find a Grave, "Kidla Rebecca Idlout (1916–1965)." My thanks to Madeleine d'Argencourt and Lucie Idlout for information about their grandmother.
121 Susan Salluviniq, interview by Augatnaaq Eccles and Carol Payne, Ottawa, 22 March 2023.
122 Amagoalik, *Changing the Face of Canada*, 32.

Chapter Seven

1 Bank of Canada, press release, 31 July 1975, Bank of Canada Archives, press releases. Much has been written about the two-dollar bill. In writing this section of the chapter, I have benefited from publications by Graham Iddon, Kenn Harper, and Ellen Bond, from references in the documentary *Between Two Worlds* (1990), and from Idlout's daughter Leah Idlout d'Argencourt Paulson's writing. Iddon, "Story behind the Engraving"; Harper, "'Our Picture Was Once'"; Bond, "Inuit of the 1975 Canadian"; Idlout d'Argencourt, "First Inuit Picture."
2 It had originally been intended for the $100 bill. Bank of Canada, *Art and Design*, 75.
3 Wilson, "Relationality."
4 Qitsualik, "Inummarik," 31.
5 Nunavut Department of Education, Curriculum and School Services Division, *Inuit Qaujimajatuqangit*, 22–4.
6 Elsewhere, she uses the term "social objects." Edwards, "Photographs and the Sound," 27.
7 Again, in Edwards's words, photographs are "active within [social relationships], maintaining, reproducing and articulating shifting relations." Edwards, "Photographs and the Sound," 29. Edwards's discussion is informed by actor-network theory as well as by the work of Alfred Gell.
8 Langford, *Suspended Conversations*.
9 Edwards, "Photographs and the Sound," 31.
10 Edwards, "Objects of Affect," 223. See also Edwards, "Exchanging Photographs."
11 These images differ from "frame enlargements," stills made from a single frame of the actual motion picture stock. Production stills were basically tableaux vivants, being reperformed action from the film.
12 Among them was a 1964 NFB "photostory" on the board's own filmmaking that featured a large promotional image from *Land of the Long Day*. National Gallery of Canada, "Photostory 378." See also Payne, *Official Picture*.
13 Iddon, "Story behind the Engraving."
14 Wilkinson, "National Film Board Arctic Project," 37.
15 Howell, "Inuit Want."
16 Jane Boyko, email correspondence with author, 24 June 2020. See Bank of Canada, "Scenes of Canada Series."
17 "Memorandum – Selection of Pictorial Subjects for the Backs of Notes," 25 March 1969, Bank of Canada Archives, Secretary's Department fonds, 240-75-12, vol. 2:

> It is believed that security is assisted by limiting subjects to photographic presentations as compared to painting, art treatments, drawings, etc. The elements of artistic style involved in these forms tend to prevent the eye from seeing the representation in a "neutral" way. We believe that the imperfections of counterfeit reproduction of a photographic scene are more likely to trigger suspicion than those of a scene involving a "personal" factor of artistic style. In other words, most people would have difficulty in determining whether – say – the sky in a rendering of Tom Thompson's [*sic*: Thomson's] "North Wind" was too light or too dark in mental comparison with the original, whereas a counterfeit of a photographic rendering with a too dark sky would tend to look more unfamiliar and unnatural.

18 Bank of Canada, *Art and Design*, 71.
19 For a discussion of the engraving, see Iddon, "Story behind the Engraving."

20 "Memorandum – Selection of Pictorial Subjects for the Backs of Notes," 25 March 1969, Bank of Canada Archives, Secretary's Department fonds, 240-75-12, vol. 2.
21 Bank of Canada, *Art and Design*, 79.
22 In short, these images – and indeed national currency itself – reflect what Michael Billig terms "banal nationalism," the routine "flagging" of national belonging. As I have argued elsewhere, Canadian government photography of the mid-twentieth century can be understood productively in terms of "banal nationalism." Billig, *Banal Nationalism*; Payne, *Official Picture*.
23 On St-Laurent and Massey, see the introductory chapter and chapter 5.
24 Idlout d'Argencourt, "First Inuit Picture." My thanks to Sandra Dyck for discussions about this article.
25 Carleton University Art Gallery, *Alootook Ipellie*.
26 Martin, *Stories in a New Skin*. There is a rich body of literature on Inuit memory and oral tradition. See, among others, McGrath, "*Isumaksaqsiurutigijakka*"; Collignon, Therrien, and Duchemin-Pelletier, *Orality/Oralité*; Dorais, *Language of the Inuit*; Laugrand and Oosten, *Inuit Shamanism and Christianity*; Nakasuk et al., *Inuit Worldviews*, vol. 1; Bennett and Rowley, eds, *Uqalurait*; and Kublu, Laugrand, and Oosten, "Listening to Our Past." Among publications drawing on material from the Igloolik Oral History Project, see Igloolik Oral History Centre, *Stories from Igloolik*.
27 Payne et al., eds, *Atiqput*.
28 Qitsualik, "Inummarik," 31.
29 Wilson, "Relationality," 80.
30 Wilkinson also identified the figures to bank officials using his own spellings of their names: "Kitsooalik, Paneeluk, Kadluk, Oodleteetuk, Idlouk, Elijah." Doug Wilkinson, note, signed and dated September 1975, attached to G.K. Bouey to Major S. Carroll, 12 April 1976, Bank of Canada Archives, Secretary's Department fonds, 240-75-12, vol. 8.
31 Thank you to John MacDonald for permission to reproduce the image and to Kenn Harper for his help.
32 Idlout d'Argencourt, "First Inuit Picture," 33.
33 Idlout d'Argencourt, "First Inuit Picture," 43.
34 "$2 Bill Has His Picture." This *Ottawa Citizen* article was posted at Gjoa Haven by hunter Gideon Qitsualik.
35 Nellie Erkloo's interview with Kadluk was reprinted and renarrated by Kenn Harper. See Erkloo, "Mint Replaces"; and Harper, "'Our Picture Was Once.'"
36 See Erkloo, "Mint Replaces"; Harper, "'Our Picture Was Once.'"
37 In a humorous, if costly, anecdote, the popular historian Kenn Harper, then owner of the Arctic Ventures store in Iqaluit/Frobisher Bay, tells of saving 1,000 two-dollar banknotes in 1996 when they were put out of circulation, with a plan to sell them in a few years. The hidden notes were never seen again. Harper, "Inuit Two-Dollar Bill."
38 Crust, "Inuits [*sic*] on $2 Bill."
39 Howell, "Inuit Want." Gideon Qitsualik repeated a similar sentiment to Nellie Erkloo in a *Nunatsiaq News* article: "When I saw the $2 bill, I never gave it much thought. I just laughed about it. Even though I had no money myself, here I was on the $2 bill – I just found it humorous. To me it wasn't such a monumental thing." Quoted in Erkloo, "Mint Replaces." See also Harper, "'Our Picture Was Once.'"
40 See Erkloo, "Mint Replaces"; and Harper, "'Our Picture Was Once."
41 Wilkinson did not disclose publicly how much he received for the sale. Crust, "Inuits [*sic*] on $2 Bill"; Howell, "Inuit Want."
42 Crust, "Inuits [*sic*] on $2 Bill."
43 Among recent discussions, see Harper, "'Our Picture Was Once'"; Bond, "Inuit of the 1975 Canadian"; and Iddon, "Story behind the Engraving."
44 The interview with Lucie Idlout originally aired on CBC Radio's popular arts program *Definitely Not the Opera*. Lucie Idlout, "Stories behind the Pictures." See also Friesen, "'Human Flagpoles.'"
45 In 1986, the Bank of Canada issued a new series, Birds of Canada, and retired the 1975 two-dollar bill. Bank of Canada, "Birds of

Canada Series." The Royal Canadian Mint first issued the toonie coin in 1996. Royal Canadian Mint, "Balance and Composition."

46 See below for a discussion of the concept of survivance. Vizenor, ed., *Survivance.*

47 Lucie Idlout, "Stories behind the Pictures." See also Friesen, "'Human Flagpoles.'"

48 Greenwald, dir., *Between Two Worlds.*

49 The film was screened at the 15th Toronto Festival of Festivals, Festival International du Nouveau Cinéma de Montréal, Atlantic Film Festival (Halifax), Celebration of Canadian Cinema (Calgary), Dixième-Bilan du Film Ethnographique (Paris), Leningrad International Film Festival, 15th Margaret Mead Film Festival (New York), Pamu Film Festival (Estonia), 12th Hawaii International Film Festival, and 8th Native American Film Festival (New York). It was also broadcast on the Global Television Network (Canada), Channel Four Television (UK), Australian Broadcasting Corporation, NHK (Japan), Sveriges Television (Sweden), Premiere Cable (Germany), and Access Alberta–BC Knowledge Network–Manitoba Educational Television (METV). *Between Two Worlds* promotional flyer, National Film Board of Canada Archives (hereafter NFB Archives), 55-390, *Between Two Worlds* production file.

50 *Between Two Worlds* list of requested stock footage, 20 July 1990, NFB Archives, 55-390, *Between Two Worlds* production file.

51 Raymont, dir., *Magic in the Sky.* I am grateful to the NFB Archives, especially Olivier Lamothe, for securing access to this film.

52 The brief sequence on the history of how Inuit have been imaged reflects an earlier proposal that Raymont and the anthropologist Asen Balikci had made to the NFB. The proposed film, tentatively titled "Nanook and His Brothers," drew on Balikci's extensive research, including film footage, with the Netsilik Inuit to critically examine southern media images of Inuit as a whole. As the filmmakers summarized, "*Nanook and His Brothers* will examine the origins and development of the Inuit stereotype and explore why we have created this idealized image of life on the roof of the world." However, the proposal was not well received at the NFB. On 10 August 1988, the NFB's Ontario Women's Film officer, Pat Hacker, wrote a scathing memo to John Taylor of the board about the proposal's inherent sexism:

> I recall that the author's intent in the proposed film was to eliminate bad, old myths and stereotypes about the "noble save," and to portray Inuit life as it is lived. Unfortunately, I find that their entire proposal is itself a sexist myth and stereotype. In examining Inuit life "honestly" they are unconscious of their sexist bias. There is an implicit assumption that all life is male; all societal values are male; all significant Inuit activities are male. Women are absent almost entirely from participation in the proposal, and, one might extrapolate, from Inuit life ... Since the film is about communication and the proposal is society as it truly is, the people proposing this film are falling short of sensitivity, understanding, and analysis.

Asen Balikci and Peter Raymont, *Nanook and His Brothers: The Image of the Inuit in the Western Imagination,* film proposal, May 1988, 1, NFB Archives, 55-390, *Between Two Worlds* production file; Pat Hacker to John Taylor, "Subject: Nanook and His Brothers," memo, 10 August 1988, NFB Archives, 55-390, *Between Two Worlds* production file.

53 Four versions of the newsreel were released under various titles, which are included among the entries for Wilkinson in the Bibliography. These versions are the Warner Pathé release *Eskimo Gets Medal from the Queen* (0:36) and three British Pathé releases: *Canada: Eskimos Award* (0:22), *Canada: Eskimo Medal* (0:49), and *Eskimo Receives Coronation Medal* (3:29).

54 One order alone requested that twenty-four films be screened. Initially, twenty-seven films were requested, but three were withdrawn: Boulton, dir., *Eskimo Arts and Crafts*; Newman, dir., *Arctic Jungle*; and Rasmussen, dir., *Hunters of the North Pole.* John Taylor (NFB), internal memo, n.d., NFB Archives, 55-390, *Between Two Worlds* production file.

55 Investigative Productions Inc., "Nanook and His Brothers: List of NFB Archival Films to Screen," memo, 31 August 1988, NFB Archives, 55-390, *Between Two Worlds* production file.

56 Wilkinson, dir., *Easter in Canadian Arctic*; Wilkinson, dir., *Resolute: Eskimo Village*.

57 Peter Raymont to John Taylor (NFB), 12 October 1990, NFB Archives, 55-390, *Between Two Worlds* production file.

58 Although *Between Two Worlds* was an independent production (using NFB archival material and later distributed educationally within Canada), it is instructive to consider approaches at the NFB. For a detailed discussion of Indigenous films at the NFB, see Arnaquq-Baril, *Indigenous Filmmaking*. Zoë Druick argues that these shifts at the NFB reflected not only broader changes in the social sciences, particularly internal critiques of ethnography, but also Canada's growing emphasis on the concept of multiculturalism. As she demonstrates, these critiques were limited structurally. Druick, *Projecting Canada*; Druick, "Documenting Difference."

59 In this way, the film also reflects NFB film production since the 1970s. As Sara Blair, Joseph Entin, and Franny Nudelman broadly characterize interdisciplinary US documentary practice after the Second World War, documentarians "reconceived reality as the site of political conflict and collaboration, and documentation as instrumental to anti-institutional struggles for justice." Blair, Entin, and Nudelman, "Introduction," 1.

60 *Between Two Worlds* transcript of final mix, 18 September 1990, NFB Archives, 55-390, *Between Two Worlds* production file.

61 *Between Two Worlds* transcript of final mix, 18 September 1990, NFB Archives, 55-390, *Between Two Worlds* production file.

62 These films, discussed in chapter 6, are *Resolute – Hub of the Arctic* (1961); and *Eskimo Village, Resolute* (1963). NFB Archives, 61-323-28, *Resolute – Hub of the Arctic* film and production files; NFB Archives, 62-323-20, *Eskimo Village, Resolute*, production files and film.

63 Quill, "Inuit Tragedy"; Griffin, "'Worlds' Is Cold Look." John Haslett Cuff of *The Globe and Mail* was less glowing than most, describing the film as "well-crafted, sympathetic and politically correct, but thoroughly unprovocative." Haslett Cuff, "Bittersweet but Predictable Tale." Copies of these reviews are in NFB Archives, 55-390, *Between Two Worlds* production file.

64 Tuck, "Suspending Damage," 416.

65 *Between Two Worlds* transcript of final mix, 18 September 1990, NFB Archives, 55-390, *Between Two Worlds* production file.

66 Vizenor, "Aesthetics of Survivance," 1.

67 As discussed earlier, "visual excesses," a concept coined by anthropologist Deborah Poole, are uncontrolled elements that seep into images, suggesting alternative meanings. Poole, "Excess of Description."

68 Peter Raymont, email correspondence with author, 9 September 2025.

69 The NFB collaborated on the initiative with the Inuit Relations Secretariat of what was then known as Aboriginal Affairs and Northern Development Canada, with the Government of Nunavut's Department of Education, and with other Inuit organizations. National Film Board of Canada, "Unikkausivut – Sharing Our Stories."

70 See chapter 3 for a detailed discussion of IQ.

71 National Film Board of Canada, *Unikkausivut – Sharing Our Stories: An Interdisciplinary Educational Resource*, 15.

72 This approach is a model for the online exhibition of Idlout's photographs curated by Augatnaaq Eccles with my participation.

73 *Between Two Worlds* transcript of final mix, 18 September 1990, NFB Archives, 55-390, *Between Two Worlds* production file.

74 Pond Inlet/Mittimalik, *Pond Inlet Community Guidelines*.

75 Following the ethics protocols of the Nunavut Research Institute and Carleton University's Office for Research Initiatives and Services, we ensured that all Elders participating in the interviews were paid for their time. In addition, we gave out copies of the photographs to anyone interested. As noted above, the photograph of Paul Ullatitaq Idlout with the dying polar bear proved to be the most popular.

76 Qitsualik, "Inummarik," 31.

77 Paul Ullatitaq Idlout, interview by Christina Williamson and Carol Payne, Apex, Baffin Island, 10 May 2018.

78 Quoted in Bell, "Ludy Pudluk."

79 See also Boudaud, "Les photos de famille."

80 Ludy Pudluk, interview by Alexandra Anaviapik, Christina Williamson, and Carol Payne, Pond Inlet/Mittimatalik, 7 May 2018.

81 Elijah Erkloo worked for the federal government and, from 1983 to 1987, as a member of the Northwest Territories government. During the 1960s, while working as a translator for the federal government, he regularly corresponded with Idlout, as discussed in chapter 6. The group identification session was organized by Alexandra Anaviapik, Christina Williamson, and me at Pond Inlet/Mittimatalik on 7 May 2018.

82 In addition to producing an Inuktitut dictionary (Tununiq dialect), Elisapee Ootoova has participated in a number of oral history initiatives, particularly in association with Nunavut Arctic College. Among her publications, see Ootoova, *Inuktitut Dictionary*; and Nakasuk et al., *Inuit Worldviews*, vol. 1. Elisapee Ootoova, interview by Alexandra Anaviapik, Christina Williamson, and Carol Payne, Pond Inlet/Mittimatalik, 9 May 2018.

83 Jacob Anaviapik, interview by Alexandra Anaviapik, Christina Williamson, and Carol Payne, Pond Inlet/Mittimatalik, 8 May 2018.

84 Solomon Awa, interview by Christina Williamson and Carol Payne, Iqaluit/Frobisher Bay, 11 May 2018.

85 Joshua Idlout, interview by Alexandra Anaviapik, Christina Williamson, and Carol Payne, Pond Inlet/Mittimatalik, 8 May 2018.

86 Susan Salluviniq, interview by Augatnaaq Eccles and Carol Payne, Ottawa, 22 March 2023.

87 Susan Salluviniq, interview by Augatnaaq Eccles and Carol Payne, Ottawa, 22 March 2023.

88 Susan Salluviniq, interview by Augatnaaq Eccles and Carol Payne, Ottawa, 22 March 2023.

89 Nunavut Tunngavik, "Apology for the Inuit." See also Wakeham, "At the Intersection"; and Henderson and Wakeham, *Reconciling Canada*.

90 Eccles, "Teacher's Guide."

91 Cameron, *Far Off Metal River*, 27.

92 Qitsualik, "Inummarik."

93 Mitchell, "Showing Seeing," 175.

Bibliography

Archives

Anglican Church of Canada Archives, Toronto, M96-7, Diocese of the Arctic, series 1
– Archibald Lang Fleming Records, subseries 1-1, Clergy files 1927–72, box 1, boxes 17 1a–d, 2, 3.
– Daulby, Thomas, Rev. (Pond Inlet), 1944–61, box 2.
– Flint, Maurice Sidney, Rev. (Pond Inlet), 1937–56, box 2, file 2.
– Turner, John Hudspith, Rev. (Pond Inlet, Moffet Inlet), 1 of 4 files, 1929–47, box 2, item 1.

Bank of Canada Archives and Museum, Ottawa
– Press releases.
– Secretary's Department fonds.

Hudson's Bay Company Archives, Archives of Manitoba, Winnipeg

Library and Archives Canada, Ottawa
– Arctic Institute of North America fonds.
– Canadian Broadcasting Corporation fonds.
– Department of Indian Affairs and Northern Development fonds.
– Department of Indian Affairs and Northern Development fonds.
– Department of Indian Affairs and Northern Development fonds.
– Department of Indian Affairs and Northern Development fonds.
– Department of Northern Affairs and National Resources fonds.
– Government House fonds.
– National Film Board of Canada fonds.
– Royal Canadian Mounted Police fonds.
– Roy Tash fonds.

National Film Board of Canada Archives, Montreal
– 07-035, Exercise Musk-Ox.
– 11-207, Classroom Films Project.
– 12-112, "Going North."
– 51-319, *Sister Pelagie* production files.
– 51-341, *Arctic Saga* production files.
– 51-405, *Angotee* production files.
– 51-410, *Land of the Long Day* production files.
– 52-106, *Arctic Lifeline* production files.
– 54-321-13, *White Eskimo* production files.
– 55-390, *Between Two Worlds* production files.
– 61-323-28, *Resolute – Hub of the Arctic* production files and film.
– 62-323-20, *Eskimo Village, Resolute* production files and film.

Nunavut Archives, Iqaluit
– Douglas E. Wilkinson fonds

Pond Inlet Library and Archives Society, Nattinak Visitors Centre, Pond Inlet/Mittimatalik

Scott Polar Research Institute, Thomas H. Manning Polar Archive, Cambridge, United Kingdom
– Harold Duncan Papers, MS1576

University of British Columbia, Vancouver
– Social History of the Eastern Arctic Database, https://nunavutsocialhistory.arts.ubc.ca/.

University of Toronto Archives, Toronto
– Vincent Massey Papers

Author Interviews

Anaviapik, Jacob. Interview by Alexandra Anaviapik, Christina Williamson, and Carol Payne, Pond Inlet/Mittimatalik, 8 May 2018.

Awa, Solomon. Interview by Christina Williamson and Carol Payne, Iqaluit, 11 May 2018.

Erkloo, Elijah, and Daniel Komangapik. Interview by Alexandra Anaviapik, Carol Payne, and Christina Williamson, Pond Inlet/Mittimatalik, 9 May 2018.

Hanson, Ann Meekitjuk. Interview by Carol Payne, Apex, Baffin Island, 10 May 2018.

Idlout, Joshua. Interview by Alexandra Anaviapik, Christina Williamson, and Carol Payne, Pond Inlet/Mittimatalik, 8 May 2018.
Idlout, Paul Ullatitaq. Interview by Christina Williamson and Carol Payne, Apex, Baffin Island, 10 May 2018.
Ootoova, Elisapee. Interview by Alexandra Anaviapik, Christina Williamson, and Carol Payne, Pond Inlet/Mittimatalik, 9 May 2018.
Pudluk, Ludy. Interview by Alexandra Anaviapik, Christina Williamson, and Carol Payne, Pond Inlet/Mittimatalik, 7 May 2018.
Salluviniq, Susan. Interview by Augatnaaq Eccles and Carol Payne, Ottawa, 22 March 2023.
Sangoya, Ruth. Interview by Alexandra Anaviapik, Christina Williamson, and Carol Payne, Pond Inlet/Mittimatalik, 8 May 2018.
Serkoak, David. Interview by Deborah Kigjugalik Webster and Carol Payne, Ottawa, 3 July 2019.

Qikiqtani Truth Commission Interviews

Amagoalik, John. Interview by Qikiqtani Truth Commission, Iqaluit, 17–19 June 2008. https://www.qtcommission.ca/en/qtiq31.
Arreak, Malachi. Interview by Qikiqtani Truth Commission, Pond Inlet/Mittimatalik, 9–11 December 2008. https://www.qtcommission.ca/en/qtpi15.
Idlout, Joshua. Interview by Qikiqtani Truth Commission, Pond Inlet/Mittimatalik, 9–11 December 2008. https://www.qtcommission.ca/en/qtpi12.
Kadloo, Cornelius. Interview by Qikiqtani Truth Commission, Pond Inlet/Mittimatalik, 9–11 December 2008. https://www.qtcommission.ca/en/qtpi03.
Kalluk, David. Interview by Qikiqtani Truth Commission, Pond Inlet/Mittimatalik, 9–11 December 2008. https://www.qtcommission.ca/en/qtrb01.
Killiktee, Apphia. Interview by Qikiqtani Truth Commission, Pond Inlet/Mittimatalik, 9–11 December 2008. https://www.qtcommission.ca/en/qtpi01.
Killiktee, Jaykolasie. Interview by Qikiqtani Truth Commission, Pond Inlet/Mittimatalik, 9–11 December 2008. https://www.qtcommission.ca/en/qtpi10.
Komangapik, Paomee. Interview by Qikiqtani Truth Commission, Pond Inlet/Mittimatalik, 9–11 December 2008. https://www.qtcommission.ca/en/qtpi17.
Kudloo, Ham. Interview by Qikiqtani Truth Commission, Pond Inlet/Mittimatalik, 9–11 December 2008. https://www.qtcommission.ca/en/qtpi07.
Kyak, Elizabeth. Interview by Qikiqtani Truth Commission. Pond Inlet/Mittimatalik, 9–11 December 2008. https://www.qtcommission.ca/en/qtpi06.
Ootoova, Elisapee. Interview by Qikiqtani Truth Commission, Pond Inlet/Mittimatalik, 9–11 December 2008. https://www.qtcommission.ca/en/qtpi05.
Padluk, Dora. Interview by Qikiqtani Truth Commission, Resolute/Qausuittuq, 14–16 April 2008. https://www.qtcommission.ca/en/qtrb02.
Padluk (Pudluk), Ludy. Interview by Qikiqtani Truth Commission, Pond Inlet/Mittimatalik, 9–11 December 2008. https://www.qtcommission.ca/en/qtrb03.
Panipakoocho, Elijah. Interview by Qikiqtani Truth Commission, Pond Inlet/Mittimatalik, 9–11 December 2008. https://www.qtcommission.ca/en/qtpi04.
Qiyuapik, Isaac. Interview by Qikiqtani Truth Commission, Pond Inlet/Mittimatalik, 9–11 December 2008. https://www.qtcommission.ca/en/qtpi08.

Other Sources

Adams, Amy. "Arctic and Inuit Photography, Part One: An Accurate Representation of the World?" *Inuit Art Quarterly* 15, no. 2 (2000): 5–10.
Adams, Amy. "Arctic and Inuit Photography, Part Two: Through the Looking Glass: The Photographs of Robert J. Flaherty and Peter Pitseolak." *Inuit Art Quarterly* 15, no. 3 (2000): 4–19.
Agee, James, and Walker Evans. *Let Us Now Praise Famous Men*. New York: Mariner Books Classics, 2001.

Amagoalik, John. *Changing the Face of Canada: Life Stories of Northern Leaders.* Ed. Louis McComber. Iqaluit: Nunavut Arctic College, 2007.

Amagoalik, John. "Reconciliation or Conciliation? An Inuit Perspective." In *"Speaking My Truth": Reflections on Reconciliation and Residential School*, ed. Shelagh Rogers, Mike DeGagné, and Jonathan Dewar, 35–43. Ottawa: Aboriginal Healing Foundation, 2012.

Anglican Church of Canada. "General Synod Archives." n.d. https://archives.anglican.ca/.

The Arctic Circle. *Meetings of the Arctic Circle.* n.d. http://www.thearcticcircle.ca/pdf/500Meetings.pdf.

The Arctic Circle. "Welcome to the Arctic Circle." n.d. http://www.thearcticcircle.ca/index.htm.

"Arctic Holiday." *Arctic Circular* 2, no. 1 (1949): 14.

"The Arctic Note Book Series." *Arctic Circular* 3, no. 2 (1950): 14–15.

Arnakak, Jaypeetee. "Commentary: What Is Inuit Qaujimajatuqangit? Using Inuit Family and Kinship Relationships to Apply Inuit Qaujimajatuqangit." *Nunatsiaq News*, 25 August 2000.

Arnaquq-Baril, Alethea. *Indigenous Filmmaking at the NFB: An Overview.* Montreal: National Film Board of Canada, 2017.

Aubert de la Rue, E. "Geology: Geological Survey through the Ungava Peninsula." *Arctic* 1, no. 2 (1948): 135–6.

Audlaluk, Larry. *What I Remember, What I Know: The Life of a High Arctic Exile.* Iqaluit: Inhabit Media, 2020.

Azoulay, Ariella. *The Civil Contract of Photography.* New York: Zone Books, 2008.

Baird, P.D. "Land of the Long Day, by Doug Wilkinson." Book review. *Arctic* 8, no. 4 (1955): 252–3.

Bank of Canada. *The Art and Design of Canadian Bank Notes.* Ottawa: Bank of Canada, 2006.

Bank of Canada. "Birds of Canada Series." n.d. https://www.bankofcanada.ca/banknotes/bank-note-series/1986-series-birds-of-canada/.

Bank of Canada. "Inflation Calculator." n.d. https://www.bankofcanada.ca/rates/related/inflation-calculator/.

Bank of Canada. "Scenes of Canada Series." n.d. https://www.bankofcanada.ca/banknotes/bank-note-series/past-series/1969-1979/.

"Barry Pottle." *Inuit Art Quarterly*, 21 November 2017. https://www.inuitartfoundation.org/profiles/artist/Barry-Pottle.

Bauldic, Michelle. "Art and Mass Production: Federal Government Intervention in the Inuit Arts Industry during the 1960s." PhD diss., Carleton University, forthcoming.

Bell, Jim. "Ludy Pudluk, 76, Dies on Canada Day." *Nunatsiaq News*, 3 July 2019. https://nunatsiaq.com/stories/article/ludy-pudluk-76-dies-on-canada-day/.

Benjamin, Walter. "Little History of Photography." In Walter Benjamin, *Selected Writings*, vol. 2, part 2, *1931–34*, trans. Roger Livingstone et al., ed. Michael W. Jennings, Howard Eiland, and Gary Smith, 507–30. Cambridge, MA: Belknap Press of Harvard University Press, 1999.

Bennett, John, and Susan Rowley, eds. *Uqalurait: An Oral History of Nunavut.* Montreal and Kingston: McGill-Queen's University Press, 2004.

Bhabha, Homi K. "Of Mimicry and Man: The Ambivalence of Colonial Discourse." *October* 28 (1984): 125–33.

Bhabha, Homi K. "Signs Taken for Wonders: Questions of Ambivalence and Authority under a Tree outside Delhi, May 1817." *Critical Inquiry* 12, no. 1 (1985): 144–65.

Billig, Michael. *Banal Nationalism.* Thousand Oaks, CA: Sage, 1995.

Birnie-Danzker, Jo-Anne, and Taqralik Partridge. "Qikiqtaaluk: Baffin Island 1913–14." *Inuit Art Quarterly* 37, no. 1 (2024): 34–45.

Bissell, Claude T. *The Imperial Canadian: Vincent Massey in Office.* Toronto: University of Toronto Press, 1986.

Bissell, Claude T. *The Young Vincent Massey.* Toronto: University of Toronto Press, 1981.

Blair, Sara, Joseph B. Entin, and Franny Nudelman. "Introduction." In *Remaking Reality: U.S. Documentary Culture after 1945*, ed. Sara Blair, Joseph B. Entin, and Franny Nudelman, 1–13. Chapel Hill: University of North Carolina Press, 2018.

Boas, Franz. "The Eskimo of Baffin Land and Hudson Bay: From Notes Collected by Capt. George Comer, Capt. James S. Mutch, and Rev. E.J. Peck." *Bulletin of the American Museum of Natural History* 15, part 1 (1901): 1–370.

Bond, Ellen. "Inuit of the 1975 Canadian Two-Dollar Bill." *Library and Archives Canada Blog*, 29 March 2021. https://thediscoverblog.com/2021/03/29/inuit-of-the-1975-canadian-2-bill/.
Bonesteel, Sarah. *Canada's Relationship with Inuit: A History of Policy and Program Development*. Ed. Erik Anderson for Public History Inc. Ottawa: Indian and Northern Affairs Canada, 2006.
Boudaud, Laetitia. "Les photos de famille chez les Inuits de Mittimatalik au Nunavut: Une mémoire collective?" MA thesis, Laval University, 2006.
Boulton, Laura, dir. *Eskimo Arts and Crafts*. Montreal: National Film Board of Canada, 1943.
Brady, Miranda J. "Media Practices and Painful Pasts: The Public Testimonial in Canada's Truth and Reconciliation Commission." *Media International Australia* 149, no. 1 (2013): 141–50.
Brady, Miranda J., and John Kelly. *We Interrupt This Program: Indigenous Media Tactics in Canadian Culture*. Vancouver: UBC Press, 2017.
Bravo, Michael. *North Pole: Nature and Culture*. London: Reaktion Books, 2019.
British Movietone News. "Polar News – Governor General Massey." 1956. *YouTube*, 21 July 2015. https://www.youtube.com/watch?v=ivYGstjU4Ac.
Brum, Janice, and Janet Pennington. N92-012 *Douglas E. Wilkinson Fonds: An Inventory*. Yellowknife: Northwest Territory Archives, 1993.
Burant, Jim. "Using Photography to Assert Canadian Sovereignty in the Arctic: The A.P. Low Expedition of 1903–4 aboard the CGS *Neptune*." In *Imaging the Arctic*, ed. J.C.H. King and Henrietta Lidchi, 77–87. Seattle and Vancouver: University of Washington Press and UBC Press, 1998.
Cameron, Emilie. *Far Off Metal River: Inuit Lands, Settler Stories, and the Making of the Contemporary Arctic*. Vancouver: UBC Press, 2015.
Campbell, Heather, and Reilly Bishop-Stall. "An Inuit Approach to Archival Work Based on Respect and Adaptability." In *The Routledge Companion to Indigenous Art Histories in the United States and Canada*, ed. Heather Igloliorte and Carla Taunton, 53–63. New York: Routledge, 2023.
Campt, Tina. *Listening to Images*. Durham, NC: Duke University Press, 2017.
Canadian Geographic. "Roads to Reconciliation: Leah Idlout." n.d. https://pathstoreconciliation.canadiangeographic.ca/?mpfy-pin=556.
Canadian Museum of History. "Peter Pitseolak." n.d. Accessed 30 August 2023. https://www.historymuseum.ca/cmc/exhibitions/tresors/ethno/etp0300e.html.
Capitaine, Brieg, and Karine Vanthuyne. *Power through Testimony: Reframing Residential Schools in the Age of Reconciliation*. Vancouver: UBC Press, 2017.
Carleton University Art Gallery. *Alootook Ipellie: Walking Both Sides of an Invisible Border*. Exhibition catalogue. Curators Sandra Dyck, Heather Igloliorte, and Christine Lalonde. Ottawa: Carleton University, 2018.
Carter, Don. "His Excellency, the Right Honourable Vincent Massey, P.C., C.H., 1887–1967." Library and Archives Canada, n.d. https://www.collectionscanada.gc.ca/massey/h5-200-e.html.
Cheetham, Mark A. "Monumental Ephemera: British Sculpture in the Arctic, Icebergs in London, an Inuit Map," *Art History* 47, no. 2 (2024): 373–97.
Clancy, Peter. "The Making of Eskimo Policy in Canada, 1952–62: The Life and Times of the Eskimo Affairs Committee." *Arctic* 40, no. 3 (1987): 191–7.
Clancy, Peter, and P. Whitney Lackenbauer, eds. *Shaping Inuit Policy: The Minutes of the Eskimo Affairs Committee, 1952–62*. Calgary: Centre for Military, Security and Strategic Studies, University of Calgary, 2019. https://arts.ucalgary.ca/sites/default/files/teams/25/dcass-v14-eac.pdf.
Clifford, James. "On Ethnographic Allegory." In *Writing Culture: The Poetics and Politics of Ethnography*, ed. James Clifford and George E. Marcus, 98–121. Berkeley: University of California Press, 1986.
Close, Susan. *Framing Identity: Social Practice of Photography in Canada (1880–1920)*. Winnipeg: Arbeiter Ring, 2007.
Collignon, Béatrice, and Michèle Therrien, eds. *Orality/Oralité in the 21st Century: Inuit Discourse and Practices*. Proceedings of the 15th Inuit Studies Conference. Paris: Inalco-CERLOM, 2009.

Condon, Richard. "The History and Development of Arctic Photography." *Arctic Anthropology* 26, no. 1 (1989): 46–87.

"Conference on Eskimo Affairs." *Arctic Circular* 5, no. 4 (1952): 41–3.

Cook, Anna. "A Politics of Indigenous Voice: Reconciliation, Felt Knowledge, and Settler Denial." *Canadian Journal of Native Studies* 36, no. 2 (2016): 74–84.

Cook, Terry. "Canada's Arctic Islands: A Centennial Perspective." *The Archivist* 7, no. 5 (1980): 1–4. Reprinted in *The Arctic Circular* 28, nos 1–2 (1980): 32–4.

Crowe, Keith J. *A History of the Original Peoples of Northern Canada*. Montreal and Kingston: McGill-Queen's University Press, 2001.

Crown-Indigenous Relations and Northern Affairs Canada. *The James Bay and Northern Quebec Agreement (JBNQA)*. Ottawa: Indigenous and Northern Affairs Canada, 1975. https://caid.ca/AgrJamBayNorQueA1975.pdf.

Cruikshank, Julie. *Do Glaciers Listen? Local Knowledge, Colonial Encounters, and Social Imagination*. Vancouver: UBC Press, 2005.

Cruikshank, Julie. *The Social Life of Stories: Narrative and Knowledge in the Yukon Territory*. Vancouver: UBC Press, 1998.

Crust, John. "Inuits [*sic*] on $2 Bill Not Honored." *Winnipeg Sun*, 5 August 1982. Bank of Canada Archives and Museum.

Curtis, Edward S., dir. *In the Land of the Head Hunters*. Fort Lee, NJ: World Film Company, 1914.

Davis, Natalie Zemon. "Decentering History: Local Histories and Cultural Crossings in a Global World." *History and Theory* 50, no. 2 (2011): 188–202.

Dempsey, Lotta. "Young Torontonian to Show Eskimos New Way of Life." *Toronto Star*, 14 February 1953, 15.

Desjardins, Denys, dir. *Making Movie History: Jean Roy*. Montreal: National Film Board of Canada. 2014. https://www.nfb.ca/film/making_movie_history_jean_roy/.

Diumbaldo, Richard. *The Government of Canada and the Inuit, 1900–1967*. Ottawa: Corporate Policy, Research Branch, Indian and Northern Affairs Canada, 1985.

Dorais, Louis-Jacques. *The Language of the Inuit: Syntax, Semantics, and Society in the Arctic*. Montreal and Kingston: McGill-Queen's University Press, 2010.

Druick, Zoë. "Documenting Difference: The NFB in the 1980s and 1990s." In *Projecting Canada: Government Policy and Documentary Film at the National Film Board of Canada*, 163–79. Montreal and Kingston: McGill-Queen's University Press, 2007.

Druick, Zoë. *Projecting Canada: Government Policy and Documentary Film at the National Film Board of Canada*. Montreal and Kingston: McGill-Queen's University Press, 2007.

Dubois, Samuel. "'How to Build an Igloo': Deconstructing Architectural Myths in Canadian Visual Culture." Paper presented at the 50th Annual Conference of the Society for the Study of Architecture in Canada, Ottawa, 28 May 2025.

Dyck, Sandra. "Looking for Kenojuak." In *Atiqput: Inuit Oral History and Project Naming*, ed. Carol Payne, Beth Greenhorn, Deborah Kigjugalik Webster, and Christina Williamson, 187–202. Montreal and Kingston: McGill-Queen's University Press, 2022.

Dyck, Sandra. *Sanattiaqsimajut: Inuit Art from the Carleton University Art Gallery Collection*. Ottawa: Carleton University Art Gallery, 2009.

Dyer, Richard. *White*. London and New York: Routledge, 1997.

Eastman-Kodak Corporation. *History of Kodak Cameras*. Rochester: Eastman-Kodak Corporation, 1999.

Eber, Dorothy. "Peter Pitseolak and the Photographic Template." In *Imaging the Arctic*, ed. J.C.H. King and Henrietta Lidchi, 53–9. Seattle and Vancouver: University of Washington Press and UBC Press, 1998.

Eber, Dorothy. "Peter Pitseolak, an Historian for Seekooseelak." In *Peter Pitseolak (1902–1973), Inuit Historian of Seekooseelak*, ed. David Bellman, 8–33. Montreal: McCord Museum, 1980.

Eccles, Augatnaaq. "Curatorial Essay." *Ajjiliurlagit ("Let me take your picture"): The Photographs of Joseph Idlout*. n.d. https://www.josephidloutphotographs.ca/en/albums.

Eccles, Augatnaaq. "Teacher's Guide." *Ajjiliurlagit ("Let me take your picture"): The Photographs of Joseph Idlout.* n.d. https://www.josephidloutphotographs.ca/en/learning-resources.html.
Edwards, Elizabeth. "Exchanging Photographs: Preliminary Thoughts on the Currency of Photography in Collecting Anthropology." *Journal des anthropologues*, nos 80–1 (2000): 21–46.
Edwards, Elizabeth. "Objects of Affect: Photography beyond the Image." *Annual Review of Anthropology* 41 (2012): 221–34.
Edwards, Elizabeth. "Photographs and the Sound of History." *Visual Anthropology Review* 21, nos 1–2 (2006): 27–46.
Eekgeesiak, J. Okalik. "Foreword." In Qiqiktani Inuit Association, *Guide to the Community Histories and Special Studies of the Qiqiktani Truth Commission*, 8–9. Iqaluit: Inhabit Media, 2013. https://www.qtcommission.ca/sites/default/files/public/thematic_reports/web_guide_english1.pdf.
"Elijah Menarik." *Inuktitut Magazine*, May 1962, 7–8. https://www.itk.ca/wp-content/uploads/2016/10/1962-may-InuktitutMagazine-EN.pdf.
Erkloo, Nellie. "Mint Replaces Inuit $2 Bill This Month: Aulatseevingmiut Recall the Day of the Picture." *Nunatsiaq News*, 1986.
"Eskimo Dress: Massey Samples Arctic Life." *Globe and Mail*, 22 March 1956.
"Eskimo Girl Starts Own Packing Box Schoolhouse." *Globe and Mail*, 11 July 1957.
Evans, Michael Robert. *Isuma: Inuit Video Art.* Montreal and Kingston: McGill-Queen's University Press, 2008.
Fabian, Johannes. *Time and the Other: How Anthropology Makes Its Object.* New York: Columbia University Press, 1983.
"Fall 2003 Cover Identification." *Inuit Art Quarterly* 20, no. 1 (2005).
"Films of the Eastern Arctic to Be Produced by the National Film Board." *Arctic Circular* 3, no. 5 (1950): 56–7.
Find a Grave. "Kidla Rebecca Idlout (1916–1965)." n.d. https://www.findagrave.com/memorial/41106591/kidla-rebecca-idlout.
Finlay, Karen. *The Force of Culture: Vincent Massey and Canadian Sovereignty.* Toronto: University of Toronto Press, 2004.
Flaherty, Robert, dir. *Nanook of the North.* Paris: Les Frères Revillon, 1922.
Flaherty, Robert. "Preface." In *Nanook of the North.* London: Windmill Books, 1971.
Flaherty, Robert, and Frances Hubbard Flaherty. *My Eskimo Friends: "Nanook of the North."* Garden City, NJ: Doubleday, Page and Company, 1924.
Flint, Maurice S. *Operation Canon: A Short Account of the Life and Witness of the Reverend John Hudspith Turner.* London: Bible Churchmen's Missionary Society, 1949.
Folger, Napatsi. "How Did Kananginak Pootoogook Help Open Kinngait's First Print Shop?" *Inuit Art Quarterly*, 7 October 2021. https://www.inuitartfoundation.org/iaq-online/how-did-kananginak-pootoogook-help-open-kinngait-s-first-print-shop.
Foucault, Michel. *Discipline and Punish: The Birth of the Prison.* 2nd Vintage ed. Trans. Allan Sheridan. New York: Vintage Books, 1995.
Fox, Jason, and Heather Igloliorte, eds. Special issue on photography. *Inuit Art Quarterly* 37, no. 1 (2024).
Fredericks de Araujo, Carter. "Jimmy Manning." *Inuit Art Quarterly*, 14 September 2017. https://www.inuitartfoundation.org/profiles/artist/Jimmy-Manning.
Friesen, Andrew. "'Human Flagpoles': Dark Story behind Inuit Scene on $2 Bill." CBC News, 6 May 2014. https://www.cbc.ca/news/indigenous/human-flagpoles-dark-story-behind-inuit-scene-on-2-bill-1.2632380#.
Galbraith, William. "Never Be Off the Road: Lord Tweedsmuir's Visit to the North." *Canadian Parliamentary Review* 18, no. 1 (1995): 30–3.
"Geese Are Found in Grounded State." *New York Times*, 25 August 1954.
Geismar, Haidy, and Anita Herle. *Moving Images: John Layard, Fieldwork and Photography on Malakula since 1914.* Honolulu and Cambridge, UK: University of Hawai'i Press and Museum of Archaeology and Anthropology, University of Cambridge, 2010.
Geller, Peter. *Northern Exposures: Photographing and Filming the Canadian North, 1920–45.* Vancouver: UBC Press, 2004.
"A Gift for Leah: Children Save Pennies to Buy Eskimo Bible." *Globe and Mail*, 19 June 1952.

Ginzburg, Carlo. "Microhistory: Two or Three Things That I Know about It." Trans. Anne Tedeschi and John C. Tedeschi. *Critical Inquiry* 20, no. 1 (1993): 10–35.

Glass, Aaron, and Brad Evans. "Edward Curtis Meets the Kwakwaka'wakw: Cultural Encounter and Indigenous Agency in the Land of the Head Hunters." In *Return to the Land of the Head Hunters: Edward S. Curtis, the Kwakwaka'wakw, and the Making of Modern Cinema*, ed. Brad Evans and Aaron Glass, 3–39. Seattle: University of Washington Press, 2014.

Goldring, Philip, "Historians and Inuit: Learning from the Qikiqtani Truth Commission, 2007–2010." *Canadian Journal of History* 50, no. 3 (2015): 492–523.

Gordon, Holly. "Inuk Throat Singer Tanya Tagaq on Reclaiming Nanook of the North." CBC News, 25 January 2014. https://www.cbc.ca/news/indigenous/inuk-throat-singer-tanya-tagaq-on-reclaiming-nanook-of-the-north-1.2508581.

Government of Canada. "First Arctic Conference, Dept. of Northern Affairs and National Resources, Held in Ottawa." n.d. Library and Archives Canada, National Film Board of Canada fonds, RG53. http://www.bac-lac.gc.ca/eng/CollectionSearch/Pages/record.aspx?app=fonandcol&IdNumber=3519154.

Government of Canada. *House of Commons Debates*. First Session, Twenty-Second Parliament, vol. 1, 8 December 1953. https://parl.canadiana.ca/view/oop.debates_HOC2201_01/1.

Government of Canada. "Minister of Crown-Indigenous Relations Delivers Apology to Qikiqtani Inuit." 14 August 2019. https://www.canada.ca/en/crown-indigenous-relations-northern-affairs/news/2019/08/minister-of-crown-indigenous-relations-delivers-apology-to-qikiqtani-inuit.html.

Government of Nunavut. *Incorporating Inuit Societal Values*. 2013. https://www.gov.nu.ca/sites/default/files/publications/2022-01/incorporating_inuit_societal_values_report.pdf.

Government of Nunavut. "Our Guiding Principles." n.d. https://www.premier.gov.nu.ca/en/about/our-guiding-principles.

Government of Nunavut. *Qaujimatait Report*. Arviat: Department of Education, Child and Social Services, 2000.

Grace, Sheryl. *On the Art of Being Canadian*. Vancouver: UBC Press, 2010.

Grant, Shelagh D. *Arctic Justice: On Trial for Murder, Pond Inlet, 1923*. Montreal and Kingston: McGill-Queen's University Press, 2002.

Grant, Shelagh D. "A Case of Compounded Error: The Inuit Resettlement Project, 1953, and the Government Response, 1990." *Northern Perspectives* 19, no. 1 (1991): 3–29.

Grant, Shelagh D. *"Errors Exposed": Inuit Relocations to the High Arctic, 1953–60*. Calgary: Documents on Canadian Arctic Sovereignty and Security, 2016.

Greenland National Museum and Archives. "Kalaallisuut: National Dress." n.d. https://en.nka.gl/intangible-topics/kalaallisuut/.

Greenwald, Barry, dir. *Between Two Worlds*. Producer Peter Raymont. Writer/co-producer Barbara Sears. Toronto: Investigative Productions, 1990.

Griffin, John. "'Worlds' Is Cold Look at an Arctic Tragedy: Joseph Idlout Slipped from Fame to Suicide." *Montreal Gazette*, 22 October 1991, B6.

Grimshaw, Anna. "Who Has the Last Laugh? *Nanook of the North* and Some New Thoughts on an Old Classic." *Visual Anthropology* 27, no. 5 (2014): 421–35.

Hanson, Ann Meekitjuk. "A Story about Names." In *Atiqput: Inuit Oral History and Project Naming*, ed. Carol Payne, Beth Greenhorn, Deborah Kigjugalik Webster, and Christina Williamson, 125–32. Montreal and Kingston: McGill-Queen's University Press, 2022.

Harlan, Theresa. "Indigenous Photographies: A Space for Indigenous Realities." In *Native Nations: Journeys in American Photography*, ed. Jane Alison, 233–45. London: Barbican Art Gallery, 1998.

Harney, Elizabeth, and Ruth B. Phillips, eds. *Mapping Modernisms: Art, Indigeneity, Colonialism*. Durham, NC: Duke University Press, 2018.

Harper, Kenn. "Akumalik: An Inuit Religious Leader." *Nunatsiaq News*, 13 November 2020. https://nunatsiaq.com/stories/article/taissumani-nov-13/.

Harper, Kenn. "Inuktut or Inuktitut?" *Nunatsiaq News*, 8 February 2025. https://nunatsiaq.com/stories/article/inuktut-or-inuktitut/.

Harper, Kenn. "'Our Picture Was Once on a Banknote': Inuit on the Two-Dollar Bill." *Nunatsiaq News*, 30 October 2020. https://nunatsiaq.com/stories/article/taissumani-oct-30/.

Harper, Kenn. "The Inuit Two-Dollar Bill – a Bittersweet Memory." *Nunatsiaq News*, 7 April 2018. https://nunatsiaq.com/stories/article/65674taissumani_april_7/.

Haslett Cuff, John. "A Bittersweet but Predictable Tale." *Globe and Mail*, 12 October 1991.

Henderson, Jennifer, and Pauline Wakeham. *Reconciling Canada: Critical Perspectives on the Culture of Redress*. Toronto: University of Toronto Press, 2013.

Hickey, Harvey. "Eskimo Girl in Gatineau Longs for Far-Off Igloo." *Globe and Mail*, 4 June 1952.

Hickey, Harvey. "First Movies Made inside Igloo Included in 30,000 Foot Record." *Globe and Mail*, 11 February 1952.

High, Steven. "Going Beyond 'Juicy Quotes Syndrome.'" In *Going Public: The Art of Participatory Practice*, ed. Elizabeth Miller, Steven High, and Edward J. Little, 110–29. Vancouver: UBC Press, 2017.

Holloway, Caroline Forcier. "Exercise Musk-Ox: The Challenges of Filming a Military Expedition in Canada's Arctic." In *Films on Ice: Cinemas of the Arctic*, ed. Scott Mackenzie and Anna Westerstahl Stenport, 245–54. Edinburgh: Edinburgh University Press, 2016.

hooks, bell. *Black Looks: Race and Representation*. Boston: South End, 1992.

Howell, Peter. "Inuit Want Their $2 Worth: Bank of Canada Passes the Buck." *Toronto Sunday Sun*, 25 July 1982. Bank of Canada Archives and Museum.

Hudson, Anna, Heather Igloliorte, and Jan-Erik Lundström. *Qummut Qukiria!* Fredericton, NB: Goose Lane, 2022.

Hudson's Bay Company Archives. "Herodier, Gaston." https://www.gov.mb.ca/chc/archives/_assets/docs/hbca/biographical/h/herodier_gaston.pdf.

Hulan, Renée. *Northern Experience and the Myths of Canadian Culture*. Montreal and Kingston: McGill-Queen's University Press, 2002.

Iddon, Graham. "The Story behind the Engraving: Joseph Idlout and the 1975 Two-Dollar Bill." Bank of Canada Museum, 21 October 2020. https://www.bankofcanadamuseum.ca/2020/10/the-story-behind-the-engraving/.

Idlout, Joseph. "Letter to an Administrator (Idlout's 10 Uses for the Seal)." Trans. R.G.H. Williamson. *Plywood World* 1, no. 4 (1961): n.p.

Idlout, Joseph. "Resolute Bay Man Visiting Greenland." *Inuktitut Magazine*, May 1959, 11–21.

Idlout, Lucie. "Le prix du relogement." Interview. *Polar Sea 360*, n.d. Accessed 31 October 2018. http://www.polarsea360.com/fr/2014/09/page/3/.

Idlout, Lucie. "The Stories behind the Pictures." Interview by Sook-Yin Lee. *Definitely Not the Opera*, CBC Radio, 26 April 2014. https://www.cbc.ca/radio/dnto/see-the-photos-behind-the-stories-on-dnto-1.2802874.

Idlout d'Argencourt, Leah. "C.D. Howe I." *Inuit Today* 6, no. 5 (June 1977): 30–45.

Idlout d'Argencourt, Leah. "C.D. Howe II: The Hospital." *Inuit Today* 6, no. 6 (July–August 1977): 46–51, 89.

Idlout d'Argencourt, Leah. "C.D. Howe III: The Hospital." *Inuit Today* 6, no. 8 (October 1977): 26–31.

Idlout d'Argencourt, Leah. "C.D. Howe IV: Ottawa." *Inuit Today* 6, no. 9 (November 1977): 16–23, 55.

Idlout d'Argencourt, Leah. "C.D. Howe V: Trip Back Home." *Inuit Today* 6, no. 10 (December 1977): 22–9.

Idlout d'Argencourt, Leah. "First Inuit Picture on Canadian Money." *Inuit Today* 1, no. 9 (October 1975): 32–3, 43.

Idlout d'Argencourt, Leah. "Merry Christmas!" *Inuit Today* 5, no. 10 (November 1976): 38–40.

Idlout d'Argencourt, Leah. "Spring." *Inuit Today* 5, no. 6 (June 1976): 48–50.

"Idlout Family Reflections: Idlout Family Members Talk about Joseph Idlout's Photographs." n.d. https://www.josephidloutphotographs.ca/en/idlout-family-reflections.html.

Igloliorte, Heather. "Arctic Culture/Global Indigeneity." In *Negotiations in a Vacant Lot: Studying the Visual in Canada*, ed. Lynda Jessup, Erin Morton, and Kirsty Robertson, 150–70. Montreal and Kingston: McGill-Queen's University Press, 2014.

Igloliorte, Heather. "Curating Inuit Qaujimajatuqangit: Inuit Knowledge in the Qallunaat Art Museum." *Art Journal* 76, no. 2. (2017): 100–13.

Igloliorte, Heather. "'We Were So Far Away': Exhibiting Inuit Oral Histories of Residential Schools." In *Curating Difficult Knowledges: Violent Pasts in Public Places*, ed. Erica Lehrer, Cynthia E. Milton, and Monica Patterson, 23–41. New York: Palgrave, 2011.

Igloolik Oral History Centre. "Igloolik Oral History Project." n.d. Accessed 30 August 2023. http://cnnro.ca/igloolik-oral-history-centre/.

Igloolik Oral History Centre. *Stories from Igloolik*. Igloolik: Ataguttaaluk School, Igloolik Oral History Project, 1986.

Inuit Literatures/Littératures inuites. n.d. https://inuit.uqam.ca/en.

Inuit Tapiriit Kanatami. "Nanilavut." n.d. https://www.itk.ca/projects/nanilavut/.

Inuit Tapiriit Kanatami. *National Inuit Strategy on Research Roundtable: Summary Report*. 20 February 2019. https://www.itk.ca/nisr-roundtable-summary-report/.

Iqqaumavara. n.d. http://www.iqqaumavara.com/.

Iqqaumavara. "About." n.d. http://www.iqqaumavara.com/en/about/.

Iqqaumavara. "Home." n.d. https://iqqaumavara.com/en/.

Iqqaumavara. "John Amagoalik – His Story." 2011. http://www.iqqaumavara.com/en/john-amagoalik-his-story/.

Iqqaumavara. "Larry Audlaluk – His Story." 2012. http://www.iqqaumavara.com/en/larry-audlaluk/.

Iqqaumavara. "Markoosie Patsauq – His Story." 2011. http://www.iqqaumavara.com/en/familles/entrevues/markoosie-patsauq-son-histoire/.

Iqqaumavara. "Moses Idlout – His Story." 2011. http://www.iqqaumavara.com/en/moses-idlout-his-story/.

Iqqaumavara. "Susan Salluviniq – Her Story." 2012. https://www.iqqaumavara.com/en/familles/entrevues/susan-salluviniq/.

Iqqaumavara. "Team." n.d. http://www.iqqaumavara.com/en/team/.

Karetak, Joe, Frank J. Tester, and Shirley Tagalik, eds. *Inuit Qaujimajatuqangit: What Inuit Have Always Known to Be True*. Halifax: Fernwood, 2017.

"Katherine Takpannie." *Inuit Art Quarterly*, n.d. https://www.inuitartfoundation.org/profiles/artist/katherine-takpannie.

Kenney, Gerard. Untitled report. In Royal Commission on Aboriginal Peoples, *The High Arctic Relocation*, vol. 1, *Summary of Supporting Information*, 199–215. Ottawa: Minister of Supply and Services Canada, 1994. http://publications.gc.ca/collections/collection_2018/aanc-inac/Z1-1991-1-41-3-1-eng.pdf.

King, J.C.H., and Henrietta Lidchi, eds. *Imaging the Arctic*. Seattle and Vancouver: University of Washington Press and UBC Press, 1998.

Kopytoff, Igor. "The Cultural Biography of Things: Commoditization as Process." In *The Social Life of Things: Commodities in Cultural Perspective*, ed. Arjun Appadurai, 64–91. Cambridge, UK: Cambridge University Press, 1986.

Krupnik, Igor, ed. *Early Inuit Studies: Themes and Transitions, 1850–1980s*. Washington: Smithsonian Institute Press, 2016.

Kublu, Alexina, Frédéric Laugrand, and Jarich Oosten. "Listening to Our Past." Nunavut Arctic College, n.d. Accessed 10 September 2018. http://www.traditional-knowledge.ca/default.html.

Kunuk, Zacharias, dir. *One Day in the Life of Noah Piugattuk*. Igloolik: Isuma Productions, 2019.

Lackenbauer, P. Whitney, ed. *Human Flagpoles or Humanitarian Action? Discerning Government Motives behind the Inuit Relocations to the High Arctic, 1953–1960*. Calgary: Arctic Institute of North America, 2020. https://arts.ucalgary.ca/sites/default/files/teams/25/dcass16-human-flagpoles-pwl.pdf.

Lackenbauer, P. Whitney, and Ryan Shackleton. *When the Skies Rained Boxes: The Air Force and the Qikiqtani Inuit, 1941–64*. Toronto: Munk-Gordon Arctic Security Program, 2012.

Lalonde, Christine. 2015. *Pitseolak Ashoona: Life and Work*. Toronto: Art Canada Institute.

Langford, Martha. "Richard Harrington's Guide: Universality and Locality in a Canadian Photographic Document." In *Photography, History, Difference*, ed. Tanya Sheehan. 33–56. Hanover, NH: Dartmouth College Press, 2015.

Langford, Martha. "Richard Harrington's Indigenous Madonnas." *History of Photography* 40, no. 1 (2016): 28–48.

Langford, Martha. *Suspended Conversations: The Afterlife of Memory in Photographic Albums*.

Montreal and Kingston: McGill-Queen's University Press, 2008.
Lauder, John. *Tracks North: The Story of Exercise Muskox*. Ed. P. Whitney Lackenbauer and Peter Kikkert. Antigonish, NS: Mulroney Institute, St Francis Xavier University, 2018.
Laugrand, Frédéric. "Écrire pour prendre la parole: conscience historique, mémoires d'aînés et régimes d'historicité au Nunavut." *Anthropologie et Sociétés* 26, nos 2–3 (2002): 91–116.
Laugrand, Frédéric, and Jarich Oosten. *Inuit Shamanism and Christianity: Transitions and Transformations in the Twentieth Century*. Montreal and Kingston: McGill-Queen's University Press, 2010.
Laugrand, Frédéric, and Jarich Oosten. "The Case of Pelagie Inuk: The Only Inuk Woman to Become a Grey Nun." *Études Inuit Studies* 38, nos 1–2 (2014): 157–76.
Lecocq-Lemieux, Morgane. "Kananginak Pootoogook." *Inuit Art Quarterly*, 12 September 2017. https://www.inuitartfoundation.org/profiles/artist/Kananginak-Pootoogook.
Legacy of Hope Foundation. "We Were So Far Away: The Inuit Experience of Residential Schools." n.d. http://legacyofhope.ca/project/we-were-so-far-away/.
Lepage, Marquise, dir. *Martha of the North*. Montreal: National Film Board of Canada, 2008. https://www.nfb.ca/film/martha_of_the_north/.
Library and Archives Canada. "Across Arctic Ungava/À travers l'Ungava." n.d., http://www.bac-lac.gc.ca/eng/CollectionSearch/Pages/record.aspx?app=filvidandsou&IdNumber=118220.
Library and Archives Canada. "Album 37, Eastern Arctic Patrol." n.d. https://recherche-collection-search.bac-lac.gc.ca/eng/home/record?app=fonandcol&idnumber=204923&ecopy=a093102-v8.
Library and Archives Canada. "Album 66, Eastern Arctic Patrol." n.d. http://www.bac-lac.gc.ca/eng/CollectionSearch/Pages/record.aspx?app=fonandcol&IdNumber=204976.
Lien, Sigrid, and Hilde Wallem Nielssen, eds. *Adjusting the Lens: Indigenous Activism, Colonial Legacies, and Photographic Heritage*. Vancouver: UBC Press, 2021.
Liscombe, Rhodri Windsor. "Modernist Ultimate Thule." *RACAR: Revue d'art Canadienne/Canadian Art Review* 31, nos 1–2 (2006): 64–80.
Litt, Paul. *The Muses, the Masses and the Massey Commission*. Toronto: University of Toronto Press, 1992.
Lloyd, Lorna. *Diplomacy with a Difference: The Commonwealth Office of High Commissioner, 1880–2006*. London: Brill, 2007.
Lloyd, Trevor. "Changing Greenland." *The Beaver* 289 (Spring 1959): 41–4.
Lonetree, Amy. "A Heritage of Resilience: Ho-Chunk Family Photographs in the Visual Archives." *Public Historian* 41, no. 1 (2019): 34–50.
Long, Tania. "Massey to Tour Canadian Arctic." *New York Times*, 17 March 1956.
Loo, Tina. *Moved by the State: Forced Relocation and Making a Good Life in Postwar Canada*. Vancouver: UBC Press, 2019.
Lydon, Jane, ed. *Calling the Shots: Aboriginal Photographies*. Canberra: Aboriginal Studies Press, 2014.
Lydon, Jane. *Eye Contact: Photographing Indigenous Australians*. Durham, NC: Duke University Press, 2005.
MacSween, Joe. "Massey Attends Eskimo Dances at Trading Post." *Globe and Mail*, 28 March 1956.
MacSween, Joe. "No Muskox for Massey in Arctic Plane Flight." *Globe and Mail*, 27 March 1956.
Makivik Corporation. n.d. https://www.makivik.org/.
Mamers, Danielle Taschereau. *Settler Colonial Ways of Seeing: Documentation, Administration, and the Interventions of Indigenous Art*. New York: Fordham, 2023.
Manning, L.M. "Visit of Greenlanders to Baffin Island." *Arctic Circular* 9, no. 1 (1956): 2–3.
Marcus, Alan Rudolph. *Inuit Relocation Policies in Canada and Other Circumpolar Countries, 1925–1960: A Report for the Royal Commission on Aboriginal Peoples*. Ottawa: Government of Canada, 1995.
Marcus, Alan Rudolph. "Nanook of the North as Primal Drama." *Visual Anthropology* 19, nos 3–4 (2006): 201–22.
Marcus, Alan Rudolph. *Relocating Eden: The Image and Politics of Inuit Exile in the Canadian Arctic*. Hanover, NH: Dartmouth College, University Press of New England, 1995.

Martin, Keavy. "'Are We Also Here for That?': Inuit Qaujimajatuqangit – Traditional Knowledge, or Critical Theory?" *Canadian Journal of Native Studies* 29, nos 1–2 (2009): 186–92.
Martin, Keavy. *Stories in a New Skin: Approaches to Inuit Literature.* Winnipeg: University of Manitoba Press, 2012.
Massey, Vincent. *Canadians and Their Commonwealth: The Romanes Lecture, 1 June 1961.* Oxford: Clarendon, 1961.
Massey, Vincent. *On Being Canadian.* Toronto: J.M. Dent, 1948.
Massey, Vincent. "A Report on the North: From an Address at the Annual Dinner of the Canadian Press, Toronto, 18 April 1956." In *Speaking of Canada: The Canadian Club*, ed. Russell Merifield, 42–5. Toronto: McClelland and Stewart, 1993.
Massey, Vincent. "A Southerner in the North: Address to the Board of Trade and the Yellowknife Branch of the Canadian Institute of Mining and Metallurgy, Yellowknife, N.W.T., 25th February 1953." In *Speaking of Canada: Addresses by the Right Hon. Vincent Massey, C.H.* Toronto: Macmillan, 1959.
Massey, Vincent. "Vincent Massey's Dominion Day Message." CBC Archives, 30 June 1939. https://www.cbc.ca/player/play/audio/1.3625974.
Massey, Vincent. *What's Past Is Prologue: The Memoirs of the Right Honourable Vincent Massey, C.H.* Toronto: Macmillan, 1963.
Massey Ferguson. "About Us." n.d. https://www.masseyferguson.com/en_us/discover-mf.html.
"Massey Leaves a Message to Future North Pole Visitors." *Globe and Mail*, 26 March 1956.
"Massey to Fly over North Pole in 17-Day, 10,000 Mile Tour: First Hand Taste of Eskimo Life." *Ottawa Journal*, 14 March 1956.
McGrath, Janet T. "*Isumaksaqsiurutigijakka*: Conversations with Aupilaarjuk towards a Theory of Inuktitut Knowledge Renewal." PhD diss., Carleton University, 2012.
McMahon, Kevin. *Arctic Twilight: Reflections on the Destiny of Canada's Northern Land and People.* Toronto: James Lorimer, 1988.
McMaster, Gerald, ed. *Inuit Modern: The Samuel and Esther Sarick Collection.* Vancouver: Douglas and McIntyre, 2010.
McMaster, Gerald, Julia Lum, and Kaitlin McCormick. "The Entangled Gaze: Indigenous and European Views of Each Other." *ab-Original* 2, no. 2 (2018): 125–40.
Meren, David. "'Commend Me the Yak': The Columbo Plan, the Inuit of Ungava, and 'Developing' Canada's North." *Histoire sociale/Social History* 50, no. 102 (2017): 343–70.
Michéa, Jean, dir. *Across Arctic Ungava.* Montreal: National Film Board of Canada and National Museum of Canada, 1949. https://www.nfb.ca/film/across_arctic_ungava.
Million, Dian. "Felt Theory: An Indigenous Feminist Approach to Affect and History." *Wíčazo Ša Review* 24, no. 2 (2009): 53–76.
Mirzoeff, Nicholas. "On Visuality." *Journal of Visual Culture* 5, no. 1 (2006): 53–79.
Mirzoeff, Nicholas. *The Right to Look: A Counterhistory of Visuality.* Durham, NC: Duke University Press, 2011.
Mirzoeff, Nicholas. "The Subject of Visual Culture." In *The Visual Culture Reader*, ed. Nicholas Mirzoeff, 3–23. London: Routledge, 1998.
Mitchell, W.J.T. "Showing Seeing: A Critique of Visual Culture." *Journal of Visual Culture* 1, no. 2 (2002): 165–81.
Moran, Ry, director, Centre for Truth and Reconciliation. "Keynote Address." Carleton University, June 2017.
Moser, Gabrielle. *Projecting Citizenship: Photography and Belonging in the British Empire.* University Park: Pennsylvania State University Press, 2019.
Mowat, Farley. *People of the Deer.* Boston: Little, Brown and Company, 1951.
Munger, Kurt. "Kodak Duaflex IV Camera Review." *Photo Jottings*, 15 March 2018. http://photojottings.com/kodak-duaflex-iv-camera-review/.
Nakasuk, Saullu, Hervé Paiaq, Elisapee Ootoova, and Pauloosie Angmalik. *Inuit Worldviews.* Vol. 1, *An Introduction: Interviewing Elders.* Ed. Jarich Oosten and Frédéric Laugrand. Iqaluit: Nunavut Arctic College, 1999.
National Film Board of Canada. "Alethea Arnaquq-Baril." n.d. https://www.nfb.ca/directors/alethea-arnaquq-baril/.
National Film Board of Canada. "Arctic Dog Team." n.d. https://collection.nfb.ca/film/arctic-dog-team-215421.

National Film Board of Canada. "Land of the Long Day." n.d. https://collection.nfb.ca/film/land_of_the_long_day.

National Film Board of Canada. "Unikkausivut – Sharing Our Stories." Playlist. n.d. https://www.nfb.ca/playlist/unikkausivut-sharing-our-stories/.

National Film Board of Canada. *Unikkausivut – Sharing Our Stories: An Interdisciplinary Educational Resource*. https://www3.nfb.ca/sg/100778.pdf.

National Gallery of Canada. "The New Generation Photography Award." 2025. https://www.gallery.ca/whats-on/exhibitions-and-galleries/new-generation-photography-award-2024.

National Gallery of Canada. "Photostory 378." 1 December 1964.

Newman, Sydney, dir. *Arctic Jungle*. Montreal: National Film Board of Canada, 1948.

Nickels, Scot, Jamal Shirley, and Gita Laidler, eds. *Negotiating Research Relationships with Inuit Communities: A Guide for Researchers*. 2nd ed. Ottawa and Iqaluit: Inuit Tapiriit Kanatami and Nunavut Research Institute, 2007.

Nichols, Bill. *Introduction to Documentary*. 3rd ed. Bloomington: Indiana University Press, 2017.

Nichols, Bill. *Representing Reality: Issues and Concepts in Documentary*. Bloomington: Indiana University Press, 1991.

Norman, David Winfield. "Control Mapping: Peter Pitseolak and Zacharias Kunuk on Reclaiming Inuit Photographic Images and Imaging." *Decolonization: Indigeneity, Education and Society* 3, no. 1 (2014): 48–72.

Nunavut Department of Education, Curriculum and School Services Division. *Inuit Qaujimajatuqangit: Education Framework for Nunavut Curriculum*. Iqaluit: Nunavut Department of Education, 2007.

Nunavut Tunngavik. "Apology for the Inuit High Arctic Relocation." n.d. https://www.tunngavik.com/initiative_pages/arctic-exile-monument-project/apology-for-the-inuit-high-arctic-relocationmamiahugiyait-inuit-kutinikpaami-kimakhimayut.

Nungak, Zebedee. "Five Decades of *Inuktitut Magazine*." *Inuktitut Magazine*, Spring 2012, 16–25.

Olin, Margaret. *Touching Photographs*. Chicago: University of Chicago Press, 2011.

Ootoova, Elisapee. *Inuktitut Dictionary: Tununiq Dialect*. Iqaluit: Baffin Division Educational Council, 2000.

Palluq-Cloutier, Jeela. "The History of Inuktitut Writing Systems." Language Portal of Canada, 2012. Accessed 5 May 2017. https://www.noslangues-ourlanguages.gc.ca/collaborateurs-contributors/articles/inuk-eng.html.

Parsons, Sarah. "Sovereign Territories: Photographs of Inuit Canadians and Cold War Anxiety, 1951–1956." Paper presented at the Annual Conference of the American Studies Association, Toronto, 2015.

Passalacqua, Veronica, and Hulleah Tsinhnahjinnie. *Our People, Our Land, Our Images: International Indigenous Photography*. Davis, CA: C.N. Gorman Museum, 2006.

Patsauq, Markoosie. *Uumajursiutik unaatuinnamut / Hunter with Harpoon / Chasseur au harpoon*. Ed. and trans. Valerie Henitiuk and Marc-Antoine Mahieu. Montreal and Kingston: McGill-Queen's University Press, 2021.

Patterson, Monica. "The Ethical Murk of Using Testimony in Oral Historical Research in South Africa." In *Oral History Off the Record: Toward an Ethnography of Practice*, ed. Anna Sheftel and Stacey Zembrycki, 201–18. Basingstoke, UK: Palgrave Macmillan, 2013.

Payne, Carol. "Culture, Memory and Community through Photographs: Developing an Inuit-Based Methodology." *Anthropology and Photography* 5 (2016): 1–17.

Payne, Carol. "Lessons with Leah: Re-reading the Photographic Archive of Nation in The National Film Board of Canada's Still Photography Division." *Visual Studies* 21, no. 1 (2006): 4–22.

Payne, Carol. *The Official Picture: The National Film Board of Canada's Still Photography Division and the Image of Canada*. Montreal and Kingston: McGill-Queen's University Press, 2013.

Payne, Carol. "'You hear it in their voice': Photographs and Cultural Consolidation among Inuit Youths and Elders." In *The Oral History Reader*, 3rd ed., ed. Alistair Thomson and Robert Perks, 611–25. London and New York: Routledge, 2015.

Payne, Carol, and Sheena Ellison. "Views from the North: Photographs, Generations, and Inuit Cultural Memory." In *Atiqput: Inuit Oral History and Project Naming*, ed. Carol Payne, Beth Greenhorn, Deborah Kigjugalik Webster, and Christina Williamson, 173–86. Montreal and Kingston: McGill-Queen's University Press, 2022.

Payne, Carol, Beth Greenhorn, Deborah Kigjugalik Webster, and Christina Williamson, eds. *Atiqput: Inuit Oral History and Project Naming*. Montreal and Kingston: McGill-Queen's University Press, 2022.

Payne, Carol, D.R. Fraser Taylor, and Amos Hayes. *Views from the North: A Cybercartographic Atlas*. Ottawa: Nunavut Sivuniksavut Training Program, Library and Archives Canada, and Geomatics and Cartographic Research Centre of Carleton University, 2012.

Payne, Carol, and Jeffrey Thomas. "Aboriginal Interventions into the Photographic Archives: A Dialogue." *Visual Resources: An International Journal of Documentation* 18, no. 2 (2002): 109–25.

Pearson, Bryan. "Remembering Iqaluit Leader Joe Tikivik." *Nunatsiaq News*, 23 April 2012. https://nunatsiaq.com/stories/article/65674remembering_iqaluit_leader_joe_tikivik/.

Pedri-Spade, Celeste. "'But They Were Never Only the Master's Tools': The Use of Photography in De-colonial Praxis." *Alter-Native: An International Journal of Indigenous Peoples* 13, no. 2 (2017): 106–13.

Petrone, Penny, ed. *Northern Voices: Inuit Writing in English*. Toronto: University of Toronto Press, 1992.

Phillips, Mark S. *On Historical Distance*. New Haven, CT: Yale University Press, 2013.

Phillips, R.A.J., and George Franklin Parsons. *This Is the Arctic*. Ottawa: Queen's Printer, 1958.

Phillips, Ruth B. *Trading Identities: The Souvenir in Native North American Art from the Northeast, 1700–1900*. Seattle: University of Washington Press, 1998.

Pinney, Christopher. *Photography and Anthropology*. London: Reaktion Books, 2011.

Pinney, Christopher. *Photos of the Gods: The Printed Image and Political Struggle in India*. New Delhi: Oxford University Press, 2004.

Pinney, Christopher, and Nicolas Peterson. *Photography's Other Histories*. Durham, NC: Duke University Press, 2003.

Pitseolak, Peter, and Dorothy Eber. *People from Our Side: A Life Story with Photographs and Oral Biography*. Trans. Ann M. Hanson. Montreal and Kingston: McGill-Queen's University Press, 1993.

"Poliomyelitis in Keewatin District." *Arctic Circular* 2, no. 3 (1949): 33–4.

Pond Inlet/Mittimalik. *Pond Inlet Community Guidelines*. n.d. https://www.aeco.no/wp-content/uploads/2020/05/pond-inlet.pdf.

Poole, Deborah. "An Excess of Description: Ethnography, Race and Visual Technologies." *Annual Review of Anthropology* 34 (2005): 159–79.

Porsild, A.E. "A Biological Exploration of Banks and Victoria Islands." *Arctic Circular* 3, no. 1 (1950): 2–9.

Pratt, Mary Louise. *Imperial Eyes: Travel Writing and Transculturation*. London: Routledge, 1992.

Qaumajuq. n.d. https://www.wag.ca/about/qaumajuq/.

Qikiqtani Truth Commission. n.d. https://www.qtcommission.ca/en.

Qikiqtani Truth Commission. *Aaniajurliriniq: Health Care in the Qikiqtani Region, 1950–1975*. Iqaluit: Inhabit Media and Qikiqtani Inuit Association, 2013. https://www.qtcommission.ca/sites/default/files/2024_revised_reports/CW_24-110_Report-5_Health-Care_E_v4.pdf.

Qikiqtani Truth Commission. "About the Photographs." In Qiqiktani Inuit Association, *Guide to the Community Histories and Special Studies of the Qikiqtani Truth Commission*, 6–7. Iqaluit: Inhabit Media, 2015. https://www.qtcommission.ca/sites/default/files/public/thematic_reports/web_guide_english1.pdf.

Qikiqtani Truth Commission. *Analysis of the RCMP Sled Dog Report*. Iqaluit: Inhabit Media and Qikiqtani Inuit Association, 2013. https://www.qtcommission.ca/sites/default/files/public/thematic_reports/thematic_reports_english_rcmp_sled_dog.pdf.

Qikiqtani Truth Commission. *Community Histories 1950–1975: Grise Fiord (Ausuittuq)*. Iqaluit: Inhabit Media and Qikiqtani Inuit Association, 2013. https://www.qtcommission.ca/sites/default/

files/community/community_histories_grise_fiord.pdf.
Qikiqtani Truth Commission. *Community Histories 1950–1975: Pond Inlet (Mittimatalik).* Iqaluit: Inhabit Media and Qikiqtani Inuit Association, 2013. https://www.qtcommission.ca/en/communities/pond-inlet-mittimatalik.
Qikiqtani Truth Commission. *Community Histories 1950–1975: Resolute (Qausuittuq).* Iqaluit: Inhabit Media and Qikiqtani Inuit Association, 2013. https://www.qtcommission.ca/sites/default/files/community/community_histories_resolute_bay.pdf.
Qikiqtani Truth Commission. "Hearings & Interviews." n.d. https://www.qtcommission.ca/en/resources/hearings-interviews.
Qikiqtani Truth Commission. "Key Findings." n.d. https://www.qtcommission.ca/index.php/en/key-findings.
Qikiqtani Truth Commission. *Nuutauniq: Moves in Inuit Life in the Qikiqtani Region, 1950–1975.* Iqaluit: Inhabit Media and Qikiqtani Inuit Association, 2013. https://www.qtcommission.ca/sites/default/files/2024_revised_reports/CW_24-110_Report-11_Nuutauniq_E_v4.pdf.
Qikiqtani Truth Commission. *The Official Mind of Canadian Colonialism.* Iqaluit: Inhabit Media and Qikiqtani Inuit Association, 2013. https://www.qtcommission.ca/sites/default/files/2024_revised_reports/CW_24-110_Report-12_Official-Mind_E_v4.pdf.
Qikiqtani Truth Commission. *Paliisikkut: Policing in the Qikiqtani Region, 1950–1975.* Iqaluit: Inhabit Media and Qikiqtani Inuit Association, 2013. https://www.qtcommission.ca/sites/default/files/2024_revised_reports/CW_24-110_Report-14_Policing_E_v3.pdf.
Qikiqtani Truth Commission. *Qimmiliriniq: Inuit Sled Dogs in the Qikiqtani Region.* Iqaluit: Inhabit Media and Qikiqtani Inuit Association, 2013. https://www.qtcommission.ca/sites/default/files/2024_revised_reports/CW_24-110_Report-17_Qimmitt_E_v4.pdf.
Qikiqtani Truth Commission. *QTC Final Report: Achieving Saimaqatigiingniq.* Iqaluit: Inhabit Media and Qikiqtani Inuit Association, 2013. https://www.qtcommission.ca/sites/default/files/public/thematic_reports/thematic_reports_english_final_report.pdf.
Qikiqtani Truth Commission. "RCMP Self-Investigation Does Not Reveal the Truth about the Slaughter of Inuit Sled Dogs in the 1950s and 1960s." Press release. n.d. https://www.qtcommission.ca/en/news/rcmp-self-investigation-does-not-reveal-truth-about-slaughter-inuit-sled-dogs-1950s-and-1960s.
Qikiqtani Truth Commission. "Statement of Apology Regarding the Findings of the Qikiqtani Truth Commission." n.d. https://www.qtcommission.ca/index.php/en/statement-apology-regarding-findings-qikiqtani-truth-commission.
Qikiqtani Truth Commission. "Thematic Reports and Special Studies 1950–1975." n.d. https://www.qtcommission.ca/en/reports/thematic-reports-and-special-studies-1950-1975.
Qitsualik, Rachel. "Inummarik: Self-Sovereignty in Classic Inuit Thought." In *Nilliajut: Inuit Perspectives on Security, Patriotism and Sovereignty,* ed. Scot Nickels, 23–33. Ottawa: Inuit Tapiriit Kanatami, 2013.
Quill, Greg. "Inuit Tragedy a Timely Reminder." *Toronto Star,* 5 September 1990, F3.
Racette, Sherry F. "Returning Fire, Pointing the Canon: Aboriginal Photography as Resistance." In *The Cultural Work of Photography in Canada,* ed. Carol Payne and Andrea Kunard, 70–90. Montreal and Kingston: McGill-Queen's University Press, 2011.
Raheja, Michelle. "Reading Nanook's Smile: Visual Sovereignty, Indigenous Revisions of Ethnography, and Atanarjuat (The Fast Runner)." *American Quarterly* 59, no. 4 (2007): 1159–85.
Raheja, Michelle. *Reservation Reelism: Redfacing, Visual Sovereignty, and Representations of Native Americans in Film.* Lincoln: University of Nebraska Press, 2010.
Ramaswamy, Sumathi. "Introduction: The Work of Vision in the Age of European Empires." In *Empires of Vision: A Reader,* ed. Martin Jay and Sumathi Ramaswamy, 1–22. Durham, NC: Duke University Press, 2014.
Rasmussen, Nils, dir. *Hunters of the North Pole.* Montreal: National Film Board of Canada, 1950.
Raymont, Peter, dir. *Magic in the Sky.* Montreal: Investigative Productions and the National Film Board of Canada in collaboration with Inuit Tapirisat of Canada, 1981.

Regan, Paulette. *Unsettling the Settler Within: Indian Residential Schools, Truth Telling, and Reconciliation in Canada*. Vancouver: UBC Press, 2010.

Rifkin, Mark. *Beyond Settler Time: Temporal Sovereignty and Indigenous Self-Determination*. Durham, NC: Duke University Press, 2017.

"Robert Kautuk." *Inuit Art Quarterly*, n.d. https://www.inuitartfoundation.org/profiles/artist/Robert-Kautuk.

Roberts, A. Barry. *Eskimo Identification and Disc Numbers: A Brief History*. Ottawa: Social Development Division, Department of Indian and Northern Affairs, 1975. http://publications.gc.ca/collections/collection_2017/aanc-inac/R5-303-1975-eng.pdf.

Robertson, Dylan. "Canadian Inuit Head to Greenland to Show Solidarity, Attend Consulate Opening." CBC News, 5 February 2026. https://www.cbc.ca/news/canada/north/canadian-inuit-head-to-greenland-to-show-solidarity-attend-consulate-opening-9.7076032.

Rony, Fatimah Tobing. *The Third Eye: Race, Cinema and Ethnographic Spectacle*. Durham, NC: Duke University Press, 1996.

Ross, W.G. 1990. "The Use and Misuse of Historical Photographs: A Case Study from Hudson Bay, Canada." *Arctic Anthropology* 27, no. 2 (1990): 93–112.

Rousseau, Jacques. "By Canoe across the Ungava Peninsula via the Kogaluk and Payne Rivers." *Arctic* 1, no. 2 (1948): 133–5. https://pubs.aina.ucalgary.ca/arctic/Arctic1-2-131.pdf.

Rowley, Graham. *Cold Comfort: My Love Affair with the Arctic*. 2nd ed. Montreal and Kingston: McGill-Queen's University Press, 2007.

Royal Canadian Mint. "Balance and Composition – the 2-Dollar Coin." n.d. Accessed 19 May 2021. https://www.mint.ca/store/mint/about-the-mint/2-dollars-5300016.

Royal Canadian Mounted Police. *Final Report: RCMP Review of Allegations Concerning Inuit Sled Dogs*. Ottawa: Community, Contract and Aboriginal Policing Services, National Contract Policing Branch, RCMP Operational Policy Section, 2006.

Royal Commission on Aboriginal Peoples. *The High Arctic Relocation*. Vol. 1, *Summary of Supporting Information*. Ottawa: Minister of Supply and Services Canada, 1994. http://publications.gc.ca/collections/collection_2018/aanc-inac/Z1-1991-1-41-3-1-eng.pdf.

Royal Commission on Aboriginal Peoples. "The Voices of Former Officials and Others: Doug Wilkinson." In *The High Arctic Relocation*, vol. 1, *Summary of Supporting Information*, 192–6. Ottawa: Ministry of Supply and Services, 1994. http://publications.gc.ca/collections/collection_2018/aanc-inac/Z1-1991-1-41-3-1-eng.pdf.

Ruby, Jay. *Picturing Culture: Explorations of Film and Anthropology*. Chicago: University of Chicago Press, 2000.

Sangster, Joan. *The Iconic North: Cultural Constructions of Aboriginal Life in Postwar Canada*. Vancouver: UBC Press, 2016.

Scherman, Katharine. *Spring on an Arctic Island*. Boston: Little Brown, 1956.

Schiwy, Angela, and Ian Moir. *Northwest Territories Archives: A Guide to the Holdings*. Yellowknife: Northwest Territories Archives, 1994.

Secretariat on Responsible Conduct of Research. "Research Involving the First Nations, Inuit, and Métis Peoples of Canada." In *Tri-Council Policy Statement on Ethical Conduct for Research Involving Humans*, 109–37. Ottawa: Government of Canada, 2014.

Senate of Canada. *Bill H: An Act to Incorporate the Arctic Institute of North America as Passed by the Senate, 1 November 1945*. Ottawa: Edmond Cloutier, Printer to the King's Most Excellent Majesty, 1945.

Skare, Roswitha. *Nanook of the North from 1922 to Today: The Famous Arctic Documentary and Its Afterlife*. Bern, Switzerland: Peter Lang, 2019.

Skinner, Damian. "Settler Colonial Art History: A Proposition in Two Parts." *Journal of Canadian Art History* 36, no. 1 (2014): 131–75.

Smith, Shawn Michelle. "Introduction: Visual Culture and Race." *MELUS: The Society for the Study of the Multi-ethnic Literature of the United States* 39, no. 2 (2014): 1–11.

Smith, Shawn Michelle. *Photography on the Color Line: W.E.B. Du Bois, Race, and Visual Culture*. Durham, NC: Duke University Press, 2004.

"A Snow Baby is Born." Photographs by Jean Roy. *Picture Post*, 6 December 1952, 16–19.

Stern, Pamela R. *Historical Dictionary of the Inuit*. Lanham, MD: Scarecrow, 2004.

Stern, Pamela R. "The History of Canadian Arctic Photography: Issues of Territorial and Cultural Sovereignty." In *Imaging the Arctic*, ed. J.C.H. King and Henrietta Lidchi, 47–8. Seattle and Vancouver: University of Washington Press and UBC Press, 1998.

Stern, Pamela R., and Lisa Stevenson, eds. *Critical Inuit Studies: An Anthology of Contemporary Arctic Ethnography*. Lincoln: University of Nebraska Press, 2006.

Strassler, Karen. *Refracted Visions: Popular Photography and National Modernity in Java*. Durham, NC: Duke University Press, 2010.

Sturken, Marita, and Lisa Cartwright, eds. *Practices of Looking: An Introduction to Visual Culture*. 3rd ed. New York and Oxford: Oxford University Press, 2018.

Tagalik, Shirley. "*Inuit Qaujimajatuqangit*: The Role of Indigenous Knowledge in Supporting Wellness in Inuit Communities in Nunavut." National Collaborating Centre for Aboriginal Health, 2009–10. https://www.ccnsa-nccah.ca/docs/health/FS-InuitQaujimajatuqangitWellness Nunavut-Tagalik-EN.pdf.

Tash, Roy, dir. *Arctic Journey: A Photographic Record of His Excellency the Governor General's Visit to the Canadian Arctic*. Montreal: Associated Screen News, 1956. Library and Archives Canada, Roy Tash fonds, 1956.0059.

Tester, Frank, and Piita Irniq. "Inuit Qaujimajatuqangit: Social History, Politics and the Practice of Resistance." *Arctic* 61, no. 1 (2008): 48–61.

Tester, Frank J., and Peter Kulchyski. *Kiumajut (Talking Back): Game Management and Inuit Rights, 1900–70*. Vancouver: UBC Press, 2007.

Tester, Frank J., and Peter Kulchyski. *Tammarniit (Mistakes): Inuit Relocation in the Eastern Arctic, 1939–63*. Vancouver: UBC Press, 1994.

Tester, Frank J., Paule McNicoll, and Peter Irniq. "Writing for Our Lives: The Language of Homesickness, Self-Esteem, and the Inuit TB 'Epidemic.'" *Etudes Inuit Studies* 25, nos 1–2 (2001): 121–40.

Thomas, Jeff. "At the Kitchen Table with Edward Curtis." In *Return to the Land of the Head Hunters: Edward Curtis, the Kwakwaka'wakw, and the Making of Modern Cinema*, ed. Brad Evans and Aaron Glass, 128–44. Seattle: University of Washington Press, 2014.

Thomas, Nicholas. *Entangled Objects: Exchange, Material Culture, and Colonialism in the Pacific*. Cambridge, MA: Harvard University Press, 1991.

Thrasher, Kevin. "Exercise Musk Ox: Lost Opportunities." MA thesis, Carleton University, 1998.

Tippett, M. *Between Two Cultures: A Photographer among the Inuit*. Toronto: Penguin, 1994.

Toronto Metropolitan University Archives and Special Collections. "Cameras." n.d. Accessed 5 November 2018. https://library.ryerson.ca/asc/sc/holdings/heritage-cameras/.

Toronto Metropolitan University Archives and Special Collections. "Item 2005.006.05.58 – Kodak Duaflex Camera." n.d. Accessed 5 November 2018. https://archives.library.ryerson.ca/index.php/kodak-duaflex-camera-2.

Tripp, Maddy. "Asinnajaq." *Inuit Art Quarterly*, 12 September 2017. https://www.inuitartfoundation.org/profiles/artist/Asinnajaq.

Truth and Reconciliation Commission of Canada. *The Final Report of the Truth and Reconciliation Commission of Canada*. Vol. 2, *Canada's Residential Schools: The Inuit and Northern Experience*. Montreal and Kingston: McGill-Queen's University Press, 2015. https://publications.gc.ca/collections/collection_2015/trc/IR4-9-2-2015-eng.pdf.

Truth and Reconciliation Commission of Canada. *Truth and Reconciliation Commission of Canada: Calls to Action*. Winnipeg: Truth and Reconciliation Commission of Canada, 2015. http://epe.lac-bac.gc.ca/100/201/301/weekly_acquisition_lists/2015/w15-24-F-E.html/collections/collection_2015/trc/IR4-8-2015-eng.pdf.

Tsinhnahjinnie, Hulleah J. "When Is a Photograph Worth a Thousand Words?" In *Photography's Other Histories*, ed. Christopher Pinney and Nicolas Peterson, 40–51. Durham, NC: Duke University Press, 2002.

Tuck, Eve. "Suspending Damage: A Letter to Communities." *Harvard Educational Review* 79, no. 3 (2009): 409–28.

Tuck, Eve, and K. Wayne Yang. "Decolonization Is Not a Metaphor." *Decolonization: Indigeneity, Education and Society* 1, no. 1 (2012): 1–40.

Tulugarjuk, Leo, and Jaypeetee Arnakak, eds. *Unikkaaqtuat Qikiqtaniinngaaqtut: Traditional Stories from the Qikiqtani Region*. Vol. 1, *Arctic Bay and Igloolik*. Iqaluit: Inhabit Media, 2008.

"$2 Bill Has His Picture on Back." *Ottawa Citizen*, 19 July 1978. Bank of Canada Archives and Museum, Secretary's Department fonds, currency clippings, 1978.

University of Calgary. "Arctic Institute of North America." n.d. https://arctic.ucalgary.ca/.

Uummaqutik: essence de la vie at the Musée des beaux-arts de Montréal. n.d. http://www.museesmontreal.org/fr/expositions-et-evenements/expositions/uummaqutik-essence-de-la-vie.

"Vintage CBC North: Celebrating 20 Years of Northbeat, Igalaaq." CBC News, 10 November 2015. https://www.cbc.ca/news/canada/north/vintage-cbc-north-celebrating-20-years-of-northbeat-igalaaq-1.3312666.

"Vivian Wilkinson: Obituary." *Toronto Star*, 10 December 2011.

Vizenor, Gerald. "Aesthetics of Survivance: Literary Theory and Practice." In *Survivance: Narratives of Native Presence*, ed. Gerald Vizenor, 1–23. Lincoln: University of Nebraska Press, 2008

Vizenor, Gerald. "Fugitive Poses." In *Excavating Voices: Listening to Photographs of Native Americans*, ed. Michael Katakis, 7–15. Philadelphia: University of Pennsylvania Museum, 1998.

Vizenor, Gerald, ed. *Survivance: Narratives of Native Presence*. Lincoln: University of Nebraska Press, 2008.

Vorano, Norman. "Cape Dorset Cosmopolitans: Making Local Prints in Global Modernity." In *Mapping Modernisms: Art, Indigeneity, and Colonialism*, ed. Elizabeth Harney and Ruth B. Phillips, 209–34. Durham, NC: Duke University Press, 2019.

Vorano, Norman. "Creators: Negotiating the Art World for over 50 Years." *Inuit Art Quarterly* 19, 3–4 (2004): 9–17.

Wachowich, Nancy, with Apphia Agalakti Awa, Rhoda Kaukjak Katsak, and Sandra Pikujak Katsak. *Saqiyuq: Stories from the Lives of Three Inuit Women*. Montreal and Kingston: McGill-Queen's University Press, 1999.

Wakeham, Pauline. "At the Intersection of Apology and Sovereignty: The Arctic Exile Monument Project." *Cultural Critique*, no. 87 (2014): 84–143.

"Wealthier, Too: Greenland Eskimos Healthier." *Globe and Mail*, 30 September 1958.

Webster, Deborah Kigjugalik. "Unrecognized: The Wives and Children of Inuit Special Constables." *Inuktitut Magazine*, Summer 2019. https://www.itk.ca/unrecognized/.

Webster, Deborah Kigjugalik, and Carol Payne. "'Onwards': The Travels of Kiviuq in Art by Victoria Mamnguqsualuk and Nancy Pukirnak Aupaluktuq." In *Arctic Fever: Image and Narrative in North Circumpolar Voyaging in the Long 19th Century*, ed. Mark Cheetham and Isabelle Gapp. Toronto: Thomas Fisher Rare Book Library, University of Toronto, 2026.

Wilkinson, Doug, dir. *Angotee: Story of an Eskimo Boy*. Montreal: National Film Board of Canada, 1953. https://www.nfb.ca/film/angotee_story_of_an_eskimo_boy.

Wilkinson, Doug. *The Arctic Coast: The Illustrated Natural History of Canada*. Toronto: Natural Science of Canada, 1970.

Wilkinson, Doug. *Arctic Fever: The Search for the Northwest Passage*. Toronto: Clarke, Irwin, 1971.

Wilkinson, Doug, dir. *Arctic Lifeline*. Montreal: National Film Board of Canada, 1952. https://collection.onf.ca/film/eye-witness-no-39.

Wilkinson, Doug, dir. *Canada: Eskimo Medal*. Newsreel. 1954. British Pathé. https://www.britishpathe.com/asset/255499/.

Wilkinson, Doug, dir. *Canada: Eskimos Award*. Newsreel. 1954. British Pathé. https://www.britishpathe.com/asset/250002/.

Wilkinson, Doug, dir. *Easter in Canadian Arctic*. Newsreel. 1955. British Pathé. https://www.britishpathe.com/asset/59498/.

Wilkinson, Doug, dir. *Eskimo Gets Medal from the Queen*. Newsreel. 1954. Warner Pathé. https://www.gettyimages.ca/detail/video/eskimo-gets-medal-from-the-queen-superimposed-over-medal-news-footage/515381196.

Wilkinson, Doug, dir. *Eskimos Mine Their Own Coal*. Newsreel. 1954. British Pathé. https://www.britishpathe.com/asset/102307/.

Wilkinson, Doug. "The Eskimos of Frobisher Bay." *Northern Affairs Bulletin* 4, no. 1 (1957): 3–5. https://digital.scaa.sk.ca/ourlegacy/solr?query=ID:24163&start=0&rows=10&mode=results.

Wilkinson, Doug, dir. *Eskimo Receives Coronation Medal*. Newsreel. 1954. British Pathé. https://www.youtube.com/watch?v=01i8JDSaVpA.

Wilkinson, Doug, dir. *Eskimo Village, Resolute*. Newsreel. Montreal: National Film Board of Canada, 1963.

Wilkinson, Doug, dir. *Exercise Musk-Ox*. Montreal: National Film Board of Canada, 1946. https://vimeo.com/167910734.
Wilkinson, Doug, dir. *Going North*. Montreal: National Film Board of Canada, 1948.
Wilkinson, Doug. "How I Became an Eskimo." *Maclean's*, 15 November 1954, 28–30, 103–9.
Wilkinson, Doug, dir. *How to Build an Igloo*. Editor Neil Harris. Montreal: National Film Board of Canada, 1949. https://www.nfb.ca/film/how_to_build_an_igloo/.
Wilkinson, Doug. "Idlouk – Arctic Amateur." *Photography*, April 1954, 38–41, 106–7.
Wilkinson, Doug. Interview by Shelagh Mackenzie and Mary Sparling, 29 March 1985, La Have, Nova Scotia, for Inuit Art Documentation and Film Research Project. Library and Archives Canada, Department of Indian Affairs and Northern Development fonds, R216-3855-6-E, RG85-E-2.
Wilkinson, Doug. *Land of the Long Day*. London: Clarke, Irwin, 1955.
Wilkinson, Doug, dir. *Land of the Long Day*. Cinematography Jean Roy. Montreal: National Film Board of Canada, 1952.
Wilkinson, Doug. "National Film Board Arctic Project." *Arctic Circular* 5, no. 4 (1952): 36–8.
Wilkinson, Doug. "New Town of Frobisher Bay, the First Year 1955–56." Presentation at the Seventieth Meeting of the Arctic Circle, 13 November 1956. *Arctic Circular* 9, no. 2 (1956): 12.
Wilkinson, Doug, dir. *Resolute: Eskimo Village*. Newsreel. Montreal: National Film Board of Canada, 1960.
Wilkinson, Doug, dir. *Resolute – Hub of the Arctic*. Newsreel. Montreal: National Film Board of Canada, 1961.
Wilkinson, Doug, dir. *Sister Pelagie*. Cinematography Jean Roy. Newsreel. Montreal: National Film Board of Canada, 1951. https://www.nfb.ca/film/eye_witness_no30/.
Wilkinson, Doug. "A Vanishing Canadian." *The Beaver* 289 (Spring 1959): 25–9.
Wilkinson, Doug, dir. *The White Eskimo*. [Also titled *Arctic: Life in the North*]. Cinematography Joseph Idlout. Newsreel. 1954. British Pathé. https://www.britishpathe.com/asset/250143/.
Williams, Carol. "Indigenous Uses of Photography." In *Framing the West: Race, Gender, and the Photographic Frontier in the Pacific Northwest*, 138–69. New York: Oxford University Press, 2003.
Williamson, Christina. "Sewing in Arviat: Inuit Women's Work through Stories and Parkas." PhD diss., Carleton University, 2021.
Wilson, Shawn. "Relationality." In *Research Is Ceremony: Indigenous Research Methods*, 80–96. Halifax and Winnipeg: Fernwood, 2008.
Winston, Brian. *Claiming the Real: Griersonian Documentary and Its Legitimations*. London: British Film Institute, 1995.
Wintle, Pamela. "Moving Image Technology and Archives." In *Recreating First Contact: Expeditions, Anthropology, and Popular Culture*, ed. Joshua A. Bell, Alison K. Brown, and Robert J. Gordon, 31–40. Washington, DC: Smithsonian Institution Scholarly Press, 2013.
Wise, Jonathan. "Photographic Memory: Inuit Representation in the Work of Peter Pitseolak." MA thesis, Concordia University, 2000.
Wolfe, Patrick. "Settler Colonialism and the Elimination of the Native." *Journal of Genocide Research* 8, no. 4 (2006): 387–409.
Wright, Christopher. *The Echo of Things: The Lives of Photographs in the Solomon Islands*. Durham, NC: Duke University Press, 2013.
Wright, Shelley. *Our Ice Is Vanishing/Sikuvut Nunguliqtuq: A History of Inuit, Newcomers, and Climate Change*. Montreal and Kingston: McGill-Queen's University Press, 2014.
Zawadski, Krista Ulujuk. *Nuvisi: Threading Our Beads at Qatiktalik*. Exhibition catalogue. Ottawa: Carleton University Art Gallery, 2021. https://cuag.ca/wp-content/uploads/2023/04/CUAG-Nuvisi-FINAL.pdf.
Zelniker, Rachel. "Northern Researcher Digs into History of Inuit Special Constables." CBC News, 10 April 2016. https://www.cbc.ca/news/canada/north/inuit-special-constable-nunavut-deborah-webster-1.3528764.

Index

Page numbers in italics indicate references to illustrations.

McGill-Queen's/Beaverbrook Canadian Foundation Studies in Art History

MARTHA LANGFORD, SERIES EDITOR

The Practice of Her Profession
Florence Carlyle, Canadian Painter in the Age of Impressionism
Susan Butlin

Bringing Art to Life
A Biography of Alan Jarvis
Andrew Horrall

Picturing the Land
Narrating Territories in Canadian Landscape Art, 1500 to 1950
Marylin J. McKay

The Cultural Work of Photography in Canada
Edited by Carol Payne and Andrea Kunard

Newfoundland Modern
Architecture in the Smallwood Years, 1949–1972
Robert Mellin

The Codex Canadensis and the Writings of Louis Nicolas
The Natural History of the New World, Histoire Naturelle des Indes Occidentales
Edited and with an Introduction by François-Marc Gagnon, Translation by Nancy Senior, Modernization by Réal Ouellet

Museum Pieces
Toward the Indigenization of Canadian Museums
Ruth B. Phillips

The Allied Arts
Architecture and Craft in Postwar Canada
Sandra Alfoldy

Rethinking Professionalism
Essays on Women and Art in Canada, 1850–1970
Edited by Kristina Huneault and Janice Anderson

The Official Picture
The National Film Board of Canada's Still Photography Division and the Image of Canada, 1941–1971
Carol Payne

Paul-Émile Borduas
A Critical Biography
François-Marc Gagnon
Translated by Peter Feldstein

On Architecture
Melvin Charney: A Critical Anthology
Edited by Louis Martin

Making Toronto Modern
Architecture and Design, 1895–1975
Christopher Armstrong

Negotiations in a Vacant Lot
Studying the Visual in Canada
Edited by Lynda Jessup, Erin Morton, and Kirsty Robertson

Visibly Canadian
Imaging Collective Identities in the Canadas, 1820–1910
Karen Stanworth

Breaking and Entering
The Contemporary House Cut, Spliced, and Haunted
Edited by Bridget Elliott

Family Ties
Living History in Canadian House Museums
Andrea Terry

Picturing Toronto
Photography and the Making of a Modern City
Sarah Bassnett

Architecture on Ice
A History of the Hockey Arena
Howard Shubert

For Folk's Sake
Art and Economy in Twentieth-Century Nova Scotia
Erin Morton

Spaces and Places for Art
Making Art Institutions in Western Canada, 1912–1990
Anne Whitelaw

Narratives Unfolding
National Art Histories in an Unfinished World
Edited by Martha Langford

Canadian Painters in a Modern World, 1925–1955
Writings and Reconsiderations
Lora Senechal Carney

Sketches from an Unquiet Country
Canadian Graphic Satire, 1840–1940
Edited by Dominic Hardy, Annie Gérin, and
Lora Senechal Carney

I'm Not Myself at All
Women, Art, and Subjectivity in Canada
Kristina Huneault

The Global Flows of Early Scottish Photography
Encounters in Scotland, Canada, and China
Anthony W. Lee

Tear Gas Epiphanies
Protest, Culture, Museums
Kirsty Robertson

What Was History Painting and What Is It Now?
Edited by Mark Salber Phillips and Jordan Bear

Through Post-Atomic Eyes
Edited by Claudette Lauzon and John O'Brian

Jean Paul Riopelle et le mouvement automatiste
François-Marc Gagnon

Jean Paul Riopelle and the Automatiste Movement
François-Marc Gagnon
Translated by Donald Winkler

I Can Only Paint
The Story of Battlefield Artist Mary Riter Hamilton
Irene Gammel

Object Lives and Global Histories in Northern North America
Material Culture in Motion, c. 1780–1980
Edited by Beverly Lemire, Laura Peers, and
Anne Whitelaw

For the Temporary Accommodation of Settlers
Architecture and Immigrant Reception in Canada, 1870–1930
David Monteyne

Women at the Helm
How Jean Sutherland Boggs, Hsio-yen Shih, and Shirley L. Thomson Changed the National Gallery of Canada
Diana Nemiroff

Voluntary Detours
Small-Town and Rural Museums in Alberta
Lianne McTavish

Photogenic Montreal
Activisms and Archives in a Post-industrial City
Edited by Martha Langford and Johanne Sloan

Wendat Women's Arts
Annette W. de Stecher

Unsettling Canadian Art History
Edited by Erin Morton

Out of School
Information Art and the Toronto School of Communication
Adam Lauder

Jackson's Wars
A.Y. Jackson, the Birth of the Group of Seven, and the Great War
Douglas Hunter

Out of the Studio
The Photographic Innovations of Charles and John Smeaton at Home and Abroad
John Osborne and Peter Smeaton

Casa Loma
Millionaires, Medievalism, and Modernity in Toronto's Gilded Age
Edited by Matthew M. Reeve and Michael Windover

Variable Conditions
Para-computational Arts in Canada, 1965–1995
Edited by Adam Lauder

Needle Work
A History of Commercial Tattooing in Canada
Jamie Jelinski

A History of Photography in Canada
Volume 1: Anticipation to Participation, 1839–1918
Martha Langford

Toronto Edwardian
Frank Darling, Architect of Canada's Imperial Age
David E. Winterton

Classicism in Canada
Ambition, Utopia, Hubris
Edited by Joan Coutu with David A. Galbraith

The Hunter, the Crown, and the Cameras
Joseph Idlout and the Image of Sangussaqtauliqtilluta
Carol Payne
With texts and images by Joseph Idlout and Leah Idlout d'Argencourt Paulson
With contributions by Madeleine d'Argencourt and Augatnaaq Eccles
And with the words of Paul Ullatitaq Idlout, Susan Salluviniq, Moses Idlout, Joshua Idlout, Ludy Pudluk, Jacob Anaviapik, Elisapee Ootoova, Ruth Sangoya, and Solomon Awa